★★★

MANY VOICES LITERATURE

American Short Stories

Second Edition

Perfection Learning®

★★★

EDITORIAL DIRECTORS	Julie A. Schumacher, Carol Francis
SENIOR EDITORS	Rebecca Christian, Terry Ofner
EDITORIAL ASSISTANTS	Suzanne Foggia, Megan Snyder
WRITER	Rebecca Burke
PERMISSIONS	Meghan Schumacher
DESIGN	William Seabright and Associates, Glencoe, Illinois
	Emily J. Adickes
PRODUCTION MANAGER	Lisa Lorimor
TEACHER REVIEWERS	LoAnn Campbell, Retired Teacher of English, Ames High School, Ames, Iowa
	Eric D. Turley, Teacher of English, Johnsburg High School, Johnsburg, Illinois
STUDENT REVIEWERS	Luke Scheele, Hermann High School, Hermann, Missouri
	George Thompson, Hoover High School, Des Moines, Iowa

Dr. Neil E. Nakadate, consultant for this book, is a Professor of English at Iowa State University, Ames, Iowa. A recipient of the Iowa State University Foundation Award for Career Achievement in Teaching, Dr. Nakadate earned a Ph.D. in English from Indiana University and specializes in contemporary American fiction. He is the author of several books and articles, including *Understanding Jane Smiley.* Dr. Nakadate reviewed selections for this volume and helped shape the table of contents. His work also includes the essay "On Style" and the essays that introduce each unit. In addition, he wrote "The Author's Style" feature that appears before each story.

★★

American Short Stories

Second Edition

Perfection Learning®

TABLE OF CONTENTS

Unit Three
Voices of Modernism 1920s TO 1940s

Unit Four

Post-War Voices 1950s AND 1960s

Unit Five

Voices of Diversity and Disillusionment 1970s AND 1980s 528

Unit Six
Contemporary Voices 1990s AND 2000s 644

TO THE READER

A clumsy schoolteacher fleeing from the specter of a headless horeseman. An American father in search of his daughter in France. A ranchwoman in the Salinas Valley who yearns for companionship and a sense of self-worth. A postmistress in Mississippi who decides to live at the post office after feuding with her eccentric family. A terrified soldier in Vietnam who longs for his Minnesota home.

These are some of the characters and situations you will encounter in *American Short Stories.* They are as varied as the geography of the United States itself. Yet their common denominator is that each is part of a short story, a form—like jazz or baseball—that some claim is uniquely American.

Of course, thousands of American short stories have been written, and collections of them abound. What sets this volume apart is its emphasis on the authors' writing styles. By examining approaches as diverse as the spare, understated prose of Ernest Hemingway and the dazzling imagery of Louise Erdrich, you will come to recognize many elements of style. It has been said that style is comprised of the fingerprints an author leaves on a story, making it so unmistakably his or hers that a careful reader can tell who has written it without the byline.

As many of the writers in this volume have remarked, good reading comes before good writing. Reading this book and completing the activities will help you shape your own writing style.

Aside from what you will learn about style, this volume provides an overview of the American short story's development from its beginnings with Washington Irving, Nathaniel Hawthorne, and Edgar Allan Poe to the present. Indeed, many literary historians credit Poe, the master of horror, with inventing, or at least refining, the short story form. He saw the short story as different from the novel not only in length but also in intention and form. Writing when Americans were still trying to create a distinct literature for their country, Poe developed highly atmospheric, tightly constructed stories in which brevity and unity contributed to a single, focused effect.

Other American writers followed Poe's example by developing their own subjects and methods. From the beginning, a particular focus of the American short story has been the theme of personal identity, often explored in stories of personal quests that determine an individual's sense of self and relationship to others and the world.

During the 19th century, nearly all of the basic themes and issues of the American short story were introduced and developed by writers such as Nathaniel Hawthorne, Herman Melville, Mark Twain, and Kate Chopin. These and other writers focused on specifically American locations, subjects, and problems, developing a wide range of styles for storytelling. Their stories arose from local history, moral fables, character studies, and the dilemmas posed by race and class.

Against the backdrop of westward expansion, the Industrial Revolution, and wave after wave of immigration, American writers began to seek insights into the conflicts and dilemmas of the day. The short story—with its limited cast of characters, few scenes or episodes, and focus on a single effect—provided a good forum for such explorations. It was practical, besides. With Americans spread out across a continent, ten-cent magazines delivered nationwide by mail gave the country a sense of having its own literature. It also provided a mass market for short story writers.

Change was even more rapid in the 20th century. Social, political, and cultural developments included the building of transcontinental highways, the Constitutional amendment allowing women to vote, and broad recognition that World War I had introduced a new era of fears and possibilities. Many 20th-century writers whose works are represented in this book convey a firm sense of regional identity. Others focus on the lives of people in the city and the suburbs. Still others explore ethnic identity. The approaches of these writers range from the use of straightforward plots with conventional language to the creation of quirky plot lines, points of view, and narrative voices. The tone ranges from assertive pride to playful irony to sympathy for suffering and loss.

Since the United States is constantly changing, no single story could appropriately be called the American story. America is a complex whole, comprised of countless individual experiences. To read this collection of short stories is not to define the American experience so much as to learn from various pieces of it. It is to find yourself—in a phrase borrowed from John Steinbeck—in search of America.

ON STYLE

As you study this collection of short stories, you will be introduced to some of America's most important writers. Almost certainly you won't like every one, but each author has a unique message to send and a distinctive way of sending it. The way a writer conveys a message is called his or her *style*. Whether in clothing, music, visual art, or literature, style is easy to see but hard to define. You might think of style in writing as the way thoughts are *dressed*. Analyzing style will make you a more perceptive reader and help you develop your own writer's voice. A good definition of style for this book is that it is *the author's distinctive manner of expression.*

As in most arts, it takes time and familiarity to recognize distinctions among literary styles. Perhaps an analogy will help here. To the untrained eye, a forest is just a collection of indistinct trees. To the trained eye, however, the forest is composed of a grove of white oaks on the hillside, a stand of willows by the stream, and thorn-bearing hawthorn trees along its edges. As you read, follow the Literary Lens prompts and pay close attention to the information about the author's life and style that precedes each selection. Before long, clear distinctions will emerge.

In fact, some writers have such distinctive styles that they have spawned imitators. The works of authors who follow paths blazed by Ernest Hemingway and William Faulkner are sometimes called "Hemingwayesque" or "Faulknerian." Hemingway probably would have been startled by such praise. He once wrote, "In stating as fully as I could how things were, it was often very difficult and I wrote awkwardly and the awkwardness is what they called my style."

Hemingway is not alone in implying that he never deliberately set out to create a style, but only wrote as well as he could instinctively. Katherine Anne Porter once complained, "I've been called a stylist until I really could tear my hair out. And I simply don't believe in style. Style is you."

Style is hard to describe because part of it is a certain indefinable uniqueness. Some aspects of style are easier to pin down, however. That's because style includes the set of choices and techniques that enable a writer to tell a story. Choices regarding **characterization**, **setting**, and **tone**—to name a few—impact the style of a story. But there are other sources of style, such as the author's background, whether that author is a man or a woman, and the author's race or ethnicity.

For example, F. Scott Fitzgerald grew up in modest circumstances in St. Paul, Minnesota. He later left the Midwest and became fascinated with the flamboyant rich of the East Coast. Fitzgerald's descriptions often mix criticism, sympathy, and awe for the rich lifestyle, as in this one-line character sketch in his novel *The Great Gatsby*: "Her voice is full of money." The stories of Alice Walker, on the other hand, come out of her experience as a woman of color growing up in the United States. Her fiction often depicts a female character finding her way in an environment of oppression.

Personal values also determine writers' attitudes toward their characters. John Steinbeck's sympathies for those who fled the Oklahoma dust bowl of the 1930s went into his writing about the struggle of common people for economic justice. Flannery O'Connor's fiction reflects her devout Catholicism; her grotesque characters and often violent story lines express her belief in the need for salvation. The combination of background, gender, ethnicity, and values makes up the author's **worldview**.

Style also develops from writers' responses to earlier writers they have read. Some choose to work within a stylistic tradition, such as social **realism**, in which the everyday lives of characters are depicted against a social, political, and economic background that is presented as a matter of fact. John Steinbeck, Katherine Anne Porter, John Updike, and Russell Banks are among the American writers in this tradition. Other writers rebel against tradition or find it necessary to innovate. They develop new styles to convey a particular point of view. For example, William Faulkner uses **interior monologue** to narrate stories through characters whose limitations would make it impossible for them to tell their stories in the usual way. Ray Bradbury and Kurt Vonnegut use futuristic settings in order to question and probe current attitudes and trends.

Another aspect of style is **tone**, or the author's attitude toward his or her subject. Words such as "sympathetic," "comic," "passionate," or "harsh" can be used to describe the attitude of the writer. The tone helps determine the story's intellectual and emotional impact on the reader. One of the dominant tones of fiction in the 20th century is **irony**. Irony reflects the sadness or humor resulting from the gap between life as it is idealized and life as it really is. Generally irony is used to criticize some aspect of society or to reveal the silliness of people's behavior. Irony also results from unusual or unexpected points of view, oddly humorous situations, and shocking revelations or sudden turns of event. Sherman Alexie uses ironic humor to reveal the sad realities of Native American life on and off the reservation. Flannery O'Connor, Kurt Vonnegut, John Cheever, Joyce Carol Oates, and T. Coraghessan Boyle are among many whose stories use irony that is sometimes comic and sometimes bitingly satirical.

Finally, style includes the way a writer uses language. Some writers, like Thomas Wolfe, are said to be lyrical—that is, expressing intense personal emotions in much the same way as a songwriter or poet. Some, like Raymond Carver, are considered **minimalists**—that is, they let the events of the story speak for themselves without much interpretation from the author. Others, like Harry Mark Petrakis, are described as colorful, meaning full of variety and interest. Still others, such as T. Coraghessan Boyle, are labeled energetic, writing in a way that is so highly charged the reader has little choice but to go along for the ride.

Other contributions to style include the language used by the story's narrator and in the dialogue of characters; variations in **dialect** and usage that are tied to particular groups of people or regions of the country; repetitions of key words and phrases; and even the length and structure of individual sentences. Truman Capote once wrote, "I think of myself as a stylist, and stylists can become notoriously obsessed with the placing of a comma, the weight of a semicolon."

Faulkner's long, sometimes convoluted sentences convey the dynamic intensity of his characters' thoughts and emotions while the dialogue of his characters is written in the rural vernacular of his native Mississippi. The rhythm of Yiddish storytelling is reflected in the prose of Isaac Bashevis Singer. The speech of Katherine Anne Porter's characters often reflects her roots in rural Texas and the languages of Mexico and other countries in which she lived. The dialogue of the American-born daughters and native Chinese mothers in Amy Tan's stories reveal the barriers that language differences can create within a family as well as within a society.

Ultimately, how you respond to the author's style contributes greatly to the pleasure of reading. As American poet Robert Frost put it, "All the fun's in how you say a thing."

LITERARY ELEMENTS OF THE SHORT STORY

"Once upon a time" is a phrase that beckons young and old alike because it lets readers or listeners know that a story is coming. Whether it unfolds through the oral tradition, on the screen of a television, or in the pages of a book like this one, a story takes us out of our lives and helps us make sense of them at the same time.

A story can be defined simply as a telling of incidents or events. A useful definition for this book is that a story is *a fictional narrative shorter than a novel*. Whatever the definition, a story contains the following basic elements.

Plot

Simply put, the plot of a story is what happens in it. As one old saying has it, the writer gets the hero up a tree and then gets him back down again. Also known as narrative structure, a plot usually includes causality: one event causes another, which causes another, and so on, until the story ends. There are a variety of ways that stories move from beginning to end. The most common plot structure moves from **exposition** through **rising action** to a **climax**, followed by the resolution.

In the exposition we are introduced to the main character, or **protagonist**, in his or her familiar **setting**—be that a neighborhood in New York City or a farm in the Salinas Valley of California. If the narrative continued describing this "normal" life, there would be no story. A problem or **conflict** is needed to move the story forward. The conflict may be **external**—perhaps between the protagonist and a family member or between the protagonist and nature; or the problem may be **internal**—between the protagonist's sense of duty and her desire for freedom, for example. Complex stories often have both external and internal conflicts. As the conflict deepens, the story is propelled through the rising action to the climax, or high point. Here that bully of an aunt is confronted, the lifesaving campfire is started, or the inner demon is discovered. The tension of the climax is released in the **resolution**, or as it sometimes called, the *dénouement*, a French word that literally means "untying." In the resolution, the knot of the conflict is untied and everyone that is still alive goes on to a new "normal" existence.

Of course, not all stories conform to the above plot structure. Some stories start at a high point in the action, employing a technique known as *in media res*, which means "in the midst of things." Such stories will fill in the exposition along the way through **dialogue** or embedded stories. Another approach is to tell the ending first and fill in the rest through **flashbacks**, one effect of which is to make the reader pay close attention to motives and causes. Whatever the plot structure, you can be sure that there will be a problem and a character to confront it.

Character

Readers keep turning the pages of stories mainly because they are interested in what happens to the characters. The development of believable characters, called *characterization*, is perhaps the most basic task of the author. But writers have many tools at their disposal. Besides direct description of a character's traits, the author can also reveal character through actions, speeches, thoughts, feelings, and interactions with others. Depending on the type of story being told and the stylistic tradition the author is working in, characters may be fully drawn and realistic or they may be representative character types. How important they are to the story determines whether they are main or primary characters, secondary characters, or minor characters. The more crucial the character is to the plot, the more he or she will be developed by the author. Even in stories that stress realism, some minor characters might only be present as types rather than as individuals.

Another important part of characterization is **point of view**, or the eyes through which the story is told. This is determined through the author's choice of narrator. There are three main narrative points of view: **first-person**, **third-person limited**, and **third-person omniscient**. In the first person or "I" point of view, the narrator tells his or her own story as Huck does in *The Adventures of Huckleberry Finn*. The third-person limited narrator is a character in the story and only sees, hears, and knows what that character can see, hear, and know. This means that he or she might have only partial knowledge and understanding of the events and other characters. Doctor Watson of the Sherlock Holmes tales is a good example of this type of narrator. Often this limited point of view is that of the major character or protagonist, but sometimes the author chooses to tell the story from the limited point of view of a secondary character.

The third-person omniscient narrator sees all and is able to comment on any aspect of the story because he or she is an outsider, not a character in the story. Readers often like to equate the omniscient narrator with the author, but it is good to remember that any narrator or point of view is a carefully developed tool and not simply the author's voice. Some stories switch back and forth between various points of view.

Setting

A **setting** is where and when a story takes place. It is important because environment has a strong impact on what happens in a story. In this book, for example, some stories are set in Harlem, New York; a ranching area of California; and a sleepy town in the Deep South. These environments influence not only the action but also the characters' attitudes. Setting can also help to shape how characters speak and behave. Sometimes the setting of a story assumes almost as much importance in the reader's imagination as memorable characters do.

Theme

The **theme** is the underlying meaning or message of a story. A story may evoke more than one theme, depending upon your interpretation of the narrative. For example, a story in which a character struggles with a decision to lead a conventional life or seek freedom and adventure could be interpreted several ways. One person might summarize the theme of the story as "rash behavior leads to ruin," whereas another might say "it is better to have tried and failed than to have never tried at all." Whatever theme you might come up with for a story, it is important to realize that the theme statement is not the story. Authors usually don't write stories with a theme in mind. They might get an idea for a story from a news item, which gives them an idea for a character. Once the character is alive on the page, the character may take the story into places the author never dreamed. And that is the point, after all. We read stories so that they will take us to places we have never been before. Have a good trip!

For a full list of literary terms, see the Glossary of Literary Terms on pages 758–761.

Unit One
Finding an American Voice   1820s to 1850s

Falls at Catskill, Thomas Cole

Developing a National Literature

The writers in Unit One, beginning with Washington Irving and ending with Herman Melville, are considered among the most important in all of American literature. Irving was the first American to be admired abroad due to his roguish characters and amiable depiction of old New York; and he, along with Hawthorne, Poe, and Melville, has inspired and influenced every American writer since that time.

Before Washington Irving, England provided Americans with most of their reading material. Ironically, for a newly freed colony, most Americans did not deem an American writer important until England declared him so. The Frenchman Alexis de Tocqueville, who wrote the classic treatise *Democracy in America* (1835, 1840), was blunt: "The inhabitants of the United States have . . . properly speaking, no literature."

After the Revolutionary War and the War of 1812, Americans were eager to assert their own national identity. Commentators called on American writers to cease being "secondhand Englishmen" and to capture the authentic America in their fiction.

Social and Economic Changes

What did it mean to be an American during the period of 1820 to 1860?

These were years of astonishing growth and change. Americans were pushing westward, driven by the Doctrine of Manifest Destiny—a belief in their God-given right to expand the country's borders to the Pacific Ocean and to exert social and economic control throughout North America.

With the advent of the Industrial Age, stunning technological changes took place, affecting the way Americans viewed themselves as well as the rest of the world. As train tracks began to connect more towns, travel by stagecoach and horseback diminished; and with the invention of steamboats, cross-Atlantic travel became easier. Steam-powered printing presses spurred the boom in the periodical and gift book markets, providing writers with burgeoning new audiences. Even something as simple as an inexpensive postage stamp was a wondrous development.

These advances in travel and communication all ripened conditions for American writers to connect with each other and to get more of their work published. Nevertheless, writers of serious fiction found it almost impossible to make a living by their pen alone. American publishers much preferred English writers—not for content but for business reasons. Differing copyright laws between the two countries meant that U.S. publishers could profit more by "pirating" and printing the work of English writers as opposed to paying royalties to American authors.

Transcendentalism

Another significant development in the 19th century was the movement known as Transcendentalism. The philosophy of Transcendentalism was based in the belief that wisdom came from within; that there was something that transcended external experience. Its adherents—writers and philosophers such as Henry David Thoreau, Ralph Waldo Emerson, and Margaret Fuller— were free-thinking individualists, with an affinity for nature and a credo of self-sufficiency. Many were abolitionists, whose eloquent denunciations of slavery helped to hasten its end.

Writers Nathaniel Hawthorne and Herman Melville were keenly aware of the Transcendentalists' ideas and shared their concern that America, a country founded on ideals of freedom and justice, should not engage in slavery and genocide against African Americans and Native Americans. Melville was particularly horrified by slavery, calling it "man's foulest crime." By the end of this period, the Mexican-American War (1846–1848) and the Civil War (1861–1865) would further challenge America's idealistic heritage.

Romanticism

The period from 1820 to 1865 is generally considered the Romantic period in American letters, mirroring what was happening in literature and the arts in Europe. The Romantics valued the individual and intuition over society's rules and logic: the literary imagination was freed to include dreams and the supernatural, often in highly expressive language.

Edgar Allan Poe believed that a short story was the link between poetry and longer prose and so should be full of "poetic suggestion." The writing of this time was highly figurative—full of symbols and metaphors—with allusions to Scripture, myth, Shakespeare, and other classics known to most readers of the day. Writers used allegories and parables, "moralistic" literary forms their readers were comfortable with from folktales and the Bible. Fictional characters were often stand-ins for ideas, not the psychologically complex characters that would come later in the century.

All the same, Hawthorne began to explore the inner life of his characters. Mining New England Puritan history, he described the hysterical atmosphere of prejudice and persecution in the Salem witchcraft trials. In fact, much of what America knows today about the Puritans comes to us from his stories and novels. Poe derided the moral concerns of Hawthorne, firmly believing that the "job" of literature was not to provide a moral lesson. Nevertheless, Hawthorne's obsession with human arrogance, death, and depravity were themes that had much in common with his fellow mid-century writers. Melville considered Hawthorne the first American writer to truly represent the American spirit, finding a soul mate in his pessimistic predecessor.

Though all of these writers are known for other literary forms—novels, poetry, history, and literary criticism—the short stories included here represent some of their finest writing.

Before You Read

Washington Irving 1783–1859

About the Author

Born during the final days of the Revolutionary War, Washington Irving would grow up to honor his newly formed country in many ways. He served as a militia colonel and diplomat and worked as a lawyer and businessman. But his most significant contributions were as a writer. An originator of the short story, he was the first American author to cause a stir on both sides of the Atlantic.

Irving was the youngest of eleven children born to a prominent New York City family. Though a great prankster and all-around fun lover, Irving dutifully studied law and worked in the family business. He amused himself by following his true interests—reading, traveling, and writing. His first book, *A History of New York from the Beginning of the World to the End of the Dutch Dynasty* (1809), ingeniously mixed genuine history with pure hoax. It was a comic masterpiece and a huge success.

After a difficult decade in which his young fiancée died and the family business failed, Irving intensified his writing efforts. Writing from Europe, he drew on childhood memories of the upstate New York countryside to create "Rip Van Winkle" and "The Legend of Sleepy Hollow" (*The Sketch Book*, 1820). These lively stories captivated both European and American readers. Irving spent many years in Europe writing "sketches" of life in England, Spain, and France.

Upon returning home, he devoted the rest of his years to producing nonfiction works on American subjects. Shortly before his death he completed a five-volume biography of his namesake—George Washington.

★★★★★★★★★★★

The Author's Style

Irving created a recipe for what would become the classic American tale: write in clear and lively prose, "sketch" colorful images, and choose a uniquely American subject. Though short in length, his stories include abundant visual images, perhaps as a result of his interest in painting. The rich details help create vivid characters and a compelling atmosphere.

Irving avoided preaching in his fiction, but he did criticize—gently—the human tendency to conform. He had a talent for blending playfulness and satire. "The Legend of Sleepy Hollow," especially, succeeds in evoking a sense of magic while at the same time ridiculing superstition.

Figures from folktales, mythic locations, and fictional narrators, such as the befuddled Diedrich Knickerbocker—the supposed "author" of *A History of New York*—were hallmarks of his early work, as were ambiguous endings. Readers of "Sleepy Hollow," for example, are left pondering the fate of the hapless Ichabod Crane.

The Legend of
Sleepy Hollow

Washington Irving

*I*n the bosom of one of those spacious coves which indent the eastern shore of the Hudson, at that broad expansion of the river denominated by the ancient Dutch navigators the Tappan Zee,[1] and where they always pru.dently shortened sail, and implored the protection of St. Nicholas when they crossed, there lies a small market-town or rural port, which by some is called Greensburgh, but which is more generally and properly known by the name of Tarry Town. This name was given, we are told, in former days, by the good housewives of the adjacent country, from the **inveterate propensity** of their husbands to linger about the village tavern on market-days. Be that as it may, I do not vouch for the fact, but merely advert to it for the sake of being precise and authentic. Not far from this village, perhaps about two miles, there is a little valley, or rather lap of land,

inveterate:
firmly established

propensity:
tendency

---

1 **Tappan Zee:** a wide spot ("sea") in the Hudson River

among high hills, which is one of the quietest places in the whole world. A small brook glides through it, with just murmur enough to lull one to repose; and the occasional whistle of a quail, or tapping of a woodpecker, is almost the only sound that ever breaks in upon the uniform tranquillity. I recollect that, when a stripling,[2] my first exploit in squirrel-shooting was in a grove of tall walnut-trees that shades one side of the valley. I had wandered into it at noon time, when all nature is peculiarly quiet, and was startled by the roar of my own gun, as it broke the Sabbath stillness around, and was prolonged and reverberated by the angry echoes. If ever I should wish for a retreat, whither I might steal from the world and its distractions, and dream quietly away the remnant of a troubled life, I know of none more promising than this little valley.

From the listless repose of the place, and the peculiar character of its inhabitants, who are descendants from the original Dutch settlers, this **sequestered** glen has long been known by the name of SLEEPY HOLLOW, and its rustic lads are called the Sleepy Hollow Boys throughout all the neighboring country. A drowsy, dreamy influence seems to hang over the land, and to pervade the very atmosphere. Some say that the place was bewitched by a high German doctor, during the early days of the settlement; others, that an old Indian chief, the prophet or wizard of his tribe, held his powwows there before the country was discovered by Master Hendrick Hudson. Certain it is, the place still continues under the sway of some witching power, that holds a spell over the minds of the good people, causing them to walk in a continual reverie. They are given to all kinds of marvellous beliefs; are subject to trances and visions; and frequently see strange sights, and hear music and voices in the air. The whole neighborhood abounds with local tales, haunted spots, and twilight superstitions; stars shoot and meteors glare oftener across the valley than in any other part of the country, and the nightmare, with her whole nine fold[3] seems to make it the favorite scene of her gambols.

The dominant spirit, however, that haunts this enchanted region, and seems to be commander-in-chief of all the powers of the air, is the **apparition** of a figure on horseback without a head. It is said by some to be the ghost of a Hessian trooper,[4] whose head had been carried away by a cannon-ball, in some nameless battle during the Revolutionary War; and who is ever and

sequestered:
hidden; secluded

apparition:
ghost; spirit

---

2 **stripling:** a youth

3 **nightmare…nine fold:** the nightmare (female horse) was a demon in folktales, and her nine foals were imps

4 **Hessian trooper:** a German mercenary fighter hired by the British to fight American colonists

anon seen by the country folk, hurrying along in the gloom of night, as if on the wings of the wind. His haunts are not confined to the valley, but extend at times to the adjacent roads, and especially to the vicinity of a church at no great distance. Indeed certain of the most authentic historians of those parts, who have been careful in collecting and collating the floating facts concerning this spectre, allege that the body of the trooper, having been buried in the church-yard, the ghost rides forth to the scene of battle in nightly quest of his head; and that the rushing speed with which he sometimes passes along the Hollow, like a midnight blast, is owing to his being belated, and in a hurry to get back to the church-yard before daybreak.

Such is the general purport of this legendary superstition, which has furnished materials for many a wild story in that region of shadows; and the spectre is known, at all the country firesides, by the name of the Headless Horseman of Sleepy Hollow.

It is remarkable that the visionary propensity I have mentioned is not confined to the native inhabitants of the valley, but is unconsciously imbibed by every one who resides there for a time. However wide awake they may have been before they entered that sleepy region, they are sure, in a little time, to inhale the witching influence of the air, and begin to grow imaginative—to dream dreams, and see apparitions.

I mention this peaceful spot with all possible laud;[5] for it is in such little retired Dutch valleys, found here and there embosomed in the great State of New York, that population, manners, and customs remain fixed; while the great torrent of migration and improvement, which is making such incessant changes in other parts of this restless country, sweeps by them unobserved. They are like those little nooks of still water which border a rapid stream; where we may see the straw and bubble riding quietly at anchor, or slowly revolving in their mimic[6] harbor, undisturbed by the rush of the passing current. Though many years have elapsed since I trod the drowsy shades of Sleepy Hollow, yet I question whether I should not still find the same trees and the same families vegetating in its sheltered bosom.

In this by-place of nature, there abode, in a remote period of American history, that is to say, some thirty years since, a worthy wight[7] of the name of Ichabod Crane; who sojourned, or, as he expressed it, "tarried," in Sleepy

---

5 **laud:** praise

6 **mimic:** imitation

7 **wight:** a creature

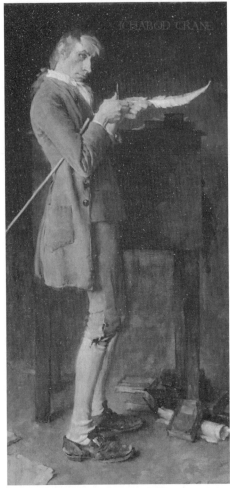

Ichabod Crane, Norman Rockwell, 1937

Hollow, for the purpose of instructing the children of the vicinity. He was a native of Connecticut, a State which supplies the Union with pioneers for the mind as well as for the forest, and sends forth yearly its legions of frontier woodsmen and country schoolmasters. The cognomen[8] of Crane was not inapplicable to his person. He was tall, but exceedingly lank, with narrow shoulders, long arms and legs, hands that dangled a mile out of his sleeves, feet that might have served for shovels, and his whole frame most loosely hung together. His head was small, and flat at top, with huge ears, large green glassy eyes, and a long snipe nose, so that it looked like a weather-cock perched upon his spindle neck, to tell which way the wind blew. To see him striding along the profile of a hill on a windy day, with his clothes bagging and fluttering about him, one might have mistaken him for the genius of famine descending upon the earth, or some scarecrow eloped from a cornfield.

His school-house was a low building of one large room, rudely constructed of logs; the windows partly glazed, and partly patched with leaves of old copy-books. It was most ingeniously secured at vacant hours by a withe[9] twisted in the handle of the door, and stakes set against the window shutters; so that, though a thief might get in with perfect ease, he would find some embarrassment in getting out: an idea most probably borrowed by the architect, Yost Van Houten, from the mystery of an eelpot. The school-house stood in a rather lonely but pleasant situation, just at the foot of a woody hill, with a brook running close by, and a formidable birch-tree growing at one end of it. From hence the low

---

8 cognomen: a name

9 withe: a thin, flexible branch or twig

murmur of his pupils' voices, conning[10] over their lessons, might be heard in a drowsy summer's day, like the hum of a bee-hive; interrupted now and then by the authoritative voice of the master, in the tone of menace or command; or, peradventure, by the appalling sound of the birch, as he urged some tardy loiterer along the flowery path of knowledge. Truth to say, he was a conscientious man, and ever bore in mind the golden maxim, "Spare the rod and spoil the child."—Ichabod Crane's scholars certainly were not spoiled.

I would not have it imagined, however, that he was one of those cruel potentates[11] of the school, who joy in the smart of their subjects; on the contrary, he administered justice with discrimination rather than severity, taking the burden off the backs of the weak, and laying it on those of the strong. Your mere puny stripling, that winced at the least flourish of the rod, was passed by with indulgence; but the claims of justice were satisfied by inflicting a double portion on some little, tough, wrong headed, broad-skirted Dutch urchin, who sulked and swelled and grew dogged and sullen beneath the birch. All this he called "doing his duty by their parents"; and he never inflicted a chastisement without following it by the assurance, so consolatory to the smarting urchin, that "he would remember it, and thank him for it the longest day he had to live."

When school hours were over, he was even the companion and playmate of the larger boys; and on holiday afternoons would convoy some of the smaller ones home, who happened to have pretty sisters, or good housewives for mothers, noted for the comforts of the cupboard. Indeed it behooved him to keep on good terms with his pupils. The revenue arising from his school was small, and would have been scarcely sufficient to furnish him with daily bread, for he was a huge feeder and, though lank, had the dilating powers of an anaconda;[12] but to help out his maintenance, he was, according to country custom in those parts, boarded and lodged at the houses of the farmers, whose children he instructed. With these he lived successively a week at a time; thus going the rounds of the neighborhood, with all his worldly effects tied up in a cotton handkerchief.

That all this might not be too **onerous** on the purses of his rustic patrons, who are apt to consider the costs of schooling a grievous burden, and schoolmasters as mere drones, he had various ways of rendering himself both

onerous: troublesome; burdensome

---

10 **conning:** studying

11 **potentates:** those who wield great power, such as kings or other rulers

12 **anaconda:** a large snake

useful and agreeable. He assisted the farmers occasionally in the lighter labors of their farms; helped to make hay; mended the fences; took the horses to water; drove the cows from pasture; and cut wood for the winter fire. He laid aside, too, all the dominant dignity and absolute sway with which he lorded it in his little empire, the school, and became wonderfully gentle and **ingratiating**. He found favor in the eyes of the mothers, by petting the children, particularly the youngest; and like the lion bold, which whilom[13] so magnanimously the lamb did hold, he would sit with a child on one knee, and rock a cradle with his foot for whole hours together.

ingratiating: disarming; charming in an oily way

In addition to his other vocations, he was the singing-master of the neighborhood, and picked up many bright shillings by instructing the young folks in psalmody.[14] It was a matter of no little vanity to him, on Sundays, to take his station in front of the church gallery, with a band of chosen singers; where, in his own mind, he completely carried away the palm from the parson. Certain it is, his voice resounded far above all the rest of the congregation; and there are peculiar quavers still to be heard in that church, and which may even be heard half a mile off, quite to the opposite side of the mill-pond, on a still Sunday morning, which are said to be legitimately descended from the nose of Ichabod Crane. Thus, by divers little make-shifts in that ingenious way which is commonly denominated "by hook and by crook," the worthy pedagogue[15] got on tolerably enough, and was thought, by all who understood nothing of the labor of headwork, to have a wonderfully easy life of it.

The schoolmaster is generally a man of some importance in the female circle of a rural neighborhood; being considered a kind of idle, gentlemanlike personage, of vastly superior taste and accomplishments to the rough country swains,[16] and, indeed, inferior in learning only to the parson. His appearance, therefore, is apt to occasion some little stir at the tea-table of a farmhouse, and the addition of a supernumerary[17] dish of cakes or sweetmeats, or, peradventure, the parade of a silver tea-pot. Our man of letters, therefore, was peculiarly happy in the smiles of all the country damsels. How he would figure among them in the churchyard, between services on Sundays!

---

13 **whilom:** formerly

14 **psalmody:** singing rhymed versions of the Psalms

15 **pedagogue:** a dull, formal teacher or schoolmaster

16 **swains:** country lads; also refers to romantic admirers

17 **supernumerary:** extra; more than is required

gathering grapes for them from the wild vines that overrun the surrounding trees; reciting for their amusement all the epitaphs on the tombstones; or sauntering, with a whole bevy of them, along the banks of the adjacent mill-pond; while the more bashful country bumpkins hung sheepishly back, envying his superior elegance and address.

From his half-itinerant life, also, he was a kind of travelling gazette, carrying the whole budget of local gossip from house to house; so that his appearance was always greeted with satisfaction. He was, moreover, esteemed by the women as a man of great **erudition**, for he had read several books quite through, and was a perfect master of Cotton Mather's "History of New England Witchcraft,"[18] in which, by the way, he most firmly and potently believed.

> **erudition:** learning; knowledge

He was, in fact, an odd mixture of small shrewdness and simple **credulity**. His appetite for the marvellous, and his powers of digesting it, were equally extraordinary; and both had been increased by his residence in this spellbound region. No tale was too gross or monstrous for his **capacious** swallow. It was often his delight, after his school was dismissed in the afternoon, to stretch himself on the rich bed of clover bordering the little brook that whimpered by his school-house, and there con over old Mather's direful tales, until the gathering dusk of the evening made the printed page a mere mist before his eyes. Then, as he wended his way, by swamp and stream, and awful woodland, to the farmhouse where he happened to be quartered, every sound of nature, at that witching hour, fluttered his excited imagination: the moan of the whippoorwill from the hillside; the boding cry of the tree-toad, that **harbinger** of storm; the dreary hooting of the screech-owl, or the sudden rustling in the thicket of birds frightened from their roost. The fire-flies, too, which sparkled most vividly in the darkest places, now and then startled him, as one of uncommon brightness would stream across his path; and if, by chance, a huge blockhead of a beetle came winging his blundering flight against him, the poor varlet[19] was ready to give up the ghost, with the idea that he was struck with a witch's token. His only resource on such occasions, either to drown thought or drive away evil spirits, was to sing psalm tunes; and the good people of Sleepy Hollow, as they sat by their doors of an evening, were often filled with awe, at hearing his nasal melody, "in linked sweetness long drawn out," floating from the distant hill, or along the dusky road.

> **credulity:** faith; trust

> **capacious:** ample; immense

> **harbinger:** precursor; foreshadower

---

18 **Cotton Mather's "History of New England Witchcraft":** books about the supernatural world published in 1689 and 1693; they point to Crane's superstitiousness

19 **varlet:** rascal

Another of his sources of fearful pleasure was, to pass long winter evenings with the old Dutch wives, as they sat spinning by the fire, with a row of apples roasting and spluttering along the hearth, and listen to their marvellous tales of ghosts and goblins, and haunted fields, and haunted brooks, and haunted bridges, and haunted houses, and particularly of the headless horseman, or Galloping Hessian of the Hollow, as they sometimes called him. He would delight them equally by his anecdotes of witchcraft, and of the direful omens and **portentous** sights and sounds in the air, which prevailed in the earlier times of Connecticut; and would frighten them woefully with speculations upon comets and shooting stars, and with the alarming fact that the world did absolutely turn round, and that they were half the time topsy-turvy!

portentous:
ominous;
prophetic

But if there was a pleasure in all this, while snugly cuddling in the chimney corner of a chamber that was all of a ruddy glow from the crackling wood fire, and where, of course, no spectre dared to show his face, it was dearly purchased by the terrors of his subsequent walk homewards. What fearful shapes and shadows beset his path amidst the dim and ghastly glare of a snowy night!—With what wistful look did he eye every trembling ray of light streaming across the waste fields from some distant window!—How often was he appalled by some shrub covered with snow, which, like a sheeted spectre, beset his very path!—How often did he shrink with curdling awe at the sound of his own steps on the frosty crust beneath his feet; and dread to look over his shoulder, lest he should behold some uncouth being tramping close behind him!—and how often was he thrown into complete dismay by some rushing blast, howling among the trees, in the idea that it was the Galloping Hessian on one of his nightly scourings!

All these, however, were mere terrors of the night, phantoms of the mind that walk in darkness; and though he had seen many spectres in his time, and been more than once beset by Satan in divers shapes, in his lonely perambulations,[20] yet daylight put an end to all these evils; and he would have passed a pleasant life of it, in despite of the devil and all his works, if his path had not been crossed by a being that causes more perplexity to mortal man than ghosts, goblins, and the whole race of witches put together, and that was- —a woman.

Among the musical disciples who assembled, one evening in each week, to receive his instructions in psalmody, was Katrina Van Tassel, the daughter and only child of a substantial Dutch farmer. She was a blooming lass of fresh

---

20 **perambulations:** wanderings

eighteen; plump as a partridge; ripe and melting and rosy-cheeked as one of her father's peaches, and universally famed, not merely for her beauty, but her vast expectations. She was withal a little of a coquette,[21] as might be perceived even in her dress, which was a mixture of ancient and modern fashions, as most suited to set off her charms. She wore the ornaments of pure yellow gold, which her great-great-grandmother had brought over from Saardam;[22] the tempting stomacher[23] of the time; and withal a provokingly short petticoat, to display the prettiest foot and ankle in the country around.

Ichabod Crane had a soft and foolish heart towards the sex; and it is not to be wondered at, that so tempting a morsel soon found favor in his eyes; more especially after he had visited her in her paternal mansion. Old Baltus Van Tassel was a perfect picture of a thriving, contented, liberal-hearted farmer. He seldom, it is true, sent either his eyes or his thoughts beyond the boundaries of his own farm; but within those everything was snug, happy, and well-conditioned. He was satisfied with his wealth, but not proud of it; and piqued[24] himself upon the hearty abundance rather than the style in which he lived. His stronghold was situated on the banks of the Hudson, in one of those green, sheltered, fertile nooks in which the Dutch farmers are so fond of nestling. A great elm-tree spread its broad branches over it; at the foot of which bubbled up a spring of the softest and sweetest water, in a little well, formed of a barrel; and then stole sparkling away through the grass, to a neighboring brook, that bubbled along among alders and dwarf willows. Hard by the farmhouse was a vast barn that might have served for a church; every window and crevice of which seemed bursting forth with the treasures of the farm; the flail[25] was busily resounding within it from morning till night; swallows and martins skimmed twittering about the eaves; and rows of pigeons, some with one eye turned up, as if watching the weather, some with their heads under their wings, or buried in their bosoms, and others swelling, and cooing, and bowing about their dames, were enjoying the sunshine on the roof. Sleek unwieldy porkers were grunting in the repose and abundance of their pens; whence sallied forth, now and then, troops of sucking pigs, as if to snuff the air. A stately squadron of snowy geese were riding in an adjoining pond, convoying whole fleets of ducks; regiments of turkeys were gobbling

---

21 **coquette:** a flirty young woman

22 **Saardam:** now Zaandam, a city near Amsterdam, Holland

23 **stomacher:** the center front piece of a dress bodice

24 **piqued:** prided

25 **flail:** a hand threshing implement

through the farmyard, and guinea fowls fretting about it, like ill-tempered housewives, with their peevish discontented cry. Before the barn door strutted the gallant cock, that pattern of a husband, a warrior, and a fine gentleman, clapping his burnished wings, and crowing in the pride and gladness of his heart—sometimes tearing up the earth with his feet, and then generously calling his ever-hungry family of wives and children to enjoy the rich morsel which he had discovered.

sumptuous: extravagant, impressive

The pedagogue's mouth watered, as he looked upon this **sumptuous** promise of luxurious winter fare. In his devouring mind's eye he pictured to himself every roasting-pig running about with a pudding in his belly, and an apple in his mouth; the pigeons were snugly put to bed in a comfortable pie, and tucked in with a coverlet of crust; the geese were swimming in their own gravy; and the ducks pairing cosily in dishes, like snug married couples, with a decent competency of onion sauce. In the porkers he saw carved out the future sleek side of bacon, and juicy relishing ham; not a turkey but he beheld daintily trussed up, with its gizzard under its wing, and, peradventure, a necklace of savory sausages; and even bright chanticleer[26] himself lay sprawling on his back, in a side-dish, with uplifted claws, as if craving that quarter which his chivalrous spirit disdained to ask while living.

As the enraptured Ichabod fancied all this, and as he rolled his great green eyes over the fat meadowlands, the rich fields of wheat, of rye, of buckwheat, and Indian corn, and the orchard burdened with ruddy fruit, which surrounded the warm tenement[27] of Van Tassel, his heart yearned after the damsel who was to inherit these domains, and his imagination expanded with the idea how they might be readily turned into cash, and the money invested in immense tracts of wild land, and shingle palaces in the wilderness. Nay, his busy fancy already realized his hopes, and presented to him the blooming Katrina, with a whole family of children, mounted on the top of a wagon loaded with household trumpery,[28] with pots and kettles dangling beneath; and he beheld himself bestriding a pacing mare, with a colt at her heels, setting out for Kentucky, Tennessee, or the Lord knows where.

When he entered the house, the conquest of his heart was complete. It was one of those spacious farmhouses, with high-ridged, but lowly sloping roofs, built in the style handed down from the first Dutch settlers; the low

---

26 **chanticleer:** a rooster

27 **tenement:** a dwelling or residence

28 **trumpery:** frivolous items; junk

projecting eaves forming a piazza along the front, capable of being closed up in bad weather. Under this were hung flails, harness, various utensils of husbandry,[29] and nets for fishing in the neighboring river. Benches were built along the sides for summer use; and a great spinning-wheel at one end, and a churn at the other, showed the various uses to which this important porch might be devoted. From this piazza the wondering Ichabod entered the hall, which formed the centre of the mansion and the place of usual residence. Here, rows of **resplendent** pewter, ranged on a long dresser, dazzled his eyes. In one corner stood a huge bag of wool ready to be spun; in another a quantity of linsey-woolsey[30] just from the loom; ears of Indian corn, and strings of dried apples and peaches, hung in gay festoons along the walls, mingled with the gaud[31] of red peppers; and a door left ajar gave him a peep into the best parlor, where the claw-footed chairs and dark mahogany tables shone like mirrors; andirons, with their accompanying shovel and tongs, glistened from their covert of asparagus tops; mock-oranges and conch-shells decorated the mantel-piece; strings of various colored birds' eggs were suspended above it; a great ostrich egg was hung from the centre of the room, and a corner cupboard, knowingly left open, displayed immense treasures of old silver and well-mended china.

resplendent: shining; glossy

From the moment Ichabod laid his eyes upon these regions of delight, the peace of his mind was at an end, and his only study was how to gain the affections of the peerless daughter of Van Tassel. In this enterprise, however, he had more real difficulties than generally fell to the lot of a knight-errant[32] of yore, who seldom had anything but giants, enchanters, fiery dragons, and such like easily conquered adversaries, to contend with; and had to make his way merely through gates of iron and brass, and walls of adamant,[33] to the castle keep, where the lady of his heart was confined; all which he achieved as easily as a man would carve his way to the centre of a Christmas pie; and then the lady gave him her hand as a matter of course. Ichabod, on the contrary, had to win his way to the heart of a country coquette, beset with a labyrinth of whims and caprices, which were forever presenting new difficulties and impediments; and he had to encounter a host of fearful adversaries of real flesh and blood, the numerous rustic admirers, who beset

---

29 **husbandry:** farming

30 **linsey-woolsey:** a coarse fabric woven from linen (or cotton) and coarse wool

31 **gaud:** a dazzling display

32 **knight-errant:** a knight who travels in search of adventure

33 **adamant:** a fabled, impenetrably hard stone

every portal to her heart; keeping a watchful and angry eye upon each other, but ready to fly out in the common cause against any new competitor.

Among these the most formidable was a burly, roaring, roistering blade,[34] of the name of Abraham, or, according to the Dutch abbreviation, Brom Van Brunt, the hero of the country round, which rang with his feats of strength and hardihood. He was broad-shouldered, and double-jointed, with short curly black hair, and a bluff, but not unpleasant **countenance**, having a mingled air of fun and arrogance. From his Herculean[35] frame and great powers of limb, he had received the nickname of BROM BONES, by which he was universally known. He was famed for great knowledge and skill in horsemanship, being as dexterous on horseback as a Tartar.[36] He was foremost at all races and cockfights; and, with the ascendancy which bodily strength acquires in rustic life, was the umpire in all disputes, setting his hat on one side, and giving his decisions with an air and tone admitting of no gainsay or appeal. He was always ready for either a fight or a frolic; but had more mischief than ill-will in his composition; and, with all his over-bearing roughness, there was a strong dash of waggish good humor at bottom. He had three or four boon[37] companions, who regarded him as their model, and at the head of whom he scoured the country, attending every scene of feud or merriment for miles round. In cold weather he was distinguished by a fur cap, surmounted with a flaunting fox's tail; and when the folks at a country gathering descried this well-known crest at a distance, whisking about among a squad of hard riders, they always stood by for a squall. Sometimes his crew would be heard dashing along past the farmhouses at midnight, with whoop and halloo, like a troop of Don Cossacks;[38] and the old dames, startled out of their sleep, would listen for a moment till the hurry-scurry had clattered by, and then exclaim, "Ay, there goes Brom Bones and his gang!" The neighbors looked upon him with a mixture of awe, admiration, and goodwill; and when any madcap prank, or rustic brawl, occurred in the vicinity, always shook their heads, and warranted Brom Bones was at the bottom of it.

This rantipole[39] hero had for some time singled out the blooming Katrina

countenance: aspect; face

---

34 **roistering blade:** a wild, dashing young man

35 **Herculean:** like Hercules, the mythical hero who possessed incredible strength

36 **Tartar:** a native of Tartary, a historical region in Central Asia, whose inhabitants were said to be of violent temperament

37 **boon:** merry; jovial

38 **Don Cossacks:** Russian cavalrymen

39 **rantipole:** wild; reckless

for the object of his uncouth gallantries; and though his amorous toyings were something like the gentle caresses and endearments of a bear, yet it was whispered that she did not altogether discourage his hopes. Certain it is, his advances were signals for rival candidates to retire, who felt no inclination to cross a lion in his amours; insomuch, that, when his horse was seen tied to Van Tassel's paling,[40] on a Sunday night, a sure sign that his master was courting, or, as it is termed, "sparking," within, all other suitors passed by in despair, and carried the war into other quarters.

Such was the formidable rival with whom Ichabod Crane had to contend, and, considering all things, a stouter man than he would have shrunk from the competition, and a wiser man would have despaired. He had, however, a happy mixture of **pliability** and perseverance in his nature; he was in form and spirit like a supple-jack[41]—yielding, but tough; though he bent, he never broke; and though he bowed beneath the slightest pressure, yet, the moment it was away—jerk! he was as erect, and carried his head as high as ever.

pliability: flexibility; suppleness

To have taken the field openly against his rival would have been madness . . .

To have taken the field openly against his rival would have been madness; for he was not a man to be thwarted in his amours, any more than that stormy lover, Achilles.[42] Ichabod, therefore, made his advances in a quiet and gently **insinuating** manner. Under cover of his character of singing-master, he made frequent visits at the farmhouse; not that he had anything to apprehend from the meddlesome interference of parents, which is so often a stumbling-block in the path of lovers. Balt Van Tassel was an easy, indulgent soul; he loved his daughter better even than his pipe, and, like a reasonable man and an excellent father, let her have her way in everything. His notable little wife, too, had enough to do to attend to her housekeeping and manage her poultry; for, as she sagely observed, ducks and geese are foolish things, and must be looked after, but girls can take care of themselves. Thus while the busy dame bustled about the house, or plied her spinning-wheel at one end of the piazza, honest Balt would sit smoking his evening pipe at the other, watching the achievements of a little wooden warrior, who, armed with a sword in each hand, was most valiantly fighting the wind on the pinnacle of the barn. In the mean time, Ichabod would carry on his suit with the

insinuating: flattering; ingratiating

---

40 **paling:** fence

41 **supple-jack:** a cane that comes from a tough, yet flexible, climbing plant

42 **Achilles:** a warrior from Homer's *Iliad*, who loses his beloved to the King, then seeks revenge

daughter by the side of the spring under the great elm, or sauntering along in the twilight, that hour so favorable to the lover's eloquence.

I profess not to know how women's hearts are wooed and won. To me they have always been matters of riddle and admiration. Some seem to have but one vulnerable point, or door of access; while others have a thousand avenues, and may be captured in a thousand different ways. It is a great triumph of skill to gain the former, but a still greater proof of generalship to maintain possession of the latter, for the man must battle for his fortress at every door and window. He who wins a thousand common hearts is therefore entitled to some renown; but he who keeps undisputed sway over the heart of a coquette, is indeed a hero. Certain it is, this was not the case with the **redoubtable** Brom Bones; and from the moment Ichabod Crane made his advances, the interests of the former evidently declined; his horse was no longer seen tied at the palings on Sunday nights, and a deadly feud gradually arose between him and the preceptor[43] of Sleepy Hollow.

Brom, who had a degree of rough chivalry in his nature, would fain have carried matters to open warfare, and have settled their pretensions to the lady according to the mode of those most concise and simple reasoners, the knights-errant of yore—by single combat; but Ichabod was too conscious of the superior might of his adversary to enter the lists against him: he had overheard a boast of Bones, that he would "double the school-master up, and lay him on a shelf of his own schoolhouse"; and he was too wary to give him an opportunity. There was something extremely provoking in this obstinately pacific system; it left Brom no alternative but to draw upon the funds of rustic waggery[44] in his disposition, and to play off **boorish** practical jokes upon his rival. Ichabod became the object of whimsical persecution to Bones and his gang of rough riders. They harried his hitherto peaceful domains; smoked out his singing school, by stopping up the chimney; broke into the school-house at night, in spite of its formidable fastenings of withe and window stakes, and turned everything topsy-turvy: so that the poor schoolmaster began to think all the witches in the country held their meetings there. But what was still more annoying, Brom took opportunities of turning him into ridicule in presence of his mistress, and had a scoundrel dog whom he taught to whine in the most ludicrous manner, and introduced as a rival of Ichabod's to instruct her in psalmody.

In this way matters went on for some time, without producing any

redoubt-able: famous; celebrated

boorish: unrefined; ill-mannered

---

43 **preceptor:** the headmaster

44 **waggery:** mischief; devilment

material effect on the relative situation of the contending powers. On a fine autumnal afternoon, Ichabod, in **pensive** mood, sat enthroned on the lofty stool whence he usually watched all the concerns of his little literary realm. In his hand he swayed a ferule,[45] that sceptre of despotic power; the birch of justice reposed on three nails, behind the throne, a constant terror to evil doers; while on the desk before him might be seen sundry contraband articles and prohibited weapons, detected upon the persons of idle urchins; such as half-munched apples, popguns, whirligigs, fly-cages, and whole legions of rampant little paper game-cocks.[46] Apparently there had been some appalling act of justice recently inflicted, for his scholars were all busily intent upon their books, or slyly whispering behind them with one eye kept upon the master; and a kind of buzzing stillness reigned throughout the schoolroom. It was suddenly interrupted by the appearance of a Negro, in tow-cloth jacket and trousers, a round-crowned fragment of a hat, like the cap of Mercury,[47] and mounted on the back of a ragged, wild, half-broken colt, which he managed with a rope by way of halter. He came clattering up to the school-door with an invitation to Ichabod to attend a merry-making or "quilting frolic," to be held that evening at Mynheer Van Tassel's; and having delivered his message with that air of importance, and effort at fine language, which a Negro is apt to display on petty embassies of the kind, he dashed over the brook, and was seen scampering away up the Hollow, full of the importance and hurry of his mission.

> **pensive:** thoughtful; reflective

All was now bustle and hubbub in the late quiet schoolroom. The scholars were hurried through their lessons, without stopping at trifles; those who were nimble skipped over half with **impunity**, and those who were tardy had a smart application now and then in the rear, to quicken their speed, or help them over a tall word. Books were flung aside without being put away on the shelves, inkstands were overturned, benches thrown down, and the whole school was turned loose an hour before the usual time, bursting forth like a legion of young imps, yelping and racketing about the green, in joy at their early emancipation.

> **impunity:** sense of privilege; feeling of permission

The gallant Ichabod now spent at least an extra half hour at his toilet,[48] brushing and furbishing up his best and indeed only suit of rusty[49] black,

---

45 **ferule:** a flat piece of wood used for punishment

46 **popguns, whirligigs, flycages, . . . game-cocks:** children's toys and treasures

47 **Mercury:** the winged messenger of the gods, symbolic of speed

48 **toilet:** grooming

49 **rusty:** discolored with age

and arranging his looks by a bit of broken looking-glass, that hung up in the school-house. That he might make his appearance before his mistress in the true style of a cavalier, he borrowed a horse from the farmer with whom he was domiciliated,[50] a choleric[51] old Dutchman, of the name of Hans Van Ripper, and, thus gallantly mounted, issued forth, like a knight-errant in quest of adventures. But it is meet I should, in the true spirit of romantic story, give some account of the looks and equipments of my hero and his steed. The animal he bestrode was a broken-down ploughhorse, that had outlived almost everything but his viciousness. He was gaunt and shagged, with a ewe neck and a head like a hammer; his rusty mane and tail were tangled and knotted with burrs; one eye had lost its pupil, and was glaring and spectral; but the other had the gleam of a genuine devil in it. Still he must have had fire and mettle in his day, if we may judge from the name he bore of Gunpowder. He had, in fact, been a favorite steed of his master's, the choleric Van Ripper, who was a furious rider, and had infused, very probably, some of his own spirit into the animal; for, old and broken-down as he looked, there was more of the lurking devil in him than in any young filly in the country.

Ichabod was a suitable figure for such a steed. He rode with short stirrups, which brought his knees nearly up to the pommel of the saddle; his sharp elbows stuck out like grasshoppers'; he carried his whip perpendicularly in his hand, like a sceptre, and, as his horse jogged on, the motion of his arms was not unlike the flapping of a pair of wings. A small wool hat rested on the top of his nose, for so his scanty strip of forehead might be called; and the skirts of his black coat fluttered out almost to the horse's tail. Such was the appearance of Ichabod and his steed, as they shambled out of the gate of Hans Van Ripper, and it was altogether such an apparition as is seldom to be met with in broad daylight.

It was, as I have said, a fine autumnal day, the sky was clear and serene, and nature wore that rich and golden livery which we always associate with the idea of abundance. The forests had put on their sober brown and yellow, while some trees of the tenderer kind had been nipped by the frosts into brilliant dyes of orange, purple, and scarlet. Streaming files of wild ducks began to make their appearance high in the air; the bark of the squirrel might be heard from the groves of beech and hickory nuts, and the pensive whistle of the quail at intervals from the neighboring stubble-field.

---

50 **domiciliated:** housed

51 **choleric:** highly irritable or angry

The small birds were taking their farewell banquets. In the fulness of their revelry, they fluttered, chirping and frolicking, from bush to bush, and tree to tree, capricious from the very profusion and variety around them. There was the honest cock-robin, the favorite game of stripling sportsmen, with its loud **querulous** note; and the twittering blackbirds flying in sable[52] clouds; and the golden-winged woodpecker, with his crimson crest, his broad black gorget, and splendid plumage; and the cedarbird, with its red-tipt wings and yellow-tipt tail, and its little monteiro cap of feathers; and the blue jay, that noisy coxcomb, in his gay light blue coat and white underclothes, screaming and chattering, nodding and bobbing and bowing, and pretending to be on good terms with every songster of the grove.

As Ichabod jogged slowly on his way, his eye, ever open to every symptom of culinary abundance, ranged with delight over the treasures of jolly autumn. On all sides he beheld vast stores of apples; some hanging in oppressive **opulence** on the trees; some gathered into baskets and barrels for the market; others heaped up in rich piles for the cider-press. Farther on he beheld great fields of Indian corn, with its golden ears peeping from their leafy coverts, and holding out the promise of cakes and hasty pudding; and the yellow pumpkins lying beneath them, turning up their fair round bellies to the sun, and giving ample prospects of the most luxurious of pies; and anon he passed the fragrant buckwheat fields, breathing the odor of the bee-hive, and as he beheld them, soft anticipations stole over his mind of dainty slapjacks,[53] well buttered, and garnished with honey or treacle,[54] by the delicate little dimpled hand of Katrina Van Tassel.

Thus feeding his mind with many sweet thoughts and "sugared suppositions," he journeyed along the sides of a range of hills which look out upon some of the goodliest scenes of the mighty Hudson. The sun gradually wheeled his broad disk down into the west. The wide bosom of the Tappan Zee lay motionless and glassy, excepting that here and there a gentle **undulation** waved and prolonged the blue shadow of the distant mountain. A few amber clouds floated in the sky, without a breath of air to move them. The horizon was of a fine golden tint, changing gradually into a pure apple green, and from that into the deep blue of the mid-heaven. A slanting ray lingered on the woody crests of the precipices that overhung some parts of the river, giving greater depth to the dark-gray and purple of their rocky sides. A

querulous: peevish; discontented

opulence: abundance; plenty

undulation: wave; ruffling

---

52 **sable:** black

53 **slapjacks:** pancakes

54 **treacle:** syrup

sloop was loitering in the distance, dropping slowly down with the tide, her sail hanging uselessly against the mast; and as the reflection of the sky gleamed along the still water, it seemed as if the vessel was suspended in the air.

It was toward evening that Ichabod arrived at the castle of the Heer Van Tassel, which he found thronged with the pride and flower of the adjacent country. Old farmers, a spare leathern-faced race, in homespun coats and breeches, blue stockings, huge shoes, and magnificent pewter buckles. Their brisk withered little dames, in close crimped caps, long waisted shortgowns, homespun petticoats, with scissors and pin-cushions, and gay calico pockets hanging on the outside. Buxom lasses, almost as antiquated as their mothers, excepting where a straw hat, a fine ribbon, or perhaps a white frock, gave symptoms of city innovation. The sons, in short square-skirted coats with rows of stupendous brass buttons, and their hair generally queued in the fashion of the times, especially if they could procure an eelskin for the purpose, it being esteemed, throughout the country, as a potent nourisher and strengthener of the hair.

Brom Bones, however, was the hero of the scene, having come to the gathering on his favorite steed, Daredevil, a creature, like himself, full of mettle and mischief, and which no one but himself could manage. He was, in fact, noted for preferring vicious animals, given to all kinds of tricks, which kept the rider in constant risk of his neck, for he held a **tractable** well-broken horse as unworthy of a lad of spirit.

tractable:
obedient; docile

Fain would I pause to dwell upon the world of charms that burst upon the enraptured gaze of my hero, as he entered the state parlor of Van Tassel's mansion. Not those of the bevy of buxom lasses, with their luxurious display of red and white; but the ample charms of a genuine Dutch country tea-table, in the sumptuous time of autumn. Such heaped-up platters of cakes of various and almost indescribable kinds, known only to experienced Dutch housewives! There was the doughty doughnut, the tenderer oly koek,[55] and the crisp and crumbling cruller; sweet cakes and short cakes, ginger cakes and honey cakes, and the whole family of cakes. And then there were apple pies and peach pies and pumpkin pies; besides slices of ham and smoked beef; and moreover delectable dishes of preserved plums, and peaches, and pears, and quinces; not to mention broiled shad and roasted chickens; together with bowls of milk and cream, all mingled higgledy-piddledy, pretty much as I have enumerated them, with the motherly tea-pot sending up its clouds of vapor from the midst—Heaven bless

---

55 **oly koek:** fried cakes

the mark! I want breath and time to discuss this banquet as it deserves, and am too eager to get on with my story. Happily, Ichabod Crane was not in so great a hurry as his historian, but did ample justice to every dainty.

He was a kind and thankful creature, whose heart dilated in proportion as his skin was filled with good cheer; and whose spirits rose with eating as some men's do with drink. He could not help, too, rolling his large eyes round him as he ate, and chuckling with the possibility that he might one day be lord of all this scene of almost unimaginable luxury and splendor. Then, he thought, how soon he'd turn his back upon the old school-house; snap his fingers in the face of Hans Van Ripper, and every other niggardly[56] patron, and kick any **itinerant** pedagogue out of doors that should dare to call him comrade!

itinerant: traveling; wandering

Old Baltus Van Tassel moved about among his guests with a face dilated with content and good humor, round and jolly as the harvest moon. His hospitable attentions were brief, but expressive, being confined to a shake of the hand, a slap on the shoulder, a loud laugh, and a pressing invitation to "fall to, and help themselves."

And now the sound of the music from the common room, or hall, summoned to the dance. The musician was an old gray-headed Negro, who had been the itinerant orchestra of the neighborhood for more than half a century. His instrument was as old and battered as himself. The greater part of the time he scraped on two or three strings accompanying every movement of the bow with a motion of the head; bowing almost to the ground and stamping with his foot whenever a fresh couple were to start.

The lady of his heart was his partner in the dance, and smiling graciously in reply to all his amorous oglings.

Ichabod prided himself upon his dancing as much as upon his vocal powers. Not a limb, not a fibre about him was idle; and to have seen his loosely hung frame in full motion, and clattering about the room, you would have thought Saint Vitus[57] himself, that blessed patron of the dance, was figuring before you in person. He was the admiration of all the Negroes; who, having gathered, of all ages and sizes, from the farm and the neighborhood, stood forming a pyramid of shining black faces at every door and window, gazing with delight at the scene, rolling their white eye-balls, and showing

---

56 **niggardly:** stingy

57 **Saint Vitus:** a Christian martyr associated with epilepsy and other nervous disorders

grinning rows of ivory from ear to ear. How could the flogger of urchins be otherwise than animated and joyous? The lady of his heart was his partner in the dance, and smiling graciously in reply to all his amorous oglings; while Brom Bones, sorely smitten with love and jealousy, sat brooding by himself in one corner.

When the dance was at an end, Ichabod was attracted to a knot of the sager folks, who, with old Van Tassel, sat smoking at one end of the piazza, gossiping over former times, and drawing out long stories about the war.

This neighborhood, at the time of which I am speaking, was one of those highly-favored places which abound with chronicle and great men. The British and American line had run near it during the war; it had, therefore, been the scene of marauding, and infested with refugees, cow-boys,[58] and all kinds of border chivalry. Just sufficient time had elapsed to enable each story-teller to dress up his tale with a little becoming fiction, and, in the indistinctness of his recollection, to make himself the hero of every exploit.

There was the story of Doffue Martling, a large blue-bearded Dutchman, who had nearly taken a British frigate with an old iron nine-pounder from a mud breastwork, only that his gun burst at the sixth discharge. And there was an old gentleman who shall be nameless, being too rich a mynheer[59] to be lightly mentioned, who, in the battle of Whiteplains, being an excellent master of defence, parried a musket ball with a small sword, insomuch that he absolutely felt it whiz round the blade, and glance off at the hilt; in proof of which he was ready at any time to show the sword, with the hilt a little bent. There were several more that had been equally great in the field, not one of whom but was persuaded that he had a considerable hand in bringing the war to a happy termination.

But all these were nothing to the tales of ghosts and apparitions that succeeded. The neighborhood is rich in legendary treasures of the kind. Local tales and superstitions thrive best in these sheltered long-settled retreats; but are trampled underfoot by the shifting throng that forms the population of most of our country places. Besides, there is no encouragement for ghosts in most of our villages, for they have scarcely had time to finish their first nap, and turn themselves in their graves, before their surviving friends have travelled away from the neighborhood; so that when they turn out at night to walk their rounds, they have no acquaintance left to call upon. This is

---

58 **cow-boys:** a name for those who worked for the British during the American Revolution

59 **mynheer:** Dutch for "sir" or "mister"

perhaps the reason why we so seldom hear of ghosts, except in our long-established Dutch communities.

The immediate cause, however, of the prevalence of supernatural stories in these parts was doubtless owing to the vicinity of Sleepy Hollow. There was a contagion in the very air that blew from that haunted region; it breathed forth an atmosphere of dreams and fancies infecting all the land. Several of the Sleepy Hollow people were present at Van Tassel's, and, as usual, were doling out their wild and wonderful legends. Many dismal tales were told about funeral trains, and mourning cries and wailings heard and seen about the great tree where the unfortunate Major André[60] was taken, and which stood in the neighborhood. Some mention was made also of the woman in white, that haunted the dark glen at Raven Rock, and was often heard to shriek on winter nights before a storm, having perished there in the snow. The chief part of the stories, however, turned upon the favorite spectre of Sleepy Hollow, the headless horseman, who had been heard several times of late, patrolling the country; and, it was said, tethered his horse nightly among the graves in the churchyard.

The sequestered situation of this church seems always to have made it a favorite haunt of troubled spirits. It stands on a knoll, surrounded by locust-trees and lofty elms, from among which its decent whitewashed walls shine modestly forth, like Christian purity beaming through the shades of retirement. A gentle slope descends from it to a silver sheet of water, bordered by high trees, between which, peeps may be caught at the blue hills of the Hudson. To look upon its grass-grown yard, where the sunbeams seem to sleep so quietly, one would think that there at least the dead might rest in peace. On one side of the church extends a wide woody dell, along which raves a large brook among broken rocks and trunks of fallen trees. Over a deep black part of the stream, not far from the church, was formerly thrown a wooden bridge; the road that led to it, and the bridge itself, were thickly shaded by overhanging trees, which cast a gloom about it, even in the daytime, but occasioned a fearful darkness at night. This was one of the favorite haunts of the headless horseman; and the place where he was most frequently encountered. The tale was told of old Brouwer, a most heretical disbeliever in ghosts, how he met the horseman returning from his foray into Sleepy Hollow, and was obliged to get up behind him; how they galloped over bush and brake, over hill and swamp, until they reached the bridge;

---

60 **Major André:** Major John André (1751–1780), a British spy

when the horseman suddenly turned into a skeleton, threw old Brouwer into the brook, and sprang away over the tree-tops with a clap of thunder.

This story was immediately matched by a thrice marvellous adventure of Brom Bones, who made light of the galloping Hessian as an arrant jockey. He affirmed that, on returning one night from the neighboring village of Sing Sing, he had been overtaken by this midnight trooper; that he had offered to race with him for a bowl of punch, and should have won it too, for Daredevil beat the goblin-horse all hollow, but, just as they came to the church-bridge, the Hessian bolted, and vanished in a flash of fire.

All these tales, told in that drowsy undertone with which men talk in the dark, the countenances of the listeners only now and then receiving a casual gleam from the glare of a pipe, sank deep in the mind of Ichabod. He repaid them in kind with large extracts from his invaluable author, Cotton Mather, and added many marvellous events that had taken place in his native State of Connecticut, and fearful sights which he had seen in his nightly walks about Sleepy Hollow.

The revel now gradually broke up. The old farmers gathered together their families in their wagons, and were heard for some time rattling along the hollow roads, and over the distant hills. Some of the damsels mounted on pillions[61] behind their favorite swains, and their light-hearted laughter, mingling with the clatter of hoofs, echoed along the silent woodlands, sounding fainter and fainter until they gradually died away—and the late scene of noise and frolic was all silent and deserted. Ichabod only lingered behind, according to the custom of country lovers, to have a tête-à-tête[62] with the heiress, fully convinced that he was now on the high road to success. What passed at this interview I will not pretend to say, for in fact I do not know. Something, however, I fear me, must have gone wrong, for he certainly sallied forth, after no very great interval, with an air quite desolate and chop-fallen.[63]—Oh, these women! these women! Could that girl have been playing off any of her coquettish tricks?—Was her encouragement of the poor pedagogue all a mere sham to secure her conquest of his rival?—Heaven only knows, not I!—Let it suffice to say, Ichabod stole forth with the air of one who had been sacking a hen-roost, rather than a fair lady's heart. Without looking to the right or left to notice the scene of rural wealth on which he had so often gloated, he went straight to the stable, and with several hearty cuffs and kicks,

---

61 **pillions:** pads put behind a man's saddle for a woman to ride on

62 **tête-à-tête:** French for "head-to-head," a one-on-one conversation

63 **chop-fallen:** depressed; crestfallen

roused his steed most uncourteously from the comfortable quarters in which he was soundly sleeping, dreaming of mountains of corn and oats, and whole valleys of timothy and clover.

It was the very witching time of night that Ichabod, heavy hearted and crestfallen, pursued his travel homewards, along the sides of the lofty hills which rise above Tarry Town, and which he had traversed so cheerily in the afternoon. The hour was as dismal as himself. Far below him, the Tappan Zee spread its dusky and indistinct waste of waters, with here and there the tall mast of a sloop, riding quietly at anchor under the land. In the dead hush of midnight he could even hear the barking of the watch dog from the opposite shore of the Hudson; but it was so vague and faint as only to give an idea of his distance from this faithful companion of man. Now and then, too, the long-drawn crowing of a cock, accidentally awakened, would sound far, far off, from some farmhouse away among the hills—but it was like a dreaming sound in his ear. No signs of life occurred near him, but occasionally the melancholy chirp of a cricket, or perhaps the guttural twang of a bull-frog, from a neighboring marsh, as if sleeping uncomfortably, and turning suddenly in his bed.

All the stories of ghosts and goblins that he had heard in the afternoon, now came crowding upon his recollection. The night grew darker and darker; the stars seemed to sink deeper in the sky, and driving clouds occasionally hid them from his sight. He had never felt so lonely and dismal. He was, moreover, approaching the very place where many of the scenes of the ghost stories had been laid. In the centre of the road stood an enormous tulip-tree, which towered like a giant above all the other trees of the neighborhood, and formed a kind of landmark. Its limbs were gnarled, and fantastic, large enough to form trunks for ordinary trees, twisting down almost to the earth, and rising again into the air. It was connected with the tragical story of the unfortunate André, who had been taken prisoner hard by; and was universally known by the name of Major André's tree. The common people regarded it with a mixture of respect and superstition, partly out of sympathy for the fate of its ill-starred namesake, and partly from the tales of strange sights and doleful lamentations told concerning it.

As Ichabod approached this fearful tree, he began to whistle: he thought his whistle was answered—it was but a blast sweeping sharply through the dry branches. As he approached a little nearer, he thought he saw something white, hanging in the midst of the tree—he paused and ceased whistling; but on looking more narrowly, perceived that it was a place where the tree had been scathed by lightning, and the white wood laid bare. Suddenly he heard a groan—his teeth chattered and his knees smote against the saddle: it was but the rubbing of one huge bough upon another, as they were swayed about by the breeze. He passed the tree in safety; but new perils lay before him.

About two hundred yards from the tree a small brook crossed the road, and ran into a marshy and thickly-wooded glen, known by the name of Wiley's swamp. A few rough logs, laid side by side, served for a bridge over this stream. On that side of the road where the brook entered the wood, a group of oaks and chestnuts, matted thick with wild grapevines, threw a cavernous gloom over it. To pass this bridge was the severest trial. It was at this identical spot that the unfortunate André was captured, and under the covert of those chestnuts and vines were the sturdy yeomen concealed who surprised him. This has ever since been considered a haunted stream, and

THE POETRY OF MOONLIGHT, RALPH BLAKELOCK, C. 1880–90

fearful are the feelings of the schoolboy who has to pass it alone after dark.

As he approached the stream, his heart began to thump; he summoned up, however, all his resolution, gave his horse half a score of kicks in the ribs, and attempted to dash briskly across the bridge; but instead of starting forward, the perverse old animal made a lateral movement, and ran broadside against the fence. Ichabod, whose fears increased with the delay, jerked the reins on the other side, and kicked lustily with the contrary foot: it was all in vain; his steed started, it is true, but it was only to plunge to the opposite side of the road into a thicket of brambles and alder bushes. The schoolmaster now bestowed both whip and heel upon the starveling ribs of old Gunpowder, who dashed forward, snuffling and snorting, but came to a stand just by the bridge, with a suddenness that had nearly sent his rider sprawling over his head. Just at this moment a plashy tramp[64] by the side of the bridge caught the sensitive ear of Ichabod. In the dark shadow of the grove, on the margin of the brook, he beheld something huge, misshapen, black, and towering. It stirred not, but seemed gathered up in the gloom, like some gigantic monster ready to spring upon the traveller.

The hair of the affrighted pedagogue rose upon his head with terror. What was to be done? To turn and fly was now too late; and besides, what chance was there of escaping ghost or goblin, if such it was, which could ride upon the wings of the wind? Summoning up, therefore, a show of courage, he demanded in stammering accents—"Who are you?" He received no reply. He repeated his demand in a still more agitated voice. Still there was no answer. Once more he cudgelled[65] the sides of the inflexible Gunpowder, and, shutting his eyes, broke forth with involuntary fervor into a psalm tune. Just then the shadowy object of alarm put itself in motion, and, with a scramble and a bound, stood at once in the middle of the road. Though the night was dark and dismal, yet the form of the unknown might now in some degree be ascertained. He appeared to be a horseman of large dimensions, and mounted on a black horse of powerful frame. He made no offer of molestation or sociability, but kept aloof on one side of the road, jogging along on the blind side of old Gunpowder, who had now got over his fright and waywardness.

Ichabod, who had no relish for this strange midnight companion, and bethought himself of the adventure of Brom Bones with the Galloping Hessian,

---

64 plashy tramp: the splashing sound of footsteps in water

65 cudgelled: beat

now quickened his steed, in hopes of leaving him behind. The stranger, however, quickened his horse to an equal pace. Ichabod pulled up, and fell into a walk, thinking to lag behind—the other did the same. His heart began to sink within him; he endeavored to resume his psalm tune, but his parched tongue clove to the roof of his mouth, and he could not utter a stave. There was something in the moody and dogged silence of this pertinacious[66] companion, that was mysterious and appalling. It was soon fearfully accounted for. On mounting a rising ground, which brought the figure of his fellow-traveller in relief against the sky, gigantic in height, and muffled in a cloak, Ichabod was horror-struck, on perceiving that he was headless!—but his horror was still more increased, on observing that the head, which should have rested on his shoulders, was carried before him on the pommel of the saddle: his terror rose to desperation; he rained a shower of kicks and blows upon Gunpowder, hoping, by a sudden movement, to give his companion the slip—but the spectre started full jump with him. Away then they dashed, through thick and thin; stones flying, and sparks flashing at every bound. Ichabod's flimsy garments fluttered in the air, as he stretched his long lank body away over his horse's head, in the eagerness of his flight.

They had now reached the road which turns off to Sleepy Hollow; but Gunpowder, who seemed possessed with a demon, instead of keeping up it, made an opposite turn, and plunged headlong downhill to the left. This road leads through a sandy hollow, shaded by trees for about a quarter of a mile, where it crosses the bridge famous in goblin story, and just beyond swells the green knoll on which stands the whitewashed church.

As yet the panic of the steed had given his unskilful rider an apparent advantage in the chase; but just as he had got half way through the hollow, the girths of the saddle gave way, and he felt it slipping from under him. He seized it by the pommel, and endeavored to hold it firm, but in vain; and had just time to save himself by clasping old Gunpowder round the neck, when the saddle fell to the earth, and he heard it trampled underfoot by his pursuer. For a moment the terror of Hans Van Ripper's wrath passed across his mind—for it was his Sunday saddle; but this was no time for petty fears; the goblin was hard on his haunches; and (unskilful rider that he was!) he had much ado to maintain his seat; sometimes slipping on one side, sometimes on another, and sometimes jolted on the high ridge of his horse's back-bone, with a violence that he verily feared would cleave him asunder.

---

66 **pertinacious:** stubborn; unyielding

ICHABOD CRANE FLYING FROM THE HEADLESS HORSEMAN, JOHN QUIDOR, C. 1828

An opening in the trees now cheered him with the hopes that the church bridge was at hand. The wavering reflection of a silver star in the bosom of the brook told him that he was not mistaken. He saw the walls of the church dimly glaring under the trees beyond. He recollected the place where Brom Bones's ghostly competitor had disappeared. "If I can but reach that bridge," thought Ichabod, "I am safe." Just then he heard the black steed panting and blowing close behind him; he even fancied that he felt his hot breath. Another convulsive kick in the ribs, and old Gunpowder sprang upon the bridge; he thundered over the resounding planks; he gained the opposite side; and now Ichabod cast a look behind to see if his pursuer should vanish, according to rule, in a flash of fire and brimstone. Just then he saw the goblin rising in his stirrups, and in the very act of hurling his head at him. Ichabod endeavored to dodge the horrible missile, but too late. It encountered his cranium with a tremendous crash—he was tumbled headlong into the dust, and Gunpowder, the black steed, and the goblin rider, passed by like a whirlwind.

The next morning the old horse was found without his saddle, and with the bridle under his feet, soberly cropping the grass at his master's gate. Ichabod did not make his appearance at breakfast—dinner-hour came, but no Ichabod. The boys assembled at the school-house, and strolled idly about the banks of the brook; but no schoolmaster. Hans Van Ripper now began to feel some uneasiness about the fate of poor Ichabod, and his saddle. An inquiry was set on foot, and after diligent investigation they came upon his traces. In one part of the road leading to the church was found the saddle trampled in the dirt; the tracks of horses' hoofs deeply dented in the road, and evidently at furious speed, were traced to the bridge, beyond which, on the bank of a broad-part of the brook, where the water ran deep and black, was found the hat of the unfortunate Ichabod, and close beside it a shattered pumpkin.

The brook was searched, but the body of the schoolmaster was not to be discovered. Hans Van Ripper, as executor of his estate, examined the bundle which contained all his worldly effects. They consisted of two shirts and a half; two stocks for the neck; a pair or two of worsted stockings; an old pair of corduroy small-clothes; a rusty razor; a book of psalm tunes, full of dogs' ears;[67] and a broken pitch-pipe. As to the books and furniture of the schoolhouse, they belonged to the community, excepting Cotton Mather's History of Witchcraft, a New England Almanac, and a book of dreams and fortune-telling; in which last was a sheet of foolscap much scribbled and blotted in several fruitless attempts to make a copy of verses in honor of the heiress of Van Tassel. These magic books and the poetic scrawl were forthwith consigned to the flames by Hans Van Ripper; who from that time forward determined to send his children no more to school; observing, that he never knew any good come of this same reading and writing. Whatever money the schoolmaster possessed, and he had received his quarter's pay but a day or two before, he must have had about his person at the time of his disappearance.

The mysterious event caused much speculation at the church on the following Sunday. Knots of gazers and gossips were collected in the churchyard, at the bridge, and at the spot where the hat and pumpkin had been found. The stories of Brouwer, of Bones, and a whole budget of others, were called to mind; and when they had diligently considered them all, and compared them with the symptoms of the present case, they shook their heads, and came to the conclusion that Ichabod had been carried off by the Galloping Hessian. As he was a bachelor, and in nobody's debt, nobody troubled his head any more about him. The school was removed to a different quarter of the Hollow, and another pedagogue reigned in his stead.

It is true, an old farmer, who had been down to New York on a visit several years after, and from whom this account of the ghostly adventure

---

67 **dogs' ears:** the turned-down corners of book pages, done to mark the reader's place

was received, brought home the intelligence that Ichabod Crane was still alive; that he had left the neighborhood, partly through fear of the goblin and Hans Van Ripper, and partly in **mortification** at having been suddenly dismissed by the heiress; that he had changed his quarters to a distant part of the country; had kept school and studied law at the same time, had been admitted to the bar, turned politician, electioneered, written for the newspapers, and finally had been made a justice of the Ten Pound Court. Brom Bones too, who shortly after his rival's disappearance conducted the blooming Katrina in triumph to the altar, was observed to look exceedingly knowing whenever the story of Ichabod was related, and always burst into a hearty laugh at the mention of the pumpkin; which led some to suspect that he knew more about the matter than he chose to tell.

mortification: shame; humiliation

The old country wives, however, who are the best judges of these matters, maintain to this day that Ichabod was spirited away by supernatural means; and it is a favorite story often told about the neighborhood round the winter evening fire. The bridge became more than ever an object of superstitious awe, and that may be the reason why the road has been altered of late years, so as to approach the church by the border of the mill-pond. The school-house, being deserted, soon fell to decay, and was reported to be haunted by the ghost of the unfortunate pedagogue; and the ploughboy, loitering homeward of a still summer evening, has often fancied his voice at a distance, chanting a melancholy psalm tune among the tranquil solitudes of Sleepy Hollow.

★ ★ ★ ★ ★

POSTSCRIPT, FOUND IN THE HANDWRITING OF MR. KNICKERBOCKER

The preceding Tale is given, almost in the precise words in which I heard it related at a Corporation meeting of the ancient city of Manhattoes, at which were present many of its sagest and most illustrious burghers. The narrator was a pleasant, shabby, gentlemanly old fellow, in pepper-and-salt clothes, with a sadly humorous face; and one whom I strongly suspected of being poor—he made such efforts to be entertaining. When his story was concluded, there was much laughter and **approbation**, particularly from two or three deputy aldermen, who had been asleep the greater part of the time. There was, however, one tall, dry-looking old gentleman, with beetling eyebrows, who maintained a grave and rather severe face throughout: now

approbation: praise; approval

and then folding his arms, inclining his head, and looking down upon the floor, as if turning a doubt over in his mind. He was one of your wary men, who never laugh, but upon good grounds—when they have reason and the law on their side. When the mirth of the rest of the company had subsided and silence was restored, he leaned one arm on the elbow of his chair, and, sticking the other akimbo,[68] demanded, with a slight but exceedingly sage motion of the head, and contraction of the brow, what was the moral of the story, and what it went to prove?

The story-teller, who was just putting a glass of wine to his lips, as a refreshment after his toils, paused for a moment, looked at his inquirer with an air of infinite deference, and, lowering the glass slowly to the table, observed, that the story was intended most logically to prove:—

"That there is no situation in life but has its advantages and pleasures—provided we will but take a joke as we find it:

"That, therefore, he that runs races with goblin troopers is likely to have rough riding of it.

"Ergo, for a country schoolmaster to be refused the hand of a Dutch heiress, is a certain step to high preferment[69] in the state."

The cautious old gentleman knit his brows tenfold closer after this explanation, being sorely puzzled by the ratiocination[70] of the syllogism;[71] while, methought, the one in pepper-and-salt eyed him with something of a triumphant leer. At length he observed, that all this was very well, but still he thought the story a little on the extravagant—there were one or two points on which he had his doubts.

"Faith, sir," replied the story-teller, "as to that matter, I don't believe one half of it myself."

---

68 **akimbo:** a position with the arm bent and the hand resting on the hip

69 **preferment:** promotion; advancement

70 **ratiocination:** train of thought; reasoning

71 **syllogism:** formal argument; premise

Read and Think Critically

Analyze, Infer, Compare

 1. **MOTIF** Analyze how Irving uses the **motif** of the Headless Horseman. Cite strong evidence to support your analysis.

2. In your own words, describe Ichabod Crane. Is he an admirable **character**? Use details from the text to back up your evaluation.

3. What **inferences** can you draw from Ichabod Crane's interest in Katrina? Name all the possible reasons for his attraction.

4. Why is Brom a good **foil** (contrasting character) for Ichabod? Compare the two men using details from the story.

5. What do you think happens to Ichabod after his disappearance?

6. **THE AUTHOR'S STYLE** Analyze the effect of Irving's language on your enjoyment of this story. Cite specific examples of the author's wordplay that you enjoyed: descriptive details and **figurative language** such as **metaphors**, **similes**, and **hyperbole** (exaggeration used for effect).

Before You Read

Nathaniel Hawthorne 1804–1864

About the Author

Hawthorne was born on July 4, 1804, in Salem, Massachusetts, to a family with a dark legacy: in the late 1600s his Puritan ancestors had participated in the notorious Salem witch trials. Hawthorne would puzzle over the nature of these moral crimes in much of his fiction and depict the era with historical accuracy. As a result, he shaped many of our present-day impressions of the early Puritans.

Hawthorne's father, a sea captain, died when his son was only four, after which the family lived with relatives in Maine. The rural setting allowed the introspective young Hawthorne to read widely and nurture literary ambitions. At Bowdoin College, where he described himself as an "idle student" but "always reading," he met poet Henry Wadsworth Longfellow.

After college Hawthorne returned to Salem and spent a decade teaching himself the writer's craft. *Twice-Told Tales*, his first story collection, impressed critics but sold poorly, forcing Hawthorne to take work at a customhouse measuring salt and coal. The income allowed him to marry Sophia Peabody, a worldly and aspiring painter.

The couple moved to Ralph Waldo Emerson's former home in Concord, where Hawthorne began an intense period of literary activity. His story collection, *Mosses from Old Manse* (1846), was followed by his masterpiece, the novel *The Scarlet Letter* (1850), and *The House of Seven Gables* (1851). Hawthorne spent several of his later years in Europe, traveling and serving as a U.S. consul. He produced biographies, travel sketches, and novels, but none received the literary acclaim of his earlier stories and novels.

The Author's Style

Hawthorne's work shares themes familiar to the Romantic period: spirituality, imagination, intellectual pride, human beings' attraction to the forbidden, and the conflict between good and evil. They also raise questions about the wisdom of trusting too much in science.

Hawthorne explored these themes in many of his works by focusing his literary lens sharply on the Puritan experience in 17th-century New England. Highly symbolic and allegorical, these works urge readers to think about the human capacity for sin, the effect of guilt on the human spirit, and the hypocrisy and arrogance of moral self-righteousness.

Simple and precise language draws readers into Hawthorne's complex stories and novels. The settings, often darkly mysterious places, mirror the emotional states of the characters. In "Young Goodman Brown," for example, it is almost impossible to separate the setting from the inner life of Goodman Brown.

Young Goodman Brown

NATHANIEL HAWTHORNE

LITERARY LENS: THEME A **theme** is an underlying meaning or message of a work of art. As you read, consider what themes run through the story.

*Y*oung Goodman Brown came forth at sunset into the street at Salem village; but put his head back, after crossing the threshold, to exchange a parting kiss with his young wife. And Faith, as the wife was aptly named, thrust her own pretty head into the street, letting the wind play with the pink ribbons of her cap while she called to Goodman Brown.

"Dearest heart," whispered she, softly and rather sadly, when her lips were close to his ear, "prithee[1] put off your journey until sunrise and sleep in your own bed to-night. A lone woman is troubled with such dreams and such thoughts that she's afeard of herself sometimes. Pray tarry with me this night, dear husband, of all nights in the year."

"My love and my Faith," replied young Goodman Brown, "of all nights in the year, this one night must I tarry away from thee. My

---

1 **prithee:** pray thee

AUGUSTA PORTER WOODBURY,
SARAH GOODRIDGE, 1828

journey, as thou callest it, forth and back again, must needs be done 'twixt now and sunrise. What, my sweet, pretty wife, dost thou doubt me already, and we but three months married?"

"Then God bless you!" said Faith, with the pink ribbons; "and may you find all well when you come back."

"Amen!" cried Goodman Brown. "Say thy prayers, dear Faith, and go to bed at dusk, and no harm will come to thee."

So they parted; and the young man pursued his way until, being about to turn the corner by the meeting-house, he looked back and saw the head of Faith still peeping after him with a melancholy air, in spite of her pink ribbons.

"Poor little Faith!" thought he, for his heart smote him. "What a wretch am I to leave her on such an errand! She talks of dreams, too. Methought as she spoke there was trouble in her face, as if a dream had warned her what work is to be done tonight. But no, no; 'twould kill her to think it. Well, she's a blessed angel on earth; and after this one night I'll cling to her skirts and follow her to heaven."

With this excellent resolve for the future, Goodman Brown felt himself justified in making more haste on his present evil purpose. He had taken a dreary road, darkened by all the gloomiest trees of the forest, which barely stood aside to let the narrow path creep through, and closed immediately behind. It was all as lonely as could be; and there is this peculiarity in such a solitude, that the traveller knows not who may be concealed by the innumerable trunks and the thick boughs overhead; so that with lonely footsteps he may yet be passing through an unseen multitude.

"There may be a devilish Indian behind every tree," said Goodman Brown to himself; and he glanced fearfully behind him as he added, "What if the devil himself should be at my very elbow!"

> "*What* if the devil himself should be at my very elbow!"

His head being turned back, he passed a crook of the road, and, looking forward again, beheld the figure of a man, in grave and decent attire, seated at the foot of an old tree. He arose at Goodman Brown's approach and walked onward side by side with him.

"You are late, Goodman Brown," said he. "The clock of the Old South was striking as I came through Boston, and that is full fifteen minutes agone."

"Faith kept me back a while," replied the young man, with a tremor in his voice, caused by the sudden appearance of his companion, though not wholly unexpected.

It was now deep dusk in the forest, and deepest in that part of it where these two were journeying. As nearly as could be **discerned**, the second traveller was about fifty years old, apparently in the same rank of life as Goodman Brown, and bearing a considerable resemblance to him, though perhaps more in expression than features. Still they might have been taken for father and son. And yet, though the elder person was as simply clad as the younger, and as simple in manner too, he had an indescribable air of one who knew the world, and who would not have felt abashed at the governor's dinner table or in King William's court, were it possible that his affairs should call him thither. But the only thing about him that could be fixed upon as remarkable was his staff, which bore the likeness of a great black snake, so curiously wrought that it might almost be seen to twist and wriggle itself like a living serpent. This, of course, must have been an **ocular** deception, assisted by the uncertain light.

"Come, Goodman Brown," cried his fellow-traveller, "this is a dull pace for the beginning of a journey. Take my staff, if you are so soon weary."

"Friend," said the other, exchanging his slow pace for a full stop, "having kept covenant[2] by meeting thee here, it is my purpose now to return whence I came. I have **scruples** touching the matter thou wot'st of."

discerned: determined; figured out

ocular: related to eyes or vision

scruples: doubts; reservations

---

2 **covenant:** agreement; promise

"Sayest thou so?" replied he of the serpent, smiling apart. "Let us walk on, nevertheless, reasoning as we go; and if I convince thee not thou shalt turn back. We are but a little way in the forest yet."

"Too far! too far!" exclaimed the goodman, unconsciously resuming his walk. "My father never went into the woods on such an errand, nor his father before him. We have been a race of honest men and good Christians since the days of the martyrs; and shall I be the first of the name of Brown that ever took this path and kept"—

"Such company, thou wouldst say," observed the elder person, interpreting his pause. "Well said, Goodman Brown! I have been as well acquainted with your family as with ever a one among the Puritans; and that's no trifle to say. I helped your grandfather, the constable, when he lashed the Quaker woman so smartly through the streets of Salem; and it was I that brought your father a pitch-pine knot, kindled at my own hearth, to set fire to an Indian village, in King Philip's war. They were my good friends, both; and many a pleasant walk have we had along this path, and returned merrily after midnight. I would fain be friends with you for their sake."

"If it be as thou sayest," replied Goodman Brown, "I marvel they never spoke of these matters; or, verily, I marvel not, seeing that the least rumor of the sort would have driven them from New England. We are a people of prayer, and good works to boot, and abide no such wickedness."

"Wickedness or not," said the traveller with the twisted staff, "I have a very general acquaintance here in New England. The deacons of many a church have drunk the communion wine with me; the selectmen of divers towns make me their chairman; and a majority of the Great and General Court are firm supporters of my interest. The governor and I, too—But these are state secrets."

"Can this be so?" cried Goodman Brown, with a stare of amazement at his undisturbed companion. "Howbeit, I have nothing to do with the governor and council; they have their own ways, and are no rule for a simple husbandman like me. But, were I to go on with thee, how should I meet the eye of that good old man, our minister, at Salem village? Oh, his voice would make me tremble both Sabbath day and lecture day."

Thus far the elder traveller had listened with due **gravity**; but now burst into a fit of **irrepressible** mirth, shaking himself so violently that his snake-like staff actually seemed to wriggle in sympathy.

gravity: seriousness; solemnity

irrepressible: uncontrollable; unrestrained

"Ha! ha! ha!" shouted he again and again; then composing himself, "Well, go on, Goodman Brown, go on; but, prithee, don't kill me with laughing."

"Well, then, to end the matter at once," said Goodman Brown, considerably nettled, "there is my wife, Faith. It would break her dear little heart; and I'd rather break my own."

"Nay, if that be the case," answered the other, "e'en go thy ways, Goodman Brown. I would not for twenty old women like the one hobbling before us that Faith should come to any harm."

As he spoke he pointed his staff at a female figure on the path, in whom Goodman Brown recognized a very **pious** and **exemplary** dame, who had taught him his catechism[3] in youth, and was still his moral and spiritual adviser, jointly with the minister and Deacon Gookin.

pious: religious; devout

exemplary: perfect; model

"A marvel, truly, that Goody Cloyse should be so far in the wilderness at nightfall," said he. "But with your leave, friend, I shall take a cut through the woods until we have left this Christian woman behind. Being a stranger to you, she might ask whom I was consorting with and whither I was going."

"Be it so," said his fellow-traveller. "Betake you the woods, and let me keep the path."

Accordingly the young man turned aside, but took care to watch his companion, who advanced softly along the road until he had come within a staff's length of the old dame. She, meanwhile, was making the best of her way, with singular speed for so aged a woman, and mumbling some indistinct words—a prayer, doubtless—as she went. The traveller put forth his staff and touched her withered neck with what seemed the serpent's tail.

"The devil!" screamed the pious old lady.

"Then Goody Cloyse knows her old friend!" observed the traveller, confronting her and leaning on his writhing stick.

"Ah, forsooth, and is it your worship indeed?" cried the good dame. "Yea, truly is it, and in the very image of my old gossip, Goodman Brown, the grandfather of the silly fellow that now is. But—would your worship believe it?—my broomstick hath strangely disappeared, stolen, as I suspect, by that unhanged witch, Goody Cory, and that, too, when I was all anointed with the juice of smallage, and cinquefoil, and wolf's bane"[4]—

---

3 **catechism:** a question-and-answer method of teaching religious doctrines

4 **smallage, and cinquefoil, and wolf's bane:** herbs and plants associated with witchcraft

"Mingled with fine wheat and the fat of a new-born babe," said the shape of old Goodman Brown.

"Ah, your worship knows the recipe," cried the old lady, cackling aloud. "So, as I was saying, being all ready for the meeting, and no horse to ride on, I made up my mind to foot it; for they tell me there is a nice young man to be taken into communion tonight. But now your good worship will lend me your arm, and we shall be there in a twinkling."

> "They tell me there is a nice young man to be taken into communion tonight."

"That can hardly be," answered her friend. "I may not spare you my arm, Goody Cloyse; but here is my staff, if you will."

So saying, he threw it down at her feet, where, perhaps, it assumed life, being one of the rods which its owner had formerly lent to the Egyptian magi.[5] Of this fact, however, Goodman Brown could not take cognizance.[6] He had cast up his eyes in astonishment, and, looking down again, beheld neither Goody Cloyse nor the serpentine staff, but this fellow-traveller alone, who waited for him as calmly as if nothing had happened.

"That old woman taught me my catechism," said the young man; and there was a world of meaning in this simple comment.

exhorted:
urged; strongly
advised

They continued to walk onward, while the elder traveller **exhorted** his companion to make good speed and persevere in the path, discoursing so aptly that his arguments seemed rather to spring up in the bosom of his auditor than to be suggested by himself. As they went, he plucked a branch of maple to serve for a walking stick, and began to strip it of the twigs and little boughs, which were wet with evening dew. The moment his fingers touched them they became strangely withered and dried up as with a week's sunshine. Thus the pair proceeded, at a good free pace, until suddenly, in a gloomy hollow of the road, Goodman Brown sat himself down on the stump of a tree and refused to go any farther.

"Friend," said he, stubbornly, "my mind is made up. Not another step will I budge on this errand. What if a wretched old woman do choose to go to the devil when I thought she was going to heaven: is that any reason why I should quit my dear Faith and go after her?"

"You will think better of this by and by," said his acquaintance, composedly. "Sit here and rest yourself a while; and when you feel like moving again, there is my staff to help you along."

---

5 **Egyptian magi:** a reference to the biblical story in which Egyptian magicians turned a rod into a serpent

6 **cognizance:** notice or acknowledgment

Without more words, he threw his companion the maple stick, and was as speedily out of sight as if he had vanished into the deepening gloom. The young man sat a few moments by the roadside, applauding himself greatly, and thinking with how clear a conscience he should meet the minister in his morning walk, nor shrink from the eye of good old Deacon Gookin. And what calm sleep would be his that very night, which was to have been spent so wickedly, but so purely and sweetly now, in the arms of Faith! Amidst these pleasant and praiseworthy meditations, Goodman Brown heard the tramp of horses along the road, and deemed it advisable to conceal himself within the verge of the forest, conscious of the guilty purpose that had brought him thither, though now so happily turned from it.

On came the hoof tramps and the voices of the riders, two grave old voices, conversing soberly as they drew near. These mingled sounds appeared to pass along the road, within a few yards of the young man's hiding-place; but, owing doubtless to the depth of the gloom at that particular spot, neither the travellers nor their steeds were visible. Though their figures brushed the small boughs by the wayside, it could not be seen that they intercepted, even for a moment, the faint gleam from the strip of bright sky athwart which they must have passed. Goodman Brown alternately crouched and stood on tiptoe, pulling aside the branches and thrusting forth his head as far as he durst without discerning so much as a shadow. It vexed him the more, because he could have sworn, were such a thing possible, that he recognized the voices of the minister and Deacon Gookin, jogging along quietly, as they were wont to do, when bound to some ordination or ecclesiastical council.[7] While yet within hearing one of the riders stopped to pluck a switch.

"Of the two, reverend sir," said the voice like the deacon's, "I had rather miss an ordination dinner than to-night's meeting. They tell me that some of our community are to be here from Falmouth and beyond, and others from Connecticut and Rhode Island, besides several of the Indian powwows, who, after their fashion, know almost as much deviltry as the best of us. Moreover, there is a goodly young woman to be taken into communion."

"Mighty well, Deacon Gookin!" replied the solemn old tones of the minister. "Spur up, or we shall be late. Nothing can be done, you know, until I get on the ground."

The hoofs clattered again; and the voices, talking so strangely in the empty air, passed on through the forest, where no church had ever been gathered or

---

7 **ecclesiastical council:** a church gathering

solitary Christian prayed. Whither, then, could these holy men be journeying so deep into the heathen wilderness? Young Goodman Brown caught hold of a tree for support, being ready to sink down on the ground, faint and overburdened with the heavy sickness of his heart. He looked up to the sky, doubting whether there really was a heaven above him. Yet there was the blue arch, and the stars brightening in it.

> "With heaven above and Faith below, I will yet stand firm against the devil!"

"With heaven above and Faith below, I will yet stand firm against the devil!" cried Goodman Brown.

While he still gazed upward into the deep arch of the firmament and had lifted his hands to pray, a cloud, though no wind was stirring, hurried across the zenith and hid the brightening stars. The blue sky was still visible, except directly overhead, where this black mass of cloud was sweeping swiftly northward. Aloft in the air, as if from the depths of the cloud, came a confused and doubtful sound of voices. Once the listener fancied that he could distinguish the accents of towns-people of his own, men and women, both pious and ungodly, many of whom he had met at the communion table, and had seen others rioting at the tavern. The next moment, so indistinct were the sounds, he doubted whether he had heard aught but the murmur of the old forest, whispering without a wind. Then came a stronger swell of those familiar tones, heard daily in the sunshine at Salem village, but never until now from a cloud of night. There was one uncertain voice, of a young woman, uttering lamentations, yet with an uncertain sorrow, and entreating for some favor, which, perhaps, it would grieve her to obtain; and all the unseen multitude, both saints and sinners, seemed to encourage her onward.

"Faith!" shouted Goodman Brown, in a voice of agony and desperation; and the echoes of the forest mocked him, crying, "Faith! Faith!" as if bewildered wretches were seeking her all through the wilderness.

The cry of grief, rage, and terror was yet piercing the night, when the unhappy husband held his breath for a response. There was a scream, drowned immediately in a louder murmur of voices, fading into far-off laughter, as the dark cloud swept away, leaving the clear and silent sky above Goodman Brown. But something fluttered lightly down through the air and caught on the branch of a tree. The young man seized it, and beheld a pink ribbon.

"My Faith is gone!" cried he, after one stupefied moment. "There is no good on earth; and sin is but a name. Come devil; for to thee is this world given."

And, maddened with despair, so that he laughed loud and long, did Goodman Brown grasp his staff and set forth again, at such a rate that he seemed to fly along the forest path rather than to walk or run. The road grew wilder and drearier and more faintly traced, and vanished at length, leaving him in the heart of the dark wilderness, still rushing onward with the instinct that guides mortal man to evil. The whole forest was peopled with frightful sounds—the creaking of the trees, the howling of wild beasts, and the yell of Indians; while sometimes the wind tolled like a distant church bell, and sometimes gave a broad roar around the traveller, as if all Nature were laughing him to scorn. But he was himself the chief horror of the scene, and shrank not from its other horrors.

"Ha! ha! ha!" roared Goodman Brown when the wind laughed at him. "Let us hear which will laugh loudest. Think not to frighten me with your deviltry. Come witch, come wizard, come Indian powwow, come devil himself, and here comes Goodman Brown. You may as well fear him as he fear you."

In truth, all through the haunted forest there could be nothing more frightful than the figure of Goodman Brown. On he flew among the black

SUNDOWN ON THE CREEK, KEN O'BRIEN, 1953

pines, brandishing his staff with frenzied gestures, now giving vent to an inspiration of horrid blasphemy, and now shouting forth such laughter as set all the echoes of the forest laughing like demons around him. The fiend in his own shape is less hideous than when he rages in the breast of man. Thus sped the demoniac on his course, until, quivering among the trees, he saw a red light before him, as when the felled trunks and branches of a clearing have been set on fire, and throw up their **lurid** blaze against the sky, at the hour of midnight. He paused, in a lull of the tempest that had driven him onward, and heard the swell of what seemed a hymn, rolling solemnly from a distance with the weight of many voices. He knew the tune; it was a familiar one in the choir of the village meeting-house. The verse died heavily away, and was lengthened by a chorus, not of human voices, but of all the sounds of the benighted wilderness pealing in awful harmony together. Goodman Brown cried out, and his cry was lost to his own ear by its unison with the cry of the desert.

In the interval of silence he stole forward until the light glared full upon his eyes. At one extremity of an open space, hemmed in by the dark wall of the forest, arose a rock, bearing some rude, natural resemblance either to an altar or a pulpit, and surrounded by four blazing pines, their tops aflame, their stems untouched, like candles at an evening meeting. The mass of foliage that had overgrown the summit of the rock was all on fire, blazing high into the night and fitfully illuminating the whole field. Each pendent twig and leafy festoon was in a blaze. As the red light arose and fell, a numerous congregation alternately shone forth, then disappeared in shadow, and again grew, as it were, out of the darkness, peopling the heart of the solitary woods at once.

"A grave and dark-clad company," quoth Goodman Brown.

In truth they were such. Among them, quivering to and fro between gloom and splendor, appeared faces that would be seen next day at the council board of the province, and others which, Sabbath after Sabbath, looked devoutly heavenward, and benignantly[8] over the crowded pews, from the holiest pulpits in the land. Some affirm that the lady of the governor was there. At least there were high dames well known to her, and wives of honored husbands, and widows, a great multitude, and ancient maidens, all of excellent repute, and fair young girls, who trembled lest their mothers should espy them. Either the sudden gleams of light flashing over the obscure field

lurid: shining with a reddish glow

---

8 **benignantly:** kindly

bedazzled Goodman Brown, or he recognized a score of the church members of Salem village famous for their especial sanctity. Good old Deacon Gookin had arrived, and waited at the skirts of that venerable saint, his revered pastor. But, irreverently consorting with these grave, reputable, and pious people, these elders of the church, these chaste dames and dewy virgins, there were men of **dissolute** lives and women of spotted fame, wretches given over to all mean and filthy vice, and suspected even of horrid crimes. It was strange to see that the good shrank not from the wicked, nor were the sinners abashed by the saints. Scattered also among their pale-faced enemies were the Indian priests, or powwows, who had often scared their native forest with more hideous incantations than any known to English witchcraft.

dissolute: wicked; evil

> *I*t was strange to see that the good shrank not from the wicked, nor were the sinners abashed by the saints.

"But where is Faith?" thought Goodman Brown; and, as hope came into his heart, he trembled.

Another verse of the hymn arose, a slow and mournful strain, such as the pious love, but joined to words which expressed all that our nature can conceive of sin, and darkly hinted at far more. **Unfathomable** to mere mortals is the love of fiends. Verse after verse was sung; and still the chorus of the desert swelled between like the deepest tone of a mighty organ; and with the final peal of that dreadful anthem there came a sound, as if the roaring wind, the rushing streams, the howling beasts, and every other voice of the unconcerted wilderness were mingling and according with the voice of guilty man in homage to the prince of all. The four blazing pines threw up a loftier flame, and obscurely discovered shapes and visages of horror on the smoke wreaths above the impious assembly. At the same moment the fire on the rock shot redly forth and formed a glowing arch above its base, where now appeared a figure. With reverence be it spoken, the figure bore no slight similitude, both in garb and manner, to some grave divine of the New England churches.

unfathomable: mysterious; unknowable

"Bring forth the converts!" cried a voice that echoed through the field and rolled into the forest.

At the word, Goodman Brown stepped forth from the shadow of the trees and approached the congregation, with whom he felt a loathful brotherhood by the sympathy of all that was wicked in his heart. He could have well-nigh sworn that the shape of his own dead father beckoned him to advance, looking downward from a smoke wreath, while a woman, with dim features of despair, threw out her hand to warn him back. Was it his mother?

But he had no power to retreat one step, nor to resist, even in thought, when the minister and good old Deacon Gookin seized his arms and led him to the blazing rock. Thither came also the slender form of a veiled female, led between Goody Cloyse, that pious teacher of the catechism, and Martha Carrier, who had received the devil's promise to be queen of hell. A rampant hag was she. And there stood the proselytes[9] beneath the canopy of fire.

"Welcome, my children," said the dark figure, "to the communion of your race. Ye have found thus young your nature and your destiny. My children, look behind you!"

They turned; and flashing forth, as it were, in a sheet of flame, the fiend worshippers were seen; the smile of welcome gleamed darkly on every visage.

"There," resumed the sable form, "are all whom ye have reverenced from youth. Ye deemed them holier than yourselves, and shrank from your own sin, contrasting it with their lives of righteousness and prayerful aspirations heavenward. Yet here are they all in my worshipping assembly. This night it shall be granted you to know their secret deeds: how hoary-bearded elders of the church have whispered **wanton** words to the young maids of their households; how many a woman, eager for widows' weeds, has given her husband a drink at bedtime and let him sleep his last sleep in her bosom; how beardless youths have made haste to inherit their fathers' wealth; and how fair damsels—blush not, sweet ones—have dug little graves in the garden, and bidden me, the sole guest, to an infant's funeral. By the sympathy of your human hearts for sin ye shall scent out all the places—whether in church, bedchamber, street, field, or forest—where crime has been committed, and shall exult to behold the whole earth one stain of guilt, one mighty blood spot. Far more than this. It shall be yours to penetrate, in every bosom, the deep mystery of sin, the fountain of all wicked arts, and which inexhaustibly supplies more evil impulses than human power—than my power at its utmost—can make **manifest** in deeds. And now, my children, look upon each other."

They did so; and, by the blaze of the hell-kindled torches, the wretched man beheld his Faith, and the wife her husband, trembling before that unhallowed altar.

"Lo, there ye stand, my children," said the figure, in a deep and solemn tone, almost sad with its despairing awfulness, as if his once angelic nature

wanton: lewd; lustful

manifest: clear; apparent

---

9 proselytes: new believers; converts

could yet mourn for our miserable race. "Depending upon one another's hearts, ye had still hoped that virtue were not all a dream. Now are ye undeceived. Evil is the nature of mankind. Evil must be your only happiness. Welcome again, my children, to the communion of your race."

"Welcome," repeated the fiend worshippers, in one cry of despair and triumph.

And there they stood, the only pair, as it seemed, who were yet hesitating on the verge of wickedness in this dark world. A basin was hollowed, naturally, in the rock. Did it contain water, reddened by the lurid light? or was it blood? or, perchance, a liquid flame? Herein did the shape of evil dip his hand and prepare to lay the mark of baptism upon their foreheads, that they might be partakers of the mystery of sin, more conscious of the secret guilt of others, both in deed and thought, than they could now be of their own. The husband cast one look at his pale wife, and Faith at him. What polluted wretches would the next glance show them to each other, shuddering alike at what they disclosed and what they saw.

"Faith! Faith!" cried the husband, "look up to heaven, and resist the wicked one."

Whether Faith obeyed he knew not. Hardly had he spoken when he found himself amid calm night and solitude, listening to a roar of the wind which died heavily away through the forest. He staggered against the rock, and felt it chill and damp; while a hanging twig, that had been all on fire, besprinkled his cheek with the coldest dew.

The next morning young Goodman Brown came slowly into the street of Salem village, staring around him like a bewildered man. The good old minister was taking a walk along the graveyard to get an appetite for breakfast and meditate his sermon, and bestowed a blessing, as he passed, on Goodman Brown. He shrank from the **venerable** saint as if to avoid an **anathema**. Old Deacon Gookin was at domestic worship, and the holy words of his prayer were heard through the open window. "What God doth the wizard pray to?" quoth Goodman Brown. Goody Cloyse, that excellent old Christian, stood in the early sunshine at her own lattice, catechizing a little girl who had brought her a pint of morning's milk. Goodman Brown snatched away the child as from the grasp of the fiend himself. Turning the corner by the meeting-house, he spied the head of Faith, with the pink ribbons, gazing anxiously forth, and bursting into such joy at sight of him that she skipped along the street and almost kissed her husband before the whole village. But Goodman Brown looked sternly and sadly into her face, and passed on without a greeting.

venerable: distinguished; esteemed

anathema: abomination; hated thing

Had Goodman Brown fallen asleep in the forest and only dreamed a wild dream of a witch-meeting?

Had Goodman Brown fallen asleep in the forest and only dreamed a wild dream of a witch-meeting?

Be it so if you will; but, alas! it was a dream of evil omen for young Goodman Brown. A stern, a sad, a darkly meditative, a distrustful, if not a desperate man did he become from the night of that fearful dream. On the Sabbath day, when the congregation were singing a holy psalm, he could not listen because an anthem of sin rushed loudly upon his ear and drowned all the blessed strain. When the minister spoke from the pulpit with power and fervid eloquence, and, with his hand on the open Bible, of the sacred truths of our religion, and of saintlike lives and triumphant deaths, and of future bliss or misery unutterable, then did Goodman Brown turn pale, dreading lest the roof should thunder down upon the gray blasphemer and his hearers. Often, awaking suddenly at midnight, he shrank from the bosom of Faith; and at morning or eventide, when the family knelt down at prayer, he scowled and muttered to himself, and gazed sternly at his wife, and turned away. And when he had lived long, and was borne to his grave a hoary corpse, followed by Faith, an aged woman, and children and grandchildren, a goodly procession, besides neighbors not a few, they carved no hopeful verse upon his tombstone, for his dying hour was gloom.

Read and Think Critically

Analyze, Determine, Explain

1. **THEME** Describe some of the **themes** of the story. Which one seems to be the central theme? Analyze how Hawthorne uses the interaction of the various themes to enhance the meanings of the story. Explain your answer using details from the text.

2. Who is the figure that Goodman Brown meets in the woods? Describe how this person is **characterized** by citing specific details from the text.

3. At a crucial point in the story, Goodman Brown says, "My Faith is gone! . . .There is no good on earth; and sin is but a name." Determine the double meaning of Brown's words, exploring their deeper significance within the overall themes of the story.

4. How does Goodman Brown act upon his return to Salem? Discuss whether you think his attitude is justified.

5. Explain the meaning of the following **symbols** in this story: Faith, pink, red, black, the staff, the rock.

6. If Brown believes he has resisted the devil, why is it that "his dying hour was gloom"?

7. **THE AUTHOR'S STYLE** In Hawthorne's stories the **setting** is particularly meaningful. Analyze how Hawthorne uses the setting to advance a theme of the story. Support your conclusions by citing examples of two or three passages in which the setting or settings add meaning to the overall story.

Before You Read

Edgar Allan Poe 1809–1849

About the Author

A fearless original, Poe was also extremely productive in his short life. Although most famous as a master of terror, he also pioneered the modern detective story and early science fiction, and was a first-rate editor and critic.

Orphaned at age three, Poe was raised by the Allans, a wealthy family in Richmond, Virginia. He performed well in school and displayed literary aspirations in college. Poe's gambling debts and drinking episodes, however, caused Mr. Allan to withdraw support. After brief stints in the army and a military academy, Poe lived with an aunt and cousin in Baltimore. His cousin, Virginia, whom he married when she was thirteen, reportedly resembled the heroines in much of his fiction.

As an editor and critic, Poe became well-acquainted with the current literature, studied it carefully, and eventually developed a formula of his own. His first successful story collection included the detective classic "The Murders in the Rue Morgue." Fame followed with publication of "The Raven," one of the most widely read American poems. Despite fame, Poe still struggled financially.

Poe, the writer, has been described as "a wolf chained by the leg among a lot of domestic dogs." Yet he reportedly was gentle with loved ones, and even humorous at times. (He once apologized to a visitor for not keeping a pet raven.) After Virginia's premature death, he became even more unstable, yet managed to continue writing and to regain some fame by reciting "The Raven" to huge crowds. At age 40 the enigmatic writer met his own premature end. The precise cause remains a mystery.

★★★★★★★★★★★

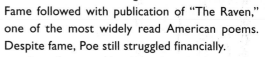

The Author's Style

Poe's work contains familiar Gothic elements: melodramatic plots, mysterious settings, grotesque characters, and surreal situations. But Poe is credited with elevating this popular genre into the realm of literature. His works explore more than the dark recesses of the outer world; they also probe the dark recesses of the human psyche. His characters grapple with dark pasts, hideous crimes, and their own deaths. Repressed emotions erupt, and psychological balance breaks down.

Structurally, a Poe story is a tightly controlled unit in which every element, every sentence, contributes to the whole. The voices of unreliable and often deranged first-person narrators reveal characters' psyches. Inventive sentence structures and sound techniques enhance a sense of terror. Irony is a major element in "The Masque of the Red Death," the story you are about to read. Will the prince and his guests meet the fate they so elaborately seek to avoid?

The Masque
of the
Red Death

EDGAR ALLAN POE

LITERARY LENS: SETTING **Setting** is the time and place of the action of a story. In Poe's fiction, the setting is always crucial to plot and meaning. Note the details that contribute to the setting's effectiveness in this story.

The "Red Death" had long devastated the country. No pestilence[1] had ever been so fatal, or so hideous. Blood was its Avatar[2] and its seal—the redness and the horror of blood. There were sharp pains, and sudden dizziness, and then **profuse** bleeding at the pores, with dissolution.[3] The scarlet stains upon the body and especially upon the face of the victim, were the pest ban[4] which shut him out from the aid and from the sympathy of his fellow-men. And the whole seizure, progress and termination of the disease, were the incidents of half an hour.

But the Prince Prospero was happy and **dauntless** and sagacious. When his dominions were half depopulated, he summoned to his

profuse: excessive; abundant

dauntless: bold; daring

---

1 **pestilence:** a fatal epidemic; plague

2 **Avatar:** the physical embodiment of something

3 **dissolution:** death

4 **pest ban:** a notice that someone is afflicted with the plague

presence a thousand hale and light-hearted friends from among the knights and dames of his court, and with these retired to the deep seclusion of one of his castellated[5] abbeys. This was an extensive and magnificent structure, the creation of the prince's own eccentric yet august taste. A strong and lofty wall girdled it in. This wall had gates of iron. The courtiers, having entered, brought furnaces and massy hammers and welded the bolts. They resolved to leave means neither of ingress or egress to the sudden impulses of despair or of frenzy from within. The abbey was amply provisioned. With such precautions the courtiers might bid defiance to contagion. The external world could take care of itself. In the meantime it was folly to grieve, or to think. The prince had provided all the appliances of pleasure. There were buffoons, there were improvisatori,[6] there were ballet-dancers, there were musicians, there was Beauty, there was wine. All these and security were within. Without was the "Red Death."

It was toward the close of the fifth or sixth month of his seclusion, and while the pestilence raged most furiously abroad, that the Prince Prospero entertained his thousand friends at a masked ball of the most unusual magnificence.

voluptuous:
extravagant;
hedonistic

It was a **voluptuous** scene, that masquerade. But first let me tell of the rooms in which it was held. There were seven—an imperial suite. In many palaces, however, such suites form a long and straight vista, while the folding doors slide back nearly to the walls on either hand, so that the view of the whole extent is scarcely **impeded**. Here the case was very different; as might have been expected from the duke's love of the *bizarre*. The apartments were so irregularly disposed that the vision embraced but little more than one at a time. There was a sharp turn at every twenty or thirty yards, and at each turn a novel effect. To the right and left, in the middle of each wall, a tall and narrow Gothic window looked out upon a closed corridor which pursued the windings of the suite. These windows were of stained glass whose color varied in accordance with the prevailing hue of the decorations of the chamber into which it opened. That at the eastern extremity was hung, for example, in blue—and vividly blue were its windows. The second chamber was purple in its ornaments and tapestries, and here the panes were purple. The third was green throughout, and so were the casements. The fourth was furnished and lighted with orange—the fifth with white—the sixth with violet. The seventh apartment was closely shrouded in black velvet tapestries that hung all over

impeded:
impaired;
hampered

5 **castellated:** built like a castle, with turrets and battlements

6 **improvisatori:** Italian for *improvisators*, entertainers who recite impromptu verse

the ceiling and down the walls, falling in heavy folds upon a carpet of the same material and hue. But in this chamber only, the color of the windows failed to correspond with the decorations. The panes here were scarlet—a deep blood color. Now in no one of the seven apartments was there any lamp or candelabrum, amid the profusion of golden ornaments that lay scattered to and fro or depended from the roof. There was no light of any kind emanating from lamp or candle within the suite of chambers. But in the corridors that followed the suite, there stood, opposite to each window, a heavy tripod, bearing a brazier of fire that projected its rays through the tinted glass and so glaringly illumined the room. And thus were produced a multitude of gaudy and fantastic appearances. But in the western or black chamber the effect of the fire-light that streamed upon the dark hangings through the blood-tinted panes, was ghastly in the extreme, and produced so wild a look upon the countenances of those who entered, that there were few of the company bold enough to set foot within its precincts at all.

It was in this apartment, also, that there stood against the western wall, a gigantic clock of ebony. Its pendulum swung to and fro with a dull, heavy, monotonous clang; and when the minute-hand made the circuit of the face, and the hour was to be stricken, there came from the brazen lungs of the clock a sound which was clear and loud and deep and exceedingly musical, but of so peculiar a note and emphasis that, at each lapse of an hour, the musicians of the orchestra were constrained to pause, momentarily, in their performance, to hearken to the sound; and thus the waltzers perforce ceased their evolutions; and there was a brief disconcert of the whole gay company; and, while the chimes of the clock yet rang, it was observed that the giddiest grew pale, and the more aged and **sedate** passed their hands over their brows as if in confused revery or meditation. But when the echoes had fully ceased, a light laughter at once pervaded the assembly; the musicians looked at each other and smiled as if at their own nervousness and folly, and made whispering vows, each to the other, that the next chiming of the clock should produce in them no similar emotion; and then, after the lapse of sixty minutes (which embrace three thousand and six hundred seconds of the Time that flies), there came yet another chiming of the clock, and then were the same disconcert and **tremulousness** and meditation as before.

But, in spite of these things, it was a gay and magnificent revel. The tastes of the duke were peculiar. He had a fine eye for colors and effects. He disregarded the decora of mere fashion. His plans were bold and fiery, and

sedate: calm; dignified

tremulousness: fear; timidity

his conceptions glowed with barbaric lustre. There are some who would have thought him mad. His followers felt that he was not. It was necessary to hear and see and touch him to be *sure* that he was not.

He had directed, in great part, the moveable embellishments of the seven chambers, upon occasion of this great *fete*; and it was his own guiding taste which had given character to the masqueraders. Be sure they were grotesque. There were much glare and glitter and piquancy and phantasm—much of what has been since seen in "Hernani."[7] There were arabesque[8] figures with unsuited limbs and appointments. There were delirious fancies such as the madman fashions. There were much of the beautiful, much of the wanton, much of the *bizarre*, something of the terrible, and not a little of that which might have excited disgust. To and fro in the seven chambers there stalked, in fact, a multitude of dreams. And these—the dreams—writhed in and about, taking hue from the rooms, and causing the wild music of the orchestra to seem as the echo of their steps. And, anon, there strikes the ebony clock which stands in the hall of velvet. And then, for a moment, all is still, and all is silent save the voice of the clock. The dreams are stiff-frozen as they stand. But the echoes of the chime die away—they have endured but an instant—and a light, half-subdued laughter floats after them as they depart. And now again the music swells, and the dreams live, and writhe to and fro more merrily than ever, taking hue from the many tinted windows through which stream the rays from the tripods. But to the chamber which lies most westwardly of the seven, there are now none of the maskers who venture; for the night is waning away; and there flows a ruddier light through the blood-colored panes; and the blackness of the sable drapery appalls; and to him whose foot falls upon the sable carpet, there comes from the near clock of ebony a muffled peal more solemnly **emphatic** than any which reaches *their* ears who indulge in the more remote gaieties of the other apartments.

emphatic:
forceful; striking

But these other apartments were densely crowded, and in them beat feverishly the heart of life. And the revel went whirlingly on, until at length there commenced the sounding of midnight upon the clock. And then the music ceased, as I have told; and the evolutions of the waltzers were quieted; and there was an uneasy cessation of all things as before. But now there were twelve strokes to be sounded by the bell of the clock; and thus it happened, perhaps, that more of thought crept, with more of time, into the meditations of the thoughtful among those who revelled. And thus, too, it happened,

---

7 **"Hernani":** a play by French writer Victor Hugo (1802–1885)

8 **arabesque:** highly decorated

★★

perhaps, that before the last echoes of the last chime had utterly sunk into silence, there were many individuals in the crowd who had found leisure to become aware of the presence of a masked figure which had **arrested** the attention of no single individual before. And the rumor of this new presence having spread itself whisperingly around, there arose at length from the whole company a buzz, or murmur, expressive of **disapprobation** and surprise—then, finally, of terror, of horror, and of disgust.

arrested: stopped; halted

disapprobation: disapproval; criticism

In an assembly of phantasms such as I have painted, it may well be supposed that no ordinary appearance could have excited such sensation. In truth the masquerade license of the night was nearly unlimited; but the figure in question had out-Heroded Herod,[9] and gone beyond the bounds of even the prince's indefinite decorum. There are chords in the hearts of the most reckless which cannot be touched without emotion. Even with the utterly lost, to whom life and death are equally jests, there are matters of which no jest can be made. The whole company, indeed, seemed now deeply to feel that in the costume and bearing of the stranger neither wit nor **propriety** existed. The figure was tall and gaunt, and shrouded from head to foot in the habiliments[10] of the grave. The mask which concealed the visage was made so nearly to resemble the countenance of a stiffened corpse that the closest scrutiny must have had difficulty in detecting the cheat. And yet all this might have been endured, if not approved, by the mad revellers around. But the mummer[11] had gone so far as to assume the type of the Red Death. His vesture was dabbled in *blood*—and his broad brow, with all the features of the face, was besprinkled with the scarlet horror.

propriety: decency; suitability

When the eyes of Prince Prospero fell upon this spectral image (which, with a slow and solemn movement, as if more fully to sustain its *role*, stalked to and fro among the waltzers) he was seen to be convulsed, in the first moment with a strong shudder either of terror or distaste; but, in the next, his brow reddened with rage.

"Who dares?"—he demanded hoarsely of the courtiers who stood near him—"who dares insult us with this blasphemous mockery? Seize him and unmask him—that we may know whom we have to hang, at sunrise, from the battlements!"

---

9 **out-Heroded Herod:** associated with the story of the slaughter of the innocents in the Bible, Herod is synonymous with "cruel." Anyone who outdoes him is extremely cruel.

10 **habiliments:** dress; clothing

11 **mummer:** a person in costume

★★★

It was in the eastern or blue chamber in which stood the Prince Prospero as he uttered these words. They rang throughout the seven rooms loudly and clearly, for the prince was a bold and robust man, and the music had become hushed at the waving of his hand.

It was in the blue room where stood the prince, with a group of pale courtiers by his side. At first, as he spoke, there was a slight rushing movement of this group in the direction of the intruder, who, at the moment was also near at hand, and now, with deliberate and stately step, made closer approach to the speaker. But from a certain nameless awe with which the mad assumptions of the mummer had inspired the whole party, there were found none who put

unimpeded:
unstopped

forth hand to seize him; so that, **unimpeded**, he passed within a yard of the prince's person; and, while the vast assembly, as if with one impulse, shrank from the centres of the rooms to the walls, he made his way uninterruptedly, but with the same solemn and measured step which had distinguished him from the first, through the blue chamber to the purple—through the purple to the green—through the green to the orange—through this again to the white—and even thence to the violet, ere a decided movement had been made to arrest him. It was then, however, that the Prince Prospero, maddening with rage and the shame of his own momentary cowardice, rushed hurriedly through the six chambers, while none followed him on account of a deadly terror that had seized upon all. He bore aloft a drawn dagger, and had approached,

impetuosity:
spontaneity;
abandon

in rapid **impetuosity**, to within three or four feet of the retreating figure, when the latter, having attained the extremity of the velvet apartment, turned suddenly and confronted his pursuer. There was a sharp cry—and the dagger dropped gleaming upon the sable carpet, upon which, instantly afterwards, fell prostrate in death the Prince Prospero. Then, summoning the wild courage of despair, a throng of the revellers at once threw themselves into the black apartment, and, seizing the mummer, whose tall figure stood erect and motionless within the shadow of the ebony clock, gasped in unutterable horror at finding the grave cerements[12] and corpse-like mask, which they handled with so violent a rudeness, untenanted[13] by any tangible form.

And now was acknowledged the presence of the Red Death. He had come like a thief in the night. And one by one dropped the revellers in the blood-bedewed halls of their revel, and died each in the despairing posture of his fall. And the life of the ebony clock went out with that of the last of the gay. And the flames of the tripods expired. And Darkness and Decay and the Red Death held illimitable dominion over all.

12 **cerements:** shrouds or coverings for the dead
13 **untenanted:** uninhabited

Read and Think Critically

Analyze, Explain, Evaluate

1. **SETTING** The **setting**—Prospero's castle—is vividly described. Analyze the author's choices of the lighting, room colors, and clock. What meanings do they suggest?

2. Analyze Poe's word choice in the first paragraph of the story. Which words create the **tone** of the story? Look up the word *Avatar* and consider its multiple meanings. What meaning did it have in Poe's story? How is it most often used today?

3. How would you describe Prospero? Determine his primary **character** trait by citing specific examples from the story.

4. When Prospero prepares for the party, the **narrator** says, "The external world could take care of itself. In the meantime it was folly to grieve, or to think." What happens later in the story when the guests stop to think?

5. Explain the emotions of the guests each time the clock strikes and later when the music resumes.

6. **THE AUTHOR'S STYLE** In a few sentences, summarize the **plot** of the story. Then read the quotation below. Evaluate the complexity of the plot versus the emotional impact of the story. Based upon what you know about Poe's style, what do you think Poe's primary goal was in writing the story?

Consideration of an Effect

I prefer commencing with the consideration of an effect. Keeping originality always in view—for he is false to himself who ventures to dispense with so obvious and so easily attainable a source of interest—I say to myself, in the first place, "Of the innumerable effects, or impressions, of which the heart, the intellect, or (more generally) the soul is susceptible, what one shall I, on the present occasion, select?"

—Edgar Allan Poe, "The Philosophy of Composition"

Before You Read

Herman Melville 1819–1891

About the Author

By the time he died, Herman Melville was chiefly thought of as "that writer who lived with the cannibals." He was celebrated in the 1840s and produced a masterpiece, *Moby-Dick*, in 1851. But for most of his career, he did not write what the public wanted or the critics esteemed. As a result, he spent the last part of his life toiling in obscurity.

The author suffered many disappointments in his life. Born to a once-wealthy New York family, his father's bankruptcy and death forced Melville to quit school at 15 and work to support his mother and seven siblings. After stints as a bank clerk and schoolteacher, the young man shipped out to sea as a cabin boy on the whaler *Acushnet*. His lengthy voyages on the Atlantic and South Seas provided him with all the adventures he needed to write his first novels. His capture by friendly cannibals in the South Seas contributed to the South Sea novel *Typee* (1846) and later *Omoo* (1847), romantic adventure stories that the public devoured.

With *Moby-Dick*, however, the public and critical reception cooled. People found the long, highly symbolic story about the pursuit of a white whale "too dull, poorly written, or incoherently metaphysical."

By the middle of the 20th century, Melville had become the focus of more literary scholarship than any other American writer. His short story, "Bartleby the Scrivener" is widely thought to be one of his most important fictions, a predecessor of existentialist and absurdist literature.

****

The Author's Style

Melville's early works are lighthearted tales of his adventures at sea. In their depiction of abuses by both the U.S. Navy and Christian missionaries, they also express the very beginnings of Melville's disillusionment with Western civilization. Melville created the epic novel *Moby-Dick* after reading works by Shakespeare and Hawthorne. A dark, morally ambiguous, and stylistically experimental work, *Moby-Dick* explores such themes as man's struggle against his destiny and the powerful downfalls and victories of the human spirit. Ahead of his time, Melville also explored the tension between faith and doubt and the concept of existentialism.

Stylistically, Melville was a master at using classic rhetorical devices to emphasize ideas or evoke moods. In *Moby-Dick*, he experimented with combining genres and styles. The fictional story is mixed with whaling information, autobiography, metaphysical musings, dramatic stage directions, and even art criticism. In "Bartleby the Scrivener," Melville uses imagery, symbolism, and inventive narration to explore the effects of materialism on the individual. Wall Street's tragic effect on Bartleby is magnified by the narrator's own struggle to understand the dehumanized scrivener.

Bartleby
the Scrivener
A Tale of Wall Street

HERMAN MELVILLE

> **LITERARY LENS: CONFLICT** **Conflict** can be described as a struggle between opposing forces, the basis of all suspense. Writers use conflict to fuel the plot and reveal character traits. As you read, observe the nature and progress of the conflict between Bartleby and his employer.

I am a rather elderly man. The nature of my avocations[1] for the last thirty years has brought me into more than ordinary contact with what would seem an interesting and somewhat singular set of men, of whom as yet nothing that I know of has ever been written: —I mean the law-copyists, or scriveners. I have known very many of them, professionally and privately, and if I pleased, could relate divers histories, at which good-natured gentlemen might smile, and sentimental souls might weep. But I waive the biographies of all other scriveners for a few passages in the life of Bartleby, who was a scrivener, the strangest I ever saw, or heard of. While of other law-copyists, I might write the complete life, of Bartleby nothing of that sort can be done. I believe that no materials exist for a full and satisfactory biography of this man. It is an irreparable

---

1 **avocations:** regular or customary employment

loss to literature. Bartleby was one of those beings of whom nothing is **ascertainable**, except from the original sources, and in his case those are very small. What my own astonished eyes saw of Bartleby, *that* is all I know of him, except, indeed, one vague report which will appear in the sequel.

Ere introducing the scrivener, as he first appeared to me, it is fit I make some mention of myself, my *employés*, my business, my chambers, and general surroundings; because some such description is **indispensable** to an adequate understanding of the chief character about to be presented.

Imprimis:[2] I am a man who, from his youth upward, has been filled with a profound conviction that the easiest way of life is the best. Hence, though I belong to a profession proverbially energetic and nervous, even to turbulence, at times, yet nothing of that sort have I ever suffered to invade my peace. I am one of those unambitious lawyers who never addresses a jury, or in any way draws down public applause; but in the cool tranquillity of a snug retreat, do a snug business among rich men's bonds and mortgages and title-deeds. All who know me, consider me an eminently *safe* man. The late John Jacob Astor,[3] a personage little given to poetic enthusiasm, had no hesitation in pronouncing my first grand point to be **prudence**; my next, method. I do not speak it in vanity, but simply record the fact, that I was not unemployed in my profession by the late John Jacob Astor; a name which, I admit, I love to repeat, for it hath a rounded and orbicular[4] sound to it, and rings like unto bullion.[5] I will freely add, that I was not insensible to the late John Jacob Astor's good opinion.

Some time prior to the period at which this little history begins, my avocations had been largely increased. The good old office, now extinct in the State of New York, of a Master in Chancery, had been conferred upon me. It was not a very **arduous** office, but very pleasantly **remunerative**. I seldom lose my temper; much more seldom indulge in dangerous indignation at wrongs and outrages; but I must be permitted to be rash here and declare, that I consider the sudden and violent abrogation[6] of the office of Master in Chancery, by the new Constitution, as a—premature act; inasmuch as I had counted upon a life-lease of the profits, whereas I only received those of a few short years. But this is by the way.

ascertainable: able to be known

indispensable: essential; necessary

prudence: caution; carefulness

arduous: tough; difficult
remunerative: profitable; lucrative

---

2 **Imprimis:** Latin for "in the first place"

3 **John Jacob Astor:** (1763–1848), a merchant with the largest fortune in America at the time

4 **orbicular:** circular

5 **bullion:** gold or silver bars

6 **abrogation:** cancellation; annulment

My chambers were upstairs at No.—Wall Street. At one end they looked upon the white wall of the interior of a spacious sky-light shaft, penetrating the building from top to bottom. This view might have been considered rather tame than otherwise, deficient in what landscape painters call "life." But if so, the view from the other end of my chambers offered, at least, a contrast, if nothing more. In that direction my windows commanded an unobstructed view of a lofty brick wall, black by age and everlasting shade; which wall required no spy-glass to bring out its lurking beauties, but for the benefit of all near-sighted spectators, was pushed up to within ten feet of my window panes. Owing to the great height of the surrounding buildings, and my chambers being on the second floor, the interval between this wall and mine not a little resembled a huge square cistern.[7]

At the period just preceding the advent of Bartleby, I had two persons as copyists in my employment, and a promising lad as an office-boy. First, Turkey; second, Nippers; third, Ginger Nut. These may seem names, the like of which are not usually found in the Directory. In truth they were nicknames, mutually conferred upon each other by my three clerks, and were deemed expressive of their respective persons or characters. Turkey was a short, pursy[8] Englishman of about my own age, that is, somewhere not far from sixty. In the morning, one might say, his face was of a fine florid hue, but after twelve o'clock, meridian[9]—his dinner hour—it blazed like a grate full of Christmas coals; and continued blazing—but, as it were, with a gradual wane—till 6 o'clock P.M. or thereabouts, after which I saw no more of the proprietor of the face, which, gaining its meridian with the sun, seemed to set with it, to rise, culminate, and decline the following day, with the like regularity and undiminished glory.

There are many singular coincidences I have known in the course of my life, not the least among which was the fact, that exactly when Turkey displayed his fullest beams from his red and radiant countenance, just then, too, at that critical moment, began the daily period when I considered his business capacities as seriously disturbed for the remainder of the twenty-four hours. Not that he was absolutely idle, or averse to business then; far from it. The difficulty was, he was apt to be altogether too energetic. There was a strange, inflamed, flurried, flighty recklessness of activity about him. He would be incautious in dipping his pen into his inkstand. All his blots

---

7 **cistern:** water tank

8 **pursy:** fat

9 **meridian:** noon

upon my documents, were dropped there after twelve o'clock, meridian. Indeed, not only would he be reckless and sadly given to making blots in the afternoon, but some days he went further, and was rather noisy. At such times, too, his face flamed with **augmented** blazonry, as if cannel coal had been heaped on anthracite.[10] He made an unpleasant racket with his chair; spilled his sand-box;[11] in mending his pens, impatiently split them all to pieces, and threw them on the floor in a sudden passion; stood up and leaned over his table, boxing his papers about in a most indecorous manner, very sad to behold in an elderly man like him. Nevertheless, as he was in many ways a most valuable person to me, and all the time before twelve o'clock, meridian, was the quickest, steadiest creature, too, accomplishing a great deal of work in a style not easy to be matched—for these reasons, I was willing to overlook his eccentricities, though indeed, occasionally, I **remonstrated** with him. I did this very gently, however, because, though the civilest, nay, the blandest and most reverential of men in the morning, yet in the afternoon he was disposed, upon **provocation**, to be slightly rash with his tongue, in fact, **insolent**. Now, valuing his morning services as I did, and resolving not to lose them—yet, at the same time, made uncomfortable by his inflamed ways after twelve o'clock; and being a man of peace, unwilling by my **admonitions** to call forth unseemly **retorts** from him—I took upon me, one Saturday noon (he was always worse on Saturdays), to hint to him, very kindly, that perhaps now that he was growing old, it might be well to abridge his labors; in short, he need not come to my chambers after twelve o'clock, but, dinner over, had best go home to his lodgings and rest himself till tea-time. But no; he insisted upon his afternoon devotions. His countenance became intolerably fervid, as he oratorically assured me—gesticulating, with a long ruler, at the other side of the room—that if his services in the morning were useful, how indispensable, then, in the afternoon?

"With submission, sir," said Turkey on this occasion, "I consider myself your right-hand man. In the morning I but marshal and deploy my columns; but in the afternoon I put myself at their head, and gallantly charge the foe, thus!"—and he made a violent thrust with the ruler.

"But the blots, Turkey," intimated I.

"True,—but, with submission, sir, behold these hairs! I am getting old. Surely, sir, a blot or two of a warm afternoon is not to be severely urged

---

10 **cannel coal . . . anthracite:** cannel is a bright-burning, smoky coal; anthracite burns with little light or smoke

11 **sand-box:** a shaker or receptacle for sprinkling sand on wet ink to help it dry

augmented: exaggerated; heightened

remonstrated: protested; scolded

provocation: aggravation; goad

insolent: rude; insulting

admonitions: warnings; scoldings

retorts: responses

Herman Melville   Unit 1

against grey hairs. Old age—even if it blot the page—is honorable. With submission, sir, we *both* are getting old."

This appeal to my fellow-feeling was hardly to be resisted. At all events, I saw that go he would not. So I made up my mind to let him stay, resolving, nevertheless, to see to it, that during the afternoon he had to do with my less important papers.

Nippers, the second on my list, was a whiskered, sallow, and, upon the whole, rather piratical-looking man of about five and twenty. I always deemed him the victim of two evil powers—ambition and indigestion. The ambition was evinced by a certain impatience of the duties of a mere copyist—an unwarrantable usurpation[12] of strictly professional affairs, such as the original drawing up of legal documents. The indigestion seemed betokened in an occasional nervous testiness and grinning irritability, causing the teeth to audibly grind together over mistakes committed in copying; unnecessary maledictions,[13] hissed, rather than spoken, in the heart of business; and especially a continual discontent with the height of the table where he worked. Though of a very ingenious mechanical turn, Nippers could never get this table to suit him. He put chips under it, blocks of various sorts, bits of pasteboard, and at last went so far as to attempt an exquisite adjustment by final pieces of folded blotting-paper. But no invention would answer. If, for the sake of easing his back, he brought the table lid at a sharp angle well up towards his chin, and wrote there like a man using the steep roof of a Dutch house for his desk—then he declared that it stopped the circulation in his arms. If now he lowered the table to his waistbands, and stooped over it in writing, then there was a sore aching in his back. In short, the truth of the matter was, Nippers knew not what he wanted. Or, if he wanted anything, it was to be rid of a scrivener's table altogether. Among the manifestations of his diseased ambition was a fondness he had for receiving visits from certain ambiguous-looking fellows in seedy coats, whom he called his clients. Indeed I was aware that not only was he, at times, considerable of a ward-politician, but he occasionally did a little business at the Justices' courts, and was not unknown on the steps of the Tombs.[14] I have good reason to believe, however, that one individual who called upon him at my chambers, and who, with a grand air, he insisted was his client, was no other than a dun,[15] and the alleged

---

12 **unwarrantable usurpation:** an unjustified takeover

13 **maledictions:** curses

14 **Tombs:** an old prison in New York

15 **dun:** a bill collector

title-deed, a bill. But with all his failings, and the annoyances he caused me, Nippers, like his compatriot Turkey, was a very useful man to me; wrote a neat, swift hand; and, when he chose, was not deficient in a gentlemanly sort of deportment.[16] Added to this, he always dressed in a gentlemanly sort of way; and so, incidentally, reflected credit upon my chambers. Whereas with respect to Turkey, I had much ado to keep him from being a reproach to me. His clothes were apt to look oily and smell of eating-houses. He wore his pantaloons very loose and baggy in summer. His coats were execrable;[17] his hat not to be handled. But while the hat was a thing of indifference to me, inasmuch as his natural civility and deference, as a dependent Englishman, always led him to doff[18] it the moment he entered the room, yet his coat was another matter. Concerning his coats, I reasoned with him; but with no effect. The truth was, I suppose, that a man with so small an income, could not afford to sport such a lustrous face and a lustrous coat at one and the same time. As Nippers once observed, Turkey's money went chiefly for red ink. One winter day I presented Turkey with a highly respectable-looking coat of my own, a padded grey coat, of a most comfortable warmth, and which buttoned straight up from the knee to the neck. I thought Turkey would appreciate the favor, and abate his rashness and obstreperousness of afternoons. But no. I verily believe that buttoning himself up in so downy and blanket-like a coat had a **pernicious** effect upon him; upon the same principle that too much oats are bad for horses. In fact, precisely as a rash, restive horse is said to feel his oats, so Turkey felt his coat. It made him insolent. He was a man whom prosperity harmed.

pernicious: harmful; dangerous

Though concerning the self-indulgent habits of Turkey I had my own private surmises,[19] yet touching Nippers I was well persuaded that whatever might be his faults in other respects, he was, at least, a temperate young man. But, indeed, nature herself seemed to have been his vintner,[20] and at his birth charged him so thoroughly with an irritable, brandy-like disposition, that all subsequent potations[21] were needless. When I consider how, amid the stillness of my chambers, Nippers would sometimes impatiently rise from his seat, and stooping over his table, spread his arms wide apart, seize the whole

---

16 **deportment:** manners; personal behavior

17 **execrable:** offensive; disgusting

18 **doff:** take off

19 **surmises:** guesses

20 **vintner:** one who makes or sells wine

21 **potations:** alcoholic drinks

desk, and move it, and jerk it, with a grim, grinding motion on the floor, as if the table were a perverse voluntary agent, intent on thwarting and vexing him; I plainly perceive that for Nippers, brandy-and-water were altogether superfluous.

It was fortunate for me that, owing to its peculiar cause—indigestion—the irritability and consequent nervousness of Nippers, were mainly observable in the morning, while in the afternoon he was comparatively mild. So that Turkey's **paroxysms** only coming on about twelve o'clock, I never had to do with their eccentricities at one time. Their fits relieved each other like guards. When Nippers' was on, Turkey's was off; and vice versa. This was a good natural arrangement under the circumstances.

paroxysms: fits; spasms

Ginger Nut, the third on my list, was a lad some twelve years old. His father was a car-man, ambitious of seeing his son on the bench instead of a cart, before he died. So he sent him to my office as a student at law, errand-boy, and cleaner and sweeper, at the rate of one dollar a week. He had a little desk to himself, but he did not use it much. Upon inspection, the drawer exhibited a great array of the shells of various sorts of nuts. Indeed, to this quickwitted youth the whole noble science of the law was contained in a nutshell. Not the least among the employments of Ginger Nut, as well as one which he discharged with the most **alacrity**, was his duty as cake and apple purveyor[22] for Turkey and Nippers. Copying law papers being proverbially a dry, husky sort of business, my two scriveners were fain to moisten their mouths very often with Spitzenbergs to be had at the numerous stalls nigh the Custom House and Post Office. Also, they sent Ginger Nut very frequently for that peculiar cake—small, flat, round, and very spicy after which he had been named by them. Of a cold morning, when business was but dull, Turkey would gobble up scores of these cakes, as if they were mere wafers—indeed they sell them at the rate of six or eight for a penny—the scrape of his pen blending with the crunching of the crisp particles in his mouth. Of all the fiery afternoon blunders and flurried rashnesses of Turkey, was his once moistening a ginger-cake between his lips, and clapping it on to a mortgage for a seal. I came within an ace of dismissing him then. But he **mollified** me by making an oriental bow and saying—"With submission, sir, it was generous of me to find you in[23] stationery on my own account."

alacrity: quickness; alertness

mollified: pleased; gratified

Now my original business—that of a conveyancer and title hunter, and

---

22 **purveyor:** a supplier

23 **find you in:** supply you with

recondite:
obscure;
scholarly

drawer-up of **recondite** documents of all sorts—was considerably increased by receiving the master's office. There was now great work for scriveners. Not only must I push the clerks already with me, but I must have additional help. In answer to my advertisement, a motionless young man one morning stood upon my office threshold, the door being open, for it was summer. I can see that figure now—pallidly neat, pitiably respectable, incurably forlorn! It was Bartleby.

After a few words touching his qualifications, I engaged him, glad to have among my corps of copyists a man of so singularly sedate an aspect, which I thought might operate beneficially upon the flighty temper of Turkey, and the fiery one of Nippers.

I should have stated before that ground glass folding-doors divided my premises into two parts, one of which was occupied by my scriveners, the other by myself. According to my humor I threw open these doors, or closed them. I resolved to assign Bartleby a corner by the folding-doors, but on my side of them, so as to have this quiet man within easy call, in case any trifling thing was to be done. I placed his desk close up to a small side-window in that part of the room, a window which originally had afforded a lateral view of certain grimy back-yards and bricks, but which, owing to subsequent erections, commanded at present no view at all, though it gave some light. Within three feet of the panes was a wall, and the light came down from far above, between two lofty buildings, as from a very small opening in a dome. Still further to a satisfactory arrangement, I procured a high green folding screen, which might entirely isolate Bartleby from my sight, though not remove him from my voice. And thus, in a manner, privacy and society were conjoined.

At first Bartleby did an extraordinary quantity of writing. As if long famishing for something to copy, he seemed to gorge himself on my documents. There was no pause for digestion. He ran a day and night line, copying by sun-light and by candle-light. I should have been quite delighted with his application, had he been cheerfully industrious. But he wrote on silently, palely, mechanically.

It is, of course, an indispensable part of a scrivener's business to verify the accuracy of his copy, word by word. Where there are two or more scriveners in an office, they assist each other in this examination, one reading from the copy, the other holding the original. It is a very dull, wearisome, and **lethargic** affair. I can readily imagine that to some **sanguine** temperaments it would

lethargic:
sleep-inducing

sanguine:
confident; high-
spirited

be altogether intolerable. For example, I cannot credit that the mettlesome poet Byron would have contentedly sat down with Bartleby to examine a law document of, say five hundred pages, closely written in a crimpy hand.[24]

Now and then, in the haste of business, it had been my habit to assist in comparing some brief document myself, calling Turkey or Nippers for this purpose. One object I had in placing Bartleby so handy to me behind the screen, was to avail myself of his services on such trivial occasions. It was on the third day, I think, of his being with me, and before any necessity had arisen for having his own writing examined, that, being much hurried to complete a small affair I had in hand, I abruptly called to Bartleby. In my haste and natural expectancy of instant compliance, I sat with my head bent over the original on my desk, and my right hand sideways, and somewhat nervously extended with the copy, so that immediately upon emerging from his retreat, Bartleby might snatch and proceed to business without the least delay.

VERMONT LAWYER, HORACE BUNDY, 1841

In this very attitude did I sit when I called to him, rapidly stating what it was I wanted him to do—namely, to examine a small paper with me. Imagine my surprise, nay, my consternation, when without moving from his privacy, Bartleby in a singularly mild, firm voice, replied, "I would prefer not to."

I sat awhile in perfect silence, rallying my stunned faculties. Immediately it occurred to me that my ears had deceived me, or Bartleby had entirely misunderstood my meaning. I repeated my request in the clearest tone I could assume. But in quite as clear a one came the previous reply, "I would prefer not to."

"Prefer not to," echoed I, rising in high excitement, and crossing the room with a stride. "What do you mean? Are you moon-struck? I want you to help me compare this sheet—here take it," and I thrust it towards him.

---

24 **crimpy hand:** cramped handwriting

"I would prefer not to," said he.

I looked at him steadfastly. His face was leanly composed; his grey eye dimly calm. Not a wrinkle of agitation rippled him. Had there been the least uneasiness, anger, impatience or impertinence in his manner; in other words, had there been anything ordinarily human about him; doubtless I should have violently dismissed him from the premises. But as it was, I should have as soon thought of turning my pale plaster-of-Paris bust of Cicero[25] out of doors. I stood gazing at him awhile, as he went on with his own writing, and then reseated myself at my desk. This is very strange, thought I. What had one best do? But my business hurried me. I concluded to forget the matter for the present, preserving it for my future leisure. So calling Nippers from the other room, the paper was speedily examined.

A few days after this, Bartleby concluded four lengthy documents, being quadruplicates of a week's testimony taken before me in my High Court of Chancery. It became necessary to examine them. It was an important suit, and great accuracy was imperative. Having all things arranged, I called Turkey, Nippers and Ginger Nut from the next room, meaning to place the four copies in the hands of my four clerks, while I should read from the original. Accordingly, Turkey, Nippers and Ginger Nut had taken their seats in a row, each with his document in hand, when I called to Bartleby to join this interesting group.

"Bartleby! quick, I am waiting."

I heard a slow scrape of his chair legs on the uncarpeted floor, and soon he appeared standing at the entrance of his hermitage.[26]

"What is wanted?" said he mildly.

"The copies, the copies," said I hurriedly. "We are going to examine them. There"—and I held towards him the fourth quadruplicate.

"I would prefer not to," he said, and gently disappeared behind the screen.

For a few moments I was turned into a pillar of salt, standing at the head of my seated column of clerks. Recovering myself, I advanced towards the screen, and demanded the reason for such extraordinary conduct.

"*Why* do you refuse?"

"I would prefer not to."

With any other man I should have flown outright into a dreadful passion,

25 **bust of Cicero:** a sculpture of the head of the Roman statesman and orator (106–42 B.C.)

26 **hermitage:** place inhabited by a hermit or loner

scorned all further words, and thrust him **ignominiously** from my presence. But there was something about Bartleby that not only strangely disarmed me, but in a wonderful manner touched and disconcerted me. I began to reason with him.

ignominiously: in a dishonorable fashion

"These are your own copies we are about to examine. It is labor saving to you, because one examination will answer for your four papers. It is common usage. Every copyist is bound to help examine his copy. Is it not so? Will you not speak? Answer!"

"I prefer not to," he replied in a flute-like tone. It seemed to me that while I had been addressing him, he carefully revolved every statement that I made; fully comprehended the meaning: could not gainsay[27] the irresistible conclusion; but, at the same time, some paramount consideration prevailed with him to reply as he did.

"You are decided, then, not to comply with my request—a request made according to common usage and common sense?"

He briefly gave me to understand that on that point my judgment was sound. Yes: his decision was irreversible.

It is not seldom the case that when a man is browbeaten in some unprecedented and violently unreasonable way, he begins to stagger in his own plainest faith. He begins, as it were, vaguely to surmise that, wonderful as it may be, all the justice and all the reason are on the other side. Accordingly, if any disinterested persons are present, he turns to them for some reinforcement for his own faltering mind.

"Turkey," said I, "what do you think of this? Am I not right?"

"With submission, sir," said Turkey, with his blandest tone, "I think that you are."

"Nippers," said I, "what do *you* think of it?"

"I think I should kick him out of the office."

(The reader of nice perceptions will perceive that, it being morning, Turkey's answer is couched in polite and tranquil terms but Nippers' reply in ill-tempered ones. Or, to repeat a previous sentence, Nippers' ugly mood was on duty, and Turkey's off.)

"Ginger Nut," said I, willing to enlist the smallest suffrage[28] in my behalf, "what do *you* think of it?"

"I think, sir, he's a little *luny*," replied Ginger Nut, with a grin.

---

27 **gainsay:** deny

28 **suffrage:** a vote

"You hear what they say," said I, turning towards the screen, "come forth and do your duty."

But he vouchsafed[29] no reply. I pondered a moment in sore perplexity. But once more business hurried me. I determined again to postpone the consideration of this dilemma to my future leisure. With a little trouble we made out to examine the papers without Bartleby, though at every page or two, Turkey **deferentially** dropped his opinion that this proceeding was quite out of the common; while Nippers, twitching in his chair with a dyspeptic[30] nervousness, ground out between his set teeth occasional hissing maledictions against the stubborn oaf behind the screen. And for his (Nippers') part, this was the first and the last time he would do another man's business without pay.

Meanwhile Bartleby sat in his hermitage, oblivious to everything but his own peculiar business there.

Some days passed, the scrivener being employed upon another lengthy work. His late remarkable conduct led me to regard his ways narrowly. I observed that he never went to dinner; indeed that he never went anywhere. As yet I had never of my personal knowledge known him to be outside of my office. He was a perpetual sentry in the corner. At about eleven o'clock though, in the morning, I noticed that Ginger Nut would advance towards the opening in Bartleby's screen, as if silently beckoned thither by a gesture invisible to me where I sat. The boy would then leave the office jingling a few pence, and reappear with a handful of ginger-nuts which he delivered in the hermitage, receiving two of the cakes for his trouble.

He lives, then, on ginger-nuts, thought I; never eats a dinner, properly speaking; he must be a vegetarian then; but no; he never eats even vegetables, he eats nothing but ginger-nuts. My mind then ran on in reveries concerning the probable effects upon the human constitution of living entirely on ginger-nuts. Ginger-nuts are so called because they contain ginger as one of their peculiar constituents, and the final flavoring one. Now what was ginger? A hot, spicy, thing. Was Bartleby hot and spicy? Not at all. Ginger, then, had no effect upon Bartleby. Probably he preferred it should have none.

Nothing so aggravates an earnest person as a passive resistance. If the individual so resisted be of a not inhumane temper, and the resisting one perfectly harmless in his passivity; then, in the better moods of the former, he will endeavor charitably to construe to his imagination what

deferentially: respectfully; politely

---

29 **vouchsafed:** gave or awarded as an act of charity or a favor

30 **dyspeptic:** bad-tempered

proves impossible to be solved by his judgment. Even so, for the most part, I regarded Bartleby and his ways. Poor fellow! thought I, he means no mischief; it is plain he intends no insolence: his aspect sufficiently evinces[31] that his **eccentricities** are involuntary. He is useful to me. I can get along with him. If I turn him away, the chances are he will fall in with some less indulgent employer, and then he will be rudely treated, and perhaps driven forth miserably to starve. Yes. Here I can cheaply purchase a delicious self-approval. To befriend Bartleby; to humor him in his strange willfulness, will cost me little or nothing, while I lay up in my soul what will eventually prove a sweet morsel for my conscience. But this mood was not invariable with me. The passiveness of Bartleby sometimes irritated me. I felt strangely goaded on to encounter him in new opposition, to elicit some angry spark from him answerable to my own. But indeed I might as well have essayed to strike fire with my knuckles against a bit of Windsor soap. But one afternoon the evil impulse in me mastered me, and the following little scene ensued:

"Bartleby," said I, "when those papers are all copied, I will compare them with you."

"I would prefer not to."

"How? Surely you do not mean to persist in that mulish vagary?"

No answer.

I threw open the folding-doors near by, and turning upon Turkey and Nippers, exclaimed in an excited manner:

"He says, a second time, he won't examine his papers. What do you think of it, Turkey?"

It was afternoon, be it remembered. Turkey sat glowing like a brass boiler, his bald head steaming, his hands reeling among his blotted papers.

"Think of it?" roared Turkey; "I think I'll just step behind his screen, and black his eyes for him!"

So saying, Turkey rose to his feet and threw his arms into a pugilistic[32] position. He was hurrying away to make good his promise, when I detained him, alarmed at the effect of incautiously rousing Turkey's combativeness after dinner.

"Sit down, Turkey," said I, "and hear what Nippers has to say. What do you think of it, Nippers? Would I not be justified in immediately dismissing Bartleby?"

> **eccentricities:** odd habits; strange behaviors

---

31 **evinces:** demonstrates, shows

32 **pugilistic:** like a boxer or combatant

"Excuse me, that is for you to decide, sir. I think his conduct quite unusual, and indeed unjust, as regards Turkey and myself. But it may only be a passing whim."

"Ah," exclaimed I, "you have strangely changed your mind then—you speak very gently of him now."

"All beer," cried Turkey; "gentleness is effects of beer—Nippers and I dined together today. You see how gentle I am, sir. Shall I go and black his eyes?"

"You refer to Bartleby, I suppose. No, not today, Turkey," I replied; "pray, put up your fists."

I closed the doors, and again advanced towards Bartleby. I felt additional incentives tempting me to my fate. I burned to be rebelled against again. I remembered that Bartleby never left the office.

"Bartleby," said I, "Ginger Nut is away; just step round to the Post Office, won't you? (it was but a three minutes' walk), and see if there is anything for me."

"I would prefer not to."

"You *will* not?"

"I *prefer* not."

I staggered to my desk, and sat there in a deep study. My blind inveteracy returned. Was there any other thing in which I could procure myself to be ignominiously repulsed by this lean, penniless wight?—my hired clerk? What added thing is there, perfectly reasonable, that he will be sure to refuse to do?

"Bartleby!"

No answer.

"Bartleby," in a louder tone.

No answer.

"Bartleby," I roared.

Like a very ghost, agreeably to the laws of magical invocation, at the third summons, he appeared at the entrance of his hermitage.

"Go to the next room, and tell Nippers to come to me."

"I prefer not to," he respectfully and slowly said, and mildly disappeared.

"Very good, Bartleby," said I, in a quiet sort of serenely-severe self-possessed tone, intimating the unalterable purpose of some terrible **retribution** very close at hand. At the moment I half intended something of the kind. But upon the

retribution:
revenge;
retaliation

whole, as it was drawing towards my dinner-hour, I thought it best to put on my hat and walk home for the day, suffering much from perplexity and distress of mind.

Shall I acknowledge it? The conclusion of this whole business was, that it soon became a fixed fact of my chambers, that a pale young scrivener, by the name of Bartleby, had a desk there; that he copied for me at the usual rate of four cents a folio (one hundred words); but he was permanently exempt from examining the work done by him, that duty being transferred to Turkey and Nippers, out of compliment doubtless to their superior acuteness; moreover, said Bartleby was never on any account to be dispatched on the most trivial errand of any sort; and that even if entreated to take upon him such a matter, it was generally understood that he would prefer not to—in other words, that he would refuse point-blank.

As days passed on, I became considerably reconciled to Bartleby. His steadiness, his freedom from all **dissipation**, his incessant industry (except when he chose to throw himself into a standing revery behind his screen), his great stillness, his unalterableness of demeanor[33] under all circumstances, made him a valuable acquisition. One prime thing was this— *he was always there*—first in the morning, continually through the day, and the last at night. I had a singular confidence in his honesty. I felt my most precious papers perfectly safe in his hands. Sometimes to be sure I could not, for the very soul of me, avoid falling into sudden spasmodic passions with him. For it was exceeding difficult to bear in mind all the time those strange peculiarities, privileges, and unheard of exemptions, forming the tacit stipulations[34] on Bartleby's part under which he remained in my office. Now and then, in the eagerness of despatching[35] pressing business, I would **inadvertently** summon Bartleby, in a short, rapid tone, to put his finger, say, on the **incipient** tie of a bit of red tape with which I was about compressing some papers. Of course, from behind the screen the usual answer, "I prefer not to," was sure to come; and then, how could a human creature with the common infirmities of our nature, refrain from bitterly exclaiming upon such **perverseness**—such unreasonableness. However, every added repulse of this sort which I received only tended to lessen the probability of my repeating the inadvertence.

Here it must be said, that according to the custom of most legal gentlemen

dissipation: indulgences; debauchery

inadvertently: accidentally; mistakenly

incipient: first; beginning

perverseness: contrariness; cantankerousness

---

33 **unalterableness of demeanor:** unchangeable behavior

34 **tacit stipulations:** unspoken conditions

35 **despatching:** sending off

occupying chambers in densely-populated law buildings, there were several keys to my door. One was kept by a woman residing in the attic, which person weekly scrubbed and daily swept and dusted my apartments. Another was kept by Turkey for convenience' sake. The third I sometimes carried in my own pocket. The fourth I knew not who had.

Now, one Sunday morning I happened to go to Trinity Church, to hear a celebrated preacher, and finding myself rather early on the ground, I thought I would walk round to my chambers for awhile. Luckily I had my key with me; but upon applying it to the lock, I found it resisted by something inserted from the inside. Quite surprised, I called out; when to my consternation a key was turned from within; and thrusting his lean visage at me, and holding the door ajar, the apparition of Bartleby appeared, in his shirt sleeves, and otherwise in a strangely tattered dishabille,[36] saying quietly that he was deeply engaged just then, and—preferred not admitting me at present. In a brief word or two, he moreover added, that perhaps I had better walk round the block two or three times, and by that time he would probably have concluded his affairs.

Now, the utterly unsurmised appearance of Bartleby, tenanting my law-chambers of a Sunday morning, with his cadaverously gentlemanly **nonchalance:** *nonchalance*, yet withal firm and self possessed, had such a strange effect calm; indifference upon me, that incontinently I slunk away from my own door, and did as desired. But not without sundry twinges of impotent rebellion against the **effrontery:** mild **effrontery** of this unaccountable scrivener. Indeed, it was his wonderful boldness; mildness chiefly, which not only disarmed me, but unmanned me, as it impudence were. For I consider that one, for the time, is in a way unmanned when he tranquilly permits his hired clerk to dictate to him, and order him away from his own premises. Furthermore, I was full of uneasiness as to what Bartleby could possibly be doing in my office in his shirt sleeves, and in an otherwise dismantled condition of a Sunday morning. Was anything amiss going on? Nay, that was out of the question. It was not to be thought of for a moment that Bartleby was an immoral person. But what could he be doing there—copying? Nay again, whatever might be his eccentricities, Bartleby was an eminently decorous person. He would be the last man to sit down to his desk in any state approaching to nudity. Besides, it was Sunday; and there was something about Bartleby that forbade the supposition that he would by any secular occupation violate the proprieties of the day.

---

36 **dishabille:** a state of undress or careless dress

Nevertheless, my mind was not pacified; and full of a restless curiosity, at last I returned to the door. Without hindrance I inserted my key, opened it, and entered. Bartleby was not to be seen. I looked round anxiously, peeped behind his screen; but it was very plain that he was gone. Upon more closely examining the place, I surmised that for an indefinite period Bartleby must have ate, dressed, and slept in my office, and that too without plate, mirror, or bed. The cushioned seat of a rickety old sofa in one corner bore the faint impress of a lean, reclining form. Rolled away under his desk, I found a blanket; under the empty grate, a blacking box and brush; on a chair, a tin basin, with soap and a ragged towel; in a newspaper a few crumbs of ginger-nuts and a morsel of cheese. Yes, thought I, it is evident enough that Bartleby has been making his home here, keeping bachelor's hall all by himself. Immediately then the thought came sweeping across me, what miserable friendlessness and loneliness are here revealed! His poverty is great; but his solitude, how horrible! Think of it. Of a Sunday, Wall Street is deserted as Petra;[37] and every night of every day it is an emptiness. This building too, which of week-days hums with industry and life, at nightfall echoes with sheer vacancy, and all through Sunday is forlorn. And here Bartleby makes his home; sole spectator of a solitude which he has seen all populous—a sort of innocent and transformed Marius brooding among the ruins of Carthage![38]

For the first time in my life a feeling of overpowering stinging melancholy seized me. Before, I had never experienced aught but a not-unpleasing sadness. The bond of a common humanity now drew me irresistibly to gloom. A fraternal melancholy! For both I and Bartleby were sons of Adam. I remembered the bright silks and sparkling faces I had seen that day, in gala trim, swan-like sailing down the Mississippi of Broadway; and I contrasted them with the pallid copyist, and thought to myself, Ah, happiness courts the light, so we deem the world is gay; but misery hides aloof, so we deem that misery there is none. These sad fancyings—chimeras,[39] doubtless, of a sick and silly brain—led on to other and more special thoughts, concerning the eccentricities of Bartleby. **Presentiments** of strange discoveries hovered round me. The scrivener's pale form appeared to me laid out, among uncaring strangers, in its shivering winding sheet.[40]

presentiments: misgivings; apprehensions

---

37 **Petra:** an ancient city near the Dead Sea, with walls of towering rocks

38 **Marius . . . Carthage!:** A Roman general (157–86 B.C.) who took part in the sacking of Carthage, in northern Africa. Unsuccessful in his nonmilitary life, he took to wandering about the ruined city like a sort of outlaw.

39 **chimeras:** illusions or visions

40 **winding sheet:** a sheet in which a corpse is wrapped

Suddenly I was attracted by Bartleby's closed desk, the key in open sight left in the lock.

I mean no mischief, seek the gratification of no heartless curiosity, thought I; besides, the desk is mine, and its contents, too, so I will make bold to look within. Everything was methodically arranged, the papers smoothly placed. The pigeon holes were deep, and, removing the files of documents, I groped into their recesses. Presently I felt something there, and dragged it out. It was an old bandana handkerchief, heavy and knotted. I opened it, and saw it was a savings bank. I now recalled all the quiet mysteries which I had noted in the man. I remembered that he never spoke but to answer; that though at intervals he had considerable time to himself, yet I had never seen him reading—no, not even a newspaper; that for long periods he would stand looking out, at his pale window behind the screen, upon the dead brick wall; I was quite sure he never visited any refectory or eating-house; while his pale face clearly indicated that he never drank beer like Turkey, or tea and coffee even, like other men; that he never went anywhere in particular that I could learn; never went out for a walk, unless indeed that was the case at present: that he had declined telling who he was, or whence he came or whether he had any relatives in the world; that though so thin and pale, he never complained of ill health. And more than all, I remembered a certain unconscious air of pallid—how shall I call it?—of pallid haughtiness, say, or rather an austere reserve about him, which had positively awed me into my tame compliance with his eccentricities, when I had feared to ask him to do the slightest incidental thing for me, even though I might know, from his long-continued motionlessness, that behind his screen he must be standing in one of those dead-wall reveries of his.

Revolving all these things, and coupling them with the recently discovered fact that he made my office his constant abiding place and home, and not forgetful of his morbid moodiness; revolving all these things, a prudential feeling began to steal over me. My first emotions had been those of pure melancholy and sincerest pity; but just in proportion as the forlornness of Bartleby grew and grew to my imagination, did that same melancholy merge into fear, that pity into repulsion. So true it is, and so terrible, too, that up to a certain point the thought or sight of misery enlists our best affections: but, in certain special cases, beyond that point it does not. They err who would assert that invariably this is owing to the inherent selfishness of the human heart. It rather proceeds from a certain hopelessness of remedying excessive and organic ill. To a sensitive being, pity is not seldom pain. And when at last it is perceived that such pity cannot lead to effectual **succor**, common sense bids the soul be rid of it. What I saw that morning persuaded me that the scrivener was the victim of innate and incurable disorder. I might give alms to his body; but his body did not pain him; it was his soul that suffered, and his soul I could not reach.

succor: relief; assistance

I did not accomplish the purpose of going to Trinity Church that morning. Somehow, the things I had seen disqualified me for the time from church-going. I walked homeward, thinking what I would do with Bartleby. Finally, I resolved upon this:—I would put certain calm questions to him the next morning, touching his history, etc., and if he declined to answer them openly and unreservedly (and I suppose he would prefer not), then to give him a twenty dollar bill over and above whatever I might owe him, and tell him his services were no longer required; but that if in any other way I could assist him, I would be happy to do so, especially if he desired to return to his native place, wherever that might be, I would willingly help to defray the expenses. Moreover, if, after reaching home, he found himself at any time in want of aid, a letter from him would be sure of a reply.

The next morning came.

"Bartleby," said I, gently calling to him behind his screen.

No reply.

"Bartleby," said I, in a still gentler tone, "come here; I am not going to ask you to do anything you would prefer not to do—I simply wish to speak to you."

TRINITY CHURCH AND WALL STREET, c. 1890

Upon this he noiselessly slid into view.

"Will you tell me, Bartleby, where you were born?"

"I would prefer not to."

"Will you tell me *anything* about yourself?"

"I would prefer not to."

"But what reasonable objection can you have to speak to me? I feel friendly towards you."

He did not look at me while I spoke, but kept his glance fixed upon my bust of Cicero, which, as I then sat, was directly behind me, some six inches above my head.

"What is your answer, Bartleby?" said I, after waiting a considerable time for a reply, during which his countenance remained immovable, only there was the faintest conceivable tremor of the white, attenuated[41] mouth.

"At present I prefer to give no answer," he said, and retired into his hermitage.

It was rather weak in me I confess, but his manner on this occasion nettled me. Not only did there seem to lurk in it a certain calm disdain, but his perverseness seemed ungrateful, considering the undeniable good usage and indulgence he had received from me.

Again I sat ruminating[42] what I should do. Mortified as I was at his behavior, and resolved as I had been to dismiss him when I entered my office, nevertheless I strangely felt something superstitious knocking at my heart, and forbidding me to carry out my purpose, and denouncing me for a villain if I dared to breathe one bitter word against this forlornest of mankind. At last, familiarly drawing my chair behind his screen, I sat down and said: "Bartleby, never mind then about revealing your history; but let me entreat you, as a friend, to comply as far as may be with the usages of this office. Say now you will help to examine papers tomorrow or next day: in short, say now that in a day or two you will begin to be a little reasonable:—say so,—Bartleby."

"At present I would prefer not to be a little reasonable," was his mildly cadaverous reply.

Just then the folding-doors opened, and Nippers approached. He seemed suffering from an unusually bad night's rest, induced by severer indigestion than common. He overheard those final words of Bartleby.

"*Prefer not*, eh?" gritted Nippers—"I'd prefer him, if I were you, sir," addressing me—"I'd *prefer* him; I'd give him preferences, the stubborn mule! What is it, sir, pray, that he *prefers* not to do now?"

Bartleby moved not a limb.

"Mr. Nippers," said I, "I'd prefer that you would withdraw for the present."

Somehow, of late I had got into the way of involuntarily using this word prefer upon all sorts of not exactly suitable occasions. And I trembled to

---

41 **attenuated:** thin

42 **ruminating:** reflecting on

think that my contact with the scrivener had already and seriously affected me in a mental way. And what further and deeper **aberration** might it not yet produce? This apprehension had not been without **efficacy** in determining me to summary[43] means.

aberration: deviation; alteration

efficacy: effect

As Nippers, looking very sour and sulky, was departing, Turkey blandly and deferentially approached.

"With submission, sir," said he, "yesterday I was thinking about Bartleby here, and I think that if he would but prefer to take a quart of good ale every day, it would do much towards mending him, and enabling him to assist in examining his papers."

"So you have got the word, too," said I, slightly excited.

"With submission, what word, sir?" asked Turkey, respectfully crowding himself into the contracted space behind the screen, and by so doing, making me jostle the scrivener. "What word, sir?"

"I would prefer to be left alone here," said Bartleby, as if offended at being mobbed in his privacy.

"*That's* the word, Turkey," said I—"*that's* it."

"Oh, *prefer*? oh, yes—queer word. I never use it myself. But sir, as I was saying, if he would but prefer—"

"Turkey," interrupted I, "you will please withdraw."

"Oh, certainly, sir, if you prefer that I should."

As he opened the folding-door to retire, Nippers at his desk caught a glimpse of me, and asked whether I would prefer to have a certain paper copied on blue paper or white. He did not in the least roguishly accent the word prefer. It was plain that it involuntarily rolled from his tongue. I thought to myself, surely I must get rid of a demented man, who already has in some degree turned the tongues, if not the heads, of myself and clerks. But I thought it prudent not to break the dismission at once.

The next day I noticed that Bartleby did nothing but stand at his window in his dead-wall revery. Upon asking him why he did not write, he said that he had decided upon doing no more writing.

"Why, how now? what next?" exclaimed I, "do no more writing?"

"No more."

"And what is the reason?"

"Do you not see the reason for yourself?" he indifferently replied.

---

43 **summary:** quick-acting

I looked steadfastly at him, and perceived that his eyes looked dull and glazed. Instantly it occurred to me, that his unexampled diligence in copying by his dim window for the first few weeks of his stay with me might have temporarily impaired his vision.

I was touched. I said something in condolence with him. I hinted that, of course, he did wisely in abstaining from writing for a while, and urged him to embrace that opportunity of taking wholesome exercise in the open air. This, however, he did not do. A few days after this, my other clerks being absent, and being in a great hurry to despatch certain letters by the mail, I thought that, having nothing else earthly to do, Bartleby would surely be less inflexible than usual, and carry these letters to the Post Office. But he blankly declined. So, much to my inconvenience, I went myself.

Still added days went by. Whether Bartleby's eyes improved or not, I could not say. To all appearance, I thought they did. But when I asked him if they did, he vouchsafed no answer. At all events, he would do no copying. At last, in reply to my urgings, he informed me that he had permanently given up copying.

"What!" exclaimed I; "suppose your eyes should get entirely well—better than ever before—would you not copy then?"

"I have given up copying," he answered and slid aside.

He remained, as ever, a fixture in my chamber. Nay—if that were possible—he became still more of a fixture than before. What was to be done? He would do nothing in the office: why should he stay there? Yet I was sorry for him. I speak less than truth when I say that, on his own account, he occasioned me uneasiness. If he would have but named a single relative or friend, I would instantly have written, and urged their taking the poor fellow away to some convenient retreat. But he seemed alone, absolutely alone in the universe. A bit of wreckage in the mid-Atlantic. At length, necessities connected with my business tyrannized over all other considerations. Decently as I could, I told Bartleby that in six days' time he must unconditionally leave the office. I warned him to take measures, in the interval, for procuring some other abode. I offered to assist him in this endeavour, if he himself would but take the first step towards a removal. "And when you finally quit me, Bartleby," added I, "I shall see that you go away not entirely unprovided. Six days from this hour, remember."

At the expiration of that period, I peeped behind the screen, and lo! Bartleby was there.

I buttoned up my coat, balanced myself; advanced slowly towards him, touched his shoulder, and said, "The time has come; you must quit this place; I am sorry for you; here is money; but you must go."

"I would prefer not," he replied, with his back still towards me.

"You *must*."

He remained silent.

Now I had an unbounded confidence in this man's common honesty. He had frequently restored to me sixpences and shillings carelessly dropped upon the floor, for I am apt to be very reckless in such shirt-button affairs. The proceeding then which followed will not be deemed extraordinary.

"Bartleby," said I, "I owe you twelve dollars on account; here are thirty-two; the odd twenty are yours.—Will you take it?" and I handed the bills towards him.

But he made no motion.

"I will leave them here then," putting them under a weight on the table. Then taking my hat and cane and going to the door, I tranquilly turned and added—"After you have removed your things from these offices, Bartleby, you will of course lock the door—since every one is now gone for the day but you—and if you please, slip your key underneath the mat, so that I may have it in the morning. I shall not see you again; so good-bye to you. If hereafter, in your new place of abode I can be any service to you, do not fail to advise me by letter. Good-bye, Bartleby, and fare you well."

But he answered not a word; like the last column of some ruined temple, he remained standing mute and solitary in the middle of the otherwise deserted room.

As I walked home in a pensive mood, my vanity got the better of my pity. I could not but highly plume myself on my masterly management in getting rid of Bartleby. Masterly I call it, and such it must appear to any dispassionate thinker. The beauty of my procedure seemed to consist in its perfect quietness. There was no vulgar bullying, no bravado of any sort, no choleric **hectoring**, no striding to and fro across the apartment, jerking out **vehement** commands for Bartleby to bundle himself off with his beggarly traps.[44] Nothing of the kind. Without loudly bidding Bartleby depart—as an inferior genius might have done—I assumed the ground that depart he must;

> "*The* time has come; you must quit this place; I am sorry for you; here is money; but you must go."

hectoring: harassing; tormenting

vehement: fierce; angry

---

44 traps: personal belongings

and upon that assumption built all I had to say. The more I thought over my procedure, the more I was charmed with it. Nevertheless, next morning, upon awakening, I had my doubts, I had somehow slept off the fumes of vanity. One of the coolest and wisest hours a man has, is just after he awakes in the morning. My procedure seemed as sagacious as ever—but only in theory. How it would prove in practice—there was the rub. It was truly a beautiful thought to have assumed Bartleby's departure; but, after all, that assumption was simply my own, and none of Bartleby's. The great point was, not whether I had assumed that he would quit me, but whether he would prefer so to do. He was more a man of preferences than assumptions.

After breakfast I walked down town, arguing the probabilities *pro* and *con*. One moment I thought it would prove a miserable failure, and Bartleby would be found all alive at my office as usual; the next moment it seemed certain that I should see his chair empty. And so I kept veering about. At the corner of Broadway and Canal Street, I saw quite an excited group of people standing in earnest conversation.

"I'll take odds he doesn't," said a voice as I passed.

"Doesn't go?—done!—" said I, "put up your money."

I was instinctively putting my hand in my pocket to produce my own, when I remembered that this was an election day. The words I had overheard bore no reference to Bartleby, but the success or non-success of some candidate for the mayoralty. In my intent frame of mind, I had, as it were, imagined that all Broadway shared in my excitement, and were debating the same question with me. I passed on, very thankful that the uproar of the street screened my momentary absent-mindedness.

As I had intended, I was earlier than usual at my office door. I stood listening for a moment. All was still. He must be gone. I tried the knob. The door was locked. Yes, my procedure had worked to a charm; he indeed must be vanished. Yet a certain melancholy mixed with this: I was almost sorry for my brilliant success. I was fumbling under the door mat for the key, which Bartleby was to have left there for me, when accidently my knee knocked against a panel, producing a summoning sound, and in response a voice came to me from within "Not yet; I am occupied."

It was Bartleby.

I was thunderstruck. For an instant I stood like the man who, pipe in mouth, was killed one cloudless afternoon long ago in Virginia, by summer lightning; at his own warm open window he was killed, and remained leaning out there upon the dreamy afternoon, till some one touched him, and he fell.

Herman Melville

★★

"Not gone!" I murmured at last. But again obeying that wondrous **ascendency** which the **inscrutable** scrivener had over me—and from which ascendency, for all my chafing, I could not completely escape—I slowly went down stairs and out into the street, and while walking round the block, considered what I should next do in this unheard-of perplexity. Turn the man out by an actual thrusting I could not; to drive him away by calling him hard names would not do; calling in the police was an unpleasant idea; and yet, permit him to enjoy his cadaverous triumph over me—this too I could not think of. What was to be done? Or, if nothing could be done, was there anything further that I could *assume* in the matter? Yes, as before I had prospectively assumed that Bartleby would depart, so now I might retrospectively assume that departed he was. In the legitimate carrying out of this assumption, I might enter my office in a great hurry, and pretending not to see Bartleby at all, walk straight against him as if he were air. Such a proceeding would in a singular degree have the appearance of a home-thrust. It was hardly possible that Bartleby would withstand such an application of the doctrine of assumptions. But, upon second thought, the success of the plan seemed rather dubious. I resolved to argue the matter over with him again.

ascendency: domination

inscrutable: mysterious

"Bartleby," said I, entering the office, with a quietly severe expression, "I am seriously displeased. I am pained, Bartleby. I had thought better of you. I had imagined you of such a gentlemanly organization, that in any delicate dilemma a slight hint would suffice—in short, an assumption; but it appears I am deceived. Why," I added, unaffectedly starting, "you have not even touched that money yet," pointing to it, just where I had left it the evening previous.

He answered nothing.

"Will you, or will you not, quit me?" I now demanded in a sudden passion, advancing close to him.

"I would prefer not to quit you," he replied, gently emphasizing the not.

"What earthly right have you to stay here? Do you pay any rent? Do you pay my taxes? Or is this property yours?"

He answered nothing.

"Are you ready to go on and write now? Are your eyes recovered? Could you copy a small paper for me this morning? or help examine a few lines? or step round to the Post Office? In a word, will you do any thing at all, to give a coloring to your refusal to depart the premises?"

He silently retired into his hermitage.

I was now in such a state of nervous resentment that I thought it but prudent to check myself, at present, from further demonstrations. Bartleby and I were alone. I remembered the tragedy of the unfortunate Adams and the still more unfortunate Colt in the solitary office of the latter; and how poor Colt, being dreadfully incensed by Adams, and imprudently permitting himself to get wildly excited, was at unawares hurried into his fatal act—an act which certainly no man could possibly deplore more than the actor himself. Often it had occurred to me in my ponderings upon the subject, that had that altercation taken place in the public street, or at a private residence, it would not have terminated as it did. It was the circumstance of being alone in a solitary office, upstairs, of a building entirely unhallowed by humanizing domestic associations—an uncarpeted office, doubtless, of a dusty, haggard sort of appearance;—this it must have been, which greatly helped to enhance the irritable desperation of the hapless Colt.

But when this old Adam of resentment rose in me and tempted me concerning Bartleby, I grappled him and threw him. How? Why, simply by recalling the divine injunction: "A new commandment give I unto you, that ye love one another." Yes, this it was that saved me. Aside from higher considerations, charity often operates as a vastly wise and prudent principle—a great safeguard to its possessor. Men have committed murder for jealousy's sake, and anger's sake, and hatred's sake, and selfishness' sake, and spiritual pride's sake; but no man that ever I heard of, ever committed a diabolical murder for sweet charity's sake. Mere self-interest, then, if no better motive can be enlisted, should, especially with high-tempered men, prompt all beings to charity and philanthropy. At any rate, upon the occasion in question, I strove to drown my exasperated feelings towards the scrivener by benevolently construing his conduct. Poor fellow, poor fellow! thought I, he doesn't mean anything; and besides, he has seen hard times, and ought to be indulged.

I endeavored also immediately to occupy myself, and at the same time to comfort my despondency.[45] I tried to fancy that in the course of the morning, at such time as might prove agreeable to him, Bartleby, of his own free accord, would emerge from his hermitage, and take up some decided line of march in the direction of the door. But no. Half-past twelve o'clock came; Turkey began to glow in the face, overturn his inkstand, and become generally **obstreperous**; Nippers abated down into quietude and courtesy; Ginger Nut munched his noon apple; and Bartleby remained standing at his window

obstreperous: unruly; loud-mouthed

---

45 **despondency:** depression

in one of his profoundest dead-wall reveries. Will it be credited? Ought I to acknowledge it? That afternoon I left the office without saying one further word to him.

Some days now passed, during which at leisure intervals I looked a little into "Edwards on the Will," and "Priestley on Necessity." Under the circumstances, those books induced a salutary feeling. Gradually I slid into the persuasion that these troubles of mine, touching the scrivener, had been all predestinated[46] from eternity, and Bartleby was billeted[47] upon me for some mysterious purpose of an all-wise Providence, which it was not for a mere mortal like me to fathom. Yes, Bartleby, stay there behind your screen, thought I; I shall persecute you no more; you are harmless and noiseless as any of these old chairs; in short, I never feel so private as when I know you are here. At least I see it, I feel it; I penetrate to the predestinated purpose of my life. I am content. Others may have loftier parts to enact; but my mission in this world, Bartleby, is to furnish you with office-room for such period as you may see fit to remain.

I believe that this wise and blessed frame of mind would have continued with me had it not been for the unsolicited and uncharitable remarks obtruded upon me by my professional friends who visited the rooms. But thus it often is, that the constant friction of illiberal minds wears out at last the best resolves of the more generous. Though to be sure, when I reflected upon it, it was not strange that people entering my office should be struck by the peculiar aspect of the unaccountable Bartleby, and so be tempted to throw out some sinister observations concerning him. Sometimes an attorney having business with me, and calling at my office, and finding no one but the scrivener there, would undertake to obtain some sort of precise information from him touching my whereabouts; but without heeding his idle talk, Bartleby would remain standing immovable in the middle of the room. So, after contemplating him in that position for a time, the attorney would depart, no wiser than he came.

Also, when a reference was going on, and the room full of lawyers and witnesses, and business was driving fast, some deeply-occupied legal gentleman present, seeing Bartleby wholly unemployed, would request him to run round to his (the legal gentleman's) office and fetch some papers for him. Thereupon, Bartleby would tranquilly decline, and yet remain idle as before. Then the lawyer would give a great stare, and turn to me. And

---

46 **predestinated:** fated; predetermined

47 **billeted:** housed

what could I say? At last I was made aware that all through the circle of my professional acquaintance, a whisper of wonder was running round, having reference to the strange creature I kept at my office. This worried me very much. And as the idea came upon me of his possibly turning out a long-lived man, and keep occupying my chambers, and denying my authority; and perplexing my visitors; and scandalizing my professional reputation; and casting a general gloom over the premises; keeping soul and body together to the last upon his savings (for doubtless he spent but half a dime a day), and in the end perhaps outlive me, and claim possession of my office by right of his perpetual occupancy: as all these dark anticipations crowded upon me more and more, and my friends continually intruded their relentless remarks upon the apparition in my room, a great change was wrought in me. I resolved to gather all my faculties together, and forever rid me of this intolerable incubus.[48] Ere revolving any complicated project, however, adapted to this end, I first simply suggested to Bartleby the propriety of his permanent departure. In a calm and serious tone, I commended the idea to his careful and mature consideration. But having taken three days to meditate upon it, he apprised me that his original determination remained the same; in short, that he still preferred to abide with me.

What shall I do? I now said to myself, buttoning up my coat to the last button. What shall I do? what does conscience say I *should* do with this man, or, rather, ghost? Rid myself of him, I must; go, he shall. But how? You will not thrust him, the poor, pale, passive mortal—you will not thrust such a helpless creature out of your door? you will not dishonor yourself by such cruelty? No, I will not, I cannot do that. Rather would I let him live and die here, and then mason up his remains in the wall. What then will you do? For all your coaxing, he will not budge. Bribes he leaves under your own paper-weight on your table; in short, it is quite plain that he prefers to cling to you.

Then something severe, something unusual must be done. What! surely you will not have him collared by a constable, and commit his innocent pallor to the common jail? And upon what ground could you procure such a thing to be done?—a vagrant, is he? What! he a vagrant, a wanderer, who refuses to budge? It is because he will *not* be a vagrant, then, that you seek to count him as a vagrant. That is too absurd. No visible means of support: there I have him. Wrong again: for indubitably he *does* support himself, and that is the only unanswerable proof that any man can show of his possessing the

---

48 incubus: evil spirit or fiend

means so to do. No more then. Since he will not quit me, I must quit him. I will change my offices; I will move elsewhere; and give him fair notice, that if I find him on my new premises I will then proceed against him as a common trespasser.

Acting accordingly, next day I thus addressed him: "I find these chambers too far from the City Hall; the air is unwholesome. In a word, I propose to remove my offices next week, and shall no longer require your services. I tell you this now, in order that you may seek another place."

He made no reply, and nothing more was said.

On the appointed day I engaged carts and men, proceeded to my chambers, and having but little furniture, everything was removed in a few hours. Throughout all, the scrivener remained standing behind the screen, which I directed to be removed the last thing. It was withdrawn; and being folded up like a huge folio, left him the motionless occupant of a naked room. I stood in the entry watching him a moment, while something from within me upbraided me.

I re-entered, with my hand in my pocket—and—and my heart in my mouth.

"Good-bye, Bartleby; I am going—good-bye, and God some way bless you; and take that," slipping something in his hand. But it dropped upon the floor and then—strange to say—I tore myself from him whom I had so longed to be rid of.

Established in my new quarters, for a day or two I kept the door locked, and started at every footfall in the passages. When I returned to my rooms after any little absence, I would pause at the threshold for an instant, and attentively listen, ere applying my key. But these fears were needless. Bartleby never came nigh me.

Established in my new quarters, for a day or two I kept the door locked, and started at every footfall in the passages.

I thought all was going well, when a perturbed-looking stranger visited me, inquiring whether I was the person who had recently occupied rooms at No.—Wall Street.

Full of forebodings, I replied that I was.

"Then, sir," said the stranger, who proved a lawyer, "you are responsible for the man you left there. He refuses to do any copying, he refuses to do anything; and he says he prefers not to; and he refuses to quit the premises."

"I am very sorry, sir," said I, with assumed tranquillity, but an inward tremor, "but, really, the man you allude to is nothing to me—he is no relation or apprentice of mine, that you should hold me responsible for him."

"In mercy's name, who is he?"

"I certainly cannot inform you. I know nothing about him. Formerly I employed him as a copyist; but he has done nothing for me now for some time past."

"I shall settle him then—good morning, sir."

Several days passed, and I heard nothing more; and though I often felt a charitable prompting to call at the place and see poor Bartleby, yet a certain squeamishness of I know not what withheld me.

All is over with him, by this time, thought I at last, when through another week no further intelligence reached me. But coming to my room the day after, I found several persons waiting at my door in a high state of nervous excitement.

"That's the man—here he comes," cried the foremost one, whom I recognized as the lawyer who had previously called upon me alone.

"You must take him away, sir, at once," cried a portly person among them, advancing upon me, and whom I knew to be the landlord of No.—Wall Street. "These gentlemen, my tenants, cannot stand it any longer; Mr. B——," pointing to the lawyer, "has turned him out of his room, and he now persists in haunting the building generally, sitting upon the banisters of the stairs by day, and sleeping in the entry by night. Everybody here is concerned; clients are leaving the offices; some fears are entertained of a mob; something you must do, and that without delay."

Aghast at this torrent, I fell back before it, and would fain[49] have locked myself in my new quarters. In vain I persisted that Bartleby was nothing to me—no more than to any one else there. In vain:—I was the last person known to have anything to do with him, and they held me to the terrible account. Fearful then of being exposed in the papers (as one person present obscurely threatened) I considered the matter, and at length said, that if the lawyer would give me a confidential interview with the scrivener, in his (the lawyer's) own room, I would that afternoon strive my best to rid them of the nuisance they complained of.

Going upstairs to my old haunt, there was Bartleby silently sitting upon the banister at the landing.

"What are you doing here, Bartleby?" said I.

"Sitting upon the banister," he mildly replied.

I motioned him into the lawyer's room, who then left us.

---

49 fain: willingly

"Bartleby," said I, "are you aware that you are the cause of a great tribulation to me, by persisting in occupying the entry after being dismissed from the office?"

No answer.

"Now one of two things must take place. Either you must do something, or something must be done to you. Now what sort of business would you like to engage in? Would you like to re-engage in copying for some one?"

"No; I would prefer not to make any change."

"Would you like a clerkship in a dry-goods store?"

"There is too much confinement about that. No, I would not like a clerkship; but I am not particular."

"Too much confinement," I cried, "why, you keep yourself confined all the time!"

"I would prefer not to take a clerkship," he rejoined, as if to settle that little item at once.

"How would a bartender's business suit you? There is no trying of the eye-sight in that."

"I would not like it at all; though, as I said before, I am not particular."

His unwonted wordiness inspirited me. I returned to the charge.

"Well then, would you like to travel through the country collecting bills for the merchants? That would improve your health."

"No, I would prefer to be doing something else."

"How then would going as a companion to Europe to entertain some young gentleman with your conversation—how would that suit you?"

"Not at all. It does not strike me that there is anything definite about that. I like to be stationary. But I am not particular."

"Stationary you shall be then," I cried, now losing all patience, and for the first time in all my exasperating connection with him fairly flying into a passion. "If you do not go away from these premises before night, I shall feel bound—indeed I *am* bound—to—to—to quit the premises myself." I rather absurdly concluded, knowing not with what possible threat to try to frighten his immobility into compliance. Despairing of all further efforts, I was precipitately leaving him, when a final thought occurred to me—one which had not been wholly unindulged before.

"Bartleby," said I, in the kindest tone I could assume under such exciting circumstances, "will you go home with me now—not to my office, but my dwelling—and remain there till we can conclude upon some convenient arrangement for you at our leisure? Come, let us start now, right away."

"No: at present I would prefer not to make any change at all."

I answered nothing; but effectually dodging everyone by the suddenness and rapidity of my flight, rushed from the building, ran up Wall Street towards Broadway, and then jumping into the first omnibus, was soon removed from pursuit. As soon as tranquillity returned I distinctly perceived that I had now done all that I possibly could, both in respect to the demands of the landlord and his tenants, and with regard to my own desire and sense of duty, to benefit Bartleby, and shield him from rude persecution. I now strove to be entirely care-free and **quiescent**; and my conscience justified me in the attempt; though indeed it was not so successful as I could have wished. So fearful was I of being again hunted out by the incensed landlord and his exasperated tenants, that, surrendering my business to Nippers, for a few days I drove about the upper part of the town and through the suburbs, in my rockaway;[50] crossed over to Jersey City and Hoboken, and paid fugitive visits to Manhattanville and Astoria. In fact I almost lived in my rockaway for the time.

quiescent: calm; untroubled

When again I entered my office, lo, a note from the landlord lay upon the desk. I opened it with trembling hands. It informed me that the writer had sent to the police, and had Bartleby removed to the Tombs as a vagrant. Moreover, since I knew more about him than any one else, he wished me to appear at that place, and make a suitable statement of the facts. These tidings had a conflicting effect upon me. At first I was indignant; but at last almost approved. The landlord's energetic, summary disposition had led him to adopt a procedure which I do not think I would have decided upon myself; and yet as a last resort, under such peculiar circumstances, it seemed the only plan.

As I afterwards learned, the poor scrivener, when told that he must be conducted to the Tombs, offered not the slightest obstacle, but in his own pale, unmoving way silently acquiesced.

Some of the compassionate and curious bystanders joined the party; and headed by one of the constables, arm-in-arm with Bartleby, the silent procession filed its way through all the noise, and heat, and joy of the roaring thoroughfares at noon. The same day I received the note I went to the Tombs, or, to speak more properly, the Halls of Justice. Seeking the right officer, I stated the purpose of my call, and was informed that the individual I described was indeed within. I then assured the functionary that Bartleby was a perfectly honest man, and greatly to be compassionated, however

---

50 **rockaway:** a light, low, four-wheeled carriage

THE TOMBS, 1871

unaccountably eccentric. I narrated all I knew, and closed by suggesting the idea of letting him remain in as indulgent confinement as possible till something less harsh might be done—though indeed I hardly knew what. At all events, if nothing else could be decided upon, the alms-house[51] must receive him. I then begged to have an interview.

Being under no disgraceful charge, and quite serene and harmless in all his ways, they had permitted him freely to wander about the prison, and especially in the inclosed grass-platted yards thereof. And so I found him there, standing all alone in the quietest of the yards, his face towards a high wall—while all around, from the narrow slits of the jail windows, I thought I saw peering out upon him the eyes of murderers and thieves.

"Bartleby!"

"I know you," he said, without looking round—"and I want nothing to say to you."

"It was not I that brought you here, Bartleby," said I, keenly pained at his implied suspicion. "And to you, this should not be so vile a place. Nothing reproachful attaches to you by being here. And see, it is not so sad a place as one might think. Look, there is the sky and here is the grass."

"I know where I am," he replied, but would say nothing more, and so I left him.

As I entered the corridor again, a broad, meat-like man in an apron accosted me, and jerking his thumb over his shoulder said—"Is that your friend?"

"Yes."

"Does he want to starve? If he does, let him live on the prison fare, that's all."

"Who are you?" asked I, not knowing what to make of such an unofficially speaking person in such a place.

"I am the grub-man. Such gentlemen as have friends here, hire me to provide them with something good to eat."

"Is this so?" said I, turning to the turnkey.

He said it was. "Well then," said I, slipping some silver into the grubman's hands (for so they called him), "I want you to give particular attention to my friend there; let him have the best dinner you can get. And you must be as polite to him as possible."

"Introduce me, will you?" said the grub-man, looking at me with an expression which seemed to say he was all impatience for an opportunity to

---

51 **alms-house:** a home for the poor

give a specimen of his breeding.

Thinking it would prove of benefit to the scrivener, I acquiesced; and asking the grub-man his name, went up with him to Bartleby.

"Bartleby, this is Mr. Cutlets; you will find him very useful to you."

"Your sarvant, sir, your sarvant," said the grub-man, making a low salutation behind his apron. "Hope you find it pleasant here, sir;—spacious grounds—cool apartments, sir—hope you'll stay with us some time—try to make it agreeable. May Mrs. Cutlets and I have the pleasure of your company to dinner, sir, in Mrs. Cutlets' private room?"

"I prefer not to dine today," said Bartleby, turning away. "It would disagree with me; I am unused to dinners." So saying, he slowly moved to the other side of the inclosure and took up a position fronting the dead-wall. "How's this?" said the grub-man, addressing me with a stare of astonishment. "He's odd, ain't he?"

"I think he is a little deranged," said I, sadly.

"Deranged? deranged is it? Well now, upon my word, I thought that friend of yourn was a gentleman forger; they are always pale and genteel-like, them forgers. I can't help pity 'em—can't help it, sir. Did you know Monroe Edwards?" he added touchingly, and paused. Then, laying his hand pityingly on my shoulder, sighed, "He died of the consumption at Sing-Sing. So you weren't acquainted with Monroe?"

"No, I was never socially acquainted with any forgers. But I cannot stop longer. Look to my friend yonder. You will not lose by it. I will see you again."

Some few days after this, I again obtained admission to the Tombs, and went through the corridors in quest of Bartleby; but without finding him.

"I saw him coming from his cell not long ago," said a turnkey, "maybe he's gone to loiter in the yards."

So I went in that direction.

"Are you looking for the silent man?" said another turnkey passing me. "Yonder he lies—sleeping in the yard there. 'Tis not twenty minutes since I saw him lie down."

The yard was entirely quiet. It was not accessible to the common prisoners. The surrounding walls, of amazing thickness, kept off all sounds behind them. The Egyptian character of the masonry weighed upon me with its gloom. But a soft imprisoned turf grew under foot. The heart of the eternal pyramids, it seemed, wherein by some strange magic, through the clefts, grass-seed, dropped by birds, had sprung.

Strangely huddled at the base of the wall—his knees drawn up, and lying on his side, his head touching the cold stones—I saw the wasted Bartleby. But nothing stirred. I paused; then went close up to him: stooped over, and saw that his dim eyes were open; otherwise he seemed profoundly sleeping. Something prompted me to touch him. I felt his hand, when a tingling shiver ran up my arm and down my spine to my feet.

The round face of the grub-man peered upon me now. "His dinner is ready. Won't he dine today, either? Or does he live without dining?"

"Lives without dining," said I, and closed the eyes.

"Eh!—He's asleep, ain't he?"

"With kings and counsellors," murmured I.

There would seem little need for proceeding further in this history. Imagination will readily supply the meagre recital of poor Bartleby's interment. But ere parting with the reader, let me say, that if this little narrative has sufficiently interested him, to awaken curiosity as to who Bartleby was, and what manner of life he led prior to the present narrator's making his acquaintance, I can only reply, that in such curiosity I fully share—but am wholly unable to gratify it. Yet here I hardly know whether I should divulge one little item of rumor, which came to my ear a few months after the scrivener's decease. Upon what basis it rested, I could never ascertain; and hence, how true it is I cannot now tell. But inasmuch as this vague report has not been without a certain strange suggestive interest to me, however sad, it may prove the same with some others; and so I will briefly mention it. The report was this: that Bartleby had been a subordinate clerk in the Dead Letter Office at Washington, from which he had been suddenly removed by a change in the administration. When I think over this rumor I cannot adequately express the emotions which seize me. Dead letters! does it not sound like dead men? Conceive a man by nature and misfortune prone to a pallid hopelessness: can any business seem more fitted to heighten it than that of continually handling these dead letters, and assorting them for the flames? For by the cart-load they are annually burned. Sometimes from out the folded paper the pale clerk takes a ring:—the finger it was meant for, perhaps, moulders in the grave; a bank-note sent in swiftest charity:—he whom it would relieve, nor eats nor hungers any more; pardon for those who died despairing; hope for those who died unhoping; good tidings for those who died stifled by unrelieved calamities. On errands of life, these letters speed to death.

Ah, Bartleby! Ah, humanity!

Read and Think Critically

Explain, Conclude, Analyze

1. **CONFLICT** What is the main **conflict** in this story? Explain your response with references to specific passages.

2. Why doesn't the **narrator** fire Bartleby when he stops working? Support your answer with evidence from the text.

3. The narrator asks Bartleby, "What earthly right have you to stay here? Do you pay any rent? Do you pay my taxes? Or is this property yours?" Explain the meaning of this passage.

4. The story is subtitled "A Tale of Wall Street." Draw a conclusion about the significance of this larger **setting**.

5. What do you think is the possible meaning of the last line of the story, "Ah, Bartleby! Ah, humanity!"?

6. **THE AUTHOR'S STYLE** Throughout his career, Melville made innovative choices of narrators for his fiction. For example, the narrator of his novel *Moby-Dick* is called Ishmael, a name that connotes "outcast" or "outsider." Analyze the choice of narrator in "Bartleby the Scrivener." You might consider the following questions.

   • Is the narrator an insider or outsider in relation to the dominant society?
   • Does the narrator change during the course of the narration?
   • Does the subject of his narration (Bartleby) change?
   • Do the two main **characters** (the narrator and Bartleby) represent different parts of society? If so, which parts?

Responding to Unit One

Key Ideas and Details

1. Who is your favorite **character** in Unit One? Explain three of this character's qualities that are explicitly stated in the text and three that are implied by the character's words and actions. Support your description with evidence from the text.

2. Several authors in Unit One use ambiguity in their stories. Give three examples where the author purposely leaves matters uncertain. Offer an explanation of why the author does this and what effect it has on the reader.

Craft and Structure

3. In 19th-century **Romanticism, allegory** and **symbolism** are used frequently, and morality is often addressed in an obvious way. Choose a story in Unit One and decide how it fits the definition of Romanticism. Use evidence from the text to support your view.

4. In fiction, the mysterious stranger is a basic ingredient of many **plots**. In the traditional form, a mysterious stranger appears in the life of an individual or a community, and everyone is affected as a result. Examine "The Legend of Sleepy Hollow," "The Masque of the Red Death," or "Bartleby the Scrivener" and explain how the **archetype** of the mysterious stranger is employed.

 5. Poe believed that good short stories require a single, unifying effect. Analyze one of the stories in Unit One using Poe's standard of unity. Do the descriptions, incidents, structure, and images all contribute to the single effect of the story? Is there a single effect? Feel free to evaluate Poe's own story.

Integration of Knowledge and Ideas

6. Many writers of the early 19th-century Romantic era were drawn to the **Gothic** writing style, which relies on grotesque **imagery**, morbid **settings**, and plots heavy in horror and the supernatural. Compare and contrast the Gothic elements found in two of the stories in this unit.

7. Modern authors and filmmakers have reinterpreted Washington Irving's stories, often for a younger audience. Analyze a modern film or book version of "The Legend of Sleepy Hollow." Evaluate how the adaption reinterprets the characters, the plot, and the setting to appeal to its targeted audience.

Writing About the Literature

Trouble Everywhere

Conflict, simply put, means "trouble." Without trouble, there is usually no story. Choose one of the stories in Unit One and analyze the ways in which the author introduces, develops, and resolves the conflict.

Writing with Style

Choose one of these two assignments.

"I prefer not to . . ."

Using Melville's style, write a short scene from a modern-day version of "Bartleby the Scrivener." Invent a modern-day workplace with its employees and employer. Then have the employer narrate the scene of his or her encounter with Bartleby the _____ .

Diary

As one of the characters in Unit One, write a personal diary for the time period of the story. Provide more information than we get in the story about the "real" you. Use the writing style you think the character would use.

★★

IN YOUR OWN STYLE

Hubris, the character trait of pride or excessive self-confidence, is a theme that comes up repeatedly in Unit One. Consider your own life. Have you or someone you know suffered from, or experienced the effects of, hubris? Write about this in your own style. Choose between taking a humorous approach or creating a dark and serious mood.

Unit Two
New American Voices 1860s to 1910s

THE REAPER, WINSLOW HOMER, 1878

Changing Times

Washington Irving, whose writing introduced Unit One, would have hardly recognized the America of Mark Twain, the first author in Unit Two.

Before the American Civil War (1861–1865), the country was largely rural and agricultural; after the war, Northern industrial cities became magnets for millions of newcomers—European immigrants, rural Americans, and Southern blacks—seeking jobs in refineries and factories.

Pre-1861, much of the country was still "empty." But the Homestead Act of 1862, which offered free land to settlers, and the completion of the cross-country railroad in 1869 spurred on western migration. As a result, more settlement occurred in the three decades following the war than in all the rest of American history.

The pace of change was breathtaking, spurred on by amazing technologies such as electricity, the telephone, and the transcontinental telegraph. Americans began to consider progress their birthright.

From a humanitarian standpoint, the end of slavery was unquestionably the most positive change brought by the war. But the conflict also enacted a steep price: the lives of 620,000 Americans. The rebuilding and reunification process called Reconstruction officially ended in 1877; however, the scars of the Civil War may never fully heal.

Corruption riddled American commerce and politics in the era that followed Reconstruction, known as the Gilded Age. Vast fortunes were made via aggressive, sometimes shady business practices, and factory workers and farmers were ruthlessly exploited by industrialists, land speculators, and financiers. Not surprisingly, with so much wealth coinciding with so much dire poverty, the era also spawned the popular "rags-to-riches" novels of Horatio Alger. Speeches, sermons, and editorials touted the virtues of industry, ambition, and optimism—traits American writers such as Mark Twain and Ambrose Bierce often mocked in their fiction.

Popular authors were able to make a living from their writing. Advances in printing and transportation meant more magazines and books for the larger and more literate population to read. Writers could also prosper on the lecture circuit. Twain became a bona fide celebrity in this way, delighting huge audiences with his hilarious stories and irreverent commentary.

Realism

In literature, the period from 1865 to 1895 was dominated by the Realist movement, led by Mark Twain and Henry James, and joined by Ambrose Bierce and most other important writers of the day. Their "cheerleader" was William Dean Howells, the influential editor of *The Atlantic Monthly*, who believed that realism was the best way to represent these new developments in American life. And in his words, "Realism is nothing more and nothing less than the truthful treatment of material."

Techniques that characterized the short stories of the Romantic period—allegories, symbolism, and the heavy presence of the author's voice—did not fit these new times. As the country became more comfortable with democracy, and the middle class began to expand, there needed to be a literature to address this new era.

In general, realistic fiction elevates character and setting over plot and theme. The characters are ordinary men and women speaking authentic local dialect in recognizable settings. The events of the stories are not as dramatic or sensationalistic as in Romantic fiction, but closer to what does or could happen in everyday life. The characters tend to act instead of merely react to their situations (recall Young Goodman Brown and Bartleby).

Regionalism

Americans were intrigued by other parts of their vast country. What would it be like to live in a mining camp on the frontier or on a homestead in the Dakotas? Regionalist writing—a branch of realism—brought to life the frontier and Mississippi River, New England villages and sea ports, and the farms of the upper Midwest. The terms "regionalism" and "local color" in writing are often used interchangeably, though the latter is charged with being somewhat more sentimental and exaggerated.

Naturalism

During this period, naturalism became a definable offshoot of American fiction. It has been called "realism-plus-pessimism." Stephen Crane and Jack London—leading naturalist writers—believed that outside forces such as heredity and the environment controlled people's destinies. Humans were up against an indifferent universe, one filled with social conflicts and Darwinian struggles ("survival of the fittest").

Writers in Unit Two came from all sorts of backgrounds and looked at every corner of the country for their inspiration. African American Charles W. Chesnutt, along with Stephen Crane and O. Henry, had modest origins. Willa Cather came from the solid middle class, while Kate Chopin began life as a rich society girl who surprised everyone by becoming an important writer.

These writers set their stories in places they were familiar with—the Midwest, South, and far Northwest, in addition to the East. Their subject matter was far-reaching as well, often stretching the boundaries of the acceptable. Chopin scandalized the public when she wrote about women's desires for artistic and sexual freedom. Chesnutt's career came to a halt because of his uncompromising attention to racial themes. Cather attacked the ills of the age, chiefly its greed and timid conformism.

In their fiction and often in their personal lives, they displayed a very American idealism and resolve to push boundaries. All were master story-tellers who knew that whatever its variations, the basic themes of literature remained the same. "Times may change, inventions may alter a world, but birth, love, maternity, and death cannot be changed," Cather reminded her readers.

Before You Read

Mark Twain (Samuel Clemens) 1835–1910

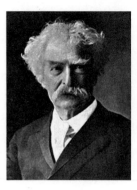

About the Author

Two exceptional events happened in 1835: the appearance of Halley's Comet, and the birth of Samuel Longhorne Clemens. Samuel grew up in Hannibal, Missouri, right on the Mississippi River. After the death of his father, the teenaged Samuel was forced to go to work, and various jobs finally led to a favorite—piloting a riverboat on the Mississippi. Clemens' next job as a journalist in Nevada uncovered a talent for writing satire and hoaxes. When he signed one story with the pseudonym "Mark Twain"—riverboat jargon for the "safe waters" of twelve feet—a literary personality was born.

With publication of "The Celebrated Jumping Frog of Calaveras County," Twain became an overnight celebrity. Twain's colorful childhood near the Mississippi, his young adulthood in the "wild" West, and his restless wanderings around the globe provided rich and varied material for humorous pieces.

After the publication of his masterpiece, *The Adventures of Huckleberry Finn* (1885), Twain's outlook became progressively more pessimistic. His family suffered serious health problems, and his business ventures failed. He managed to pull himself out of bankruptcy by lecturing and playing the role of an American sage on stage. He died in 1910, the year in which Halley's Comet made its next rare appearance.

★★★★★★★★★★★

The Author's Style

Twain's comic genius stamped nearly everything he wrote, but unforgettable characters and vivid vernacular speech distinguish his fiction. With his early short stories, Twain introduced the West to East Coast readers by combining regional oral tales with a blunt journalistic style. He often mixed elements of the tall tale—hyperbole and larger-than-life characters—with a new style featuring lively nouns and verbs. Twain's fiction is not driven by complex plots. Instead, he uses an inventive and consistent narrative voice to link a series of anecdotes and sharply focused episodes. With wit and humor he presented the weaknesses of American society—its pretenses, greed, and political errors. Though cynicism runs beneath the surface of Twain's work, so does his affection for America's dreams and, perhaps most of all, for its quirky, free-spirited citizens.

The Celebrated Jumping Frog
of Calaveras County

MARK TWAIN

🔍 **LITERARY LENS: FRAME NARRATOR** Note that there are two narrators in this story: one who tells the overall story (the **frame narrator**) and one who tells the story-within-the-story. As you read, consider how Twain's use of the frame narrator contributes to the overall effect of the story.

*I*n compliance with the request of a friend of mine, who wrote me from the East, I called on good-natured, **garrulous** old Simon Wheeler, and inquired after my friend's friend, *Leonidas* W. Smiley, as requested to do, and I hereunto append the result. I have a lurking suspicion that *Leonidas* W. Smiley is a myth; that my friend never knew such a personage; and that he only conjectured that if I asked old Wheeler about him, it would remind him of his infamous *Jim* Smiley, and he would go to work and bore me nearly to death with some exasperating reminiscence of him as long and tedious as it should be useless to me. If that was the design, it succeeded.

    I found Simon Wheeler dozing comfortably by the bar-room stove of the **dilapidated** tavern in the decayed mining camp of Angel's, and I noticed that he was fat and bald-headed, and had an expression of winning gentleness and simplicity upon his **tranquil** countenance. He roused up and gave me good-day. I told him that a friend of mine had commissioned me to

garrulous: talkative; chatty

dilapidated: worn down

tranquil: calm; peaceful

make some inquiries about a cherished companion of his boyhood named *Leonidas* W. Smiley—*Rev. Leonidas* W. Smiley—a young minister of the Gospel, who he had heard was at one time a resident of Angel's Camp. I added that if Mr. Wheeler could tell me anything about this Rev. Leonidas W. Smiley, I would feel under many obligations to him.

Simon Wheeler backed me into a corner and blockaded me there with his chair, and then sat me down and reeled off the **monotonous** narrative which follows this paragraph. He never smiled, he never frowned, he never changed his voice from the gentle-flowing key to which he tuned his initial sentence, he never betrayed the slightest suspicion of enthusiasm; but all through the **interminable** narrative there ran a vein of impressive earnestness and sincerity, which showed me plainly that, so far from his imagining that there was anything ridiculous or funny about his story, he regarded it as a really important matter, and admired its two heroes as men of **transcendent** genius in *finesse.*[1] To me the spectacle of a man drifting serenely along through such a queer yarn without ever smiling was exquisitely absurd. As I said before, I asked him to tell me what he knew of Rev. Leonidas W. Smiley, and he replied as follows. I let him go on in his own way, and never interrupted him once:

"Rev. Leonidas W. H'm, Reverend Le—there was a feller here once by the name of *Jim* Smiley, in the winter of '49—or maybe it was the spring of '50—I don't recollect exactly, somehow, though what makes me think it was one or the other is because I remember the big flume[2] wasn't finished when he first came to the camp; but anyway he was the curiousest man about always betting on anything that turned up you ever see, if he could get anybody to bet on the other side; and if he couldn't, he'd change sides. Any way that suited the other man would suit *him*—any way just so's he got a bet, *he* was satisfied. But still he was lucky, uncommon lucky; he most always come out winner. He was always ready and laying for a chance; there couldn't be no solit'ry thing mentioned but that feller'd offer to bet on it, and take any side you please, as I was just telling you. If there was a horse-race, you'd find him flush, or you'd find him busted at the end of it; if there was a dog-fight, he'd bet on it; if there was a cat-fight, he'd bet on it; if there was a chicken-fight, he'd bet on it; why, if there was two birds setting on a fence, he would bet you which one would fly first; or if there was a camp-meeting, he would

---

1 **finesse:** impressive style or skill

2 **flume:** a waterway miners used for gold-mining

monotonous: dull; tedious

interminable: endless; ceaseless

transcendent: superior; extraordinary

be there reg'lar, to bet on Parson Walker, which he judged to be the best exhorter[3] about here, and so he was, too, and a good man. If he even seen a straddle-bug start to go anywheres, he would bet you how long it would take him to get to—to wherever he was going to, and if you took him up, he would foller that straddle-bug to Mexico but what he would find out where he was bound for and how long he was on the road. Lots of the boys here has seen that Smiley, and can tell you about him. Why, it never made no difference to *him*—he would bet on *any* thing—the dangdest feller. Parson Walker's wife laid very sick once, for a good while, and it seemed as if they warn't going to save her; but one morning he come in, and Smiley up and asked how she was, and he said she was considerable better—thank the Lord for His inf'nite mercy—and coming on so smart that, with the blessing of Prov'dence, she'd get well yet; and Smiley, before he thought, says, 'Well, I'll resk two-and-a-half that she don't, anyway.'

"Thish-yer Smiley had a mare—the boys called her the fifteen-minute nag, but that was only in fun, you know, because of course she was faster than that—and he used to win money on that horse, for all she was so slow and always had the asthma, or the distemper, or the consumption, or something of that kind. They used to give her two or three hundred yards' start, and then pass her under way; but always at the fag-end of the race she'd get excited and desperate-like, and come cavorting and straddling up, and scattering her legs around limber, sometimes in the air, and sometimes out to one side among the fences, and kicking up m-o-r-e dust, and raising m-o-r-e racket with her coughing and sneezing and blowing her nose—and *always* fetch up at the stand just about a neck ahead, as near as you could cipher it down.

"And he had a little small bull-pup, that to look at him you'd think he warn't worth a cent but to set around and look ornery and lay for a chance to steal something. But as soon as money was up on him he was a different dog; his under-jaw'd begin to stick out like the fo'castle[4] of a steamboat, and his teeth would uncover, and shine savage like the furnaces. And a dog might tackle him and bully-rag him, and bite him, and throw him over his shoulder two or three times, and Andrew Jackson[5]—which was the name of the pup—Andrew Jackson would never let on but what *he* was satisfied, and hadn't expected nothing else—and the bets being doubled and doubled on the

---

3 **exhorter:** dialect for orator or speaker

4 **fo'castle:** dialect for *forecastle*, the front of a ship's upper deck

5 **Andrew Jackson:** seventh president of the United States, known for his strong will

other side all the time, till the money was all up; and then all of a sudden he would grab that other dog jest by the j'int of his hind leg and freeze to it—not chaw, you understand, but only jest grip and hang on till they throwed up the sponge, if it was a year. Smiley always come out winner on that pup, till he harnessed a dog once that didn't have no hind legs, because they'd been sawed off in a circular saw, and when the thing had gone along far enough, and the money was all up, and he come to make a snatch for his pet holt, he saw in a minute how he'd been imposed on, and how the other dog had him in the door, so to speak, and he 'peared surprised, and then he looked sorter discouraged-like, and didn't try no more to win the fight, and so he got shucked out bad. He give Smiley a look, as much as to say his heart was broke, and it was *his* fault, for putting up a dog that hadn't no hind legs for him to take holt of, which was his main dependence in a fight, and then he limped off a piece and laid down and died. It was a good pup, was that Andrew Jackson, and would have made a name for hisself if he'd lived, for the stuff was in him and he had genius—I know it, because he hadn't had no opportunities to speak of, and it don't stand to reason that a dog could make such a fight as he could under them circumstances if he hadn't no talent. It always makes me feel sorry when I think of that last fight of his'n, and the way it turned out.

"Well, thish-yer Smiley had rat-tarriers, and chicken cocks, and tom-cats and all them kind of things, till you couldn't rest, and you couldn't fetch nothing for him to bet on but he'd match you. He ketched a frog one day, and took him home, and said he cal'klated to educate him; and so he never done nothing for three months but set in his back yard and learn that frog to jump. And you bet you he did learn him, too. He'd give him a little punch behind, and the next minute you'd see that frog whirling in the air like a doughnut—see him turn one summerset, or maybe a couple, if he got a good start, and come down flat- footed and all right, like a cat. He got him up so in the matter of ketching flies, and kep' him in practice so constant, that he'd nail a fly every time as fur as he could see him. Smiley said all a frog wanted was education, and he could do 'most anything—and I believe him. Why, I've seen him set Dan'l Webster[6] down here on this floor—Dan'l Webster was the name of the frog—and sing out, 'Flies, Dan'l, flies!' and quicker'n you could wink, he'd spring straight up, and snake a fly off'n the counter there, and flop down on the floor again as solid as a gob of mud, and fall to scratching the side of his head with his hind foot as indifferent as if he hadn't no idea he'd

---

6 **Dan'l Webster:** American statesman (1782–1852)

been doin' any more'n any frog might do. You never see a frog so modest and straightfor'ard as he was, for all he was so gifted. And when it come to fair and square jumping on a dead level, he could get over more ground at one straddle than any animal of his breed you ever see. Jumping on a dead level was his strong suit, you understand; and when it come to that, Smiley would ante up money on him as long as he had a red.[7] Smiley was monstrous proud of his frog, and well he might be, for fellers that had traveled and been everywheres, all said he laid over any frog that ever *they* see.

"Well, Smiley kep' the beast in a little lattice box, and he used to fetch him down-town sometimes and lay for a bet. One day a feller—a stranger in the camp, he was—come acrost him with his box, and says:

" 'What might it be that you've got in the box?'

"And Smiley says, sorter indifferent-like, 'It might be a parrot, or it might be a canary, maybe, but it ain't—it's only just a frog.'

"And the feller took it, and looked at it careful, and turned it round this way and that, and says, 'H'm, so 'tis. Well, what's *he* good for?'

" 'Well,' Smiley says, easy and careless, 'he's good enough for *one* thing, I should judge—he can outjump any frog in Calaveras County.'

"The feller took the box again, and took another long, particular look, and give it back to Smiley, and says, very deliberate, 'Well,' he says, 'I don't see no p'ints about that frog that's any better'n any other frog.'

" 'Maybe you don't,' Smiley says. 'Maybe you understand frogs, and maybe you don't understand 'em; maybe you've had experience, and maybe you ain't, only a amature, as it were. Anyways, I've got *my* opinion, and I'll resk forty dollars that he can outjump any frog in Calaveras County.'

"And the feller studied a minute, and then says, kinder sadlike, 'Well, I'm only a stranger here, and I ain't got no frog; but if I had a frog, I'd bet you.'

"And then Smiley says, 'That's all right—that's all right—if you'll hold my box a minute, I'll go and get you a frog.' And so the feller took the box, and put up his forty dollars along with Smiley's and set down to wait.

"So he set there a good while thinking and thinking to hisself, and then he got the frog out and prized his mouth open and took a teaspoon and filled him full of quail shot[8]—filled him pretty near up to his chin—and set him on the floor. Smiley he went to the swamp and slopped around in the mud for a long time, and finally he ketched a frog, and fetched him in, and

---

7 **red:** short for *red cent*, an idiomatic expression meaning "any money at all"

8 **quail shot:** the lead pellets in a shotgun shell. Quail are small game birds.

AN ILLUSTRATION FROM THE ORIGINAL PRINTING OF "THE CELEBRATED JUMPING FROG OF CALAVERAS COUNTY," 1867

give him to this feller, and says:

" 'Now, if you're ready, set him alongside of Dan'l, with his fore-paws just even with Dan'l's, and I'll give the word.' Then he says, 'One—two—three—*git*!' and him and the feller touched up the frogs from behind, and the new frog hopped off lively, but Dan'l give a heave, and hysted up his shoulders—so—like a Frenchman, but it warn't no use—he couldn't budge; he was planted as solid as a church, and he couldn't no more stir than if he was anchored out. Smiley was a good deal surprised, and he was disgusted too, but he didn't have no idea what the matter was, of course.

"The feller took the money and started away; and when he was going out at the door, he sorter jerked his thumb over his shoulder—so—at Dan'l, and says again, very deliberate, 'Well' he says, '*I* don't see no p'ints about that frog that's any better'n any other frog.'

"Smiley he stood scratching his head and looking down at Dan'l a long time, and at last he says, 'I wonder what in the nation that frog throw'd off for—I wonder if there ain't something the matter with him—he 'pears to look mighty baggy, somehow.' And he ketched Dan'l by the nap of the neck, and hefted him and says, 'Why, blame my cats, if he don't weigh five pound!' and turned him upside down and he belched out a double handful of shot. And then he see how it was, and he was the maddest man—he set the frog down and took out after that feller, but he never ketched him. And—"

(Here Simon Wheeler heard his name called from the front yard, and got up to see what was wanted.) And turning to me as he moved away, he said: "Just set where you are, stranger, and rest easy—I ain't going to be gone a second."

But, by your leave, I did not think that a continuation of the history of the **enterprising** vagabond *Jim* Smiley would be likely to afford me much information concerning the Rev. Leonidas W. Smiley, and so I started away.

At the door I met the sociable Wheeler returning, and he button-holed me and recommenced:

"Well, thish-yer Smiley had a yaller one-eyed cow that didn't have no tail, only just a short stump like a bannanner, and—"

However, lacking both time and inclination, I did not wait to hear about the **afflicted** cow, but took my leave.

enterprising: energetic or bold, especially in commercial matters

afflicted: troubled; unfortunate

Read and Think Critically

Analyze, Compare, Explain

 1. **FRAME NARRATOR** Use a chart like the one below to analyze the two **narrators** of this story. How does the narrative structure contribute to the story's comic effect?

Points of Comparison	Frame Narrator	Story-within-the-story Narrator
Narrative **point of view**		
Attitude toward story		
Use of **dialogue**		
Descriptions of **characters'** thoughts and feelings		

2. What do you find comical in this story? Give specific examples of wordplay, situation, characters, etc., that work together to produce a humorous effect.

3. Compare the social standing of the **frame narrator** with that of Simon Wheeler. Analyze how Twain's word choice contributes to your understanding of the characters. Support your comparison with examples from the text.

 4. **THE AUTHOR'S STYLE** This story marks one of Twain's first attempts to capture the "flavor" of the American West in fiction. Consider the quotation below by Willa Cather about writers who portray a particular community or region. Explain how Twain's choice of subject matter, **genre**, and style for this story reflect the "flavor" of the West. Could Twain "think and feel" in the speech of this region's residents?

A Gift from Heart to Heart

The "sayings" of a community, its proverbs, are its characteristic comment upon life; they imply its history, suggest its attitude toward the world and its way of accepting life. Such an idiom makes the finest language any writer can have; and he can never get it with a notebook. He himself must be able to think and feel in that speech—it is a gift from heart to heart.

—Willa Cather, from *Willa Cather on Writing*

Before You Read

Ambrose Bierce 1842–1914

About the Author

Ambrose Bierce was known as "Bitter Bierce," as famous for his misanthropy as for his literary accomplishments. Raised in Indiana by pious disciplinarians, Bierce developed a lifelong contempt for religion. He fought in some of the bloodiest battles of the Civil War, and later found himself in the outlaw atmosphere of San Francisco. Legend has it that he tossed a coin to choose between soldiering and reporting, and turned to writing. Bierce's biting humor landed him a column called the "Town Crier." He had to carry a gun to protect himself from those he mocked. A master of hoax, he once published a tongue-in-cheek treatise about the dangers of the waltz. Gullible preachers began warning their flocks about this "suggestive" dance, and the waltz surged in popularity.

Most famous for his *Devil's Dictionary*, a satirical lexicon of definitions, Bierce is also still admired for the ghost tales and stories set during the Civil War written late in his career.

With literary success came the collapse of Bierce's domestic life. One son was killed in a senseless duel, another died from alcoholism, and his wife died of heart failure. The writer's grief was masked in ever more cynicism. He made a final tour of the former Civil War battlefields, traveled to Mexico to serve with Pancho Villa's forces, and was never heard from again.

★★★★★★★★★★★

The Author's Style

Ambrose Bierce's fiction is admired for its ironic plot twists and weird, supernatural effects. His ghost tales owe a debt to Poe with their vivid, sometimes grisly images, striking language, and lasting themes about mortality, hypocrisy, guilt, and obsession. He excelled in taut, suspense-filled plots and shocking or surprising endings.

The human psyche—the source of all real terror—is usually the culprit in Bierce's stories. Some critics speculate that the author's wartime experiences and tragic family life left him obsessed with death. His tales demonstrate this obsession.

The critic Edmund Wilson once remarked that death is Bierce's "only real character." Characters in his stories can seem like unimportant players whose choices and actions prove ineffective.

In "An Occurrence at Owl Creek Bridge," Bierce blends reality with fantasy as the story moves toward its surprise ending. Structure helps the story succeed: the brief flashback provides essential information that elicits the reader's sympathy, and a long, dreamlike sequence ends with an abrupt return to reality.

An Occurrence at Owl Creek Bridge

AMBROSE BIERCE

LITERARY LENS: SENSORY DETAILS Sensory details are descriptions that rely on the five senses (sight, hearing, smell, touch, and taste). Pay attention to the effect of the sensory details in this story.

A man stood upon a railroad bridge in northern Alabama, looking down into the swift water twenty feet below. The man's hands were behind his back, the wrists bound with a cord. A rope closely encircled his neck. It was attached to a stout cross-timber above his head and the slack fell to the level of his knees. Some loose boards laid upon the sleepers[1] supporting the metals of the railway supplied a footing for him and his executioners—two private soldiers of the Federal army,[2] directed by a sergeant who in civil life may have been a deputy sheriff. At a short remove upon the same temporary platform was an officer in the uniform of his rank, armed. He was a captain. A sentinel at each end of the bridge

---

1 **sleepers:** railroad ties

2 **Federal army:** Union forces

RAILROAD BRIDGE, C. 1870

stood with his rifle in the position known as "support," that is to say, vertical in front of the left shoulder, the hammer resting on the forearm thrown straight across the chest—a formal and unnatural position, enforcing an erect **carriage** of the body. It did not appear to be the duty of these two men to know what was occurring at the center of the bridge; they merely blockaded the two ends of the foot planking that traversed it.

carriage: posture; stance

    Beyond one of the sentinels nobody was in sight; the railroad ran straight away into a forest for a hundred yards, then, curving, was lost to view. Doubtless there was an outpost farther along. The other bank of the stream was open ground—a gentle acclivity[3] topped with a stockade of vertical tree trunks, loopholed for rifles, with a single embrasure[4] through which protruded the muzzle of a brass cannon commanding the bridge. Midway of the slope between the bridge and fort were the spectators—a single company of infantry in line, at "parade rest," the butts of the rifles on the ground, the barrels inclining slightly backward against the right shoulder, the hands crossed upon the stock. A lieutenant stood at the right of the line, the point of his sword upon the ground, his left hand resting upon his right. Excepting the group of four at the center of the bridge, not a man moved. The company

3 **acclivity:** slope

4 **embrasure:** opening

    Ambrose Bierce   Unit 2

faced the bridge, staring stonily, motionless. The sentinels, facing the banks of the stream, might have been statues to adorn the bridge. The captain stood with folded arms, silent, observing the work of his subordinates, but making no sign. Death is a dignitary who when he comes announced is to be received with formal **manifestations** of respect, even by those most familiar with him. In the code of military etiquette silence and fixity are forms of deference.

The man who was engaged in being hanged was apparently about thirty-five years of age. He was a civilian, if one might judge from his habit, which was that of a planter. His features were good—a straight nose, firm mouth, broad forehead, from which his long, dark hair was combed straight back, falling behind his ears to the collar of his well-fitting frock coat. He wore a mustache and pointed beard, but no whiskers; his eyes were large and dark gray, and had a kindly expression which one would hardly have expected in one whose neck was in the hemp. Evidently this was no vulgar assassin. The liberal military code makes provision for hanging many kinds of persons, and gentlemen are not excluded.

The preparations being complete, the two private soldiers stepped aside and each drew away the plank upon which he had been standing. The sergeant turned to the captain, saluted and placed himself immediately behind that officer, who in turn moved apart one pace. These movements left the condemned man and the sergeant standing on the two ends of the same plank, which spanned three of the cross-ties of the bridge. The end upon which the civilian stood almost, but not quite, reached a fourth. This plank had been held in place by the weight of the captain; it was now held by that of the sergeant. At a signal from the former the latter would step aside, the plank would tilt and the condemned man go down between two ties. The arrangement commended itself to his judgment as simple and effective. His face had not been covered nor his eyes bandaged. He looked a moment at his "unsteadfast footing," then let his gaze wander to the swirling water of the stream racing madly beneath his feet. A piece of dancing driftwood caught his attention and his eyes followed it down the current. How slowly it appeared to move! What a sluggish stream!

He closed his eyes in order to fix his last thoughts upon his wife and children. The water, touched to gold by the early sun, the brooding mists under the banks at some distance down the stream, the fort, the soldiers, the piece of drift—all had distracted him. And now he became conscious of a new disturbance. Striking through the thought of his dear ones was a sound which he could neither ignore nor understand, a sharp, distinct, metallic percussion

manifestations: demonstrations

recurrence:
repetition

like the stroke of a blacksmith's hammer upon the anvil; it had the same ringing quality. He wondered what it was, and whether immeasurably distant or near by—it seemed both. Its **recurrence** was regular, but as slow as the tolling of a death knell. He awaited each stroke with impatience and—he knew not why—apprehension. The intervals of silence grew progressively longer, the delays became maddening. With their greater infrequency the sounds increased in strength and sharpness. They hurt his ear like the thrust of a knife; he feared he would shriek. What he heard was the ticking of his watch.

> "*If* I could free my hands," he thought, "I might throw off the noose . . ."

He unclosed his eyes and saw again the water below him. "If I could free my hands," he thought, "I might throw off the noose and spring into the stream. By diving I could evade the bullets and, swimming vigorously, reach the bank, take to the woods and get away home. My home, thank God, is as yet outside their lines; my wife and little ones are still beyond the invader's farthest advance."

As these thoughts, which have here to be set down in words, were flashed into the doomed man's brain rather than evolved from it, the captain nodded to the sergeant. The sergeant stepped aside.

II

Peyton Farquhar was a well-to-do planter,[5] of an old and highly respected Alabama family. Being a slave owner, and like other slave owners, a politician, he was naturally an original secessionist[6] and ardently devoted to the Southern cause. Circumstances of an imperious nature, which it is unnecessary to relate here, had prevented him from taking service[7] with the gallant army that had fought the disastrous campaigns ending with the fall of Corinth,[8] and he **chafed** under the inglorious restraint, longing for the release of his energies, the larger life of the soldier, the opportunity for distinction. That opportunity, he felt, would come, as it comes to all in war time. Meanwhile he did what he could. No service was too humble for him to perform in aid of the South, no adventure too perilous for him to undertake if consistent with the character of a civilian who was at heart a soldier, and who in good faith and without too

chafed: was annoyed or irritated

---

5 **planter:** Southern plantation owner

6 **secessionist:** one who believed in the Southern states leaving the Union shortly before the beginning of the U.S. Civil War

7 **taking service:** joining the army

8 **fall of Corinth:** the seizure of Corinth, Mississippi, in the Battle of Shiloh (1862)

much qualification assented to at least a part of the frankly villainous dictum[9] that all is fair in love and war.

One evening while Farquhar and his wife were sitting on a rustic bench near the entrance to his grounds, a gray-clad soldier rode up to the gate and asked for a drink of water. Mrs. Farquhar was only too happy to serve him with her own white hands. While she was fetching the water her husband approached the dusty horseman and inquired eagerly for news from the front.

"The Yanks are repairing the railroads," said the man, "and are getting ready for another advance. They have reached the Owl Creek bridge, put it in order and built a stockade on the north bank. The commandant has issued an order, which is posted everywhere, declaring that any civilian caught interfering with the railroad, its bridges, tunnels or trains will be **summarily** hanged. I saw the order."

summarily: instantly; immediately

"How far is it to the Owl Creek bridge?" Farquhar asked.

"About thirty miles."

"Is there no force on this side the creek?"

"Only a picket post half a mile out, on the railroad, and a single sentinel at this end of the bridge."

"Suppose a man—a civilian and student of hanging—should elude the picket post and perhaps get the better of the sentinel," said Farquhar, smiling, "what could he accomplish?"

The soldier reflected. "I was there a month ago," he replied. "I observed that the flood of last winter had lodged a great quantity of driftwood against the wooden pier at this end of the bridge. It is now dry and would burn like tow."[10]

The lady had now brought the water, which the soldier drank. He thanked her ceremoniously, bowed to her husband and rode away. An hour later, after nightfall, he repassed the plantation, going northward in the direction from which he had come. He was a Federal scout.

III

As Peyton Farquhar fell straight downward through the bridge, he lost consciousness and was as one already dead. From this state he was awakened—ages later, it seemed to him—by the pain of a sharp pressure

---

9 **dictum:** saying

10 **tow:** loose fibers such as that of hemp or flax

upon his throat, followed by a sense of suffocation. Keen, poignant agonies seemed to shoot from his neck downward through every fiber of his body and limbs. These pains appeared to flash along well-defined lines of ramification and to beat with an inconceivably rapid periodicity.[11] They seemed like streams of **pulsating** fire heating him to an intolerable temperature. As to his head, he was conscious of nothing but a feeling of fullness—of congestion. These sensations were unaccompanied by thought. The intellectual part of his nature was already **effaced**; he had power only to feel, and feeling was torment. He was conscious of motion. Encompassed in a luminous cloud, of which he was now merely the fiery heart, without material substance, he swung through unthinkable arcs of oscillation, like a vast pendulum. Then all at once, with terrible suddenness, the light about him shot upward with the noise of a loud splash; a frightful roaring was in his ears, and all was cold and dark. The power of thought was restored; he knew that the rope had broken and he had fallen into the stream. There was no additional strangulation; the noose about his neck was already suffocating him and kept the water from his lungs. To die of hanging at the bottom of a river!—the idea seemed to him ludicrous. He opened his eyes in the darkness and saw above him a gleam of light, but how distant, how inaccessible! He was still sinking, for the light became fainter and fainter until it was a mere glimmer. Then it began to grow and brighten, and he knew that he was rising toward the surface—knew it with reluctance, for he was now very comfortable. "To be hanged and drowned," he thought? "that is not so bad; but I do not wish to be shot. No; I will not be shot; that is not fair."

He was not conscious of an effort, but a sharp pain in his wrist apprised him that he was trying to free his hands. He gave the struggle his attention, as an idler might observe the feat of a juggler, without interest in the outcome. What splendid effort!—what magnificent, what superhuman strength! Ah, that was a fine endeavor! Bravo! The cord fell away; his arms parted and floated upward, the hands dimly seen on each side in the growing light. He watched them with a new interest as first one and then the other pounced upon the noose at his neck. They tore it away and thrust it fiercely aside, its undulations resembling those of a water snake. "Put it back, put it back!" He thought he shouted these words to his hands, for the undoing of the noose had been succeeded by the direst pang that he had yet experienced.

pulsating: throbbing; vibrating

effaced: destroyed; wiped out

> *H*e knew that the rope had broken and he had fallen into the stream.

---

11 **periodicity:** regularity

His neck ached horribly; his brain was on fire; his heart, which had been fluttering faintly, gave a great leap, trying to force itself out at his mouth. His whole body was racked and wrenched with an insupportable anguish! But his disobedient hands gave no heed to the command. They beat the water vigorously with quick, downward strokes, forcing him to the surface. He felt his head emerge; his eyes were blinded by the sunlight; his chest expanded convulsively, and with a supreme and crowning agony his lungs engulfed a great draught[12] of air, which instantly he expelled in a shriek!

He was now in full possession of his physical senses. They were, indeed, **preternaturally** keen and alert. Something in the awful disturbance of his organic system had so exalted and refined them that they made record of things never before perceived. He felt the ripples upon his face and heard their separate sounds as they struck. He looked at the forest on the bank of the stream, saw the individual trees, the leaves and the veining of each leaf—saw the very insects upon them: the locusts, the brilliant-bodied flies, the grey spiders stretching their webs from twig to twig. He noted the prismatic colors in all the dewdrops upon a million blades of grass. The humming of the gnats that danced above the eddies of the stream, the beating of the dragon flies' wings, the strokes of the water-spiders' legs, like oars which had lifted their boat—all these made audible music. A fish slid along beneath his eyes and he heard the rush of its body parting the water.

preternaturally: extraordinarily; exceptionally

He had come to the surface facing down the stream; in a moment the visible world seemed to wheel slowly round, himself the pivotal point, and he saw the bridge, the fort, the soldiers upon the bridge, the captain, the sergeant, the two privates, his executioners. They were in silhouette against the blue sky. They shouted and **gesticulated**, pointing at him. The captain had drawn his pistol, but did not fire; the others were unarmed. Their movements were grotesque and horrible, their forms gigantic.

gesticulated: motioned; gestured

Suddenly he heard a sharp report[13] and something struck the water smartly within a few inches of his head, spattering his face with spray. He heard a second report, and saw one of the sentinels with his rifle at his shoulder, a light cloud of blue smoke rising from the muzzle. The man in the water saw the eye of the man on the bridge gazing into his own through the sights of the rifle. He observed that it was a grey eye and remembered having read that grey eyes were keenest, and that all famous marksmen had them. Nevertheless, this one had missed.

12 **draught:** draft

13 **report:** an explosive noise

A counter-swirl had caught Farquhar and turned him half round; he was again looking into the forest on the bank opposite the fort. The sound of a clear, high voice in a monotonous singsong now rang out behind him and came across the water with a distinctness that pierced and **subdued** all other sounds, even the beating of the ripples in his ears. Although no soldier, he had frequented camps enough to know the dread significance of that deliberate, drawling, aspirated chant; the lieutenant on shore was taking a part in the morning's work. How coldly and pitilessly—with what an even, calm intonation, **presaging**, and enforcing tranquility in the men—with what accurately measured intervals fell those cruel words:

subdued: quieted; muted

presaging: warning

"Attention, company! . . . Shoulder arms! . . . Ready! . . . Aim! . . . Fire!"

Farquhar dived—dived as deeply as he could. The water roared in his ears like the voice of Niagara, yet he heard the dulled thunder of the volley and, rising again toward the surface, met shining bits of metal, singularly flattened, oscillating slowly downward. Some of them touched him on the face and hands, then fell away, continuing their descent. One lodged between his collar and neck; it was uncomfortably warm and he snatched it out.

As he rose to the surface, gasping for breath, he saw that he had been a long time under water; he was perceptibly farther down stream nearer to safety. The soldiers had almost finished reloading; the metal ramrods flashed all at once in the sunshine as they were drawn from the barrels, turned in the air, and thrust into their sockets. The two sentinels fired again, independently and ineffectually.

The hunted man saw all this over his shoulder; he was now swimming vigorously with the current. His brain was as energetic as his arms and legs; he thought with the rapidity of lightning.

"The officer," he reasoned, "will not make that martinet's[14] error a second time. It is as easy to dodge a volley as a single shot. He has probably already given the command to fire at will. God help me, I cannot dodge them all!"

An appalling splash within two yards of him was followed by a loud, rushing sound, *diminuendo*,[15] which seemed to travel back through the air to the fort and died in an explosion which stirred the very river to its deeps!

A rising sheet of water curved over him, fell down upon him, blinded him, strangled him! The cannon had taken a hand in the game. As he shook his head free from the commotion of the smitten water he heard the deflected

---

14 **martinet's:** a strong disciplinarian, especially in the military

15 *diminuendo:* diminishing in volume

shot humming through the air ahead, and in an instant it was cracking and smashing the branches in the forest beyond.

"They will not do that again," he thought; "the next time they will use a charge of grape[16] I must keep my eye upon the gun; the smoke will apprise me—the report arrives too late; it lags behind the missile. That is a good gun."

Suddenly he felt himself whirled round and round—spinning like a top. The water, the banks, the forests, the now distant bridge, fort and men—all were commingled and blurred. Objects were represented by their colors only; circular horizontal streaks of color—that was all he saw. He had been caught in a vortex and was being whirled on with a velocity of advance and **gyration** that made him giddy and sick. In a few moments he was flung upon the gravel at the foot of the left bank of the stream—the southern bank—and behind a projecting point which concealed him from his enemies. The sudden arrest of his motion, the abrasion of one of his hands on the gravel, restored him, and he wept with delight. He dug his fingers into the sand, threw it over himself in handfuls and audibly blessed it. It looked like diamonds, rubies, emeralds; he could think of nothing beautiful which it did not resemble. The trees upon the bank were giant garden plants; he noted a definite order in their arrangement, inhaled the fragrance of their blooms. A strange, roseate light shone through the spaces among their trunks and the wind made in their branches the music of æolian harps.[17] He had no wish to perfect his

gyration: whirling; coiling

escape—was content to remain in that enchanting spot until retaken.

A whiz and rattle of grapeshot among the branches high above his head roused him from his dream. The baffled cannoneer had fired him a random farewell. He sprang to his feet, rushed up the sloping bank, and plunged into the forest.

All that day he traveled, laying his course by the rounding sun. The forest seemed

ALAN BALL IN THE ROLE OF PEYTON FARQUHAR, CHAMBER REPERTORY THEATRE

---

16 **grape:** grapeshot—clusters of iron balls used as cannon charge

17 **æolian harps:** musical instruments sounded by the wind

interminable; nowhere did he discover a break in it, not even a woodman's road. He had not known that he lived in so wild a region. There was something uncanny in the revelation.

By nightfall he was fatigued, footsore, famishing. The thought of his wife and children urged him on. At last he found a road which led him in what he knew to be the right direction. It was as wide and straight as a city street, yet it seemed untravelled. No fields bordered it, no dwelling anywhere. Not so much as the barking of a dog suggested human habitation. The black bodies of the trees formed a straight wall on both sides, terminating on the horizon in a point, like a diagram in a lesson in perspective. Overhead, as he looked up through this rift in the wood, shone great golden stars looking unfamiliar and grouped in strange constellations. He was sure they were arranged in some order which had a secret and malign significance. The wood on either side was full of **singular** noises, among which—once, twice, and again—he distinctly heard whispers in an unknown tongue.

singular: unusual; peculiar

His neck was in pain and lifting his hand to it found it horribly swollen. He knew that it had a circle of black where the rope had bruised it. His eyes felt congested; he could no longer close them. His tongue was swollen with thirst; he relieved its fever by thrusting it forward from between his teeth into the cold air. How softly the turf had carpeted the untraveled avenue—he could no longer feel the roadway beneath his feet!

Doubtless, despite his suffering, he had fallen asleep while walking, for now he sees another scene—perhaps he has merely recovered from a delirium. He stands at the gate of his own home. All is as he left it, and all bright and beautiful in the morning sunshine. He must have traveled the entire night. As he pushes open the gate and passes up the wide white walk, he sees a flutter of female garments; his wife, looking fresh and cool and sweet, steps down from the veranda to meet him. At the bottom of the steps she stands waiting, with a smile of **ineffable** joy, an attitude of matchless grace and dignity. Ah, how beautiful she is! He springs forward with extended arms. As he is about to clasp her he feels a stunning blow upon the back of the neck; a blinding white light blazes all about him with a sound like the shock of a cannon—then all is darkness and silence!

ineffable: indescribable; inexpressible

Peyton Farquhar was dead; his body, with a broken neck, swung gently from side to side beneath the timbers of the Owl Creek bridge.

Read and Think Critically

Analyze, Examine, Describe

 1. **SENSORY DETAILS** are especially important in the telling of this story. Find three details, one from each of the sections of the story. In a short paragraph, write an analysis of how these details contribute to the effect of the section.

2. Why do you think the author begins the story with a highly detailed description of the **setting** and method of execution? Consider the impact the author is desiring to have on the reader.

3. What kind of a man is Peyton Farquhar? Examine every element of his **character**, including his cultural background, and decide how each characteristic might help explain his actions.

4. Why is Peyton Farquhar deceived? Determine how this deception relates to the larger **themes** of the story. Explain several of these themes in detail.

5. Time is handled in a fairly complex way in this **plot**. Why did Bierce choose to structure his story by dividing it into three parts? Describe the function served by each of the three parts of the narrative. What impact does each have on the reader?

6. **THE AUTHOR'S STYLE** Bierce is known for his use of **surprise endings**. In what way does the ending in this story surprise the reader? What writing techniques does Bierce use to heighten the surprise?

Before You Read

Henry James 1843–1916

About the Author

Henry James was born into a cultured American family. He was schooled in both America and Europe and later dropped out of Harvard Law School to write full-time. From his sheltered life experiences emerged an astounding number of acclaimed novels, stories, plays, biographies, and essays. He was also the first American to develop a theory of fictional technique.

After seeking the ideal place to work as a writer, James settled on Europe. His transatlantic status gave him one of his many great literary themes—the conflict between the Old and New Worlds. He is famous for portraying naïve Americans introduced to a corrupt European society.

In England, James wrote his first internationally acclaimed novel, *Daisy Miller*

(1878). In the masterpiece that followed, *A Portrait of a Lady* (1881), he portrays a spirited young American woman in Europe who rejects the Victorian notion of her as a mere "marriageable object." Both novels illustrate James' profound insight into the often-subtle play of power in human relationships. With these works, James became a prominent figure in Victorian society and a frequent guest of lords, poets, and artists. He eventually became a British citizen in protest of America's reluctance to engage in World War I. His ashes, however, lie buried in Cambridge, Massachusetts, where a headstone memorializes him as "interpreter of his generation on both sides of the sea."

****

The Author's Style

Like Hawthorne, James explored the interior world of his characters. Unlike Hawthorne, however, James was a social realist. His psychological explorations are more complex, and his characters react to more subtle social constraints. His ability to survey his characters' inner worlds, in addition to his long, nuanced sentences, are thought to foretell the "stream of consciousness" writing of the early part of the 20th century. Some compare the style of his later works to impressionist painting.

James experimented with new points of

view, setting, and symbolism to depict the fast-changing world of his era. His works are not, however, fast-paced or action-packed. The characters' thoughts provide the drama, often by leading to an epiphany—a powerful moment in which a situation or problem becomes suddenly clear. With this approach James also explored such themes as the supernatural and the effects of evil on idealism. In "The Real Thing," the unreliable narrator offers a view of yet another James theme—artists and writers attempting to distinguish the "real" from artifice.

The Real Thing

HENRY JAMES

 LITERARY LENS: PARADOX A **paradox** is a person, thing, or situation that expresses a seemingly contradictory nature. Look for some of the paradoxes that occur in "The Real Thing."

Part I

When the porter's wife, who used to answer the house-bell, announced "A gentleman and a lady, sir" I had, as I often had in those days—the wish being father to the thought—an immediate vision of sitters. Sitters my visitors in this case proved to be; but not in the sense I should have preferred. There was nothing at first however to indicate that they mightn't have come for a portrait. The gentleman, a man of fifty, very high and very straight, with a moustache slightly grizzled[1] and a dark grey walking-coat admirably fitted, both of which I noted professionally—I don't mean as a barber or yet as a tailor—would have struck me as a celebrity if celebrities often were striking. It was a truth of which I had for some time been conscious that a figure with a good deal

---

1 **grizzled:** touched with gray

paradoxical:
seemingly
contradictory

of frontage was, as one might say, almost never a public institution. A glance at the lady helped to remind me of this **paradoxical** law: she also looked too distinguished to be a "personality." Moreover one would scarcely come across two variations together.

Neither of the pair immediately spoke—they only prolonged the preliminary gaze suggesting that each wished to give the other a chance. They were visibly shy; they stood there letting me take them in—which, as I afterwards perceived, was the most practical thing they could have done. In this way their embarrassment served their cause. I had seen people painfully reluctant to mention that they desired anything so gross as to be represented on canvas; but the scruples of my new friends appeared almost insurmountable. Yet the gentlemen might have said "I should like a portrait of my wife," and the lady might have said "I should like a portrait of my husband." Perhaps they weren't husband and wife—this naturally would make the matter more delicate. Perhaps they wished to be done together—in which case they ought to have brought a third person to break the news.

"We come from Mr. Rivet," the lady finally said with a dim smile that had the effect of a moist sponge passed over a "sunk" piece of painting, as well as of a vague allusion to vanished beauty. She was as tall and straight, in her degree, as her companion, and with ten years less to carry. She looked as sad as a woman could look whose face was not charged with expression; that is her tinted oval mask showed waste as an exposed surface shows friction. The hand of time had played over her freely, but to an effect of elimination. She was slim and stiff, and so well-dressed, in dark blue cloth, with lappets[2] and pockets and buttons, that it was clear she employed the same tailor as her husband. The couple had an indefinable air of prosperous thrift—they evidently got a good deal of luxury for their money. If I was to be one of their luxuries it would behove me to consider my terms.

"Ah, Claude Rivet recommended me?" I echoed; and I added that it was very kind of him, though I could reflect that, as he only painted landscape, this wasn't a sacrifice.

The lady looked very hard at the gentleman, and the gentleman looked round the room. Then staring at the floor a moment and stroking his moustache, he rested his pleasant eyes on me with the remark: "He said you were the right one."

"I try to be, when people want to sit."

"Yes, we should like to," said the lady anxiously.

---

2 **lappets:** flaps or folds

"Do you mean together?"

My visitors exchanged a glance. "If you could do anything with *me* I suppose it would be double," the gentleman stammered.

"Oh yes, there's naturally a higher charge for two figures than for one."

"We should like to make it pay," the husband confessed.

"That's very good of you," I returned, appreciating so unwonted[3] a sympathy—for I supposed he meant pay the artist.

A sense of strangeness seemed to draw on the lady.

"We mean for the illustrations—Mr. Rivet said you might put one in."

"Put in—an illustration?" I was equally confused.

"Sketch her off, you know," said the gentleman, colouring.

It was only then that I understood the service Claude Rivet had rendered me; he had told them how I worked in black-and-white, for magazines, for storybooks, for sketches of contemporary life, and consequently had **copious** employment for models. These things were true, but it was not less true—I may confess it now; whether because the **aspiration** was to lead to everything or to nothing I leave the reader to guess—that I couldn't get the honours, to say nothing of the emoluments,[4] of a great painter of portraits out of my head. My "illustrations" were my pot-boilers;[5] I looked to a different branch of art—far and away the most interesting it had always seemed to me—to perpetuate my fame. There was no shame in looking to it to also make my fortune; but that fortune was by so much further from being made from the moment my visitors wished to be "done" for nothing. I was disappointed; for in the pictorial sense I had immediately *seen* them. I had seized their type—I had already settled what I would do with it. Something that wouldn't absolutely have pleased them, I afterwards reflected.

"Ah you're—you're—a—?" I began as soon as I had mastered my surprise. I couldn't bring out the dingy word "models": it seemed so little to fit the case.

"We haven't had much practice," said the lady.

"We've got to do something, and we've thought that an artist in your line might perhaps make something of us," her husband threw off. He further mentioned that they didn't know many artists and that they had gone first, on the off-chance—he painted views of course, but sometimes put in figures; perhaps I remembered—to Mr. Rivet, whom they had met a few years before

copious: plentiful; abundant

aspiration: goal; ambition

---

3 **unwonted:** surprising; unasked for

4 **emoluments:** compensation

5 **pot-boilers:** mediocre works of art produced solely for money

Mr. and Mrs. Isaac Newton Phelps Stokes,
John Singer Sargent, 1897

at a place in Norfolk where he was sketching.

"We used to sketch a little ourselves," the lady hinted.

"It's very awkward, but we absolutely must do something," her husband went on.

"Of course we're not so *very* young," she admitted with a wan smile.

With the remark that I might as well know something more about them the husband had handed me a card extracted from a neat new pocket-book—their appurtenances[6] were all of the freshest—and inscribed with the words "Major Monarch." Impressive as these words were they didn't carry my knowledge much further; but my visitor presently added: "I've left the army and we've had the misfortune to lose our money. In fact our means are dreadfully small."

"It's awfully trying—a regular strain," said Mrs. Monarch.

They evidently wished to be discreet—to take care not to swagger because they were gentlefolk. I felt them willing to recognise this as something of a drawback, at the same time that I guessed at an underlying sense—their consolation in adversity—that they *had* their points. They certainly had; but these advantages struck me as preponderantly[7] social; such for instance as would help

---

6 **appurtenances:** accessories

7 **preponderantly:** mainly

to make a drawing-room[8] look well. However, a drawing-room was always, or ought to be, a picture.

In consequence of his wife's allusion to their age Major Monarch observed: "Naturally it's more for the figure that we thought of going in. We can still hold ourselves up." On the instant I saw that the figure was indeed their strong point. His "naturally" didn't sound vain, but it lighted up the question. "*She* has the best one," he continued, nodding at his wife with a pleasant after-dinner absence of circumlocution.[9] I could only reply, as if we were in fact sitting over our wine, that this didn't prevent his own from being very good; which led him in turn to make answer: "We thought that if you ever have to do people like us we might be something like it. She particularly—for a lady in a book, you know."

I was so amused by them that, to get more of it, I did my best to take their point of view; and though it was an embarrassment to find myself appraising physically, as if they were animals on hire or useful blacks, a pair whom I should have expected to meet only in one of the relations in which criticism is tacit, I looked at Mrs. Monarch judicially enough to be able to exclaim after a moment with conviction: "Oh yes, a lady in a book!" She was singularly like a bad illustration.

"We'll stand up, if you like," said the Major; and he raised himself before me with a really grand air.

I could take his measure at a glance—he was six feet two, and a perfect gentleman. I would have paid any club in process of formation and in want of a stamp to engage him at a salary to stand in the principal window. What struck me at once was that in coming to me they had rather missed their vocation; they could surely have been turned to better account for advertising purposes. I couldn't of course see the thing in detail, but I could see them make somebody's fortune—I don't mean their own. There was something in them for a waistcoat-maker, an hotel-keeper or a soap-vendor. I could imagine "We always use it" pinned on their bosoms with the greatest effect; I had a vision of the brilliancy with which they would launch a *table d'hôte*.[10]

Mrs. Monarch sat still, not from pride but from shyness, and presently her husband said to her; "Get up, my dear, and show how smart you are." She obeyed, but she had no need to get up to show it. She walked to the end of the studio and then came back blushing, her fluttered eyes on the partner of

---

8 **drawing-room:** a formal reception room

9 **circumlocution:** in conversation, an unnecessarily large number of words used to express an idea

10 *table d'hôte:* a fixed-price meal

her appeal. I was reminded of an incident I had accidentally had a glimpse of in Paris—being with a friend there, a dramatist about to produce a play, when an actress came to him to ask to be entrusted with a part. She went through her paces before him, walked up and down as Mrs. Monarch was doing. Mrs. Monarch did it quite as well, but I abstained from applauding. It was very odd to see such people apply for such poor pay. She looked as if she had ten thousand a year. Her husband had used the word that described her: she was in the London current **jargon** essentially and typically "smart." Her figure was, in the same order of ideas, **conspicuously** and irreproachably "good." For a woman of her age her waist was surprisingly small; her elbow moreover had the orthodox crook. She held her head at the conventional angle, but why did she come to me? She ought to have tried on jackets at a big shop. I feared my visitors were not only destitute but "artistic"—which would be a great complication. When she sat down again I thanked her, observing that what a draughtsman[11] most valued in his model was the faculty of keeping quiet.

"Oh *she* can keep quiet," said Major Monarch. Then he added **jocosely**: "I've always kept her quiet."

"I'm not a nasty fidget, am I?" It was going to wring tears from me, I felt, the way she hid her head, ostrich-like, in the other broad bosom.

The owner of this expanse addressed his answer to me. "Perhaps it isn't out of place to mention—because we ought to be quite business-like, oughtn't we?—that when I married her she was known as the Beautiful Statue."

"Oh dear!" said Mrs. Monarch ruefully.

"Of course I should want a certain amount of expression," I rejoined.

"Of *course*!"—and I had never heard such **unanimity**.

"And then I suppose you know that you'll get awfully tired."

"Oh we *never* get tired!" they eagerly cried.

"Have you had any kind of practice?"

They hesitated—they looked at each other. "We've been photographed—immensely," said Mrs. Monarch.

"She means the fellows have asked us themselves," added the Major.

"I see—because you're so good-looking."

"I don't know what they thought, but they were always after us."

"We always got our photographs for nothing," smiled Mrs. Monarch.

"We might have brought some, my dear," her husband remarked.

jargon: language; terminology

conspicuously: noticeably; obviously

jocosely: jokingly; amusingly

unanimity: agreement

---

11 **draughtsman:** variant of draftsman, one who excels at fine drawing

"I'm not sure we have any left. We've given quantities away," she explained to me.

"With our autographs and that sort of thing," said the Major.

"Are they to be got in the shops?" I enquired as a harmless pleasantry.

"Oh yes, *hers*—they used to be."

"Not now," said Mrs. Monarch with her eyes on the floor.

Part II

I could fancy the "sort of thing" they put on the presentation copies of their photographs, and I was sure they wrote a beautiful hand. It was odd how quickly I was sure of everything that concerned them. If they were now so poor as to have to earn shillings and pence[12] they could never have had much of a margin. Their good looks had been their capital, and they had good-humouredly made the most of the career that this resource marked out for them. It was in their faces, the blankness, the deep intellectual repose of the twenty years of country-house visiting that had given them pleasant intonations. I could see the sunny drawing-rooms, sprinkled with periodicals she didn't read, in which Mrs. Monarch had continuously sat; I could see the wet shrubberies in which she had walked, equipped to admiration for either exercise. I could see the rich covers the Major had helped to shoot and the wonderful garments in which, late at night, he repaired to the smoking-room to talk about them. I could imagine their leggings and waterproofs, their knowing tweeds and rugs, their rolls of sticks and cases of tackle and neat umbrellas;[13] and I could evoke the exact appearance of their servants and the compact variety of their luggage on the platforms of country stations.

They gave small tips, but they were liked; they didn't do anything themselves, but they were welcome. They looked so well everywhere; they gratified the general **relish** for stature, complexion and "form." They knew it without fatuity or vulgarity, and they respected themselves in consequence. They weren't superficial; they were thorough and kept themselves up—it had been their line. People with such a taste for activity had to have some line. I could feel how even in a dull house they could have been counted on for the joy of life. At present something had happened—it didn't matter what, their little income had grown less, it had grown least—and they had to do something

relish: desire

---

12 **shillings and pence:** British coins

13 **I could . . . umbrellas:** descriptions and terminology referring to parties at English country manors that included hunting and fishing

for pocket-money. Their friends could like them, I made out, without liking to support them. There was something about them that represented credit— their clothes, their manners, their type; but if credit is a large empty pocket in which an occasional chink reverberates, the chink at least must be audible. What they wanted of me was to help to make it so. Fortunately they had no children—I soon divined that. They would also perhaps wish our relations to be kept secret: this was why it was "for the figure"—the reproduction of the face would betray them.

I liked them—I felt, quite as their friends must have done—they were so simple; and I had no objection to them if they would suit. But somehow with all their perfections I didn't easily believe in them. After all they were amateurs, and the ruling passion of my life was the detestation of the amateur. Combined with this was another **perversity**—an innate preference for the represented subject over the real one: the defect of the real one was so apt to be a lack of representation. I liked things that appeared; then one was sure. Whether they *were* or not was a subordinate and almost always a profitless question. There were other considerations, the first of which was that I already had two or three recruits in use, notably a young person with big feet, in alpaca,[14] from Kilburn, who for a couple of years had come to me regularly for my illustrations and with whom I was still—perhaps **ignobly**—satisfied. I frankly explained to my visitors how the case stood, but they had taken more precautions than I supposed. They had reasoned out their opportunity, for Claude Rivet had told them of the projected edition de luxe of one of the writers of our day—the rarest of the novelists—who, long neglected by the multitudinous vulgar[15] and dearly prized by the attentive (need I mention Philip Vincent?) had had the happy fortune of seeing, late in life, the dawn and then the full light of a higher criticism; an estimate in which on the part of the public there was something really of **expiation**. The edition preparing, planned by a publisher of taste, was practically an act of high reparation; the wood-cuts with which it was to be enriched were the **homage** of English art to one of the most independent representatives of English letters. Major and Mrs. Monarch confessed to me they had hoped I might be able to work *them* into my branch of the enterprise. They knew I was to do the first of the books, "Rutland Ramsay," but I had to make clear to them that my participation in the rest of the affair—this first book was to be a test—must depend on the satisfaction I should give. If this should be limited

perversity: act of stubbornness

ignobly: meanly

expiation: making up for past offenses

homage: tribute; respect

---

14 **alpaca:** thin fabric made or appearing to be made from the wool of a llama-like animal

15 **vulgar:** common people

my employers would drop me with scarce common forms. It was therefore a crisis for me, and naturally I was making special preparations, looking about for new people, should they be necessary, and securing the best types. I admitted however that I should like to settle down to two or three good models who would do for everything.

"Should we have often to—a—put on special clothes?" Mrs. Monarch timidly demanded.

"Dear yes—that's half the business."

"And should we be expected to supply our own costumes?"

"Oh no; I've got a lot of things. A painter's models put on—or put off—anything he likes."

"And you mean—a—the same?"

"The same?"

Mrs. Monarch looked at her husband again.

"Oh she was just wondering," he explained, "if the costumes are in *general* use." I had to confess that they were, and I mentioned further that some of them—I had a lot of genuine greasy last-century things—had served their time, a hundred years ago, on living world-stained men and women; on figures not perhaps so far removed, in that vanished world, from *their* type, the Monarchs', *quoi!*[16] of a breeched and bewigged age. "We'll put on anything that *fits*," said the Major.

"Oh I arrange that—they fit in the pictures."

"I'm afraid I should do better for the modern books. I'd come as you like," said Mrs. Monarch.

"She has got a lot of clothes at home: they might do for contemporary life," her husband continued.

"Oh I can fancy scenes in which you'd be quite natural." And indeed I could see the slipshod rearrangements of stale properties—the stories I tried to produce pictures for without the exasperation of reading them—whose sandy tracts[17] the good lady might help to people. But I had to return to the fact that for this sort of work—the daily mechanical grind—I was already equipped: the people I was working with were fully adequate.

"We only thought we might be more like *some* characters," said Mrs. Monarch mildly, getting up.

Her husband also rose; he stood looking at me with a dim wistfulness that was touching in so fine a man. "Wouldn't it be rather a pull sometimes

---

16 *quoi:* French for "what"

17 **tracts:** pieces of writing

The Real Thing

to have—a—to have—?" He hung fire; he wanted me to help him by phrasing what he meant. But I couldn't—I didn't know. So he brought it out awkwardly: "The *real* thing: a gentleman, you know, or a lady." I was quite ready to give a general assent—I admitted that there was a great deal in that. This encouraged Major Monarch to say, following up his appeal with an unacted gulp: "It's awfully hard—we've tried everything." The gulp was communicative; it proved too much for his wife. Before I knew it Mrs. Monarch had dropped again upon a divan[18] and burst into tears. Her husband sat down beside her, holding one of her hands; whereupon she quickly dried her eyes with the other, while I felt embarrassed as she looked up at me. "There isn't a confounded job I haven't applied for—waited for—prayed for. You can fancy we'd be pretty bad first. Secretaryships and that sort of thing? You might as well ask for a peerage.[19] I'd be *anything*—I'm strong; a messenger or a coal-heaver. I'd put on a gold-laced cap and open carriage-doors in front of the haberdasher's;[20] I'd hang about a station to carry portmanteaux;[21] I'd be a postman. But they won't *look* at you; there are thousands as good as yourself already on the ground. *Gentlemen*, poor beggars, who've drunk their wine, who've kept their hunters!"

I was as reassuring as I knew how to be, and my visitors were presently on their feet again while, for the experiment, we agreed on an hour. We were discussing it when the door opened and Miss Churm came in with a wet umbrella. Miss Churm had to take the omnibus to Maida Vale and then walk half a mile. She looked a trifle blowsy and slightly splashed. I scarcely ever saw her come in without thinking afresh how odd it was that, being so little in herself, she should yet be so much in others. She was a meager little Miss Churm, but was such an ample heroine of romance. She was only a freckled cockney,[22] but she could represent everything, from a fine lady to a shepherdess; she had the faculty as she might have had a fine voice or long hair. She couldn't spell and she loved beer, but she had two or three "points," and practice, and a knack, and mother-wit, and a whimsical sensibility, and a love of the theatre, and seven sisters, and not an ounce of respect, especially for the *h*.[23] The first thing my visitors saw was that her umbrella was wet, and

---

18 **divan:** a couch, usually without a back or arms

19 **peerage:** the rank and title of a British peer (baron, duke, and so on)

20 **haberdasher:** a dealer in men's clothing

21 **portmanteaux:** large suitcases

22 **cockney:** those who lived in London's East End slums

23 **the *h*:** the letter *h* is not pronounced in the Cockney dialect

in their spotless perfection they visibly winced at it. The rain had come on since their arrival.

"I'm all in a soak; there *was* a mess of people in the 'bus. I wish you lived near a stytion," said Miss Churm. I requested her to get ready as quickly as possible, and she passed into the room in which she always changed her dress. But before going out she asked me what she was to get into this time.

"It's the Russian princess, don't you know?" I answered; "the one with the 'golden eyes,' in black velvet, for the long thing in the *Cheapside.*"

"Golden eyes? I *say*!" cried Miss Churm, while my companions watched her with intensity as she withdrew. She always arranged herself, when she was late, before I could turn around; and I kept my visitors a little on purpose, so that they might get an idea, from seeing her, what would be expected of themselves. I mentioned that she was quite my notion of an excellent model—she was really very clever.

"Do you think she looks like a Russian princess?" Major Monarch asked with lurking alarm.

"When I make her, yes."

"Oh if you have to make her—!" he reasoned, not without point.

La Dame aux Éventail—Nina de Callias, Edouard Manet, 1873–74

"That's the most you can ask. There are so many who are not makeable."

"Well now, *here's* a lady"—and with a persuasive smile he passed his arm into his wife's—"who's already made!"

"Oh I'm not a Russian princess," Mrs. Monarch protested a little coldly. I could see she had known some and didn't like them. There at once was a complication of a kind I never had to fear with Miss Churm.

This young lady came back in black velvet—the gown was rather rusty[24] and very low on her lean shoulders—and with a Japanese fan in her red hands. I reminded her that in the scene I was doing she had to look over someone's head. "I forget whose it is; but it doesn't matter. Just look over a head."

"I'd rather look over a stove," said Miss Churm; and she took her station near the fire. She fell into position, settled herself into a tall attitude, gave a certain backward inclination to her head and a certain forward droop to her fan, and looked, at least to my prejudiced sense, distinguished and charming, foreign and dangerous. We left her looking so while I went downstairs with Major and Mrs. Monarch.

"I believe I could come about as near it as that," said Mrs. Monarch.

"Oh, you think she's shabby, but you must allow for the **alchemy** of art."

However, they went off with an evident increase of comfort founded on their demonstrable advantage in being the real thing. I could fancy them shuddering over Miss Churm. She was very **droll** about them when I went back, for I told her what they wanted.

"Well, if she can sit I'll tyke to bookkeeping," said my model.

"She's very ladylike," I replied as an innocent form of aggravation.

"So much the worse for *you*. That means she can't turn round."

"She'll do for the fashionable novels."

"Oh yes, she'll *do* for them!" my model humorously declared. "Ain't they bad enough without her?" I had often sociably denounced them to Miss Churm.

Part III

It was for the **elucidation** of a mystery in one of these works that I first tried Mrs. Monarch. Her husband came with her, to be useful if necessary—it was sufficiently clear that as a general thing he would prefer to come with her. At first I wondered if this were for "propriety's" sake—if he were going to be jealous and meddling. The idea was too tiresome, and if it had been confirmed

alchemy:
the process of turning something common into something precious

droll: humorous; witty

elucidation:
explanation; clarification

---

24 **rusty:** dulled in color or appearance through age and use

it would speedily have brought our acquaintance to a close. But I soon saw there was nothing in it and that if he accompanied Mrs. Monarch it was—in addition to the chance of being wanted—simply because he had nothing else to do. When they were separate his occupation was gone and they never *had* been separate. I judged rightly that in their awkward situation their close union was their main comfort and that this union had no weak spot. It was a real marriage, an encouragement to the hesitating, a nut for pessimists to crack. Their address was humble—I remember afterwards thinking it had been the only thing about them that was really professional—and I could fancy the **lamentable** lodgings in which the Major would have been left alone. He could sit there more or less grimly with his wife—he couldn't sit there anyhow without her.

lamentable: sad; unfortunate

He had too much tact to try and make himself agreeable when he couldn't be useful; so when I was too absorbed in my work to talk he simply sat and waited. But I liked to hear him talk—it made my work, when not interrupting it, less mechanical, less special. To listen to him was to combine the excitement of going out with the economy of staying at home. There was only one hindrance—that I seemed not to know any of the people this brilliant couple had known. I think he wondered extremely, during the term of our intercourse,[25] whom the deuce I *did* know. He hadn't a stray sixpence of an idea to fumble for, so we didn't spin it very fine; we confined ourselves to questions of leather and even of liquor—saddlers and breeches-makers and how to get excellent claret[26] cheap—and matters like "good trains" and the habits of small game. His lore on these last subjects was astonishing—he managed to interweave the station-master with the ornithologist.[27] When he couldn't talk about greater things he could talk cheerfully about smaller, and since I couldn't accompany him into reminiscences of the fashionable world he could lower the conversation without a visible effort to my level.

So earnest a desire to please was touching in a man who could so easily have knocked one down. He looked after the fire and had an opinion on the draught of the stove without my asking him, and I could see that he thought many of my arrangements not half knowing. I remember telling him that if I were only rich I'd offer him a salary to come and teach me how to live. Sometimes he gave a random sigh of which the essence might have been: "Give me even such a bare old barrack as this, and I'd do something with it!"

---

25 **intercourse:** dealings; business

26 **claret:** a kind of red wine

27 **ornithologist:** one who studies birds

When I wanted to use him he came alone; which was an illustration of the superior courage of women. His wife could bear her solitary second floor, and she was in general more discreet; showing by various small reserves that she was alive to the propriety of keeping our relations markedly professional—not letting them slide into sociability. She wished to remain clear that she and the Major were employed, not cultivated, and if she approved of me as a superior, who could be kept in his place, she never thought me quite good enough for an equal.

She sat with great intensity, giving the whole of her mind to it, and was capable of remaining for an hour almost as motionless as before a photographer's lens. I could see that she had been photographed often, but somehow the very habit that made her good for that purpose unfitted her for mine. At first I was extremely pleased with her ladylike air, and it was a satisfaction, on coming to follow her lines, to see how good they were and how far they could lead the pencil. But after a little skirmishing I began to find her too insurmountably stiff; do what I would with it my drawing looked like a photograph or a copy of a photograph. Her figure had no variety of expression—she herself had no sense of variety. You may say that this was my business and was only a question of placing her. Yet I placed her in every conceivable position and she managed to obliterate their differences. She was always a lady certainly, and into the bargain was always the same lady. She was the real thing, but always the same thing. There were moments when I rather writhed under the serenity of her confidence that she *was* the real thing. All her dealings with me and all her husband's were an implication that this was lucky for *me*. Meanwhile I found myself trying to invent types that approached her own, instead of making her own transform itself—in the clever way that was not impossible for instance to poor Miss Churm. Arrange as I would and take the precautions I would, she always came out, in my pictures, too tall—landing me in the dilemma of having represented a fascinating woman as seven feet high, which (out of respect perhaps to my own very much scantier inches) was far from my idea of such a personage.

The case was worse with the Major—nothing I could do would keep *him* down, so that he became useful only for representation of brawny giants. I adored variety and range, I cherished human accidents, the illustrative note; I wanted to characterise closely, and the thing in the world I most hated was the danger of being ridden by a type. I had quarreled with some of my friends about it; I had parted company with them for maintaining that one *had* to be, and that if the type was beautiful—witness Raphael and Leonardo—the servitude was only a gain. I was neither Leonardo nor Raphael—I might only be a **presumptuous** young modern searcher; but I held that everything was to be sacrificed sooner than character. When they claimed that the obsessional form could easily be character I retorted, perhaps superficially, "Whose?" It couldn't be everybody's—it might end in being nobody's.

After I had drawn Mrs. Monarch a dozen times I felt surer even than before that the value of such a model as Miss Churm resided precisely in the fact that she had no positive stamp, combined of course with the other fact that what she did have was a curious and **inexplicable** talent for imitation. Her usual appearance was like a curtain which she could draw up at request for a capital performance. This performance was simply suggestive; but it was a word to the wise—it was vivid and pretty. Sometimes even I thought it, though she was plain herself, too **insipidly** pretty; I made it a reproach to her that the figures drawn from her were monotonously (*bêtement*,[28] as we used to say) graceful. Nothing made her more angry: it was so much her pride to feel she could sit for characters that had nothing in common with each other. She would accuse me at such moments of taking away her "reputytion."

It suffered a certain shrinkage, this queer quantity, from the repeated visits of my new friends. Miss Churm was greatly in demand, never in want of employment, so I had no scruple in putting her off occasionally, to try them more at my ease. It was certainly amusing at first to do the real thing—it was amusing to do Major Monarch's trousers. They *were* the real thing, even if he did come out colossal. It was amusing to do his wife's back hair—it was so mathematically neat—and the particular "smart" tension of her tight stays. She lent herself especially to position in which the face was somewhat averted or blurred; she abounded in ladylike back views and *profils perdus*.[29] When she stood erect she took naturally one of the attitudes in which court-painters represent queens and princesses; so that I found myself wondering whether, to draw out this accomplishment, I couldn't get the editor of the *Cheapside* to publish a really royal romance, "A Tale of Buckingham Palace." Sometimes however the real thing and the make-believe came into contact; by which I mean that Miss Churm, keeping an appointment or coming to make one on days when I had much work in hand, encountered her **invidious** rivals. The encounter was not on their part, for they noticed her no more than if she had been the housemaid; not from intentional loftiness, but simply

presumptuous: overconfident; brash

inexplicable: unexplainable; mysterious

insipidly: boringly; blandly

invidious: causing resentment or envy

---

28 *bêtement:* French for "foolishly"

29 *profils perdus:* French for views from behind that "lose" most of a profile

because as yet, professionally, they didn't know how to fraternise,[30] as I could imagine they would have liked—or at least that the Major would. They couldn't talk about the omnibus—they always walked; and they didn't know what else to try—she wasn't interested in good trains or cheap claret. Besides, they must have felt—in the air—that she was amused at them, secretly derisive of their ever knowing how. She wasn't a person to conceal the limits of her faith if she had had a chance to show them. On the other hand Mrs. Monarch didn't think her tidy; for why else did she take pains to say to me—it was going out of the way, for Mrs. Monarch—that she didn't like dirty women?

One day when my young lady happened to be present with my other sitters—she even dropped in, when it was convenient, for a chat—I asked her to be so good as to lend a hand in getting tea, a service with which she was familiar and which was one of a class that, living as I did in a small way, with slender domestic resources, I often appealed to my models to render. They liked to lay hands on my property, to break the sitting, and sometimes the china—it made them feel Bohemian. The next time I saw Miss Churm after this incident she surprised me greatly by making a scene about it—she accused me of having wished to humiliate her. She hadn't resented the outrage at the time, but had seemed obliging and amused, enjoying the comedy of asking Mrs. Monarch, who sat vague and silent, whether she would have cream and sugar, and putting an exaggerated simper[31] into the question. She had tried intonations—as if she too wished to pass for the real thing—till I was afraid my other visitors would take offense.

Oh they were determined not to do this, and their touching patience was the measure of their great need. They would sit by the hour, uncomplaining, till I was ready to use them; they would come back on the chance of being wanted and would walk away cheerfully if it failed. I used to go to the door with them to see in what magnificent order they retreated. I tried to find other employment for them—I introduced them to several artists. But they didn't "take," for reasons I could appreciate, and I became rather anxiously aware that after such disappointments they fell back upon me with a heavier weight. They did me the honour to think me most their form. They weren't romantic enough for the painters, and in those days there were few serious workers in black-and-white.

Besides, they had an eye to the great job I had mentioned to them—they

---

30 **fraternise:** socialize

31 **simper:** a coy or silly smile

★★★

had secretly set their hearts on supplying the right essence for my pictorial **vindication** of our fine novelist. They knew that for this undertaking I should want no costume-effects, none of the frippery[32] of past ages—that it was a case in which everything would be contemporary and satirical and presumably genteel. If I could work them into it their future would be assured, for the labour would of course be long and the occupation steady.

One day Mrs. Monarch came without her husband—she explained his absence by his having to go to the City. While she sat there in her usual relaxed majesty there came at the door a knock which I immediately recognized as the subdued appeal of a model out of work. It was followed by the entrance of a young man whom I at once saw to be a foreigner and who proved in fact an Italian acquainted with no English word but my name, which he uttered in a way that made it seem to include all others. I hadn't then visited his country, nor was I proficient in his tongue; but as he was not so meanly constituted—what Italian is?—as to depend only on that member for expression he conveyed to me, in familiar but graceful mimicry, that he was in search of exactly the employment in which the lady before me was engaged. I was not struck with him at first, and while I continued to draw I dropped few signs of interest or encouragement. He stood his ground however—not importunately, but with a dumb dog-like fidelity in his eyes that amounted to innocent impudence, the manner of a devoted servant—he might have been in the house for years—unjustly suspected. Suddenly it struck me that this very attitude and expression made a picture; whereupon I told him to sit down and wait till I should be free. There was another picture in the way he obeyed me, and I observed as I worked that there were others still in the way he looked wonderingly, with his head thrown back, about the high studio. He might have been crossing himself in Saint Peter's. Before I finished I said to myself "The fellow's a bankrupt orangemonger,[33] but a treasure."

When Mrs. Monarch withdrew he passed across the room like a flash to open the door for her, standing there with the rapt pure gaze of the young Dante spellbound by the young Beatrice.[34] As I never insisted, in such situations, on the blankness of the British domestic, I reflected that he had the making of a servant—and I needed one, but couldn't pay him to be only that—as well as of a model; in short I resolved to adopt my bright

---

32 **frippery:** decorative garments

33 **orangemonger:** orange seller

34 **Dante . . . Beatrice:** Dante (1265–1321) was the Italian author of the *Divine Comedy*. Beatrice was a young woman Dante idealized both in real life and in his fiction.

adventurer if he would agree to officiate in the double capacity. He jumped at my offer, and in the event my rashness—for I had really known nothing about him—wasn't brought home to me. He proved a sympathetic though a desultory ministrant,[35] and had in a wonderful degree the *sentiment de la pose*.[36] It was uncultivated, instinctive, a part of the happy instinct that had guided him to my door and helped him to spell out my name on the card nailed to it. He had had no other introduction to me than a guess, from the shape of my high north window, seen outside, that my place was a studio and that as a studio it would contain an artist. He had wandered to England in search of fortune, like other itinerants, and had embarked, with a partner and a small green hand-card, on the sale of penny ices. The ices had melted away and the partner had dissolved in their train. My young man wore tight yellow trousers with reddish stripes and his name was Oronte. He was sallow but fair, and when I put him into some old clothes of my own, he looked like an Englishman. He was as good as Miss Churm, who could look, when requested, like an Italian.

Part IV

I thought Mrs. Monarch's face slightly convulsed when, on her coming back with her husband, she found Orante installed. It was strange to have to recognise in a scrap of a *lazzarone*[37] a competitor to her magnificent Major. It was she who scented danger first, for the Major was anecdotally unconscious. But Oronte gave us tea, with a hundred eager confusions—he had never been concerned in so queer a process—and I think she thought better of me for having at last an "establishment." They saw a couple of drawings that I had made of the establishment, and Mrs. Monarch hinted that it never would have struck her he had sat for them. "Now the drawings you make from *us*, they look exactly like us," she reminded me, smiling in triumph; and I recognized that this was indeed just their defect. When I drew the Monarchs I couldn't anyhow get away from them—get into the character I wanted to represent; and I hadn't the least desire my model should be discoverable in my picture. Miss Churm never was, and Mrs. Monarch thought I hid her, very properly, because she was vulgar; whereas if she was lost it was only as the dead who go to heaven are lost—in the gain of an angel the more.

---

35 **desultory ministrant:** sluggish, slow-moving servant

36 *sentiment de la pose:* an instinct for posing

37 *lazzarone:* Italian for someone who works at odd jobs

By this time I had got a certain start with "Rutland Ramsay," the first novel in the great projected series; that is I had produced a dozen drawings, several with the help of the Major and his wife, and I had sent them in for approval. My understanding with the publishers, as I have already hinted, had been that I was to be left to do my work, in this particular case, as I liked, with the whole book committed to me; but my connections with the rest of the series was only contingent. There were moments when, frankly, it was a comfort to have the real thing under one's hand; for there were characters in "Rutland Ramsay" that were very much like it. There were people presumably as erect as the Major and women of as good a fashion as Mrs. Monarch. There was a great deal of country-house life—treated, it is true, in a fine fanciful ironical generalized way—and there was a considerable implication of knickerbockers and kilts. There were certain things I had to settle at the outset; such things for instance as the exact appearance of the hero and the particular bloom and figure of the heroine. The author of course gave me a lead, but there was a margin for interpretation. I took the Monarchs into my confidence. I told them frankly what I was about, I mentioned my embarrassments and alternatives. "Oh take him!" Mrs. Monarch murmured sweetly, looking at her husband; and "What could you want better than my wife?" the Major enquired with the comfortable candour that now prevailed between us.

I wasn't obliged to answer these remarks—I was only obliged to place my sitters. I wasn't easy in mind, and I postponed a little timidly perhaps the solving of my question. The book was a large canvas, the other figures were numerous, and I worked off at first some of the episodes in which the hero and the heroine were not concerned. When once I had set them up I should have to stick to them—I couldn't make my young man seven feet high in one place and five feet nine in another. I inclined on the whole to the latter measurement, though the Major more than once reminded me that he looked about as young as any one. It was indeed quite possible to arrange him, for the figure, so that it would have been difficult to detect his age. After the spontaneous Oronte had been with me a month, and after I had given him to understand several times over that his native exuberance would presently constitute an insurmountable barrier to our further intercourse, I waked to a sense of his heroic capacity. He was only five feet seven, but the remaining inches were **latent**. I tried him almost secretly at first, for I was really rather afraid of the judgment my other models would pass on such a choice. If they regarded Miss Churm as little better than a snare what

latent:
hidden

THE ARTISTS,
HERMANN KAUFFMANN

would they think of the representation by a person so little the real thing as an Italian street-vendor of a protagonist formed by a public school?

If I went a little in fear of them it wasn't because they bullied me, because they had got an oppressive foothold, but because in their really pathetic **decorum** and mysteriously permanent newness they counted on me so intensely. I was therefore very glad when Jack Hawley came home: he was always of such good counsel. He painted badly himself, but there was no one like him for putting his finger on the place. He had been absent from England for a year; he had been somewhere—I don't remember where—to get a fresh eye. I was in a good deal of dread of any such organ, but we were old friends; he had been away for months and a sense of emptiness was creeping into my life. I hadn't dodged a missile for a year.

decorum: good manners; politeness

He came back with a fresh eye, but with the same old black velvet blouse, and the first evening he spent in my studio we smoked cigarettes till the small hours. He had done no work himself, he had only got the eye; so the field was clear for the production of my little things. He wanted to see what I had produced for the *Cheapside*, but he was disappointed in the exhibition. That at least seemed the meaning of two or three comprehensive groans which, as he lounged on my big divan, his leg folded under him, looking at my latest drawings, issued from his lips with the smoke of the cigarette.

"What's the matter with you?" I asked.

"What's the matter with you?"

"Nothing save that I'm mystified."

"You are indeed. You're quite off the hinge. What's the meaning of this new fad?" And he tossed me, with visible irreverence, a drawing in which I happened to have depicted both my elegant models. I asked if he didn't think it good, and he replied that it struck him as execrable, given the sort of thing I had always represented myself to him as wishing to arrive at; but I let that pass—I was so anxious to see exactly what he meant. The two figures in the picture looked colossal, but I supposed that this was not what he meant, inasmuch as, for ought he knew the contrary. I might have been trying for some such effect. I maintained that I was working exactly in the same way as when he last had done me the honour to tell me I might do something some day. "Well, there's a screw loose somewhere," he answered; "wait a bit and I'll discover it." I depended upon him to do so: where else was the fresh eye? But he produced at last nothing more **luminous** than "I don't know—I don't like your types." This was lame for a critic who had never consented to discuss with me anything but the question of execution, the direction of strokes and the mystery of values.

luminous: brilliant; enlightening

"In the drawings you've been looking at I think my types are very handsome."

"Oh they won't do!"

"I've been working with new models."

"I see you have. *They* won't do."

"Are you very sure of that?"

"Absolutely—they're stupid."

"You mean I am—for I ought to get round that."

"You can't—with such people. Who are they?"

I told him, so far as was necessary, and he concluded heartlessly: "*Ce sont des gens qu'il faut mettre á la porte.*"[38]

---

38 **"Ce sont des gens qu'il faut mettre á la porte.":** French for "They are the kind of people one must get rid of."

"You've never seen them; they're awfully good"—I flew to their defence.

"Not seen them? Why all this recent work of yours drops to pieces with them. It's all I want to see of them."

"No one else has said anything against it—the *Cheapside* people are pleased."

"Everyone else is an ass, and the *Cheapside* people the biggest asses of all. Come, don't pretend at this time of day to have pretty illusions about the public, especially about publishers and editors. It's not for *such* animals you work—it's for those who know, *color che sanno;*[39] so keep straight for me if you can't keep straight for yourself. There was a certain sort of thing you used to try for—and a very good thing it was, but this twaddle isn't in it." When I talked with Hawley later about "Rutland Ramsay" and its possible successors he declared that I must get back into my boat again or I should go to the bottom. His voice in short was the voice of a warning.

I noted the warning, but I didn't turn my friends out of doors. They bored me a good deal; but the very fact that they bored me admonished me not to sacrifice them—if there was anything to be done with them—simply to irritation. As I look back at this phase they seem to me to have pervaded my life not a little. I have a vision of them as most of the time in my studio, seated against the wall on an old velvet bench to be out of the way, and resembling the while a pair of patient courtiers in a royal ante-chamber. I'm convinced that during the coldest weeks of the winter they held their ground because it saved them fire. Their newness was losing its gloss, and it was impossible not to feel them objects of charity. Whenever Miss Churm arrived they went away, and after I was fairly launched in "Rutland Ramsay" Miss Churm arrived pretty often. They managed to express to me tacitly that they supposed I wanted her for the low life of the book, and I let them suppose it, since they had attempted to study the work—it was lying about the studio—without discovering that it dealt only with the highest circles. They had dipped into the most brilliant of our novelists without deciphering many passages. I still took an hour from them, now and again, in spite of Jack Hawley's warning: it would be time enough to dismiss them, if dismissal should be necessary, when the rigour of the season was over. Hawley had made their acquaintance—he had met them at my fireside—and thought them a ridiculous pair. Learning that he was a painter they tried to approach him, to show him too that they were the real thing; but he looked at them,

---

39 **color che sanno:** Italian phrase from Dante's reference to the philosopher Aristotle: "*Vidi il Maestro di color che sanno*"—"I saw the master of those who know."

across the big room, as if they were miles away: they were a **compendium** of everything he most objected to in the social system of his country. Such people as that, all convention and patent-leather, with ejaculations that stopped conversation, had no business in a studio. A studio was a place to learn to see, and how could you see through a pair of feather-beds?

compendium: collection

The main inconvenience I suffered at their hands was that at first I was shy of letting it break upon them that my artful little servant had begun to sit to me for "Rutland Ramsay." They knew I had been odd enough—they were prepared by this time to allow oddity to artists—to pick a foreign vagabond out of the streets when I might have had a person with whiskers and credentials, but it was some time before they learned how high I rated his accomplishments. They found him in an attitude more than once, but they never doubted I was doing him as an organ-grinder. There were several things they never guessed, and one of them was that for a striking scene in the novel, in which a footman briefly figured, it occurred to me to make sure of Major Monarch as the **menial**. I kept putting this off, I didn't like to ask him to don the livery—besides the difficulty of finding a livery to fit him. At last, one day late in the winter, when I was at work on the despised Oronte, who caught one's idea on the wing, and was in the glow of feeling myself go very straight, they came in, the Major and his wife, with their society laugh about nothing (there was less and less to laugh at); came in like country-callers—they always reminded me of that—who have walked across the park after church and are presently persuaded to stay to luncheon. Luncheon was over, but they could stay to tea—I knew they wanted it. The fit was on me, however, and I couldn't let my ardour cool and my work wait, with the fading daylight, while my model prepared it. So I asked Mrs. Monarch if she would mind laying it out—a request which for an instant brought all the blood to her face. Her eyes were on her husband's for a second, and some mute telegraphy passed between them. Their folly was over the next instant; his cheerful shrewdness put an end to it. So far from pitying their wounded pride, I must add, I was moved to give it as complete a lesson as I could. They bustled about together and got out the cups and saucers and made the kettle boil. I know they felt as if they were waiting on my servant, and when the tea was prepared I said: "He'll have a cup, please—he's tired." Mrs. Monarch brought him one where he stood, and he took it from her as if he had been a gentleman at a party squeezing a crush-hat with an elbow.

menial: servant

Then it came over me that she had made a great effort for me—made it with a kind of nobleness—and that I owed her a compensation. Each time

I saw her after this I wondered what the compensation could be. I couldn't go on doing the wrong thing to oblige them. Oh it *was* the wrong thing, the stamp of the work for which they sat—Hawley was not the only person to say it now. I sent in a large number of the drawings I had made for "Rutland Ramsay," and I received a warning that was more to the point than Hawley's. The artistic advisor of the house for which I was working was of opinion that many of my illustrations were not what had been looked for. Most of these illustrations were the subjects in which the Monarchs had figured. Without going into the question of what had been looked for, I had to face the fact that at this rate I shouldn't get the other books to do. I hurled myself in despair on Miss Churm—I put her through all her paces. I not only adopted Oronte publicly as my hero, but one morning when the Major looked in to see if I didn't require him to finish a *Cheapside* figure for which he had begun to sit the week before, I told him I had changed my mind—I'd do the drawing from my man. At this my visitor turned pale and stood looking at me. "Is he your idea of an English gentleman?" he asked.

I was disappointed. I was nervous, I wanted to get on with my work; so I replied with irritation: "Oh my dear Major—I can't be ruined for *you!*"

It was a horrid speech, but he stood another moment—after which, without a word, he quitted the studio. I drew a long breath, for I said to myself that I shouldn't see him again. I hadn't told him definitely that I was in danger of having my work rejected, but I was vexed at his not having felt the catastrophe in the air, read with me the moral of our fruitless collaboration, the lesson that in the deceptive atmosphere of art even the highest respectability may fail of being plastic.

I didn't owe my friends money, but I did see them again. They reappeared together three days later, and, given all the other facts, there was something tragic in that one. It was a clear proof they could find nothing else in life to do. They had threshed the matter out in a dismal conference—they had digested the bad news that they were not in for the series. If they weren't useful to me even for the *Cheapside* their function seemed difficult to determine, and I could only judge at first that they had come, forgivingly, decorously, to take a last leave. This made me rejoice in secret that I had little leisure for a scene; for I had placed both my other models in position together and I was pegging away at a drawing from which I hoped to derive glory. It had been suggested by the passage in which Rutland Ramsay, drawing up a chair to Artemisia's piano-stool, says extraordinary things to her while she ostensibly fingers out a difficult piece of music. I had done Miss Churm at the piano before—it was an attitude in which she knew how to take on an absolutely poetic grace. I wished the two figures to "compose" together with intensity, and my little Italian had entered perfectly into my conception. The pair were vividly before me, the piano had been pulled out; it was a charming show of blended youth and murmured love, which I had only to catch and keep. My visitors stood and looked at it, and I was friendly to them over my shoulder.

They made no response, but I was used to silent company and went on with my work, only a little **disconcerted**—even though exhilarated by the sense that this was at least the ideal thing—at not having got rid of them after all. Presently I heard Mrs. Monarch's sweet voice beside or rather above me: "I wish her hair were a little better done." I looked up and she was staring with a strange fixedness at Miss Churm, whose back was turned to her. "Do you mind my just touching it?" she went on—a question which made me spring up for an instant as with the instinctive fear that she might do the young lady a harm. But she quieted me with a glance I shall never forget—I confess I should like to have been able to paint that—and went for a moment to my model. She spoke to her softly, laying a hand on her shoulder and bending over her; and as the girl, understanding, gratefully assented, she disposed her rough curls, with a few quick passes, in such a way to make Miss Churm's head twice as charming. It was one of the most heroic personal services I've ever seen rendered. Then Mrs. Monarch turned away with a low sign and, looking about her as if for something to do, stooped to the floor with a noble humility and picked up a dirty rag that had dropped out of my paint-box.

disconcerted: unsettled; perturbed

A Corner of the Painter's Studio, Claude Monet, 1861

The Major meanwhile had also been looking for something to do, and, wandering to the other end of the studio, saw before him my breakfast-things neglected, unremoved. "I say, can't I be useful *here?*" he called out to me with an irrepressible quaver. I assented with a laugh that I fear was awkward, and for the next ten minutes, while I worked, I heard the light clatter of china and the tinkle of spoons and glass. Mrs. Monarch assisted her husband—they washed up my crockery, they put it away. They wandered off into my little scullery,[40] and I afterwards found that they had cleaned my knives and that my slender stock of plate had an unprecedented surface. When it came over me, the latent eloquence of what they were doing, I confess that my drawing was blurred for a moment—the picture swam. They had accepted their failure, but they couldn't accept their fate. They had bowed their heads in bewilderment to the perverse and cruel law in virtue of which the real thing could be so much less precious than the unreal; but they didn't want to starve. If my servants were my models; then my models might be my servants. They would reverse the parts—the others would sit for the ladies and gentlemen and *they* would do the work. They would still be in the studio—it was an intense dumb appeal to me not to turn them out. "Take us on," they wanted to say—"we'll do *anything.*"

My pencil dropped from my hand; my sitting was spoiled and I got rid of my sitters, who were also evidently rather mystified and awestruck. Then, alone with the Major and his wife I had a most uncomfortable moment. He put their prayer into a single sentence: "I say, you know—just let *us* do for you, can't you?" I couldn't—it was dreadful to see them emptying my slops; but I pretended I could, to oblige them, for about a week. Then I gave them a sum of money to go away, and I never saw them again. I obtained the remaining books, but my friend Hawley repeats that Major and Mrs. Monarch did me a permanent harm, got me into false ways. If it be true I'm content to have paid the price—for the memory.

---

40 **scullery:** pantry; a room to store dishes and kitchen utensils

Read and Think Critically

Consider, Infer, Analyze

1. **PARADOX** What are some of the **paradoxes** in "The Real Thing"? You might start with the passage on page 150 that describes the artist's first impressions of the Monarchs: "After all they were amateurs . . . "

2. Consider the significance of the author's choice of names for the Monarchs and Miss Churm. What is the double meaning of the word *Monarch*? What **connotations** do their names imply?

3. Do you think the **narrator** is reliable? In light of the final sentence of the story, does the reader really understand the narrator's feelings toward the Monarchs? Make an **inference** about the objectivity of the narrator, citing his own words for support.

4. Analyze how the **theme** of **realism** in art interacts with the theme of class structure. What conclusion about class structure can you draw from the story?

5. **THE AUTHOR'S STYLE** Henry James was interested in the relationship of outer physical reality to inner psychological reality. Consider this quotation from one of Henry James' essays on writing fiction in which he explores this topic. How does his discussion of reality and "writing from experience" relate to his short story "The Real Thing"?

Writing from Experience

It goes without saying that you will not write a good novel unless you possess the sense of reality; but it will be difficult to give you a recipe for calling that sense into being. Humanity is immense and reality has a myriad forms. . . . It is equally . . . inconclusive to say that one must write from experience. . . . What kind of experience is intended, and where does it begin and end? Experience is never limited and it is never complete; it is an immense sensibility, a kind of huge spider-web, of the finest silken threads, suspended in the chamber of consciousness and catching every air-borne particle in its tissue. It is the very atmosphere of the mind; and when the mind is imaginative . . . it takes to itself the faintest hints of life, it converts the very pulses of the air into revelations. The young lady living in a village has only to be a damsel upon whom nothing is lost to make it quite unfair (as it seems to me) to declare to her that she shall have nothing to say about the military.

—Henry James, "The Art of Fiction"

Before You Read

Kate Chopin 1851–1904

About the Author

Chopin was born in St. Louis to an Irish-American businessman and his well-connected Creole wife. She wed Alfred Chopin, a Creole cotton broker from the New Orleans area. When her husband died, Kate was only 32 years old and had six children to support. After managing his business for a short time, she and her children moved back to St. Louis, where she began to write fiction. She was especially interested in portraying the richly diverse Cajun and Creole culture of Louisiana.

Chopin wrote nearly 100 popular and critically praised stories. But she is most famous for her novel *The Awakening* (1899). Ironically, it was this book that put an end to her high-flying career. In the story, a woman falls in love and abandons her family in pursuit of sexual and artistic liberation—a scandalous idea in Chopin's day, when most female protagonists were limited to conventional notions of romance. She was stunned at her critics'

reactions and soon stopped publishing. Her literary reputation never recovered during her lifetime.

Chopin's writing is now celebrated for its modern attitudes about women's independence as well as its elegant writing. Though often described as a feminist who rebelled against the roles of daughter, wife, and mother, others contend that Chopin was quite happy in these roles. Instead, her works may express the broader human quest for freedom of spirit, soul, and character in a life full of constraints. Perhaps her father's death when she was a young girl and her upbringing by well-educated women influenced her strong interest in a woman's quest for these freedoms. In *The Awakening*, Chopin states her philosophy frankly: "Perhaps it is better to wake up after all, even to suffer, rather than to remain a dupe to illusions all one's life."

****

The Author's Style

Set chiefly in the Deep South after the Civil War, Chopin's stories depict the racial, class, and gender tensions of that region and era. Racially mixed marriages, divorce, a woman's choice between marriage and career, and "modern" marriages (in which women wield more power) are some of her themes. Chopin's protagonists, mostly female, yearn for purpose and pleasures apart from those offered in their traditional roles. Third-person narrators most often reveal these characters' feelings by reporting key

actions and interactions. Influenced by French realist Guy de Maupassant, Chopin exposes hidden realities and false perceptions by ending many of her stories with ironic twists.

A Chopin story is concise, simply plotted, and rich in natural imagery. Her keen ear for dialect and her focus on uniquely Southern settings and situations earned her a reputation as a writer who aptly captured the local color, or flavor, of that region.

A Pair of
Silk Stockings

KATE CHOPIN

🔍 **LITERARY LENS: TURNING POINT** The **turning point** of a plot is when a significant change happens. What is the turning point of this story?

*L*ittle Mrs. Sommers one day found herself the unexpected possessor of fifteen dollars. It seemed to her a very large amount of money, and the way in which it stuffed and bulged her worn old *porte-monnaie*[1] gave her a feeling of importance such as she had not enjoyed for years.

The question of investment was one that occupied her greatly. For a day or two she walked about apparently in a dreamy state, but really absorbed in speculation and calculation. She did not wish to act hastily, to do anything she might afterward regret. But it was during the still hours of the night when she lay awake revolving plans in her mind that she seemed to see her way clearly toward a proper and **judicious** use of the money.

judicious: wise

A dollar or two should be added to the price usually paid for Janie's shoes, which would insure their lasting an appreciable

---

1 *porte-monnaie:* French meaning "pocketbook"

time longer than they usually did. She would buy so and so many yards of percale for new shirt waists[2] for the boys and Janie and Mag. She had intended to make the old ones do by skilful patching. Mag should have another gown. She had seen some beautiful patterns, **veritable** bargains in the shop windows. And still there would be left enough for new stockings—two pairs apiece—and what darning[3] that would save for a while! She would get caps for the boys and sailor-hats for the girls. The vision of her little brood looking fresh and dainty and new for once in their lives excited her and made her restless and wakeful with anticipation.

The neighbors sometimes talked of certain "better days" that little Mrs. Sommers had known before she had ever thought of being Mrs. Sommers. She herself indulged in no such **morbid retrospection**. She had no time— no second of time to devote to the past. The needs of the present absorbed her every **faculty**. A vision of the future like some dim, gaunt monster sometimes appalled her, but luckily to-morrow never comes.

Mrs. Sommers was one who knew the value of bargains; who could stand for hours making her way inch by inch toward the desired object that was selling below cost. She could elbow her way if need be; she had learned to clutch a piece of goods and hold it and stick to it with persistence and determination till her turn came to be served, no matter when it came.

But that day she was a little faint and tired. She had swallowed a light luncheon—no! when she came to think of it, between getting the children fed and the place righted, and preparing herself for the shopping bout, she had actually forgotten to eat any luncheon at all!

She sat herself upon a revolving stool before a counter that was comparatively deserted, trying to gather strength and courage to charge through an eager multitude that was **besieging** breastworks[4] of shirting and figured lawn. An all-gone limp feeling had come over her and she rested her hand aimlessly upon the counter. She wore no gloves. By degrees she grew aware that her hand had encountered something very soothing, very pleasant to touch. She looked down to see that her hand lay upon a pile of silk stockings. A placard nearby announced that they had been reduced in price from two dollars and fifty cents to one dollar and ninety-eight cents; and a young girl who stood behind the counter asked her if she wished to

veritable: true

morbid: gloomy; morose

retrospection: thinking or observations about the past

faculty: mental ability

besieging: crowding around; surrounding

---

2 **shirt waists:** tailored blouses with details copied from men's shirts

3 **darning:** mending holes in clothing

4 **breastworks:** temporary fortifications or strongholds

examine their line of silk hosiery. She smiled, just as if she had been asked to inspect a tiara of diamonds with the ultimate view of purchasing it. But she went on feeling the soft, sheeny luxurious things—with both hands now, holding them up to see them glisten, and to feel them glide serpent-like through her fingers.

Two hectic blotches came suddenly into her pale cheeks. She looked up at the girl.

"Do you think there are any eights-and-a-half among these?"

There were any number of eights-and-a-half. In fact, there were more of that size than any other. Here was a light-blue pair; there were some lavender, some all black and various shades of tan and gray. Mrs. Sommers selected a black pair and looked at them very long and closely. She pretended to be examining their texture, which the clerk assured her was excellent.

"A dollar and ninety-eight cents," she mused aloud. "Well, I'll take this pair." She handed the girl a five-dollar bill and waited for her change and for her parcel. What a very small parcel it was! It seemed lost in the depths of her shabby old shopping-bag.

Mrs. Sommers after that did not move in the direction of the bargain

LETTER WITH SKETCH OF LEGS, EDOUARD MANET, 1880

counter. She took the elevator, which carried her to an upper floor into the region of the ladies' waiting-rooms. Here, in a retired corner, she exchanged her cotton stockings for the new silk ones which she had just bought. She was not going through any acute mental process or reasoning with herself, nor was she striving to explain to her satisfaction the motive of her action. She was not thinking at all. She seemed for the time to be taking a rest from that laborious and fatiguing function and to have abandoned herself to some mechanical impulse that directed her actions and freed her of responsibility.

How good was the touch of the raw silk to her flesh! She felt like lying back in the cushioned chair and reveling for a while in the luxury of it. She did for a little while. Then she replaced her shoes, rolled the cotton stockings together and thrust them into her bag. After doing this she crossed straight over to the shoe department and took her seat to be fitted.

She was fastidious. The clerk could not make her out; he could not reconcile her shoes with her stockings.

reconcile: make consistent or compatible

She was fastidious. The clerk could not make her out; he could not **reconcile** her shoes with her stockings, and she was not too easily pleased. She held back her skirts and turned her feet one way and her head another way as she glanced down at the polished, pointed-tipped boots. Her foot and ankle looked very pretty. She could not realize that they belonged to her and were a part of herself. She wanted an excellent and stylish fit, she told the young fellow who served her, and she did not mind the difference of a dollar or two more in the price so long as she got what she desired.

It was a long time since Mrs. Sommers had been fitted with gloves. On rare occasions when she had bought a pair they were always "bargains," so cheap that it would have been **preposterous** and unreasonable to have expected them to be fitted to the hand.

preposterous: outrageous; outlandish

Now she rested her elbow on the cushion of the glove counter, and a pretty, pleasant young creature, delicate and **deft** of touch, drew a long-wristed "kid"[5] over Mrs. Sommers's hand. She smoothed it down over the wrist and buttoned it neatly, and both lost themselves for a second or two in admiring contemplation of the little symmetrical gloved hand. But there were other places where money might be spent.

deft: nimble; dexterous

There were books and magazines piled up in the window of a stall a few paces down the street. Mrs. Sommers bought two high-priced magazines

---

5 **"kid":** short for *kidskin*, a soft fine leather from young goats

such as she had been accustomed to read in the days when she had been accustomed to other pleasant things. She carried them without wrapping. As well as she could she lifted her skirts at the crossings. Her stockings and boots and well fitting gloves had worked marvels in her bearing—had given her a feeling of assurance, a sense of belonging to the well-dressed multitude.

She was very hungry. Another time she would have stilled the cravings for food until reaching her own home, where she would have brewed herself a cup of tea and taken a snack of anything that was available. But the impulse that was guiding her would not suffer[6] her to entertain any such thought.

There was a restaurant at the corner. She had never entered its doors; from the outside she had sometimes caught glimpses of spotless damask and shining crystal, and soft-stepping waiters serving people of fashion.

When she entered her appearance created no surprise, no consternation, as she had half feared it might. She seated herself at a small table alone, and an attentive waiter at once approached to take her order. She did not want a profusion; she craved a nice and tasty bite—a half dozen blue-points,[7] a plump chop with cress, a something sweet—a creme-frappee, for instance; a glass of Rhine wine, and after all a small cup of black coffee.

While waiting to be served she removed her gloves very leisurely and laid them beside her. Then she picked up a magazine and glanced through it, cutting the pages with a blunt edge of her knife.[8] It was all very agreeable. The damask was even more spotless than it had seemed through the window, and the crystal more sparkling. There were quiet ladies and gentlemen, who did not notice her, lunching at the small tables like her own. A soft, pleasing strain of music could be heard, and a gentle breeze, was blowing through the window. She tasted a bite, and she read a word or two, and she sipped the amber wine and wiggled her toes in the silk stockings. The price of it made no difference. She counted the money out to the waiter and left an extra coin on his tray, whereupon he bowed before her as before a princess of royal blood.

There was still money in her purse, and her next temptation presented itself in the shape of a matinee poster.

It was a little later when she entered the theatre, the play had begun and the house seemed to her to be packed. But there were vacant seats here and

---

6 **suffer:** allow; endure

7 **blue-points:** small oysters

8 **cutting . . . knife:** at one time, book and magazine pages were bound in folded sections that needed to be cut open before reading

THEATRE,
HONORE DAUMIER
C. 1857–60

there, and into one of them she was ushered, between brilliantly dressed women who had gone there to kill time and eat candy and display their gaudy attire. There were many others who were there solely for the play and acting. It is safe to say there was no one present who bore quite the attitude which Mrs. Sommers did to her surroundings. She gathered in the whole— stage and players and people in one wide impression, and absorbed it and enjoyed it. She laughed at the comedy and wept—she and the gaudy woman next to her wept over the tragedy. And they talked a little together over it. And the gaudy woman wiped her eyes and sniffled on a tiny square of filmy, perfumed lace and passed little Mrs. Sommers her box of candy.

The play was over, the music ceased, the crowd filed out. It was like a dream ended. People scattered in all directions. Mrs. Sommers went to the corner and waited for the cable car.

A man with keen eyes, who sat opposite to her, seemed to like the study of her small, pale face. It puzzled him to decipher what he saw there. In truth, he saw nothing—unless he were wizard enough to detect a poignant wish, a powerful longing that the cable car would never stop anywhere, but go on and on with her forever.

Read and Think Critically

Explain, Infer, Analyze

 1. **TURNING POINT** What do you think is the **turning point** of this story? Explain why.

2. How do you explain the "mechanical impulse" that propels Mrs. Sommers to spend her windfall? Share how you felt as you read about each of her purchases.

3. On a scale of 1 to 5, evaluate whether you felt her purchases were justified (1) or unjustified (5). Explain your answers.

4. How important are the silk stockings of the **title** to Mrs. Sommers? Explain what you think they mean to her. Suggest another title for the story.

5. Look at the description of Mrs. Sommers's meal in the restaurant. List some details from the text. What can you infer about her background prior to her marriage?

6. At the story's end, the **narrator** says, "It was like a dream ended." Do you think Mrs. Sommers will regret her actions on this day? Support your answer with details from the story.

 7. **THE AUTHOR'S STYLE** In many of Chopin's stories, a third-person narrator reveals the **character's** feelings by reporting key actions and interactions. Analyze Chopin's use of this technique in the last paragraph of the story. How does the action she chooses to report in that paragraph affect the story?

★★★

Before You Read

Charles Waddell Chesnutt 1858–1932

About the Author

Charles Waddell Chesnutt—a teacher, newspaperman, and lawyer—was also the first African American to achieve widespread literary acclaim. His fiction dealt mainly with the black experience in post–Civil War America. His masterwork was a story collection, *The Wife of His Youth and Other Stories of the Color Line* (1899), which portrayed the mixed-race characters who straddled the "color-line"—neither white nor black in the eyes of society. Chesnutt, himself of mixed heritage, understood the prejudice that often arose between light- and dark-skinned blacks.

Chesnutt's parents were free Southern blacks who spent the Civil War period in Ohio. Chesnutt was born in Cleveland but was raised

in North Carolina, where he attended school, married, and became a school principal by the time he was 25. But he aspired to be a writer in a time and place that did not nourish the careers of black men. So, Chesnutt moved back to Ohio, passed the bar exam, and opened up a successful court reporting business. In a few years, he was able to devote himself to writing.

Eventually his frank treatment of racial subjects began to trouble white readers, and his work fell out of favor. He gave up writing fiction for publication, instead writing essays about the status of African Americans. In both his fiction and nonfiction, Chesnutt was not only an innovator but a writer of conscience.

★★★★★★★★★★★

The Author's Style

Chesnutt's work explored groundbreaking themes. While his contemporaries portrayed romantic versions of plantation life, he addressed the tragic effects of the institution on which that way of life depended—slavery. By depicting slaves of exceptional determination and creativity as they survived a wide range of experiences, he dispelled prevailing stereotypes. In exploring the unique difficulties of people of mixed race, including issues of interracial marriage, he exposed the prejudices that existed within the African American community itself.

Chesnutt's early fiction draws on the folk characters and superstitions of African American culture and uses a white frame

narrator who recounts stories told by an ex-slave. The stories involve a "conjure woman" who magically transforms slaves into trees, plants, and animals, thus evoking the black Americans' less-than-human status in American society.

In later, more realistic stories such as "The Wife of His Youth," Chesnutt uses irony to draw attention to the psychological and social problems of African Americans. His characters' actions subtly present the story's powerful message. Local color techniques, especially the use of dialects, emphasize the unique characteristics of the North Carolina region and its people.

The Wife of His Youth

CHARLES WADDELL CHESNUTT

LITERARY LENS: CHARACTERIZATION Notice how the author creates and develops the character of Mr. Ryder in the following story.

I

*M*r. Ryder was going to give a ball. There were several reasons why this was an opportune time for such an event.

Mr. Ryder might aptly be called the dean of the Blue Veins. The original Blue Veins were a little society of colored persons organized in a certain Northern city shortly after the war. Its purpose was to establish and maintain correct social standards among a people whose social condition presented almost unlimited room for improvement. By accident, combined perhaps with some natural **affinity**, the society consisted of individuals who were, generally speaking, more white than black. Some envious outsider made the suggestion that no one was eligible for membership who was not white enough to show blue veins. The suggestion was readily adopted by those who were not of the favored few, and since that

affinity: special attraction

pretentious:
conceited; showy

time the society, though possessing a longer and more **pretentious** name, had been known far and wide as the "Blue Vein Society" and its members as the "Blue Veins."

The Blue Veins did not allow that any such requirement existed for admission to their circle, but, on the contrary, declared that character and culture were the only things considered; and that if most of their members were light-colored, it was because such persons, as a rule, had had better opportunities to qualify themselves for membership. Opinions differed, too, as to the usefulness of the society. There were those who had been

assail: attack; assault

known to **assail** it violently as a glaring example of the very prejudice from which the colored race had suffered most; and later, when such critics had succeeded in getting on the inside, they had been heard to maintain with

earnestness:
seriousness;
sincerity

zeal and **earnestness** that the society was a lifeboat, an anchor, a bulwark and a shield,—a pillar of cloud by day and of fire by night, to guide their people through the social wilderness. Another **alleged prerequisite** for Blue

alleged:
suspected;
so-called

Vein membership was that of free birth; and while there was really no such requirement, it is doubtless true that very few of the members would have been unable to meet it if there had been. If there were one or two of the older

prerequisite:
requirement;
qualification

members who had come up from the South and from slavery, their history presented enough romantic circumstances to rob their servile origin of its grosser aspects.

While there were no such tests of eligibility, it is true that the Blue Veins had their notions on these subjects, and that not all of them were equally liberal in regard to the things they collectively disclaimed. Mr. Ryder was one of the most conservative. Though he had not been among the founders of the society, but had come in some years later, his genius for social leadership was such that he had speedily become its recognized adviser and head, the custodian of its standards, and the preserver of its traditions. He shaped its social policy, was active in providing for its entertainment, and when the interest fell off, as it sometimes did, he fanned the embers until they burst again into a cheerful flame.

There were still other reasons for his popularity. While he was not as white as some of the Blue Veins, his appearance was such as to confer distinction upon them. His features were of a refined type, his hair was almost straight; he was always neatly dressed; his manners were irreproachable, and his morals above suspicion. He had come to Groveland a young man, and obtaining employment in the office of a railroad company as messenger had in time worked himself up to the position of stationery clerk, having charge of the distribution of the office supplies for the whole company. Although the lack of early training had hindered the orderly development of a naturally fine mind, it had not prevented him from doing a great deal of reading or from forming decidedly literary tastes. Poetry was his passion. He could repeat whole pages of the great English poets; and if his pronunciation was sometimes faulty, his eye, his voice, his gestures, would respond to the changing **sentiment** with a precision that revealed a poetic soul and **disarmed** criticism. He was economical, and had saved money; he owned and occupied a very comfortable

Yale student, c. 1885

house on a respectable street. His residence was handsomely furnished, containing among other things a good library, especially rich in poetry, a piano, and some choice engravings. He generally shared his house with some young couple, who looked after his wants and were company for him; for Mr. Ryder was a single man. In the early days of his connection with the Blue Veins he had been regarded as quite a catch, and young ladies and their mothers had **manoeuvred** with much **ingenuity** to capture him. Not, however, until Mrs. Molly Dixon visited Groveland had any woman ever made him wish to change his condition to that of a married man.

Mrs. Dixon had come to Groveland from Washington in the spring, and before the summer was over she had won Mr. Ryder's heart. She possessed many attractive qualities. She was much younger than he; in fact, he was old enough to have been her father, though no one knew exactly how old he was. She was whiter than he, and better educated. She had moved in the best colored society of the country, at Washington, and had taught in the schools

sentiment: emotion; feeling

disarmed: won over; charmed

manoeuvred: plotted; schemed

ingenuity: cleverness; skillfulness

of that city. Such a superior person had been eagerly welcomed to the Blue Vein Society, and had taken a leading part in its activities. Mr. Ryder had at first been attracted by her charms of person, for she was very good looking and not over twenty-five; then by her refined manners and the **vivacity** of her wit. Her husband had been a government clerk, and at his death had left a considerable life insurance. She was visiting friends in Groveland, and, finding the town and the people to her liking, had prolonged her stay indefinitely. She had not seemed displeased at Mr. Ryder's attentions, but on the contrary had given him every proper encouragement; indeed, a younger and less cautious man would long since have spoken. But he had made up his mind, and had only to determine the time when he would ask her to be his wife. He decided to give a ball in her honor, and at some time during the evening of the ball to offer her his heart and hand. He had no special fears about the outcome, but, with a little touch of romance, he wanted the surroundings to be in harmony with his own feelings when he should have received the answer he expected.

Mr. Ryder resolved that this ball should mark an epoch in the social history of Groveland. He knew, of course,—no one could know better,—the entertainments that had taken place in past years, and what must be done to surpass them. His ball must be worthy of the lady in whose honor it was to be given, and must, by the quality of its guests, set an example for the future. He had observed of late a growing liberality, almost a **laxity**, in social matters, even among members of his own set, and had several times been forced to meet in a social way persons whose complexions and callings in life were hardly up to the standard which he considered proper for the society to maintain. He had a theory of his own.

"I have no race prejudice," he would say, "but we people of mixed blood are ground between the upper and the nether millstone. Our fate lies between absorption by the white race and extinction in the black. The one doesn't want us yet, but may take us in time. The other would welcome us, but it would be for us a backward step. 'With **malice** towards none, with charity for all,' we must do the best we can for ourselves and those who are to follow us. Self-preservation is the first law of nature."

His ball would serve by its exclusiveness to counteract leveling tendencies, and his marriage with Mrs. Dixon would help to further the upward process of absorption he had been wishing and waiting for.

> **vivacity:** liveliness; energy

> **laxity:** looseness; carelessness

> **malice:** hatred; cruelty

Charles Waddell Chesnutt · Unit 2

II

The ball was to take place on Friday night. The house had been put in order, the carpets covered with canvas, the halls and stairs decorated with palms and potted plants; and in the afternoon Mr. Ryder sat on his front porch, which the shade of a vine running up over a wire netting made a cool and pleasant lounging place. He expected to respond to the toast "The Ladies" at the supper, and from a volume of Tennyson—his favorite poet—was fortifying himself with apt quotations. The volume was open at "A Dream of Fair Women." His eyes fell on these lines, and he read them aloud to judge better of their effect:—

> "At length I saw a lady within call,
> Stiller than chisell'd marble, standing there;
> A daughter of the gods, divinely tall,
> And most divinely fair."

He marked the verse, and turning the page read the stanza beginning,—

> "O sweet pale Margaret,
> O rare pale Margaret."

He weighed the passage a moment, and decided that it would not do. Mrs. Dixon was the palest lady he expected at the ball, and she was of a rather ruddy complexion, and of lively disposition and buxom build. So he ran over the leaves until his eye rested on the description of Queen Guinevere:—

> "She seem'd a part of joyous Spring:
> A gown of grass-green silk she wore,
> Buckled with golden clasps before;
> A light-green tuft of plumes she bore
> Closed in a golden ring.
>
> . . . . . .
> "She look'd so lovely, as she sway'd
> The rein with dainty finger-tips,
> A man had given all other bliss,
> And all his worldly worth for this,
> To waste his whole heart in one kiss
> Upon her perfect lips."

As Mr. Ryder murmured these words audibly, with an appreciative thrill, he heard the latch of his gate click, and a light footfall sounding on the steps. He turned his head, and saw a woman standing before his door.

She was a little woman, not five feet tall, and proportioned to her height. Although she stood erect, and looked around her with very bright and restless eyes, she seemed quite old; for her face was crossed and recrossed with a hundred wrinkles, and around the edges of her bonnet could be seen protruding here and there a tuft of short gray wool. She wore a blue calico gown of ancient cut, a little red shawl fastened around her shoulders with an old-fashioned brass brooch, and a large bonnet profusely ornamented with faded red and yellow artificial flowers. And she was very black,—so black that her toothless gums, revealed when she opened her mouth to speak, were not red, but blue. She looked like a bit of the old plantation life, summoned up from the past by the wave of a magician's wand, as the poet's fancy had called into being the gracious shapes of which Mr. Ryder had just been reading.

> *S*he looked like a bit of the old plantation life, summoned up from the past by the wave of a magician's wand . . .

He rose from his chair and came over to where she stood.

"Good-afternoon, madam," he said.

"Good-evenin', suh," she answered, ducking suddenly with a quaint curtsy. Her voice was shrill and piping, but softened somewhat by age. "Is dis yere whar Mistuh Ryduh lib, suh?" she asked, looking around her doubtfully, and glancing into the open windows, through which some of the preparations for the evening were visible.

patronage: support; aid

"Yes," he replied, with an air of kindly **patronage**, unconsciously flattered by her manner, "I am Mr. Ryder. Did you want to see me?"

"Yas, suh, ef I ain't 'sturbin' of you too much."

"Not at all. Have a seat over here behind the vine, where it is cool. What can I do for you?"

" 'Scuse me, suh," she continued, when she had sat down on the edge of a chair, " 'scuse me, suh, I 's lookin' for my husban'. I heerd you wuz a big man an' had libbed heah a long time, an' I 'lowed you would n't min' ef I'd come roun' an' ax you ef you'd ever heerd of a merlatter man by de name er Sam Taylor 'quirin' roun' in de chu'ches ermongs' de people fer his wife 'Liza Jane?"

Mr. Ryder seemed to think for a moment.

"There used to be many such cases right after the war," he said, "but it has been so long that I have forgotten them. There are very few now. But tell me your story, and it may refresh my memory."

She sat back farther in her chair so as to be more comfortable, and folded her withered hands in her lap.

"My name's 'Liza," she began, " 'Liza Jane. W'en I wuz young I us'ter b'long ter Marse Bob Smif, down in ole Missoura. I wuz bawn down dere. W'en I wuz a gal I wuz married ter a man named Jim. But Jim died, an' after dat I married a merlatter man named Sam Taylor. Sam wuz freebawn, but his mammy and daddy died, an' de w'ite folks 'prenticed him ter my marster fer ter work fer 'im 'tel he wuz growed up. Sam worked in de fiel', an' I wuz de cook. One day Ma'y Ann, ole miss's maid, came rushin' out ter de kitchen, an' says she, ' 'Liza Jane, ole marse gwine sell yo' Sam down de ribber.'

" 'Go way f'm yere,' says I; ' my husban' 's free! '

" 'Don' make no diff'ence. I heerd ole marse tell ole miss he wuz gwine take yo' Sam 'way wid 'im ter-morrow, fer he needed money, an' he knowed whar he could git a t'ousan' dollars fer Sam an' no questions axed.'

"W'en Sam come home f'm de fiel' dat night, I tole him 'bout ole marse gwine steal 'im, an' Sam run erway. His time wuz mos up, an' he swo' dat w'en he wuz twenty-one he would come back an' he'p me run erway, er else save up de money ter buy my freedom. An' I know he'd 'a' done it, fer he thought a heap er me, Sam did. But w'en he come back he did n' fin' me, fer I wuz n' dere. Ole marse had heerd dat I warned Sam, so he had me whip' an' sol' down de ribber.

> " *He* swo' dat w'en he wuz twenty-one he would come back an' he'p me run erway, er else save up de money ter buy my freedom."

"Den de wah broke out, an' w'en it wuz ober de cullud folks wuz scattered. I went back ter de ole home; but Sam wuz n' dere, an' I could n' l'arn nuffin' 'bout 'im. But I knowed he 'd be'n dere to look fer me an' had n' foun' me, an' had gone erway ter hunt fer me.

"I's be'n lookin' fer 'im eber sence," she added simply, as though twenty-five years were but a couple of weeks, "an' I knows he 's be'n lookin' fer me. Fer he sot a heap er sto' by me, Sam did, an' I know he 's be'n huntin' fer me all dese years, — 'less'n he 's be'n sick er sump'n, so he could n' work, er out'n his head, so he could n' 'member his promise. I went back down de ribber, fer I 'lowed he 'd gone down dere lookin' fer me. I's be'n ter Noo Orleens, an' Atlanty, an' Charleston, an' Richmon'; an' w'en I 'd be'n all ober de Souf I come ter de Norf. Fer I knows I'll fin' 'im some er dese days," she added softly,

★★

New Orleans Vendor c. 1900

"er he'll fin' me, an' den we'll bofe be as happy in freedom as we wuz in de ole days befo' de wah." A smile stole over her withered countenance as she paused a moment, and her bright eyes softened into a faraway look.

This was the substance of the old woman's story. She had wandered a little here and there. Mr. Ryder was looking at her curiously when she finished.

"How have you lived all these years?" he asked.

"Cookin', suh. I's a good cook. Does you know anybody w'at needs a good cook, suh? I 's stoppin' wid a cullud fam'ly roun' de corner yonder 'tel I kin git a place."

"Do you really expect to find your husband? He may be dead long ago."

She shook her head emphatically. "Oh no, he ain' dead. De signs an' de tokens tells me. I dremp three nights runnin' on'y dis las' week dat I foun' him."

"He may have married another woman. Your slave marriage would not have prevented him, for you never lived with him after the war, and without that your marriage doesn't count."

"Would n' make no diff'ence wid Sam. He would n' marry no yuther 'ooman 'tel he foun' out 'bout me. I knows it," she added. "Sump'n's be'n tellin' me all dese years dat I's gwine fin' Sam 'fo' I dies."

"Perhaps he's outgrown you, and climbed up in the world where he wouldn't care to have you find him."

"No, indeed, suh," she replied, "Sam ain' dat kin' er man. He wuz good ter me, Sam wuz, but he wuz n' much good ter nobody e'se, fer he wuz one er de triflin'es' han's on de plantation. I 'spec's ter haf ter suppo't 'im w'en I fin' 'im, fer he nebber would work 'less'n he had ter. But den he wuz free, an' he did n' git no pay fer his work, an' I don' blame 'im much. Mebbe he's done better sence he run erway, but I ain' 'spectin' much."

"You may have passed him on the street a hundred times during the twenty-five years, and not have known him; time works great changes."

She smiled incredulously. "I 'd know 'im 'mongs' a hund'ed men. Fer dey wuz n' no yuther merlatter man like my man Sam, an' I could n' be mistook. I 's toted his picture roun' wid me twenty-five years."

"May I see it?" asked Mr. Ryder. "It might help me to remember whether I have seen the original."

As she drew a small parcel from her bosom he saw that it was fastened to a string that went around her neck. Removing several wrappers, she brought to light an old fashioned daguerreotype[1] in a black case. He looked long and intently at the portrait. It was faded with time, but the features were still distinct, and it was easy to see what manner of man it had represented.

He closed the case, and with a slow movement handed it back to her.

"I don't know of any man in town who goes by that name," he said, "nor have I heard of any one making such inquiries. But if you will leave me your address, I will give the matter some attention, and if I find out anything I will let you know."

She gave him the number of a house in the neighborhood, and went away, after thanking him warmly.

He wrote the address on the fly-leaf of the volume of Tennyson, and, when she had gone, rose to his feet and stood looking after her curiously. As she walked down the street with mincing step, he saw several persons whom she passed turn and look back at her with a smile of kindly amusement.

When she had turned the corner, he went upstairs to his bedroom, and stood for a long time before the mirror of his dressing-case,[2] gazing thoughtfully at the reflection of his own face.

> The occasion was long memorable among the colored people of the city . . . for the high average of intelligence and culture that distinguished the gathering as a whole.

III

At eight o'clock the ballroom was a blaze of light and the guests had begun to assemble; for there was a literary program and some routine business of the society to be gone through with before the dancing. A black servant in evening dress waited at the door and directed the guests to the dressing-rooms.

The occasion was long memorable among the colored people of the city; not alone for the dress and display, but for the high average of intelligence and culture that distinguished the gathering as a whole. There were a number of school-teachers, several young doctors, three or four lawyers, some professional singers, an editor, a lieutenant in the United States army spending his furlough[3] in the city, and others in

---

1 **daguerreotype:** a photograph made from a 19th-century method

2 **dressing-case:** a dresser or chest of drawers

3 **furlough:** a vacation for someone enlisted in the U.S. military

various polite callings; these were colored, though most of them would not have attracted even a casual glance because of any marked difference from white people. Most of the ladies were in evening costume, and dress coats and dancing pumps were the rule among the men. A band of string music, stationed in an alcove behind a row of palms, played popular airs while the guests were gathering.

The dancing began at half past nine. At eleven o'clock supper was served. Mr. Ryder had left the ballroom some little time before the intermission, but reappeared at the supper-table. The spread was worthy of the occasion, and the guests did full justice to it. When the coffee had been served, the toastmaster,[4] Mr. Solomon Sadler, rapped for order. He made a brief introductory speech, complimenting host and guests, and then presented in their order the toasts of the evening. They were responded to with a very fair display of after-dinner wit.

> "*The* last toast," said the toastmaster . . . "is one which must appeal to us all. There is no one of us of the sterner sex who is not at some time dependent upon woman . . . "

"The last toast," said the toastmaster, when he reached the end of the list, "is one which must appeal to us all. There is no one of us of the sterner sex who is not at some time dependent upon woman,—in infancy for protection, in manhood for companionship, in old age for care and comforting. Our good host has been trying to live alone, but the fair faces I see around me to-night prove that he too is largely dependent upon the gentler sex for most that makes life worth living,—the society and love of friends,—and rumor is at fault if he does not soon yield entire subjection to one of them. Mr. Ryder will now respond to the toast,—The Ladies."

There was a **pensive** look in Mr. Ryder's eyes as he took the floor and adjusted his eyeglasses. He began by speaking of woman as the gift of Heaven to man, and after some general observations on the relations of the sexes he said: "But perhaps the quality which most distinguishes woman is her **fidelity** and devotion to those she loves. History is full of examples, but has recorded none more striking than one which only today came under my notice."

He then related, simply but effectively, the story told by his visitor of the afternoon. He gave it in the same soft dialect, which came readily to his lips, while the company listened attentively and sympathetically. For the story had awakened a responsive thrill in many hearts. There were some present

pensive:
thoughtful

fidelity:
faithfulness;
loyalty

---

4 **toastmaster:** one who introduces speakers at a dinner

who had seen, and others who had heard their fathers and grandfathers tell, the wrongs and sufferings of this past generation, and all of them still felt, in their darker moments, the shadow hanging over them. Mr. Ryder went on:—

"Such devotion and confidence are rare even among women. There are many who would have searched a year, some who would have waited five years, a few who might have hoped ten years; but for twenty-five years this woman has retained her affection for and her faith in a man she has not seen or heard of in all that time.

"She came to me today in the hope that I might be able to help her find this long-lost husband. And when she was gone I gave my fancy rein, and imagined a case I will put to you.

"Suppose that this husband, soon after his escape, had learned that his wife had been sold away, and that such inquiries as he could make brought no information of her whereabouts. Suppose that he was young, and she much older than he; that he was light, and she was black; that their marriage was a slave marriage, and legally binding only if they chose to make it so after the war. Suppose, too, that he made his way to the North as some of us have done, and there, where he had larger opportunities, had improved them, and had in the course of all these years grown to be as different from the ignorant boy who ran away from fear of slavery as the day is from the night. Suppose, even, that he had qualified himself, by industry, by thrift, and by study, to win the friendship and be considered worthy of the society of such people as these I see around me to-night, gracing my board and filling my heart with gladness; for I am old enough to remember the day when such a gathering would not have been possible in this land. Suppose, too, that, as the years went by, this man's memory of the past grew more and more indistinct, until at last it was rarely, except in his dreams, that any image of this bygone period rose before his mind. And then suppose that accident should bring to his knowledge the fact that the wife of his youth, the wife he had left behind him,—not one who had walked by his side and kept pace with him in his upward struggle, but one upon whom advancing years and

> "For twenty-five years this woman has retained her affection for and her faith in a man she has not seen or heard of in all that time."

> "And then suppose that accident should bring to his knowledge the fact that the wife of his youth . . . was alive and seeking him . . . . My friends, what would the man do?"

a laborious life had set their mark,—was alive and seeking him, but that he was absolutely safe from recognition or discovery, unless he chose to reveal himself. My friends, what would the man do? I will presume that he was one who loved honor, and tried to deal justly with all men. I will even carry the case further, and suppose that perhaps he had set his heart upon another, whom he had hoped to call his own. What would he do, or rather what ought he to do, in such a crisis of a lifetime?

"It seemed to me that he might hesitate, and I imagined that I was an old friend, a near friend, and that he had come to me for advice; and I argued the case with him. I tried to discuss it impartially. After we had looked upon the matter from every point of view, I said to him, in words that we all know:—

HARRIET SCOTT, 1857

'This above all: to thine own self be true,
And it must follow, as the night the day,
Thou canst not then be false to any man.' [5]

Then, finally, I put the question to him, 'Shall you acknowledge her?'

"And now, ladies and gentlemen, friends and companions, I ask you, what should he have done?"

There was something in Mr. Ryder's voice that stirred the hearts of those who sat around him. It suggested more than mere sympathy with an imaginary situation; it seemed rather in the nature of a personal appeal. It was observed, too, that his look rested more especially upon Mrs. Dixon, with a mingled expression of **renunciation** and inquiry.

renunciation: a formal separation from someone

---

5 **"This above all . . . any man.":** a famous quotation from Shakespeare's play, *Hamlet*

She had listened, with parted lips and streaming eyes. She was the first to speak: "He should have acknowledged her."

"Yes," they all echoed, "he should have acknowledged her."

"My friends and companions," responded Mr. Ryder, "I thank you, one and all. It is the answer I expected, for I knew your hearts."

He turned and walked toward the closed door of an adjoining room, while every eye followed him in wondering curiosity. He came back in a moment, leading by the hand his visitor of the afternoon, who stood startled and trembling at the sudden plunge into this scene of brilliant gayety. She was neatly dressed in gray, and wore the white cap of an elderly woman.

"Ladies and gentlemen," he said, "this is the woman, and I am the man, whose story I have told you. Permit me to introduce to you the wife of my youth."

Read and Think Critically

Describe, Analyze, Explain

 1. **CHARACTERIZATION** Describe the **characterization** of Mr. Ryder. Why do you think he is so concerned with skin color?

2. In what ways does Mr. Ryder consider Mrs. Dixon a desirable mate?

3. This story is filled with **irony**: the discrepancy between what people appear to be and what they truly are. Analyze the author's use of irony in the story.

4. Does Mr. Ryder recall his past when 'Liza Jane first comes calling? Explain what his reaction implies.

5. Explain the impact of the author's choice to have Mr. Ryder's wife speak in Southern black **dialect**. Does this help or hinder your appreciation of the story?

6. Throughout the story Chesnutt includes **allusions** to great works of literature, including the Bible and works by Tennyson and Shakespeare. Choose an allusion from the story, explain its meaning, and describe how the beauty of the language impacts the reader.

7. **THE AUTHOR'S STYLE** In this story Chesnutt uses **juxtaposition**, the placing of two or more things side by side to heighten their similarities and differences. What does Chesnutt juxtapose, and what does he accomplish through this juxtaposition?

Before You Read

Stephen Crane 1871–1900

About the Author

Stephen Crane's life rivaled any work of fiction. Born in Newark, New Jersey, he was the youngest of 14 children of a minister who wrote pious attacks on drinking, novels, and baseball. When Crane's father died, Stephen experimented with every activity his father had condemned. At Syracuse University, he excelled at sports, especially baseball.

Crane eventually abandoned college to try his hand at journalism. His style—short on facts but long on sensory details—attracted a prominent writer who urged Crane to experience real life and write fiction. Crane took the advice and, after spending time in urban slums, wrote the novel *Maggie: A Girl of the Streets*. When its sordid subject matter proved unpopular, Crane sought a more marketable subject. His next novel, *A Red Badge of Courage* (1895), caused a sensation with its powerfully spare style and realistic portrayal of the Civil War.

Success brought Crane steady work as a feature writer and war correspondent. While traveling on assignment, Crane spent many agonizing hours in a lifeboat after his ship capsized. This experience inspired him to write "The Open Boat," a story that conveys the then-bold idea that people have little control, if any, over the forces of an uncaring, natural world. A few years later, Crane was dead from tuberculosis. In his mere 28 years he had managed to rock the literary world with his realistic subject matter and innovative style.

****

The Author's Style

Crane sought to create a "direct impression of life" in his fiction, much like an impressionist painter creates a unified image with a multitude of small strokes of paint. He achieved this in *The Red Badge of Courage* with disjointed sentences and disconnected images that work together to evoke the chaotic reality of a battle.

Crane explored inner truths with spare, poetic language. His prose brims with powerful, sensory images that often represent broad concepts and ideas. In "The Bride Comes to Yellow Sky," Crane parodies the prevailing perception of the Wild West largely through irony. As in much of his fiction, the characters perceive themselves as having a power and importance they actually lack.

The Bride Comes to Yellow Sky

S T E P H E N   C R A N E

LITERARY LENS: COLOR IMAGERY Crane has been called an Impressionist writer because his technique is comparable to that of the 19th-century Impressionist painters. Using bold brushstrokes to capture natural light and colors, these artists were able to evoke a scene's mood. In this story, notice Crane's frequent use of **color imagery**.

I

*T*he great Pullman[1] was whirling onward with such dignity of motion that a glance from the window seemed simply to prove that the plains of Texas were pouring eastward. Vast flats of green grass, dull-hued spaces of mesquite and cactus, little groups of frame houses, woods of light and tender trees, all were sweeping into the east, sweeping over the horizon, a precipice.

A newly married pair had boarded this coach at San Antonio. The man's face was reddened from many days in the wind and sun, and a direct result of his new black clothes was that his brick-colored hands were constantly performing in a most conscious fashion. From time to time he looked down respectfully at his attire. He sat with a hand on each knee, like a man waiting in a barber's shop. The glances he devoted to other passengers were furtive and shy.

The bride was not pretty, nor was she very young. She wore a

---

[1] **Pullman:** a railroad car with sleeping quarters

dress of blue cashmere, with small reservations[2] of velvet here and there and with steel buttons abounding. She continually twisted her head to regard her puff sleeves, very stiff, straight, and high. They embarrassed her. It was quite apparent that she had cooked, and that she expected to cook, dutifully. The blushes caused by the careless scrutiny of some passengers as she had entered the car were strange to see upon this plain, under-class countenance, which was drawn in placid, almost emotionless lines.

They were evidently very happy. "Ever been in a parlor-car before?" he asked, smiling with delight.

"No," she answered, "I never was. It's fine, ain't it?"

"Great! And then after a while we'll go forward to the diner and get a big layout. Finest meal in the world. Charge a dollar."

"Oh, do they?" cried the bride. "Charge a dollar? Why, that's too much—for us—ain't it, Jack?"

"Not this trip, anyhow," he answered bravely. "We're going to go the whole thing."

Later, he explained to her about the trains. "You see, it's a thousand miles from one end of Texas to the other, and this train runs right across it and never stops but four times." He had the pride of an owner. He pointed out to her the dazzling fittings of the coach, and in truth her eyes opened wider as she contemplated the sea-green figured velvet, the shining brass, silver, and glass, the wood that gleamed as darkly brilliant as the surface of a pool of oil. At one end a bronze figure sturdily held a support for a separated chamber, and at convenient places on the ceiling were frescoes in olive and silver.

To the minds of the pair, their surroundings reflected the glory of their marriage that morning in San Antonio. This was the environment of their new estate, and the man's face in particular beamed with an elation that made him appear ridiculous to the negro porter. This individual at times surveyed them from afar with an amused and superior grin. On other occasions he bullied them with skill in ways that did not make it exactly plain to them that they were being bullied. He subtly used all the manners of the most unconquerable kind of snobbery. He oppressed them, but of this oppression they had small knowledge, and they speedily forgot that infrequently a number of travelers covered them with stares of derisive enjoyment. Historically there was supposed to be something infinitely humorous in their situation.

---

2 reservations: patches

"We are due in Yellow Sky at 3:42," he said, looking tenderly into her eyes.

"Oh, are we?" she said, as if she had not been aware of it. To **evince** surprise at her husband's statement was part of her wifely **amiability**. She took from a pocket a little silver watch, and as she held it before her and stared at it with a frown of attention, the new husband's face shone.

"I bought it in San Anton' from a friend of mine," he told her gleefully.

"It's seventeen minutes past twelve," she said, looking up at him with a kind of shy and clumsy coquetry. A passenger, noting this play, grew excessively **sardonic**, and winked at himself in one of the numerous mirrors.

At last they went to the dining-car. Two rows of negro waiters, in glowing white suits, surveyed their entrance with the interest and also the **equanimity** of men who had been forewarned. The pair fell to the lot of a waiter who happened to feel pleasure in steering them through their meal. He viewed them with the manner of a fatherly pilot, his countenance radiant with benevolence. The patronage, entwined with the ordinary deference, was not plain to them. And yet, as they returned to their coach, they showed in their faces a sense of escape.

To the left, miles down a long purple slope, was a little ribbon of mist where moved the keening[3] Rio Grande. The train was approaching it at an angle, and the apex was Yellow Sky. Presently it was apparent that, as the distance from Yellow Sky grew shorter, the husband became **commensurately** restless. His brick-red hands were more insistent in their prominence. Occasionally he was even rather absent-minded and far-away when the bride leaned forward and addressed him.

As a matter of truth, Jack Potter was beginning to find the shadow of a deed weigh upon him like a leaden slab. He, the town marshal of Yellow Sky, a man known, liked, and feared in his corner, a prominent person, had gone to San Antonio to meet a girl he believed he loved, and there, after the usual prayers, had actually induced her to marry him, without consulting Yellow Sky for any part of the transaction. He was now bringing his bride before an innocent and unsuspecting community.

Of course, people in Yellow Sky married as it pleased them, in accordance with a general custom; but such was Potter's thought of his duty to his friends, or of their idea of his duty, or of an unspoken form which does not control

"*We* are due in Yellow Sky at 3:42," he said, looking tenderly into her eyes.

evince: demonstrate; show

amiability: friendliness

sardonic: mocking; derisive

equanimity: poise; composure

commensurately: in equal measure; correspondingly

---

3 **keening:** wailing, lamenting

★★★

heinous:
scandalous

men in these matters, that he felt he was **heinous**. He had committed an extraordinary crime. Face to face with this girl in San Antonio, and spurred by his sharp impulse, he had gone headlong over all the social hedges. At San Antonio he was like a man hidden in the dark. A knife to sever any friendly duty, any form, was easy to his hand in that remote city. But the hour of Yellow Sky, the hour of daylight, was approaching.

He knew full well that his marriage was an important thing to his town. It could only be exceeded by the burning of the new hotel. His friends could not forgive him. Frequently he had reflected on the advisability of telling them by telegraph, but a new cowardice had been upon him. He feared to do it. And now the train was hurrying him toward a scene of amazement, glee, and reproach. He glanced out of the window at the line of haze swinging slowly in towards the train.

If the citizens could dream of his prospective arrival with his bride, they would parade the band at the station and escort them, amid cheers and laughing congratulations, to his adobe home.

Yellow Sky had a kind of brass band, which played painfully, to the delight of the populace. He laughed without heart as he thought of it. If the citizens could dream of his prospective arrival with his bride, they would parade the band at the station and escort them, amid cheers and laughing congratulations, to his adobe home.

He resolved that he would use all the devices of speed and plains-craft in making the journey from the station to his house. Once within that safe citadel he could issue some sort of a vocal bulletin, and then not go among the citizens until they had time to wear off a little of their enthusiasm.

The bride looked anxiously at him. "What's worrying you, Jack?"

He laughed again. "I'm not worrying, girl. I'm only thinking of Yellow Sky."

She flushed in comprehension.

A sense of mutual guilt invaded their minds and developed a finer tenderness. They looked at each other with eyes softly aglow. But Potter often laughed the same nervous laugh. The flush upon the bride's face seemed quite permanent.

The traitor to the feelings of Yellow Sky narrowly watched the speeding landscape. "We're nearly there," he said.

Presently the porter came and announced the proximity of Potter's home. He held a brush in his hand and, with all his airy superiority gone, he brushed Potter's new clothes as the latter slowly turned this way and that way. Potter fumbled out a coin and gave it to the porter, as he had seen others do. It was a heavy and muscle-bound business, as that of a man shoeing his first horse.

The porter took their bag, and as the train began to slow they moved forward to the hooded platform of the car. Presently the two engines and their long string of coaches rushed into the station of Yellow Sky.

"They have to take water here," said Potter, from a constricted throat and in mournful cadence, as one announcing death. Before the train stopped, his eye had swept the length of the platform, and he was glad and astonished to see there was none upon it but the station-agent, who, with a slightly hurried and anxious air, was walking toward the water-tanks. When the train had halted, the porter alighted first and placed in position a little temporary step.

"Come on, girl," said Potter hoarsely. As he helped her down they each laughed on a false note. He took the bag from the negro, and bade his wife cling to his arm. As they slunk rapidly away, his hang-dog glance perceived that they were unloading the two trunks, and also that the station-agent far ahead near the baggage-car had turned and was running toward him, making gestures. He laughed, and groaned as he laughed, when he noted the first effect of his marital bliss upon Yellow Sky. He gripped his wife's arm firmly to his side, and they fled. Behind them the porter stood chuckling **fatuously**.

fatuously: foolishly

II

The California Express on the Southern Railway was due at Yellow Sky in twenty-one minutes. There were six men at the bar of the "Weary Gentleman" saloon. One was a drummer[4] who talked a great deal and rapidly; three were Texans who did not care to talk at that time; and two were Mexican sheep-herders who did not talk as a general practice in the "Weary Gentleman" saloon. The barkeeper's dog lay on the board walk that crossed in front of the door. His head was on his paws, and he glanced drowsily here and there with the constant vigilance of a dog that is kicked on occasion. Across the sandy street were some vivid green grass plots, so wonderful in appearance amid the sands that burned near them in a blazing sun that they caused a doubt in the mind. They exactly resembled the grass mats used to represent lawns on the stage. At the cooler end of the railway station a man without a coat sat in a tilted chair and smoked his pipe. The fresh-cut bank of the Rio Grande circled

---

4 **drummer:** a traveling salesman

THE HORSESHOE SALOON, C. 1900

near the town, and there could be seen beyond it a great, plum-colored plain of mesquite.[5]

Save for the busy drummer and his companions in the saloon, Yellow Sky was dozing. The new-comer leaned gracefully upon the bar, and recited many tales with the confidence of a bard[6] who has come upon a new field.

" —and at the moment that the old man fell down stairs with the bureau in his arms, the old woman was coming up with two scuttles of coal, and, of course— "

The drummer's tale was interrupted by a young man who suddenly appeared in the open door. He cried: "Scratchy Wilson's drunk, and has turned loose with both hands." The two Mexicans at once set down their glasses and faded out of the rear entrance of the saloon.

jocular: merry; jovial

The drummer, innocent and **jocular**, answered: "All right, old man. S'pose he has. Come in and have a drink, anyhow."

But the information had made such an obvious cleft in every skull in the room that the drummer was obliged to see its importance. All had become instantly solemn. "Say," said he, mystified, "what is this?" His three

---

5 mesquite: a shrub found in the southwestern United States

6 bard: poet; storyteller

companions made the introductory gesture of eloquent speech, but the young man at the door forestalled them.

"It means, my friend," he answered, as he came into the saloon, "that for the next two hours this town won't be a health resort."

The barkeeper went to the door and locked and barred it. Reaching out of the window, he pulled in heavy wooden shutters and barred them. Immediately a solemn, chapel-like gloom was upon the place. The drummer was looking from one to another.

"But, say," he cried, "what is this, anyhow? You don't mean there is going to be a gun-fight?"

"Don't know whether there'll be a fight or not," answered one man grimly. "But there'll be some shootin'—some good shootin'."

The young man who had warned them waved his hand. "Oh, there'll be a fight fast enough if anyone wants it. Anybody can get a fight out there in the street. There's a fight just waiting."

The drummer seemed to be swayed between the interest of a foreigner and a perception of personal danger.

"What did you say his name was?" he asked.

"Scratchy Wilson," they answered in chorus.

"And will he kill anybody? What are you going to do? Does this happen often? Does he rampage around like this once a week or so? Can he break in that door?"

"No, he can't break down that door," replied the barkeeper. "He's tried it three times. But when he comes you'd better lay down on the floor, stranger. He's dead sure to shoot at it, and a bullet may come through."

Thereafter the drummer kept a strict eye upon the door. The time had not yet been called for him to hug the floor, but, as a minor precaution, he sidled near to the wall. "Will he kill anybody?" he said again.

The men laughed low and scornfully at the question.

"He's out to shoot, and he's out for trouble. Don't see any good in experimentin' with him."

"But what do you do in a case like this? What do you do?"

A man responded: "Why, he and Jack Potter— "

"But," in chorus, the other men interrupted, "Jack Potter's in San Anton'."

"Well, who is he? What's he got to do with it?"

"Oh, he's the town marshal. He goes out and fights Scratchy when he gets on one of these tears."

"Wow," said the drummer, mopping his brow. "Nice job he's got."

The voices had toned away to mere whisperings. The drummer wished to ask further questions which were born of an increasing anxiety and bewilderment; but when he attempted them, the men merely looked at him in irritation and motioned him to remain silent. A tense waiting hush was upon them. In the deep shadows of the room their eyes shone as they listened for sounds from the street. One man made three gestures at the barkeeper, and the latter, moving like a ghost, handed him a glass and a bottle. The man poured a full glass of whisky, and set down the bottle noiselessly. He gulped the whisky in a swallow, and turned again toward the door in immovable silence. The drummer saw that the barkeeper, without a sound, had taken a Winchester[7] from beneath the bar. Later he saw this individual beckoning to him, so he tiptoed across the room.

"You better come with me back of the bar."

"No, thanks," said the drummer, perspiring. "I'd rather be where I can make a break for the back door."

peremptory:
authoritative;
decisive

Whereupon the man of bottles made a kindly but **peremptory** gesture. The drummer obeyed it, and finding himself seated on a box with his head below the level of the bar, balm was laid upon his soul at sight of various zinc and copper fittings that bore a resemblance to armor-plate. The barkeeper took a seat comfortably upon an adjacent box.

> *"He's about the last one of the old gang that used to hang out along the river here. He's a terror when he's drunk."*

"You see," he whispered, "this here Scratchy Wilson is a wonder with a gun—a perfect wonder—and when he goes on the war trail, we hunt our holes—naturally. He's about the last one of the old gang that used to hang out along the river here. He's a terror when he's drunk. When he's sober he's all right—kind of simple— wouldn't hurt a fly—nicest fellow in town. But when he's drunk—whoo!"

There were periods of stillness. "I wish Jack Potter was back from San Anton'," said the barkeeper. "He shot Wilson up once—in the leg—and he would sail in and pull out the kinks in this thing."

Presently they heard from a distance the sound of a shot, followed by three wild yowls. It instantly removed a bond from the men in the darkened saloon. There was a shuffling of feet. They looked at each other. "Here he comes," they said.

---

7 **Winchester:** a rifle

★★★

III

A man in a maroon-colored flannel shirt, which had been purchased for purposes of decoration and made, principally, by some Jewish women on the east side of New York, rounded a corner and walked into the middle of the main street of Yellow Sky. In either hand the man held a long, heavy, blue-black revolver. Often he yelled, and these cries rang through a semblance of a deserted village, shrilly flying over the roofs in a volume that seemed to have no relation to the ordinary vocal strength of a man. It was as if the surrounding stillness formed the arch of a tomb over him. These cries of ferocious challenge rang against walls of silence. And his boots had red tops with gilded imprints, of the kind beloved in winter by little sledding boys on the hillsides of New England.

The man's face flamed in a rage begot of whisky. His eyes, rolling and yet keen for ambush, hunted the still doorways and windows. He walked with the creeping movement of the midnight cat. As it occurred to him, he roared menacing information. The long revolvers in his hands were as easy as straws; they were moved with an electric swiftness. The little fingers of each hand played sometimes in a musician's way. Plain from the low collar of the shirt, the cords of his neck straightened and sank, straightened and sank, as passion moved him. The only sounds were his terrible invitations. The calm adobes preserved their demeanor at the passing of this small thing in the middle of the street.

There was no offer of fight; no offer of fight. The man called to the sky. There were no attractions. He bellowed and fumed and swayed his revolvers here and everywhere.

The dog of the barkeeper of the "Weary Gentleman" saloon had not appreciated the advance of events. He yet lay dozing in front of his master's door. At sight of the dog, the man paused and raised his revolver humorously. At sight of the man, the dog sprang up and walked diagonally away, with a sullen head, and growling. The man yelled, and the dog broke into a gallop. As it was about to enter an alley, there was a loud noise, a whistling, and something spat the ground directly before it. The dog screamed, and, wheeling in terror, galloped headlong in a new direction. Again there was a noise, a whistling, and sand was kicked viciously before it. Fear-stricken, the dog turned and flurried like an animal in a pen. The man stood laughing, his weapons at his hips.

New American Voices   The Bride Comes to Yellow Sky   **203**

Ultimately the man was attracted by the closed door of the "Weary Gentleman" saloon. He went to it, and hammering with a revolver, demanded drink.

The door remaining imperturbable, he picked a bit of paper from the walk and nailed it to the framework with a knife. He then turned his back contemptuously upon this popular resort, and walking to the opposite side of the street, and spinning there on his heel quickly and lithely, fired at the bit of paper. He missed it by a half inch. He swore at himself, and went away. Later, he comfortably fusilladed[8] the windows of his most intimate friend. The man was playing with this town. It was a toy for him.

But still there was no offer of fight. The name of Jack Potter, his ancient antagonist, entered his mind, and he concluded that it would be a glad thing if he should go to Potter's house and by bombardment induce him to come out and fight. He moved in the direction of his desire, chanting Apache scalp-music.

When he arrived at it, Potter's house presented the same still front as had the other adobes. Taking up a strategic position, the man howled a challenge. But this house regarded him as might a great stone god. It gave no sign. After a decent wait, the man howled further challenges, mingling with them wonderful epithets.

Presently there came the spectacle of a man churning himself into deepest rage over the immobility of a house. He fumed at it as the winter wind attacks a prairie cabin in the North. To the distance there should have gone the sound of a tumult like the fighting of two hundred Mexicans. As necessity bade him, he paused for breath or to reload his revolvers.

IV

Potter and his bride walked sheepishly[9] and with speed. Sometimes they laughed together shamefacedly and low.

"Next corner, dear," he said finally.

They put forth the efforts of a pair walking bowed against a strong wind. Potter was about to raise a finger to point the first appearance of the new home when, as they circled the corner, they came face to face with a man in a maroon-colored shirt who was feverishly pushing cartridges into a large revolver. Upon the instant the man dropped his revolver to the ground, and,

---

8 **fusilladed:** bombarded; showered with bullets

9 **sheepishly:** with embarrassment

★★★

like lightning, whipped another from its holster. The second weapon was aimed at the bridegroom's chest.

There was silence. Potter's mouth seemed to be merely a grave for his tongue. He exhibited an instinct to at once loosen his arm from the woman's grip, and he dropped the bag to the sand. As for the bride, her face had gone as yellow as old cloth. She was a slave to hideous rites gazing at the apparitional[10] snake.

The two men faced each other at a distance of three paces. He of the revolver smiled with a new and quiet ferocity.

"Tried to sneak up on me," he said. "Tried to sneak up on me!" His eyes grew more **baleful**. As Potter made a slight movement, the man thrust his revolver venomously forward. "No, don't you do it, Jack Potter. Don't you move a finger toward a gun just yet. Don't you move an eyelash. The time has come for me to settle with you, and I'm goin' to do it my own way and loaf along with no interferin'. So if you don't want a gun bent on you, just mind what I tell you."

Potter looked at his enemy. "I ain't got a gun on me, Scratchy," he said. "Honest, I ain't." He was stiffening and steadying, but yet somewhere at the back of his mind a vision of the Pullman floated, the sea-green figured velvet, the shining brass, silver, and glass, the wood that gleamed as darkly brilliant as the surface of a pool of oil—all the glory of the marriage, the environment of the new estate. "You know I fight when it comes to fighting, Scratchy Wilson, but I ain't got a gun on me. You'll have to do all the shootin' yourself."

His enemy's face went livid. He stepped forward and lashed his weapon to

baleful: ominous; evil

Western Gunfighter

10 **apparitional:** unexpected; suddenly visible

The Bride Comes to Yellow Sky

and fro before Potter's chest. "Don't you tell me you ain't got no gun on you, you whelp. Don't tell me no lie like that. There ain't a man in Texas ever seen you without no gun. Don't take me for no kid." His eyes blazed with light, and his throat worked like a pump.

"I ain't takin' you for no kid," answered Potter. His heels had not moved an inch backward. "I'm takin' you for a———fool. I tell you I ain't got a gun, and I ain't. If you're goin' to shoot me up, you better begin now. You'll never get a chance like this again."

So much enforced reasoning had told on Wilson's rage. He was calmer. "If you ain't got a gun, why ain't you got a gun?" he sneered. "Been to Sunday-school?"

"I ain't got a gun because I've just come from San Anton' with my wife. I'm married," said Potter. "And if I'd thought there was going to be any galoots[11] like you prowling around when I brought my wife home, I'd had a gun, and don't you forget it."

"Married!" said Scratchy, not at all comprehending.

"Yes, married. I'm married," said Potter distinctly.

"Married?" said Scratchy. Seemingly for the first time he saw the drooping, drowning woman at the other man's side. "No!" he said. He was like a creature allowed a glimpse of another world. He moved a pace backward, and his arm with the revolver dropped to his side. "Is this the lady?" he asked.

"Yes, this is the lady," answered Potter.

There was another period of silence.

"Well," said Wilson at last, slowly, "I s'pose it's all off now."

"It's all off if you say so, Scratchy. You know I didn't make the trouble." Potter lifted his valise.

"Well, I 'low it's off, Jack," said Wilson. He was looking at the ground. "Married!" He was not a student of chivalry;[12] it was merely that in the presence of this foreign condition he was a simple child of the earlier plains. He picked up his starboard revolver, and placing both weapons in their holsters, he went away. His feet made funnel-shaped tracks in the heavy sand.

---

11 **galoots:** fellows

12 **chivalry:** courtesy toward one's enemies; gallantry

Read and Think Critically

Describe, Characterize, Analyze

 1. **COLOR IMAGERY** Find a passage in the story containing **color imagery** that is particularly engaging or beautiful. Describe what Crane is able to suggest with the image.

2. Explain why Jack feels that he has betrayed Yellow Sky.

3. The **narrator** says of the newlyweds, "Historically there was supposed to be something infinitely humorous in their situation." What significance does this statement have universally and for the story?

4. How are Jack Potter, his bride, and Scratchy Wilson **characterized**? Use details from the text to fill out a chart similar to the one below. Then use one or two adjectives to summarize each character.

Name	Details	Adjectives
Jack Potter		
Potter's Bride		
Scratchy Wilson		

5. Describe the Weary Gentleman Saloon. Does its depiction of the Old West seem **realistic** or **romantic**?

6. In your opinion, what is the main **theme** of the story?

7. **THE AUTHOR'S STYLE** Crane occasionally adds details to a description that seem out of place. Consider the following detail from the first description of Scratchy Wilson on page 203. Analyze the effect of this detail on the meaning of the story.

"... his boots had red tops with gilded imprints, of the kind beloved in winter by little sledding boys on the hillsides of New England."

Before You Read

Willa Cather 1873–1947

About the Author

Willa Cather found human stories among Nebraska homesteaders, stifled artists, and missionaries in far-flung parts of North America. Virginia-born, Cather grew up in Red Cloud, Nebraska, where her parents settled among European immigrants and homesteaders. Despite the small size of Red Cloud, Cather studied classical music and read classic literature. After graduation from the University of Nebraska, she went east to pursue her interest in an artistic life. There she edited and managed various newspapers and magazines, taught high school, and began to write and publish stories and poems. By 1912 she was focusing only on writing and published her first novel, *Alexander's Bridge*, a story of cosmopolitan life.

After befriending and reading the regional fiction of Sarah Orne Jewett, Cather gained a new appreciation for the Midwest prairie of her youth. Her novels *O Pioneers!* (1913) and *My Antonia* (1918) evoke the beauty of the region and the pioneer spirit of its settlers.

Cather's fiction eventually came to seem like an argument with the 20th century. Her distaste for the growing mass culture and materialism matched the feelings of other writers. The fiction that resulted from this "argument," however, was highly acclaimed. In addition to the Pulitzer Prize for her World War I novel, *One of Ours* (1922), Cather also became the first woman to receive an honorary doctorate from Princeton University.

✦✦✦✦✦✦✦✦✦✦✦

✐ The Author's Style

Early in her career, Cather wrote judgmentally about the prairie towns of her youth. These stories feature artistic souls in conflict with the narrow-minded and conformist attitudes found in small towns. "Paul's Case," the story you are about to read, explores this conflict.

As she became a regionalist writer, Cather strove to create stories like those of fellow writer Sarah Orne Jewett, stories Cather described as "living things" which "melt into the land and the life of the land until they are not stories at all, but life itself." Cather's classic Midwest fiction features characters of strong body, spirit, vitality, and courage struggling to

create meaningful lives on various frontiers. In these lands of promise, the characters develop a deep relationship with their place and often with the earth itself.

In all her writing, Cather devoted herself to the most significant moments in her characters' lives. A realist, she did not embellish or exaggerate; rather, she used the power of suggestion to convey her characters' feelings, moods, and wishes. In "Paul's Case," for example, Cather subtly suggests Paul's inner turmoil by describing images of his surroundings from his perspective. Yet the story's narrator also offers objective analysis of the troubled young man.

Paul's Case

A Study in Temperament

WILLA CATHER

🔍 **LITERARY LENS: ALLUSIONS** An **allusion** is a reference to an artistic, literary, or historical figure, happening, or event. Notice all of the allusions in this story and consider how they may be meaningful.

*I*t was Paul's afternoon to appear before the faculty of the Pittsburgh High School to account for his various misdemeanors. He had been suspended a week ago, and his father had called at the Principal's office and confessed his **perplexity** about his son. Paul entered the faculty room suave and smiling. His clothes were a trifle outgrown, and the tan velvet on the collar of his open overcoat was frayed and worn; but for all that there was something of the **dandy** about him, and he wore an opal pin in his neatly knotted black four-in-hand,[1] and a red carnation in his buttonhole. This latter adornment the faculty somehow felt was not properly significant of the **contrite** spirit befitting a boy under the ban of suspension.

Paul was tall for his age and very thin, with high, cramped shoulders and a narrow chest. His eyes were remarkable for a certain hysterical brilliancy, and he continually used them in a conscious,

perplexity: bewilderment; puzzlement

dandy: a man who gives exaggerated attention to his appearance

contrite: apologetic; remorseful

---

1 **four-in-hand:** a necktie

theatrical sort of way, peculiarly offensive in a boy. The pupils were abnormally large, as though he were addicted to belladonna,[2] but there was a glassy glitter about them which that drug does not produce.

When questioned by the Principal as to why he was there Paul stated, politely enough, that he wanted to come back to school. This was a lie, but Paul was quite accustomed to lying; found it, indeed, indispensable for overcoming friction. His teachers were asked to state their respective charges against him, which they did with such a **rancor** and **aggrievedness** as **evinced** that this was not a usual case. Disorder and impertinence were among the offenses named, yet each of his instructors felt that it was scarcely possible to put into words the real cause of the trouble, which lay in a sort of hysterically defiant manner of the boy's; in the contempt which they all knew he felt for them, and which he seemingly made not the least effort to conceal. Once, when he had been making a synopsis of a paragraph at the blackboard, his English teacher had stepped to his side and attempted to guide his hand. Paul had started back with a shudder and thrust his hands violently behind him. The astonished woman could scarcely have been more hurt and embarrassed had he struck at her. The Insult was so involuntary and definitely personal as to be unforgettable. In one way and another he had made all his teachers, men and women alike, conscious of the same feeling of physical aversion. In one class he **habitually** sat with his hand shading his eyes; in another he always looked out of the window during the recitation; in another he made a running commentary on the lecture, with humorous intention.

His teachers felt this afternoon that his whole attitude was symbolized by his shrug and his **flippantly** red carnation flower, and they fell upon him without mercy, his English teacher leading the pack. He stood through it smiling, his pale lips parted over his white teeth. (His lips were continually twitching, and he had a habit of raising his eyebrows that was contemptuous and irritating to the last degree.) Older boys than Paul had broken down and shed tears under that baptism of fire,[3] but his set smile did not once desert him, and his only sign of discomfort was the nervous trembling of the fingers that toyed with the buttons of his overcoat, and an occasional jerking of the other hand that held his hat. Paul was always smiling, always glancing about

rancor: resentment; ill will
aggrievedness: distress
evinced: demonstrated; revealed

habitually: regularly; frequently

flippantly: lacking respect or seriousness

---

2 **belladonna:** a drug used as a stimulant

3 **baptism of fire:** an initial experience that is severe and difficult, e.g., a soldier experiencing the first gunfire

him, seeming to feel that people might be watching him and trying to detect something. This conscious expression, since it was as far as possible from boyish mirthfulness,[4] was usually attributed to insolence or "smartness."

As the inquisition proceeded one of his instructors repeated an impertinent remark of the boy's, and the Principal asked him whether he thought that a courteous speech to have made a woman. Paul shrugged his shoulders slightly and his eyebrows twitched.

"I don't know," he replied. "I didn't mean to be polite or impolite, either. I guess it's a sort of way I have of saying things regardless."

The Principal, who was a sympathetic man, asked him whether he didn't think that a way it would be well to get rid of. Paul grinned and said he guessed so. When he was told that he could go he bowed gracefully and went out. His bow was but a repetition of the scandalous red carnation.

His teachers were in despair, and his drawing master voiced the feeling of them all when he declared there was something about the boy which none of them understood. He added: "I don't really believe that smile of his comes altogether from insolence; there's something sort of haunted about it. The boy is not strong, for one thing. I happen to know that he was born in Colorado, only a few months before his mother died out there of a long illness. There is something wrong about the fellow."

The drawing master had come to realize that, in looking at Paul, one saw only his white teeth and the forced animation of his eyes. One warm afternoon the boy had gone to sleep at his drawing board, and his master had noted with amazement what a white, blue-veined face it was; drawn and wrinkled like an old man's about the eyes, the lips twitching even in his sleep, and stiff with a nervous tension that drew them back from his teeth.

His teachers left the building dissatisfied and unhappy; humiliated to have felt so **vindictive** toward a mere boy, to have uttered this feeling in cutting terms, and to have set each other on, as it were, in the gruesome game of **intemperate reproach**. Some of them remembered having seen a miserable street cat set at bay by a ring of tormentors.

vindictive: mean; hurtful

intemperate: hotheaded; unrestrained
reproach: blame; scolding

As for Paul, he ran down the hill whistling the "Soldiers' Chorus" from *Faust*,[5] looking wildly behind him now and then to see whether some of his teachers were not there to writhe under his lightheartedness. As it was now late in the afternoon and Paul was on duty that evening as usher at Carnegie

---

4 **mirthfulness:** joy

5 **"Soldiers' Chorus" from *Faust*:** a showpiece song in the famous opera by Gounod

Hall, he decided that he would not go home to supper. When he reached the concert hall the doors were not yet open and, as it was chilly outside, he decided to go up into the picture gallery—always deserted at this hour—where there were some of Raffelli's gay studies of Paris streets and an airy blue Venetian scene or two that always **exhilarated** him. He was delighted to find no one in the gallery but the old guard, who sat in one corner, a newspaper on his knee, a black patch over one eye and the other closed. Paul possessed himself of the peace and walked confidently up and down, whistling under his breath. After a while he sat down before a blue Rico and lost himself. When he bethought him to look at his watch, it was after seven o'clock, and he rose with a start and ran downstairs, making a face at Augustus Caesar, peering out from the cast room, and an evil gesture at the Venus de Milo[6] as he passed her on the stairway.

exhilarated: energized; excited

When Paul reached the ushers' dressing room half a dozen boys were there already, and he began excitedly to tumble into his uniform. It was one of the few that at all approached fitting, and Paul thought it very becoming—though he knew that the tight, straight coat accentuated his narrow chest, about which he was exceedingly sensitive. He was always considerably excited while he dressed, twanging all over to the tuning of the strings and the preliminary flourishes of the horns in the music room; but tonight he seemed quite beside himself, and he teased and plagued the boys until, telling him that he was crazy, they put him down on the floor and sat on him.

Somewhat calmed by his suppression, Paul dashed out to the front of the house to seat the early comers. He was a model usher; gracious and smiling he ran up and down the aisles; nothing was too much trouble for him; he carried messages and brought programs as though it were his greatest pleasure in life, and all the people in his section thought him a charming boy, feeling that he remembered and admired them. As the house filled, he grew more and more vivacious and animated, and the color came to his cheeks and lips. It was very much as though this were a great reception and Paul were the host. Just as the musicians came out to take their places, his English teacher arrived with checks for the seats which a prominent manufacturer had taken for the season. She betrayed some embarrassment when she handed Paul the tickets, and a *hauteur*[7] which subsequently made her feel very foolish. Paul was startled for a moment, and had the feeling of wanting to put her out; what business had she here among all these fine people and gay colors? He

---

6 **Raffelli . . . Rico . . . Augustus Caesar . . . Venus de Milo:** artists and classic sculptural representations

7 *hauteur:* French for "haughtiness of manner"

THE ORCHESTRA
OF THE OPERA,
EDGAR DE GAS,
C. 1870

looked her over and decided that she was not appropriately dressed and must be a fool to sit downstairs in such togs. The tickets had probably been sent her out of kindness, he reflected as he put down a seat for her, and she had about as much right to sit there as he had.

When the symphony began Paul sank into one of the rear seats with a long sigh of relief, and lost himself as he had done before the Rico. It was not that symphonies, as such, meant anything in particular to Paul, but the first sigh of the instruments seemed to free some hilarious and potent spirit within him; something that struggled there like the genie in the bottle found by the Arab fisherman.[8] He felt a sudden zest of life; the lights danced before his eyes and the concert hall blazed into unimaginable splendor. When the soprano soloist came on Paul forgot even the nastiness of his teacher's being there and gave himself up to the peculiar stimulus such personages always

---

8 **genie . . . fisherman:** a reference to an Arabian folktale in which a bottle containing a wish-granting genie is found by a fisherman

had for him. The soloist chanced to be a German woman, by no means in her first youth, and the mother of many children; but she wore an elaborate gown and a tiara, and above all she had that indefinable air of achievement, that worldshine upon her, which, in Paul's eyes, made her a veritable queen of Romance.

After a concert was over Paul was always irritable and wretched until he got to sleep, and tonight he was even more than usually restless. He had the feeling of not being able to let down, of its being impossible to give up this delicious excitement which was the only thing that could be called living at all. During the last number he withdrew and, after hastily changing his clothes in the dressing room, slipped out to the side door where the soprano's carriage stood. Here he began pacing rapidly up and down the walk, waiting to see her come out.

Over yonder, the Schenley, in its vacant stretch, loomed big and square through the fine rain, the windows of its twelve stories glowing like those of a lighted cardboard house under a Christmas tree. All the actors and singers of the better class stayed there when they were in the city, and a number of the big manufacturers of the place lived there in the winter. Paul had often hung about the hotel, watching the people go in and out, longing to enter and leave schoolmasters and dull care behind him forever.

At last the singer came out, accompanied by the conductor, who helped her into her carriage and closed the door with a cordial *auf wiedersehen*[9] which set Paul to wondering whether she were not an old sweetheart of his. Paul followed the carriage over to the hotel, walking so rapidly as not to be far from the entrance when the singer alighted, and disappeared behind the swinging glass doors that were opened by a Negro in a tall hat and a long coat. In the moment that the door was ajar it seemed to Paul that he, too, entered. He seemed to feel himself go after her up the steps, into the warm, lighted building, into an exotic, tropical world of shiny, glistening surfaces and basking ease. He reflected upon the mysterious dishes that were brought into the dining room, the green bottles in buckets of ice, as he had seen them in the supper party pictures of the *Sunday World* supplement. A quick gust of wind brought the rain down with sudden vehemence, and Paul was startled to find that he was still outside in the slush of the gravel

> *P*aul had often hung about the hotel, watching the people go in and out.

---

9 auf wiedersehen: German farewell meaning "till we meet again"

driveway; that his boots were letting in the water and his scanty overcoat was clinging wet about him; that the lights in front of the concert hall were out and that the rain was driving in sheets between him and the orange glow of the windows above him. There it was, what he wanted—tangibly before him, like the fairy world of a Christmas pantomime—but mocking spirits stood guard at the doors, and, as the rain beat in his face, Paul wondered whether he were destined always to shiver in the black night outside, looking up at it.

He turned and walked reluctantly toward the car[10] tracks. The end had to come sometime; his father in his nightclothes at the top of the stairs, explanations that did not explain, hastily improvised fictions that were forever tripping him up, his upstairs room and its horrible yellow wallpaper, the creaking bureau with the greasy plush collarbox, and over his painted wooden bed the pictures of George Washington and John Calvin,[11] and the framed motto, "Feed my Lambs," which had been worked in red worsted by his mother.

Half an hour later Paul alighted from his car and went slowly down one of the side streets off the main thoroughfare. It was a highly respectable street, where all the houses were exactly alike, and where businessmen of moderate means begot and reared large families of children, all of whom went to Sabbath school and learned the shorter catechism,[12] and were interested in arithmetic; all of whom were as exactly alike as their homes, and of a piece with the monotony in which they lived. Paul never went up Cordelia Street without a shudder of loathing. His home was next to the house of the Cumberland minister. He approached it tonight with the nerveless sense of defeat, the hopeless feeling of sinking back forever into ugliness and commonness that he had always had when he came home. The moment he turned into Cordelia Street he felt the waters close above his head. After each of these orgies of living he experienced all the physical depression which follows a debauch;[13] the loathing of respectable beds, of common food, of a house penetrated by kitchen odors; a shuddering repulsion for the flavorless, colorless mass of everyday existence; a morbid desire for cool things and soft lights and fresh flowers.

---

10 **car:** streetcar

11 **John Calvin:** 16th-century French Protestant reformer and theologian. His work informs the Protestant ethic, which preaches hard work and piety and downplays pleasure and frivolity.

12 **catechism:** oral instruction in religion based on questions and answers

13 **debauch:** an orgy

The nearer he approached the house, the more absolutely unequal Paul felt to the sight of it all: his ugly sleeping chamber; the cold bathroom with the grimy zinc tub, the cracked mirror, the dripping spiggots; his father, at the top of the stairs, his hairy legs sticking out from his nightshirt, his feet thrust into carpet slippers. He was so much later than usual that there would certainly be inquiries and reproaches. Paul stopped short before the door. He felt that he could not be **accosted** by his father tonight; that he could not toss again on that miserable bed. He would not go in. He would tell his father that he had no carfare and it was raining so hard he had gone home with one of the boys and stayed all night.

accosted:
confronted;
stopped

Meanwhile, he was wet and cold. He went around to the back of the house and tried one of the basement windows, found it open, raised it cautiously, and scrambled down the cellar wall to the floor. There he stood, holding his breath, terrified by the noise he had made, but the floor above him was silent, and there was no creak on the stairs. He found a soapbox, and carried it over to the soft ring of light that streamed from the furnace door, and sat down. He was horribly afraid of rats, so he did not try to sleep, but sat looking distrustfully at the dark, still terrified lest he might have awakened his father. In such reactions, after one of the experiences which made days and nights out of the dreary blanks of the calendar, when his senses were deadened, Paul's head was always singularly clear. Suppose his father had heard him getting in at the window and had come down and shot him for a burglar? Then, again, suppose his father had come down, pistol in hand, and he had cried out in time to save himself, and his father had been horrified to think how nearly he had killed him? Then, again, suppose a day should come when his father would remember that night, and wish there had been no warning cry to stay his hand? With this last supposition Paul entertained himself until daybreak.

The following Sunday was fine; the sodden November chill was broken by the last flash of autumnal summer. In the morning Paul had to go to church and Sabbath school, as always. On seasonable Sunday afternoons the burghers[14] of Cordelia Street always sat out on their front stoops[15] and talked to their neighbors on the next stoop, or called to those across the street in neighborly fashion. The men usually sat on gay cushions placed upon the steps that led down to the sidewalk, while the women, in their Sunday

---

14 **burghers:** middle-class citizens

15 **stoops:** front steps; porches

"waists,"[16] sat in rockers on the cramped porches, pretending to be greatly at their ease. The children played in the streets; there were so many of them that the place resembled the recreation grounds of a kindergarten. The men on the steps—all in their shirt sleeves, their vests unbuttoned—sat with their legs well apart, their stomachs comfortably protruding, and talked of the prices of things, or told anecdotes of the sagacity of their various chiefs and overlords. They occasionally looked over the multitude of squabbling children, listened affectionately to their high-pitched, nasal voices, smiling to see their own **proclivities** reproduced in their offspring, and interspersed their legends of the iron kings with remarks about their sons' progress at school, their grades in arithmetic, and the amounts they had saved in their toy banks.

proclivities: habits; tendencies

On this last Sunday of November Paul sat all the afternoon on the lowest step of his stoop, staring into the street, while his sisters, in their rockers, were talking to the minister's daughters next door about how many shirtwaists they had made in the last week, and how many waffles someone had eaten at the last church supper. When the weather was warm, and his father was in a particularly jovial frame of mind, the girls made lemonade, which was always brought out in a red-glass pitcher, ornamented with forget-me-nots in blue enamel. This the girls thought very fine, and the neighbors always joked about the suspicious color of the pitcher.

Today Paul's father sat on the top step, talking to a young man who shifted a restless baby from knee to knee. He happened to be the young man who was daily held up to Paul as a model, and after whom it was his father's dearest hope that he would pattern. This young man was of a ruddy complexion, with a compressed, red mouth, and faded, nearsighted eyes, over which he wore thick spectacles, with gold bows that curved about his ears. He was clerk to one of the **magnates** of a great steel corporation, and was looked upon in Cordelia Street as a young man with a future. There was a story that, some five years ago—he was now barely twenty-six—he had been a trifle dissipated, but in order to curb his appetites and save the loss of time and strength that a sowing of wild oats might have entailed, he had taken his chief's advice, oft **reiterated** to his employees, and at twenty-one had married the first woman whom he could persuade to share his fortunes. She happened to be an angular schoolmistress, much older than he, who also wore thick glasses, and who had now borne him four children, all nearsighted, like herself.

magnates: powerful businessmen

reiterated: repeated; said again

The young man was relating how his chief, now cruising in the

---

16 **"waists":** blouses

Mediterranean, kept in touch with all the details of the business, arranging his office hours on his yacht just as though he were at home, and "knocking off work enough to keep two stenographers busy." His father told, in turn, the plan his corporation was considering, of putting in an electric railway plant in Cairo. Paul snapped his teeth; he had an awful apprehension that they might spoil it all before he got there. Yet he rather liked to hear these legends of the iron kings that were told and retold on Sundays and holidays; these stories of palaces in Venice, yachts on the Mediterranean, and high play at Monte Carlo[17] appealed to his fancy, and he was interested in the triumphs of these cash boys who had become famous, though he had no mind for the cash-boy stage.

After supper was over and he had helped to dry the dishes, Paul nervously asked his father whether he could go to George's to get some help in his geometry, and still more nervously asked for carfare. This latter request he had to repeat, as his father, on principle, did not like to hear requests for money, whether much or little. He asked Paul whether he could not go to some boy who lived nearer, and told him that he ought not to leave his schoolwork until Sunday; but he gave him the dime. He was not a poor man, but he had a worthy ambition to come up in the world. His only reason for allowing Paul to usher was that he thought a boy ought to be earning a little.

Paul bounded upstairs, scrubbed the greasy odor of the dishwater from his hands with the ill-smelling soap he hated, and then shook over his fingers a few drops of violet water from the bottle he kept hidden in his drawer. He left the house with his geometry conspicuously under his arm, and the moment he got out of Cordelia Street and boarded a downtown car, he shook off the **lethargy** of two deadening days and began to live again.

lethargy: stupor; sluggishness

The leading juvenile[18] of the permanent stock company which played at one of the downtown theaters was an acquaintance of Paul's, and the boy had been invited to drop in at the Sunday-night rehearsals whenever he could. For more than a year Paul had spent every available moment loitering about Charley Edwards's dressing room. He had won a place among Edwards's following not only because the young actor, who could not afford to employ a dresser, often found him useful, but because he recognized in Paul something akin to what churchmen term "vocation."

---

17 **high play at Monte Carlo:** heavy gambling in a famous European casino

18 **juvenile:** a young male actor

It was at the theater and at Carnegie Hall that Paul really lived; the rest was but a sleep and a forgetting. This was Paul's fairy tale, and it had for him all the allurement of a secret love. The moment he inhaled the gassy, painty, dusty odor behind the scenes, he breathed like a prisoner set free, and felt within him the possibility of doing or saying splendid, brilliant, poetic things. The moment the cracked orchestra beat out the overture from *Martha*, or jerked at the serenade from *Rigoletto*,[19] all stupid and ugly things slid from him, and his senses were deliciously, yet delicately fired.

Perhaps it was because, in Paul's world, the natural nearly always wore the guise of ugliness, that a certain element of artificiality seemed to him necessary in beauty. Perhaps it was because his experience of life elsewhere was so full of Sabbath-school picnics, petty economies, wholesome advice as to how to succeed in life, and the inescapable odors of cooking, that he found this existence so alluring, these smartly clad men and women so attractive, that he was so moved by these starry apple orchards that bloomed perennially under the limelight.

It would be difficult to put it strongly enough how convincingly the stage entrance of that theater was for Paul the actual portal of Romance. Certainly none of the company ever suspected it, least of all Charley Edwards. It was very like the old stories that used to float about London of fabulously rich Jews, who had subterranean halls there, with palms, and fountains, and soft lamps and richly appareled women who never saw the disenchanting light of London day. So, in the midst of that smoke-palled city, enamored of figures and grimy toil, Paul had his secret temple, his wishing carpet, his bit of blue-and- white Mediterranean shore bathed in perpetual sunshine.

Several of Paul's teachers had a theory that his imagination had been perverted by garish fiction, but the truth was that he scarcely ever read at all. The books at home were not such as would either tempt or corrupt a youthful mind, and as for reading the novels that some of his friends urged upon him—well, he got what he wanted much more quickly from music; any sort of music, from an orchestra to a barrel organ. He needed only the spark, the indescribable thrill that made his imagination master of his senses, and he could make plots and pictures enough of his own. It was equally true that he was not stagestruck—not, at any rate, in the usual acceptation[20] of that expression. He had no desire to become an actor, any more than he had to become a musician. He felt no necessity to do any of these things; what he

---

19 ***Martha . . . Rigoletto:*** well-known operas

20 **acceptation:** acceptance

STUDENT,
AMEDEO MODIGLIANI,
1917

wanted was to see, to be in the atmosphere, float on the wave of it, to be carried out, blue league after blue league, away from everything.

After a night behind the scenes Paul found the schoolroom more than ever repulsive; the bare floors and naked walls; the prosy men who never wore frock coats, or violets in their buttonholes; the women with their dull gowns, shrill voices, and pitiful seriousness about prepositions that govern the dative.[21] He could not bear to have the other pupils think, for a moment, that he took these people seriously; he must convey to them that he considered it all trivial, and was there only by way of a jest, anyway. He had autographed pictures of all the members of the stock company which he showed his classmates, telling them the most incredible stories of his familiarity with these people, of his acquaintance with the soloists who

---

21 **dative:** a grammatical term referring to the indirect object of a verb

came to Carnegie Hall, his suppers with them and the flowers he sent them. When these stories lost their effect, and his audience grew listless, he became desperate and would bid all the boys good-by, announcing that he was going to travel for a while; going to Naples, to Venice, to Egypt. Then, next Monday, he would slip back, conscious and nervously smiling; his sister was ill, and he should have to defer his voyage until spring.

Matters went steadily worse with Paul at school. In the itch to let his instructors know how heartily he despised them and their homilies,[22] and how thoroughly he was appreciated elsewhere, he mentioned once or twice that he had no time to fool with theorems; adding—with a twitch of the eyebrows and a touch of that nervous bravado which so perplexed them— that he was helping the people down at the stock company; they were old friends of his.

The upshot of the matter was that the Principal went to Paul's father, and Paul was taken out of school and put to work. The manager at Carnegie Hall was told to get another usher in his stead; the doorkeeper at the theater was warned not to admit him to the house; and Charley Edwards remorsefully promised the boy's father not to see him again.

The members of the stock company were vastly amused when some of Paul's stories reached them—especially the women. They were hardworking women, most of them supporting indigent husbands or brothers, and they laughed rather bitterly at having stirred the boy to such fervid and **florid** inventions. They agreed with the faculty and with his father that Paul's was a bad case.

florid: elaborate; ornate

𝒯he eastbound train was plowing through a January snowstorm; the dull dawn was beginning to show gray when the engine whistled a mile out of Newark. Paul started up from the seat where he had lain curled in uneasy slumber, rubbed the breath-misted window glass with his hand, and peered out. The snow was whirling in curling eddies above the white bottom lands, and the drifts lay already deep in the fields and along the fences, while here and there the long dead grass and dried weed stalks protruded black above it. Lights shone from the scattered houses, and a gang of laborers who stood beside the track waved their lanterns.

Paul had slept very little, and he felt grimy and uncomfortable. He had made the all-night journey in a day coach, partly because he was ashamed, dressed as he was, to go into a Pullman, and partly because he was afraid of

22 **homilies:** sermons or moralizing

being seen there by some Pittsburgh businessman, who might have noticed him in Denny & Carson's office. When the whistle awoke him, he clutched quickly at his breast pocket, glancing about him with an uncertain smile. But the little, clay-bespattered Italians were still sleeping, the slatternly women across the aisle were in open-mouthed **oblivion**, and even the crumby, crying babies were for the nonce[23] stilled. Paul settled back to struggle with his impatience as best he could.

oblivion:
unconsciousness;
mental
withdrawal

When he arrived at the Jersey City station he hurried through his breakfast, manifestly ill at ease and keeping a sharp eye about him. After he reached the Twenty-third Street station, he consulted a cabman and had himself driven to a men's-furnishings establishment that was just opening for the day. He spent upward of two hours there, buying with endless reconsidering and great care. His new street suit he put on in the fitting room; the frock coat and dress clothes he had bundled into the cab with his linen. Then he drove to a hatter's and a shoe house. His next errand was at Tiffany's, where he selected his silver and a new scarf pin. He would not wait to have his silver marked, he said. Lastly, he stopped at a trunk shop on Broadway and had his purchases packed into various traveling bags.

THE WALDORF-ASTORIA HOTEL IN NEW YORK CITY AS IT
APPEARED IN 1903

It was a little after one o'clock when he drove up to the Waldorf, and after settling with the cabman, went into the office. He registered from Washington; said his mother and father had been abroad, and that he had come down to await the arrival of their steamer. He told his story plausibly and had no trouble, since he volunteered to pay for

---

23 **nonce:** for the time being

them in advance, in engaging his rooms; a sleeping room, sitting room, and bath.

Not once, but a hundred times, Paul had planned this entry into New York. He had gone over every detail of it with Charley Edwards, and in his scrapbook at home there were pages of description about New York hotels, cut from the Sunday papers. When he was shown to his sitting room on the eighth floor he saw at a glance that everything was as it should be; there was but one detail in his mental picture that the place did not realize, so he rang for the bellboy and sent him down for flowers. He moved about nervously until the boy returned, putting away his new linen and fingering it delightedly as he did so. When the flowers came he put them hastily into water, and then tumbled into a hot bath. Presently he came out of his white bathroom, resplendent in his new silk underwear, and playing with the tassels of his red robe. The snow was whirling so fiercely outside his windows that he could scarcely see across the street, but within the air was deliciously soft and fragrant. He put the violets and jonquils on the taboret[24] beside the couch, and threw himself down, with a long sigh, covering himself with a Roman blanket. He was thoroughly tired; he had been in such haste, he had stood up to such a strain, covered so much ground in the last twenty-four hours, that he wanted to think how it had all come about. Lulled by the sound of the wind, the warm air, and the cool fragrance of the flowers, he sank into deep, drowsy retrospection.

It had been wonderfully simple; when they had shut him out of the theater and concert hall, when they had taken away his bone, the whole thing was virtually determined. The rest was a mere matter of opportunity. The only thing that at all surprised him was his own courage—for he realized well enough that he had always been tormented by fear, a sort of apprehensive dread that, of late years, as the meshes of the lies he had told closed about him, had been pulling the muscles of his body tighter and tighter. Until now he could not remember the time when he had not been dreading something. Even when he was a little boy it was always there—behind him, or before, or on either side. There had always been the shadowed corner, the dark place into which he dared not look, but from which something seemed always to be watching him—and Paul had done things that were not pretty to watch, he knew.

But now he had a curious sense of relief, as though he had at last thrown

---

24 **taboret:** a small cabinet or stand

down the gauntlet[25] to the thing in the corner.

Yet it was but a day since he had been sulking in the traces;[26] but yesterday afternoon that he had been sent to the bank with Denny & Carson's deposit, as usual—but this time he was instructed to leave the book to be balanced. There was above two thousand dollars in checks, and nearly a thousand in the bank notes which he had taken from the book and quietly transferred to his pocket. At the bank he had made out a new deposit slip. His nerves had been steady enough to permit of his returning to the office, where he had finished his work and asked for a full day's holiday tomorrow, Saturday, giving a perfectly reasonable pretext. The bankbook, he knew, would not be returned before Monday or Tuesday, and his father would be out of town for the next week. From the time he slipped the bank notes into his pocket until he boarded the night train for New York, he had not known a moment's hesitation. It was not the first time Paul had steered through treacherous waters. How astonishingly easy it had all been; here he was, the thing done; and this time there would be no awakening, no figure at the top of the stairs. He watched the snowflakes whirling by his window until he fell asleep.

When he awoke, it was three o'clock in the afternoon. He bounded up with a start; half of one of his precious days gone already! He spent more than an hour in dressing, watching every stage of his toilet carefully in the mirror. Everything was quite perfect; he was exactly the kind of boy he had always wanted to be.

When he went downstairs Paul took a carriage and drove up Fifth Avenue toward the Park. The snow had somewhat abated; carriages and tradesmen's wagons were hurrying soundlessly to and fro in the winter twilight; boys in woolen mufflers were shoveling off the doorsteps; the avenue stages made fine spots of color against the white street. Here and there on the corners were stands, with whole flower gardens blooming under glass cases, against the sides of which the snowflakes stuck and melted; violets, roses, carnations, lilies of the valley—somehow vastly more lovely and alluring that they blossomed thus unnaturally in the snow. The Park itself was a wonderful stage winterpiece.

When he returned, the pause of the twilight had ceased and the tune of the streets had changed. The snow was falling faster, lights streamed from the hotels that reared their dozen stories fearlessly up into the storm, defying the raging Atlantic winds. A long, black stream of carriages poured down the

---

25 **thrown down the gauntlet:** challenged

26 **traces:** harness

avenue, intersected here and there by other streams, tending horizontally. There were a score of cabs about the entrance of his hotel, and his driver had to wait. Boys in livery were running in and out of the awning stretched across the sidewalk, up and down the red velvet carpet laid from the door to the street. Above, about, within it all was the rumble and roar, the hurry and toss of thousands of human beings as hot for pleasure as himself, and on every side of him towered the glaring affirmation of the **omnipotence** of wealth.

omnipotence: unlimited power

The boy set his teeth and drew his shoulders together in a spasm of realization; the plot of all dramas, the text of all romances, the nerve-stuff of all sensations was whirling about him like the snowflakes. He burnt like a faggot[27] in a tempest.

When Paul went down to dinner the music of the orchestra came floating up the elevator shaft to greet him. His head whirled as he stepped into the thronged corridor, and he sank back into one of the chairs against the wall to get his breath. The lights, the chatter, the perfumes, the bewildering medley of color—he had, for a moment, the feeling of not being able to stand it. But only for a moment; these were his own people, he told himself. He went slowly about the corridors, through the writing rooms, smoking rooms, reception rooms, as though he were exploring the chambers of an enchanted palace, built and peopled for him alone.

> *T*his was what all the world was fighting for, he reflected; this was what all the struggle was about.

When he reached the dining room he sat down at a table near a window. The flowers, the white linen, the many-colored wineglasses, the gay toilettes of the women, the low popping of corks, the undulating repetitions of the *Blue Danube*[28] from the orchestra, all flooded Paul's dream with bewildering radiance. When the roseate tinge of his champagne was added—that cold, precious, bubbling stuff that creamed and foamed in his glass—Paul wondered that there were honest men in the world at all. This was what all the world was fighting for, he reflected; this was what all the struggle was about. He doubted the reality of his past. Had he ever known a place called Cordelia Street, a place where fagged-looking businessmen got on the early car; mere rivets in a machine they seemed to Paul,—sickening men, with combings of children's hair always hanging to their coats, and the smell of cooking in their clothes. Cordelia Street—Ah, that

---

27 **faggot:** a bundle of sticks

28 ***Blue Danube:*** a waltz composed by Johann Strauss (1825–1899)

belonged to another time and country; had he not always been thus, had he not sat here night after night, from as far back as he could remember, looking pensively over just such shimmering textures and slowly twirling the stem of a glass like this one between his thumb and middle finger? He rather thought he had.

He was not in the least abashed or lonely. He had no especial desire to meet or to know any of these people; all he demanded was the right to look on and conjecture, to watch the pageant. The mere stage properties were all he contended for. Nor was he lonely later in the evening, in his lodge at the Metropolitan.[29] He was now entirely rid of his nervous misgivings, of his forced aggressiveness, of the imperative desire to show himself different from his surroundings. He felt now that his surroundings explained him. Nobody questioned the purple;[30] he had only to wear it passively. He had only to glance down at his attire to reassure himself that here it would be impossible for anyone to humiliate him.

PAUL WAYLAND BARTLETT,
CHARLES PEARCE, 1890

---

29 **lodge at the Metropolitan:** a box at the Metropolitan Opera House in New York City

30 **purple:** a color historically reserved for royalty

He found it hard to leave his beautiful sitting room to go to bed that night, and sat long watching the raging storm from his turret window. When he went to sleep it was with the lights turned on in his bedroom; partly because of his old timidity, and partly so that, if he should wake in the night, there would be no wretched moment of doubt, no horrible suspicion of yellow wallpaper, or of Washington and Calvin above his bed.

Sunday morning the city was practically snowbound. Paul breakfasted late, and in the afternoon he fell in with a wild San Francisco boy, a freshman at Yale, who said he had run down for a "little flyer" over Sunday. The young man offered to show Paul the night side of the town, and the two boys went out together after dinner, not returning to the hotel until seven o'clock the next morning. They had started out in the confiding warmth of a champagne friendship, but their parting in the elevator was singularly cool. The freshman pulled himself together to make his train, and Paul went to bed. He awoke at two o'clock in the afternoon, very thirsty and dizzy, and rang for icewater, coffee, and the Pittsburgh papers.

On the part of the hotel management, Paul excited no suspicion. There was this to be said for him, that he wore his spoils with dignity and in no way made himself conspicuous. Even under the glow of his wine he was never boisterous, though he found the stuff like a magician's wand for wonder-building. His chief greediness lay in his ears and eyes, and his excesses were not offensive ones. His dearest pleasures were the gray winter twilights in his sitting room; his quiet enjoyment of his flowers, his clothes, his wide divan, his cigarette, and his sense of power. He could not remember a time when he had felt so at peace with himself. The mere release from the necessity of petty lying, lying every day and every day, restored his self-respect. He had never lied for pleasure, even at school; but to be noticed and admired, to assert his difference from other Cordelia Street boys; and he felt a good deal more manly, more honest, even, now that he had no need for boastful pretensions, now that he could, as his actor friends used to say, "dress the part." It was characteristic that remorse did not occur to him. His golden days went by without a shadow, and he made each as perfect as he could.

On the eighth day after his arrival in New York he found the whole affair exploited in the Pittsburgh papers, exploited with a wealth of detail which indicated that local news of a sensational nature was at a low ebb. The firm of Denny & Carson announced that the boy's father had refunded the full amount of the theft and that they had no intention of prosecuting. The Cumberland minister had been interviewed, and expressed his hope of yet reclaiming the motherless lad, and his Sabbath-school teacher declared that she would spare no effort to that end. The rumor had reached Pittsburgh that the boy had been seen in a New York hotel, and his father had gone East to find him and bring him home.

Paul had just come in to dress for dinner; he sank into a chair, weak to the knees, and clasped his head in his hands. It was to be worse than jail, even; the tepid waters of Cordelia Street were to close over him finally and forever. The gray monotony stretched before him in hopeless, unrelieved years; Sabbath school, Young People's Meeting, the yellow-papered room, the damp dishtowels; it all rushed back upon him with a sickening vividness. He had the old feeling that the orchestra had suddenly stopped, the sinking sensation that the play was over. The sweat broke out on his face, and he sprang to his feet, looked about him with his white, conscious smile, and winked at himself in the mirror. With something of the old childish belief in miracles with which he had so often gone to class, all his lessons unlearned, Paul dressed and dashed whistling down the corridor to the elevator.

He had no sooner entered the dining room and caught the measure of the music than his remembrance was lightened by his old elastic power of claiming the moment, mounting with it, and finding it all-sufficient. The glare and glitter about him, the mere scenic accessories had again, and for the last time, their old potency. He would show himself that he was game, he would finish the thing splendidly. He doubted, more than ever, the existence of Cordelia Street, and for the first time he drank his wine recklessly. Was he not, after all, one of those fortunate beings born to the purple, was he not still himself and in his own place? He drummed a nervous accompaniment to the Pagliacci music and looked about him, telling himself over and over that it had paid.

He reflected drowsily, to the swell of the music and the chill sweetness of his wine, that he might have done it more wisely. He might have caught an outbound steamer and been well out of their clutches before now. But the other side of the world had seemed too far away and too uncertain then; he could not have waited for it; his need had been too sharp. If he had to choose over again, he would do the same thing tomorrow. He looked affectionately about the dining room, now gilded with a soft mist. Ah, it had paid indeed!

Paul was awakened next morning by a painful throbbing in his head and feet. He had thrown himself across the bed without undressing, and had slept with his shoes on. His limbs and hands were lead heavy, and his tongue and throat were parched and burnt. There came upon him one of those fateful attacks of clearheadedness that never occurred except when he was physically exhausted and his nerves hung loose. He lay still, closed his eyes, and let the tide of things wash over him.

His father was in New York; "stopping at some joint or other," he told himself. The memory of successive summers on the front stoop fell upon him like a weight of black water. He had not a hundred dollars left; and he knew now, more than ever, that money was everything, the wall that stood between all he loathed and all he wanted. The thing was winding itself up; he had thought of that on his first glorious day in New York, and had even provided a way to snap the thread. It lay on his dressing table now; he had got it out last night when he came blindly up from dinner, but the shiny metal hurt his eyes, and he disliked the looks of it.

> *P*aul took one of the blossoms carefully from his coat and scooped a little hole in the snow, where he covered it up.

He rose and moved about with a painful effort, succumbing now and again to attacks of nausea. It was the old depression exaggerated; all the world had become Cordelia Street. Yet somehow he was not afraid of anything, was absolutely calm; perhaps because he had looked into the dark corner at last and knew. It was bad enough, what he saw there, but somehow not so bad as his long fear of it had been. He saw everything clearly now. He had a feeling that he had made the best of it, that he had lived the sort of life he was meant to live, and for half an hour he sat staring at the revolver. But he told himself that was not the way, so he went downstairs and took a cab to the ferry.

When Paul arrived in Newark he got off the train and took another cab, directing the driver to follow the Pennsylvania tracks out of the town. The snow lay heavy on the roadways and had drifted deep in the open fields. Only here and there the dead grass or dried weed stalks projected, singularly black, above it. Once well into the country, Paul dismissed the carriage and walked, floundering along the tracks, his mind a medley of irrelevant things. He seemed to hold in his brain an actual picture of everything he had seen that morning. He remembered every feature of both his drivers, of the toothless old woman from whom he had bought the red flowers in his coat, the agent from whom he had got his ticket, and all of his fellow passengers on the ferry. His mind, unable to cope with vital matters near at hand, worked feverishly and deftly at sorting and grouping these images. They made for him a part of the ugliness of the world, of the ache in his head, and the bitter burning on his tongue. He stooped and put a handful of snow into his mouth as he walked, but that, too, seemed hot. When he reached a little hillside, where the tracks ran through a cut some twenty feet below him, he stopped and sat down.

The carnations in his coat were drooping with the cold, he noticed, their red glory all over. It occurred to him that all the flowers he had seen in the glass cases that first night must have gone the same way, long before this. It was only one splendid breath they had, in spite of their brave mockery at the winter outside the glass; and it was a losing game in the end, it seemed, this revolt against the homilies by which the world is run. Paul took one of the blossoms carefully from his coat and scooped a little hole in the snow, where he covered it up. Then he dozed awhile, from his weak condition, seemingly insensible to the cold.

The sound of an approaching train awoke him, and he started to his feet, remembering only his resolution, and afraid lest he should be too late. He stood watching the approaching locomotive, his teeth chattering, his lips drawn away from them in a frightened smile; once or twice he glanced nervously sidewise, as though he were being watched. When the right moment came, he jumped. As he fell, the folly of his haste occurred to him with merciless clearness, the vastness of what he had left undone. There flashed through his brain, clearer than ever before, the blue of Adriatic water, the yellow of Algerian sands.

He felt something strike his chest, and that his body was being thrown swiftly through the air, on and on, immeasurably far and fast, while his limbs were gently relaxed. Then, because the picture-making mechanism was crushed, the disturbing visions flashed into black, and Paul dropped back into the immense design of things.

Read and Think Critically

Explain, Analyze, Summarize

 1. **ALLUSIONS** List two or three **allusions** in the story and explain their possible significance.

2. Paul's teachers "fell upon him without mercy, his English teacher leading the pack" (page 210). Why do they have this reaction to him, and how do they feel afterward?

3. Consider the contrasts in this story listed below. Analyze how Cather uses the contrast in **settings** to develop the **plot**.

Paul's school	the concert hall
Paul's room at home	his room at the hotel
Pittsburgh	New York City

4. Analyze the **character** of Paul, looking at what seems to **motivate** his behavior, how he presents himself, how he regards and treats people he knows, and how he feels about himself. Support your opinion with details from the text.

 5. **THE AUTHOR'S STYLE** A *case study* is a focused and in-depth examination of a single group or community, usually over a period of time. For example, a researcher doing a case study of the study habits of teenage boys might follow five boys through the four years of high school, noting the development (or lack thereof) of their study habits. Consider the **title** and subtitle of this short story: "Paul's Case: A Study in Temperament." In what ways does the style of writing reflect a research report, and in what ways does it differ? Write two summaries of the story: one as an objective case study, and the other as a subjective account of the events narrated by Paul.

★★★

Before You Read

O. Henry (pseudonym for William Sydney Porter) 1862–1910

About the Author

During his lifetime, O. Henry was America's most popular writer, known all over the world for his humorous stories with twist endings.

The facts of O. Henry's life were as melodramatic as his fiction. After his mother died when he was three, he was raised by a grandmother in North Carolina. As a young man, he traveled to Texas and worked as a licensed pharmacist, sheep rancher, publisher of a humor periodical, and—after getting married—bank teller.

When bank audits revealed a large sum of money missing, Porter was indicted for embezzlement. To avoid trial, he fled to New Orleans and hopped on a steamer to Honduras. When he learned that his wife was dying, he left Central America to return to her side in the States. He was promptly tried, found guilty, and sentenced to three years in the Ohio State Penitentiary.

"The Ransom of Red Chief" is one of O. Henry's funniest stories and is still a favorite of anthologies, as is "The Gift of the Magi"—a Christmas standard. "A Retrieved Reformation" has inspired plays and several films. O. Henry can be criticized for being sentimental, but his engaging characters and situations are entirely to the liking of most readers.

★★★★★★★★★★★

The Author's Style

O. Henry was a great champion of the commonplace. Many of his stories grew from his observance of ordinary New Yorkers in such ordinary places as restaurants, subways, and park benches. Once caught in O. Henry's imagination, these commonplace "subjects" pursued fictional romance and adventure in the author's economical, ironic tales. O. Henry also drew on his experience in other regions to spin tales set in the South, West, and Central America. Critics often note his adept use of local color descriptions and dialects to portray the distinct characteristics of these regions.

O. Henry is also known for his "warm" characterizations. He avoided commenting on moral or political issues in his fiction, preferring humor, satire, romance, and burlesque.

O. Henry strongly believed in determinism, the conviction that everything is the result of a predetermined cause and that humans have no real free will. One critic notes that, consistent with this belief, O. Henry's characters are often "mere pawns in a large, indifferent world." His hallmark ironic, surprise endings, besides being highly entertaining, also reflect this belief.

A Retrieved Reformation

O. Henry

LITERARY LENS: ANTIHERO An **antihero** is a protagonist who displays traits opposite to the qualities associated with a traditional hero. In the story, note the qualities that make Jimmy Valentine unlike a classic, "true-blue" American hero.

A guard came to the prison shoe-shop, where Jimmy Valentine was assiduously stitching uppers, and escorted him to the front office. There the warden handed Jimmy his pardon, which had been signed that morning by the governor. Jimmy took it in a tired kind of way. He had served nearly ten months of a four-year sentence. He had expected to stay only about three months, at the longest. When a man with as many friends on the outside as Jimmy Valentine had is received in the "stir" it is hardly worth while to cut his hair.

"Now, Valentine," said the warden, "you'll go out in the morning. Brace up, and make a man of yourself. You're not a bad fellow at heart. Stop cracking safes, and live straight. "

"Me?" said Jimmy, in surprise. "Why, I never cracked a safe in my life."

"Oh, no," laughed the warden. "Of course not. Let's see, now.

How was it you happened to get sent up on that Springfield job? Was it because you wouldn't prove an alibi for fear of compromising somebody in extremely high-toned society? Or was it simply a case of a mean old jury that had it in for you? It's always one or the other with you innocent victims."

"Me?" said Jimmy, still blankly virtuous. "Why, warden, I never was in Springfield in my life!"

"Take him back, Cronin," smiled the warden, "and fix him up with outgoing clothes. Unlock him at seven in the morning, and let him come to the bull-pen.[1] Better think over my advice, Valentine."

At a quarter past seven on the next morning Jimmy stood in the warden's outer office. He had on a suit of the villainously fitting, ready-made clothes and a pair of the stiff, squeaky shoes that the state furnishes to its discharged **compulsory** guests.

compulsory: required; enforced

The clerk handed him a railroad ticket and the five-dollar bill with which the law expected him to rehabilitate himself into good citizenship and prosperity. The warden gave him a cigar, and shook hands. Valentine, 9762, was chronicled on the books "Pardoned by Governor," and Mr. James Valentine walked out into the sunshine.

Disregarding the song of the birds, the waving green trees, and the smell of the flowers, Jimmy headed straight for a restaurant. There he tasted the first sweet joys of liberty in the shape of a broiled chicken and a bottle of white wine, followed by a cigar a grade better than the one the warden had given him. From there he proceeded leisurely to the depot. He tossed a quarter into the hat of a blind man sitting by the door, and boarded his train. Three hours set him down in a little town near the state line. He went to the café of one Mike Dolan and shook hands with Mike, who was alone behind the bar.

"Sorry we couldn't make it sooner, Jimmy, me boy," said Mike. "But we had that protest from Springfield to buck against, and the governor nearly **balked**. Feeling all right?"

balked: refused

"Fine," said Jimmy. "Got my key?"

He got his key and went upstairs, unlocking the door of a room at the rear. Everything was just as he had left it. There on the floor was still Ben Price's collar-button that had been torn from that **eminent** detective's shirt-band when they had overpowered Jimmy to arrest him.

eminent: well-known; distinguished

Pulling out from the wall a folding-bed, Jimmy slid back a panel in the wall and dragged out a dust-covered suit-case.

---

1 **bull-pen:** temporary holding area for prisoners

He opened this and gazed fondly at the finest set of burglar's tools in the East. It was a complete set, made of specially tempered steel, the latest design in drills, punches, braces and bits, jimmies, clamps, and augers, with two or three novelties, invented by Jimmy himself, in which he took pride.

Over nine hundred dollars they had cost him to have made at—, a place where they make such things for the profession.

In half an hour Jimmy went down stairs and through the cafe. He was now dressed in tasteful and well-fitting clothes, and carried his dusted and cleaned suit-case in his hand.

"Got anything on?" asked Mike Dolan, genially.

"Me?" said Jimmy, in a puzzled tone. "I don't understand. I'm representing the New York Amalgamated Short Snap Biscuit Cracker and Frazzled Wheat Company."

This statement delighted Mike to such an extent that Jimmy had to take a seltzer-and-milk on the spot. He never touched "hard" drinks.

A week after the release of Valentine, 9762, there was a neat job of safe-burglary done in Richmond, Indiana, with no clue to the author. A scant eight hundred dollars was all that was secured. Two weeks after that a patented, improved, burglar-proof safe in Logansport was opened like a cheese to the tune of fifteen hundred dollars, currency; securities and silver untouched. That began to interest the rogue-catchers. Then an old-fashioned bank-safe in Jefferson City became active and threw out of its crater an eruption of bank-notes amounting to five thousand dollars. The losses were now high enough to bring the matter up into Ben Price's class of work. By comparing notes, a remarkable similarity in the methods of the burglaries was noticed. Ben Price investigated the scenes of the robberies, and was heard to remark:

"*That's Dandy Jim Valentine's autograph. He's resumed business.*"

"That's Dandy Jim Valentine's autograph. He's resumed business. Look at that combination knob—jerked out as easy as pulling up a radish in wet weather. He's got the only clamps that can do it. And look how clean those tumblers[2] were punched out! Jimmy never has to drill but one hole. Yes, I guess I want Mr. Valentine. He'll do his bit next time without any short-time or clemency[3] foolishness."

Ben Price knew Jimmy's habits. He had learned them while working up the Springfield case. Long jumps, quick get-aways, no confederates,[4] and a taste

---

2 **tumblers:** parts of a locking mechanism

3 **clemency:** act of forgiveness

for good society—these ways had helped Mr. Valentine to become noted as a successful dodger of retribution. It was given out that Ben Price had taken up the trail of the **elusive** cracksman, and other people with burglar-proof safes felt more at ease.

elusive: mysterious; hard to pin down

One afternoon Jimmy Valentine and his suit-case climbed out of the mail-hack in Elmore, a little town five miles off the railroad down in the black-jack country of Arkansas. Jimmy, looking like an athletic young senior just home from college, went down the board side-walk toward the hotel.

A young lady crossed the street, passed him at the corner and entered a door over which was the sign "The Elmore Bank." Jimmy Valentine looked into her eyes, forgot what he was, and became another man. She lowered her eyes and colored slightly. Young men of Jimmy's style and looks were scarce in Elmore.

Jimmy collared a boy that was loafing on the steps of the bank as if he were one of the stockholders, and began to question him about the town, feeding him dimes at intervals. By and by the young lady came out, looking royally unconscious of the young man with the suit-case, and went her way.

"Isn't that young lady Miss Polly Simpson?" asked Jimmy, with **specious guile**.

specious: false; phony

guile: slyness; cunning

"Naw," said the boy, "She's Annabel Adams. Her pa owns this bank. What'd you come to Elmore for? Is that a gold watch-chain? I'm going to get a bulldog. Got any more dimes?"

Jimmy went to the Planters' Hotel, registered as Ralph D. Spencer, and engaged a room. He leaned on the desk and declared his platform to the clerk. He said he had come to Elmore to look for a location to go into business. How was the shoe business, now, in the town? He had thought of the shoe business. Was there an opening?

The clerk was impressed by the clothes and manner of Jimmy. He, himself, was something of a pattern of fashion to the thinly gilded youth of Elmore, but he now perceived his shortcomings. While trying to figure out Jimmy's manner of tying his four-in-hand he cordially gave information.

Yes, there ought to be a good opening in the shoe line. There wasn't an exclusive shoe-store in the place. The dry goods and general stores

---

4 **confederates:** partners or sidekicks

handled them. Business in all lines was fairly good. Hoped Mr. Spencer would decide to locate in Elmore. He would find it a pleasant town to live in, and the people very sociable.

Mr. Spencer thought he would stop over in the town a few days and look over the situation. No, the clerk needn't call the boy. He would carry up his suit-case, himself; it was rather heavy.

Mr. Ralph Spencer, the phoenix[5] that arose from Jimmy Valentine's ashes— ashes left by the flame of a sudden and alternative attack of love—remained in Elmore, and prospered. He opened a shoe-store and secured a good run of trade.

Socially he was also a success, and made many friends. And he accomplished the wish of his heart. He met Miss Annabel Adams, and became more and more captivated by her charms.

At the end of a year the situation of Mr. Ralph Spencer was this: he had won the respect of the community, his shoe-store was flourishing, and he and Annabel were engaged to be married in two weeks. Mr. Adams, the typical, plodding, country banker, approved of Spencer. Annabel's pride in him almost equaled her affection. He was as much at home in the family of Mr. Adams and that of Annabel's married sister as if he were already a member.

One day Jimmy sat down in his room and wrote this letter, which he mailed to the safe address of one of his old friends in St. Louis:

DEAR OLD PAL:

I want you to be at Sullivan's place, in Little Rock, next Wednesday night, at nine o'clock. I want you to wind up some little matters for me. And, also, I want to make you a present of my kit of tools. I know you'll be glad to get them—you couldn't duplicate the lot for a thousand dollars. Say, Billy, I've quit the old business—a year ago. I've got a nice store. I'm making an honest living, and I'm going to marry the finest girl on earth two weeks from now. It's the only life, Billy—the straight one. I wouldn't touch a dollar of another man's money now for a million. After I get married I'm going to sell out and go West, where there won't be so much danger of having old scores brought up against me. I tell you, Billy, she's an angel. She believes in me; and I wouldn't do another crooked thing for the whole world. Be sure to be at Sully's, for I must see you. I'll bring the tools with me.

Your old friend,
Jimmy

---

5 phoenix: a mythical bird that supposedly rose from its funeral ashes to live again

On the Monday night after Jimmy wrote this letter, Ben Price jogged unobtrusively into Elmore in a livery[6] buggy. He lounged about town in his quiet way until he found out what he wanted to know. From the drug-store across the street from Spencer's shoe-store he got a good look at Ralph D. Spencer.

"Going to marry the banker's daughter are you, Jimmy?" said Ben to himself, softly. "Well, I don't know!"

The next morning Jimmy took breakfast at the Adamses. He was going to Little Rock that day to order his wedding suit and buy something nice for Annabel. That would be the first time he had left town since he came to Elmore. It had been more than a year now since those last professional "jobs," and he thought he could safely venture out.

After breakfast quite a family party went downtown together—Mr. Adams, Annabel, Jimmy, and Annabel's married sister with her two little girls, aged five and nine. They came by the hotel where Jimmy still boarded, and he ran up to his room and brought along his suit-case. Then they went on to the bank. There stood Jimmy's horse and buggy and Dolph Gibson, who was going to drive him over to the railroad station.

PHOTOGRAPH OF A TRAVELING SALESMAN

---

6 **livery:** rented

All went inside the high, carved oak railings into the banking-room—Jimmy included, for Mr. Adams's future son-in-law was welcome anywhere. The clerks were pleased to be greeted by the good-looking, agreeable young man who was going to marry Miss Annabel. Jimmy set his suit-case down. Annabel, whose heart was bubbling with lively youth, put on Jimmy's hat, and picked up the suit-case. "Wouldn't I make a nice drummer?" said Annabel. "My! Ralph, how heavy it is. Feels like it was full of gold bricks."

"Lot of nickel-plated shoe-horns in there," said Jimmy, coolly, "that I'm going to return. Thought I'd save express charges by taking them up. I'm getting awfully economical. "

The Elmore Bank had just put in a new safe and vault. Mr. Adams was very proud of it, and insisted on an inspection by every one. The vault was a small one, but it had a new, patented door. It fastened with three solid steel bolts thrown simultaneously with a single handle, and had a time-lock. Mr. Adams beamingly explained its workings to Mr. Spencer, who showed a courteous but not too intelligent interest. The two children, May and Agatha, were delighted by the shining metal and funny clock and knobs.

While they were thus engaged Ben Price sauntered in and leaned on his elbow, looking casually inside between the railings. He told the teller that he didn't want anything; he was just waiting for a man he knew.

Suddenly there was a scream or two from the women, and a commotion. Unperceived by the elders, May, the nine-year-old girl, in a spirit of play, had shut Agatha in the vault. She had then shot the bolts and turned the knob of the combination as she had seen Mr. Adams do.

The old banker sprang to the handle and tugged at it for a moment. "The door can't be opened," he groaned. "The clock hasn't been wound nor the combination set."

Agatha's mother screamed again, hysterically.

"Hush!" said Mr. Adams, raising his trembling hand. "All be quiet for a moment. Agatha!" he called as loudly as he could. "Listen to me." During the following silence they could just hear the faint sound of the child wildly shrieking in the dark vault in a panic of terror.

"My precious darling!" wailed the mother. "She will die of fright! Open the door! Oh, break it open! Can't you men do something?"

"There isn't a man nearer than Little Rock who can open that door," said Mr. Adams, in a shaky voice. "My God! Spencer, what shall we do? That child—she can't stand it long in there. There isn't enough air, and, besides, she'll go into convulsions from fright."

Agatha's mother, frantic now, beat the door of the vault with her hands. Somebody wildly suggested dynamite. Annabel turned to Jimmy, her large eyes full of anguish, but not yet despairing. To a woman nothing seems quite impossible to the powers of the man she worships.

"Can't you do something, Ralph—try, won't you?"

He looked at her with a queer, soft smile on his lips and in his keen eyes.

"Annabel," he said, "give me that rose you are wearing, will you?"

Hardly believing that she heard him aright, she unpinned the bud from the bosom of her dress, and placed it in his hand. Jimmy stuffed it into his vest-pocket, threw off his coat and pulled up his shirt-sleeves. With that act Ralph D. Spencer passed away and Jimmy Valentine took his place.

"Get away from the door, all of you," he commanded, shortly.

He set his suit-case on the table, and opened it out flat. From that time on he seemed to be unconscious of the presence of any one else. He laid out the shining, queer implements swiftly and orderly, whistling softly to himself as he always did when at work. In a deep silence and immovable, the others watched him as if under a spell.

In a minute Jimmy's pet drill was biting smoothly into the steel door. In ten minutes—breaking his own burglarious record—he threw back the bolts and opened the door.

Agatha, almost collapsed, but safe, was gathered into her mother's arms.

Jimmy Valentine put on his coat, and walked outside the railings toward the front door. As he went he thought he heard a far-away voice that he once knew call "Ralph!" But he never hesitated.

At the door a big man stood somewhat in his way.

"Hello, Ben!" said Jimmy, still with his strange smile. "Got around at last, have you? Well, let's go. I don't know that it makes much difference, now."

And then Ben Price acted rather strangely.

"Guess you're mistaken, Mr. Spencer," he said. "Don't believe I recognize you. Your buggy's waiting for you, ain't it?"

And Ben Price turned and strolled down the street.

> *B*reaking his own burglarious record—he threw back the bolts and opened the door.

Read and Think Critically

Analyze, Contrast, Predict

1. **ANTIHERO** Is rescuing Agatha Adams from the bank vault a heroic action on Jimmy Valentine's part? Explain.

2. Much of the story is told through **dialogue**. Good dialogue moves the **plot** forward, shows **characters** and relationships, provides authenticity, and entertains. Analyze the author's use of dialogue in the story. Cite one or more passages of conversation that illustrate your evaluation.

3. Contrast Jimmy Valentine's negative character traits with his positive traits. Which do you think say more about the kind of man he is?

4. Is this a **realistic** story? Explain your answer.

5. Predict how Jimmy's fiancée and future in-laws will react after having seen this new side of the man.

6. **THE AUTHOR'S STYLE** O. Henry is known for his warm characterizations. Explain which characters O. Henry portrays with unexpected sympathy. How does he create a sense of sympathy for characters that might typically be portrayed negatively?

Responding to Unit Two

Key Ideas and Details

1. What can you infer about the authors' view of women in "A Pair of Silk Stockings" and "The Wife of His Youth"? Support your conclusions with details from the stories.

2. Analyze the use of **setting** in any story in Unit Two. Is it integral to the story or merely a backdrop? Does it **symbolize** anything?

Craft and Structure

3. In **realistic fiction**, ordinary **characters** speak authentic **dialect** in recognizable settings. The author's **voice** is usually objective and the **tone** of presentation is matter-of-fact. The events of the stories are close to what does or could happen in everyday life. Choose a story in Unit Two and decide how it fits the definition of realistic writing. Use evidence from the text to support your view.

4. **Regionalism** is a form of **realism** that emphasizes realistic settings, using local dialect, customs, and other specific details of place. Identify the regional stories in Unit Two. Analyze how the author uses setting, word choice, and structure to portray a specific region of America.

Integration of Knowledge and Ideas

5. Writing in the middle of the 19th century, political philosopher Alexis de Tocqueville claimed, "The inhabitants of the United States have . . . properly speaking, no literature." Evaluate the contributions of two of the writers in this unit to the development of a uniquely American literature.

6. Some critics believe that late 19th-century writers were more pessimistic than their predecessors. Choose two or more stories from Unit Two that reflect a pessimistic tone and jot down words, phrases, sentences, or **themes** that illustrate this dark outlook.

7. What similar themes do you see in the stories of this unit? Choose two stories and compare and contrast the authors' treatment of a similar theme through **plot**, setting, **characterization**, and tone.

Writing About the Literature

Realism

Mark Twain and Henry James have distinctive styles and subject matter, yet each is considered a realist writer. How do they fit into this tradition? Write a paper that evaluates their contribution to realism.

Writing with Style

Choose one of these two assignments.

Voice for the Voiceless

Rewrite part of a story using the perspective of someone who is not given a voice in it. For example, you could rewrite an opening scene from "The Real Thing" from the point of view of Mr. or Mrs. Monarch or from the point of view of one of the nameless soldiers in "An Occurrence at Owl Creek Bridge."

Your Own Local Color

Write a "local color" description of your own home state or region. Play up the dialect, the typical characters you meet, and situations you might encounter.

In Your Own Style

Willa Cather believed that "Art must have freedom. Some people seem afraid to say or do anything that is the least bit different from the things everyone else says and does." Do you agree that most people are conformists? Who or what influences you to conform? Write about the ways in which you give in to this pressure, and describe how you would behave differently if you could.

Unit Three
Voices of Modernism   1920s to 1940s

THE FIGURE 5 IN GOLD, CHARLES DEMUTH, 1928

If 19th-century writers put America on the world literary map, early 20th-century American writers were part of an artistic exchange program. Visual artists, musicians, and writers from both sides of the Atlantic Ocean inspired one another. Some of them met on the battlefields of World War I. After the war, a number of American writers congregated in Parisian bistros to soak up the new artistic sensibility flourishing there. At the same time, American jazz and blues music invaded European nightclubs.

In poetry, short stories, and novels, American writers described a party atmosphere spiraling out of control and a generation losing itself in the excesses of alcohol and overspending. As the Roaring Twenties crashed into the economic disaster known as the Great Depression, these writers pondered how America's promise had been squandered. Through the thirties and during the forties and World War II, gripping tales of isolation and unendurable poverty were matched by comic jaunts that developed America's peculiar, self-deprecating brand of humor.

Modernism

After the turn of the 20th century, the movement called modernism was carried on the winds of war in Europe and revolution in Russia. Fueled by political unrest, artists in all genres rejected the traditional and embraced the disruptive. Modernism was based in part on psychoanalytical theories of the unconscious mind and on the philosophy of existentialism. Existentialism stresses a person's free will and the individual struggle to create meaning and order out of the chaos of an indifferent universe. Modernist writers such as France's Albert Camus, Ireland's James Joyce, England's Virginia Woolf, and America's T. S. Eliot, William Faulkner, and Ernest Hemingway emphasized internal experience over social structures. They sought to expose fractured social and political structures while at the same time creating meaning and unity through their art. They experimented with new as well as ancient languages and art forms. Several modernist writers explored stream of consciousness, a form of writing that replaces realistic narrative with a flow of impressions—visual, auditory, or psychological—to reveal the mind and heart of a character.

The Lost Generation

Many Americans struggled to make meaning out of World War I's carnage by partying—even as a constitutional amendment banned all alcohol. Homemade gin flowed in bathtubs and riotous jazz inspired scandalous dances such as the Charleston. It seemed to some that women got the right to vote in 1920 only to pick up their skirt hems and kick up their heels. Stock prices and wealth rose along with the skyscrapers, and then dropped with terrifying speed into the Great Depression.

American writers witnessed the frenzy and the fall. Writing from France at the time, Ernest Hemingway became known for his uniquely clipped prose and simple declarative sentences. Fellow expatriate F. Scott Fitzgerald's work was marked by rich descriptions and precise use of metaphor. Home from his time in Europe, Thomas Wolfe wrote autobiographical novels and stories that reflect the turbulence of the time and are filled with a sense of longing. All three conveyed the pain of what came to be known as the Lost Generation: rich in bravado, deprived of spirit.

Harlem Renaissance

A different party raged in New York City, with guests of another color. In the early 1900s, hundreds of thousands of African Americans left rural southern areas for northern cities, seeking factory jobs and an escape from segregation. Though racism thrived in northern cities, too, this new concentration of blacks launched an artistic explosion that drew worldwide attention. Most influential was the Harlem Renaissance, named for the famous black neighborhood in New York. Blues and jazz musicians drew huge white audiences to the black enclave, while black writers found acceptance in white publishing houses and new black literary magazines. Though styles were diverse, in general, their literary works did away with black stereotypes and invoked the ghosts of slavery and the burdens of racism.

Though the Stock Market Crash of 1929 brought an end to Harlem's greatest artistic swell, its impact was felt into the thirties and forties with the emergence of writers such as Richard Wright and Ralph Ellison. Through their fiction they sought to expose the color lines that meant the difference between finding acceptance or derision in America.

America Faces Itself

The American art and literature of the thirties and forties portray the harsh realities of America's rural landscapes and bustling cities. During the Depression, photographers chronicled the widespread poverty in brutally stark black-and-white images. Using similarly gritty journalistic prose, writer John Steinbeck depicted the plight of drought-stricken farmers. While Steinbeck explored his home turf, the American West, an informal southern school of writers rose to prominence—including several women writers. Katherine Anne Porter, from Texas, and Carson McCullers, from Georgia, turned their knack for writing realistic dialogue in local dialects into moving characterizations of dysfunctional families and outcasts.

Even as so many American writers found a beauty in life's grimness, others looked for the lightness. Turning the mirror to face all Americans, writers such as James Thurber and Eudora Welty showed us that we could do more than mourn our losses and regret our weaknesses. We could laugh at ourselves.

Before You Read

Ernest Hemingway 1899–1961

About the Author

An innovative writing style and an adventurous, much-publicized life made Ernest Hemingway not only one of the most influential writers of the 20th century but also a cultural icon. A leader of the post-World War I group of artists known as the Lost Generation, Hemingway was a big game hunter and fisherman, world traveler, and war correspondent. These pursuits influenced his work, which is often set in Africa or Europe.

Born to a doctor's family in Oak Park, Illinois, Hemingway edited his high school newspaper and worked as a reporter at *The Kansas City Star*. He served as an ambulance driver during World War I and was seriously wounded at the age of eighteen.

Like the heroes of his fiction, the author courted danger to prove his courage. Two plane crashes late in life left him in a state of chronic pain that some say prompted his suicide. Like his father before him, he died of a self-inflicted gunshot wound. Among his best-known works are the novels *A Farewell to Arms* and *The Old Man and the Sea*, the latter of which earned the Pulitzer Prize.

★★★★★★★★★★★

The Author's Style

Many of Hemingway's stories involve initiations or tests, both of which stress codes of conduct that typically require courage and endurance. His characters are involved in violent activities such as boxing, hunting, bullfighting, and combat, where they are in a position to suffer both physical and psychological wounds.

Spare, understated prose is a hallmark of the Hemingway style. It emphasizes carefully pared-down declarative sentences based on simple syntax, strategic repetition, and a minimum of explanatory material. This style nevertheless conveys his characters' situations and feelings. It is considered by many to be his most important contribution to 20th-century American fiction.

Hemingway mistrusted flowery and official-sounding language, preferring to use much simpler, concrete language in both narration and dialogue.

The ironic tone of Hemingway's storytelling is also crucial. In his war stories, it reflects his cynicism about authorities who use notions such as duty in pushing naïve soldiers to sacrifice themselves. Sometimes a Hemingway character uses irony to protect himself from fully acknowledging the depth of his pain. So it is particularly important whenever a Hemingway character does make a direct statement about his feelings or his situation. The story you are about to read owes its insight to the author's personal war experiences.

In Another Country

ERNEST HEMINGWAY

🔍 **LITERARY LENS: MOOD Mood** is related to the emotional tone of a story. Pay attention to the mood of this story.

*I*n the fall the war was always there, but we did not go to it any more. It was cold in the fall in Milan[1] and the dark came very early. Then the electric lights came on, and it was pleasant along the streets looking in the windows. There was much game hanging outside the shops, and the snow powdered in the fur of the foxes and the wind blew their tails. The deer hung stiff and heavy and empty, and small birds blew in the wind and the wind turned their feathers. It was a cold fall and the wind came down from the mountains.

We were all at the hospital every afternoon, and there were different ways of walking across the town through the dusk to the hospital. Two of the ways were alongside canals, but they were long. Always, though, you crossed a bridge across a canal to enter the hospital. There was a choice of three bridges. On one of them a woman

---

1 **Milan:** a large city in northern Italy

pavilions:
annexes;
outbuildings

sold roasted chestnuts. It was warm, standing in front of her charcoal fire, and the chestnuts were warm afterward in your pocket. The hospital was very old and very beautiful, and you entered through a gate and walked across a courtyard and out a gate on the other side. There were usually funerals starting from the courtyard. Beyond the old hospital were the new brick **pavilions**, and there we met every afternoon and were all very polite and interested in what was the matter, and sat in the machines that were to make so much difference.

The doctor came up to the machine where I was sitting and said: "What did you like best to do before the war? Did you practice a sport?"

I said: "Yes, football."

"Good," he said. "You will be able to play football again better than ever."

My knee did not bend and the leg dropped straight from the knee to the ankle without a calf, and the machine was to bend the knee and make it move as in riding a tricycle. But it did not bend yet, and instead the machine lurched when it came to the bending part. The doctor said: "That will all pass. You are a fortunate young man. You will play football again like a champion."

In the next machine was a major who had a little hand like a baby's. He winked at me when the doctor examined his hand, which was between two leather straps that bounced up and down and flapped the stiff fingers, and said: "And will I too play football, captain-doctor?" He had been a very great fencer, and before the war the greatest fencer in Italy.

The doctor went to his office in a back room and brought a photograph which showed a hand that had been withered almost as small as the major's, before it had taken a machine course, and after was a little larger. The major held the photograph with his good hand and looked at it very carefully. "A wound?" he asked.

"An industrial accident," the doctor said.

"Very interesting, very interesting," the major said, and handed it back to the doctor.

"You have confidence?"

"No," said the major.

There were three boys who came each day who were about the same age I was. They were all three from Milan, and one of them was to be a lawyer, and one was to be a painter, and one had intended to be a soldier, and after we were finished with the machines, sometimes we walked back together to the Café Cova, which was next door to the Scala.[2] We walked the short way through the communist quarter because we were four together. The people hated us because we were officers, and from a wine-shop someone would call out, *"A basso gli ufficiali!"*[3] as we passed. Another boy who walked with us sometimes and made us five wore a black silk hand-

kerchief across his face because he had no nose then and his face was to be rebuilt. He had gone out to the front from the military academy and been wounded within an hour after he had gone into the front line for the first time. They rebuilt his face, but he came from a very old family and they could never get the nose exactly right. He went to South America and worked in a bank. But this was a long time ago, and then we did not any of us know how it was going to be afterward. We only knew then that there was always the war, but that we were not going to it any more.

We all had the same medals, except the boy with the black silk bandage across his face, and he had not been at the front long enough to get any medals. The tall boy with the very pale face who was to be a lawyer had been lieutenant of *Arditi*[4] and had three medals of the sort we each had only one of. He had lived a very long time with death and was a little detached. We were all a little detached, and there was nothing that held us together except that we

ERNEST HEMINGWAY RECOVERING FROM WWI WOUNDS, ITALY, 1919

met every afternoon at the hospital. Although, as we walked to the Cova through the tough part of town, walking in the dark, with light and singing coming out of the wine-shops, and sometimes having to walk into the street when the

---

2 **Scala:** La Scala, a famous opera house in Milan

3 ***"A basso gli ufficiali!":*** Italian for "Down with the officers!"

4 ***Arditi:*** heavily armed and highly trained soldiers who were given the most dangerous combat assignments

men and women would crowd together on the sidewalk so that we would have had to jostle them to get by, we felt held together by there being something that had happened that they, the people who disliked us, did not understand.

We ourselves all understood the Cova, where it was rich and warm and not too brightly lighted, and noisy and smoky at certain hours, and there were always girls at the tables and the illustrated papers on a rack on the wall. The girls at the Cova were very patriotic, and I found that the most patriotic people in Italy were the café girls—and I believe they are still patriotic.

The boys at first were very polite about my medals and asked me what I had done to get them. I showed them the papers, which were written in very beautiful language and full of *fratellanza*[5] and *abnegazione*,[6] but which really said, with the adjectives removed, that I had been given the medals because I was an American. After that their manner changed a little toward me, although I was their friend against outsiders. I was a friend, but I was never really one of them after they had read the citations, because it had been different with them and they had done very different things to get their medals. I had been wounded, it was true; but we all knew that being wounded, after all, was really an accident. I was never ashamed of the ribbons, though, and sometimes, after the cocktail hour, I would imagine myself having done all the things they had done to get their medals; but walking home at night through the empty streets with the cold wind and all the shops closed, trying to keep near the street lights, I knew that I would never have done such things, and I was very much afraid to die, and often lay in bed at night by myself, afraid to die and wondering how I would be when I went back to the front again.

The three with the medals were like hunting-hawks;[7] and I was not a hawk, although I might seem a hawk to those who had never hunted; they, the three, knew better and so we drifted apart. But I stayed good friends with the boy who had been wounded his first day at the front, because he would

---

5 *fratellanza:* brotherhood

6 *abnegazione:* sacrifice

7 **hunting-hawks:** Literally, hunting hawks are birds trained to hunt and kill prey; with reference to war, "hawks" are people who are pro-military.

never know now how he would have turned out; so he could never be accepted either, and I liked him because I thought perhaps he would not have turned out to be a hawk either.

The major, who had been the great fencer, did not believe in bravery, and spent much time while we sat in the machines correcting my grammar. He had complimented me on how I spoke Italian, and we talked together very easily. One day I had said that Italian seemed such an easy language to me that I could not take a great interest in it; everything was so easy to say. "Ah, yes," the major said. "Why, then, do you not take up the use of grammar?" So we took up the use of grammar, and soon Italian was such a difficult language that I was afraid to talk to him until I had the grammar straight in my mind.

The major came very regularly to the hospital. I do not think he ever missed a day, although I am sure he did not believe in the machines. There was a time when none of us believed in the machines, and one day the major said it was all nonsense. The machines were new then and it was we who were to prove them. It was an idiotic idea, he said, "a theory, like another." I had not learned my grammar, and he said I was a stupid impossible disgrace, and he was a fool to have bothered with me. He was a small man and he sat straight up in his chair with his right hand thrust into the machine and looked straight ahead at the wall while the straps thumped up and down with his fingers in them.

"What will you do when the war is over if it is over?" he asked me. "Speak grammatically!"

"I will go to the States."

"Are you married?"

"No, but I hope to be."

"The more of a fool you are," he said. He seemed very angry. "A man must not marry."

"Why, Signor Maggiore?"

"Don't call me 'Signor Maggiore.'"

"Why must not a man marry?"

"He cannot marry. He cannot marry," he said angrily. "If he is to lose everything, he should not place himself in a position to lose that. He should not place himself in a position to lose. He should find things he cannot lose."

He spoke very angrily and bitterly, and looked straight ahead while he talked.

"But why should he necessarily lose it?"

"He'll lose it," the major said. He was looking at the wall. Then he looked down at the machine and jerked his little hand out from between the straps and slapped it hard against his thigh. "He'll lose it," he almost shouted. "Don't argue with me!" Then he called to the attendant who ran the machines. "Come and turn this damned thing off."

He went back into the other room for the light treatment and the massage. Then I heard him ask the doctor if he might use his telephone and he shut the door. When he came back into the room, I was sitting in another machine. He was wearing his cape and had his cap on, and he came directly toward my machine and put his arm on my shoulder.

"I am sorry," he said, and patted me on the shoulder with his good hand. "I would not be rude. My wife has just died. You must forgive me."

"Oh—" I said, feeling sick for him. "I am *so* sorry."

He stood there biting his lower lip. "It is very difficult," he said. "I cannot resign myself."

He looked straight past me and out through the window. Then he began to cry. "I am utterly unable to resign myself," he said and choked. And then crying, his head up looking at nothing, carrying himself straight and soldierly, with tears on both cheeks and biting his lips, he walked past the machines and out the door.

The doctor told me that the major's wife, who was very young and whom he had not married until he was definitely invalided out of the war,[8] had died of pneumonia. She had been sick only a few days. No one expected her to die. The major did not come to the hospital for three days. Then he came at the usual hour, wearing a black band on the sleeve of his uniform. When he came back, there were large framed photographs around the wall, of all sorts of wounds before and after they had been cured by the machines. In front of the machine the major used were three photographs of hands like his that were completely restored. I do not know where the doctor got them. I always understood we were the first to use the machines. The photographs did not make much difference to the major because he only looked out of the window.

---

8 **invalided out of the war:** meaning that the major was injured and could no longer fight in the war

Read and Think Critically

Analyze, Explain, Describe

1. **MOOD** is conveyed through descriptions of the **setting**, through the author's (or **narrator's**) attitude toward the story, and through **imagery**. Analyze the first paragraph of the story. How does Hemingway's imagery and word choice influence the **mood** of the story?

2. **Existentialism** is the belief that humans exist in an empty universe that does not care about human existence. In the face of this nothingness and loneliness, humans must create their own meaning and purpose. Explain how the story reflects the idea of existentialism.

3. One of the major **themes** of the story is the futility of war. Describe another theme from the story and analyze how Hemingway weaves the two themes together throughout the story.

4. **THE AUTHOR'S STYLE** After reading the quotation below, locate two sentences in the story that seem to fit Hemingway's description of the "true simple declarative sentence."

One True Sentence

Sometimes when I was starting a new story and I could not get it going . . . I would stand and look out over the roofs of Paris and think, "Do not worry. You have always written before and you will write now. All you have to do is write one true sentence. Write the truest sentence that you know." So finally I would write one true sentence, and then go on from there . . . If I started to write elaborately, or like someone introducing or presenting something, I found that I could cut that scrollwork or ornament out and throw it away and start with the first true simple declarative sentence I had written.

—Ernest Hemingway, *A Moveable Feast*

Before You Read

Katherine Anne Porter 1890–1980

About the Author

Born in Indian Creek, Texas, Katherine Anne Porter led a long and full life. The glamorous blonde author married for the first of four times at 16. A world traveler, she acted in two movies and moved frequently, both within the States and overseas. She also enjoyed a long writing career, living to the age of 90 and thus outlasting most of her contemporaries.

Because her mother died when Porter was two, the author was reared afterward by her beloved grandmother. It amused Porter that although she was to teach at many prestigious universities, she never went to college herself.

She began her career as a theatre and music critic, publishing her first story in 1922.

Porter was known mostly for her short stories and was awarded the National Book Award and the Pulitzer Prize for *Collected Short Stories*, published in 1965. While traveling to Germany in 1931 for a fellowship, Porter was horrified by the rise of the Nazis to power. This trip provided her with the background for her only novel, *Ship of Fools*, which was published 31 years later and made into a popular film.

★★★★★★★★★★★

✏ The Author's Style

Katherine Anne Porter's stories always convey a strong sense of place, revealing her understanding of the practical impact of social and economic conditions on people's lives. Her primary focus, however, is on the hidden motives and emotions of her characters.

Porter understood that everyday people and uncomplicated events can still provide powerful stories of individual personality, character, and moral choice. Her often simple characters are typified by conflicted feelings and unexpressed tensions. She brings their perspectives out by clarifying and respecting their points of view. Many of Porter's most memorable characters are women.

Known as a careful planner of her novel and stories, the author revised each one many times to produce precise phrasing, concentrated action, and emotional focus. Her stories also reflect her careful attention to the idioms and dialects of particular times and places, making her writing representative of what came to be known as "the local color movement." A native Texan, Porter eventually lived and worked in Dallas, Denver, Chicago, and New York, and she traveled and lived for extended periods in Mexico and in Europe, including several years in Paris.

He

KATHERINE ANNE PORTER

 LITERARY LENS: CONFLICT Watch for internal as well as external **conflicts** in this family drama.

*L*ife was very hard for the Whipples. It was hard to feed all the hungry mouths, it was hard to keep the children in flannels[1] during the winter, short as it was: "God knows what would become of us if we lived north," they would say: keeping them decently clean was hard. "It looks like our luck won't never let up on us," said Mr. Whipple, but Mrs. Whipple was all for taking what was sent and calling it good, anyhow when the neighbors were in earshot. "Don't ever let a soul hear us complain," she kept saying to her husband. She couldn't stand to be pitied. "No, not if it comes to it

---

1 **flannels:** underwear made of soft cloth

that we have to live in a wagon and pick cotton around the country," she said, "nobody's going to get a chance to look down on us."

Mrs. Whipple loved her second son, the simple-minded one, better than she loved the other two children put together. She was forever saying so, and when she talked with certain of her neighbors, she would even throw in her husband and her mother for good measure.

FARMER'S WIFE, HORACE BRISTOL, 1939

"You needn't keep on saying it around," said Mr. Whipple, "you'll make people think nobody else has any feelings about Him but you."

"It's natural for a mother," Mrs. Whipple would remind him. "You know yourself it's more natural for a mother to be that way. People don't expect so much of fathers, some way."

This didn't keep the neighbors from talking plainly among themselves. "A Lord's pure mercy if He should die," they said. "It's the sins of the fathers," they agreed among themselves. "There's bad blood and bad doings somewhere, you can bet on that." This behind the Whipples' backs. To their faces everybody said, "He's not so bad off. He'll be all right yet. Look how He grows!"

Mrs. Whipple hated to talk about it, she tried to keep her mind off it, but every time anybody set foot in the house, the subject always came up, and she had to talk about Him first, before she could get on to anything else. It seemed to ease her mind. "I wouldn't have anything happen to Him for all the world, but it just looks like I can't keep Him out of mischief. He's so strong and active, He's always into everything; He was like that since He could walk. It's actually funny sometimes, the way He can do anything; it's laughable to see Him up to His tricks. Emly has more accidents; I'm forever tying up her bruises, and Adna can't fall a foot without cracking a bone. But

He can do anything and not get a scratch. The preacher said such a nice thing once when he was here. He said, and I'll remember it to my dying day, 'The innocent walk with God— that's why He don't get hurt.'" Whenever Mrs. Whipple repeated these words, she always felt a warm pool spread in her breast, and the tears would fill her eyes, and then she could talk about something else.

"*It's* the neighbors," said Mrs. Whipple to her husband. "Oh, I do mortally wish they would keep out of our business."

He did grow and He never got hurt. A plank blew off the chicken house and struck Him on the head and He never seemed to know it. He had learned a few words, and after this He forgot them. He didn't whine for food as the other children did, but waited until it was given Him. He ate squatting in the corner, smacking and mumbling. Rolls of fat covered Him like an overcoat, and He could carry twice as much wood and water as Adna. Emly had a cold in the head most of the time—"she takes that after me," said Mrs. Whipple—so in bad weather they gave her the extra blanket off His cot. He never seemed to mind the cold.

Just the same, Mrs. Whipple's life was a torment for fear something might happen to Him. He climbed the peach trees much better than Adna and went skittering along the branches like a monkey, just a regular monkey. "Oh, Mrs. Whipple, you hadn't ought to let Him do that. He'll lose His balance sometime. He can't rightly know what He's doing."

Mrs. Whipple almost screamed out at the neighbor. "He *does* know what He's doing! He's as able as any other child! Come down out of there, you!" When He finally reached the ground she could hardly keep her hands off Him for acting like that before people, a grin all over His face and her worried sick about Him all the time.

"It's the neighbors," said Mrs. Whipple to her husband. "Oh, I do **mortally** wish they would keep out of our business. I can't afford to let Him do anything for fear they'll come nosing around about it. Look at the bees, now. Adna can't handle them, they sting him up so; I haven't got time to do everything, and now I don't dare let Him. But if He gets a sting He don't really mind."

"It's just because He ain't got sense enough to be scared of anything," said Mr. Whipple.

"You ought to be ashamed of yourself," said Mrs. Whipple, "talking that

mortally: intensely; unremittingly

way about your own child. Who's to take up for Him if we don't, I'd like to know? He sees a lot that goes on, He listens to things all the time. And anything I tell Him to do He does it. Don't never let anybody hear you say such things. They'd think you favored the other children over Him."

"Well, now I don't, and you know it, and what's the use of getting all worked up about it? You always think the worst of everything. Just let Him alone, He'll get along somehow. He gets plenty to eat and wear, don't He?" Mr. Whipple suddenly felt tired out. "Anyhow, it can't be helped now."

Mrs. Whipple felt tired too, she complained in a tired voice. "What's done can't never be undone, I know that good as anybody; but He's my child, and I'm not going to have people say anything. I get sick of people coming around saying things all the time."

> "*It's a waste and I don't hold with waste the way we are now*," said Mr. Whipple. "That pig'll be worth money by Christmas."

In the early fall Mrs. Whipple got a letter from her brother saying he and his wife and two children were coming over for a little visit next Sunday week.[2] "Put the big pot in the little one," he wrote at the end. Mrs. Whipple read this part out loud twice, she was so pleased. Her brother was a great one for saying funny things. "We'll just show him that's no joke," she said, "we'll just butcher one of the sucking pigs."

"It's a waste and I don't hold with waste the way we are now," said Mr. Whipple. "That pig'll be worth money by Christmas."

vittles:
food

"It's a shame and a pity we can't have a decent meal's **vittles** once in a while when my own family comes to see us," said Mrs. Whipple. "I'd hate for his wife to go back and say there wasn't a thing in the house to eat. My God, it's better than buying up a great chance of meat in town. There's where you'd spend the money!"

"All right, do it yourself then," said Mr. Whipple. "Christamighty, no wonder we can't get ahead!"

The question was how to get the little pig away from his ma, a great fighter, worse than a Jersey cow. Adna wouldn't try it: "That sow'd rip my insides out all over the pen." "All right, old fraidy," said Mrs. Whipple, "*He's* not scared. Watch *Him* do it." And she laughed as though it was all a good joke and gave Him a little push towards the pen. He sneaked up and snatched the

---

2 **Sunday week:** the Sunday of the following week

pig right away from the teat and galloped back and was over the fence with the sow raging at His heels. The little black squirming thing was screeching like a baby in a tantrum, stiffening its back and stretching its mouth to the ears. Mrs. Whipple took the pig with her face stiff and sliced its throat with one stroke. When He saw the blood He gave a great jolting breath and ran away. "But He'll forget and eat plenty, just the same," thought Mrs. Whipple. Whenever she was thinking, her lips moved making words. "He'd eat it all if I didn't stop Him. He'd eat up every mouthful from the other two if I'd let Him."

And she boxed Him on the ears, hard. He blinked and blinked and rubbed His head, and His face hurt Mrs. Whipple's feelings.

She felt badly about it. He was ten years old now and a third again as large as Adna, who was going on fourteen. "It's a shame, a shame," she kept saying under her breath, "and Adna with so much brains!"

She kept on feeling badly about all sorts of things. In the first place it was the man's work to butcher; the sight of the pig scraped pink and naked made her sick. He was too fat and soft and pitiful-looking. It was simply a shame the way things had to happen. By the time she had finished it up, she almost wished her brother would stay at home.

Early Sunday morning Mrs. Whipple dropped everything to get Him all cleaned up. In an hour He was dirty again, with crawling under fences after a possum, and straddling along the rafters of the barn looking for eggs in the hayloft. "My Lord, look at you now after all my trying! And here's Adna and Emly staying so quiet. I get tired trying to keep you decent. Get off that shirt and put on another, people will say I don't half dress you!" And she boxed Him on the ears, hard. He blinked and blinked and rubbed His head, and His face hurt Mrs. Whipple's feelings. Her knees began to tremble, she had to sit down while she buttoned His shirt. "I'm just all gone before the day starts."

The brother came with his plump healthy wife and two great roaring hungry boys. They had a grand dinner, with the pig roasted to a crackling in the middle of the table, full of dressing, a pickled peach in his mouth and plenty of gravy for the sweet potatoes.

"This looks like prosperity all right," said the brother; "you're going to have to roll me home like I was a barrel when I'm done."

Everybody laughed out loud; it was fine to hear them laughing all at once around the table. Mrs. Whipple felt warm and good about it. "Oh, we've got six more of these; I say it's as little as we can do when you come to see us so seldom." He wouldn't come into the dining room, and Mrs. Whipple passed it off very well. "He's timider than my other two," she said, "He'll just have to get used to you. There isn't everybody He'll make up with, you know how it is with some children, even cousins." Nobody said anything out of the way.

"Just like my Alfy here," said the brother's wife. "I sometimes got to lick him to make him shake hands with his own grand-mammy."

So that was over, and Mrs. Whipple loaded up a big plate for Him first, before everybody. "I always say He ain't to be slighted, no matter who else goes without," she said, and carried it to Him herself.

"He can chin Himself on the top of the door," said Emly, helping along.

"That's fine, He's getting along fine," said the brother.

They went away after supper. Mrs. Whipple rounded up the dishes, and sent the children to bed and sat down and unlaced her shoes. "You see?" she said to Mr. Whipple. "That's the way my whole family is. Nice and considerate about everything. No out-of-the-way remarks—they *have* got refinement. I get awfully sick of people's remarks. Wasn't that pig good?"

Mr. Whipple said, "Yes, we're out three hundred pounds of pork, that's all. It's easy to be polite when you come to eat. Who knows what they had in their minds all along?"

"Yes, that's like you," said Mrs. Whipple. "I don't expect anything else from you. You'll be telling me next that my own brother will be saying around that we made Him eat in the kitchen! Oh, my God!" She rocked her head in her hands, a hard pain started in the very middle of her forehead. "Now it's all spoiled, and everything was so nice and easy. All right, you don't like them and you never did—all right, they'll not come here again soon, never you mind! But they *can't* say He wasn't dressed every lick as good as Adna—oh, honest, sometimes I wish I was dead!"

"I wish you'd let up," said Mr. Whipple. "It's bad enough as it is."

It was a hard winter. It seemed to Mrs. Whipple that they hadn't ever known anything but hard times, and now to cap it all a winter like this.

The crops were about half of what they had a right to expect; after the cotton was in it didn't do much more than cover the grocery bill. They swapped off one of the plow horses, and got cheated, for the new one died of the heaves.[3] Mrs. Whipple kept thinking all the time it was terrible to have a man you couldn't depend on not to get cheated. They cut down on everything, but Mrs. Whipple kept saying there are things you can't cut down on, and they cost money. It took a lot of warm clothes for Adna and Emly, who walked four miles to school during the three-months session. "He sets around the fire a lot, He won't need so much," said Mr. Whipple. "That's so," said Mrs. Whipple, "and when He does the outdoor chores He can wear your tarpaullion[4] coat. I can't do no better, that's all."

In February He was taken sick, and lay curled up under His blanket looking very blue in the face and acting as if He would choke. Mr. and Mrs. Whipple did everything they could for Him for two days, and then they were scared and sent for the doctor. The doctor told them they must keep Him warm and give Him plenty of milk and eggs. "He isn't as stout as He looks, I'm afraid," said the doctor. "You've got to watch them when they're like that. You must put more cover onto Him, too."

"I just took off His big blanket to wash," said Mrs. Whipple, ashamed. "I can't stand dirt."

"Well, you'd better put it back on the minute it's dry," said the doctor, "or He'll have pneumonia."

Mr. and Mrs. Whipple took a blanket off their own bed and put His cot in by the fire. "They can't say we didn't do everything for Him," she said, "even to sleeping cold ourselves on His account."

When the winter broke He seemed to be well again, but He walked as if His feet hurt Him. He was able to run a cotton planter during the season.

"I got it all fixed up with Jim Ferguson about breeding the cow next time," said Mr. Whipple. "I'll pasture the bull this summer and give Jim some fodder in the fall. That's better than paying out money when you haven't got it."

"I hope you didn't say such a thing before Jim Ferguson," said Mrs. Whipple. "You oughtn't to let him know we're so down as all that."

"Godamighty, that ain't saying we're down. A man is got to look ahead sometimes. *He* can lead the bull over today. I need Adna on the place."

At first Mrs. Whipple felt easy in her mind about sending Him for the

---

3 heaves: a type of emphysema that causes difficulty breathing and a persistent cough

4 tarpaullion: a durable, heavy material

bull. Adna was too jumpy and couldn't be trusted. You've got to be steady around animals. After He was gone she started thinking, and after a while she could hardly bear it any longer. She stood in the lane and watched for Him. It was nearly three miles to go and a hot day, but He oughtn't to be so long about it. She shaded her eyes and stared until colored bubbles floated in her eyeballs. It was just like everything else in life, she must always worry and never know a moment's peace about anything. After a long time she saw Him turn into the side lane, limping. He came on very slowly, leading the big hulk of an animal by a ring in the nose, twirling a little stick in His hand, never looking back or sideways, but coming on like a sleepwalker with His eyes half shut.

It was no use trying to keep up, Mrs. Whipple couldn't bear another thing. She sat down and rocked and cried with her apron over her head.

Mrs. Whipple was scared sick of bulls; she had heard awful stories about how they followed on quietly enough, and then suddenly pitched on with a bellow and pawed and gored a body to pieces. Any second now that black monster would come down on Him, my God, He'd never have sense enough to run.

She mustn't make a sound nor a move; she mustn't get the bull started. The bull heaved his head aside and horned the air at a fly. Her voice burst out of her in a shriek, and she screamed at Him to come on, for God's sake. He didn't seem to hear her clamor, but kept on twirling His switch and limping on, and the bull lumbered along behind him as gently as a calf. Mrs. Whipple stopped calling and ran towards the house, praying under her breath: "Lord, don't let anything happen to Him. Lord, you *know* people will say we oughtn't to have sent Him. You *know* they'll say we didn't take care of Him. Oh, get Him home, safe home, safe home, and I'll look out for Him better! Amen."

She watched from the window while He led the beast in, and tied him up in the barn. It was no use trying to keep up, Mrs. Whipple couldn't bear another thing. She sat down and rocked and cried with her apron over her head.

From year to year the Whipples were growing poorer and poorer. The place just seemed to run down of itself, no matter how hard they worked. "We're losing our hold," said Mrs. Whipple. "Why can't we do like other people and watch for our best chances? They'll be calling us poor white trash next."

"When I get to be sixteen I'm going to leave," said Adna. "I'm going to get a job in Powell's grocery store. There's money in that. No more farm for me."

"I'm going to be a schoolteacher," said Emly. "But I've got to finish the eighth grade, anyhow. Then I can live in town. I don't see any chances here."

"Emly takes after my family," said Mrs. Whipple. "Ambitious every last one of them, and they don't take second place for anybody."

When fall came Emly got a chance to wait on table in the railroad eating-house in the town near by, and it seemed such a shame not to take it when the wages were good and she could get her food too, that Mrs. Whipple decided to let her take it, and not bother with school until the next session. "You've got plenty of time," she said. "You're young and smart as a whip."

With Adna gone too, Mr. Whipple tried to run the farm with just Him to help. He seemed to get along fine, doing His work and part of Adna's without noticing it. They did well enough until Christmas time, when one morning He slipped on the ice coming up from the barn. Instead of getting up He thrashed round and round, and when Mr. Whipple got to Him, He was having some sort of fit.

They brought Him inside and tried to make Him sit up, but He blubbered and rolled, so they put Him to bed and Mr. Whipple rode to town for the doctor. All the way there and back he worried about where the money was to come from: it sure did look like he had about all the troubles he could carry.

From then on He stayed in bed. His legs swelled up double their size, and the fits kept coming back. After four months, the doctor said, "It's no use, I think you'd better put Him in the County Home for treatment right away. I'll see about it for you. He'll have good care there and be off your hands."

"We don't begrudge Him any care, and I won't let Him out of my

PUBLIC SALE
1943
ANDREW WYETH
THE PHILADELPHIA MUSEUM OF ART

sight," said Mrs. Whipple. "I won't have it said I sent my sick child off among strangers."

"I know how you feel," said the doctor. "You can't tell me anything about that, Mrs. Whipple. I've got a boy of my own. But you'd better listen to me. I can't do anything more for Him, that's the truth."

Mr. and Mrs. Whipple talked it over a long time that night after they went to bed. "It's just charity," said Mrs. Whipple, "that's what we've come to, charity! I certainly never looked for this."

"We pay taxes to help support the place just like everybody else," said Mr. Whipple, "and I don't call that taking charity. I think it would be fine to have Him where He'd get the best of everything . . . and besides, I can't keep up with these doctor bills any longer."

"Maybe that's why the doctor wants us to send Him—he's scared he won't get his money," said Mrs. Whipple.

"Don't talk like that," said Mr. Whipple, feeling pretty sick, "or we won't be able to send Him."

"Oh, but we won't keep Him there long," said Mrs. Whipple. "Soon's He's better, we'll bring Him right back home."

"The doctor has told you and told you time and again He can't ever get

better, and you might as well stop talking," said Mr. Whipple.

"Doctors don't know everything," said Mrs. Whipple, feeling almost happy. "But anyhow, in the summer Emly can come home for a vacation, and Adna can get down for Sundays: we'll all work together and get on our feet again, and the children will feel they've got a place to come to."

All at once she saw it full summer again, with the garden going fine, and new white roller shades up all over the house, and Adna and Emly home, so full of life, all of them happy together. Oh, it could happen, things would ease up on them.

They didn't talk before Him much, but they never knew just how much He understood. Finally the doctor set the day and a neighbor who owned a double-seated carryall[5] offered to drive them over. The hospital would have sent an ambulance, but Mrs. Whipple couldn't stand to see Him going away looking so sick as all that. They wrapped Him in blankets, and the neighbor and Mr. Whipple lifted Him into the back seat of the carryall beside Mrs. Whipple, who had on her black shirtwaist.[6] She couldn't stand to go looking like charity.

---

5 **carryall:** a covered carriage for four people

6 **shirtwaist:** a tailored blouse or dress

"You'll be all right, I guess I'll stay behind," said Mr. Whipple. "It don't look like everybody ought to leave the place at once."

"Besides, it ain't as if He was going to stay forever," said Mrs. Whipple to the neighbor. "This is only for a little while."

They started away, Mrs. Whipple holding to the edges of the blankets to keep Him from sagging sideways. He sat there blinking and blinking. He worked His hands out and began rubbing His nose with His knuckles, and then with the end of the blanket. Mrs. Whipple couldn't believe what she saw; He was scrubbing away big tears that rolled out of the corners of His eyes. He sniveled and made a gulping noise. Mrs. Whipple kept saying, "Oh, honey, you don't feel so bad, do you? You don't feel so bad, do you?" for He seemed to be accusing her of something. Maybe He remembered that time she boxed His ears, maybe He had been scared that day with the bull, maybe He had slept cold and couldn't tell her about it; maybe He knew they were sending Him away for good and all because they were too poor to keep Him. Whatever it was, Mrs. Whipple couldn't bear to think of it. She began to cry, frightfully, and wrapped her arms tight around Him. His head rolled on her shoulder: she had loved Him as much as she possibly could, there were Adna and Emly who had to be thought of too, there was nothing she could do to make up to Him for His life. Oh, what a mortal pity He was ever born.

They came in sight of the hospital, with the neighbor driving very fast, not daring to look behind him.

Read and Think Critically

Analyze, Evaluate, Compare and Contrast

1. **CONFLICT** Analyze the use of **conflict** in the story. Explain what you think the major conflict is.

2. Porter chooses to leave some critical elements of the story uncertain, including the name of the disabled son. What other elements of the story are ambiguous? Explain why the author purposely leaves things unclear.

3. Evaluate Mrs. Whipple as a parent. Do you think Mrs. Whipple failed her son in any way? If so, what could she have done differently?

4. Do you think that attitudes toward mentally disabled people have changed very much since this story was written? Compare and contrast current attitudes with those in the story.

5. **THE AUTHOR'S STYLE** Porter is known for her ability to bring complex **characters** to life. Select a passage that you think demonstrates Porter's skill at **characterization**. Give reasons for your choice.

Before You Read

F. Scott Fitzgerald 1896–1940

About the Author

One of the most important writers of his generation, F. Scott Fitzgerald coined the term "the Jazz Age" for the prosperous twenties. He was born in St. Paul, Minnesota, to an established family and was named for Francis Scott Key, the author of "The Star-Spangled Banner" and an ancestor of his father. In 1913, he went east to prestigious Princeton University, later dropping out of college to join the army. He never saw combat, and instead spent most of his army time writing a spectacularly successful first novel, *This Side of Paradise*, published in 1920.

That same year Fitzgerald married a temperamental Southern belle, Zelda Sayre. Their sophisticated, globetrotting life became the backdrop for his work as the Fitzgeralds flitted between the Riviera, Paris, and New York. By 1930, the lifestyle took its toll; Fitzgerald had become an alcoholic and his wife was mentally ill. Afterward, when Fitzgerald was struggling to recover, he became known as the spokesman for the Lost Generation. This was a group of artists who rode the roller coaster of the times and reflected on its aftermath in their work. One of his best-known works is his novel *The Great Gatsby*.

★★★★★★★★★★★

𝒪 The Author's Style

F. Scott Fitzgerald's fiction conveys the contrasts and extremes of the Jazz Age of the twenties. He was equally adept at chronicling the period of deflation and regret that followed it after the Stock Market Crash of 1929. Fitzgerald, like many of his protagonists, was a participant in a wild culture that led to excesses of many kinds. His prose is both subtle and richly descriptive. Through the precise rendering of dialogue, gesture, metaphor, and crucial detail, his style captures the subtle distinctions of setting, character, and tone. Fitzgerald was particularly good at rendering the glossy social lives of the affluent. He also revealed how the close attention rich people pay to manners and customs can mask their moral inadequacies. Often his characters are both shaped by wealth and injured by its loss.

The mood of many Fitzgerald stories is one of tragic regret—not only for fortunes squandered, but for bad behavior, opportunities lost, and nagging reminders of past mistakes that follow people into the future.

Babylon Revisited

F. SCOTT FITZGERALD

LITERARY LENS: IN MEDIAS RES Watch for Fitzgerald's use of **in medias res** in this story. Literally meaning "in the midst of things," *in medias res* refers to the technique of opening a story in the middle of the action, without letting the reader know who the main character is or where and when the story is taking place.

I

"And where's Mr. Campbell?" Charlie asked.

"Gone to Switzerland. Mr. Campbell's a pretty sick man, Mr. Wales."

"I'm sorry to hear that. And George Hardt?" Charlie inquired.

"Back in America, gone to work."

"And where is the Snow Bird?"

"He was in here last week. Anyway, his friend, Mr. Schaeffer, is in Paris."

Two familiar names from the long list of a year and a half ago. Charlie scribbled an address in his notebook and tore out the page.

"If you see Mr. Schaeffer, give him this," he said. "It's my brother-in-law's address. I haven't settled on a hotel yet."

He was not really disappointed to find Paris was so empty.

portentous:
ominous; full
of meaning

But the stillness in the Ritz bar was strange and **portentous**. It was not an American bar any more—he felt polite in it, and not as if he owned it. It had gone back into France. He felt the stillness from the moment he got out of the taxi and saw the doorman, usually in a frenzy of activity at this hour, gossiping with a *chasseur*[1] by the servants' entrance.

Passing through the corridor, he heard only a single, bored voice in the once-clamorous women's room. When he turned into the bar he traveled the twenty feet of green carpet with his eyes fixed straight ahead by old habit; and then, with his foot firmly on the rail, he turned and surveyed the room, encountering only a single pair of eyes that fluttered up from a newspaper in the corner. Charlie asked for the head barman, Paul, who in the latter days of the bull market[2] had come to work in his own custom-built car—disem-

nicety:
correctness;
propriety

barking, however, with due **nicety** at the nearest corner. But Paul was at his country house today and Alix giving him information.

"No, no more," Charlie said. "I'm going slow these days."

Alix congratulated him: "You were going pretty strong a couple of years ago."

"I'll stick to it all right," Charlie assured him. "I've stuck to it for over a year and a half now."

"How do you find conditions in America?"

"I haven't been to America for months. I'm in business in Prague, representing a couple of concerns there. They don't know about me down there."

Alix smiled.

"Remember the night of George Hardt's bachelor dinner here?" said Charlie. "By the way, what's become of Claude Fessenden?"

Alix lowered his voice confidentially: "He's in Paris, but he doesn't come here any more. Paul doesn't allow it. He ran up a bill of thirty thousand francs, charging all his drinks and his lunches, and usually his dinner, for more than a year. And when Paul finally told him he had to pay, he gave him a bad check."

Alix shook his head sadly.

"I don't understand it, such a dandy fellow. Now he's all bloated up—" he made a plump apple of his hands.

strident:
commanding
attention

Charlie watched a group of **strident** queens installing themselves in a corner.

"Nothing affects them," he thought "Stocks rise and fall, people loaf

---

1 *chasseur:* French for "messenger boy"

2 **bull market:** a period when the stock market is rising

or work, but they go on forever." The place oppressed him. He called for the dice and shook with Alix for the drink.

"Here for long, Mr. Wales?"

"I'm here for four or five days to see my little girl."

"Oh-h! You have a little girl?"

Outside, the fire-red, gas-blue, ghost-green signs shone smokily through the tranquil rain. It was late afternoon and the streets were in movement; the *bistros*[3] gleamed. At the corner of the Boulevard des Capucines he took a taxi. The Place de la Concorde moved by in pink majesty; they crossed the logical Seine,[4] and Charlie felt the sudden provincial[5] quality of the Left Bank.[6]

Charlie directed his taxi to the Avenue de l'Opéra, which was out of his way. But he wanted to see the blue hour spread over the magnificent façade, and imagine that the cab horns, playing endlessly the first few bars of *Le Plus que Lente*,[7] were the trumpets of the Second Empire.[8] They were closing the iron grill in front of Brentano's Bookstore, and people were already at dinner behind the trim little **bourgeois** hedge of Duval's. He had never eaten at a really cheap restaurant in Paris. Five-course dinner, four francs fifty, eighteen cents, wine included. For some odd reason he wished that he had.

As they rolled on to the Left Bank and he felt its sudden provincialism, he thought, "I spoiled this city for myself. I didn't realize it, but the days came along one after another, and then two years were gone, and everything was gone, and I was gone."

He was thirty-five, and good to look at. The Irish mobility of his face was sobered by a deep wrinkle between his eyes. As he rang his brother-in-law's bell in the Rue Palatine, the wrinkle deepened till it pulled down his brows; he felt a cramping sensation in his belly. From behind the maid who opened the door darted a lovely little girl of nine, who shrieked "Daddy!" and flew

> They were closing the iron grill in front of Brentano's Bookstore, and people were already at dinner behind the trim little bourgeois hedge of Duval's.

bourgeois: middle-class; conventional

---

3 *bistros:* French for "taverns"

4 **Seine:** a river in France

5 **provincial:** regional; in this case, rural or small-town

6 **Left Bank:** the southern shore of the Seine in Paris, less stylish than the Right Bank

7 *Le Plus que Lente:* a waltz by Claude Debussy

8 **Second Empire:** refers to the reign of Napoleon III from 1852 until 1871

up, struggling like a fish, into his arms. She pulled his head around by one ear and set her cheek against his.

"My old pie," he said.

"Oh, daddy, daddy, daddy, daddy, dads, dads, dads!"

She drew him into the salon, where the family waited, a boy and girl his daughter's age, his sister-in-law and her husband. He greeted Marion with his voice pitched carefully to avoid either **feigned** enthusiasm or dislike, but her response was more frankly **tepid**, though she minimized her expression of unalterable distrust by directing her regard toward his child. The two men clasped hands in a friendly way and Lincoln Peters rested his for a moment on Charlie's shoulder.

The room was warm and comfortably American. The three children moved intimately about, playing through the yellow oblongs that led to other rooms; the cheer of six o'clock spoke in the eager smacks of the fire and the sounds of French activity in the kitchen. But Charlie did not relax; his heart sat up rigidly in his body and he drew confidence from his daughter, who from time to time came close to him, holding in her arms the doll he had brought.

"Really extremely well," he declared in answer to Lincoln's question. "There's a lot of business there that isn't moving at all, but we're doing even better than ever. In fact, damn well. I'm bringing my sister over from America next month to keep house for me. My income last year was bigger than it was when I had money. You see, the Czechs—"

His boasting was for a specific purpose; but after a moment, seeing a faint **restiveness** in Lincoln's eye, he changed the subject:

"Those are fine children of yours, well brought up, good manners."

"We think Honoria's a great little girl too."

Marion Peters came back from the kitchen. She was a tall woman with worried eyes, who had once possessed a fresh American loveliness. Charlie had never been sensitive to it and was always surprised when people spoke of how pretty she had been. From the first there had been an instinctive **antipathy** between them.

"Well, how do you find Honoria?" she asked.

"Wonderful. I was astonished how much she's grown in ten months. All the children are looking well."

"We haven't had a doctor for a year. How do you like being back in Paris?"

---

feigned: pretended

tepid: lukewarm; unenthusiastic

restiveness: uneasiness

antipathy: intense dislike

---

274   F. Scott Fitzgerald   Unit 3

THE CATHEDRALS OF BROADWAY, FLORINE STETTHEIMER, 1929, THE METROPOLITAN MUSEUM OF ART

vehemently: forcefully; with conviction

"It seems very funny to see so few Americans around."

"I'm delighted," Marion said **vehemently**. "Now at least you can go into a store without their assuming you're a millionaire. We've suffered like everybody, but on the whole it's a good deal pleasanter."

"But it was nice while it lasted," said Charlie. "We were a sort of royalty, almost infallible, with a sort of magic around us. In the bar this afternoon"—he stumbled, seeing his mistake—"there wasn't a man I knew."

She looked at him keenly. "I should think you'd have had enough of bars."

"I only stayed a minute. I take one drink every afternoon, and no more."

"Don't you want a cocktail before dinner?" Lincoln asked.

"I take only one drink every afternoon, and I've had that."

"I hope you keep to it," said Marion.

Her dislike was evident in the coldness with which she spoke, but Charlie only smiled; he had larger plans. Her very aggressiveness gave him an advantage, and he knew enough to wait. He wanted them to initiate the discussion of what they knew had brought him to Paris.

At dinner he couldn't decide whether Honoria was most like him or her mother. Fortunate if she didn't combine the traits of both that had brought them to disaster. A great wave of protectiveness went over him. He thought he knew what to do for her. He believed in character; he wanted to jump back a whole generation and trust in character again as the eternally valuable element. Everything else wore out.

He left soon after dinner, but not to go home. He was curious to see Paris by night with clearer and more judicious eyes than those of other days. He bought a *strapontin*[9] for the Casino and watched Josephine Baker[10] go through her chocolate arabesques.[11]

After an hour he left and strolled toward Montmartre,[12] up the Rue Pigalle[13] into the Place Blanche.[14] The rain had stopped and there were a few people in evening clothes disembarking from taxis in front of cabarets, and *cocottes*[15] prowling singly or in pairs, and many Negroes. He passed a lighted door

---

9 *strapontin*: French for "cheap seat"

10 Josephine Baker: popular African American dancer in Paris in the 1920s

11 arabesques: ballet moves

12 Montmartre: a hill in northern Paris known for its artists and breathtaking view of the city

13 Rue Pigalle: French for "Pigalle Street"

14 Place Blanche: French for "White Square"

15 *cocottes*: French for "tarts," meaning "prostitutes"

from which issued music, and stopped with the sense of familiarity; it was Bricktop's, where he had parted with so many hours and so much money. A few doors farther on he found another ancient rendezvous and incautiously put his head inside. Immediately an eager orchestra burst into sound, a pair of professional dancers leaped to their feet and a maître d'hôtel swooped toward him, crying, "Crowd just arriving, sir!" But he withdrew quickly.

"You have to be damn drunk," he thought.

Zelli's was closed, the bleak and **sinister** cheap hotels surrounding it were dark; up in the Rue Blanche there was more light and a local, **colloquial** French crowd. The Poet's Cave had disappeared, but the two great mouths of the Café of Heaven and the Café of Hell still yawned— even devoured, as he watched, the meager contents of a tourist bus—a German, a Japanese, and an American couple who glanced at him with frightened eyes.

So much for the effort and ingenuity of Montmartre. All the catering to vice and waste was on an utterly childish scale, and he suddenly realized the meaning of the word "dissipate"—to dissipate into thin air; to make nothing out of something. In the little hours of the night every move from place to place was an enormous human jump, an increase of paying for the privilege of slower and slower motion.

He remembered thousand-franc notes given to an orchestra for playing a single number, hundred-franc notes tossed to a doorman for calling a cab.

But it hadn't been given for nothing.

It had been given, even the most wildly squandered sum, as an offering to destiny that he might not remember the things most worth remembering, the things that now he would always remember—his child taken from his control, his wife escaped to a grave in Vermont.

In the glare of a *brasserie*[16] a woman spoke to him. He bought her some eggs and coffee, and then, eluding her encouraging stare, gave her a twenty-franc note and took a taxi to his hotel.

> **sinister:** dangerous-looking
>
> **colloquial:** familiar; ordinary

> *He* remembered thousand-franc notes given to an orchestra for playing a single number, hundred-franc notes tossed to a doorman for calling a cab.

---

16 *brasserie:* French for a tavern that also serves as a restaurant

II

He woke up on a fine fall day—football weather. The depression of yesterday was gone and he liked the people on the streets. At noon he sat opposite Honoria at Le Grand Vatel, the only restaurant he could think of not reminiscent of champagne dinners and long luncheons that began at two and ended in a blurred and vague twilight.

"Now, how about vegetables? Oughtn't you to have some vegetables?"

"Well, yes."

"Here's *épinards* and *chou-fleur* and carrots and *haricots*."[17]

"I'd like chou-fleur."

"Wouldn't you like to have two vegetables?"

"I usually have only one at lunch."

The waiter was pretending to be inordinately fond of children. *"Qu'elle est mignonne, la petite! Elle parle exactement comme une française."*[18]

"How about dessert? Shall we wait and see?"

The waiter disappeared. Honoria looked at her father expectantly.

"What are we going to do?"

"First, we're going to that toy store in the Rue Saint-Honoré and buy you anything you like. And then we're going to the vaudeville at the Empire."

She hesitated. "I like it about the vaudeville, but not the toy store."

"Why not?"

"Well, you brought me this doll." She had it with her. "And I've got lots of things. And we're not rich any more, are we?"

"We never were. But today you are to have anything you want."

"All right," she agreed resignedly.

When there had been her mother and a French nurse he had been inclined to be strict; now he extended himself, reached out for a new tolerance; he must be both parents to her and not shut any of her out of communication.

"I want to get to know you," he said gravely. "First let me introduce myself. My name is Charles J. Wales, of Prague."

"Oh, daddy!" her voice cracked with laughter.

"And who are you, please?" he persisted, and she accepted a rôle immediately: "Honoria Wales, Rue Palatine, Paris."

"Married or single?"

"No, not married. Single."

---

17 *épinards . . . chou-fleur . . . haricots:* French for "spinach," "cauliflower," "beans"

18 *"Qu'elle . . . française.":* French for "She is charming, the little one! She speaks exactly like a French girl."

He indicated the doll. "But I see you have a child, madame."

Unwilling to disinherit it, she took it to her heart and thought quickly: "Yes, I've been married, but I'm not married now. My husband is dead."

He went on quickly, "And the child's name?"

"Simone. That's after my best friend at school."

"I'm very pleased that you're doing so well at school."

"I'm third this month," she boasted. "Elsie"—that was her cousin—"is only about eighteenth, and Richard is about at the bottom."

"You like Richard and Elsie, don't you?"

"Oh, yes. I like them all right."

Cautiously and casually he asked: "And Aunt Marion and Uncle Lincoln—which do you like best?"

"Oh, Uncle Lincoln, I guess."

He was increasingly aware of her presence. As they came in, a murmur of ". . . adorable" followed them, and now the people at the next table bent all their silences upon her, staring as if she were something no more conscious than a flower.

"Why don't I live with you?" she asked suddenly. "Because mamma's dead?"

"You must stay here and learn more French. It would have been hard for daddy to take care of you so well."

"I don't really need much taking care of any more. I do everything for myself."

Going out of the restaurant, a man and a woman unexpectedly hailed him.

"Well, the old Wales!"

"Hello there, Lorraine . . . Dunc."

Sudden ghosts out of the past: Duncan Schaeffer, a friend from college. Lorraine Quarles, a lovely, pale blonde of thirty; one of a crowd who had helped them make months into days in the lavish times of three years ago.

"My husband couldn't come this year," she said, in answer to his question. "We're poor as hell. So he gave me two hundred a month, and told me I could do my worst on that. . . . This your little girl?"

"What about coming back and sitting down?" Duncan asked.

"Can't do it." He was glad for an excuse. As always, he felt Lorraine's passionate, **provocative** attraction, but his own rhythm was different now.

"Well, how about dinner?" she asked.

provocative: suggestive; exciting

judicially:
critically; with
judgment

"I'm not free. Give me your address and let me call you."

"Charlie, I believe you're sober," she said **judicially**. "I honestly believe he's sober, Dunc. Pinch him and see if he's sober."

Charlie indicated Honoria with his head. They both laughed.

"What's your address?" said Duncan skeptically.

He hesitated, unwilling to give the name of his hotel.

> *S*he was already an individual with a code of her own, and Charlie was more and more absorbed by the desire of putting a little of himself into her before she crystallized utterly.

"I'm not settled yet. I'd better call you. We're going to see the vaudeville at the Empire."

"There! That's what I want to do," Lorraine said. "I want to see some clowns and acrobats and jugglers. That's just what we'll do, Dunc."

"We've got to do an errand first," said Charlie. "Perhaps we'll see you there."

"All right, you snob. . . . Good-by, beautiful little girl."

"Good-by."

Honoria bobbed politely.

Somehow, an unwelcome encounter. They liked him because he was functioning, because he was serious; they wanted to see him, because he was stronger than they were now, because they wanted to draw a certain **sustenance** from his strength.

sustenance:
nourishment;
support

At the Empire, Honoria proudly refused to sit upon her father's folded coat. She was already an individual with a code of her own, and Charlie was more and more absorbed by the desire of putting a little of himself into her before she crystallized utterly. It was hopeless to try to know her in so short a time.

Between the acts they came upon Duncan and Lorraine in the lobby where the band was playing.

"Have a drink?"

"All right; but not up at the bar. We'll take a table."

"The perfect father."

Listening abstractedly to Lorraine, Charlie watched Honoria's eyes leave their table, and he followed them wistfully about the room, wondering what they saw. He met her glance and she smiled.

"I liked that lemonade," she said.

What had she said? What had he expected? Going home in a taxi afterward, he pulled her over until her head rested against his chest.

"Darling, do you ever think about your mother?"

"Yes, sometimes," she answered vaguely.

"I don't want you to forget her. Have you got a picture of her?"

"Yes, I think so. Anyhow, Aunt Marion has. Why don't you want me to forget her?"

"She loved you very much."

"I loved her too."

They were silent for a moment.

"Daddy, I want to come and live with you," she said suddenly.

His heart leaped; he had wanted it to come like this.

"Aren't you perfectly happy?"

"Yes, but I love you better than anybody. And you love me better than anybody, don't you, now that mummy's dead?"

"Of course I do. But you won't always like me best, honey. You'll grow up and meet somebody your own age and go marry him and forget you ever had a daddy."

"Yes, that's true," she agreed **tranquilly**.

He didn't go in. He was coming back at nine o'clock and he wanted to keep himself fresh and new for the thing he must say then.

"When you're safe inside, just show yourself in that window."

"All right. Good-by, dads, dads, dads, dads."

He waited in the dark street until she appeared, all warm and glowing, in the window above and kissed her fingers out into the night.

III

They were waiting: Marion sat behind the coffee service in a dignified black dinner dress that just faintly suggested mourning. Lincoln was walking up and down with the animation of one who had already been talking. They were as anxious as he was to get into the question. He opened it almost immediately:

"I suppose you know what I want to see you about—why I really came to Paris."

Marion played with the black stars on her necklace and frowned.

"I'm awfully anxious to have a home," he continued. "And I'm awfully anxious to have Honoria in it. I appreciate your taking in Honoria for her mother's sake, but things have changed now"—he hesitated and then continued more forcibly—"changed radically with me, and I want to ask you to reconsider the matter. It would be silly for me to deny that about three years ago I was acting badly—"

Marion looked up at him with hard eyes.

"—But all that's over. As I told you, I haven't had more than a drink a day for over a year, and I take that drink deliberately, so that the idea of alcohol won't get too big in my imagination. You see the idea?"

"No," said Marion succinctly.

"It's a sort of stunt I set myself. It keeps the matter in proportion."

"I get you," said Lincoln. "You don't want to admit it's got any attraction for you."

"Something like that. Sometimes I forget and don't take it. But I try to take it. Anyhow, I couldn't afford to drink in my position. The people I represent are more than satisfied with what I've done, and I'm bringing my sister over from Burlington to keep house for me, and I want awfully to have Honoria too. You know that even when her mother and I weren't getting along well we never let anything that happened touch Honoria. I know she's fond of me and I know I'm able to take care of her—well, there you are. How do you feel about it?"

He knew that now he would have to take a beating. It would last an hour or two hours, and it would be difficult, but if he **modulated** his inevitable resentment to the **chastened** attitude of the reformed sinner, he might win his point in the end.

Keep your temper, he told himself. You don't want to be justified. You want Honoria.

Lincoln spoke first: "We've been talking it over ever since we got your letter last month. We're happy to have Honoria here. She's a dear little thing, and we're glad to be able to help her, but of course that isn't the question—"

Marion interrupted suddenly. "How long are you going to stay sober, Charlie?" she asked.

"Permanently, I hope."

"How can anybody count on that?"

"You know I never did drink heavily until I gave up business and came over here with nothing to do. Then Helen and I began to run around with—"

"Please leave Helen out of it. I can't bear to hear you talk about her like that."

He stared at her grimly; he had never been certain how fond of each

modulated:
adjusted;
modified

chastened:
humbled;
disciplined

other the sisters were in life.

"My drinking only lasted about a year and a half—from the time we came over until I—collapsed."

"It was time enough—"

"It was time enough," he agreed.

"My duty is entirely to Helen," she said. "I try to think what she would have wanted me to do. Frankly, from the night you did that terrible thing you haven't really existed for me. I can't help that. She was my sister."

"Yes."

"When she was dying she asked me to look out for Honoria. If you hadn't been in a sanitarium then, it might have helped matters."

He had no answer.

"I'll never in my life be able to forget the morning when Helen knocked at my door, soaked to the skin and shivering, and said you'd locked her out."

Charlie gripped the sides of the chair. This was more difficult than he expected: he wanted to launch out into a long **expostulation** and explanation, but he only said: "The night I locked her out—" and she interrupted, "I don't feel up to going over that again."

After a moment's silence Lincoln said: "We're getting off the subject. You want Marion to set aside her legal guardianship and give you Honoria. I think the main point for her is whether she has confidence in you or not."

"I don't blame Marion," Charlie said slowly, "but I think she can have entire confidence in me. I had a good record up to three years ago. Of course, it's within human possibilities I may go wrong again. But if we wait much longer I'll lose Honoria's childhood and my chance for a home." He shook his head. "I'll simply lose her, don't you see?"

"Yes, I see," said Lincoln.

"Why didn't you think of all this before?" Marion asked.

"I suppose I did, from time to time, but Helen and I were getting along badly. When I consented to the guardianship, I was flat on my back in a sanitarium, and the market had cleaned me out. I knew I'd acted badly, and I thought if it would bring any peace to Helen, I'd agree to anything. But now it's different. I'm functioning, I'm behaving damn well, so far as—"

"Please don't swear at me," Marion said.

> *He* shook his head. "I'll simply lose her, don't you see?"

expostulation:
justification

He looked at her, startled. With each remark the force of her dislike became more and more apparent. She had built up all her fear of life into one wall and faced it toward him. This trivial **reproof** was possibly the result of some trouble with the cook several hours before. Charlie became increasingly alarmed at leaving Honoria in this atmosphere of hostility against himself; sooner or later it would come out, in a word here, a shake of the head there, and some of that distrust would be **irrevocably** implanted in Honoria. But he pulled his temper down out of his face and shut it up inside him; he had won a point, for Lincoln realized the absurdity of Marion's remark, and asked her lightly since when she had objected to the word "damn."

"Another thing," Charlie said: "I'm able to give her certain advantages now. I'm going to take a French governess to Prague with me. I've got a lease on a new apartment—"

He stopped, realizing that he was blundering. They couldn't be expected to accept with **equanimity** the fact that his income was again twice as large as their own.

"I suppose you can give her more luxuries than we can," said Marion. "When you were throwing away money we were living along watching every ten francs. . . . I suppose you'll start doing it again."

"Oh, no," he said. "I've learned. I worked hard for ten years, you know—until I got lucky in the market, like so many people. Terribly lucky. It didn't seem any use working any more, so I quit. It won't happen again."

There was a long silence. All of them felt their nerves straining, and for the first time in a year Charlie wanted a drink. He was sure now that Lincoln Peters wanted him to have his child.

Marion shuddered suddenly; part of her saw that Charlie's feet were planted on the earth now, and her own maternal feeling recognized the naturalness of his desire; but she had lived for a long time with a prejudice—a prejudice founded on a curious disbelief in her sister's happiness, which, in the shock of one terrible night, had turned to hatred for him. It had all happened at a point in her life where the discouragement of ill health and adverse circumstances made it necessary for her to believe in tangible villainy and a tangible villain.

"I can't help what I think!" she cried out suddenly. "How much you were responsible for Helen's death, I don't know. It's something you'll have to square with your own conscience."

reproof: criticism; reprimand

irrevocably: permanently; unchangeably

equanimity: pleasant calmness

An electric current of agony surged through him; for a moment he was almost on his feet, an unuttered sound echoing in his throat.

He hung on to himself for a moment, another moment.

"Hold on there," said Lincoln uncomfortably. "I never thought you were responsible for that."

"Helen died of heart trouble," Charlie said dully.

"Yes, heart trouble." Marion spoke as if the phrase had another meaning for her.

Then, in the flatness that followed her outburst, she saw him plainly and she knew he had somehow arrived at control over the situation. Glancing at her husband, she found no help from him, and as abruptly as if it were a matter of no importance, she threw up the sponge.

"Do what you like!" she cried, springing up from her chair. "She's your child. I'm not the person to stand in your way. I think if it were my child I'd rather see her—" She managed to check herself. "You two decide it. I can't stand this. I'm sick. I'm going to bed."

She hurried from the room; after a moment Lincoln said:

"This has been a hard day for her. You know how strongly she feels—" His voice was almost apologetic: "When a woman gets an idea in her head."

"Of course."

"It's going to be all right. I think she sees now that you—can provide for the child, and so we can't very well stand in your way or Honoria's way."

"Thank you, Lincoln."

"I'd better go along and see how she is."

"I'm going."

He was still trembling when he reached the street, but a walk down the Rue Bonaparte to the quais[19] set him up, and as he crossed the Seine, fresh and new by the quai lamps, he felt exultant. But back in his room he couldn't sleep. The image of Helen haunted him. Helen whom he had loved so until they had senselessly begun to abuse each other's love, tear it into shreds. On that terrible February night that Marion remembered so vividly, a slow quarrel had gone on for hours. There was a scene at the Florida, and then he attempted to take her home, and then she kissed young Webb at a table; after that there was what she had hysterically said. When he arrived home alone he turned the key in the lock in wild anger. How could he know she would arrive an hour later alone, that there would be a snowstorm in which she

19 **quais:** French for "shores"

wandered about in slippers, too confused to find a taxi? Then the after-math, her escaping pneumonia by a miracle, and all the attendant horror. They were "reconciled," but that was the beginning of the end, and Marion, who had seen with her own eyes and who imagined it to be one of many scenes from her sister's martyrdom, never forgot.

Going over it again brought Helen nearer, and in the white, soft light that steals upon half sleep near morning he found himself talking to her again. She said that he was perfectly right about Honoria and that she wanted Honoria to be with him. She said she was glad he was being good and doing better. She said a lot of other things—very friendly things—but she was in a swing in a white dress, and swinging faster and faster all the time, so that at the end he could not hear clearly all that she said.

IV

He woke up feeling happy. The door of the world was open again. He made plans, vistas, futures for Honoria and himself, but suddenly he grew sad, remembering all the plans he and Helen had made. She had not planned to die. The present was the thing—work to do, and some one to love. But not to love too much, for he knew the injury that a father can do to a daughter or a mother to a son by attaching them too closely; afterward, out in the world, the child would seek in the marriage partner the same blind tenderness and, failing probably to find it, turn against love and life.

It was another bright, crisp day. He called Lincoln Peters at the bank where he worked and asked if he could count on taking Honoria when he left for Prague. Lincoln agreed that there was no reason for delay. One thing—the legal guardianship. Marion wanted to retain that a while longer. She was upset by the whole matter, and it would oil things if she felt that the situation was still in her control for another year. Charlie agreed, wanting only the tangible, visible child.

Then the question of a governess. Charlie sat in a gloomy agency and talked to a cross Bernaise and to a **buxom** Breton[20] peasant neither of whom he could have endured. There were others whom he would see tomorrow.

buxom:
full-figured

He lunched with Lincoln Peters at Griffons, trying to keep down his exultation.

"There's nothing quite like your own child," Lincoln said. "But you understand how Marion feels too."

---

20 **Bernaise . . . Breton:** persons from the French regions Béarn and Brittany, respectively

"She's forgotten how hard I worked for seven years there," Charlie said. "She just remembers one night."

"There's another thing," Lincoln hesitated. "While you and Helen were tearing around Europe throwing money away, we were just getting along. I didn't touch any of the prosperity because I never got ahead enough to carry anything but my insurance. I think Marion felt there was some kind of injustice in it—you not even working toward the end, and getting richer and richer."

"It went just as quick as it came," said Charlie.

"Yes, a lot of it stayed in the hands of chasseurs and saxophone players and maîtres d'hôtel—well, the big party's over now. I just said that to explain Marion's feeling about those crazy years. If you drop in about six o'clock tonight before Marion's too tired, we'll settle the details on the spot."

Back at his hotel, Charlie found a *pneumatique*[21] that had been redirected from the Ritz bar where Charlie had left his address for the purpose of finding a certain man.

> DEAR CHARLIE:
>
> You were so strange when we saw you the other day that I wondered if I did something to offend you. If so, I'm not conscious of it. In fact, I have thought about you too much for the last year, and it's always been in the back of my mind that I might see you if I came over here. We *did* have such good times that crazy spring, like the night you and I stole the butcher's tricycle, and the time we tried to call on the president and you had the old derby rim[22] and the wire cane. Everybody seems so old lately, but I don't feel old a bit. Couldn't we get together some time today for old time's sake? I've got a vile hang-over for the moment, but will be feeling better this afternoon and will look for you about five in the sweetshop at the Ritz.
>
> Always devotedly,
> LORRAINE.

His first feeling was one of awe that he had actually, in his mature years, stolen a tricycle and pedaled Lorraine all over the Étoile[23] between the small hours and dawn. In retrospect it was a nightmare. Locking out Helen didn't fit in with any other act of his life, but the tricycle incident did—it was one

---

21 **pneumatique:** French for "message"

22 **derby rim:** rim of a stiff felt cap called a *derby*

23 **Étoile:** the square in Paris where the Arc de Triomphe is located

of many. How many weeks or months of dissipation to arrive at that condition of utter irresponsibility?

He tried to picture how Lorraine had appeared to him then—very attractive; Helen was unhappy about it, though she said nothing. Yesterday, in the restaurant, Lorraine had seemed trite, blurred, worn away. He emphatically did not want to see her, and he was glad Alix had not given away his hotel address. It was a relief to think, instead, of Honoria, to think of Sundays spent with her and of saying good morning to her and of knowing she was there in his house at night, drawing her breath in the darkness.

piquant:
charming

At five he took a taxi and bought presents for all the Peters—a **piquant** cloth doll, a box of Roman soldiers, flowers for Marion, big linen handkerchiefs for Lincoln.

recalcitrant:
difficult to
manage

He saw, when he arrived in the apartment, that Marion had accepted the inevitable. She greeted him now as though he were a **recalcitrant** member of the family, rather than a menacing outsider. Honoria had been told she was going; Charlie was glad to see that her tact made her conceal her excessive happiness. Only on his lap did she whisper her delight and the question "When?" before she slipped away with the other children.

He and Marion were alone for a minute in the room, and on an impulse he spoke out boldly:

"Family quarrels are bitter things. They don't go according to any rules. They're not like aches or wounds; they're more like splits in the skin that won't heal because there's not enough material. I wish you and I could be on better terms."

"Some things are hard to forget," she answered. "It's a question of confidence." There was no answer to this and presently she asked, "When do you propose to take her?"

"As soon as I can get a governess. I hoped the day after tomorrow."

"That's impossible. I've got to get her things in shape. Not before Saturday."

He yielded. Coming back into the room, Lincoln offered him a drink.

"I'll take my daily whisky," he said.

It was warm here, it was a home, people together by a fire. The children felt very safe and important; the mother and father were serious, watchful. They had things to do for the children more important than his visit here. A spoonful of medicine was, after all, more important than the strained relations between Marion and himself. They were not dull people, but they were very much in the grip of life and circumstances. He wondered if he couldn't do something to get Lincoln out of his rut at the bank.

A long peal at the door-bell; the *bonne à tout faire*[24] passed through and went down the corridor. The door opened upon another long ring, and then voices, and the three in the salon looked up expectantly; Richard moved to bring the corridor within his range of vision, and Marion rose. Then the maid came back along the corridor, closely followed by the voices, which developed under the light into Duncan Schaeffer and Lorraine Quarles.

They were gay, they were hilarious, they were roaring with laughter. For a moment Charlie was astounded; unable to understand how they had **ferreted** out the Peters' address.

ferreted: searched

"Ah-h-h!" Duncan wagged his finger **roguishly** at Charlie. "Ah-h-h!"

roguishly: mischievously

They both slid down another cascade of laughter. Anxious and at a loss, Charlie shook hands with them quickly and presented them to Lincoln and Marion. Marion nodded, scarcely speaking. She had drawn back a step toward the fire; her little girl stood beside her, and Marion put an arm about her shoulder.

With growing annoyance at the intrusion, Charlie waited for them to explain themselves. After some concentration Duncan said:

"We came to invite you out to dinner. Lorraine and I insist that all this shishi business 'bout your address got to stop."

Charlie came closer to them, as if to force them backward down the corridor.

"Sorry, but I can't. Tell me where you'll be and I'll phone you in half an hour."

This made no impression. Lorraine sat down suddenly on the side of a chair, and focussing her eyes on Richard, cried, "Oh, what a nice little boy! Come here, little boy." Richard glanced at his mother, but did not move. With a perceptible shrug of her shoulders, Lorraine turned back to Charlie.

"Come and dine. Sure your cousins won' mine. See you so sel'om. Or solemn."

"I can't," said Charlie sharply. "You two have dinner and I'll phone you."

Her voice became suddenly unpleasant. "All right, we'll go. But I remember once when you hammered on my door at four A.M. I was enough of a good sport to give you a drink. Come on, Dunc." Still in slow motion, with blurred, angry faces, with uncertain feet, they retired along the corridor.

"Good night," Charlie said.

"Good night!" responded Lorraine emphatically.

---

24 *bonne à tout faire:* French for "maid"

When he went back into the salon Marion had not moved, only now her son was standing in the circle of her other arm. Lincoln was still swinging Honoria back and forth like a pendulum from side to side.

"What an outrage!" Charlie broke out. "What an absolute outrage!"

Neither of them answered. Charlie dropped into an armchair, picked up his drink, set it down again and said:

"People I haven't seen for two years having the colossal nerve—" He broke off. Marion had made the sound "Oh!" in one swift, furious breath, turned her body from him with a jerk and left the room.

Lincoln set down Honoria carefully.

"You children go in and start your soup," he said, and when they obeyed, he said to Charlie:

"Marion's not well and she can't stand shocks. That kind of people make her really physically sick."

"I didn't tell them to come here. They wormed your name out of somebody. They deliberately—"

"Well, it's too bad. It doesn't help matters. Excuse me a minute."

Left alone, Charlie sat tense in his chair. In the next room he could **monosyllables:** hear the children eating, talking in **monosyllables,** already oblivious to **one-syllable words** the scene between their elders. He heard a murmur of conversation from a farther room and then the ticking bell of a telephone receiver picked up, and in a panic he moved to the other side of the room and out of earshot.

In a minute Lincoln came back. "Look here, Charlie. I think we'd better call off dinner for tonight. Marion's in bad shape."

"Is she angry with me?"

"Sort of," he said, almost roughly. "She's not strong and—"

"You mean she's changed her mind about Honoria."

"She's pretty bitter right now. I don't know. You phone me at the bank tomorrow."

"I wish you'd explain to her I never dreamed these people would come here. I'm just as sore as you are."

"I couldn't explain anything to her now."

Charlie got up. He took his coat and hat and started down the corridor.

Then he opened the door of the dining room and said in a strange voice, "Good night, children."

Honoria rose and ran around the table to hug him.

"Good night, sweetheart," he said vaguely, and then trying to make his voice more tender, trying to **conciliate** something, "Good night, dear children."

conciliate:
soothe; appease

V

Charlie went directly to the Ritz bar with the furious idea of finding Lorraine and Duncan, but they were not there, and he realized that in any case there was nothing he could do. He had not touched his drink at the Peters', and now he ordered a whisky-and-soda. Paul came over to say hello.

"It's a great change," he said sadly. "We do about half the business we did. So many fellows I hear about back in the States lost everything, maybe not in the first crash, but then in the second. Your friend George Hardt lost every cent, I hear. Are you back in the States?"

"No. I'm in business in Prague."

"I heard that you lost a lot in the crash."

"I did," and he added grimly, "but I lost everything I wanted in the boom."

"Selling short?"

"Something like that."

Again the memory of those days swept over him like a nightmare—the people they had met travelling; the people who couldn't add a row of figures or speak a coherent sentence. The little man Helen had consented to dance with at the ship's party, who had insulted her ten feet from the table, the women and girls carried screaming with drink or drugs out of public places . . . the men who locked their wives out in the snow because the snow of '29 wasn't real snow. If you didn't want it to be snow, you just paid some money.

He went to the phone and called the Peters apartment; Lincoln answered.

"I called up because this thing is on my mind. Has Marion said anything definite?"

"Marion's sick," Lincoln answered shortly. "I know this thing isn't altogether your fault, but I can't have her go to pieces about it. I'm afraid we'll have to let it slide for six months; I can't take the chance of working her up to this state again."

"I see."

"I'm sorry, Charlie."

He went back to his table. His whisky glass was empty, but he shook his head when Alix looked at it questioningly. There wasn't much he could do now except send Honoria some things; he would send her a lot of things tomorrow. He thought rather angrily that this was just money—he had given so many people money. . . .

"No, no more," he said to another waiter. "What do I owe you?"

He would come back some day; they couldn't make him pay forever. But he wanted his child, and nothing was much good now, beside that fact. He wasn't young any more, with a lot of nice thoughts and dreams to have by himself. He was absolutely sure Helen wouldn't have wanted him to be so alone.

Read and Think Critically

Interpret, Explain, Analyze

 1. **IN MEDIAS RES** What impact does being plunged into the middle of the story without much setup have on the reader?

2. Babylon was one of the greatest cities in the ancient world; now only ruins remain. How would you interpret the **title** "Babylon Revisited"?

3. One of the **themes** of this story is that everything we say or do has consequences. Using a chart like the one below, identify some of the actions (words and deeds) and their consequences in this story. Explain whether you think there is any one comment or deed that led inevitably to the story's conclusion.

Words and Deeds	Consequences

4. Analyze the **characters** of Charlie and Marion. How are they alike? How are they different? Which do you think would be a better parent for Honoria? Why?

 5. **THE AUTHOR'S STYLE** Fitzgerald was often singled out as the spokesman for the Lost Generation of the twenties. This was the group of artists and writers who seemed to lose their purpose as the excesses of the era led up to the stock market crash and its aftermath. His work is infused with a sense of time passing and of opportunities lost. Select a passage that you think demonstrates this sense of loss. Be prepared to explain your choice.

Before You Read

Thomas Wolfe 1900–1938

About the Author

Growing up in Asheville, North Carolina, as the youngest of eight children, Thomas Wolfe became an observer of human nature early in life. The characters he encountered in the boardinghouse his mother ran turned up in his autobiographical novel, *Look Homeward, Angel*. Acclaimed by critics, the novel was nonetheless banned in the Asheville library because some of the characters so closely resembled people in the town.

A precocious student, Wolfe entered the University of North Carolina at Chapel Hill at 16 and later graduated from Harvard with a master's degree, intending to become a playwright. Eventually he became a writer of prose instead. His work was greatly influenced by Aline Bernstein, a married set and costume designer from New York with whom he had a long and turbulent relationship and upon whom he based characters in his novels.

In 1938, Wolfe died of a brain tumor caused by an undetected case of tuberculosis. He left behind large manuscripts of unpublished work from which editors gleaned two novels and a collection of short stories. One of these novels is *You Can't Go Home Again*. People familiar with Wolfe's work believe that when the first President Bush made an often-quoted reference to "a thousand points of light" in a speech, the phrase was borrowed from Wolfe's description of "ten thousand points of light" in that novel.

****

The Author's Style

Thomas Wolfe was an intensely emotional person who poured his heart and soul onto the page. Thousands of his rapidly typed and handwritten pages were eventually shaped into stories and novels, many of them recognizable as having been drawn from his own life. Wolfe's writing is full of energy, turbulence, and extremes of feeling; he has been referred to as a writer of romance and doom. The sensitive presentation of childhood and adolescence in his novel *Look Homeward,* *Angel* has been widely recognized and praised.

Wolfe was more interested in expressing his longing and passion for experience than in taking the time to carefully shape his prose—just the opposite of Hemingway's approach to fiction writing. Because the short story requires a writer to complete a coherent narrative in a limited number of pages, some readers prefer Wolfe's more carfully shaped stories to his intense but sprawling novels.

The Far
and the Near

THOMAS WOLFE

LITERARY LENS: THE FABLE A **fable** is a story meant to give the reader a single useful truth, often through marvelous elements such as talking animals. Look for the elements of a fable in this story.

On the outskirts of a little town upon a rise of land that swept back from the railway there was a tidy little cottage of white boards, trimmed vividly with green blinds. To one side of the house there was a garden neatly patterned with plots of growing vegetables, and an arbor for the grapes which ripened late in August. Before the house there were three mighty oaks which sheltered it in their clean and massive shade in summer, and to the other side there was a border of gay flowers. The whole place had an air of tidiness, thrift, and modest comfort.

Every day, a few minutes after two o'clock in the afternoon, the limited express between two cities passed this spot. At that moment the great train, having halted for a breathing-space at the town near by, was beginning to lengthen evenly into its stroke, but it had not yet reached the full drive of its terrific speed. It swung into view deliberately, swept past with a powerful swaying motion of the engine, a low smooth rumble of its heavy cars upon pressed steel, and then it vanished in the cut. For a moment the progress of the engine could be marked by heavy bellowing puffs of smoke that burst at spaced intervals above the edges of the meadow grass, and finally nothing could be heard but the solid clacking tempo of the wheels receding into the drowsy stillness of the afternoon.

Every day for more than twenty years, as the train had approached this house, the engineer had blown on the whistle, and every day, as soon as she heard this signal, a woman had appeared on the back porch of the little house and waved to him. At first she had a small child clinging to her skirts, and now this child had grown to full womanhood, and every day she, too, came with her mother to the porch and waved.

The engineer had grown old and gray in service. He had driven his great train, loaded with its weight of lives, across the land ten thousand times. His own children had grown up and married, and four times he had seen before him on the tracks the ghastly dot of tragedy converging like a cannon ball to its eclipse of horror at the boiler head[1]—a light spring wagon filled with children, with its clustered row of small stunned faces; a cheap automobile stalled upon the tracks, set with the wooden figures of people paralyzed with fear; a battered hobo walking by the rail, too deaf and old to hear the whistle's warning; and a form flung past his window with a scream—all this the man had seen and known. He had known all the grief, the joy, the peril and the labor such a man could know; he had grown seamed and weathered in his loyal service, and now, schooled by the qualities of faith and courage and humbleness that attended his labor, he had grown old, and had the grandeur and the wisdom these men have.

But no matter what peril or tragedy he had known, the vision of the little house and the women waving to him with a brave free motion of the arm had become fixed in the mind of the engineer as something beautiful and enduring, something beyond all change and ruin, and something that would always be the same, no matter what mishap, grief or error might break the iron schedule of his days.

The sight of the little house and of these two women gave him the most extraordinary happiness he had ever known. He had seen them in a thousand lights, a hundred weathers. He had seen them through the harsh bare

---

I **boiler head:** front of an engine, where water is converted into steam

light of wintry gray across the brown and frosted stubble of the earth, and he had seen them again in the green luring **sorcery** of April.

sorcery: magic

He felt for them and for the little house in which they lived such tenderness as a man might feel for his own children, and at length the picture of their lives was carved so sharply in his heart that he felt that he knew their lives completely, to every hour and moment of the day, and he resolved that one day, when his years of service should be ended, he would go and find these people and speak at last with them whose lives had been so wrought into his own.

That day came. At last the engineer stepped from a train onto the station platform of the town where these two women lived. His years upon the rail had ended. He was a pensioned[2] servant of his company, with no more work to do. The engineer walked slowly through the station and out into the streets of the town. Everything was as strange to him as if he had never seen this town before. As he walked on, his sense of bewilderment and confusion grew. Could this be the town

Train on the Desert, Thomas Hart Benton, c. 1926–28

he had passed ten thousand times? Were these the same houses he had seen so often from the high windows of his cab? It was all as unfamiliar, as disquieting as a city in a dream, and the perplexity of his spirit increased as he went on.

Presently the houses thinned into the straggling outposts of the town, and the street faded into a country road—the one on which the women lived. And the man plodded on slowly in the heat and dust. At length he stood before the house he sought. He knew at once that he had found the proper place. He saw the lordly oaks before the house, the flower beds, the garden and the arbor, and farther off, the glint of rails.

---

2 pensioned: having a pension, or retirement, fund

Yes, this was the house he sought, the place he had passed so many times, the destination he had longed for with such happiness. But now that he had found it, now that he was here, why did his hand falter on the gate; why had the town, the road, the earth, the very entrance to this place he loved turned unfamiliar as the landscape of some ugly dream? Why did he now feel this sense of confusion, doubt and hopelessness?

At length he entered by the gate, walked slowly up the path and in a moment more had mounted three short steps that led up to the porch, and was knocking at the door. Presently he heard steps in the hall, the door was opened, and a woman stood facing him.

And instantly, with a sense of bitter loss and grief, he was sorry he had come. He knew at once that the woman who stood there looking at him with a mistrustful eye was the same woman who had waved to him so many thousand times. But her face was harsh and pinched and meager, the flesh sagged wearily in sallow folds, and the small eyes peered at him with timid suspicion and uneasy doubt. All the brave freedom, the warmth and the affection that he had read into her gesture, vanished in the moment that he saw her and heard her unfriendly tongue.

And now his own voice sounded unreal and ghastly to him as he tried to explain his presence, to tell her who he was and the reason he had come. But he faltered on, fighting stubbornly against the horror of regret, confusion, disbelief that surged up in his spirit, drowning all his former joy and making his act of hope and tenderness seem shameful to him.

At length the woman invited him almost unwillingly into the house, and called her daughter in a harsh shrill voice. Then, for a brief agony of time, the man sat in an ugly little parlor, and he tried to talk while the two women stared at him with a dull, bewildered hostility, a sullen, **timorous** restraint.

timorous:
fearful

And finally, stammering a crude farewell, he departed. He walked away down the path and then along the road toward town, and suddenly he knew that he was an old man. His heart, which had been brave and confident when it looked along the familiar **vista** of the rails, was now sick with doubt and horror as it saw the strange and unsuspected visage of an earth which had always been within a stone's throw of him, and which he had never seen or known. And he knew that all the magic of that bright lost way, the vista of that shining line, the imagined corner of that small good universe of hope's desire, was gone forever, could never be got back again.

vista:
view

Read and Think Critically

Explain, Analyze, Compare and Contrast

 1. **THE FABLE** In what ways is this story both like and unlike a **fable**?

2. William Faulkner, whom you will read later in this book, once said that Wolfe's stories "put all the experience of the human heart on the head of a pin." Explain how the story demonstrates Wolfe's ability to summarize the human experience.

3. "The Far and the Near" begins with a faraway view, and then, like a movie camera, draws nearer. How does the **mood** of the story change as the focus narrows and sharpens?

4. A common **theme** of **realistic fiction** is the exposure of a dark, even evil, "reality" hiding behind the mask of a pleasant appearance. Using a chart like the one below, identify and analyze the contrasts between the themes of appearance and reality in this story.

Appearance	Reality

5. **THE AUTHOR'S STYLE** As in poetry, word choice is often crucial to the success of a short story. Compare and contrast Wolfe's choice of descriptive words in the opening three paragraphs to the descriptive words in the closing three paragraphs. Analyze the impact of Wolfe's word choice on the **mood** at these points in the story.

★★★

Before You Read

Carson McCullers 1917–1967

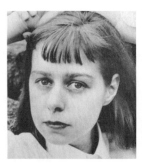

About the Author

Although her first dream was to study music at Julliard School of Music in New York City, Carson McCullers set her sights on writing instead because her parents could not afford to send her to the expensive private music school. Despite her ill health—the author contracted rheumatic fever as an adolescent and was consequently an invalid most of her life—she nonetheless focused her energies on her writing and published her first fiction, a short story, at 19. Although she lived for a time in New York and Paris after leaving home, McCullers set most of her work in the South of her youth—she was reared in Georgia.

As an adult, McCullers led a turbulent life. She was married twice to the same man. An alcoholic, she also battled severe depression. She attempted suicide but ultimately died of natural causes at the age of 50.

McCullers' work leant itself well to the stage and screen. Her novella *The Ballad of the Sad Café* and her novel *The Member of the Wedding* became stage plays. Her novels *The Heart Is a Lonely Hunter* and *Reflections in a Golden Eye* were both adapted to the screen.

****

The Author's Style

Carson McCullers began writing fiction as an adolescent, the age of many of her main characters. A key to her work is the sensitive presentation of the inner reality of these young protagonists—their needs, fears, and jealousies. The effect is particularly poignant when these characters do not fit easily into the expectations of their communities. Frankie Addams, the central character of *The Member of the Wedding*, is a young girl who "belonged to no club and was a member of nothing in the world." Such characters are rebellious, contradictory, vulnerable, and lonely; they struggle to find love and their place in life.

The narration and the dialogue in McCullers' stories develop out of common speech, precisely phrased to fit her characters. Their dialogue enables the reader to see how these characters see themselves and the world around them. McCullers uses both third-person and first-person narration, but always conveys effectively the inner moods of her "outsider" characters. Conflicts are not always acted out but shown only to the reader through naïve observations, simple descriptions, and plain, direct judgments of people and events. These are often expressed in terms of everyday comparisons and figures of speech.

Sucker

Carson McCullers

LITERARY LENS: POINT OF VIEW The author's choice of narrator, or **point of view**, determines how we learn about the characters in a short story. In "Sucker," the narrator is the main character who shares his thoughts, feelings, and story through an interior monologue. Be aware of these thoughts and feelings as you read.

It was always like I had a room to myself. Sucker slept in my bed with me but that didn't interfere with anything. The room was mine and I used it as I wanted to. Once I remember sawing a trap door in the floor. Last year when I was a sophomore in high school I tacked on my wall some pictures of girls from magazines and one of them was just in her underwear. My mother never bothered me because she had the younger kids to look after. And Sucker thought anything I did was always swell.

Whenever I would bring any of my friends back to my room all I had to do was just glance once at Sucker and he would get up from whatever he was busy with and maybe half smile at me, and leave without saying a word. He never brought kids back there. He's

★★

*N*ow that Sucker has changed so much it is a little hard to remember him as he used to be. I never imagined anything would suddenly happen that would make us both very different.

twelve, four years younger than I am, and he always knew without me even telling him that I didn't want kids that age meddling with my things.

Half the time I used to forget that Sucker isn't my brother. He's my first cousin but practically ever since I remember he's been in our family. You see his folks were killed in a wreck when he was a baby. To me and my kid sisters he was like our brother.

Sucker used to always remember and believe every word I said. That's how he got his nick-name. Once a couple of years ago I told him that if he'd jump off our garage with an umbrella it would act as a parachute and he wouldn't fall hard. He did it and busted his knee. That's just one instance. And the funny thing was that no matter how many times he got fooled he would still believe me. Not that he was dumb in other ways—it was just the way he acted with me. He would look at everything I did and quietly take it in.

There is one thing I have learned, but it makes me feel guilty and is hard to figure out. If a person admires you a lot you despise him and don't care— and it is the person who doesn't notice you that you are apt to admire. This is not easy to realize. Maybelle Watts, this senior at school, acted like she was the Queen of Sheba and even humiliated me. Yet at this same time I would have done anything in the world to get her attentions. All I could think about day and night was Maybelle until I was nearly crazy. When Sucker was a little kid and on up until the time he was twelve I guess I treated him as bad as Maybelle did me.

Now that Sucker has changed so much it is a little hard to remember him as he used to be. I never imagined anything would suddenly happen that would make us both very different. I never knew that in order to get what has happened straight in my mind I would want to think back on him as he used to be and compare and try to get things settled. If I could have seen ahead maybe I would have acted different.

I never noticed him much or thought about him and when you consider how long we have had the same room together it is funny the few things I remember. He used to talk to himself a lot when he'd think he was alone—

all about him fighting gangsters and being on ranches and that sort of kids' stuff. He'd get in the bathroom and stay as long as an hour and sometimes his voice would go up high and excited and you could hear him all over the house. Usually, though, he was very quiet. He didn't have many boys in the neighborhood to buddy with and his face had the look of a kid who is watching a game and waiting to be asked to play. He didn't mind wearing the sweaters and coats that I outgrew, even if the sleeves did flop down too big and make his wrists look as thin and white as a little girl's. That is how I remember him—getting a little bigger every year but still being the same. That was Sucker up until a few months ago when all this trouble began.

Maybelle was somehow mixed up in what happened so I guess I ought to start with her. Until I knew her I hadn't given much time to girls. Last fall she sat next to me in General Science class and that was when I first began to notice her. Her hair is the brightest yellow I ever saw and occasionally she will wear it set into curls with some sort of gluey stuff. Her fingernails are pointed and manicured and painted a shiny red. All during class I used to watch Maybelle, nearly all the time except when I thought she was going to look my way or when the teacher called on me. I couldn't keep my eyes off her hands, for one thing. They are very little and white except for that red stuff, and when she would turn the pages of her book she always licked her thumb and held out her little finger and turned very slowly. It is impossible to describe Maybelle. All the boys are crazy about her but she didn't even notice me. For one thing she's almost two years older than I am. Between periods I used to try and pass very close to her in the halls but she would hardly ever smile at me. All I could do was sit and look at her in class—and sometimes it was like the whole room could hear my heart beating and I wanted to holler or light out and run for Hell.

At night, in bed, I would imagine about Maybelle. Often this would keep me from sleeping until as late as one or two o'clock. Sometimes Sucker would wake up and ask me why I couldn't get settled and I'd tell him to hush his mouth. I suppose I was mean to him lots of times. I guess I wanted to ignore somebody like Maybelle did me. You could always tell by Sucker's face when his feelings were hurt. I don't remember all the ugly remarks I must have made because even when I was saying them my mind was on Maybelle.

That went on for nearly three months and then somehow she began to change. In the halls she would speak to me and every morning she copied my homework. At lunch time once I danced with her in the gym. One afternoon

I got up nerve and went around to her house with a carton of cigarettes. I knew she smoked in the girls' basement and sometimes outside of school—and I didn't want to take her candy because I think that's been run into the ground. She was very nice and it seemed to me everything was going to change.

It was that night when this trouble really started. I had come into my room late and Sucker was already asleep. I felt too happy and keyed up to get in a comfortable position and I was awake thinking about Maybelle a long time. Then I dreamed about her and it seemed I kissed her. It was a surprise to wake up and see the dark. I lay still and a little while passed before I could come to and understand where I was. The house was quiet and it was a very dark night.

Sucker's voice was a shock to me. "Pete? . . ."

I didn't answer anything or even move.

"You do like me as much as if I was your own brother, don't you, Pete?"

I couldn't get over the surprise of everything and it was like this was the real dream instead of the other.

"You have liked me all the time like I was your own brother, haven't you?"

"Sure," I said.

Then I got up for a few minutes. It was cold and I was glad to come back to bed. Sucker hung on to my back. He felt little and warm and I could feel his warm breathing on my shoulder.

"No matter what you did I always knew you liked me."

I was wide awake and my mind seemed mixed up in a strange way. There was this happiness about Maybelle and all that—but at the same time something about Sucker and his voice when he said these things made me take notice. Anyway I guess you understand people better when you are happy than when something is worrying you. It was like I had never really thought about Sucker until then. I felt I had always been mean to him. One night a few weeks before I had heard him crying in the dark. He said he had lost a boy's beebee gun and was scared to let anybody know. He wanted me to tell him what to do. I was sleepy and tried to make him hush and when he wouldn't I kicked at him. That was just one of the things I remembered. It seemed to me he had always been a lonesome kid. I felt bad.

There is something about a dark cold night that makes you feel close to someone you're sleeping with. When you talk together it is like you are the only people awake in the town.

"You're a swell kid, Sucker," I said.

It seemed to me suddenly that I did like him more than anybody else I knew—more than any other boy, more than my sisters, more in a certain way even than Maybelle. I felt good all over and it was like when they play sad music in the movies. I wanted to show Sucker how much I really thought of him and make up for the way I had always treated him.

We talked for a good while that night. His voice was fast and it was like he had been saving up these things to tell me for a long time. He mentioned that he was going to try to build a canoe and that the kids down the block wouldn't let him in on their football team and I don't know what all. I talked some too and it was a good feeling to think of him taking in everything I said so seriously. I even spoke of Maybelle a little, only I made out like it was her who had been running after me all this time. He asked questions about high school and so forth. His voice was excited and he kept on talking fast like he could never get the words out in time. When I went to sleep he was still talking and I could still feel his breathing on my shoulder, warm and close.

During the next couple of weeks I saw a lot of Maybelle. She acted as though she really cared for me a little. Half the time I felt so good I hardly knew what to do with myself.

But I didn't forget about Sucker. There were a lot of old things in my bureau drawer I'd been saving—boxing gloves and Tom Swift books and second rate fishing tackle. All this I turned over to him. We had some more talks together and it was really like I was knowing him for the first time. When there was a long cut on his cheek I knew he had been monkeying around with this new first razor set of mine, but I didn't say anything. His face seemed different now. He used to look timid and sort of like he was afraid of a whack over the head. That expression was gone. His face, with those wide-open eyes and his ears sticking out and his mouth never quite shut, had the look of a person who is surprised and expecting something swell.

Once I started to point him out to Maybelle and tell her he was my kid brother. It was an afternoon when a murder mystery was on at the movie. I had earned a dollar working for my Dad and I gave Sucker a quarter to go and get candy and so forth. With the rest I took Maybelle. We were sitting near the back and I saw Sucker come in. He began to stare at the screen the minute he stepped past the ticket man and he stumbled down the aisle without noticing where he was going. I started to punch Maybelle but couldn't quite make up my mind. Sucker looked a little silly—walking like a drunk with his eyes glued to the movie. He was wiping his reading glasses on his shirt tail and his knickers flopped down. He went on until he got to the first few rows where the kids usually sit. I never did punch Maybelle. But I got to thinking it was good to have both of them at the movie with the money I earned.

I guess things went on like this for about a month or six weeks. I felt so good I couldn't settle down to study or put my mind on anything. I wanted to be friendly with everybody. There were times when I just had to talk to some person. And usually that would be Sucker. He felt as good as I did. Once he said: "Pete, I am gladder that you are like my brother than anything else in the world."

Then something happened between Maybelle and me. I never have figured out just what it was. Girls like her are hard to understand. She began to act different toward me. At first I wouldn't let myself believe this and tried to think it was just my imagination. She didn't act glad to see me anymore. Often she went out riding with this fellow on the football team who owns this yellow roadster. The car was the color of her hair and after school she would ride off with him, laughing and looking into his face. I couldn't think of anything to do about it and she was on my mind all day and night. When I did get a chance to go out with her she was snippy and didn't seem to notice me. This made me feel like something was the matter—I would worry about my shoes clopping too loud on the floor or the fly of my pants, or the bumps on my chin. Sometimes when Maybelle was around, a devil would get into me and I'd hold my face stiff and call grown men by their last names without the Mister and say rough things. In the night I would wonder what made me do all this until I was too tired for sleep.

At first I was so worried I just forgot about Sucker. Then later he began to get on my nerves. He was always hanging around until I would get back from high school, always looking like he had something to say to me or wanted me to tell him. He made me a magazine rack in his Manual Training class and one week he saved his lunch money and bought me three packs of cigarettes. He couldn't seem to take it in that I had things on my mind and didn't want to fool with him. Every afternoon it would be the same—him in my room with this waiting expression on his face. Then I wouldn't say anything or I'd maybe answer him rough-like and he would finally go on out.

I can't divide that time up and say this happened one day and that the next. For one thing I was so mixed up the weeks just slid along into each other and I felt like Hell and didn't care. Nothing definite was said or done. Maybelle still rode around with this fellow in his yellow roadster and sometimes she would smile at me and sometimes not. Every afternoon I went from one place to another where I thought she would be. Either she would act almost nice and I would begin thinking how things would finally clear up and she would care for me—or else she'd behave so that if she hadn't been a girl I'd have wanted to grab her by that white little neck and choke her. The more ashamed I felt for making a fool of myself the more I ran after her.

Sucker kept getting on my nerves more and more. He would look at me as though he sort of blamed me for something, but at the same time knew that it wouldn't last long. He was growing fast and for some reason began to stutter when he talked. Sometimes he had nightmares or would throw up his breakfast. Mom got him a bottle of cod liver oil.

Then the finish came between Maybelle and me. I met her going to the drug store and asked for a date. When she said no I remarked something sarcastic. She told me she was sick and tired of my being around and that she had never cared a rap about me. She said all that. I just stood there and didn't answer anything. I walked home very slowly.

For several afternoons I stayed in my room by myself. I didn't want to go anywhere or talk to anyone. When Sucker would come in and look at me sort of funny I'd yell at him to get out. I didn't want to think of Maybelle and I sat at my desk reading *Popular Mechanics* or whittling at a toothbrush rack I was making. It seemed to me I was putting that girl out of my mind pretty well.

But you can't help what happens to you at night. That is what made things how they are now.

You see a few nights after Maybelle said those words to me I dreamed about her again. It was like that first time and I was squeezing Sucker's arm so tight I woke him up. He reached for my hand.

"Pete, what's the matter with you?"

All of a sudden I felt so mad my throat choked—at myself and the dream and Maybelle and Sucker and every single person I knew. I remembered all the times Maybelle had humiliated me and everything bad that had ever happened. It seemed to me for a second that nobody would ever like me but a sap like Sucker.

"Why is it we aren't buddies like we were before? Why—?"

"Shut your damn trap!" I threw off the cover and got up and turned on the light. He sat in the middle of the bed, his eyes blinking and scared.

Afterward I could remember the change in Sucker's face. Slowly that blank look went away and he closed his mouth. His eyes got narrow and his fists shut.

There was something in me and I couldn't help myself. I don't think anybody ever gets that mad but once. Words came without me knowing what they would be. It was only afterward that I could remember each thing I said and see it all in a clear way.

"Why aren't we buddies? Because you're the dumbest slob I ever saw! Nobody cares anything about you! And just because I felt sorry for you sometimes and tried to act decent don't think I give a damn about a dumb-bunny like you!"

If I'd talked loud or hit him it wouldn't have been so bad. But my voice was slow and like I was very calm. Sucker's mouth was part way open and he looked as though he'd knocked his funny bone. His face was white and sweat came out on his forehead. He wiped it away with the back of his hand and for a minute his arm stayed raised that way as though he was holding something away from him.

"Don't you know a single thing? Haven't you ever been around at all? Why don't you get a girl friend instead of me? What kind of a sissy do you want to grow up to be anyway?"

I didn't know what was coming next. I couldn't help myself or think.

Sucker didn't move. He had on one of my pajama jackets and his neck stuck out skinny and small. His hair was damp on his forehead.

"Why do you always hang around me? Don't you know when you're not wanted?"

Afterward I could remember the change in Sucker's face. Slowly that blank look went away and he closed his mouth. His eyes got narrow and his fists shut. There had never been such a look on him before. It was like every second he was getting older. There was a hard look to his eyes you don't see usually in a kid. A drop of sweat rolled down his chin and he didn't notice. He just sat there with those eyes on me and he didn't speak and his face was hard and didn't move.

"No you don't know when you're not wanted. You're too dumb. Just like your name—a dumb Sucker."

It was like something had busted inside me. I turned off the light and sat down in the chair by the window. My legs were shaking and I was so tired I could have bawled. The room was cold and dark. I sat there for a long time

Winter, Andrew Wyeth, 1946, The North Carolina Museum of Art, Raleigh

and smoked a squashed cigarette I had saved. Outside the yard was black and quiet. After a while I heard Sucker lie down.

I wasn't mad any more, only tired. It seemed awful to me that I had talked like that to a kid only twelve. I couldn't take it all in. I told myself I would go over to him and try to make it up. But I just sat there in the cold until a long time had passed. I planned how I could straighten it out in the morning. Then, trying not to squeak the springs, I got back in bed.

Sucker was gone when I woke up the next day. And later when I wanted to apologize as I had planned he looked at me in this new hard way so that I couldn't say a word.

All of that was two or three months ago. Since then Sucker has grown faster than any boy I ever saw. He's almost as tall as I am and his bones have gotten heavier and bigger. He won't wear any of my old clothes any more and has bought his first pair of long pants—with some leather suspenders to hold them up. Those are just the changes that are easy to see and put into words.

Our room isn't mine at all any more. He's gotten up this gang of kids and they have a club. When they aren't digging trenches in some vacant lot and fighting they are always in my room. On the door there is some foolishness written in Mercurochrome[1] saying "Woe to the Outsider who Enters" and signed with crossed bones and their secret initials. They have rigged up a radio and every afternoon it blares out music. Once as I was coming in I heard a boy telling something in a loud voice about what he saw in the back of his big brother's automobile. I could guess what I didn't hear. *That's what her and my brother do. It's the truth—parked in the car.* For a minute Sucker looked surprised and his face was almost like it used to be. Then he got hard and tough again. "Sure, dumbbell. We know all that." They didn't notice me. Sucker began telling them how in two years he was planning to be a trapper in Alaska.

But most of the time Sucker stays by himself. It is worse when we are alone together in the room. He sprawls across the bed in those long corduroy pants with the suspenders and just stares at me with that hard, half-sneering look. I fiddle around my desk and can't get settled because of those eyes of his. And the thing is I just have to study because I've gotten three bad cards this term already. If I flunk English I can't graduate next year. I don't want to be a bum and I just have to get my mind on it. I don't care a flip for Maybelle or any particular girl any more and it's only this thing between Sucker and me that is the trouble now. We never speak except when we have to before the family. I don't even want to call him Sucker any more and unless I forget I call him by his real name, Richard. At night I can't study with him in the room and I have to hang around the drug store, smoking and doing nothing, with the fellows who loaf there.

More than anything I want to be easy in my mind again. And I miss the way Sucker and I were for a while in a funny, sad way that before this I never would have believed. But everything is so different that there seems to be nothing I can do to get it right. I've sometimes thought if we could have it out in a big fight that would help. But I can't fight him because he's four years younger. And another thing—sometimes this look in his eyes makes me almost believe that if Sucker could he would kill me.

---

1 **Mercurochrome:** trademark name for a red antiseptic that is meant to be brushed on skin

Read and Think Critically

Explain, Describe, Analyze

1. **POINT OF VIEW** Occasionally, the **narrator** stops telling his story and expresses his feelings directly. For example, near the end of the story he says, "More than anything I want to be easy in my mind again." Find another example of the narrator's sharing of his feelings. Explain what these statements tell you about the narrator.

2. The **plot** of a story is usually built around a problem or issue facing the main **character**. Describe the problem that drives the plot in "Sucker."

3. "There was something in me and I couldn't help myself," Pete says of the incident with his cousin. Do you think it is true that people sometimes can't help themselves from doing or saying things they later deeply regret? Why or why not?

4. Why does Pete, the narrator, start addressing his cousin by his given name, Richard, instead of the nickname Sucker near the end of the story?

5. **THE AUTHOR'S STYLE** Critics consider McCullers a master of showing the inner lives of lonely people. Analyze how **point of view**, **dialogue**, and **characterization** help create an atmosphere of isolation and loneliness.

Before You Read

John Steinbeck 1902–1968

About the Author

"The ancient commission of the writer has not changed," John Steinbeck said when he received the Nobel Prize for Literature in 1962. "He is charged with exposing our many grievous faults and failures, with dredging up to the light our dark and dangerous dreams for the purpose of improvement."

Reared in a middle-class family in California, the setting for much of his fiction, Steinbeck learned about hard work and the potential for failure. He attended Stanford University but dropped out and worked as a caretaker, fruit picker, and fisherman before achieving success as a novelist. He was a passionate writer of the Proletarian Literature of the thirties, literature in which the most important characters are working class.

Steinbeck's *The Grapes of Wrath*, considered a landmark of 20th-century literature, won the Pulitzer Prize despite the controversy it caused. The book follows a poor family traveling from Oklahoma to California in search of work during the Depression. It displeased officials in both states with its depiction of labor conditions. Other well-known works include *Of Mice and Men, East of Eden,* and *The Red Pony.*

★★★★★★★★★★★

The Author's Style

Factual, unemotional descriptions of setting are typical of Steinbeck's style. In his work, the natural world often defines the terms under which his characters live. The author's flat, matter-of-fact tone is created by relatively short, declarative sentences. It is clear from the outset that the lives of Steinbeck's people are determined by external forces as much as human will. In part for this reason, and in part because they usually lack extensive education, these characters speak briefly and simply. Their eloquence comes from simple language and everyday dialect used without apology. Some Steinbeck characters express themselves through gestures as much as through speech itself.

Occasionally, Steinbeck develops an object from nature into a controlling symbol in a story or novel—a pearl, a turtle, and, in the story you are about to read, chrysanthemums.

The Chrysanthemums

JOHN STEINBECK

LITERARY LENS: SYMBOLISM A **symbol** is an object that has meaning in itself, but it also has a deeper, more abstract meaning within the context of a work of literature. Pay attention to the **symbolism** in this story.

The high grey-flannel fog of winter closed off the Salinas Valley[1] from the sky and from all the rest of the world. On every side it sat like a lid on the mountains and made of the great valley a closed pot. On the broad, level land floor the gang ploughs bit deep and left the black earth shining like metal where the shares had cut. On the foot-hill ranches across the Salinas River, the yellow stubble fields seemed to be bathed in pale cold sunshine, but there was no sunshine in the valley now in December. The thick willow scrub along the river flamed with sharp and positive yellow leaves.

It was a time of quiet and of waiting. The air was cold and tender. A light wind blew up from the southwest so that the farmers

---

1 **Salinas Valley:** a region in western California

were mildly hopeful of a good rain before long; but fog and rain do not go together.

Across the river, on Henry Allen's foot-hill ranch there was little work to be done, for the hay was cut and stored and the orchards were ploughed up to receive the rain deeply when it should come. The cattle on the higher slopes were becoming shaggy and rough-coated.

Elisa Allen, working in her flower garden, looked down across the yard and saw Henry, her husband, talking to two men in business suits. The three of them stood by the tractor-shed, each man with one foot on the side of the little Fordson. They smoked cigarettes and studied the machine as they talked.

Elisa watched them for a moment and then went back to her work. She was thirty-five. Her face was lean and strong and her eyes were as clear as water. Her figure looked blocked and heavy in her gardening costume, a man's black hat pulled low down over her eyes, clod-hopper shoes, a figured print dress almost completely covered by a big corduroy apron with four big pockets to hold the snips, the trowel and scratcher, the seeds and the knife she worked with. She wore heavy leather gloves to protect her hands while she worked.

She was cutting down the old year's chrysanthemum stalks with a pair of short and powerful scissors. She looked down toward the men by the tractor-shed now and then. Her face was eager and mature and handsome; even her work with the scissors was overeager, over-powerful. The chrysanthemum stems seemed too small and easy for her energy.

She brushed a cloud of hair out of her eyes with the back of her glove, and left a smudge of earth on her cheek in doing it. Behind her stood the neat white farmhouse with red geraniums close-banked around it as high as the windows. It was a hard-swept-looking little house, with hard-polished windows, and a clean mud-mat on the front steps.

Elisa cast another glance toward the tractor-shed. The strangers were getting into their Ford coupé. She took off a glove and put her strong fingers down into the forest of new green chrysanthemum sprouts that were growing around the old roots. She spread the leaves and looked down among the close-growing stems. No aphids were there, no sow bugs or snails or cutworms. Her terrier fingers destroyed such pests before they could get started.

Elisa started at the sound of her husband's voice. He had come near quietly, and he leaned over the wire fence that protected her flower garden from cattle and dogs and chickens.

"At it again," he said. "You've got a strong new crop coming."

Elisa straightened her back and pulled on the gardening glove again. "Yes. They'll be strong this coming year." In her tone and on her face there was a little smugness.

"You've got a gift with things," Henry observed. "Some of those yellow chrysanthemums you had this year were ten inches across. I wish you'd work out in the orchard and raise some apples that big."

Her eyes sharpened. "Maybe I could do it, too. I've a gift with things, all right. My mother had it. She could stick anything in the ground and make it grow. She said it was having planters' hands that knew how to do it."

"Well, it sure works with flowers," he said.

"Henry, who were those men you were talking to?"

"Why, sure, that's what I came to tell you. They were from the Western Meat Company. I sold those thirty head of three-year-old steers. Got nearly my own price, too."

"Good," she said. "Good for you."

"And I thought," he continued, "I thought how it's Saturday afternoon, and we might go into Salinas for dinner at a restaurant, and then to a picture show—to celebrate, you see."

"Good," she repeated. "Oh, yes. That will be good."

Henry put on his joking tone. "There's fights tonight. How'd you like to go to the fights?"

"Oh, no," she said breathlessly. "No, I wouldn't like fights."

"Just fooling, Elisa. We'll go to a movie. Let's see. It's two now. I'm going to take Scotty and bring down those steers from the hill. It'll take us maybe two hours. We'll go in town about five and have dinner at the Cominos Hotel. Like that?"

"Of course I'll like it. It's good to eat away from home."

"All right, then. I'll go get up a couple of horses."

She said: "I'll have plenty of time to transplant some of these sets, I guess."

She heard her husband calling Scotty down by the barn. And a little later she saw the two men ride up the pale yellow hillside in search of the steers.

There was a little square sandy bed kept for rooting the chrysanthemums. With her trowel she turned the soil over and over, and smoothed it and patted it firm. Then she dug ten parallel trenches to receive the sets. Back at the chrysanthemum bed she pulled out the little crisp shoots, trimmed off the leaves of each one with her scissors and laid it on a small orderly pile.

A squeak of wheels and plod of hoofs came from the road. Elisa looked up. The country road ran along the dense bank of willows and cottonwoods that bordered the river, and up this road came a curious vehicle, curiously drawn. It was an old spring-wagon, with a round canvas top on it like the cover of a prairie schooner. It was drawn by an old bay horse and a little grey-and-white burro. A big stubble-bearded man sat between the cover flaps and drove the crawling team. Underneath the wagon, between the hind wheels, a lean and rangy mongrel dog walked sedately. Words were painted on the canvas, in clumsy, crooked letters. "Pots, pans, knives, sisors, lawn mores, Fixed." Two rows of articles, and the triumphantly definitive "Fixed" below. The black paint had run down in little sharp points beneath each letter.

Elisa, squatting on the ground, watched to see the crazy, loose-jointed wagon pass by. But it didn't pass. It turned into the farm road in front of her house, crooked old wheels **skirling** and squeaking. The rangy dog darted from between the wheels and ran ahead. Instantly the two ranch shepherds flew out at him. Then all three stopped, and with stiff and quivering tails, with taut straight legs, with **ambassadorial** dignity, they slowly circled, sniffing daintily. The caravan pulled up to Elisa's wire fence and stopped. Now the newcomer dog, feeling outnumbered, lowered his tail and retired under the wagon with raised hackles and bared teeth.

skirling: making a shrill sound

ambassadorial: formal; diplomatic

The man on the wagon seat called out: "That's a bad dog in a fight when he gets started."

Elisa laughed. "I see he is. How soon does he generally get started?"

The man caught up her laughter and echoed it heartily. "Sometimes not for weeks and weeks," he said. He climbed stiffly down, over the wheel. The horse and the donkey drooped like unwatered flowers.

Elisa saw that he was a very big man. Although his hair and beard were greying, he did not look old. His worn black suit was wrinkled and spotted with grease. The laughter had disappeared from his face and eyes the moment his laughing voice ceased. His eyes were dark, and they were full of the brooding that gets in the eyes of teamsters and of sailors. The calloused hands he rested on the wire fence were cracked, and every crack

The laughter had disappeared from his face and eyes the moment his laughing voice ceased. His eyes were dark, and they were full of the brooding that gets in the eyes of teamsters and of sailors.

was a black line. He took off his battered hat.

"I'm off my general road, ma'am," he said. "Does this dirt road cut over across the river to the Los Angeles highway?"

Elisa stood up and shoved the thick scissors in her apron pocket. "Well, yes, it does, but it winds around and then fords the river. I don't think your team could pull through the sand."

He replied with some **asperity**: "It might surprise you what them beasts can pull through."

asperity: roughness

"When they get started?" she asked.

He smiled for a second. "Yes. When they get started."

"Well," said Elisa, "I think you'll save time if you go back to the Salinas road and pick up the highway there."

He drew a big finger down the chicken wire and made it sing. "I ain't in any hurry, ma'am. I go from Seattle to San Diego and back every year. Takes all my time. About six months each way. I aim to follow nice weather."

Elisa took off her gloves and stuffed them in the apron pocket with the scissors. She touched the under edge of her man's hat, searching for fugitive hairs. "That sounds like a nice kind of way to live," she said.

He leaned confidentially over the fence. "Maybe you noticed the writing on my wagon. I mend pots and sharpen knives and scissors. You got any of them things to do?"

"Oh, no," she said quickly. "Nothing like that." Her eyes hardened with resistance.

"Scissors is the worst thing," he explained. "Most people just ruin scissors trying to sharpen 'em, but I know how. I got a special tool. It's a little bobbit kind of thing, and patented. But it sure does the trick."

"No. My scissors are all sharp."

"All right, then. Take a pot," he continued earnestly, "a bent pot, or a pot with a hole. I can make it like new so you don't have to buy no new ones. That's a saving for you."

"No," she said shortly. "I tell you I have nothing like that for you to do."

His face fell to an exaggerated sadness. His voice took on a whining undertone. "I ain't had a thing to do today. Maybe I won't have no supper tonight. You see I'm off my regular road. I know folks on the highway clear from Seattle to San Diego. They save their things for me to sharpen up because they know I do it so good and save them money."

"I'm sorry," Elisa said irritably. "I haven't anything for you to do."

His eyes left her face and fell to searching the ground. They roamed about until they came to the chrysanthemum bed where she had been working. "What's them plants, ma'am?"

The irritation and resistance melted from Elisa's face. "Oh, those are chrysanthemums, giant whites and yellows. I raise them every year, bigger than anybody around here."

"Kind of a long-stemmed flower? Looks like a quick puff of colored smoke?" he asked.

"That's it. What a nice way to describe them."

"They smell kind of nasty till you get used to them," he said.

"It's a good bitter smell," she retorted, "not nasty at all."

He changed his tone quickly. "I like the smell myself."

"I had ten-inch blooms this year," she said.

The man leaned farther over the fence. "Look. I know a lady down the road a piece, has got the nicest garden you ever seen. Got nearly every kind of flower but not chrysanthemums. Last time I was mending a copper-bottom washtub for her (that's a hard job but I do it good), she said to me: 'If you ever run acrost some nice chrysanthemums I wish you'd try to get me a few seeds.' That's what she told me."

Elisa's eyes grew alert and eager. "She couldn't have known much about chrysanthemums. You *can* raise them from seed, but it's much easier to root the little sprouts you see here."

"Oh," he said. "I s'pose I can't take none to her, then."

"Why yes you can," Elisa cried. "I can put some in damp sand, and you can carry them right along with you. They'll take root in the pot if you keep them damp. And then she can transplant them."

"She'd sure like to have some, ma'am. You say they're nice ones?"

"Beautiful," she said. "Oh, beautiful." Her eyes shone. She tore off the battered hat and shook out her dark pretty hair. "I'll put them in a flower-pot, and you can take them right with you. Come into the yard."

While the man came through the picket gate Elisa ran excitedly along the geranium-bordered path to the back of the house. And she returned carrying a big red flower-pot. The gloves were forgotten now. She kneeled on the ground by the starting bed and dug up the sandy soil with her fingers and scooped it into the bright new flower-pot. Then she picked up the little pile of shoots she had prepared. With her strong fingers she pressed them into the sand and **tamped** around them with her knuckles. The man stood over her. "I'll tell you what to do," she said. "You remember so you can tell the lady."

"Yes, I'll try to remember."

"Well, look. These will take root in about a month. Then she must set them out, about a foot apart in good rich earth like this, see?" She lifted a handful of dark soil for him to look at. "They'll grow fast and tall. Now remember this: In July tell her to cut them down, about eight inches from the ground."

"Before they bloom?" he asked.

"Yes, before they bloom." Her face was tight with eagerness. "They'll grow right up again. About the last of September the buds will start."

She stopped and seemed perplexed. "It's the budding that takes the most care," she said hesitantly. "I don't know how to tell you." She looked deep into his eyes, searchingly. Her mouth opened a little, and she seemed to be listening. "I'll try to tell you," she said. "Did you ever hear of planting hands?"

*T*he man leaned farther over the fence. "Look. I know a lady down the road a piece, has got the nicest garden you ever seen. Got nearly every kind of flower but not chrysanthemums."

"Can't say I have, ma'am."

"Well, I can only tell you what it feels like. It's when you're picking off the buds you don't want. Everything goes right down into your fingertips. You watch your fingers work. They do it themselves. You can feel how it is. They pick and pick the buds. They never make a mistake. They're with the plant. Do you see? Your fingers and the plant. You can feel that, right up your arm. They know. They never make a mistake. You can feel it. When you're like that you can't do anything wrong. Do you see that? Can you understand that?"

She was kneeling on the ground looking up at him. Her breast swelled passionately.

The man's eyes narrowed. He looked away self-consciously.

"Maybe I know," he said. "Sometimes in the night in the wagon there—"

Elisa's voice grew husky. She broke in on him: "I've never lived as you do, but I know what you mean. When the night is dark—why, the stars are sharp-pointed, and there's quiet. Why, you rise up and up! Every pointed star gets driven into your body. It's like that. Hot and sharp and—lovely."

Kneeling there, her hand went out toward his legs in the greasy black trousers. Her hesitant fingers almost touched the cloth. Then her hand dropped to the ground. She crouched low like a **fawning** dog.

fawning:
cringing

He said: "It's nice, just like you say. Only when you don't have no dinner, it ain't."

She stood up then, very straight, and her face was ashamed. She held the flower-pot out to him and placed it gently in his arms. "Here. Put it in your wagon, on the seat, where you can watch it. Maybe I can find something for you to do."

At the back of the house she dug in the can pile and found two old and battered aluminum saucepans. She carried them back and gave them to him. "Here, maybe you can fix these."

His manner changed. He became professional. "Good as new I can fix them." At the back of his wagon he set a little anvil, and out of an oily toolbox dug a small machine hammer. Elisa came through the gate to watch him while he pounded out the dents in the kettles. His mouth grew sure and knowing. At a difficult part of the work he sucked his underlip.

"You sleep right in the wagon?" Elisa asked.

"Right in the wagon, ma'am. Rain or shine I'm dry as a cow in there."

"It must be nice," she said. "It must be very nice. I wish women could do such things."

"It ain't the right kind of a life for a woman."

Her upper lip raised a little, showing her teeth. "How do you know? How can you tell?" she said.

"I don't know, ma'am," he protested. "Of course I don't know. Now here's your kettles, done. You don't have to buy no new ones."

"How much?"

"Oh, fifty cents'll do. I keep my prices down and my work good. That's why I have all them satisfied customers up and down the highway."

Elisa brought him a fifty-cent piece from the house and dropped it in his hand. "You might be surprised to have a rival some time. I can sharpen scissors, too. And I can beat the dents out of little pots. I could show you what a woman might do."

He put his hammer back in the oily box and shoved the little anvil out of sight. "It would be a lonely life for a woman, ma'am, and a scarey life, too, with animals creeping under the wagon all night." He climbed over the single-tree, steadying himself in the seat, picked up the lines. "Thank you kindly ma'am," he said. "I'll do like you told me; I'll go back and catch the Salinas road."

"Mind," she called, "if you're long in getting there, keep the sand damp."

"Sand, ma'am? . . . Sand? Oh, sure. You mean around the chrysanthemums. Sure I will." He clucked his tongue. The beasts leaned luxuriously into their collars. The mongrel dog took his place between the back wheels. The wagon turned and crawled out the entrance road and back the way it had come, along the river.

Elisa stood in front of her wire fence watching the slow progress of the caravan. Her shoulders were straight, her head thrown back, her eyes half-closed, so that the scene came vaguely into them. Her lips moved silently, forming the words "Good-bye—good-bye." Then she whispered: "That's a bright direction. There's a glowing there." The sound of her whisper startled her. She shook herself free and looked about to see whether anyone had been listening. Only the dogs had heard. They lifted their heads toward her from their sleeping in the dust, and then stretched out their chins and settled asleep again. Elisa turned and ran hurriedly into the house.

In the kitchen she reached behind the stove and felt the water tank. It was full of hot water from the noonday cooking. In the bathroom she tore off her soiled clothes and flung them into the corner. And then she scrubbed herself with a little block of pumice,[2] legs and thighs, loins and chest and arms, until her skin was scratched and red. When she had dried herself she stood in front of a mirror in her bedroom and looked at her body. She tightened her stomach and threw out her chest. She turned and looked over her shoulders at her back.

After a while she began to dress, slowly. She put on her newest underclothing and her nicest stockings and the dress which was the symbol of her prettiness. She worked carefully on her hair, penciled her eyebrows and rouged her lips.

Before she was finished she heard the little thunder of hoofs and the shouts of Henry and his helper as they drove the red steers into the corral. She heard the gate bang shut and set herself for Henry's arrival.

> *E*lisa stood in front of her wire fence watching the slow progress of the caravan. Her shoulders were straight, her head thrown back, her eyes half-closed, so that the scene came vaguely into them.

---

2 **pumice:** finely powdered volcanic glass used to smooth and polish

The Chrysanthemums

His step sounded on the porch. He entered the house calling: "Elisa, where are you?"

"In my room, dressing. I'm not ready. There's hot water for your bath. Hurry up. It's getting late."

When she heard him splashing in the tub, Elisa laid his dark suit on the bed, and shirt and socks and tie beside it. She stood his polished shoes on

EARTH PATTERNS, RINALDO CUNEO, 1932, THE OAKLAND MUSEUM OF CALIFORNIA

the floor beside the bed. Then she went to the porch and sat primly and stiffly down. She looked toward the river road where the willow-line was still yellow with frosted leaves so that under the high grey fog they seemed a thin band of sunshine. This was the only color in the grey afternoon. She sat unmoving for a long time. Her eyes blinked rarely.

Henry came banging out of the door, shoving his tie inside his vest as he came. Elisa stiffened and her face grew tight. Henry stopped short and looked at her. "Why—why, Elisa. You look so nice!"

"Nice? You think I look nice? What do you mean by 'nice'?"

Henry blundered on. "I don't know. I mean you look different, strong and happy."

"I am strong? Yes, strong. What do you mean 'strong'?"

He looked bewildered. "You're playing some kind of a game," he said helplessly. "It's a kind of a play. You look strong enough to break a calf over your knee, happy enough to eat it like a watermelon."

For a second she lost her rigidity. "Henry! Don't talk like that. You didn't know what you said." She grew complete again. "I'm strong," she boasted. "I never knew before how strong."

Henry looked down toward the tractor-shed, and when he brought his eyes back to her, they were his own again. "I'll get out the car. You can put on your coat while I'm starting."

Elisa went into the house. She heard him drive to the gate and idle down his motor, and then she took a long time to put on her hat. She pulled it here and pressed it there. When Henry turned the motor off she slipped into her coat and went out.

The little roadster bounced along on the dirt road by the river, raising the birds and driving the rabbits into the brush. Two cranes flapped heavily over the willow-line and dropped into the river-bed.

Far ahead on the road Elisa saw a dark speck. She knew.

She tried not to look as they passed it, but her eyes would not obey. She whispered to herself sadly: "He might have thrown them off the road. That wouldn't have been much trouble, not very much. But he kept the pot," she explained. "He had to keep the pot. That's why he couldn't get them off the road."

> "*I'm strong*," she boasted. "I never knew before how strong."

The roadster turned a bend and she saw the caravan ahead. She swung full around toward her husband so she could not see the little covered wagon and the mismatched team as the car passed them.

In a moment it was over. The thing was done. She did not look back.

She said loudly, to be heard above the motor: "It will be good, tonight, a good dinner."

"Now you've changed again," Henry complained. He took one hand from the wheel and patted her knee. "I ought to take you in to dinner oftener. It would be good for both of us. We get so heavy out on the ranch."

"Henry," she asked, "could we have wine at dinner?"

"Sure we could. Say! That will be fine."

She was silent for a while; then she said: "Henry, at those prizefights, do the men hurt each other very much?"

"Sometimes a little, not often. Why?"

"Well, I've read how they break noses, and blood runs down their chests. I've read how the fighting gloves get heavy and soggy with blood."

He looked around at her. "What's the matter, Elisa? I didn't know you read things like that." He brought the car to a stop, then turned to the right over the Salinas River bridge.

"Do any women ever go to the fights?" she asked.

"Oh, sure, some. What's the matter, Elisa? Do you want to go? I don't think you'd like it, but I'll take you if you really want to go."

She relaxed limply in the seat. "Oh, no. No. I don't want to go. I'm sure I don't." Her face was turned away from him. "It will be enough if we can have wine. It will be plenty." She turned up her coat collar so he could not see that she was crying weakly—like an old woman.

Read and Think Critically

Conclude, Infer, Analyze

 1. **SYMBOLISM** What do you think are some of the ideas or feelings the chrysanthemums might **symbolize**? Support your conclusions with examples from the text.

2. Make an **inference** about why Elisa is so anxious to share her chrysanthemums with the woman up the road.

3. Steinbeck begins creating an ominous atmosphere as soon as the pot fixer approaches. Use a chart like the one below to trace clues from the text such as **dialogue** and gestures. In the second column, chart what the readers' resulting expectations are. An example has been done for you.

Clue	Expectation
The fixer's manner is jovial, but his eyes are brooding.	*He is a dangerous person who will harm Elisa.*

4. Analyze how the **character** of Elisa changes over the course of the story. What does she gain and then lose? Support your answer with details from the text.

5. **THE AUTHOR'S STYLE** People's lives in Steinbeck's fiction are often ruled by outside forces. Thus, **setting** is very important. How do the land and the ranch govern the characters' lives in this story? Find two specific examples.

Before You Read

Eudora Welty 1909–2001

About the Author

An illness at the age of seven had an influence on Eudora Welty's decision to become a writer. In her autobiography, *One Writer's Beginnings,* the beloved Southern writer recalls the months she was confined to bed: "As I read away, I was Rapunzel, or the Goose Girl, or the Princess Labam in one of the *Thousand and One Nights* who mounted the roof of her palace every night and of her own radiance faithfully lighted the whole city. . . ."

Born in Jackson, Mississippi, where she lived most of her life, Welty set much of her work in the South. She worked early in her career as a newspaper reporter and photographer.

Welty was known as an unassuming writer

who had an instinctive style, a profound empathy for others, and a down-to-earth sense of humor. In the introduction to her collection of stories *A Curtain of Green*, the author is reported to have said: "I haven't a literary life at all . . . I do feel that the people and things I love are of a true and human world, and there is no clutter about them. . . . I would not understand a literary life." The email software program Eudora is named in tribute to the author and to the story you are about to read.

****

The Author's Style

Eudora Welty's fiction always conveys a distinct sense of personality and place. Her characters—often quirky, obsessive, introspective, and disconcerting—typically live in small-town, rural Mississippi. This "local color" aspect of her work is created in part through her skillful use of dialect and everyday language. Her creation of a narrative tone that we associate with gossip and innuendo helps intensify the local color.

In reading Welty's stories it is always helpful to pay close attention to what family and community conversation reveal in the way of hostility and affection. Welty's families are peculiar and universal at the same time—in their dreams, funny habits, jealousies, and expressions of human nature. The humor and comic ironies of her stories have much to do with her characters understanding considerably less about what their own words reveal than do Welty's readers.

Sometimes Welty's characters behave so oddly that we are inclined to write them off as crackpots. But when we find their comments and conversations compelling enough to eavesdrop on, we find ourselves asking what Welty might be saying about the rest of us through this particular family.

Why I Live at the P.O.

E U D O R A   W E L T Y

> **LITERARY LENS: CHARACTERIZATION** Welty is known for her
> skillful **characterization**. Take a close look at the personal qualities
> of this story's narrator.

I was getting along fine with Mama, Papa-Daddy, and Uncle
Rondo until my sister Stella-Rondo just separated from her
husband and came back home again. Mr. Whitaker! Of course
I went with Mr. Whitaker first, when he first appeared here in
China Grove, taking "Pose Yourself" photos, and Stella-Rondo
broke us up. Told him I was one-sided. Bigger on one side
than the other, which is a deliberate, calculated falsehood: I'm
the same. Stella-Rondo is exactly twelve months to the day younger
than I am and for that reason she's spoiled.

She's always had anything in the world she wanted and then
she'd throw it away. Papa-Daddy give her this gorgeous Add-a-Pearl
necklace when she was eight years old and she threw it away playing baseball when she was nine, with only two pearls.

So as soon as she got married and moved away from home the first thing she did was separate! From Mr. Whitaker! This photographer with the popeyes she said she trusted. Came home from one of those towns up in Illinois and to our complete surprise brought this child of two.

Mama said she like to made her drop dead for a second. "Here you had this marvelous blonde child and never so much as wrote your mother a word about it," says Mama. "I'm thoroughly ashamed of you." But of course she wasn't.

So Papa-Daddy l-a-y-s down his knife and fork! He's real rich. Mama says he is, he says he isn't. So he says, "Have I heard correctly? You don't understand why I don't cut off my beard?"

Stella-Rondo just calmly takes off this *hat*, I wish you could see it. She says, "Why, Mama, Shirley-T.'s adopted, I can prove it."

"How?" says Mama, but all I says was, "H'm!" There I was over the hot stove, trying to stretch two chickens over five people and a completely unexpected child into the bargain, without one moment's notice.

"What do you mean—'H'm'?" says Stella-Rondo, and Mama says, "I heard that, Sister."

I said that oh, I didn't mean a thing, only that whoever Shirley-T. was, she was the spit-image of Papa-Daddy if he'd cut off his beard, which of course he'd never do in the world. Papa-Daddy's Mama's papa and sulks.

Stella-Rondo got furious! She said, "Sister, I don't need to tell you you got a lot of nerve and always did have and I'll thank you to make no future reference to my adopted child whatsoever."

"Very well," I said. "Very well, very well. Of course I noticed at once she looks like Mr. Whitaker's side too. That frown. She looks like a cross between Mr. Whitaker and Papa-Daddy."

"Well, all I can say is she isn't."

"She looks exactly like Shirley Temple to me," says Mama, but Shirley-T. just ran away from her.

So the first thing Stella-Rondo did at the table was turn Papa-Daddy against me.

"Papa-Daddy," she says. He was trying to cut up his meat. "Papa-Daddy!" I was taken completely by surprise. Papa-Daddy is about a million years old and's got this long-long beard. "Papa-Daddy, Sister says she fails to under-stand why you don't cut off your beard."

So Papa-Daddy l-a-y-s down his knife and fork! He's real rich. Mama says he is, he says he isn't. So he says, "Have I heard correctly? You don't understand why I don't cut off my beard?"

"Why," I says, "Papa-Daddy, of course I understand, I did not say any such a thing, the idea!"

He says, "Hussy!"

I says, "Papa-Daddy, you know I wouldn't any more want you to cut off your beard than the man in the moon. It was the farthest thing from my mind! Stella-Rondo sat there and made that up while she was eating breast of chicken."

But he says, "So the postmistress fails to understand why I don't cut off my beard. Which job I got you through my influence with the government. 'Bird's nest'—is that what you call it?"

Not that it isn't the next to smallest P.O. in the entire state of Mississippi.

I says, "Oh, Papa-Daddy," I says, "I didn't say any such a thing, I never dreamed it was a bird's nest, I have always been grateful though this is the next to smallest P.O. in the state of Mississippi, and I do not enjoy being referred to as a hussy by my own grandfather."

But Stella-Rondo says, "Yes, you did say it too. Anybody in the world could of heard you, that had ears."

"Stop right there," says Mama, looking at *me*.

So I pulled my napkin straight back through the napkin ring and left the table.

As soon as I was out of the room Mama says, "Call her back, or she'll starve to death," but Papa-Daddy says, "This is the beard I started growing on the Coast when I was fifteen years old." He would of gone on till night-fall if Shirley-T. hadn't lost the Milky Way she ate in Cairo.[1]

So Papa-Daddy says, "I am going out and lie in the hammock, and you can all sit here and remember my words: I'll never cut off my beard as long as I live, even one inch, and I don't appreciate it in you at all." Passed right by me in the hall and went straight out and got in the hammock.

It would be a holiday. It wasn't five minutes before Uncle Rondo sud-denly appeared in the hall in one of Stella-Rondo's flesh-colored kimonos,[2]

---

1 **Cairo:** Cairo, Illinois

2 **kimono:** a loose robe worn as a dressing gown, imitated from robes originally worn by the Japanese

all cut on the bias, like something Mr. Whitaker probably thought was gorgeous.

"Uncle Rondo!" I says. "I didn't know who that was! Where are you going?"

"Sister," he says, "get out of my way, I'm poisoned."

"If you're poisoned stay away from Papa-Daddy," I says. "Keep out of the hammock. Papa-Daddy will certainly beat you on the head if you come within forty miles of him. He thinks I deliberately said he ought to cut off his beard after he got me the P.O., and I've told him and told him and told him, and he acts like he just don't hear me. Papa-Daddy must of gone stone deaf."

"He picked a fine day to do it then," says Uncle Rondo, and before you could say "Jack Robinson"[3] flew out in the yard.

What he'd really done, he'd drunk another bottle of that prescription. He does it every single Fourth of July as sure as shooting, and it's horribly expensive. Then he falls over in the hammock and snores. So he insisted on zigzagging right on out to the hammock, looking like a half-wit.

Papa-Daddy woke up with this horrible yell and right there without moving an inch he tried to turn Uncle Rondo against me. I heard every word he said. Oh, he told Uncle Rondo I didn't learn to read till I was eight years old and he didn't see how in the world I ever got the mail put up at the P.O., much less read it all, and he said if Uncle Rondo could only fathom the lengths he had gone to get me that job! And he said on the other hand he thought Stella-Rondo had a brilliant mind and deserved credit for getting out of town. All the time he was just lying there swinging as pretty as you please and looping out his beard, and poor Uncle Rondo was *pleading* with him to slow down the hammock, it was making him as dizzy as a witch to watch it. But that's what Papa-Daddy likes about a hammock. So Uncle Rondo was too dizzy to get turned against me for the time being. He's Mama's only brother and is a good case of a one-track mind. Ask anybody. A certified pharmacist.

Just then I heard Stella-Rondo raising the upstairs window. While she was married she got this peculiar idea that it's cooler with the windows shut and locked. So she has to raise the window before she can make a soul hear her outdoors.

So she raises the window and says, "*Oh!*" You would have thought she was mortally wounded.

---

3 **before you could say "Jack Robinson":** an idiom that indicates immediacy. Jack Robinson was disputably a man who changed his mind frequently, dropping in on neighbors and leaving almost before they realized he was there.

Uncle Rondo and Papa-Daddy didn't even look up, but kept right on with what they were doing. I had to laugh.

I flew up the stairs and threw the door open! I says, "What in the wide world's the matter, Stella-Rondo? You mortally wounded?"

"No," she says, "I am not mortally wounded but I wish you would do me the favor of looking out that window there and telling me what you see."

So I shade my eyes and look out the window.

"I see the front yard," I says.

"Don't you see any human beings?" she says.

> *All* the time he was just lying there swinging as pretty as you please and looping out his beard, and poor Uncle Rondo was pleading with him to slow down the hammock, it was making him as dizzy as a witch to watch it.

"I see Uncle Rondo trying to run Papa-Daddy out of the hammock," I says. "Nothing more. Naturally, it's so suffocating-hot in the house, with all the windows shut and locked, everybody who cares to stay in their right mind will have to go out and get in the hammock before the Fourth of July is over."

"Don't you notice anything different about Uncle Rondo?" asks Stella-Rondo.

"Why, no, except he's got on some terrible-looking flesh-colored contraption I wouldn't be found dead in, is all I can see," I says.

"Never mind, you won't be found dead in it, because it happens to be part of my trousseau,[4] and Mr. Whitaker took several dozen photographs of me in it," says Stella-Rondo. "What on earth could Uncle Rondo *mean* by wearing part of my trousseau out in the broad open daylight without saying so much as 'Kiss my foot,' *knowing* I only got home this morning after my separation and hung my negligee[5] up on the bathroom door, just as nervous as I could be?"

"I'm sure I don't know, and what do you expect me to do about it?" I says. "Jump out the window?"

"No, I expect nothing of the kind. I simply declare that Uncle Rondo looks like a fool in it, that's all," she says. "It makes me sick to my stomach."

---

4 **trousseau:** the clothing and linens provided by her family and assembled by a bride before her marriage

5 **negligee:** a loose dressing gown made of soft fabric and worn by women

"Well, he looks as good as he can," I says. "As good as anybody in reason could." I stood up for Uncle Rondo, please remember. And I said to Stella-Rondo, "I think I would do well not to criticize so freely if I were you and came home with a two-year-old child I had never said a word about, and no explanation whatever about my separation."

"I asked you the instant I entered this house not to refer one more time to my adopted child, and you gave me your word of honor you would not," was all Stella-Rondo would say, and started pulling out every one of her eyebrows with some cheap Kress[6] tweezers.

So I merely slammed the door behind me and went down and made some green-tomato pickle. Somebody had to do it. Of course Mama had turned both the Negroes loose; she always said no earthly power could hold one anyway on the Fourth of July, so she wouldn't even try. It turned out that Jaypan fell in the lake and came within a very narrow limit of drowning.

So Mama trots in. Lifts up the lid and says, "H'm! Not very good for your Uncle Rondo in his precarious condition, I must say. Or poor little adopted Shirley-T. Shame on you!"

That made me tired. I says, "Well, Stella-Rondo had better thank her lucky stars it was her instead of me came trotting in with that very peculiar-looking child. Now if it had been me that trotted in from Illinois and brought a peculiar-looking child of two, I shudder to think of the reception I'd of got, much less controlled the diet of an entire family."

"But you must remember, Sister, that you were never married to Mr. Whitaker in the first place and didn't go up to Illinois to live," says Mama, shaking a spoon in my face. "If you had I would of been just as overjoyed to see you and your little adopted girl as I was to see Stella-Rondo, when you wound up with your separation and came on back home."

"You would not," I says.

"Don't contradict me, I would," says Mama.

But I said she couldn't convince me though she talked till she was blue in the face. Then I said, "Besides, you know as well as I do that that child is not adopted."

"She most certainly is adopted," says Mama, stiff as a poker.

I says, "Why, Mama, Stella-Rondo had her just as sure as anything in this world, and just too stuck up to admit it."

"Why, Sister," said Mama. "Here I thought we were going to have a

---

6 **Kress:** a chain of dime stores

pleasant Fourth of July, and you start right out not believing a word your own baby sister tells you!"

"Just like Cousin Annie Flo. Went to her grave denying the facts of life," I reminded Mama.

"I told you if you ever mentioned Annie Flo's name I'd slap your face," says Mama, and slaps my face.

"All right, you wait and see," I says.

"I," says Mama, "I prefer to take my children's word for anything when it's humanly possible." You ought to see Mama, she weighs two hundred pounds and has real tiny feet.

Just then something perfectly horrible occurred to me.

"Mama," I says, "can that child talk?" I simply had to whisper! "Mama, I wonder if that child can be—you know—in any way? Do you realize?" I says, "that she hasn't spoken one single, solitary word to a human being up to this minute? This is the way she looks," I says, and I looked like this.

Well, Mama and I just stood there and stared at each other. It was horrible!

"I remember well that Joe Whitaker frequently drank like a fish," says Mama. "I believed to my soul he drank *chemicals*." And without another word she marches to the foot of the stairs and calls Stella-Rondo.

"Stella-Rondo? O-o-o-o-o! Stella-Rondo!"

"What?" says Stella-Rondo from upstairs. Not even the grace to get up off the bed.

"Can that child of yours talk?" asks Mama.

Stella-Rondo says, "Can she what?"

"Talk! Talk!" says Mama. "Burdyburdyburdyburdy!"

So Stella-Rondo yells back, "Who says she can't talk?"

"Sister says so," says Mama.

"You didn't have to tell me, I know whose word of honor don't mean a thing in this house," says Stella-Rondo.

And in a minute the loudest Yankee voice I ever heard in my life yells out, "OE'm Pop-OE the Sailor-r-r-r Ma-a-an!" and then somebody jumps up and down in the upstairs hall. In another second the house would of fallen down.

> "*I* remember well that Joe Whitaker frequently drank like a fish," says Mama. "I believed to my soul he drank *chemicals*." And without another word she marches to the foot of the stairs and calls Stella-Rondo.

"Not only talks, she can tap-dance!" calls Stella-Rondo. "Which is more than some people I won't name can do."

"Why, the little precious darling thing!" Mama says, so surprised. "Just as smart as she can be!" Starts talking baby talk right there. Then she turns on me. "Sister, you ought to be thoroughly ashamed! Run upstairs this instant and apologize to Stella-Rondo and Shirley-T."

"Apologize for what?" I says. "I merely wondered if the child was normal, that's all. Now that she's proved she is, why, I have nothing further to say."

But Mama just turned on her heel and flew out, furious. She ran right upstairs and hugged the baby. She believed it was adopted. Stella-Rondo hadn't done a thing but turn her against me from upstairs while I stood there helpless over the hot stove. So that made Mama, Papa-Daddy and the baby all on Stella-Rondo's side.

Next, Uncle Rondo.

I must say that Uncle Rondo has been marvelous to me at various times in the past and I was completely unprepared to be made to jump out of my skin, the way it turned out. Once Stella-Rondo did something perfectly horrible to him—broke a chain letter from Flanders Field[7]—and he took the radio back he had given her and gave it to me. Stella-Rondo was furious! For six months we all had to call her Stella instead of Stella-Rondo, or she wouldn't answer. I always thought Uncle Rondo had all the brains of the entire family. Another time he sent me to Mammoth Cave,[8] with all expenses paid.

But this would be the day he was drinking that prescription, the Fourth of July.

So at supper Stella-Rondo speaks up and says she thinks Uncle Rondo ought to try to eat a little something. So finally Uncle Rondo said he would try a little cold biscuits and ketchup, but that was all. So *she* brought it to him.

disport:
frolic; play
around

"Do you think it wise to **disport** with ketchup in Stella-Rondo's flesh-colored kimono?" I says. Trying to be considerate! If Stella-Rondo couldn't watch out for her trousseau, somebody had to.

"Any objections?" asks Uncle Rondo, just about to pour out all the ketchup.

"Don't mind what she says, Uncle Rondo," says Stella-Rondo. "Sister has

---

7 Flanders Field: WWI battlefield in Belgium where American soldiers are buried. In 1927, nine days after making his trans-Atlantic flight, Charles Lindbergh flew over the cemetery during Memorial Day ceremonies, dropping poppies.

8 Mammoth Cave: Located in Mammoth Cave National Park in southcentral Kentucky, the Mammoth Cave system is the largest known cave system in the world.

been devoting this solid afternoon to sneering out my bedroom window at the way you look."

"What's that?" says Uncle Rondo. Uncle Rondo has got the most terrible temper in the world. Anything is liable to make him tear the house down if it comes at the wrong time.

So Stella-Rondo says, "Sister says, 'Uncle Rondo certainly does look like a fool in that pink kimono!'"

Do you remember who it was really said that?

Uncle Rondo spills out all the ketchup and jumps out of his chair and tears off the kimono and throws it down on the dirty floor and puts his foot on it. It had to be sent all the way to Jackson to the cleaners and repleated.

"So that's your opinion of your Uncle Rondo, is it?" he says. "I look like a fool, do I? Well, that's the last straw. A whole day in this house with nothing to do, and then to hear you come out with a remark like that behind my back!"

"I didn't say any such of a thing, Uncle Rondo," I says, "and I'm not saying who did, either. Why, I think you look all right. Just try to take care of yourself and not talk and eat at the same time," I says. "I think you better go lie down."

"Lie down my foot," says Uncle Rondo. I ought to of known by that he was fixing to do something perfectly horrible.

So he didn't do anything that night in the **precarious** state he was in— just played Casino with Mama and Stella-Rondo and Shirley-T. and gave Shirley-T. a nickel with a head on both sides. It tickled her nearly to death, and she called him "Papa." But at 6:30 A.M. the next morning, he threw a whole five-cent package of some unsold one-inch firecrackers from the store as hard as he could into my bedroom and then every one went off. Not one bad one in the string. Anybody else, there'd be one that wouldn't go off.

> **precarious:** uncertain; dangerous

Well, I'm just terribly susceptible to noise of any kind, the doctor has always told me I was the most sensitive person he had ever seen in his whole life, and I was simply **prostrated**. I couldn't eat! People tell me they heard it as far as the cemetery, and old Aunt Jep Patterson, that had been holding her own so good, thought it was Judgment Day and she was going to meet her whole family. It's usually so quiet here.

> **prostrated:** exhausted; flattened

And I'll tell you it didn't take me any longer than a minute to make up my mind what to do. There I was with the whole entire house on Stella-Rondo's side and turned against me. If I have anything at all I have pride.

So I just decided I'd go straight down to the P.O. There's plenty of room there in the back, I says to myself.

Well! I made no bones about letting the family catch on to what I was up to. I didn't try to conceal it.

The first thing they knew, I marched in where they were all playing Old Maid and pulled the electric oscillating fan out by the plug, and everything got real hot. Next I snatched the pillow I'd done the needlepoint on right off the davenport from behind Papa-Daddy. He went "Ugh!" I beat Stella-Rondo up the stairs and finally found my charm bracelet in her bureau drawer under a picture of Nelson Eddy[9].

piecing:
picking at;
snacking on

"So that's the way the land lies," says Uncle Rondo. There he was, **piecing** on the ham. "Well, Sister, I'll be glad to donate my army cot if you got any place to set it up, providing you'll leave right this minute and let me get some peace." Uncle Rondo was in France.

"Thank you kindly for the cot and 'peace' is hardly the word I would select if I had to resort to firecrackers at 6:30 A.M. in a young girl's bedroom," I says to him. "And as to where I intend to go, you seem to forget my position as postmistress of China Grove, Mississippi," I says. "I've always got the P.O."

Well, that made them all sit up and take notice.

I went out front and started digging up some four-o'clocks to plant around the P.O.

"Ah-ah-ah!" says Mama, raising the window. "Those happen to be my four-o'clocks. Everything planted in that star is mine. I've never known you to make anything grow in your life."

"Very well," I says. "But I take the fern. Even you, Mama, can't stand there and deny that I'm the one watered that fern. And I happen to know where I can send in a box top and get a packet of one thousand mixed seeds, no two the same kind, free."

"Oh, where?" Mama wants to know.

But I says, "Too late. You 'tend to your house, and I'll 'tend to mine. You hear things like that all the time if you know how to listen to the radio. Perfectly marvelous offers. Get anything you want free."

So I hope to tell you I marched in and got that radio, and they could of all bit a nail in two, especially Stella-Rondo, that it used to belong to, and she well knew she couldn't get it back, I'd sue for it like a shot. And I very politely took the sewing-machine motor I helped pay the most on to give Mama for Christmas back in 1929, and a good big calendar, with the first-aid remedies

---

9 **Nelson Eddy:** (1901–1967) an opera and Hollywood musical star of the 1920s and '30s who went on to perform as part of a famous traveling nightclub trio

on it. The thermometer and the Hawaiian ukulele certainly were rightfully mine, and I stood on the step-ladder and got all my watermelon-rind preserves and every fruit and vegetable I'd put up, every jar. Then I began to pull the tacks out of the bluebird wall vases on the archway to the dining room.

"Who told you you could have those, Miss Priss?" says Mama, fanning as hard as she could.

INTERIOR, WALKER EVANS, 1934, THE METROPOLITAN MUSEUM OF ART

"I bought 'em and I'll keep track of 'em," I says. "I'll tack 'em up one on each side the post-office window, and you can see 'em when you come to ask me for your mail, if you're so dead to see 'em."

"Not I! I'll never darken the door to that post office again if I live to be a hundred," Mama says. "Ungrateful child! After all the money we spent on you at the Normal."

"Me either," says Stella-Rondo. "You can just let my mail lie there and *rot*, for all I care. I'll never come and relieve you of a single, solitary piece."

"I should worry," I says. "And who you think's going to sit down and write you all those big fat letters and postcards, by the way? Mr. Whitaker? Just because he was the only man ever dropped down in China Grove and you got him—unfairly—is he going to sit down and write you a lengthy correspondence after you come home giving no rhyme nor reason whatsoever for your separation and no explanation for the presence of that child? I may not have your brilliant mind, but I fail to see it."

So Mama says, "Sister, I've told you a thousand times that Stella-Rondo simply got homesick, and this child is far too big to be hers," and she says, "Now, why don't you all just sit down and play Casino?"

Then Shirley-T. sticks out her tongue at me in this perfectly horrible way. She has no more manners than the man in the moon. I told her she was going to cross her eyes like that some day and they'd stick.

"It's too late to stop me now," I says. "You should have tried that yesterday. I'm going to the P.O. and the only way you can possibly see me is to visit me there."

So Papa-Daddy says, "You'll never catch me setting foot in that post office, even if I should take a notion into my head to write a letter some place." He says, "I won't have you reachin' out of that little old window with a pair of shears and cuttin' off any beard of mine. I'm too smart for you!"

"We all are," says Stella-Rondo.

But I said, "If you're so smart, where's Mr. Whitaker?"

So then Uncle Rondo says, "I'll thank you from now on to stop reading all the orders I get on postcards and telling everybody in China Grove what you think is the matter with them," but I says, "I draw my own conclusions and will continue in the future to draw them." I says, "If people want to write their inmost secrets on penny postcards, there's nothing in the wide world you can do about it, Uncle Rondo."

"And if you think we'll ever *write* another postcard you're sadly mistaken," says Mama.

"Cutting off your nose to spite your face then," I says. "But if you're all determined to have no more to do with the U.S. mail, think of this: What will Stella-Rondo do now, if she wants to tell Mr. Whitaker to come after her?"

"Wah!" says Stella-Rondo. I knew she'd cry. She had a conniption fit right there in the kitchen.

"It will be interesting to see how long she holds out," I says. "And now— I am leaving."

"Good-bye," says Uncle Rondo.

"Oh, I declare," says Mama, "to think that a family of mine should quarrel on the Fourth of July, or the day after, over Stella-Rondo leaving old Mr. Whitaker and having the sweetest little adopted child! It looks like we'd all be glad!"

"Wah!" says Stella-Rondo, and has a fresh conniption fit.

"He left *her*—you mark my words," I says. "That's Mr. Whitaker. I know

FRAME HOUSES,
WALKER EVANS, 1936,
THE METROPOLITAN
MUSEUM OF ART

Mr. Whitaker. After all, I knew him first. I said from the beginning he'd up and leave her. I foretold every single thing that's happened."

"Where did he go?" asks Mama.

"Probably to the North Pole, if he knows what's good for him," I says.

But Stella-Rondo just bawled and wouldn't say another word. She flew to her room and slammed the door.

"Now look what you've gone and done, Sister," says Mama. "You go apologize."

"I haven't got time, I'm leaving," I says.

"Well, what are you waiting around for?" asks Uncle Rondo.

So I just picked up the kitchen clock and marched off, without saying "Kiss my foot" or anything, and never did tell Stella-Rondo good-bye.

There was a Cnigger[10] girl going along on a little wagon right in front.

"Nigger girl," I says, "come help me haul these things down the hill, I'm going to live in the post office."

Took her nine trips in her express wagon. Uncle Rondo came out on the porch and threw her a nickel.

*A*nd that's the last I've laid eyes on any of my family or my family laid eyes on me for five solid days and nights. Stella-Rondo may be telling the most horrible tales in the world about Mr. Whitaker, but I haven't heard them. As I tell everybody, I draw my own conclusions.

But oh, I like it here. It's ideal, as I've been saying. You see, I've got everything cater-cornered, the way I like it. Hear the radio? All the war news. Radio, sewing machine, book ends, ironing board and that great big piano lamp—peace, that's what I like. Butter-bean vines planted all along the front where the strings are.

Of course, there's not much mail. My family are naturally the main people in China Grove, and if they prefer to vanish from the face of the earth, for all the mail they get or the mail they write, why, I'm not going to open my mouth. Some of the folks here in town are taking up for me and some turned against me. I know which is which. There are always people who will quit buying stamps just to get on the right side of Papa-Daddy.

But here I am, and here I'll stay. I want the world to know I'm happy.

And if Stella-Rondo should come to me this minute, on bended knees, and *attempt* to explain the incidents of her life with Mr. Whitaker, I'd simply put my fingers in both my ears and refuse to listen.

---

10 **nigger:** Although used by authors to reflect common speech of earlier time periods, this term for African Americans is extremely offensive and racist.

Read and Think Critically

Judge, Explain, Analyze

1. **CHARACTERIZATION** Some readers have said that Sister, the teller of this story, is an "**unreliable narrator**"—one who twists the truth and comes to false conclusions. Do you agree? Make a judgment about the reliability of the narrator. Support your answer with evidence from the story.

2. Readers of this story often wonder what, if anything, has caused Sister's hostility toward her family members, and why she chooses to dwell on her grievances. Use a chart like the one below to note how Sister relates to each member of her family. Explain why you think she feels and acts as she does.

Family Member	Sister's Attitude, Descriptions, and Actions
Papa-Daddy	*Sister wants to find favor with him but also seems to resent him.*
Stella-Rondo	
Shirley Temple	
Mama	
Uncle Rondo	

3. Besides her writing, Welty also worked as a photographer for the Works Progress Administration. A photographer's interest in focus and detail can be seen in her fiction. Find a scene in the story that you think would make a telling snapshot of this eccentric family. Be prepared to explain how your "snapshot" reveals the **characters** in it.

4. The members of the family in this story are memorably eccentric, yet they share some of the problems and concerns of all families. Analyze the story and explain some **universal** problems you find.

5. **THE AUTHOR'S STYLE** Welty is known as a **local color** writer. Local color writing had its origins in the 1880s with such writers as Mark Twain and Bret Harte. They attempted to accurately depict the speech, dress, and mannerisms of a certain place. Local color writers often emphasized eccentric characters and used humor and innuendo to distinguish the region they were depicting. Detail some of the aspects of "Why I Live at the P.O." that make it an example of local color writing.

Before You Read

Ralph Ellison 1914–1994

About the Author

Ralph Ellison's father had such high literary hopes for him that he named him after the poet Ralph Waldo Emerson. Unfortunately, Ellison's father died when the author was a boy and so couldn't witness his son's success. After his father died, Ellison's mother went to work as a house cleaner in Oklahoma City, where Ellison grew up. She brought home used books from her employers, encouraging a love of reading.

As a young man, Ellison studied music and became a fine trumpet player but was denied entrance into the navy band. Such early experiences with racism helped shape his fiction.

After a move to New York, he studied sculpture and was mentored in his writing by Richard Wright, author of *Black Boy*, who helped him publish his early work. This led to a period in Rome as a fellow of the American Academy of Arts and Letters, followed by a return to the United States, where Ellison continued to write while teaching at colleges.

Known primarily as a short story writer and essayist, Ellison's only novel, *Invisible Man*, won the National Book Award for fiction in 1953.

★★★★★★★★★★★

The Author's Style

Ralph Ellison was a path-breaking writer with a talent for addressing the issue of race in America in imaginative ways. His stories often develop complex metaphors to explore racial conflict, especially in the stories "King of the Bingo Game" and "The Black Ball," as well as in his novel *Invisible Man*.

A key feature of Ellison's style is a tone of pathos, a sense of the helplessness and frustration his African American characters experience because of bigotry. Often discrimination in Ellison's stories is based on arbitrary distinctions of "blackness," "brownness," and "whiteness." The author's frustration is expressed in the irony that pervades his stories. This is especially true when his first-person narrators are naively unaware of, or stubbornly resistant to, the messages they are being sent by those around them, both black and white. In the following story, "black ball" is used as both a noun and a verb.

In essays and in his novel *Invisible Man,* Ellison shows the sustaining power of music, particularly jazz and the blues, for forging identity and sustaining African American life.

The Black Ball

RALPH ELLISON

LITERARY LENS: WORD CHOICE Ellison wrote this short story before the Civil Rights movement addressed issues of race and class in American society. Consider how his **word choice** helps you understand the precarious social standing of the narrator.

I had rushed through the early part of the day mopping the lobby, placing fresh sand in the tall green jars, sweeping and dusting the halls, and emptying the trash to be burned later on in the day into the incinerator. And I had stopped only once to chase out after a can of milk for Mrs. Johnson, who had a new baby and who was always nice to my boy. I had started at six o'clock, and around eight I ran out to the quarters where we lived over the garage to dress the boy and give him his fruit and cereal. He was very thoughtful sitting there in his high chair and paused several times with his spoon midway to his mouth to watch me as I chewed my toast.

"What's the matter, son?"

"Daddy, am I black?"

Voices of Modernism

The Black Ball

343

"Of course not, you're brown. You know you're not black."

"Well yesterday Jackie said I was so black."

"He was just kidding. You mustn't let them kid you, son."

"Brown's much nicer than white, isn't it, Daddy?"

[He was four, a little brown boy in blue rompers,[1] and when he talked and laughed with imaginary playmates, his voice was soft and round in its accents like those of most Negro Americans.]

"Some people think so. But American is better than both, son."

"Is it, Daddy?"

"Sure it is. Now forget this talk about you being black, and Daddy will be back as soon as he finishes his work."

I gave special attention to that brass because for Berry, the manager, the luster of these brass panels and door handles was the measure of all my industry. It was near time for him to arrive.

I left him to play with his toys and a book of pictures until I returned. He was a pretty nice fellow, as he used to say after particularly quiet afternoons while I tried to study, and for which quietness he expected a treat of candy or a "picture movie," and I often let him alone while I attended to my duties in the apartments.

I had gone back and started doing the brass on the front doors when a fellow came up and stood watching from the street. He was lean and red in the face with that redness that comes from a long diet of certain foods. You see much of it in the deep South, and here in the Southwest it is not uncommon. He stood there watching, and I could feel his eyes in my back as I polished the brass.

I gave special attention to that brass because for Berry, the manager, the luster of these brass panels and door handles was the measure of all my industry. It was near time for him to arrive.

"Good morning, John," he would say, looking not at me but at the brass.

"Good morning, sir," I would say, looking not at him but at the brass. Usually his face was reflected there. For him, I *was* there. Besides that brass, his money, and the half-dozen or so plants in his office, I don't believe he had any other real interests in life.

---

1 **rompers:** a one-piece outfit worn by children, mostly for play

There must be no flaws this morning. Two fellows who worked at the building across the street had already been dismissed because whites had demanded their jobs, and with the boy at that age needing special foods and me planning to enter school again next term, I couldn't afford to allow something like that out on the sidewalk to spoil my chances. Especially since Berry had told one of my friends in the building that he didn't like that "damned educated nigger."

I was so concerned with the brass that when the fellow spoke, I jumped with surprise.

"Howdy," he said. The expected drawl was there. But something was missing, something usually behind that kind of drawl.

"Good morning."

"Looks like you working purty hard over that brass."

"It gets pretty dirty overnight."

That part wasn't missing. When they did have something to say to us, they always became familiar.

"You been working here long?" he asked, leaning against the column with his elbow.

"Two months."

I turned my back to him as I worked.

"Any other colored folks working here?"

As I turned, picking up the bottle to pour more polish into my rag, he pulled a tobacco sack from the pocket of his old blue coat. I noticed his hands were scarred as though they had been burned.

"I'm the only one," I lied. There were two others. It was none of his business anyway.

"Have much to do?"

"I have enough," I said. Why, I thought, doesn't he go on in and ask for the job? Why bother me? Why tempt me to choke him? Doesn't he know we aren't afraid to fight his kind out this way?

As I turned, picking up the bottle to pour more polish into my rag, he pulled a tobacco sack from the pocket of his old blue coat. I noticed his hands were scarred as though they had been burned.

"Ever smoke Durham?" he asked.

"No thank you," I said.

He laughed.

"Not used to anything like that, are you?"

"Not used to what?"

A little more from this guy and I would see red.

"Fellow like me offering a fellow like you something besides a rope."

I stopped to look at him. He stood there smiling with the sack in his outstretched hand. There were many wrinkles around his eyes, and I had to smile in return. In spite of myself I had to smile.

UNTITLED
RUTH MARTEN

"Sure you won't smoke some Durham?"

"No thanks," I said.

He was fooled by the smile. A smile couldn't change things between my kind and his.

"I'll admit it ain't much," he said. "But it's a helluva lot different."

I stopped the polishing again to see what it was he was trying to get after.

"But," he said, "I've got something really worth a lot; that is, if you're interested."

"Let's hear it," I said.

Here, I thought, is where he tries to put one over on old "George."

"You see, I come out from the union and we intend to organize all the building-service help in this district. Maybe you been reading 'bout it in the papers?"

"I saw something about it, but what's it to do with me?"

"Well, first place we'll make 'em take some of this work off you. It'll mean shorter hours and higher wages, and better conditions in general."

"What you really mean is that you'll get in here and bounce me out. Unions don't want Negro members."

"You mean *some* unions don't. It used to be that way, but things have changed."

"Listen, fellow. You're wasting your time and mine. Your damn unions are like everything else in the country—for whites only. What ever caused *you* to give a damn about a Negro anyway? Why should *you* try to organize Negroes?"

His face had become a little white.

"See them hands?"

He stretched out his hands.

"Yes," I said, looking not at his hands but at the color draining from his face.

"Well, I got them scars in Macon County, Alabama, for saying a colored friend of mine was somewhere else on a day he was supposed to have raped a woman. He was, too, 'cause I was with him. Me and him was trying to borrow some seed fifty miles away when it happened—if it did happen. They made them scars with a gasoline torch and run me out of the county 'cause they said I tried to help a nigger make a white woman out a lie. That same night they lynched him and burned down his house. They did that to him and this to me, and both of us was fifty miles away."

> "I quit the country and came to town. First it was in Arkansas and now it's here. And the more I move around, the more I see, and the more I see, the more I work."

He was looking down at his outstretched hands as he talked.

"God," was all I could say. I felt terrible when I looked closely at his hands for the first time. It must have been hell. The skin was drawn and puckered and looked as though it had been fried. Fried hands.

"Since that time I learned a lot," he said, "I been at this kinda thing. First it was the croppers, and when they got to know me and made it too hot, I quit the country and came to town. First it was in Arkansas and now it's here. And the more I move around, the more I see, and the more I see, the more I work."

He was looking into my face now, his eyes blue in his red skin. He was looking very earnestly. I said nothing. I didn't know what to say to that. Perhaps he was telling the truth; I didn't know. He was smiling again.

"Listen," he said. "Now, don't you go trying to figger it all out right now. There's going to be a series of meetings at this number starting tonight, and I'd like mighty much to see you there. Bring any friends along you want to."

★★★

He handed me a card with a number and 8 P.M. sharp written on it. He smiled as I took the card and made as if to shake my hand but turned and walked down the steps to the street. I noticed that he limped as he moved away.

"*G*ood morning, John," Mr. Berry said. I turned, and there he stood; derby, long black coat, stick, nose glasses, and all. He stood gazing into the brass like the wicked queen into her looking glass in the story which the boy liked so well.

"Good morning, sir," I said.

I should have finished long before.

"Did the man I saw leaving wish to see me, John?"

"Oh no, sir. He only wished to buy old clothes."

Satisfied with my work for the day, he passed inside, and I walked around to the quarters to look after the boy. It was near twelve o'clock.

I found the boy pushing a toy back and forth beneath a chair in the little room which I used for a study.

"Hi, Daddy," he called.

"Hi, son," I called. "What are you doing today?"

"Oh, I'm trucking."

"I thought you had to stand up to truck."

"Not that kind, Daddy, this kind."

He held up the toy.

"Ooh," I said. "*That* kind."

"Aw, Daddy, you're kidding. You always kid, don't you, Daddy?"

"No. When you're bad I don't kid, do I?"

"I guess not."

In fact, he wasn't—only enough to make it unnecessary for me to worry because he wasn't.

The business of trucking soon absorbed him, and I went back to the kitchen to fix his lunch and to warm up the coffee for myself.

The boy had a good appetite, so I didn't have to make him eat. I gave him his food and settled into a chair to study, but my mind wandered away, so I got up and filled a pipe hoping that would help, but it didn't, so I threw the book aside and picked up Malraux's *Man's Fate*, which Mrs. Johnson had given me, and tried to read it as I drank a cup of coffee. I had to give that up also. Those hands were on my brain, and I couldn't forget that fellow.

"Daddy," the boy called softly; it's always softly when I'm busy.

"Yes, son."

"When I grow up I think I'll drive a truck."

"You do?"

"Yes, and then I can wear a lot of buttons on my cap like the men that bring the meat to the grocery. I saw a colored man with some today, Daddy. I looked out the window, and a colored man drove the truck today, and, Daddy, he had two buttons on his cap. I could see 'em plain."

He had stopped his play and was still on his knees, beside the chair in his blue overalls. I closed the book and looked at the boy a long time. I must have looked queer.

"What's the matter, Daddy?" he asked. I explained that I was thinking, and got up and walked over to stand looking out the front window. He was quiet for a while; then he started rolling his truck again.

The only nice feature about the quarters was that they were high up and offered a view in all directions. It was afternoon and the sun was brilliant. Off to the side, a boy and girl were playing tennis in a driveway. Across the street a group of little fellows in bright sunsuits were playing on a long stretch of lawn before a white stone building. Their nurse, dressed completely in white except for her dark glasses, which I saw when she raised her head, sat still as a picture, bent over a book on her knees. As the children played, the wind blew their cries over to where I stood, and as I watched, a flock of pigeons swooped down into the driveway near the stretch of green, only to take flight again wheeling in a mass as another child came skipping up the drive pulling some sort of toy. The children saw him and were running toward him in a group when the nurse looked up and called them back. She called something to the child and pointed back in the direction of the garages where he had just come from. I could see him turn slowly around and drag his toy, some kind of bird that flapped its wings like an eagle, slowly after him. He stopped and pulled a flower from one of the bushes that lined the drive, turning to look hurriedly at the nurse, and then ran back down the drive. The child had been Jackie, the little son of the white gardener who worked across the street.

As I turned away I noticed that my boy had come to stand beside me.

"What you looking at, Daddy?" he said.

"I guess Daddy was just looking out on the world."

I picked up the book to read again, and must have fallen asleep immediately, for when I came to it was almost time to go water the lawn. When I got downstairs the boy was not there.

Then he asked if he could go out and play with his ball, and since I would soon have to go down myself to water the lawn, I told him it would be all right. But he couldn't find the ball; I would have to find it for him.

"All right now," I told him. "You stay in the back out of everybody's way, and you mustn't ask anyone a lot of questions."

I always warned about the questions, even though it did little good. He ran down the stairs, and soon I could hear the *bump bump bump* of his ball bouncing against the garage doors underneath. But since it didn't make a loud noise, I didn't ask him to stop.

I picked up the book to read again, and must have fallen asleep immediately, for when I came to it was almost time to go water the lawn. When I got downstairs the boy was not there. I called, but no answer. Then I went out into the alley in back of the garages to see if he was playing there. There were three older white boys sitting talking on a pile of old packing cases. They looked uneasy when I came up. I asked if they had seen a little Negro boy, but they said they hadn't. Then I went farther down the alley behind the grocery store where the trucks drove up, and asked one of the fellows working there if he had seen my boy. He said he had been working on the platform all afternoon and that he was sure the boy had not been there. As I started away, the four o'clock whistle blew and I had to go water the lawn. I wondered where the boy could have gone. As I came back up the alley I was becoming alarmed. Then it occurred to me that he might have gone out in front in spite of my warning not to. Of course, that was where he would go, out in front to sit on the grass. I laughed at myself for becoming alarmed and decided not to punish him, even though Berry had given instructions that he was not to be seen out in the front without me. A boy that size will make you do that.

As I came around the building past the tall new evergreens, I could hear the boy crying in just that note no other child has, and when I came completely around I found him standing looking up into a window with tears on his face.

"What is it, son?" I asked. "What happened?"

"My ball, my ball, Daddy. My ball," he cried, looking up at the window.

"Yes, son. But what about the ball?"

"He threw it up in the window."

"Who did? Who threw it, son? Stop crying and tell Daddy about it."

He made an effort to stop, wiping the tears away with the back of his hand.

"A big white boy asked me to throw him my ball an', an' he took it and threw it up in that window and ran," he said, pointing.

I looked up just as Berry appeared at the window. The ball had gone into his private office.

"John, is that your boy?" he snapped.

He was red in the face.

"Yessir, but—"

"Well, he's taken his damned ball and ruined one of my plants."

"Yessir."

"You know he's got no business around here in front, don't you?"

"Yes!"

"Well, if I ever see him around here again, you're going to find yourself behind the black ball. Now get him on round to the back and then come up here and clean up this mess he's made."

I gave him one long hard look and then felt for the boy's hand to take him back to the quarters. I had a hard time seeing as we walked back, and scratched myself by stumbling into the evergreens as we went around the building.

The boy was not crying now, and when I looked down at him, the pain in my hand caused me to notice that it was bleeding. When we got upstairs, I sat the boy in a chair and went looking for iodine to doctor my hand.

"If anyone should ask me, young man, I'd say your face needed a good washing."

He didn't answer then, but when I came out of the bathroom, he seemed more inclined to talk.

"Daddy, what did that man mean?"

"Mean how, son?"

"About a black ball. You know, Daddy."

"Oh—that."

"You know, Daddy. What'd he mean?"

"He meant, son, that if your ball landed in his office again, Daddy would go after it behind the old black ball."

"Oh," he said, very thoughtful again. Then, after a while he told me: "Daddy, that white man can't see very good, can he, Daddy?"

"Why do you say that, son?"

"Daddy," he said impatiently. "Anybody can see my ball is white."

For the second time that day I looked at him a long time.

"Yes, son," I said. "Your ball *is* white." Mostly white, anyway, I thought.

"Will I play with the black ball, Daddy?"

"In time, son," I said. "In time."

He had already played with the ball; that he would discover later. He was learning the rules of the game already, but he didn't know it. Yes, he would play with the ball. Indeed, poor little rascal, he would play until he grew sick of playing. My, yes, the old ball game. But I'd begin telling him the rules later.

My hand was still burning from the scratch as I dragged the hose out to water the lawn, and looking down at the iodine stain, I thought of the fellow's fried hands, and felt in my pocket to make sure I still had the card he had given me. Maybe there was a color other than white on the old ball.

Read and Think Critically

Infer, Explain, Analyze

1. **WORD CHOICE** Locate two or three words or phrases in the first paragraph from which you can infer that the **narrator** is of a low social standing.

2. The color words in this short story do more than describe objects; they are also used as code words for race, social status, and political views. Using a chart such as the one below, determine the meanings of the color words and phrases. Which words have multiple meanings or negative **connotations**?

Code Word or Phrase	Meanings
Black	
White	
Red	
Black ball	
Seeing red	

3. Several times, the narrator of this story stretches the truth, or else lies outright. Find an example and explain the narrator's **motivation** for being less than truthful.

4. List three of the narrator's reactions to, and concerns for, his son. Then decide which are **universal** among fathers and which are attributable mainly to race.

5. **THE AUTHOR'S STYLE** Ellison is often noted for his use of **pathos** in his short stories and novels. *Pathos* is the quality in art or literature that stimulates pity, compassion, or sorrow. Analyze Ellison's use of pathos in the story. List at least two examples.

Before You Read

James Thurber 1894–1961

About the Author

Writer, reporter, cartoonist, and humorist James Thurber developed his famous sense of humor under the influence of his practical joker mother. An accident had an influence on his choice of career, too. After a stray arrow struck his eye when he was a child, Thurber had lifelong vision problems that eventually led to total blindness. Poor vision kept him from participating in sports when he was growing up. Instead he turned to reading and writing. After leaving his hometown of Columbus, Ohio, he held several jobs as a newspaper reporter both at home and abroad. In 1927, his career was launched when he went to work at *The New Yorker*.

The weekly magazine became influential, and Thurber helped set the tone with his polished writing and whimsical cartoons. Often his subjects were nagging wives, timid husbands, and placid, observant animals. A typical caption is "Well if I called the wrong number, then why did you answer the phone?" With E. B. White he wrote and illustrated a spoof of pop psychology called *Is Sex Necessary?* He also wrote autobiographical sketches, a memoir of his time at *The New Yorker*, a play, and fantasies for children.

In *The Secret Life of Walter Mitty*, Thurber created the widely recognized character of a hen-pecked man so befuddled by modern urban life that he escapes into a world of fantasy. In fact, the Walter Mitty Syndrome was described in a British medical journal as a diagnosable condition.

★★★★★★★★★★★

The Author's Style

James Thurber's stories often read as contemporary fables that make use of simple, familiar story lines. Though his endings are often comical or far-cical, his final purpose was to create a balance between whimsicality and sober reality. He often explored the tension between the human inclination toward confusion on one hand and the need for order on the other. He once wrote, "Humor is emotional chaos remembered in tranquility." In other words, some experiences aren't funny until afterward.

Though the tone in Thurber's work is often sardonic and sophisticated, his stories generally end by affirming the power of love in a troubled world. His work manages to have a gentle tone yet still take a clear-eyed look at human foibles. In typical self-deprecating style, he once wrote, "I myself have accomplished nothing of excellence except a remarkable and, to some of my friends, unaccountable expertness in hitting empty ginger ale bottles with small rocks at a distance of thirty paces."

The Secret Life of Walter Mitty

JAMES THURBER

LITERARY LENS: ANTIHERO An **antihero** is a protagonist who is lacking in the qualities usually associated with being a hero, such as courage, honesty, and a willingness to sacrifice. Look for the antihero in this story.

"We're going through!" The Commander's voice was like thin ice breaking. He wore his full-dress uniform, with the heavily braided white cap pulled down nakishly over one cold gray eye. "We can't make it, sir. It's spoiling for a hurricane, if you ask me." "I'm not asking you, Lieutenant Berg," said the Commander. "Throw on the power lights! Rev her up to 8,500! We're going through!" The pounding of the cylinders increased: ta-pocketa-pocketa-pocketa-*pocketa-pocketa*. The Commander stared at the ice forming on the pilot window. He walked over and twisted a row of complicated dials. "Switch on No. 8 auxiliary!" he shouted. "Switch on No. 8 auxiliary!" repeated Lieutenant Berg. "Full strength in No. 3 turret!" shouted the commander. "Full strength in No. 3 turret!" The crew, bending to their various tasks in the huge, hurtling eight-engined Navy hydroplane, looked at each other and grinned. "The Old Man'll get us through," they said to one another. "The Old Man ain't afraid of Hell!"...

BLAM, ROY LICHTENSTEIN, 1962, YALE UNIVERSITY ART GALLERY

"Not so fast! You're driving too fast!" said Mrs. Mitty. "What are you driving so fast for?"

"Hmm?" said Walter Mitty. He looked at his wife, in the seat beside him, with shocked astonishment. She seemed grossly unfamiliar, like a strange woman who had yelled at him in a crowd. "You were up to fifty-five," she said. "You know I don't like to go more than forty. You were up to fifty-five." Walter Mitty drove on toward Waterbury in silence, the roaring of the SN202 through the worst storm in twenty years of Navy flying fading in the remote, intimate airways of his mind. "You're tensed up again," said Mrs. Mitty. "It's one of your days. I wish you'd let Dr. Renshaw look you over."

Walter Mitty stopped the car in front of the building where his wife went to have her hair done. "Remember to get those overshoes while I'm having my hair done," she said. "I don't need overshoes," said Mitty. She put her mirror back into her bag. "We've been all through that," she said, getting out of the car. "You're not a young man any longer." He raced the engine a little. "Why don't you wear your gloves? Have you lost your gloves?" Walter Mitty reached in a pocket and brought out the gloves. He put them on, but after she had turned and gone into the building and he had driven on to a red light, he took them off again. "Pick it up, brother!" snapped a cop as the light changed, and Mitty hastily pulled on his gloves and lurched ahead. He drove around the streets aimlessly for a time, and then he drove past the hospital on his way to the parking lot.

. . . "It's the millionaire banker, Wellington McMillan," said the pretty nurse. "Yes?" said Walter Mitty, removing his gloves slowly. "Who has the case?" "Dr. Renshaw and Dr. Benbow, but there are two specialists here, Dr. Remington from New York and Mr. Pritchard-Mitford from London. He flew over." A door opened down a long, cool corridor and Dr. Renshaw came out. He looked distraught and haggard. "Hello, Mitty," he said. "We're having the devil's own time with McMillan, the mil-

In the operating room there were whispered introductions: "Dr. Remington, Dr. Mitty. Mr. Pritchard-Mitford, Dr. Mitty." "I've read your book on streptothricosis," said Pritchard-Mitford, shaking hands.

lionaire banker and close personal friend of Roosevelt. Obstreosis of the ductal tract. Tertiary. Wish you'd take a look at him." "Glad to," said Mitty.

In the operating room there were whispered introductions: "Dr. Remington, Dr. Mitty. Mr. Pritchard-Mitford, Dr. Mitty." "I've read your book on streptothricosis," said Pritchard-Mitford, shaking hands. "A brilliant performance, sir." "Thank you," said Walter Mitty. "Didn't know you were in the States, Mitty," grumbled Remington. "Coals to Newcastle,[1] bringing Mitford and me up here for a tertiary." "You are very kind," said Mitty. A huge, complicated machine, connected to the operating table, with many tubes and wires, began at this moment to go pocketa-pocketa-pocketa. "The new anesthetizer is giving way!" shouted an interne. "There is no one in the East who knows how to fix it!" "Quiet, man!" said Mitty, in a low, cool voice. He sprang to the machine, which was now going pocketa-pocketa-queep-pocketa-queep. He began fingering delicately a row of glistening dials: "Give me a fountain pen!" he snapped. Someone handed him a fountain pen. He pulled a faulty piston out of the machine and inserted the pen in its place. "That will hold for ten minutes," he said. "Get on with the operation." A nurse hurried over and whispered to Renshaw, and Mitty saw the man turn pale. "Coreopsis has set in," said Renshaw nervously. "If you would take over, Mitty?" Mitty looked at him and at the **craven** figure of Benbow, who

craven: cowardly; contemptible

---

1 **Coals to Newcastle:** an expression meaning an unnecessary act. (Because Newcastle is a coal-mining city, there is no reason to take coals to it.)

drank, and at the grave uncertain faces of the two great specialists. "If you wish," he said. They slipped a white gown on him, he adjusted a mask and drew on thin gloves; nurses handed him shining . . .

"Back it up, Mac! Look out for that Buick!" Walter Mitty jammed on the brakes. "Wrong lane, Mac," said the parking-lot attendant, looking at Mitty closely. "Gee. Yeh," muttered Mitty. He began cautiously to back out of the lane marked "Exit Only." "Leave her sit there," said the attendant: "I'll put her away." Mitty got out of the car. "Hey, better leave the key." "Oh," said Mitty, handing the man the ignition key. The attendant vaulted into the car, backed it up with insolent skill, and put it where it belonged.

They're so damn cocky, thought Walter Mitty, walking along Main Street; they think they know everything. Once he had tried to take his chains off, outside New Milford, and he had got them wound around the axles. A man had had to come out in a wrecking car and unwind them, a young, grinning garageman. Since then Mrs. Mitty always made him drive to a garage to have the chains taken off. The next time, he thought, I'll wear my right arm in a sling; they won't grin at me then. I'll have my right arm in a sling and they'll see I couldn't possibly take the chains off myself. He kicked at the slush on the sidewalk. "Overshoes," he said to himself, and he began looking for a shoe store.

When he came out into the street again, with the overshoes in a box under his arm, Walter Mitty began to wonder what the other thing was his wife had told him to get. She had told him, twice, before they set out from their house for Waterbury. In a way he hated these weekly trips to town—he was always getting something wrong. Kleenex, he thought, Squibb's, razor blades? No. Toothpaste, toothbrush, bicarbonate, carborundum, initiative and referendum? He gave it up. But she would remember it. "Where's the what's-its-name?" she would ask. "Don't tell me you forgot the what's-its-name." A newsboy went by shouting something about the Waterbury trial.

. . . "Perhaps this will refresh your memory." The District Attorney suddenly thrust a heavy automatic at the quiet figure on the witness stand. "Have you ever seen this before?" Walter Mitty took the gun and examined it expertly. "This is my Webley-Vickers 50.80," he said calmly. An excited buzz ran around the courtroom. The Judge rapped for order. "You are a crack shot with any sort of firearms, I believe?" said the District Attorney, insinuatingly. "Objection!" shouted Mitty's attorney. "We have shown that the defendant could not have fired the shot. We have shown that he wore his right arm in a sling on the night of the fourteenth of July." Walter Mitty raised his hand briefly and the bickering attorneys were stilled. "With any known make of gun," he said evenly, "I could have killed Gregory Fitzhurst at three hundred feet *with my left hand*." Pandemonium broke loose in the courtroom. A woman's scream rose above the bedlam and suddenly a lovely, dark-haired girl was in Walter Mitty's arms. The District Attorney struck at her savagely. Without rising from his chair, Mitty let the man have it on the point of the chin. "You miserable cur!" . . .

"Puppy biscuit," said Walter Mitty. He stopped walking and the buildings of Waterbury rose up out of the misty courtroom and surrounded him again. A woman who was passing laughed. "He said 'Puppy biscuit,'" she said to her companion. "That man said 'Puppy biscuit' to himself." Walter Mitty hurried on. He went into an A & P, not the first one he came to but a smaller one farther up the street. "I want some buscuit for small, young dogs," he said to the clerk. "Any special brand, sir?" The greatest pistol shot in the world thought a moment. "It says 'Puppies Bark for It' on the box," said Walter Mitty.

*"H*e said 'Puppy biscuit,' " she said to her companion. "That man said 'Puppy biscuit' to himself." Walter Mitty hurried on. He went into an A & P, not the first one he came to but a smaller one farther up the street.

*H*is wife would be through at the hairdresser's in fifteen minutes, Mitty saw in looking at his watch, unless they had trouble drying it; sometimes they had trouble drying it. She didn't like to get to the hotel first; she would want him to be there waiting for her as usual. He found a big leather chair in the lobby, facing a window, and he put the overshoes and the puppy biscuit on the floor beside it. He picked up an old copy of *Liberty* and sank down into the chair. "Can Germany Conquer the World Through the Air?" Walter Mitty looked at the pictures of bombing planes and of ruined streets.

. . . "The cannonading[2] has got the wind up in young Raleigh, sir," said the sergeant. Captain Mitty looked up at him through tousled hair. "Get him to bed," he said wearily. "With the others. I'll fly alone." "But you can't sir," said the sergeant anxiously. "It takes two men to handle that bomber and the Archies are pounding hell out of the air. Von Richtman's circus is between

---

2 **cannonading:** heavily firing with artillery

here and Saulier." "Somebody's got to get that ammunition dump," said Mitty. "I'm going over. Spot of brandy?" He poured a drink for the sergeant and one for himself. War thundered and whined around the dugout and battered at the door. There was a rending of wood and splinters flew through the room. "A bit of a near thing," said Captain Mitty carelessly. "The box barrage is closing in," said the sergeant. "We only live once, Sergeant," said Mitty, with his faint, fleeting smile. "Or do we?" He poured another brandy and tossed it off. "I never see a man could hold his brandy like you, sir," said the sergeant. "Begging your pardon, sir." Captain Mitty stood up and strapped on his huge Webley-Vickers automatic. "It's forty kilometers through hell, sir," said the sergeant. Mitty finished one last brandy. "After all," he said softly, "what isn't?" The pounding of the cannon increased; there was the rat-tat-tatting of machine guns, and from somewhere came the menacing pocketa-pocketa-pocketa of the new flame-throwers. Walter Mitty walked to the door of the dugout humming "Auprès de Ma Blonde." He turned and waved to the sergeant. "Cheerio!" he said. . . .

Something struck his shoulder. "I've been looking all over this hotel for you," said Mrs. Mitty. "Why do you have to hide in this old chair? How did you expect me to find you?" "Things close in," said Walter Mitty vaguely. "What?" Mrs. Mitty said. "Did you get the what's-its-name? The puppy biscuit? What's in that box?" "Overshoes," said Mitty. "Couldn't you have put them on in the store?" "I was thinking," said Walter Mitty. "Does it ever occur to you that I am sometimes thinking?" She looked at him. "I'm going to take your temperature when I get you home," she said.

They went out through the revolving doors that made a faintly derisive whistling sound when you pushed them. It was two blocks to the parking lot. At the drugstore on the corner she said, "Wait here for me. I forgot something. I won't be a minute." She was more than a minute. Walter Mitty lighted a cigarette. It began to rain, rain with sleet in it. He stood up against the wall of the drugstore, smoking. . . . He put his shoulders back and his heels together. "To hell with the handkerchief," said Walter Mitty scornfully. He took one last drag on his cigarette and snapped it away. Then, with a faint, fleeting smile playing about his lips, he faced the firing squad; erect and motionless, proud and disdainful, Walter Mitty the Undefeated, inscrutable to the last.

Read and Think Critically

Analyze, Evaluate, Explain

1. **ANTIHERO** Analyze the qualities that make Walter Mitty a humorous **antihero**.

2. James Thurber was a renowned cartoonist as well as a writer. What specific qualities of the writing make this story seem cartoonish?

3. The author of this story once said, "All men should strive to learn before they die, what they are running from, and to, and why." What do you think Walter Mitty is running from, and why?

4. Analyze how **point of view** adds to the humor and the **irony** of the story.

5. Walter Mitty lives in two worlds: a **fantasy** world and the real world. Each world is represented by its own language, or *register*. For example, in his fantasy sequences, the language is often "hyped up," consisting of jargon and a liberal use of exclamation points. In the reality scenes, on the other hand, the language is down-to-earth and mundane. Select one fantasy passage and one mundane passage. Then rewrite each one using the other style and register. An example has been done for you. Evaluate how Thurber's choice of words influences the **tone** of the writing.

Original	Rewrite in Opposite Register
"Switch on No. 8 auxiliary!" he shouted.	*"Please turn on the engine," he said.*

6. **THE AUTHOR'S STYLE** "Nowadays most men lead lives of noisy desperation," James Thurber once quipped. This was a paraphrase of Henry David Thoreau's famous observation that "The mass of men lead lives of quiet desperation. An unconscious despair is concealed even under what are the games and amusements of mankind." The quip is typical of James Thurber's style: whimsicality contrasted with sober reality. Explain the qualities that make "The Secret Life of Walter Mitty" both funny and serious.

★★

Before You Read

Shirley Jackson 1916–1965

About the Author

Shirley Jackson knew she wanted to be a writer at an early age. Her mother said she started composing verse nearly as soon as she could form letters. In 1935 she enrolled at Syracuse University, where she first edited the campus humor magazine and then launched a literary magazine with Stanley Edgar Hyman, a fellow student who would become both her husband and a well-known literary critic.

A versatile writer, Jackson is best remembered for horror stories and novels with a tone of dark pessimism. Yet she also enjoyed writing humor, publishing two volumes of memoirs that took a comic look at the couple's family life

rearing four children in a small Vermont town.

The Lottery, which provoked public outrage along with critical praise, remains Jackson's best-known work. This chilling tale was published originally as a short story in *The New Yorker* in 1948 and was later adapted for both the stage and television. For many years it was one of the most frequently performed plays in the country, particularly in productions put on by small theatre groups and high schools. It is still so popular that probably somewhere a high school theatre group is in rehearsal for it even as you read.

★★★★★★★★★★★

The Author's Style

Some critics consider Shirley Jackson a master of horror and psychological suspense. The deceptively casual tone of her writing is one of its most important stylistic features. This casualness helps to disguise the dark motives in her characters and the even darker truths behind her plots.

Jackson's novels and stories sometimes read as moral allegories, parables, or fable-like commentaries on collective social behavior. Her writing often takes the form of a cautionary tale— that is, a story that carries with it a warning, such

as blind obedience to tradition can be dangerous, or people are not what they seem.

The author is often more interested in showing how people behave in groups than in examining the lives of individuals. Thus her characters might strike readers less as fully drawn characters than as types. Sometimes their names reflect this fact. In the story you are about to read, for example, Old Man Warner sounds more like a type representing all old men than a unique individual.

The
Lottery

Shirley Jackson

Literary Lens: The Parable A **parable** is a story in which the events point to a deeper moral lesson. Look for the deeper meaning, or lesson, in this parable.

The morning of June 27th was clear and sunny, with the fresh warmth of a full-summer day; the flowers were blossoming profusely and the grass was richly green. The people of the village began to gather in the square, between the post office and the bank, around ten o'clock; in some towns there were so many people that the lottery took two days and had to be started on June 26th, but in this village, where there were only about three hundred people, the whole lottery took less than two hours, so it could begin at ten o'clock in the morning and still be through in time to allow the villagers to get home for noon dinner.

The children assembled first, of course. School was recently over for the summer, and the feeling of liberty sat uneasily on most of them; they tended to gather together quietly for a while before they

Soon the men began to gather, surveying their own children, speaking of planting and rain, tractors and taxes. They stood together, away from the pile of stones in the corner, and their jokes were quiet and they smiled rather than laughed.

broke into boisterous play, and their talk was still of the classroom and the teacher, of books and reprimands. Bobby Martin had already stuffed his pockets full of stones, and the other boys soon followed his example, selecting the smoothest and roundest stones; Bobby and Harry Jones and Dickie Delacroix—the villagers pronounced this name "Dellacroy"—eventually made a great pile of stones in one corner of the square and guarded it against the raids of the other boys. The girls stood aside, talking among themselves, looking over their shoulders at the boys, and the very small children rolled in the dust or clung to the hands of their older brothers or sisters.

Soon the men began to gather, surveying their own children, speaking of planting and rain, tractors and taxes. They stood together, away from the pile of stones in the corner, and their jokes were quiet and they smiled rather than laughed. The women, wearing faded house dresses and sweaters, came shortly after their menfolk. They greeted one another and exchanged bits of gossip as they went to join their husbands. Soon the women, standing by their husbands, began to call to their children, and the children came reluctantly, having to be called four or five times. Bobby Martin ducked under his mother's grasping hand and ran, laughing, back to the pile of stones. His father spoke up sharply, and Bobby came quickly and took his place between his father and his oldest brother.

The lottery was conducted—as were the square dances, the teenage club, the Halloween program—by Mr. Summers, who had time and energy to devote to civic activities. He was a round-faced, jovial man and he ran the coal business, and people were sorry for him, because he had no children and his wife was a scold. When he arrived in the square, carrying the black wooden box, there was a murmur of conversation among the villagers, and he waved and called, "Little late today, folks." The postmaster, Mr. Graves, followed him, carrying a three-legged stool, and the stool was put in the center of the square and Mr. Summers set the black box down on it. The villagers kept their distance, leaving a space between themselves and the stool, and when Mr. Summers said, "Some of you fellows want to give me a hand?" there was a hesitation before two men, Mr. Martin and his oldest son, Baxter, came forward to hold the box steady on the stool while Mr. Summers stirred up the papers inside it.

The original paraphernalia for the lottery had been lost long ago, and the black box now resting on the stool had been put into use even before Old Man Warner, the oldest man in town, was born. Mr. Summers spoke frequently to the villagers about making a new box, but no one liked to upset even as much tradition as was represented by the black box. There was a story that the present box had been made with some pieces of the box that had preceded it, the one that had been constructed when the first people settled down to make a village here. Every year, after the lottery, Mr. Summers began talking again about a new box, but every year the subject was allowed to fade

Stone City Iowa, Grant Wood, 1930, Joslyn Art Museum

off without anything's being done. The black box grew shabbier each year; by now it was no longer completely black but splintered badly along one side to show the original wood color, and in some places faded or stained.

Mr. Martin and his oldest son, Baxter, held the black box securely on the stool until Mr. Summers had stirred the papers thoroughly with his hand. Because so much of the ritual had been forgotten or discarded, Mr. Summers had been successful in having slips of paper substituted for the chips of wood that had been used for generations. Chips of wood, Mr. Summers had argued, had been all very well when the village was tiny, but now that the population was more than three hundred and likely to keep on growing, it was necessary to use something that would fit more easily into the black box. The night before the lottery, Mr. Summers and Mr. Graves made up the slips of paper and put them in the box, and it was then taken to the safe of Mr. Summers's coal company and locked up until Mr. Summers was ready to take it to the square next morning. The rest of the year, the box was put away, sometimes one place, sometimes another; it had spent one year in Mr. Graves's barn and another year underfoot in the post office, and sometimes it was set on a shelf in the Martin grocery and left there. There was a great deal of fussing to be done before Mr. Summers declared the lottery open.

There were the lists to make up—of heads of families, heads of households in each family, members of each household in each family. There was the proper swearing-in of Mr. Summers by the postmaster, as the official of the lottery; at one time, some people remembered, there had been a recital of some sort, performed by the official of the lottery, a perfunctory, tuneless chant that had been rattled off duly each year; some people believed that the official of the lottery used to stand just so when he said or sang it, others believed that he was supposed to walk among the people, but years and years ago this part of the ritual had been allowed to lapse. There had been, also, a ritual salute, which the official of the lottery had had to use in addressing each person who came up to draw from the box, but this also had changed with time, until now it was felt necessary only for the official to speak to each person approaching. Mr. Summers was very good at all this; in his clean white shirt and blue jeans, with one hand resting carelessly on the black box, he seemed very proper and important as he talked **interminably** to Mr. Graves and the Martins.

Just as Mr. Summers finally left off talking and turned to the assembled

interminably: endlessly

villagers, Mrs. Hutchinson came hurriedly along the path to the square, her sweater thrown over her shoulders, and slid into place in the back of the crowd. "Clean forgot what day it was," she said to Mrs. Delacroix, who stood next to her, and they both laughed softly. "Thought my old man was out back stacking wood," Mrs. Hutchinson went on, "and then I looked out the window and the kids was gone, and then I remembered it was the twenty-seventh and came a-running." She dried her hands on her apron, and Mrs. Delacroix said, "You're in time, though. They're still talking away up there."

Mrs. Hutchinson craned her neck to see through the crowd and found her husband and children standing near the front. She tapped Mrs. Delacroix on the arm as a farewell and began to make her way through the crowd. The people separated good-humoredly to let her through; two or three people said, in voices just loud enough to be heard across the crowd, "Here comes your Missus, Hutchinson," and "Bill, she made it after all." Mrs. Hutchinson reached her husband, and Mr. Summers, who had been waiting, said cheerfully, "Thought we were going to have to get on without you, Tessie." Mrs. Hutchinson said, grinning, "Wouldn't have me leave m'dishes in the sink, now, would you, Joe?" and soft laughter ran through the crowd as the people stirred back into position after Mrs. Hutchinson's arrival.

"Well, now," Mr. Summers said soberly, "guess we better get started, get this over with, so's we can go back to work. Anybody ain't here?"

"Dunbar," several people said. "Dunbar, Dunbar."

Mr. Summers consulted his list. "Clyde Dunbar," he said. "That's right. He's broke his leg, hasn't he? Who's drawing for him?"

"Me, I guess," a woman said, and Mr. Summers turned to look at her. "Wife draws for her husband," Mr. Summers said. "Don't you have a grown boy to do it for you, Janey?" Although Mr. Summers and everyone else in the village knew the answer perfectly well, it was the business of the official of the lottery to ask such questions formally. Mr. Summers waited with an expression of polite interest while Mrs. Dunbar answered.

> "Wife draws for her husband," Mr. Summers said. "Don't you have a grown boy to do it for you, Janey?" Although Mr. Summers and everyone else in the village knew the answer perfectly well, it was the business of the official of the lottery to ask such questions formally.

"Horace's not but sixteen yet," Mrs. Dunbar said regretfully. "Guess I gotta fill in for the old man this year."

"Right," Mr. Summers said. He made a note on the list he was holding. Then he asked, "Watson boy drawing this year?"

A tall boy in the crowd raised his hand. "Here," he said. "I'm drawing for m' mother and me." He blinked his eyes nervously and ducked his head as several voices in the crowd said things like "Good fellow, Jack," and "Glad to see your mother's got a man to do it."

"Well," Mr. Summers said, "guess that's everyone. Old Man Warner make it?"

"Here," a voice said, and Mr. Summers nodded.

> By now, all through the crowd there were men holding the small folded papers in their large hands, turning them over and over nervously.

A sudden hush fell on the crowd as Mr. Summers cleared his throat and looked at the list. "All ready?" he called. "Now, I'll read the names—heads of families first—and the men come up and take a paper out of the box. Keep the paper folded in your hand without looking at it until everyone has had a turn. Everything clear?"

The people had done it so many times that they only half listened to the directions; most of them were quiet, wetting their lips, not looking around. Then Mr. Summers raised one hand high and said, "Adams." A man disengaged himself from the crowd and came forward. "Hi, Steve," Mr. Summers said, and Mr. Adams said, "Hi, Joe." They grinned at one another humorlessly and nervously. Then Mr. Adams reached into the black box and took out a folded paper. He held it firmly by one corner as he turned and went hastily back to his place in the crowd, where he stood a little apart from his family, not looking down at his hand.

"Allen," Mr. Summers said. "Anderson. . . . Bentham."

"Seems like there's no time at all between lotteries any more." Mrs. Delacroix said to Mrs. Graves in the back row. "Seems like we got through with the last one only last week."

"Time sure goes fast," Mrs. Graves said.

"Clark. . . . Delacroix."

"There goes my old man," Mrs. Delacroix said. She held her breath while her husband went forward.

"Dunbar," Mr. Summers said, and Mrs. Dunbar went steadily to the box while one of the women said, "Go on, Janey," and another said, "There she goes."

"We're next," Mrs. Graves said. She watched while Mr. Graves came around from the side of the box, greeted Mr. Summers gravely, and selected a slip of paper from the box. By now, all through the crowd there were men holding the small folded papers in their large hands, turning them over and over nervously. Mrs. Dunbar and her two sons stood together, Mrs. Dunbar holding the slip of paper.

"Harburt. . . . Hutchinson."

"Get up there, Bill," Mrs. Hutchinson said, and the people near her laughed.

"Jones."

"They do say," Mr. Adams said to Old Man Warner, who stood next to him, "that over in the north village they're talking of giving up the lottery."

Old Man Warner snorted. "Pack of crazy fools," he said. "Listening to the young folks, nothing's good enough for *them*. Next thing you know, they'll be wanting to go back to living in caves, nobody work any more, live *that* way for a while. Used to be a saying about 'Lottery in June, corn be heavy soon.' First thing you know, we'd all be eating stewed chickweed and acorns. There's *always* been a lottery," he added petulantly. "Bad enough to see young Joe Summers up there joking with everybody."

"Some places have already quit lotteries," Mrs. Adams said.

"Nothing but trouble in *that*," Old Man Warner said stoutly. "Pack of young fools."

"Martin." And Bobby Martin watched his father go forward. "Overdyke. . . . Percy."

"I wish they'd hurry," Mrs. Dunbar said to her older son. "I wish they'd hurry."

"They're almost through," her son said.

"You get ready to run tell Dad," Mrs. Dunbar said.

Mr. Summers called his own name and then stepped forward precisely and selected a slip from the box. Then he called, "Warner."

"Seventy-seventh year I been in the lottery," Old Man Warner said as he went through the crowd. "Seventy-seventh time."

"Watson." The tall boy came awkwardly through the crowd. Someone said, "Don't be nervous, Jack," and Mr. Summers said, "Take your time, son."

"Zanini."

After that, there was a long pause, a breathless pause, until Mr. Summers,

*P*eople began to look around to see the Hutchinsons. Bill Hutchinson was standing quiet, staring down at the paper in his hand.

holding his slip of paper in the air, said, "All right, fellows." For a minute, no one moved, and then all the slips of paper were opened. Suddenly, all the women began to speak at once, saying, "Who is it?," "Who's got it?," "Is it the Dunbars?," "Is it the Watsons?" Then the voices began to say, "It's Hutchinson. It's Bill," "Bill Hutchinson's got it."

"Go tell your father," Mrs. Dunbar said to her older son.

People began to look around to see the Hutchinsons. Bill Hutchinson was standing quiet, staring down at the paper in his hand. Suddenly, Tessie Hutchinson shouted to Mr. Summers, "You didn't give him time enough to take any paper he wanted. I saw you. It wasn't fair!"

"Be a good sport, Tessie," Mrs. Delacroix called, and Mrs. Graves said, "All of us took the same chance."

"Shut up, Tessie," Bill Hutchinson said.

"Well, everyone," Mr. Summers said, "that was done pretty fast, and now we've got to be hurrying a little more to get done in time." He consulted his next list. "Bill," he said, "you draw for the Hutchinson family. You got any other households in the Hutchinsons?"

"There's Don and Eva," Mrs. Hutchinson yelled. "Make *them* take their chance!"

"Daughters draw with their husbands' families, Tessie," Mr. Summers said gently. "You know that as well as anyone else."

"It wasn't *fair*," Tessie said.

"I guess not, Joe," Bill Hutchinson said regretfully. "My daughter draws with her husband's family, that's only fair. And I've got no other family except the kids."

"Then, as far as drawing for families is concerned, it's you," Mr. Summers said in explanation, "and as far as drawing for households is concerned, that's you, too. Right?"

"Right," Bill Hutchinson said.

"How many kids, Bill?" Mr. Summers asked formally.

"Three," Bill Hutchinson said. "There's Bill, Jr., and Nancy, and little Dave. And Tessie and me."

"All right, then," Mr. Summers said. "Harry, you got their tickets back?"

Mr. Graves nodded and held up the slips of paper. "Put them in the box, then," Mr. Summers directed. "Take Bill's and put it in."

"I think we ought to start over," Mrs. Hutchinson said, as quietly as she could. "I tell you it wasn't *fair*. You didn't give him time enough to choose. *Every*body saw that."

Mr. Graves had selected the five slips and put them in the box, and he dropped all the papers but those onto the ground, where the breeze caught them and lifted them off.

"Listen, everybody," Mrs. Hutchinson was saying to the people around her.

"Ready, Bill?" Mr. Summers asked, and Bill Hutchinson, with one quick glance around at his wife and children, nodded.

"Remember," Mr. Summers said, "take the slips and keep them folded until each person has taken one. Harry, you help little Dave." Mr. Graves took the hand of the little boy, who came willingly with him up to the box. "Take a paper out of the box, Davy," Mr. Summers said. Davy put his hand into the box and laughed. "Take just *one* paper," Mr. Summers said. "Harry, you hold it for him." Mr. Graves took the child's hand and removed the folded paper from the tight fist and held it while little Dave stood next to him and looked up at him wonderingly.

"Nancy next," Mr. Summers said. Nancy was twelve, and her school friends breathed heavily as she went forward, switching her skirt, and took a slip daintily from the box. "Bill, Jr.," Mr. Summers said, and Billy, his face red and his feet overlarge, nearly knocked the box over as he got a paper out. "Tessie," Mr. Summers said. She hesitated for a minute, looking around defiantly, and then set her lips and went up to the box. She snatched a paper out and held it behind her.

*S*he hesitated for a minute, looking around defiantly, and then set her lips and went up to the box. She snatched a paper out and held it behind her.

"Bill," Mr. Summers said, and Bill Hutchinson reached into the box and felt around, bringing his hand out at last with the slip of paper in it.

The crowd was quiet. A girl whispered, "I hope it's not Nancy," and the sound of the whisper reached the edges of the crowd.

"It's not the way it used to be," Old Man Warner said clearly. "People ain't the way they used to be."

"All right," Mr. Summers said. "Open the papers. Harry, you open little Dave's."

Mr. Graves opened the slip of paper and there was a general sigh through the crowd as he held it up and everyone could see that it was blank. Nancy and Bill, Jr., opened theirs at the same time, and both beamed and laughed, turning around to the crowd and holding their slips of paper above their heads.

"Tessie," Mr. Summers said. There was a pause, and then Mr. Summers looked at Bill Hutchinson, and Bill unfolded his paper and showed it. It was blank.

"It's Tessie," Mr. Summers said, and his voice was hushed. "Show us her paper, Bill."

Bill Hutchinson went over to his wife and forced the slip of paper out of her hand. It had a black spot on it, the black spot Mr. Summers had made the night before with the heavy pencil in the coal-company office. Bill Hutchinson held it up, and there was a stir in the crowd.

"All right, folks," Mr. Summers said. "Let's finish quickly."

Although the villagers had forgotten the ritual and lost the original black box, they still remembered to use stones. The pile of stones the boys had made earlier was ready; there were stones on the ground with the blowing scraps of paper that had come out of the box. Mrs. Delacroix selected a stone so large she had to pick it up with both hands and turned to Mrs. Dunbar. "Come on," she said. "Hurry up."

Mrs. Dunbar had small stones in both hands, and she said, gasping for breath, "I can't run at all. You'll have to go ahead and I'll catch up with you."

The children had stones already. And someone gave little Davy Hutchinson a few pebbles.

Tessie Hutchinson was in the center of a cleared space by now, and she held her hands out desperately as the villagers moved in on her. "It isn't fair," she said. A stone hit her on the side of the head.

Old Man Warner was saying, "Come on, come on, everyone." Steve Adams was in the front of the crowd of villagers, with Mrs. Graves beside him.

"It isn't fair, it isn't right," Mrs. Hutchinson screamed, and then they were upon her.

Read and Think Critically

Explain, Analyze, Evaluate

1. **THE PARABLE** Explain several lessons from the story. What do you think is the main **theme** of this story?

2. Explain what this story implies about the author's attitude toward the concepts of tradition, conformity, and obedience. Support your answer with evidence from the text.

3. This story provoked outrage from many when it first appeared in *The New Yorker* in 1948. What do you think were some reasons for this response?

4. In what ways does the author set you up to be shocked by the ending of the story? Analyze the author's use of **setting**, **tone**, **imagery**, and even the **title** of the story. Evaluate the effectiveness of her choices.

5. **THE AUTHOR'S STYLE** Critics often refer to Jackson as a master of horror and psychological suspense. Would you agree? Explain.

★★★

Before You Read

Truman Capote 1924–1984

About the Author

Flamboyant. Gifted. Social. Unique. These qualities helped catapult Truman Capote into literary fame early and kept him there until his death of a drug overdose at 60. Born in New Orleans to a 16-year-old beauty queen, Capote stayed in the South with relatives when his mother moved to New York after her divorce from his father. As a child, Capote was a neighbor of Harper Lee, who would also become a writer; in *To Kill a Mockingbird,* Lee modeled the precocious character "Dill" after Capote. Capote published his first novel, *Other Voices, Other Rooms,* the story of a boy's search for his father, at 24. Living in New York for most of his adult life, Capote published screenplays and a musical as well as prose. His best-known book is *In Cold Blood,* based on an actual multiple murder. The book blended the techniques of fiction and journalism; Capote called it a "nonfiction novel."

Capote himself was perhaps the most famous character he created. He often turned up on talk shows wearing outrageous hats and criticizing other writers. After he published an excerpt from a novel he was working on that thinly disguised his rich friends, he was shunned by them. He later succumbed to drug addiction and alcoholism.

★★★★★★★★★★★

The Author's Style

"What I am trying to achieve is a voice sitting by a fireplace telling you a story on a winter's evening," Truman Capote is quoted as saying in the 1990 collection *Writers on Writing.* Capote is more interested in personality and mood—that is, character—than in logic and plot. Often he puts his eccentric, "outsider" characters into odd situations that have a poetic and dream-like aura. For this reason his short pieces are sometimes referred to as tales.

Capote's fiction often involves either children or adults who have a childlike way of looking at and interacting with the "real" world. Generally they are in search of security and a sense of identity.

His style is brilliantly descriptive, using precise phrases to reveal character and mood. A careful writer, Capote once said that because what is taken out is as important as what is put in, he believed in using scissors more than pencils.

Capote is interested in human psychology, and the fantasies of his characters often concern love, understanding, and acceptance. In this and other respects his work has been compared to that of fellow southern writers Carson McCullers and Eudora Welty.

Miriam

Truman Capote

LITERARY LENS: VOICE Every writer has a **voice**, or a distinct way of expressing himself or herself. As you read, consider what elements of the story seem distinctive to Capote.

For several years, Mrs. H. T. Miller had lived alone in a pleasant apartment (two rooms with kitchenette) in a remodeled brownstone near the East River. She was a widow: Mr. H. T. Miller had left a reasoable amount of insurance. Her interests were narrow, she had no friends to speak of, and she rarely journeyed farther than the corner grocery. The other people in the house never seemed to notice her: her clothes were matter-of-fact, her hair iron-gray, clipped and casually waved; she did not use cosmetics, her features were plain and inconspicuous, and on her last birthday she was sixty-one. Her activities were seldom spontaneous: she kept the two rooms immaculate, smoked an occasional cigarette, prepared her own meals, and tended a canary.

Then she met Miriam. It was snowing that night. Mrs. Miller had finished drying the supper dishes and was thumbing through an afternoon paper when she saw an advertisement of a picture playing at a neighborhood theater. The title sounded good, so she struggled into her beaver coat, laced her galoshes, and left the apartment, leaving one light burning in the foyer: she found nothing more disturbing than a sensation of darkness.

The snow was fine, falling gently, not yet making an impression on the pavement. The wind from the river cut only at street crossings. Mrs. Miller hurried, her head bowed, oblivious as a mole burrowing a blind path. She stopped at a drugstore and bought a package of peppermints.

A long line stretched in front of the box office; she took her place at the end. There would be (a tired voice groaned) a short wait for all seats. Mrs. Miller rummaged in her leather handbag till she collected exactly the correct change for admission. The line seemed to be taking its own time and, looking around for some distraction, she suddenly became conscious of a little girl standing under the edge of the marquee.

Her hair was the longest and strangest Mrs. Miller had ever seen: absolutely silver-white, like an albino's.

Her hair was the longest and strangest Mrs. Miller had ever seen: absolutely silver-white, like an albino's. It flowed waistlength in smooth, loose lines. She was thin and fragilely constructed. There was a simple, special elegance in the way she stood with her thumbs in the pockets of a tailored plum-velvet coat.

Mrs. Miller felt oddly excited, and when the little girl glanced toward her, she smiled warmly. The little girl walked over and said, "Would you care to do me a favor?"

"I'd be glad to, if I can," said Mrs. Miller.

"Oh, it's quite easy. I merely want you to buy a ticket for me; they won't let me in otherwise. Here, I have the money." And gracefully she handed Mrs. Miller two dimes and a nickel.

They went into the theater together. An usherette directed them to a lounge; in twenty minutes the picture would be over.

"I feel just like a genuine criminal," said Mrs. Miller gaily, as she sat down. "I mean that sort of thing's against the law, isn't it? I do hope I haven't done the wrong thing. Your mother knows where you are, dear? I mean she does, doesn't she?"

The little girl said nothing. She unbuttoned her coat and folded it across her lap. Her dress underneath was prim and dark blue. A gold chain dangled about her neck, and her fingers, sensitive and musical-looking, toyed with it. Examining her more attentively, Mrs. Miller decided the truly distinctive feature was not her hair, but her eyes; they were hazel, steady, lacking any childlike quality whatsoever and, because of their size, seemed to consume her small face.

Mrs. Miller offered a peppermint. "What's your name, dear?"

"Miriam," she said, as though, in some curious way, it were information already familiar.

"Why, isn't that funny—my name's Miriam, too. And it's not a terribly common name either. Now, don't tell me your last name's Miller!"

"Just Miriam."

"But isn't that funny?"

"Moderately," said Miriam, and rolled the peppermint on her tongue.

Mrs. Miller flushed and shifted uncomfortably. "You have such a large vocabulary for such a little girl."

"Do I?"

"Well, yes," said Mrs. Miller, hastily changing the topic to: "Do you like the movies?"

"I really wouldn't know," said Miriam. "I've never been before."

Women began filling the lounge; the rumble of the newsreel bombs[1] exploded in the distance. Mrs. Miller rose, tucking her purse under her arm. "I guess I'd better be running now if I want to get a seat," she said. "It was nice to have met you."

Miriam nodded ever so slightly.

*I*t snowed all week. Wheels and footsteps moved soundlessly on the street, as if the business of living continued secretly behind a pale but impenetrable curtain. In the falling quiet there was no sky or earth, only snow lifting in the wind, frosting the window glass, chilling the rooms, deadening and hushing the city. At all hours it was necessary to keep a lamp lighted, and Mrs. Miller lost track of the days: Friday was no different from Saturday and on Sunday she went to the grocery: closed, of course.

That evening she scrambled eggs and fixed a bowl of tomato soup. Then, after putting on a flannel robe and cold-creaming her face, she propped

---

1 **newsreel bombs:** Newsreels were brief news stories on film, shown before a movie; in this instance, the newsreel covered war news.

herself up in bed with a hot-water bottle under her feet. She was reading the *Times* when the doorbell rang. At first she thought it must be a mistake and whoever it was would go away. But it rang and rang and settled to a persistent buzz. She looked at the clock: a little after eleven; it did not seem possible, she was always asleep by ten.

Climbing out of bed, she trotted barefoot across the living room. "I'm coming, please be patient." The latch was caught; she turned it this way and that way and the bell never paused an instant. "Stop it," she cried. The bolt gave way and she opened the door an inch. "What in heaven's name?"

"Hello," said Miriam.

"Oh . . . why, hello," said Mrs. Miller, stepping hesitantly into the hall. "You're that little girl."

"I thought you'd never answer, but I kept my finger on the button; I knew you were home. Aren't you glad to see me?"

Mrs. Miller did not know what to say. Miriam, she saw, wore the same plum-velvet coat and now she had also a beret to match; her white hair was braided in two shining plaits and looped at the ends with enormous white ribbons.

"Since I've waited so long, you could at least let me in," she said.

"It's awfully late. . . ."

Miriam regarded her blankly. "What difference does that make? Let me in. It's cold out here and I have on a silk dress." Then, with a gentle gesture, she urged Mrs. Miller aside and passed into the apartment.

She dropped her coat and beret on a chair. She was indeed wearing a silk dress. White silk. White silk in February. The skirt was beautifully pleated and the sleeves long; it made a faint rustle as she strolled about the room. "I like your place," she said. "I like the rug, blue's my favorite color." She touched a paper rose in a vase on the coffee table. "Imitation," she commented wanly. "How sad. Aren't imitations sad?" She seated herself on the sofa, daintily spreading her skirt.

"What do you want?" asked Mrs. Miller.

"Sit down," said Miriam. "It makes me nervous to see people stand."

> *W*hite silk. White silk in February. The skirt was beautifully pleated and the sleeves long; it made a faint rustle as she strolled about the room.

*KATIE IN AN
ARMCHAIR
1954
FAIRFIELD PORTER*

Mrs. Miller sank to a hassock.[2] "What do you want?" she repeated.
"You know, I don't think you're glad I came."
For a second time Mrs. Miller was without an answer; her hand motioned

---

2 hassock: a thickly padded cushion or low stool that serves as a small seat or footrest vaguely. Miriam giggled and pressed back on a mound of chintz pillows. Mrs. Miller observed that the girl was less pale than she remembered; her cheeks were flushed.

"How did you know where I lived?"

Miriam frowned. "That's no question at all. What's your name? What's mine?"

"But I'm not listed in the phone book."

"Oh, let's talk about something else."

Mrs. Miller said, "Your mother must be insane to let a child like you wander around at all hours of the night—and in such ridiculous clothes. She must be out of her mind."

Miriam got up and moved to a corner where a covered bird cage hung from a ceiling chain. She peeked beneath the cover. "It's a canary," she said. "Would you mind if I woke him? I'd like to hear him sing."

"Leave Tommy alone," said Mrs. Miller, anxiously. "Don't you dare wake him."

"Certainly," said Miriam. "But I don't see why I can't hear him sing." And then, "Have you anything to eat? I'm starving! Even milk and a jam sandwich would be fine."

"Look," said Mrs. Miller, rising from the hassock, "look—if I make some nice sandwiches will you be a good child and run along home? It's past midnight, I'm sure."

"It's snowing," reproached Miriam. "And cold and dark."

"Well, you shouldn't have come here to begin with," said Mrs. Miller, struggling to control her voice. "I can't help the weather. If you want anything to eat you'll have to promise to leave."

Miriam brushed a braid against her cheek. Her eyes were thoughtful, as if weighing the proposition. She turned toward the bird cage. "Very well," she said, "I promise."

How old is she? Ten? Eleven? Mrs. Miller, in the kitchen, unsealed a jar of strawberry preserves and cut four slices of bread. She poured a glass of milk and paused to light a cigarette. *And why has she come?* Her hand shook as she held the match, fascinated, till it burned her finger. The canary was singing; singing as he did in the morning and at no other time. "Miriam," she called, "Miriam, I told you not to disturb Tommy." There was no answer. She called again; all she heard was the canary. She inhaled the cigarette and discovered she had lighted the cork-tip end and—oh, really, she mustn't lose her temper.

She carried the food in on a tray and set it on the coffee table. She saw first that the bird cage still wore its night cover. And Tommy was singing. It gave her a queer sensation. And no one was in the room. Mrs. Miller went through an alcove leading to her bedroom: at the door she caught her breath.

She saw first that the bird cage still wore its night cover. And Tommy was singing. It gave her a queer sensation.

"What are you doing?" she asked.

Miriam glanced up and in her eyes there was a look that was not ordinary. She was standing by the bureau, a jewel case opened before her. For a minute she studied Mrs. Miller, forcing their eyes to meet, and she smiled. "There's nothing good here," she said. "But I like this." Her hand held a cameo brooch. "It's charming."

"Suppose—perhaps you'd better put it back," said Mrs. Miller, feeling suddenly the need of some support. She leaned against the door frame; her head was unbearably heavy; a pressure weighted the rhythm of her heartbeat. The light seemed to flutter defectively. "Please, child—a gift from my husband . . ."

"But it's beautiful and I want it," said Miriam. *"Give it to me."*

As she stood, striving to shape a sentence which would somehow save the brooch, it came to Mrs. Miller there was no one to whom she might turn; she was alone; a fact that had not been among her thoughts for a long time. Its sheer emphasis was stunning. But here in her own room in the hushed snow-city were evidences she could not ignore or, she knew with startling clarity, resist.

Miriam ate ravenously, and when the sandwiches and milk were gone, her fingers made cobweb movements over the plate, gathering crumbs. The cameo gleamed on her blouse, the blonde profile like a trick reflection of its wearer. "That was very nice," she sighed, "though now an almond cake or a cherry would be ideal. Sweets are lovely, don't you think?"

Mrs. Miller was perched precariously on the hassock, smoking a cigarette. Her hair net had slipped lopsided and loose strands straggled down her face. Her eyes were stupidly concentrated on nothing and her cheeks were mottled in red patches, as though a fierce slap had left permanent marks.

"Is there a candy—a cake?"

Mrs. Miller tapped ash on the rug. Her head swayed slightly as she tried to focus her eyes. "You promised to leave if I made the sandwiches," she said.

"Dear me, did I?"

"It was a promise and I'm tired and I don't feel well at all."

"Mustn't fret," said Miriam, "I'm only teasing."

She picked up her coat, slung it over her arm, and arranged her beret in front of a mirror. Presently she bent close to Mrs. Miller and whispered, "Kiss me good night."

"Please—I'd rather not," said Mrs. Miller.

Miriam lifted a shoulder, arched an eyebrow. "As you like," she said, and went directly to the coffee table, seized the vase containing the paper roses, carried it to where the hard surface of the floor lay bare, and hurled it downward. Glass sprayed in all directions and she stamped her foot on the bouquet.

Then slowly she walked to the door, but before closing it she looked back at Mrs. Miller with a slyly innocent curiosity.

*M*rs. Miller spent the next day in bed, rising once to feed the canary and drink a cup of tea; she took her temperature and had none, yet her dreams were feverishly agitated; their unbalanced mood lingered even as she lay staring wide-eyed at the ceiling. One dream threaded through the others like an elusively mysterious theme in a complicated symphony, and the scenes it depicted were sharply outlined, as though sketched by a hand of

> "*A*s you like," she said, and went directly to the coffee table, seized the vase containing the paper roses, carried it to where the hard surface of the floor lay bare, and hurled it downward.

gifted intensity: a small girl, wearing a bridal gown and a wreath of leaves, led a gray procession down a mountain path, and among them there was unusual silence till a woman at the rear asked, "Where is she taking us?" "No one knows," said an old man marching in front. "But isn't she pretty?" volunteered a third voice, "Isn't she like a frost flower . . . so shining and white?"

Tuesday morning she woke up feeling better; harsh slats of sunlight, slanting through Venetian blinds, shed a disrupting light on her unwholesome fancies. She opened the window to discover a thawed, mild-as-spring day; a sweep of clean new clouds crumpled against a vastly blue, out-of-season sky; and across the low line of roof-tops she could see the river and smoke curving from tug-boat stacks in a warm wind. A great silver truck plowed the snow-banked street, its machine sound humming in the air.

After straightening the apartment, she went to the grocer's, cashed a check and continued to Schrafft's where she ate breakfast and chatted happily with the waitress. Oh, it was a wonderful day—more like a holiday—and it would be so foolish to go home.

She boarded a Lexington Avenue bus and rode up to Eighty-sixth Street; it was here that she had decided to do a little shopping.

She had no idea what she wanted or needed, but she idled along, intent only upon the passers-by, brisk and preoccupied, who gave her a disturbing sense of separateness.

It was while waiting at the corner of Third Avenue that she saw the man: an old man, bowlegged and stooped under an armload of bulging packages; he wore a shabby brown coat and a checkered cap. Suddenly she realized they were exchanging a smile: there was nothing friendly about this smile, it was merely two cold flickers of recognition. But she was certain she had never seen him before.

He was standing next to an El pillar,[3] and as she crossed the street he turned and followed. He kept quite close; from the corner of her eye she watched his reflection wavering on the shop windows.

Then in the middle of the block she stopped and faced him. He stopped also and cocked his head, grinning. But what could she say? Do? Here, in broad daylight, on Eighty-sixth Street? It was useless and, despising her own helplessness, she quickened her steps.

---

3 **El pillar:** The El is the elevated sections of the New York City subway system. Pillars hold up the platforms where riders get on and off the trains.

> *But a series of unaccountable purchases had begun, as if by pre-arranged plan: a plan of which she had not the least knowledge or control.*

Now Second Avenue is a dismal street, made from scraps and ends; part cobblestone, part asphalt, part cement; and its atmosphere of desertion is permanent. Mrs. Miller walked five blocks without meeting anyone, and all the while the steady crunch of his footfalls in the snow stayed near. And when she came to a florist's shop, the sound was still with her. She hurried inside and watched through the glass door as the old man passed; he kept his eyes straight ahead and didn't slow his pace, but he did one strange, telling thing: he tipped his cap.

"Six white ones, did you say?" asked the florist. "Yes," she told him, "white roses." From there she went to a glassware store and selected a vase, presumably a replacement for the one Miriam had broken, though the price was intolerable and the vase itself (she thought) grotesquely vulgar. But a series of unaccountable purchases had begun, as if by pre-arranged plan: a plan of which she had not the least knowledge or control.

She bought a bag of glazed cherries, and at a place called the Knickerbocker Bakery she paid forty cents for six almond cakes.

Within the last hour the weather had turned cold again; like blurred lenses, winter clouds cast a shade over the sun, and the skeleton of an early dusk colored the sky; a damp mist mixed with the wind and the voices of a few children who romped high on mountains of gutter snow seemed lonely and cheerless. Soon the first flake fell, and when Mrs. Miller reached the brownstone house, snow was falling in a swift screen and foot tracks vanished as they were printed.

The white roses were arranged decoratively in the vase. The glazed cherries shone on a ceramic plate. The almond cakes, dusted with sugar, awaited a hand. The canary fluttered on its swing and picked at a bar of seed.

At precisely five the doorbell rang. Mrs. Miller *knew* who it was. The hem of her housecoat trailed as she crossed the floor. "Is that you?" she called.

"Naturally," said Miriam, the word resounding shrilly from the hall. "Open this door."

"Go away," said Mrs. Miller.

"Please hurry . . . I have a heavy package."

"Go away," said Mrs. Miller. She returned to the living room, lighted a cigarette, sat down, and calmly listened to the buzzer; on and on and on. "You might as well leave. I have no intention of letting you in."

Shortly the bell stopped. For possibly ten minutes Mrs. Miller did not move. Then, hearing no sound, she concluded Miriam had gone. She tiptoed to the door and opened it a sliver; Miriam was half-reclining atop a cardboard box with a beautiful French doll cradled in her arms.

"Really, I thought you were never coming," she said peevishly. "Here, help me get this in, it's awfully heavy."

It was not spell-like compulsion that Mrs. Miller felt, but rather a curious passivity; she brought in the box, Miriam the doll. Miriam curled up on the sofa, not troubling to remove her coat or beret, and watched disinterestedly as Mrs. Miller dropped the box and stood trembling, trying to catch her breath.

"Thank you," she said. In the daylight she looked pinched and drawn, her hair less luminous. The French doll she was loving wore an exquisite powdered wig and its idiot glass eyes sought solace in Miriam's.

"Thank you," she said. In the daylight she looked pinched and drawn, her hair less luminous. The French doll she was loving wore an exquisite powdered wig and its idiot glass eyes sought solace in Miriam's. "I have a surprise," she continued. "Look into my box."

Kneeling, Mrs. Miller parted the flaps and lifted out another doll; then a blue dress which she recalled as the one Miriam had worn that first night at the theater; and of the remainder she said, "It's all clothes. Why?"

"Because I've come to live with you," said Miriam, twisting a cherry stem. "Wasn't it nice of you to buy me the cherries . . . ?"

"But you can't! For God's sake go away—go away and leave me alone!"

". . . and the roses and the almond cakes? How really wonderfully generous. You know, these cherries are delicious. The last place I lived was with an old man; he was terribly poor and we never had good things to eat. But I think I'll be happy here." She paused to snuggle her doll closer. "Now, if you'll just show me where to put my things . . ."

Mrs. Miller's face dissolved into a mask of ugly red lines; she began to cry, and it was an unnatural, tearless sort of weeping, as though, not having wept for a long time, she had forgotten how. Carefully she edged backward till she touched the door.

*S*he fumbled through the hall and down the stairs to a landing below. She pounded frantically on the door of the first apartment she came to; a short, red-headed man answered and she pushed past him. "Say, what the hell is this?" he said. "Anything wrong, lover?" asked a young woman who appeared from the kitchen, drying her hands. And it was to her that Mrs. Miller turned.

"Listen," she cried, "I'm ashamed behaving this way but—well, I'm Mrs. H. T. Miller and I live upstairs and . . ." She pressed her hands over her face. "It sounds so absurd . . . ."

The woman guided her to a chair, while the man excitedly rattled pocket change. "Yeah?"

"I live upstairs and there's a little girl visiting me, and I suppose that I'm afraid of her. She won't leave and I can't make her and—she's going to do something terrible. She's already stolen my cameo, but she's about to do something worse— something terrible!"

The man asked, "Is she a relative, huh?"

> *M*rs. Miller's face dissolved into a mask of ugly red lines; she began to cry, and it was an unnatural, tearless sort of weeping, as though, not having wept for a long time, she had forgotten how.

Mrs. Miller shook her head. "I don't know who she is. Her name's Miriam, but I don't know for certain who she is."

"You gotta calm down, honey," said the woman, stroking Mrs. Miller's arm. "Harry here'll tend to this kid. Go on, lover." And Mrs. Miller said, "The door's open—5A."

After the man left, the woman brought a towel and bathed Mrs. Miller's face. "You're very kind," Mrs. Miller said. "I'm sorry to act like such a fool, only this wicked child . . ."

"Sure, honey," consoled the woman. "Now, you better take it easy."

Mrs. Miller rested her head in the crook of her arm; she was quiet enough to be asleep. The woman turned a radio dial; a piano and a husky voice filled the silence and the woman, tapping her foot, kept excellent time. "Maybe we oughta go up too," she said.

"I don't want to see her again. I don't want to be anywhere near her."

"Uh huh, but what you shoulda done, you shoulda called a cop."

Presently they heard the man on the stairs. He strode into the room frowning and scratching the back of his neck. "Nobody there," he said, honestly embarrassed. "She musta beat it."

"Harry, you're a jerk," announced the woman. "We been sitting here the whole time and we woulda seen . . ." She stopped abruptly, for the man's glance was sharp.

"I looked all over," he said, "and there just ain't nobody there. Nobody, understand?"

"Tell me," said Mrs. Miller, rising, "tell me, did you see a large box? Or a doll?"

"No, ma'am, I didn't."

And the woman, as if delivering a verdict, said, "Well, for cryin out loud . . . "

> *The* sofa loomed before her with a new strangeness: its vacancy had a meaning that would have been less penetrating and terrible had Miriam been curled on it.

Mrs. Miller entered her apartment softly; she walked to the center of the room and stood quite still. No, in a sense it had not changed: the roses, the cakes, and the cherries were in place. But this was an empty room, emptier than if the furnishings and familiars were not present, lifeless and petrified as a funeral parlor. The sofa loomed before her with a new strangeness: its vacancy had a meaning that would have been less penetrating and terrible had Miriam been curled on it. She gazed fixedly at the space where she remembered setting the box and, for a moment, the hassock spun desperately. And she looked through the window; surely the river was real, surely snow was falling—but then, one could not be certain witness to anything: Miriam, so vividly *there*—and yet, where was she? Where, where?

As though moving in a dream, she sank to a chair. The room was losing shape; it was dark and getting darker and there was nothing to be done about it; she could not lift her hand to light a lamp.

Suddenly, closing her eyes, she felt an upward surge, like a diver emerging from some deeper, greener depth. In times of terror or immense distress, there are moments when the mind waits, as though for a revelation, while

skein:
loose coil, as of thread or yarn

a **skein** of calm is woven over thought; it is like a sleep, or a supernatural trance; and during this lull one is aware of a force of quiet reasoning: well, what if she had never really known a girl named Miriam? That she had been foolishly frightened on the street? In the end, like everything else, it was of no importance. For the only thing she had lost to Miriam was her identity, but now she knew she had found again the person who lived in this room, who cooked her own meals, who owned a canary, who was someone she could trust and believe in: Mrs. H. T. Miller.

Listening in contentment, she became aware of a double sound: a bureau drawer opening and closing: she seemed to hear it long after completion—opening and closing. Then gradually, the harshness of it was replaced by the murmur of a silk dress and this, delicately faint, was moving nearer and swelling in intensity till the walls trembled with the vibration and the room was caving under a wave of whispers. Mrs. Miller stiffened and opened her eyes to a dull, direct stare.

"Hello," said Miriam.

Read and Think Critically

Describe, Explain, Analyze

1. **VOICE** How would you describe Capote's **voice**? Use passages from the story to explain your description.

2. Mrs. Miller dreams that a girl who resembles Miriam is leading a bridal procession when one of the party asks, "Where is she taking us?" Where do you think young Miriam is taking Mrs. Miller?

3. The author purposely leaves the existence of Miriam uncertain. Do you think young Miriam really exists, or is she a figment of Mrs. Miller's imagination?

4. An *enigma* is something mysterious and difficult to explain. Miriam often delivers enigmatic statements, such as her observation upon touching the paper roses on Mrs. Miller's coffee table: "How sad. Aren't imitations sad?" Find one of these mysterious statements in the text and explain what you think it could mean.

5. **THE AUTHOR'S STYLE** Capote's short works of fiction are often referred to as **tales** instead of stories. A *tale* is a highly imaginative telling of sometimes fanciful events. Analyze Capote's use of stylistic techniques that give "Miriam" the feel of a tale rather than a story.

Responding to Unit Three

Key Ideas and Details

1. For their grotesque and macabre incidents, both "The Lottery" and "Miriam" might appear in a collection of horror stories. Analyze the **setting**, **characterization**, and **plot** of both stories. Which one do you find more more satisfyingly creepy?

2. Choose your favorite story from this unit. Write an objective summary of the story. Then write a one-page review of the story for a literary journal.

3. In three of the stories in this unit—"He," "The Far and the Near," and "The Chrysanthemums"—at least one important **character** is never given a name. Why do you think the authors leave the characters' names unclear in each instance?

Craft and Structure

4. Find a passage from this unit that you find particularly engaging or beautiful. Explain the techniques the author uses to make it so appealing to the reader.

5. Both the ball in "The Black Ball" and the black box in "The Lottery" are **symbols**. Explain both the literal meaning and the symbolic meaning of each. How do the authors use these symbols to communicate the **themes** of the stories?

Integration of Knowledge and Ideas

6. The first six stories in this unit have a theme of loss in common. In your opinion, which story evokes the most **pathos**? Give reasons to support your opinion.

7. Hemingway and Fitzgerald were both friends and competitors, moving in the same social circles and writing during the same era. Compare and contrast the styles and **themes** found in "In Another Country" and "Babylon Revisited."

8. The opening sentence of *Anna Karenina* by the Russian author Leo Tolstoy reads: "All happy families resemble one another; every unhappy family is unhappy in its own way." Consider the families in "He" and "Why I Live at the P.O." How are the families similar or different in their unhappiness?

Writing About the Literature

Staying Power

The stories in this unit were all written more than 50 years ago. Write a persuasive essay about which story you think has best stood the test of time. You may want to use passages from the story as evidence. Consider what is timeless about the style, theme, or characters of the story you choose.

Writing with Style

Choose one of these two assignments.

Sucker's Point of View

Using McCullers' style, rewrite the climax of "Sucker" as an interior monologue from the point of view of Sucker.

"The Secret Life of _____ "

Fill in the blank with the name of a seemingly ordinary character of your own creation. Using Thurber's style, put this character into an everyday situation that the character converts into a grandiose fantasy starring him- or herself.

★★

IN YOUR OWN STYLE

After reflecting on how important the theme of loss is in many of the stories in this unit, consider your own life. What have you or someone you know either already lost or would most hate to lose? Write about this in your own style. Choose between taking a nonfiction approach or using your own or others' experiences as a starting point for fiction.

Unit Four
Post-War Voices 1950s and 1960s

PAINTING NUMBER 2, FRANZ KLINE, 1954

As soldiers came home from World War II, they returned to a different America. Cities began to encroach upon the rural landscape, and farms and tractors gave way to suburban cul-de-sacs and basketball hoops. The economy boomed and the returning GIs enjoyed the cornucopia it produced: refrigerators, TVs, dishwashers, and air conditioners. Beneath the surface of calm and prosperity, however, there were troubled waters. International peace was strained in what became known as the Cold War. Americans worried about the Soviet Union, communism, and the threat of nuclear war. And of course, not everyone was stepping up into the new middle class. The Civil Rights movement would bring into focus the poverty and racism that city and rural blacks were still enduring.

American writers of the period captured the anxiety at the heart of this new economy. They showed how the society was increasingly divided between urban and suburban, North and South, black and white, rich and poor and, especially in the sixties, young and old. Characters in fiction of the period reflected a national personality split between what was felt and what was revealed, between what was said and what was done.

Postmodernism

Postmodernism was a cultural, literary, and artistic movement that emerged in the late fifties and lasted, according to some, until around the year 2000. Like the modernists, postmodern writers focused on subjective experience rather than objective cultural norms, emphasized fragmentation and collage-like effects, and rejected distinctions between high and low art forms. But where modernists mourned the loss of order and sought to create structure and meaning through their art, postmodernists seemed to play in the chaos. Rather than mourn lost forms, they celebrated diversity and fragmentation and took the opportunity to create new forms through experimentation.

Kurt Vonnegut was one of the key figures in postmodern American fiction. He lived through multiple tragedies and then wrote about them with a wicked and ironic sense of humor. As an American prisoner of war in Germany, Vonnegut was bombed by America's allies. While home on leave, his mother committed suicide on Mother's Day. Later, his sister would succumb to cancer the same day that her husband died in a train crash. Vonnegut turned such cruelly random events into dark fiction. His joy-filled observations of a terrifying world appealed to a generation grieved by the Holocaust, atomic bombings, and the assassinations of President John F. Kennedy and Civil Rights leader Martin Luther King, Jr.

Other writers of the postmodern era applied discontinuity directly to their writing, making reading strangely enjoyable work. Like Ireland's James Joyce, Nobel Prize-winner William Faulkner took readers into the chaos of the mind with the writing style called *stream of consciousness*. In this form, a character's point of view is revealed through disjointed and illogical interior monologue meant to replicate the "free association" of thoughts and emotions.

A small group of writers known as the Beat Generation appeared in the fifties and sixties with disruptive fiction and spontaneous poetry. Jack Kerouac, William Burroughs, and Allen Ginsberg led the way for a new youth culture. They merged genres, like the western and the detective story, with playful prose. They even invited readers to re-order the words of their poems and the loose pages of their fiction in order to create new meanings.

Space Race, Sci Fi, and Suburban Angst

As the United States and the Soviet Union competed to be the first to put a man on the moon, Americans became obsessed with space as a new frontier. Did the future hold a Martian home with shiny kitchen gadgets? Known for science fiction and fantasy, Ray Bradbury explored the possibilities of a society in which the gadgets were limitless but so were the unforeseen consequences. Bradbury, like Vonnegut, imagined fantastic worlds in which human inventiveness outpaced common sense, often in terrifying ways.

Bradbury's stories expressed the growing unease Americans felt with 20th-century progress. Writers such as John Updike and John Cheever joined the warning cry. Writing from the suburban front, they showed us that a bigger house didn't make a man any happier with his job or his wife. They suggested that America's worries about communism and the atom bomb couldn't compare with man's anxiety over the emptiness of everyday life. Updike has been compared to the greatest novelists of the 19th century, and Cheever has been dubbed the "Chekhov of the Suburbs" after the revered Russian writer.

If the sameness of suburbia—the persistent homogeneity of its people, cars, and houses—rattled some writers, others gave voice to problems simmering outside the new suburbs. Ernest J. Gaines describes the pain of racism as though it were the throb of an unending toothache. Flannery O'Connor takes us on a city bus ride with segregated blacks, white Dixie matriarchs, and annoyingly righteous new Southern liberals. Mixing fable, myth, and city grit, Bernard Malamud gives us a taste of the North, where immigrant sons seek peace with their ancient heritages and with what it means to be American.

Before You Read

Ray Bradbury   1920–2012

About the Author

Ray Bradbury was a writer of highly imaginative fantasies about science and technology. Yet oddly enough, he himself never flew in an airplane nor learned to drive. The author grew up in the Midwest, attended high school in California, and never went to college. Two of the most striking things about Bradbury were his sheer literary output and his legendary energy. In an introduction to *The Stories of Ray Bradbury* in 1980, he explained that ideas simply came to him: "My [stories] run up and bite me on the leg—I respond by writing down everything that goes on during the bite. When I finish, the idea lets go and runs off."

Bradbury sold his first short story at age 19. After that he wrote hundreds more, many of which he adapted for television's *Ray Bradbury's Theater*. He also worked in animated film, published more than 30 books, and served as a consultant for science-related projects, including an exhibit at Epcot Center in Florida and a space ride at Euro-Disney in France.

Among his most famous novels are *The Martian Chronicles*, *Fahrenheit 451*, and *Something Wicked This Way Comes*, all of which were made into movies. He was the recipient of many awards, including the World Fantasy Award for Lifetime Achievement.

****

The Author's Style

Bradbury's skill as a science fiction writer lies in his ability to convey a simultaneous sense of the familiar and the alien. His work reveals both the attractiveness and the dangers of science by creating contemporary settings that are fascinating but about to spin out of control. He even "predicted" scientific innovations such as virtual reality, or artificial environment technologies, by imagining them in his fiction before they became realities.

Adept at making readers laugh, marvel, or shudder, Bradbury uses eerie details to foreshadow how his stories might end. A consistent theme in the author's work is that too much of anything isn't good for anyone. The author is known for his skillful use of descriptive language, particularly for striking and memorable metaphors and similes. A versatile author, he also wrote poetry and children's stories.

Bradbury uses the technique of giving his made-up technologies general names that could be used anywhere. In the story you are about to read, for example, readers soon realize that what happens in the "Happylife Home" system may not be unique to this particular family. In fact, he implies it could happen anywhere.

The Veldt

RAY BRADBURY

 LITERARY LENS: THEME In order to communicate the **theme** of the story, Bradbury juxtaposes (or places side by side) two concepts or ideas in order to compare them. Watch for juxtapositions in this story.

"George, I wish you'd look at the nursery."

"What's wrong with it?"

"I don't know."

"Well, then."

"I just want you to look at it, is all, or call a psychologist in to look at it."

"What would a psychologist want with a nursery?"

"You know very well what he'd want." His wife paused in the middle of the kitchen and watched the stove busy humming to itself, making supper for four.

"It's just that the nursery is different now than it was."

"All right, let's have a look."

They walked down the hall of their soundproofed, Happylife

Home, which had cost them thirty thousand dollars installed, this house which clothed and fed and rocked them to sleep and played and sang and was good to them. Their approach sensitized a switch somewhere and the nursery light flicked on when they came within ten feet of it. Similarly, behind them, in the halls, lights went on and off as they left them behind, with a soft automaticity.

"Well," said George Hadley.

They stood on the thatched floor of the nursery. It was forty feet across by forty feet long and thirty feet high; it had cost half again as much as the rest of the house. "But nothing's too good for our children," George had said.

The nursery was silent. It was empty as a jungle glade at hot high noon. The walls were blank and two dimensional. Now, as George and Lydia Hadley stood in the center of the room, the walls began to purr and recede into **crystalline** distance, it seemed, and presently an African veldt[1] appeared, in three dimensions; on all sides, in colors reproduced to the final pebble and bit of straw. The ceiling above them became a deep sky with a hot yellow sun.

crystalline: sparkling; made of crystal

George Hadley felt the perspiration start on his brow.

"Let's get out of the sun," he said. "This is a little too real. But I don't see anything wrong."

"Wait a moment, you'll see," said his wife.

Now the hidden odorophonics were beginning to blow a wind of odor at the two people in the middle of the baked veldtland. The hot straw smell of lion grass, the cool green smell of the hidden water hole, the great rusty smell of animals, the smell of dust like a red paprika in the hot air. And now the sounds: the thump of distant antelope feet on grassy sod, the papery rustling of vultures. A shadow passed through the sky. The shadow flickered on George Hadley's upturned, sweating face.

"Filthy creatures," he heard his wife say.

"The vultures."

"You see, there are the lions, far over, that way. Now they're on their way to the water hole. They've just been eating," said Lydia. "I don't know what."

"Some animal." George Hadley put his hand up to shield off the burning light from his squinted eyes. "A zebra or a baby giraffe, maybe."

"Are you sure?" His wife sounded peculiarly tense.

"No, it's a little late to be sure," he said, amused. "Nothing over there I can see but cleaned bone, and the vultures dropping for what's left."

---

1 **veldt:** a grassland with scattered shrubs or trees

"Did you hear that scream?" she asked.

"No."

"About a minute ago?"

"Sorry, no."

The lions were coming. And again George Hadley was filled with admiration for the mechanical genius who had conceived this room. A miracle of efficiency selling for an absurdly low price. Every home should have one. Oh, occasionally they frightened you with their clinical accuracy, they startled you, gave you a twinge, but most of the time what fun for everyone, not only your own son and daughter, but for yourself when you felt like a quick jaunt to a foreign land, a quick change of scenery. Well, here it was!

And here were the lions now, fifteen feet away, so real, so feverishly and startlingly real that you could feel the prickling fur on your hand . . .

And here were the lions now, fifteen feet away, so real, so feverishly and startlingly real that you could feel the prickling fur on your hand, and your mouth was stuffed with the dusty upholstery smell of their heated pelts, and the yellow of them was in your eyes like the yellow of an exquisite French tapestry, the yellows of lions and summer grass, and the sound of the matted lion lungs exhaling on the silent noontide, and the smell of meat from the panting, dripping mouths.

The lions stood looking at George and Lydia Hadley with terrible green-yellow eyes.

"Watch out!" screamed Lydia.

The lions came running at them.

Lydia bolted and ran. Instinctively, George sprang after her. Outside, in the hall, with the door slammed, he was laughing and she was crying, and they both stood appalled at the other's reaction.

"George!"

"Lydia! Oh, my dear poor sweet Lydia!"

"They almost got us!"

"Walls, Lydia, remember; crystal walls, that's all they are. Oh, they look real, I must admit—Africa in your parlor—but it's all dimensional super-reactionary, supersensitive color film and mental tape film behind glass screens. It's all odorophonics and sonics, Lydia. Here's my handkerchief."

"I'm afraid." She came to him and put her body against him and cried steadily. "Did you see? Did you *feel*? It's too real."

"Now, Lydia . . . "

"You've got to tell Wendy and Peter not to read any more on Africa."

"Of course—of course." He patted her.

"Promise?"

"Sure."

"And lock the nursery for a few days until I get my nerves settled."

"You know how difficult Peter is about that. When I punished him a month ago by locking the nursery for even a few hours—the tantrum he threw! And Wendy too. They *live* for the nursery."

"It's got to be locked, that's all there is to it."

"All right." Reluctantly he locked the huge door. "You've been working too hard. You need a rest."

"I don't know—I don't know," she said, blowing her nose, sitting down in a chair that immediately began to rock and comfort her. "Maybe I don't have enough to do. Maybe I have time to think too much. Why don't we shut the whole house off for a few days and take a vacation?"

"You mean you want to fry my eggs for me?"

"Yes." She nodded.

"And darn my socks?"

"Yes." A frantic, watery-eyed nodding.

"And sweep the house?"

"Yes, yes—oh yes!"

"But I thought that's why we bought this house, so we wouldn't have to do anything?"

"That's just it. I feel like I don't belong here. The house is wife and mother now and nursemaid. Can I compete with an African veldt? Can I give a bath and scrub the children as efficiently or quickly as the automatic scrub bath can? I can not. And it isn't just me. It's you. You've been awfully nervous lately."

"I suppose I have been smoking too much."

"You look as if you didn't know what to do with yourself in this house, either. You smoke a little more every morning and drink a little more every afternoon and need a little more sedative every night. You're beginning to feel unnecessary too."

"Am I?" He paused and tried to feel into himself to see what was really there.

"Oh, George!" She looked beyond him, at the nursery door. "Those lions can't get out of there, can they?"

He looked at the door and saw it tremble as if something had jumped against it from the other side.

"Of course not," he said.

$\mathcal{A}$t dinner they ate alone, for Wendy and Peter were at a special plastic carnival across town and had televised home to say they'd be late, to go ahead eating. So George Hadley, bemused, sat watching the dining-room table produce warm dishes of food from its mechanical interior.

"We forgot the ketchup," he said.

"Sorry," said a small voice within the table, and ketchup appeared.

As for the nursery, thought George Hadley, it won't hurt for the children to be locked out of it awhile. Too much of anything isn't good for anyone. And it was clearly indicated that the children had been spending a little too much time on Africa. That sun. He could feel it on his neck, still, like a hot paw. And the lions. And the smell of blood. Remarkable how the nursery caught the telepathic **emanations** of the children's minds and created life to fill their every desire. The children thought lions, and there were lions. The children thought zebras, and there were zebras. Sun—sun. Giraffes—giraffes. Death and death.

emanations:
transmissions;
messages

That last. He chewed tastelessly on the meat that the table had cut for him. Death thoughts. They were awfully young, Wendy and Peter, for death thoughts. Or, no, you were never too young, really. Long before you knew what death was you were wishing it on someone else. When you were two years old you were shooting people with cap pistols.

But this—the long, hot African veldt—the awful death in the jaws of a lion. And repeated again and again.

"Where are you going?"

He didn't answer Lydia. Preoccupied, he let the lights glow softly on ahead of him, extinguished behind him as he padded to the nursery door. He listened against it. Far away, a lion roared.

He unlocked the door and opened it. Just before he stepped inside, he heard a faraway scream. And then another roar from the lions, which subsided quickly.

He stepped into Africa. How many times in the last year had he opened this door and found Wonderland, Alice, the Mock Turtle, or Aladdin and his

Magical Lamp, or Jack Pumpkinhead of Oz, or Dr. Doolittle, or the cow jumping over a very real-appearing moon—all the delightful contraptions of a make-believe word. How often had he seen Pegasus[2] flying in the sky ceiling, or seen fountains of red fireworks, or heard angel voices singing. But now, this yellow hot Africa, this bake oven with murder in the heat. Perhaps Lydia was right. Perhaps they needed a little vacation from the fantasy which was growing a bit too real for ten-year-old children. It was all right to exercise one's mind with gymnastic fantasies, but when the lively child mind settled on *one* pattern . . . ? It seemed that, at a distance, for the past month, he had heard lions roaring, and smelled their strong odor seeping as far away as his study door. But, being busy, he had paid it no attention.

George Hadley stood on the African grassland alone. The lions looked up from their feeding, watching him. The only flaw to the illusion was the open door through which he could see his wife, far down the dark hall, like a framed picture, eating her dinner **abstractedly**.

abstractedly: absentmindedly

"Go away," he said to the lions.

They did not go.

He knew the principle of the room exactly. You sent out your thoughts. Whatever you thought would appear.

"Let's have Aladdin and his lamp," he snapped.

The veldtland remained; the lions remained.

"Come on, room! I demand Aladdin!" he said.

Nothing happened. The lions mumbled in their baked pelts.

"Aladdin!"

He went back to dinner. "The fool room's out of order," he said. "It won't respond."

"Or—"

"Or what?"

"Or it *can't* respond," said Lydia, "because the children have thought about Africa and lions and killing so many days that the room's in a rut."

"Could be."

"Or Peter's set it to remain that way."

"*Set* it?"

"He may have got into the machinery and fixed something."

"Peter doesn't know machinery."

"He's a wise one for ten. That I.Q. of his—"

---

2 **Pegasus:** a flying horse in Greek mythology

"Nevertheless—"

"Hello, Mom. Hello, Dad."

The Hadleys turned. Wendy and Peter were coming in the front door, cheeks like peppermint candy, eyes like bright blue agate[3] marbles, a smell of ozone on their jumpers from their trip in the helicopter.

"You're just in time for supper," said both parents.

"We're full of strawberry ice cream and hot dogs," said the children, holding hands. "But we'll sit and watch."

"Yes, come tell us about the nursery," said George Hadley.

The brother and sister blinked at him and then at each other. "Nursery?"

"All about Africa and everything," said the father with false **joviality**.

"I don't understand," said Peter.

"Your mother and I were just traveling through Africa with rod and reel; Tom Swift and his Electric Lion,"[4] said George Hadley.

"There's no Africa in the nursery," said Peter simply.

"Oh, come now, Peter. We know better."

"I don't remember any Africa," said Peter to Wendy. "Do you?"

"No."

"Run see and come tell."

She obeyed.

"Wendy, come back here!" said George Hadley, but she was gone. The house lights followed her like a flock of fireflies. Too late, he realized he had forgotten to lock the nursery door after his last inspection.

"Wendy'll look and come tell us," said Peter.

"She doesn't have to tell *me*. I've seen it."

"I'm sure you're mistaken, Father."

"I'm not, Peter. Come along now."

But Wendy was back. "It's not Africa," she said breathlessly.

"We'll see about this," said George Hadley, and they all walked down the hall together and opened the nursery door.

There was a green, lovely forest, a lovely river, a purple mountain, high voices singing, and Rima,[5] lovely and mysterious, lurking in the trees with colorful flights of butterflies, like animated bouquets, lingering on her long

joviality:
cheerfulness

---

3 **agate:** having colors blended like clouds

4 **Tom Swift . . . Lion:** title of a book in a series of adventure novels by Victor Appleton

5 **Rima:** a character in *Green Mansions*, an early 20th-century romance novel by British author William Henry Hudson. Raised in a rain forest of South America, Rima is able to speak the language of the forest, including the songs of birds.

"I don't know anything," he said, "except that I'm beginning to be sorry we bought that room for the children. If children are neurotic at all, a room like that—"

hair. The African veldtland was gone. The lions were gone. Only Rima was here now, singing a song so beautiful that it brought tears to your eyes.

George Hadley looked in at the changed scene. "Go to bed," he said to the children.

They opened their mouths.

"You heard me," he said.

They went off to the air closet, where a wind sucked them like brown leaves up the flue to their slumber rooms.

George Hadley walked through the singing glade and picked up something that lay in the corner near where the lions had been. He walked slowly back to his wife.

"What is that?" she asked.

"An old wallet of mine," he said.

He showed it to her. The smell of hot grass was on it and the smell of a lion. There were drops of saliva on it, it had been chewed and there were blood smears on both sides.

He closed the nursery door and locked it, tight.

In the middle of the night he was still awake and he knew his wife was awake. "Do you think Wendy changed it?" she said at last, in the dark room.

"Of course."

"Made it from a veldt into a forest and put Rima there instead of lions?"

"Yes."

"Why?"

"I don't know. But it's staying locked until I find out."

"How did your wallet get there?"

"I don't know anything," he said, "except that I'm beginning to be sorry we bought that room for the children. If children are **neurotic** at all, a room like that—"

"It's supposed to help them work off their neuroses in a healthful way."

"I'm starting to wonder." He stared at the ceiling.

"We've given the children everything they ever wanted. Is this our reward—secrecy, disobedience?"

"Who was it said, 'Children are carpets, they should be stepped on occasionally'? We've never lifted a hand. They're insufferable—let's admit it. They

neurotic: mentally or emotionally disturbed

come and go when they like; they treat us as if *we* were offspring. They're spoiled and we're spoiled."

"They've been acting funny ever since you forbade them to take the rocket to New York a few months ago."

"They're not old enough to do that alone, I explained."

"Nevertheless, I've noticed they've been decidedly cool toward us since."

"I think I'll have Dave McClean come tomorrow morning to have a look at Africa."

"But it's not Africa now, it's Green Mansions country and Rima."

"I have a feeling it'll be Africa again before then."

A moment later they heard the screams.

Two screams. Two people screaming from downstairs. And then a roar of lions.

"Wendy and Peter aren't in their rooms," said his wife.

He lay in his bed with his beating heart. "No," he said. "They've broken into the nursery."

"Those screams—they sound familiar."

"Do they?"

"Yes, awfully."

And although their beds tried very hard, the two adults couldn't be rocked to sleep for another hour. A smell of cats was in the night air.

"*F*ather?" said Peter.

"Yes."

Peter looked at his shoes. He never looked at his father any more, nor at his mother. "You aren't going to lock up the nursery for good, are you?"

"That all depends."

"On what?" snapped Peter.

"On you and your sister. If you intersperse this Africa with a little variety—oh, Sweden perhaps, or Denmark or China—"

"I thought we were free to play as we wished."

"You are, within reasonable bounds."

"What's wrong with Africa, Father?"

"Oh, so now you admit you have been conjuring up Africa, do you?"

"I wouldn't want the nursery locked up," said Peter coldly. "Ever."

"Matter of fact, we're thinking of turning the whole house off for about a month. Live sort of a carefree one-for-all existence."

"That sounds dreadful! Would I have to tie my own shoes instead of letting the shoe tier do it? And brush my own teeth and comb my hair and give myself a bath?"

"It would be fun for a change, don't you think?"

"No, it would be horrid. I didn't like it when you took out the picture painter last month."

"That's because I wanted you to learn to paint all by yourself, son."

"I don't want to do anything but look and listen and smell; what else *is* there to do?"

"All right, go play in Africa."

"Will you shut off the house sometime soon?"

"We're considering it."

"I don't think you'd better consider it any more, Father."

"I won't have any threats from my son!"

"Very well." And Peter strolled off to the nursery.

"*A*m I on time?" said David McClean.

"Breakfast?" asked George Hadley.

"Thanks, had some. What's the trouble?"

"David, you're a psychologist."

"I should hope so."

"Well, then, have a look at our nursery. You saw it a year ago when you dropped by; did you notice anything peculiar about it then?"

"Can't say I did; the usual violences, a tendency toward a slight paranoia here or there, usual in children because they feel persecuted by parents constantly, but, oh, really nothing."

They walked down the hall. "I locked the nursery up," explained the father, "and the children broke back into it during the night. I let them stay so they could form the patterns for you to see."

There was a terrible screaming from the nursery.

"There it is," said George Hadley. "See what you make of it."

They walked in on the children without rapping.

The screams had faded. The lions were feeding.

"Run outside a moment, children," said George Hadley. "No, don't change the mental combination. Leave the walls as they are. Get!"

With the children gone, the two men stood studying the lions clustered at a distance, eating with great relish whatever it was they had caught.

"I wish I knew what it was," said George Hadley. "Sometimes I can almost see. Do you think if I brought high-powered binoculars here and—"

David McClean laughed dryly. "Hardly." He turned to study all four walls. "How long has this been going on?"

"A little over a month."

"It certainly doesn't *feel* good."

"I want facts, not feelings."

"My dear George, a psychologist never saw a fact in his life. He only hears about feelings; vague things. This doesn't feel good, I tell you. Trust my hunches and my instincts. I have a nose for something bad. This is very bad. My advice to you is to have the whole damn room torn down and your children brought to me every day during the next year for treatment."

"Is it that bad?"

"I'm afraid so. One of the original uses of these nurseries was so that we could study the patterns left on the walls by the child's mind, study at our leisure, and help the child. In this case, however, the room has become a channel toward—destructive thoughts, instead of a release away from them."

"Didn't you sense this before?"

"I sensed only that you had spoiled your children more than most. And now you're letting them down in some way. What way?"

"I wouldn't let them go to New York."

"What else?"

"I've taken a few machines from the house and threatened them, a month ago, with closing up the nursery unless they did their homework. I did close it for a few days to show I meant business."

"Ah, ha!"

"Does that mean anything?"

"Everything. Where before they had a Santa Claus now they have a Scrooge. Children prefer Santas. You've let this room and this house replace you and your wife in your children's affections. This room is their mother and father, far more important in their lives than their real parents. And now you come along and want to shut it off. No wonder there's hatred here. You can feel it coming out of the sky. Feel that sun. George, you'll have to change your life. Like too many others, you've built it around creature comforts. Why, you'd starve tomorrow if something went wrong in your kitchen. You wouldn't know how to tap an egg. Nevertheless, turn everything off. Start new. It'll take time. But we'll make good children out of bad in a year, wait and see."

"But won't the shock be too much for the children, shutting the room up abruptly, for good?"

"I don't want them going any deeper into this, that's all."

The lions were finished with their red feast.

The lions were standing on the edge of the clearing watching the two men.

"Now *I'm* feeling persecuted," said McClean. "Let's get out of here. I never have cared for these damned rooms. Make me nervous."

"The lions look real, don't they?" said George Hadley. "I don't suppose there's any way—"

"What?"

"—that they could *become* real?"

"Not that I know."

"Some flaw in the machinery, a tampering or something?"

"No."

They went to the door.

"I don't imagine the room will like being turned off," said the father.

"Nothing ever likes to die—even a room."

"I wonder if it hates me for wanting to switch it off?"

"Paranoia is thick around here today," said David McClean. "You can follow it like a spoor.[6] Hello." He bent and picked up a bloody scarf. "This yours?"

"No." George Hadley's face was rigid. "It belongs to Lydia."

They went to the fuse box together and threw the switch that killed the nursery.

The two children were in hysterics. They screamed and pranced and threw things. They yelled and sobbed and swore and jumped at the furniture.

"You can't do that to the nursery, you can't!"

"Now, children."

The children flung themselves onto a couch, weeping.

"George," said Lydia Hadley, "turn on the nursery, just for a few moments. You can't be so abrupt."

"No."

"You can't be so cruel."

"Lydia, it's off, and it stays off. And the whole damn house dies as of here and now. The more I see of the mess we've put ourselves in, the more it

---

6 spoor: a track or trail left by a wild animal

sickens me. We've been contemplating our mechanical, electronic navels for too long. My God, how we need a breath of honest air!"

And he marched about the house turning off the voice clocks, the stoves, the heaters, the shoe shiners, the shoe lacers, the body scrubbers and swabbers and massagers, and every other machine he could put his hand to.

The house was full of dead bodies, it seemed. It felt like a mechanical cemetery. So silent. None of the humming hidden energy of machines waiting to function at the tap of a button.

"Don't let them do it!" wailed Peter at the ceiling, as if he was talking to the house, the nursery. "Don't let Father kill everything." He turned to his father. "Oh, I hate you!"

"Insults won't get you anywhere."

"I wish you were dead!"

"We were, for a long while. Now we're going to really start living. Instead of being handled and massaged, we're going to *live*."

Wendy was still crying and Peter joined her again. "Just a moment, just one moment, just another moment of nursery," they wailed.

"Oh, George," said the wife, "it can't hurt."

"All right—all right, if they'll only just shut up. One minute, mind you, and then off forever."

"Daddy, Daddy, Daddy!" sang the children, smiling with wet faces.

"And then we're going on a vacation. David McClean is coming back in half an hour to help us move out and get to the airport. I'm going to dress. You turn the nursery on for a minute, Lydia, just a minute, mind you."

And the three of them went babbling off while he let himself be vacuumed upstairs through the air flue and set about dressing himself. A minute later Lydia appeared.

"I'll be glad when we get away," she sighed.

"Did you leave them in the nursery?"

"I wanted to dress too. Oh, that horrid Africa. What can they see in it?"

"Well, in five minutes we'll be on our way to Iowa. Lord, how did we ever get in this house? What prompted us to buy a nightmare?"

"Pride, money, foolishness."

"I think we'd better get downstairs before those kids get engrossed with those damned beasts again."

Just then they heard the children calling, "Daddy, Mommy, come quick—quick!"

They went downstairs in the air flue and ran down the hall. The children were nowhere in sight. "Wendy? Peter!"

They ran into the nursery. The veldtland was empty save for the lions waiting, looking at them. "Peter, Wendy?"

The door slammed.

"Wendy, Peter!"

George Hadley and his wife whirled and ran back to the door.

"Open the door!" cried George Hadley, trying the knob. "Why, they've locked it from the outside! Peter!" He beat at the door. "Open up!"

He heard Peter's voice outside, against the door.

"Don't let them switch off the nursery and the house," he was saying.

Mr. and Mrs. George Hadley beat at the door. "Now, don't be ridiculous, children. It's time to go. Mr. McClean'll be here in a minute and . . . "

And then they heard the sounds.

The lions on three sides of them, in the yellow veldt grass, padding through the dry straw, rumbling and roaring in their throats.

The lions.

Mr. Hadley looked at his wife and they turned and looked back at the beasts edging slowly forward, crouching, tails stiff.

Mr. and Mrs. Hadley screamed.

And suddenly they realized why those other screams had sounded familiar.

" *W*ell, here I am," said David McClean in the nursery doorway.

"Oh, hello." He stared at the two children seated in the center of the open glade eating a little picnic lunch. Beyond them was the water hole and the yellow veldtland; above was the hot sun. He began to perspire. "Where are your father and mother?"

The children looked up and smiled. "Oh, they'll be here directly."

"Good, we must get going." At a distance Mr. McClean saw the lions fighting and clawing and then quieting down to feed in silence under the shady trees.

He squinted at the lions with his hand up to his eyes.

Now the lions were done feeding. They moved to the water hole to drink.

A shadow flickered over Mr. McClean's hot face. Many shadows flickered. The vultures were dropping down the blazing sky.

"A cup of tea?" asked Wendy in the silence.

Read and Think Critically

Analyze, Define, Connect

 1. **THEME** Analyze how Bradbury uses **juxtaposition** to communicate the **theme** of the story. Cite examples of juxtaposition on a chart like the one below. Use these examples to determine the theme of the story.

Concept	Juxtaposed Concept
The African veldt	The beautiful forest with Rima

2. Bradbury is a master of **neologism**, or newly created words. Examine the context in which *automaticity* and *odorophonics* (page 398) are used. Based upon how they are used in the text, write dictionary definitions for each.

3. It is probably no accident that the children in this story, Wendy and Peter, have the same names as the children in *Peter Pan*. What connections are you able to make between *Peter Pan* and "The Veldt"? Analyze the impact of the author's choice for the **characters**' names on the story.

4. Look at the exchange of **dialogue** between George and Lydia on page 400. What does this dialogue tell you about their parenting?

5. **THE AUTHOR'S STYLE** Ray Bradbury credits his interest in writing to seeing a tent magic show at a carnival when he was a child. Read the quotation below. Cite examples of magic found in "The Veldt."

Bradbury the Magician

People call me a science fiction writer, but I don't think that's quite true. I think that I am a magician who is capable of making things appear and disappear right in front of you and you don't know how it happened.

—Ray Bradbury

Before You Read

William Faulkner 1897–1962

About the Author

One of the 20th century's greatest writers, William Faulkner was a high school dropout who only briefly attended college. He grew up the eldest of four sons in Oxford, Mississippi, and found success in writing about what he knew best. He once commented, ". . . I discovered my own little postage stamp of native soil was worth writing about and that I would never live long enough to exhaust it . . ."

Drawing upon family and regional history, he created the mythical Yoknapatawpha County and populated it with a gallery of memorable characters that first appeared in his novel *Sartoris* in 1929. That same year, he married his childhood sweetheart, Estelle Oldham. The couple had two daughters.

Because he felt financially responsible for a large extended family, Faulkner couldn't make enough money on his novels alone, most of which were out of print by 1945. He wrote short stories for quick publication and for 20 years worked in Hollywood as a screenwriter. Eventually his novels came back into high regard, and by the time of his death in 1962, he had won all the major prizes. He is perhaps best remembered for *The Sound and the Fury*, *As I Lay Dying*, and *Absalom, Absalom!*

★★★★★★★★★★★

The Author's Style

Faulkner's frequent themes are the burdens of Southern history, race relations in the South, and the alienation and loneliness of 20th-century life. Much of his fiction concerns powerless people, both black and white. These characters are caught between violence and injustice at one extreme, and at the other, a sense that without sympathy and equity everyone is doomed. Faulkner often spoke out against segregation.

Faulkner's fiction often involves two distinct types of people. One type is the people of a dignified pre-Civil War Southern culture who had noble convictions but were responsible for slavery. The other type is people who represent a more recent way of life that is crudely enterprising, dishonest, ruthless, and violent. He frequently uses the Sartoris and Snopes families to represent these two types.

The sense of individuals threatened by seemingly overwhelming natural and social forces is reinforced by Faulkner's prose style, which builds powerful momentum through the use of complex sentence structures. His sentences include strings of adjectives, extended figures of speech, and parenthetical statements. Another feature of Faulkner's dense style is his presentation of the thoughts of characters, such as the mentally handicapped Benjy in *The Sound and the Fury*, who have difficulty expressing themselves in a way that others can understand.

Barn Burning

WILLIAM FAULKNER

> **LITERARY LENS: STREAM OF CONSCIOUSNESS** Faulkner is a master of the **stream of consciousness** technique, the representation of a character's internal psychological and subconscious states. Watch for this in the story.

The store in which the Justice of the Peace's court was sitting smelled of cheese. The boy, crouched on his nail keg at the back of the crowded room, knew he smelled cheese, and more: from where he sat he could see the ranked shelves close-packed with the solid, squat, dynamic shapes of tin cans whose labels his stomach read, not from the lettering which meant nothing to his mind but from the scarlet devils and the silver curve of fish—this, the cheese which he knew he smelled and the **hermetic** meat which his intestines believed he smelled coming in intermittent gusts momentary and brief between the other constant one, the smell and sense just a little of fear because mostly of despair and grief, the old fierce pull of blood. He could not see the table where the Justice sat and before which his father and his

hermetic:
in an airtight seal

Hay Ledge, Andrew Wyeth, 1957, Greenville County Museum of Art

father's enemy (*our enemy* he thought in that despair; *ourn! mine and hisn both! He's my father!*) stood, but he could hear them, the two of them that is, because his father had said no word yet:

"But what proof have you, Mr. Harris?"

"I told you. The hog got into my corn. I caught it up and sent it back to him. He had no fence that would hold it. I told him so, warned him. The next time I put the hog in my pen. When he came to get it I gave him enough wire to patch up his pen. The next time I put the hog up and kept it. I rode down to his house and saw the wire I gave him still rolled on to the spool in his yard. I told him he could have the hog when he paid me a dollar pound fee. That evening a nigger[1] came with the dollar and got the hog. He was a strange nigger. He said, 'He say to tell you wood and hay kin burn.' I said,

---

1 nigger: Although used by authors to reflect common speech of earlier time periods, this term for African Americans is extremely offensive and racist.

'What?' 'That whut he say to tell you,' the nigger said. 'Wood and hay kin burn.' That night my barn burned. I got the stock out but I lost the barn."

"Where is the nigger? Have you got him?"

"He was a strange nigger, I tell you. I don't know what became of him."

"But that's not proof. Don't you see that's not proof?"

"Get that boy up here. He knows." For a moment the boy thought too that the man meant his older brother until Harris said, "Not him. The little one. The boy," and, crouching, small for his age, small and wiry like his father, in patched and faded jeans even too small for him, with straight, uncombed, brown hair and eyes gray and wild as storm scud, he saw the men between himself and the table part and become a lane of grim faces, at the end of which he saw the Justice, a shabby, collarless, graying man in spectacles, beckoning him. He felt no floor under his bare feet; he seemed to walk beneath the **palpable** weight of the grim turning faces. His father, stiff in his black Sunday coat donned not for the trial but for the moving, did not even look at him. *He aims for me to lie*, he thought, again with that frantic grief and despair. *And I will have to do hit.*

palpable: solid; touchable

"What's your name, boy?" the Justice said.

"Colonel Sartoris Snopes," the boy whispered.

"Hey?" the Justice said. "Talk louder. Colonel Sartoris? I reckon anybody named for Colonel Sartoris in this country can't help but tell the truth, can they?" The boy said nothing. *Enemy! Enemy!* he thought; for a moment he could not even see, could not see that the Justice's face was kindly nor discern that his voice was troubled when he spoke to the man named Harris: "Do you want me to question this boy?" But he could hear, and during those subsequent long seconds while there was absolutely no sound in the crowded little room save that of quiet and intent breathing it was as if he had swung outward at the end of a grape vine, over a ravine, and at the top of the swing had been caught in a prolonged instant of mesmerized gravity, weightless in time.

"No!" Harris said violently, explosively. "Damnation! Send him out of here!" Now time, the fluid world, rushed beneath him again, the voices coming to him again through the smell of cheese and sealed meat, the fear and despair and the old grief of blood.

"This case is closed. I can't find against you, Snopes, but I can give you advice. Leave this country and don't come back to it."

His father spoke for the first time, his voice cold and harsh, level, without emphasis: "I aim to. I don't figure to stay in a country among people who . . . " he said something unprintable and vile, addressed to no one.

"That'll do," the Justice said. "Take your wagon and get out of this country before dark. Case dismissed."

His father turned, and he followed the stiff black coat, the wiry figure walking a little stiffly from where a Confederate provost's[1] man's musket ball had taken him in the heel on a stolen horse thirty years ago, followed the two backs now, since his older brother had appeared from somewhere in the crowd, no taller than the father but thicker, chewing tobacco steadily, between the two lines of grim-faced men and out of the store and across the worn gallery and down the sagging steps and among the dogs and half-grown boys in the mild May dust, where as he passed a voice hissed:

"Barn burner!"

Again he could not see, whirling; there was a face in a red haze, moon-like, bigger than the full moon, the owner of it half again his size, he leaping in the red haze toward the face, feeling no blow, feeling no shock when his head struck the earth, scrabbling up and leaping again, feeling no blow this time either and tasting no blood, scrabbling up to see the other boy in full flight and himself already leaping into pursuit as his father's hand jerked him back, the harsh, cold voice speaking above him: "Go get in the wagon."

It stood in a grove of locusts and mulberries across the road. His two hulking sisters in their Sunday dresses and his mother and her sister in calico[2] and sunbonnets were already in it, sitting on and among the sorry residue of the dozen and more movings which even the boy could remember—the battered stove, the broken beds and chairs, the clock inlaid with mother-of-

---

1 **provost's:** belonging to the keeper of a prison

2 **calico:** inexpensive cotton fabric with patterned figures

pearl,[3] which would not run, stopped at some fourteen minutes past two o'clock of a dead and forgotten day and time, which had been his mother's dowry.[4] She was crying, though when she saw him she drew her sleeve across her face and began to descend from the wagon. "Get back," the father said.

"He's hurt. I got to get some water and wash his . . . "

"Get back in the wagon," his father said. He got in too, over the tail-gate. His father mounted to the seat where the older brother already sat and struck the gaunt mules two savage blows with the peeled willow, but without heat. It was not even **sadistic**; it was exactly that same quality which in later years would cause his descendants to over-run the engine before putting a motor car into motion, striking and reining back in the same movement. The wagon went on, the store with its quiet crowd of grimly watching men dropped behind; a curve in the road hid it. *Forever* he thought. *Maybe he's done satisfied now, now that he has* . . . stopping himself, not to say it aloud even to himself. His mother's hand touched his shoulder.

"Does hit hurt?" she said.

"Naw," he said. "Hit don't hurt. Lemme be."

"Can't you wipe some of the blood off before hit dries?"

"I'll wash to-night," he said. "Lemme be, I tell you."

The wagon went on. He did not know where they were going. None of them ever did or ever asked, because it was always somewhere, always a house of sorts waiting for them a day or two days or even three days away. Likely his father had already arranged to make a crop on another farm before he . . . Again he had to stop himself. He (the father) always did. There was something about his wolflike independence and even courage when the advantage was at least neutral which impressed strangers, as if they

> *His* father mounted to the seat where the older brother already sat and struck the gaunt mules two savage blows with the peeled willow, but without heat. It was not even sadistic; it was exactly that same quality which in later years would cause his descendants to over-run the engine before putting a motor car into motion, striking and reining back in the same movement.

sadistic: taking pleasure in others' pain

---

3 **mother-of-pearl:** a hard, pearly substance that lines the inside of a mollusk shell, often used in jewelry

4 **dowry:** gift or property given to the new household by the bride's family at the time of marriage

He merely ate his supper beside it and was already half asleep over his iron plate when his father called him, and once more he followed the stiff back, the stiff and ruthless limp, up the slope and on to the starlit road . . .

got from his latent ravening ferocity not so much a sense of dependability as a feeling that his ferocious conviction in the rightness of his own actions would be of advantage to all whose interest lay with his.

That night they camped, in a grove of oaks and beeches where a spring ran. The nights were still cool and they had a fire against it, of a rail lifted from a nearby fence and cut into lengths—a small fire, neat, niggard almost, a shrewd fire; such fires were his father's habit and custom always, even in freezing weather. Older, the boy might have remarked this and wondered why not a big one; why should not a man who had not only seen the waste and extravagance of war, but who had in his blood an inherent **voracious** prodigality[5] with material not his own, have burned everything in sight? Then he might have gone a step farther and thought that that was the reason: that niggard blaze was the living fruit of nights passed during those four years in the woods hiding from all men, blue or gray, with his strings of horses (captured horses, he called them). And older still, he might have **divined** the true reason: that the element of fire spoke to some deep mainspring of his father's being, as the element of steel or of powder spoke to other men, as the one weapon for the preservation of integrity, else breath were not worth the breathing, and hence to be regarded with respect and used with discretion.

But he did not think this now and he had seen those same niggard blazes all his life. He merely ate his supper beside it and was already half asleep over his iron plate when his father called him, and once more he followed the stiff back, the stiff and ruthless limp, up the slope and on to the starlit road where, turning, he could see his father against the stars but without face or depth—a shape black, flat, and bloodless as though cut from tin in the iron folds of the frockcoat which had not been made for him, the voice harsh like tin and without heat like tin:

"You were fixing to tell them. You would have told him." He didn't answer. His father struck him with the flat of his hand on the side of the head, hard but without heat, exactly as he had struck the two mules at the store, exactly as he would strike either of them with any stick in order to

voracious:
greedy; insatiable

divined:
guessed;
figured out

---

5 **prodigality:** extravagance

kill a horse fly, his voice still without heat or anger: "You're getting to be a man. You got to learn. You got to learn to stick to your own blood or you ain't going to have any blood to stick to you. Do you think either of them, any man there this morning, would? Don't you know all they wanted was a chance to get at me because they knew I had them beat? Eh?" Later, twenty years later, he was to tell himself, "If I had said they wanted only truth, justice, he would have hit me again." But now he said nothing. He was not crying. He just stood there. "Answer me," his father said.

"Yes," he whispered. His father turned.

"Get on to bed. We'll be there tomorrow."

To-morrow they were there. In the early afternoon the wagon stopped before a paintless two-room house identical almost with the dozen others it had stopped before even in the boy's ten years, and again, as on the other dozen occasions, his mother and aunt got down and began to unload the wagon, although his two sisters and his father and brother had not moved.

"Likely hit ain't fitten for hawgs," one of the sisters said.

"Nevertheless, fit it will and you'll hog it and like it," his father said. "Get out of them chairs and help your Ma unload."

The two sisters got down, big, **bovine**, in a flutter of cheap ribbons; one of them drew from the jumbled wagon bed a battered lantern, the other a worn broom. His father handed the reins to the older son and began to climb stiffly over the wheel. "When they get unloaded, take the team to the barn and feed them." Then he said, and at first the boy thought he was still speaking to his brother: "Come with me."

"Me?" he said.

"Yes," his father said. "You."

"Abner," his mother said. His father paused and looked back—the harsh level stare beneath the shaggy, graying, **irascible** brows.

"I reckon I'll have a word with the man that aims to begin to-morrow owning me body and soul for the next eight months."

They went back up the road. A week ago—or before last night, that is— he would have asked where they were going, but not now. His father had struck him before last night but never before had he paused afterward to explain why; it was as if the blow and the following calm, outrageous voice still rang, repercussed, divulging nothing to him save the terrible handicap of being young, the light weight of his few years, just heavy enough to prevent his soaring free of the world as it seemed to be ordered but not heavy

bovine: cowlike

irascible: grumpy; bad-tempered

enough to keep him footed solid in it, to resist it and try to change the course of its events.

Presently he could see the grove of oaks and cedars and the other flowering trees and shrubs where the house would be, though not the house yet. They walked beside a fence massed with honeysuckle and Cherokee roses and came to a gate swinging open between two brick pillars, and now, beyond a sweep of drive, he saw the house for the first time and at that instant he forgot his father and the terror and despair both, and even when he remembered his father again (who had not stopped) the terror and despair did not return. Because, for all the twelve movings, they had **sojourned** until now in a poor country, a land of small farms and fields and houses, and he had never seen a house like this before. *Hit's big as a courthouse* he thought quietly, with a surge of peace and joy whose reason he could not have thought into words, being too young for that: *They are safe from him. People whose lives are a part of this peace and dignity are beyond his touch, he no more to them than a buzzing wasp: capable of stinging for a little moment but that's all; the spell of this peace and dignity rendering even the barns and stable and cribs which belong to it* **impervious** *to the puny flames he might contrive . . .* this, the peace and joy, ebbing for an instant as he looked again at the stiff black back, the stiff and **implacable** limp of the figure which was not dwarfed by the house, for the reason that it had never looked big anywhere and which now, against the serene columned backdrop, had more than ever that impervious quality of something cut ruthlessly from tin, depthless, as though, sidewise to the sun, it would cast no shadow. Watching him, the boy remarked the absolutely undeviating course which his father held and saw the stiff foot come squarely down in a pile of fresh droppings where

sojourned:
wandered

> *W*atching him, the boy remarked the absolutely undeviating course which his father held and saw the stiff foot come squarely down in a pile of fresh droppings where a horse had stood in the drive and which his father could have avoided by a simple change of stride.

impervious:
invulnerable;
impenetrable

implacable:
relentless;
uncompromising

a horse had stood in the drive and which his father could have avoided by a simple change of stride. But it ebbed only for a moment, though he could not have thought this into words either, walking on in the spell of the house, which he could even want but without envy, without sorrow, certainly never with that ravening and jealous rage which unknown to him walked in the ironlike black coat before him: *Maybe he will feel it too. Maybe it will even change him now from what maybe he couldn't help but be.*

They crossed the portico.[6] Now he could hear his father's stiff foot as it came down on the boards with clocklike finality, a sound out of all proportion to the displacement of the body it bore and which was not dwarfed either by the white door before it, as though it had attained to a sort of vicious and ravening minimum not to be dwarfed by anything—the flat, wide, black hat, the formal coat of broadcloth which had once been black but which had now that friction-glazed greenish cast of the bodies of old house flies, the lifted sleeve which was too large, the lifted hand like a curled claw. The door opened so promptly that the boy knew the Negro must have been watching them all the time, an old man with neat grizzled hair, in a linen jacket, who stood barring the door with his body, saying, "Wipe yo foots, white man, fo you come in here. Major ain't home nohow."

"Get out of my way, nigger," his father said, without heat too, flinging the door back and the Negro also and entering, his hat still on his head. And now the boy saw the prints of the stiff foot on the doorjamb and saw them appear on the pale rug behind the machinelike deliberation of the foot which seemed to bear (or transmit) twice the weight which the body compassed. The Negro was shouting "Miss Lula! Miss Lula!" somewhere behind them, then the boy, **deluged** as though by a warm wave by a suave turn of carpeted stair and a pendant glitter of chandeliers and a mute gleam of gold frames, heard the swift feet and saw her too, a lady—perhaps he had never seen her like before either—in a gray, smooth gown with lace at the throat and an apron tied at the waist and the sleeves turned back, wiping cake or biscuit dough from her hands with a towel as she came up the hall, looking not at his father at all but at the tracks on the blond rug with an expression of incredulous amazement.

"I tried," the Negro cried. "I tole him to . . . "

"Will you please go away?" she said in a shaking voice. "Major de Spain is not at home. Will you please go away?"

deluged:
flooded;
overwhelmed

---

6 **portico:** a covered porch, often at the entrance to a house

His father had not spoken again. He did not speak again. He did not even look at her. He just stood stiff in the center of the rug, in his hat, the shaggy iron-gray brows twitching slightly above the pebble-colored eyes as he appeared to examine the house with brief deliberation. Then with the same deliberation he turned; the boy watched him pivot on the good leg and saw the stiff foot drag round the arc of the turning, leaving a final long and fading smear. His father never looked at it, he never once looked down at the rug. The Negro held the door. It closed behind them, upon the hysteric and indistinguishable woman-wail. His father stopped at the top of the steps and scraped his boot clean on the edge of it. At the gate he stopped again. He stood for a moment, planted stiffly on the stiff foot, looking back at the house. "Pretty and white, ain't it?" he said. "That's sweat. Nigger sweat. Maybe it ain't white enough yet to suit him. Maybe he wants to mix some white sweat with it."

Two hours later the boy was chopping wood behind the house within which his mother and aunt and the two sisters (the mother and aunt, not the two girls, he knew that; even at this distance and muffled by walls the flat loud voices of the two girls emanated an **incorrigible** idle **inertia**) were setting up the stove to prepare a meal, when he heard the hooves and saw the linen-clad man on a fine **sorrel** mare, whom he recognized even before he saw the rolled rug in front of the Negro youth following on a fat bay carriage horse—a **suffused**, angry face vanishing, still at full gallop, beyond the corner of the house where his father and brother were sitting in the two tilted chairs; and a moment later, almost before he could have put the axe down, he heard the hooves again and watched the sorrel mare go back out of the yard, already galloping again. Then his father began to shout one of the sisters' names, who presently emerged backward from the kitchen door dragging the rolled rug along the ground by one end while the other sister walked behind it.

"If you ain't going to tote, go on and set up the wash pot," the first said.

"You, Sarty!" the second shouted. "Set up the wash pot!" His father appeared at the door, framed against that shabbiness, as he had been against that other bland perfection, impervious to either, the mother's anxious face at his shoulder.

"Go on," the father said. "Pick it up." The two sisters stooped, broad, **lethargic**; stooping, they presented an incredible expanse of pale cloth and a flutter of **tawdry** ribbons.

incorrigible:
unruly; incurable

inertia:
tendency to remain in motion or at rest

sorrel:
brownish-orange

suffused:
flushed

lethargic:
lazy; sluggish

tawdry:
cheap; tasteless

"If I thought enough of a rug to have to git hit all the way from France I wouldn't keep hit where folks coming in would have to tromp on hit," the first said. They raised the rug.

"Abner," the mother said. "Let me do it."

"You go back and git dinner," his father said. "I'll tend to this."

From the woodpile through the rest of the afternoon the boy watched them, the rug spread flat in the dust beside the bubbling wash-pot, the two sisters stooping over it with that profound and lethargic reluctance, while the father stood over them in turn, implacable and grim, driving them though never raising his voice again. He could smell the harsh homemade lye they were using; he saw his mother come to the door once and look toward them with an expression not anxious now but very like despair; he saw his father turn, and he fell to with the axe and saw from the corner of his eye his father raise from the ground a flattish fragment of field stone and examine it and return to the pot, and this time his mother actually spoke: "Abner. Abner. Please don't. Please, Abner."

Then he was done too. It was dusk; the whippoorwills[7] had already begun. He could smell coffee from the room where they would presently eat the cold food remaining from the mid-afternoon meal, though when he entered the house he realized they were having coffee again probably because there was a fire on the hearth, before which the rug now lay spread over the backs of the two chairs. The tracks of his father's foot were gone. Where they had been were now long, water-cloudy **scoriations** resembling the sporadic course of a lilliputian[8] mowing machine.

scoriations: grooves; furrows

It still hung there while they ate the cold food and then went to bed, scattered without order or claim up and down the two rooms, his mother in one bed, where his father would later lie, the older brother in the other, himself, the aunt, and the two sisters on pallets on the floor. But his father was not in bed yet. The last thing the boy remembered was the depthless, harsh silhouette of the hat and coat bending over the rug and it seemed to

---

7 **whippoorwills:** nocturnal birds named for the sound of their call

8 **lilliputian:** of or relating to the miniature people on the island of Lilliput, from Jonathan Swift's *Gulliver's Travels*

him that he had not even closed his eyes when the silhouette was standing over him, the fire almost dead behind it, the stiff foot prodding him awake. "Catch up the mule," his father said.

When he returned with the mule his father was standing in the black door, the rolled rug over his shoulder. "Ain't you going to ride?" he said.

"No. Give me your foot."

He bent his knee into his father's hand, the wiry, surprising power flowed smoothly, rising, he rising with it, on to the mule's bare back (they had owned a saddle once; the boy could remember it though not when or where) and with the same effortlessness his father swung the rug up in front of him. Now in the starlight they retraced the afternoon's path, up the dusty road rife with honeysuckle, through the gate and up the black tunnel of the drive to the lightless house, where he sat on the mule and felt the rough warp of the rug drag across his thighs and vanish.

"Don't you want me to help?" he whispered. His father did not answer and now he heard again that stiff foot striking the hollow portico with that wooden and clocklike deliberation, that outrageous overstatement of the weight it carried. The rug, hunched, not flung (the boy could tell that even in the darkness) from his father's shoulder struck the angle of wall and floor with a sound unbelievably loud, thunderous, then the foot again, unhurried and enormous; a light came on in the house and the boy sat, tense, breathing steadily and quietly and just a little fast, though the foot itself did not increase its beat at all, descending the steps now; now the boy could see him.

"Don't you want to ride now?" he whispered. "We kin both ride now," the light within the house altering now, flaring up and sinking. *He's coming down the stairs now,* he thought. He had already ridden the mule up beside the horse block; presently his father was up behind him and he doubled the reins over and slashed the mule across the neck, but before the animal could begin to trot the hard, thin arm came round him, the hard knotted hand jerking the mule back to a walk.

> "*D*on't you want me to help?" he whispered. His father did not answer and now he heard again that stiff foot striking the hollow portico with that wooden and clocklike deliberation, that outrageous overstatement of the weight it carried.

In the first red rays of the sun they were in the lot, putting plow gear on the mules. This time the sorrel mare was in the lot before he heard it at all, the rider collarless and even bareheaded, trembling, speaking in a shaking voice as the woman in the house had done, his father merely looking up once before stooping again to the hame he was buckling, so that the man on the mare spoke to his stooping back:

"You must realize you have ruined that rug. Wasn't there anybody here, any of your women . . ." he ceased, shaking, the boy watching him, the older brother leaning now in the stable door, chewing, blinking slowly and steadily at nothing apparently. "It cost a hundred dollars. But you never had a hundred dollars. You never will. So I'm going to charge you twenty bushels of corn against your crop. I'll add it in your contract and when you come to the commissary[9] you can sign it. That won't keep Mrs. de Spain quiet but maybe it will teach you to wipe your feet off before you enter her house again."

Then he was gone. The boy looked at his father, who still had not spoken or even looked up again, who was now adjusting the logger-head in the hame.[10]

"Pap," he said. His father looked at him—the inscrutable face, the shaggy brows beneath which the gray eyes glinted coldly. Suddenly the boy went toward him, fast, stopping as suddenly. "You done the best you could!" he cried. "If he wanted hit done different why didn't he wait and tell you how? He won't git no twenty bushels! He won't get none! We'll gether hit and hide it! I kin watch . . ."

"Did you put the cutter back in that straight stock like I told you?"

"No, sir," he said.

"Then go do it."

That was Wednesday. During the rest of that week he worked steadily, at what was within his scope and some which was beyond it, with an industry that did not need to be driven nor even commanded twice; he had this from his mother, with the difference that some at least of what he did he liked to do, such as splitting wood with the half-size axe which his mother and aunt had earned, or saved money somehow, to present him with at Christmas. In company with the two older women (and on one afternoon, even one of the sisters), he built pens for

---

9 **commissary:** a general store for food and supplies

10 **logger-head in the hame:** parts of a horse's bridle

the shoat[11] and the cow which were a part of his father's contract with the landlord, and one afternoon, his father being absent, gone somewhere on one of the mules, he went to the field.

They were running a middle buster[12] now, his brother holding the plow straight while he handled the reins, and walking beside the straining mule, the rich black soil shearing cool and damp against his bare ankles, he thought *Maybe this is the end of it. Maybe even that twenty bushels that seems hard to have to pay for just a rug will be a cheap price for him to stop forever and always from being what he used to be*; thinking, dreaming now, so that his brother had to speak sharply to him to mind the mule: *Maybe he even won't collect the twenty bushels. Maybe it will all add up and balance and vanish—corn, rug, fire; the terror and grief, the being pulled two ways like between two teams of horses—gone, done with for ever and ever.*

> *M*aybe this is the end of it. Maybe even that twenty bushels that seems hard to have to pay for just a rug will be a cheap price for him to stop forever and always from being what he used to be ...

Then it was Saturday; he looked up from beneath the mule he was harnessing and saw his father in the black coat and hat. "Not that," his father said. "The wagon gear." And then, two hours later, sitting in the wagon bed behind his father and brother on the seat, the wagon accomplished a final curve, and he saw the weathered paintless store with its tattered tobacco- and patent-medicine posters and the tethered wagons and saddle animals below the gallery. He mounted the gnawed steps behind his father and brother, and there again was the lane of quiet, watching faces for the three of them to walk through. He saw the man in spectacles sitting at the plank table and he did not need to be told this was a Justice of the Peace; he sent one glare of fierce, exultant, **partisan** defiance at the man in collar and cravat[13] now, whom he had seen but twice before in his life, and that on a galloping horse, who now wore on his face an expression not of rage but of amazed unbelief which the boy could not have known was at the incredible circumstance of being sued by one of his own tenants,

partisan: biased; loyal to a cause

---

11 **shoat:** a young hog

12 **buster:** a plow

13 **cravat:** a necktie

William Faulkner

and came and stood against his father and cried at the Justice: "He ain't done it! He ain't burnt . . . "

"Go back to the wagon," his father said.

"Burnt?" the Justice said. "Do I understand this rug was burned too?"

"Does anybody here claim it was?" his father said. "Go back to the wagon." But he did not, he merely retreated to the rear of the room, crowded as that other had been, but not to sit down this time, instead, to stand pressing among the motionless bodies, listening to the voices:

"And you claim twenty bushels of corn is too high for the damage you did to the rug?"

"He brought the rug to me and said he wanted the tracks washed out of it. I washed the tracks out and took the rug back to him."

"But you didn't carry the rug back to him in the same condition it was in before you made the tracks on it."

His father did not answer, and now for perhaps half a minute there was no sound at all save that of breathing, the faint steady **suspiration** of complete and intent listening.

"You decline to answer that, Mr. Snopes?" Again his father did not answer. "I'm going to find against you, Mr. Snopes. I'm going to find that you were responsible for the injury to Major de Spain's rug and hold you liable for it. But twenty bushels of corn seems a little high for a man in your circumstances to have to pay. Major de Spain claims it cost a hundred dollars. October corn will be worth about fifty cents. I figure that if Major de Spain can stand a ninety-five dollar loss on something he paid cash for, you can stand a five-dollar loss you haven't earned yet. I hold you in damages to Major de Spain to the amount of ten bushels of corn over and above your contract with him, to be paid to him out of your crop at gathering time. Court adjourned."

It had taken no time hardly, the morning was but half begun. He thought they would return home and perhaps back to the field, since they were late, far behind all other farmers. But instead his father passed on behind the wagon, merely indicating with his hand for the older brother to follow with it, and crossed the road toward the blacksmith shop opposite, pressing on after his father, overtaking him, speaking, whispering up at the harsh, calm face beneath the weathered hat: "He won't git no ten bushels neither. He won't git one. We'll . . . " until his father glanced for an instant down at him, the face absolutely calm, the grizzled eyebrows tangled above the cold eyes, the voice almost pleasant, almost gentle:

"You think so? Well, we'll wait til October anyway."

suspiration:
deep breath;
sigh

The matter of the wagon—the setting of a spoke or two and the tightening of the tires—did not take long either, the business of the tires accomplished by driving the wagon into the spring branch behind the shop and letting it stand there, the mules nuzzling into the water from time to time, and the boy on the seat with the idle reins, looking up the slope and through the sooty tunnel of the shed where the slow hammer rang and where his father sat on an upended cypress bolt, easily, either talking or listening, still sitting there when the boy brought the dripping wagon up out of the branch and halted it before the door.

"Take them on to the shade and hitch," his father said. He did so and returned. His father and the smith and a third man squatting on his heels inside the door were talking, about crops and animals; the boy, squatting too in the **ammoniac** dust and hoof-parings[14] and scales of rust, heard his father tell a long and unhurried story out of the time before the birth of the older brother even when he had been a professional horsetrader. And then his father came up beside him where he stood before a tattered last year's circus poster on the other side of the store, gazing **rapt** and quiet at the scarlet horses, the incredible poisings and **convolutions** of tulle[15] and tights and the painted leers of comedians, and said, "It's time to eat."

But not at home. Squatting beside his brother against the front wall, he watched his father emerge from the store and produce from a paper sack a segment of cheese and divide it carefully and deliberately into three with his pocket knife and produce crackers from the same sack. They all three squatted on the gallery and ate, slowly, without talking; then in the store again, they drank from a tin dipper tepid water smelling of the cedar bucket and of living beech trees. And still they did not go home. It was a horse lot this time, a tall rail fence upon and along which men stood and sat and out of which one by one horses were led, to be walked and trotted and then **cantered** back and forth along the road while the slow swapping and buying went on and the sun began to slant westward, they—the three of them—watching and listening, the older brother with his muddy eyes and his steady, inevitable tobacco, the father commenting now and then on certain of the animals, to no one in particular.

It was after sundown when they reached home. They ate supper by lamp-light, then, sitting on the doorstep, the boy watched the night fully

ammoniac: foul-smelling; cough-inducing

rapt: enchanted

convolutions: twists; intricate designs

cantered: loped; trotted

---

14 **hoof-parings:** clippings that are pared away from a horse's hoof during shoeing

15 **tulle:** a netted fabric

accomplish, listening to the whippoorwills and the frogs, when he heard his mother's voice: "Abner! No! No! Oh, God. Oh, God. Abner!" and he rose, whirled, and saw the altered light through the door where a candle stub now burned in a bottle neck on the table and his father, still in the hat and coat, at once formal and **burlesque** as though dressed carefully for some shabby and ceremonial violence, emptying the reservoir of the lamp back into the five-gallon kerosene can from which it had been filled, while the mother tugged at his arm until he shifted the lamp to the other hand and flung her back, not savagely or viciously, just hard, into the wall, her hands flung out against the wall for balance, her mouth open and in her face the same quality of hopeless despair as had been in her voice. Then his father saw him standing in the door.

burlesque: comic; ridiculous

I could run on and on and never look back, never need to see his face again.

"Go to the barn and get that can of oil we were oiling the wagon with," he said. The boy did not move. Then he could speak.

"What . . . " he cried. "What are you . . . "

"Go get that oil," his father said. "Go."

Then he was moving, running, outside the house, toward the stable: this the old habit, the old blood which he had not been permitted to choose for himself, which had been **bequeathed** him willy nilly and which had run for so long (and who knew where, battening on what of outrage and savagery and lust) before it came to him. *I could keep on,* he thought. *I could run on and on and never look back, never need to see his face again. Only I can't. I can't,* the rusted can in his hand now, the liquid sploshing in it as he ran back to the house and into it, into the sound of his mother's weeping in the next room, and handed the can to his father.

bequeathed: handed down

"Ain't you going to even send a nigger?" he cried. "At least you sent a nigger before!"

This time his father didn't strike him. The hand came even faster than the blow had, the same hand which had set the can on the table with almost excruciating care flashing from the can toward him too quick for him to follow it, gripping him by the back of his shirt and on to tiptoe before he had seen it quit the can, the face stooping at him in breathless and frozen ferocity, the cold, dead voice speaking over him to the older brother who leaned against the table, chewing with that steady, curious, sidewise motion of cows:

"Empty the can into the big one and go on. I'll catch up with you."

"Better tie him up to the bedpost," the brother said.

"Do like I told you," the father said. Then the boy was moving, his bunched shirt and the hard, bony hand between his shoulder-blades, his toes just touching the floor, across the room and into the other one, past the sisters sitting with spread heavy thighs in the two chairs over the cold hearth, and to where his mother and aunt sat side by side on the bed, the aunt's arms about his mother's shoulders.

"Hold him," the father said. The aunt made a startled movement. "Not you," the father said. "Lennie. Take hold of him. I want to see you do it." His mother took him by the wrist. "You'll hold him better than that. If he gets loose don't you know what he is going to do? He will go up yonder." He jerked his head toward the road. "Maybe I'd better tie him."

"I'll hold him," his mother whispered.

"See you do then." Then his father was gone, the stiff foot heavy and measured upon the boards, ceasing at last.

Then he began to struggle. His mother caught him in both arms, he jerking and wrenching at them. He would be stronger in the end, he knew that. But he had no time to wait for it. "Lemme go!" he cried. "I don't want to have to hit you!"

"Let him go!" the aunt said. "If he don't go, before God, I am going up there myself!"

"Don't you see I can't?" his mother cried. "Sarty! Sarty! No! No! Help me, Lizzie!"

Then he was free. His aunt grasped at him but it was too late. He whirled, running, his mother stumbled forward on to her knees behind him, crying to the nearest sister: "Catch him, Net! Catch him!" But that was too late too, the sister (the sisters were twins, born at the same time, yet either of them now gave the impression of being, encompassing as much living meat and volume and weight as any other two of the family) not yet having begun to rise from the chair, her head, face, alone merely turned, presenting to him in the flying instant an astonishing expanse of young female features untroubled by any surprise even, wearing only an expression of bovine interest. Then he was out of the room, out of the house, in the mild dust of the starlit road and the heavy **rifeness** of honeysuckle, the pale ribbon unspooling with terrific slowness under his running feet, reaching the gate at last and turning in,

rifeness: abundance

> He whirled, running, his mother stumbled forward on to her knees behind him, crying to the nearest sister: "Catch him, Net! Catch him!"

running, his heart and lungs drumming, on up the drive toward the lighted house, the lighted door. He did not knock, he burst in, sobbing for breath, incapable for the moment of speech; he saw the astonished face of the Negro in the linen jacket without knowing when the Negro had appeared.

"De Spain!" he cried, panted. "Where's . . . ." then he saw the white man too emerging from a white door down the hall. "Barn!" he cried. "Barn!"

"What?" the white man said. "Barn?"

"Yes!" the boy cried. "Barn!"

"Catch him!" the white man shouted.

But it was too late this time too. The Negro grasped his shirt, but the entire sleeve, rotten with washing, carried away, and he was out that door too and in the drive again, and had actually never ceased to run even while he was screaming into the white man's face.

Behind him the white man was shouting, "My horse! Fetch my horse!" and he thought for an instant of cutting across the park and climbing the fence into the road, but he did not know the park nor how high the vine-massed fence might be and he dared not risk it. So he ran on down the drive, blood and breath roaring; presently he was in the road again though he could not see it. He could not hear either: the galloping mare was almost upon him before he heard her, and even then he held his course, as if the very urgency of his wild grief and need must in a moment more find him wings, waiting until the ultimate instant to hurl himself aside and into the weed-choked roadside ditch as the horse thundered past and on, for an instant in furious silhouette against the stars, the tranquil early summer night sky which, even before the shape of the horse and rider vanished, strained abruptly and violently upward: a long, swirling roar incredible and soundless, blotting the stars, and he springing up and into the road again, running again, knowing it was too late yet still running even after he heard the shot and, an instant later, two shots, pausing now without knowing he had ceased to run, crying "Pap! Pap!," running again before he knew he had begun to run, stumbling, tripping over something and scrabbling up again without ceasing to run, looking backward over his shoulder at the glare as he got up, running on among the invisible trees, panting, sobbing, "Father! Father!"

> "What?" the white man said. "Barn?"
>
> "Yes!" the boy cried. "Barn!"
>
> "Catch him!" the white man shouted.

At midnight he was sitting on the crest of a hill. He did not know it was midnight and he did not know how far he had come. But there was no glare behind him now and he sat now, his back toward what he had called home for four days anyhow, his face toward the dark woods which he would enter when breath was strong again, small, shaking steadily in the chill darkness, hugging himself into the remainder of his thin, rotten shirt, the grief and despair now no longer terror and fear but just grief and despair. *Father. My father*, he thought. "He was brave!" he cried suddenly, aloud but not loud, no more than a whisper: "He was! He was in the war! He was in Colonel Sartoris' cav'ry!"[16] not knowing that his father had gone to that war a private in the fine old European sense, wearing no uniform, admitting the authority of and giving fidelity to no man or army or flag, going to war as Malbrouck[17] himself did: for **booty**—it meant nothing and less than nothing to him if it were enemy booty or his own.

booty: plunder; winnings

The slow constellations wheeled on. It would be dawn and then sun-up after a while and he would be hungry. But that would be to-morrow and now he was only cold, and walking would cure that. His breathing was easier now and he decided to get up and go on, and then he found that he had been asleep because he knew it was almost dawn, the night almost over. He could tell that from the whippoorwills. They were everywhere now among the dark trees below him, constant and inflectioned and ceaseless, so that, as the instant for giving over to the day birds drew nearer and nearer, there was no interval at all between them. He got up. He was a little stiff, but walking would cure that too as it would the cold, and soon there would be the sun. He went on down the hill, toward the dark woods within which the liquid silver voices of the birds called unceasing—the rapid and urgent beating of the urgent and **quiring** heart of the late spring night. He did not look back.

quiring: questioning

16 **cav'ry:** cavalry, or soldiers mounted on horseback

17 **Malbrouck:** John Churchill, Duke of Marlborough (1650–1722); successful English general whose name evolved into Malbrough and Malbrouch in popular English and French songs

Read and Think Critically

Describe, Explain, Analyze

1. **STREAM OF CONSCIOUSNESS** Based on what you learned from following his **stream of consciousness**, write a one-paragraph description of the boy.

2. The boy views his father's clothing and even his face and body as "ironlike." Cite examples from the text that support the boy's description of his father.

3. Reread the second sentence of the story. What do you think is meant by "the old fierce pull of blood"? Explain the multiple meanings of the word *blood* as it used in this sentence.

4. Analyze the **character** of the father. What clues suggest the man's **motivation**? What do you think drives the father's need to burn things?

5. **THE AUTHOR'S STYLE** Faulkner is known for making time stand still during crystallized moments in his fiction. Identify and analyze a passage in which motion is arrested. What "artificial means," or techniques of literature, does he use to accomplish this?

Arrested Motion

The aim of every artist is to arrest motion, which is life, by artificial means.

—William Faulkner
Lion in the Garden: Interviews with William Faulkner 1926–1962

Before You Read

Bernard Malamud 1914–1986

About the Author

Born to parents who were part of the Russian Jewish immigrant community that he would grow up to write about, Bernard Malamud spent his formative years in Brooklyn. He studied at City College of New York, which was then a school for poor but bright students, and went on to earn a master's degree in English at Columbia University.

Always a careful writer, Malamud then worked for eight years as a clerk in the Bureau of Census in Washington, D.C., perfecting his writing at night. During this time he published his first short stories. Like many writers, Malamud used teaching as well as writing to support his family, returning to his alma mater, Erasmus Hall High School, to teach evening classes. He went on to teach at prestigious schools such as Harvard as his literary reputation grew.

An enthusiastic world traveler, Malamud sometimes used the places he visited as settings in his fiction. Among his best-known works are a collection of stories, *The Magic Barrel*, and his novels *The Natural* and *The Fixer*.

★★★★★★★★★★★

The Author's Style

"Life is a tragedy full of joy," Malamud said in an interview with the *New York Times*. This paradox can be seen in his characters who weep and pray, curse and rejoice. Malamud was one of several Jewish writers whose stories about exiled, vulnerable people were acclaimed by wide audiences in the decades following the Holocaust. His characters are realistic and usually unremarkable in personality and occupation. They are not always Jewish, but their drab, everyday suffering can be seen as symbolic of a struggling humanity.

Malamud's plots are fairly straightforward and often have the tone of a fable or folktale. This fable-like quality owes something to the rhythm and flavor of Yiddish speech that Malamud captures in both third-person narration and dialogue. Many of his stories have to do with questions raised by Jews who find themselves in conflict with non-Jews. More generally, though, his characters are simply trying to live in a world where they have to pay too much for making bad choices and having bad luck.

It is not uncommon for Malamud to use dreams and miracles to enable his characters to transcend their usual ways of thinking and find dignity and hope despite their constant burden of suffering. In his novel, *The Natural*, one character says to another, "We have two lives . . . the life we learn with and the life we live with after that. Suffering is what brings us toward happiness."

Angel Levine

B E R N A R D   M A L A M U D

LITERARY LENS: ARCHETYPE Malamud's stories often have the flavor of a folk-tale. Angels are **archetypes**, or frequently used characters, in myths and fables. As you read, consider how Angel Levine is different from or similar to angels in other fables you have read.

*M*anischevitz, a tailor, in his fifty-first year suffered many reverses and indignities. Previously a man of comfortable means, he overnight lost all he had when his establishment caught fire, after a metal container of cleaning fluid exploded, and burned to the ground. Although Manischevitz was insured against fire, damage suits by two customers who had been hurt in the flames deprived him of every penny he had saved. At almost the same time, his son, of much promise, was killed in the war, and his daughter, without so much as a word of warning, married a lout and disappeared with him as off the face of the earth. Thereafter Manischevitz was victimized by excruciating backaches and found himself unable to work even as a presser—the only kind of work available to him—

The bedroom was the warmest room in the house and it was here, after his outburst to God, that Manischevitz, by the light of two small bulbs overhead, sat reading his Jewish newspaper.

for more than an hour or two daily, because beyond that the pain from standing was maddening. His Fanny, a good wife and mother, who had taken in washing and sewing, began before his eyes to waste away. Suffering shortness of breath, she at last became seriously ill and took to her bed. The doctor, a former customer of Manischevitz, who out of pity treated them, at first had difficulty diagnosing her ailment, but later put it down as hardening of the arteries at an advanced stage. He took Manischevitz aside, prescribed complete rest for her, and in whispers gave him to know there was little hope.

Throughout his trials Manischevitz had remained somewhat stoic, almost unbelieving that all this had descended on his head, as if it were happening, let us say, to an acquaintance or some distant relative; it was, in sheer quantity of woe, incomprehensible. It was also ridiculous, unjust, and because he had always been a religious man, an **affront** to God. Manischevitz believed this in all his suffering. When his burden had grown too crushingly heavy to be borne he prayed in his chair with shut hollow eyes: "My dear God, sweetheart, did I deserve that this should happen to me?" Then recognizing the worthlessness of it, he set aside the complaint and prayed humbly for assistance: "Give Fanny back her health, and to me for myself that I shouldn't feel pain in every step. Help now or tomorrow is too late." And Manischevitz wept.

affront:
insult

*M*anischevitz's flat, which he had moved into after the disastrous fire, was a **meager** one, furnished with a few sticks of chairs, a table, and bed, in one of the poorer sections of the city. There were three rooms: a small, poorly papered living room; an apology for a kitchen with a wooden icebox; and the comparatively large bedroom where Fanny lay in a sagging secondhand bed, gasping for breath. The bedroom was the warmest room in the house and it was here, after his outburst to God, that Manischevitz, by the light of two small bulbs overhead, sat reading his Jewish newspaper. He was not truly reading because his thoughts were everywhere; however the print offered a convenient resting place for his eyes, and a word or two, when he permitted

meager:
poor; simple

himself to comprehend them, had the momentary effect of helping him forget his troubles. After a short while he discovered, to his
surprise, that he was actively scanning the news, searching for an
item of great interest to him. Exactly what he thought he would read
he couldn't say—until he realized, with
some astonishment, that he was expecting to discover something about himself.
Manischevitz put his paper down and
looked up with the distinct impression that
someone had come into the apartment,
though he could not remember having heard
the sound of the door opening. He looked around: the room was very still,
Fanny sleeping, for once, quietly. Half frightened, he watched her until he
was satisfied she wasn't dead; then, still disturbed by the thought of an
unannounced visitor, he stumbled into the living room and there had the
shock of his life, for at the table sat a black man reading a newspaper he had
folded up to fit into one hand.

"What do you want here?" Manischevitz asked in fright.

The Negro put down the paper and glanced up with a gentle expression.
"Good evening." He seemed not to be sure of himself, as if he had got into
the wrong house. He was a large man, bonily built, with a heavy head
covered by a hard derby,[1] which he made no attempt to remove. His eyes
seemed sad, but his lips, above which he wore a slight mustache, sought
to smile; he was not otherwise **prepossessing**. The cuffs of his sleeves,
Manischevitz noted, were frayed to the lining, and the dark suit was badly
fitted. He had very large feet. Recovering from his fright, Manischevitz
guessed he had left the door open and was being visited by a case worker
from the Welfare Department—some came at night—for he had recently
applied for welfare. Therefore he lowered himself into a chair opposite the
Negro, trying, before the man's uncertain smile, to feel comfortable. The
former tailor sat stiffly but patiently at the table, waiting for the investigator
to take out his pad and pencil and begin asking questions; but before long
he became convinced the man intended to do nothing of the sort.

"Who are you?" Manischevitz at last asked uneasily.

"If I may, insofar as one is able to, identify myself, I bear the name of
Alexander Levine."

> "What do you want here?"
> Manischevitz asked in fright.

prepossessing:
impressive

---

1 **derby:** a stiff felt hat with a narrow brim

In spite of his troubles Manischevitz felt a smile growing on his lips. "You said Levine?" he politely inquired.

The Negro nodded. "That is exactly right."

Carrying the jest further, Manischevitz asked, "You are maybe Jewish?"

"All my life I was, willingly."

The tailor hesitated. He had heard of black Jews but had never met one. It gave an unusual sensation.

Recognizing in afterthought something odd about the tense of Levine's remark, he said doubtfully, "You ain't Jewish anymore?"

Levine at this point removed his hat, revealing a very white part in his black hair, but quickly replaced it. He replied, "I have recently been disincarnated into an angel. As such, I offer you my humble assistance, if to offer is within my province and power—in the best sense." He lowered his eyes in apology. "Which calls for added explanation: I am what I am granted to be, and at present the completion is in the future."

"What kind of angel is this?" Manischevitz gravely asked.

"A bona fide angel of God, within prescribed limitations," answered Levine, "not to be confused with the members of any particular sect, order, or organization here on earth operating under a similar name."

Manischevitz was thoroughly disturbed. He had been expecting something, but not this. What sort of mockery was it—provided that Levine was an angel—of a faithful servant who had from childhood lived in the synagogues, concerned with the word of God?

To test Levine he asked, "Then where are your wings?"

The Negro blushed as well as he could. Manischevitz understood this from his altered expression. "Under certain circumstances we lose privileges and **prerogatives** upon returning to earth, no matter for what purpose or endeavoring to assist whomsoever."

"So tell me," Manischevitz said triumphantly, "how did you get here?"

"I was translated."

Still troubled, the tailor said, "If you are a Jew, say the blessing for bread."

Levine recited it in **sonorous** Hebrew.

Although moved by the familiar words Manischevitz still felt doubt he was dealing with an angel.

"If you are an angel," he demanded somewhat angrily, "give me the proof."

Levine wet his lips. "Frankly, I cannot perform either miracles or near-

prerogatives: rights; options

sonorous: full-sounding; resonant

miracles, due to the fact that I am in a condition of probation. How long that will persist or even consist depends on the outcome."

Manischevitz racked his brains for some means of causing Levine positively to reveal his true identity, when the Negro spoke again:

"It was given me to understand that both your wife and you require assistance of a **salubrious** nature?"

salubrious: health-promoting; wholesome

The tailor could not rid himself of the feeling that he was the butt of a jokester. Is this what a Jewish angel looks like? he asked himself. This I am not convinced.

He asked a last question. "So if God sends to me an angel, why a black? Why not a white that there are so many of them?"

"It was my turn to go next," Levine explained.

Manischevitz could not be persuaded. "I think you are a faker."

Levine slowly rose. His eyes indicated disappointment and worry. "Mr. Manischevitz," he said tonelessly, "if you should desire me to be of assistance to you any time in the near future, or possibly before, I can be found"—he glanced at his fingernails—"in Harlem."

He was by then gone.

$\mathscr{T}$he next day Manischevitz felt some relief from his backache and was able to work four hours at pressing. The day after, he put in six hours; and the third day four again. Fanny sat up a little and asked for some halvah[2] to suck. But after the fourth day the stabbing, breaking ache afflicted his back, and Fanny again lay **supine**, breathing with blue-lipped difficulty.

supine: passively; listlessly

Manischevitz was profoundly disappointed at the return of his active pain and suffering. He had hoped for a longer interval of easement, long enough to have a thought other than of himself and his troubles. Day by day, minute after minute, he lived in pain, pain his only memory, questioning the necessity of it, **inveighing**, though with affection, against God. Why *so much*, Gottenyu?[3] If He wanted to teach His servant a lesson for some reason, some cause—the nature of His nature—to teach him, say, for reasons of his weakness, his pride, perhaps, during his years of prosperity, his frequent neglect of God—to give him a little lesson, why then any of the tragedies that had happened to him, any *one* would have sufficed to chasten him. But *all together*—

inveighing: protesting

---

2 **halvah:** a sweet sesame candy

3 **Gottenyu:** Hebrew for "dear God"

the loss of both his children, his means of livelihood, Fanny's health and his—that was too much to ask one frail-boned man to endure. Who, after all, was Manischevitz that he had been given so much to suffer? A tailor. Certainly not a man of talent. Upon him suffering was largely wasted. It went nowhere, into nothing: into more suffering. His pain did not earn him bread, nor fill the cracks in the wall, nor lift, in the middle of the night, the kitchen table; only lay upon him, sleepless, so sharply oppressive that he could many times have cried out yet not heard himself this misery.

In this mood he gave no thought to Mr. Alexander Levine, but at moments when the pain wavered, slightly diminishing, he sometimes wondered if he had been mistaken to dismiss him. A black Jew and angel to boot—very hard to believe, but suppose he *had* been sent to **succor** him, and he, Manischevitz, was in his blindness too blind to understand? It was this thought that put him on the knife-point of agony.

succor: relieve; rescue

*W*ho, after all, was Manischevitz that he had been given so much to suffer? A tailor. Certainly not a man of talent. Upon him suffering was largely wasted.

Therefore the tailor, after much self-questioning and continuing doubt, decided he would seek the self-styled angel in Harlem. Of course he had great difficulty because he had not asked for specific directions, and movement was tedious to him. The subway took him to 116th Street, and from there he wandered in the open dark world. It was vast and its lights lit nothing. Everywhere were shadows, often moving. Manischevitz hobbled along with the aid of a cane and, not knowing where to seek in the blackened tenement[4] buildings, would look fruitlessly through store windows. In the stores he saw people and everybody was black. It was an amazing thing to observe. When he was too tired, too unhappy to go farther, Manischevitz stopped in front of a tailor's shop. Out of familiarity with the appearance of it, with some sadness he entered. The tailor, an old skinny man with a mop of woolly gray hair, was sitting cross legged on his workbench, sewing a pair of tuxedo pants that had a razor slit all the way down the seat.

"You'll excuse me, please, gentleman," said Manischevitz, admiring the tailor's deft thimbled fingerwork, "but you know maybe somebody by the name Alexander Levine?"

---

4 tenement: low-quality apartment housing

The tailor, who, Manischevitz thought, seemed a little **antagonistic** to him, scratched his scalp.

antagonistic: hostile

"Cain't say I ever heared dat name."

"Alex-ander Lev-ine," Manischevitz repeated it.

The man shook his head. "Cain't say I heared."

Manischevitz remembered to say: "He is an angel, maybe."

"Oh, *him*," said the tailor, clucking. "He hang out in dat honky tonk down here a ways." He pointed with his skinny finger and returned to sewing the pants.

Manischevitz crossed the street against a red light and was almost run down by a taxi. On the block after the next, the sixth store from the corner was a cabaret, and the name in sparkling lights was Bella's. Ashamed to go in, Manischevitz gazed through the neon lit window, and when the dancing couples had parted and drifted away, he discovered at a table on the side, toward the rear, Alexander Levine.

He was sitting alone, a cigarette butt hanging from the corner of his mouth, playing solitaire with a dirty pack of cards, and Manischevitz felt a touch of pity for him, because Levine had deteriorated in appearance. His derby hat was dented and had a gray smudge. His ill fitting suit was shabbier, as if he had been sleeping in it. His shoes and trouser cuffs were muddy, and his face covered with an impenetrable stubble the color of licorice. Manischevitz, though deeply disappointed, was about to enter, when a big-breasted Negress in a purple evening gown appeared before Levine's table, and with much laughter through many white teeth, broke into a vigorous shimmy. Levine looked at Manischevitz with a haunted expression, but the tailor was too paralyzed to move or acknowledge it. As Bella's gyrations continued Levine rose, his eyes lit in excitement. She embraced him with vigor, both his hands clasped around her restless buttocks, and they tangoed together across the floor, loudly applauded by the customers. She seemed to have lifted Levine off his feet and his large shoes hung limp as they danced. They slid past the windows where Manischevitz, white faced, stood staring in. Levine winked slyly and the tailor left for home.

*F*anny lay at death's door. Through shrunken lips she muttered concerning her childhood, the sorrow of the marriage bed, the loss of her children; yet wept to live. Manischevitz tried not to listen, but even without ears he would have heard. It was not a gift. The doctor panted up the stairs, a broad but bland, unshaven man (it was Sunday), and soon

BLUES, ARCHIBALD MOTLEY JR, 1929

shook his head. A day at most, or two. He left at once to spare himself Manischevitz's multiplied sorrow; the man who never stopped hurting. He would someday get him into a public home.

Manischevitz visited a synagogue and there spoke to God, but God had absented Himself. The tailor searched his heart and found no hope. When she died, he would live dead. He considered taking his life although he knew he wouldn't. Yet it was something to consider. Considering, you existed. He railed against God—Can you love a rock, a broom, an emptiness? Baring his chest, he smote the naked bones, cursing himself for having, beyond belief, believed.

Asleep in a chair that afternoon, he dreamed of Levine. He was standing before a faded mirror, preening small decaying **opalescent** wings. "This means," mumbled Manischevitz, as he broke out of sleep, "that it is possible he could be an angel." Begging a neighbor lady to look in on Fanny and occasionally wet her lips with water, he drew on his thin coat, gripped his walking stick, exchanged some pennies for a subway token, and rode to Harlem. He knew this act was the last desperate one of his woe: to go seeking a black magician to restore his wife to **invalidism**. Yet if there was no choice, he did at least what was chosen.

He hobbled to Bella's, but the place seemed to have changed hands. It was now, as he breathed, a synagogue in a store. In the front, toward him, were several rows of empty wooden benches. In the rear stood the Ark, its portals of rough wood covered with rainbows of sequins; under it a long table on which lay the sacred scroll unrolled, illuminated by the dim light from a bulb on a chain overhead. Around the table, as if frozen to it and the scroll, which they all touched with their fingers, sat four Negroes wearing skullcaps.[5] Now as they read the Holy Word, Manischevitz could, through the plate-glass window, hear the singsong chant of their voices. One of them was old, with a gray beard. One was bubble-eyed. One was humpbacked. The fourth was a boy, no older than thirteen. Their heads moved in rhythmic swaying. Touched by this sight from his childhood and youth, Manischevitz entered and stood silent in the rear.

"Neshoma," said bubble eyes, pointing to the word with a stubby finger. "Now what dat mean?"

"That's the word that means soul," said the boy. He wore eyeglasses.

"Let's git on wid de commentary," said the old man.

"Ain't necessary," said the humpback. "Souls is immaterial substance. That's all. The soul is derived in that manner. The immateriality is derived from the substance, and they both, causally an otherwise, derived from the soul. There can be no higher."

"That's the highest."

"Over de top."

"Wait a minute," said bubble eyes. "I don't see what is dat immaterial

opalescent: reflecting rainbow-colored light

invalidism: a disabled condition

---

5 **skullcaps:** close-fitting caps without brims, worn by many Jews

substance. How come de one gits hitched up to de odder?" He addressed the humpback.

"Ask me something hard. Because it is substanceless immateriality. It couldn't be closer together, like all the parts of the body under one skin—closer."

"Hear now," said the old man.

"All you done is switched de words."

"It's the primum mobile, the substanceless substance from which comes all things that were incepted in the idea—you, me, and every thing and -body else."

"Now how did all dat happen? Make it sound simple."

"It de speerit," said the old man. "On the face of de water moved de speerit. An dat was good. It say so in the Book. From de speerit ariz de man."

"But now listen here. How come it become substance if it all de time a spirit?"

"God alone done dat."

"Holy! Holy! Praise His Name."

"But has dis spirit got some kind of a shade or color?" asked bubble eyes, deadpan.

"Man, of course not. A spirit is a spirit."

"Then how come we is colored?" he said with a triumphant glare.

"Ain't got nothing to do wid dat."

"I still like to know."

"God put the spirit in all things," answered the boy. "He put it in the green leaves and the yellow flowers. He put it with the gold in the fishes and the blue in the sky. That's how come it came to us."

"Amen."

"Praise Lawd and utter loud His speechless Name."

"Blow de bugle till it bust the sky."

They fell silent, intent upon the next word. Manischevitz, with doubt, approached them.

"You'll excuse me," he said. "I am looking for Alexander Levine. You know him maybe?"

"That's the angel," said the boy.

"Oh, *him*," snuffed bubble eyes.

"You'll find him at Bella's. It's the establishment right down the street," the humpback said.

Manischevitz said he was sorry that he could not stay, thanked them, and limped across the street. It was already night. The city was dark and he could barely find his way.

But Bella's was bursting with jazz and the blues. Through the window Manischevitz recognized the dancing crowd and among them sought Levine. He was sitting loose-lipped at Bella's side table. They were **tippling** from an almost empty whiskey fifth.[6] Levine had shed his old clothes, wore a shiny new checkered suit, pearl-gray derby hat, cigar, and big, two-tone, button shoes. To the tailor's dismay, a drunken look had settled upon his formerly dignified face. He leaned toward Bella, tickled her earlobe with his pinky while whispering words that sent her into **gales** of raucous laughter. She fondled his knee.

Manischevitz, **girding** himself, pushed open the door and was not welcomed.

"This place reserved."

"Beat it, pale puss."

"Exit, Yankel, Semitic trash."

But he moved toward the table where Levine sat, the crowd breaking before him as he hobbled forward.

"Mr. Levine," he spoke in a trembly voice. "Is here Manischevitz."

Levine glared blearily. "Speak yo piece, son."

Manischevitz shivered. His back plagued him. Tremors tormented his legs. He looked around, everybody was all ears.

"You'll excuse me. I would like to talk to you in a private place."

"Speak, Ah is a private pusson."

Bella laughed piercingly. "Stop it, boy, you killin me."

Manischevitz, no end disturbed, considered fleeing, but Levine addressed him:

"Kindly state the pu'pose of yo communication with yo's truly."

The tailor wet his cracked lips. "You are Jewish. This I am sure."

Levine rose, nostrils flaring. "Anythin else yo got to say?"

Manischevitz's tongue lay like a slab of stone.

"Speak now or fo'ever hold off."

> **tippling:** drinking liquor

> *L*evine had shed his old clothes, wore a shiny new checkered suit, pearl-gray derby hat, cigar, and big, two-tone, button shoes. To the tailor's dismay, a drunken look had settled upon his formerly dignified face.

> **gales:** bursts

> **girding:** strengthening; preparing

---

6 whiskey fifth: one-fifth of a gallon of whiskey

Tears blinded the tailor's eyes. Was ever man so tried? Should he say he believed a half-drunk Negro was an angel?

The silence slowly petrified.

Manischevitz was recalling scenes of his youth as a wheel in his mind whirred: believe, do not, yes, no, yes, no. The pointer pointed to yes, to between yes and no, to no, no it was yes. He sighed. It moved but one still had to make a choice.

"I think you are an angel from God." He said it in a broken voice, thinking, If you said it, it was said. If you believed it, you must say it. If you believed, you believed.

The hush broke. Everybody talked but the music began and they went on dancing. Bella, grown bored, picked up the cards and dealt herself a hand.

Levine burst into tears. "How you have humiliated me."

Manischevitz apologized.

"Wait'll I freshen up." Levine went to the men's room and returned in his old suit.

No one said goodbye as they left.

They rode to the flat via subway. As they walked up the stairs Manischevitz pointed with his cane at his door.

"That's all been taken care of," Levine said. "You go in while I take off."

Disappointed that it was so soon over, but torn by curiosity, Manischevitz followed the angel up three flights to the roof. When he got there the door was already padlocked.

Luckily he could see through a small broken window. He heard an odd noise, as though of a whirring of wings, and, when he strained for a wider view, could have sworn he saw a dark figure borne aloft on a pair of strong black wings.

A feather drifted down. Manischevitz gasped as it turned white, but it was only snowing.

He rushed downstairs. In the flat Fanny wielded a dust mop under the bed, and then upon the cobwebs on the wall.

"A wonderful thing, Fanny," Manischevitz said. "Believe me, there are Jews everywhere."

Read and Think Critically

Analyze, Conclude, Explain

 1. **ARCHETYPE** Analyze Malamud's use of the angel **archetype** in the story. In what ways does Malamud change the archetypical **character** to support the **themes** of the story?

2. Angel Levine's appearance changes every time Manischevitz sees him. Use a chart like the one below to track the changes in Angel Levine's appearance. What can you conclude about the reasons for these changes?

Angel Levine's Appearance	Description
In the Manischevitz's living room	
At Bella's the first time	
At Bella's the second time, before going to the men's room	
After going to the men's room at Bella's	
While ascending	

3. What does the last line of the story reveal about the themes of the story? Analyze how several themes interact and build upon each other throughout the story.

4. **THE AUTHOR'S STYLE** Malamud's fiction has these qualities:

   • the spare prose is occasionally interrupted by sudden bursts of emotional or metaphorical language;

   • miraculous events take place in grim city neighborhoods.

   Identify an example of these two aspects of Malamud's style and explain what impact or meaning each gives to the story.

Before You Read

John Cheever 1912–1982

About the Author

"I can't write without a reader," John Cheever once said. "It's precisely like a kiss, you can't do it alone." (*Christian Science Monitor*)

The author began his relationship with readers early in life. In 1930, when he was 18, his first short story, "Expelled," was published in *The New Republic*. The story was based on a real-life incident; the year before, Cheever had been expelled from Thayer Academy in Massachusetts, a prestigious boarding school. That same year his affluent East Coast family had lost its wealth in the stock market crash. The author went on to write dozens of short stories and several novels, but before he was able to devote himself to fiction full time,

Cheever wrote synopses of films for MGM and taught in a New York State prison. Throughout his life, he suffered from alcoholism, which resulted in a stay in a rehabilitation clinic in 1975.

Cheever is best known as a writer of short stories, many of which were first published in *The New Yorker* and later collected into *The Stories of John Cheever*, which won the Pulitzer Prize, the National Book Critics Circle Award, and the American Book Award in 1978. His 1957 novel *The Wapshot Chronicle* is on the Modern Library's list of the 100 Best Novels of the 20th Century.

★★★★★★★★★★★

✎ The Author's Style

Many of Cheever's stories offer a glimpse of the moral and emotional lives of upper-middle-class people from New York City or its suburbs. Using his hometown of Quincy, Massachusetts, as a model, the author lifts the veil off suburban life, revealing the sadness and dissatisfaction beneath prosperity and success.

Cheever's characters are often extremely odd and detached from reality; generally we don't learn much about how they make a living, but the author pays close attention to how they behave socially and at home. Usually they are devoted to tradition and habit, partly because of a desperate need for status and security. Often their

behavior is exaggerated both individually and in groups. The characters' obsessions—which are revealed in fantasies or dreams as well as quirky behavior—are the author's way of enabling us to understand them even when they can't understand themselves.

Cheever conveys all of this in a polite and elegant prose style. His style includes sophisticated vocabulary and complex sentences with subordinate clauses and qualifying phrases. An ironic tone satirizes both the characters and their way of life, revealing them to be both ridiculous and sad in the end.

The Wrysons

John Cheever

 LITERARY LENS: SATIRE Cheever was an accomplished practitioner of satire, which is the exposure of vices and shortcomings through humor or exaggeration. Watch for examples of satire in this story.

The Wrysons wanted things in the suburb of Shady Hill to remain exactly as they were. Their dread of change—of irregularity of any sort—was acute, and when the Larkin estate was sold for an old people's rest home, the Wrysons went to the Village Council meeting and demanded to know what sort of old people these old people were going to be. The Wrysons' civic activities were confined to upzoning,[1] but they were very active in this field, and if you were invited to their house for cocktails, the chances were that you would be asked to sign an upzoning petition before you got away. This was something more than a natural desire to preserve the character of the community. They seemed

---

1 **upzoning:** allowing an increased population density in an area; in this case, the construction of a retirement community that houses many people as opposed to a single-family dwelling that houses only a few

There was hardly a book in their house, and, in a place where even cooks were known to have Picasso reproductions hanging above their washstands, the Wrysons' taste in painting stopped at marine sunsets and bowls of flowers.

to sense that there was a stranger at the gates—unwashed, tirelessly scheming, foreign, the father of disorderly children who would ruin their rose garden and depreciate their real-estate investment, a man with a beard, a garlic breath, and a book. The Wrysons took no part in the intellectual life of the community. There was hardly a book in their house, and, in a place where even cooks were known to have Picasso reproductions hanging above their washstands, the Wrysons' taste in painting stopped at marine sunsets and bowls of flowers. Donald Wryson was a large man with thinning fair hair and the cheerful air of a bully, but he was a bully only in the defense of **rectitude**, class distinctions, and the orderly appearance of things. Irene Wryson was not a totally unattractive woman, but she was both shy and **contentious**—especially contentious on the subject of upzoning. They had one child, a little girl named Dolly, and they lived in a pleasant house on Alewives Lane, and they went in for gardening. This was another way of keeping up the appearance of things, and Donald Wryson was very critical of a neighbor who had ragged syringa bushes and a bare spot on her front lawn. They led a limited social life; they seemed to have no ambitions or needs in this direction, although at Christmas each year they sent out about six hundred cards. The preparation and addressing of these must have occupied their evenings for at least two weeks. Donald had a laugh like a jackass, and people who did not like him were careful not to sit in the same train coach with him. The Wrysons were stiff; they were inflexible. They seemed to experience not distaste but alarm when they found quack grass in their lawn or heard of a contemplated divorce among their neighbors. They were odd, of course. They were not as odd as poor, dizzy Flossie Dolmetch, who was caught forging drug prescriptions and was discovered to have been under the influence of morphine for three years. They were not as odd as Caruthers Mason, with his collection of two thousand **lewd** photographs, or as odd as Mrs. Temon, who, with those two lovely children in the next room—But why go on? They were odd.

rectitude:
righteousness; propriety

contentious:
argumentative

lewd:
obscene

Irene Wryson's oddness centered on a dream. She dreamed once or twice a month that someone—some enemy or **hapless** American pilot—had exploded a hydrogen bomb. In the light of day, her dream was inadmissible, for she could not relate it to her garden, her interest in upzoning, or her comfortable way of life. She could not bring herself to tell her husband at breakfast that she had dreamed about the hydrogen bomb. Faced with the pleasant table

hapless: unlucky

and its view of the garden—faced even with rain and snow—she could not find it in herself to explain what had troubled her sleep. The dream cost her much in energy and composure, and often left her deeply depressed. Its sequence of events varied, but it usually went like this.

The dream was set in Shady Hill—she dreamed that she woke in her own bed. Donald was always gone. She was at once aware of the fact that the bomb had exploded. Mattress stuffing and a trickle of brown water were coming through a big hole in the ceiling. The sky was gray—lightless—although there were in the west a few threads of red light, like those charming vapor trails we see in the air after the sun has set. She didn't know if these

JANE AND ELIZABETH, FAIRFIELD PORTER, 1967, THE PARRISH ART MUSEUM

were vapor trails or some part of that force that would destroy the marrow in her bones. The gray air seemed final. The sky would never shine with light again. From her window she could see a river, and now, as she watched, boats began to come upstream. At first, there were only two or three. Then there were tens, and then there were hundreds. There were outboards, excursion boats, yachts, schooners with **auxiliary** motors; there were even rowboats. The number of boats grew until the water was covered with them, and the noise of motors rose to a loud **din**. The jockeying for position in this retreat up the river became aggressive and then savage. She saw men firing pistols at one another, and a rowboat, in which there was a family with little children, smashed and sunk by a cruiser. She cried, in her dream, to see this inhumanity as the world was ending. She cried, and she went on watching, as if some truth was being revealed to her—as if she had always known this to be the human condition, as if she had always known the world to be dangerous and the comforts of her life in Shady Hill to be the merest **palliative**.

auxiliary:
assisting; supplementary

din:
loud, persistent noise

palliative:
remedy

*A*nd how could she lean across the breakfast table and explain her pallor to her husky husband with this detailed vision of the end of the world? He would have laughed his jackass laugh.

Then in her dream she turned away from the window and went through the bathroom that connected their room and Dolly's. Her daughter was sleeping sweetly, and she woke her. At this point, her emotions were at their strongest. The force and purity of the love that she felt toward this fragrant child was an agony. She dressed the little girl and put a snowsuit on her and led her into the bathroom. She opened the medicine cabinet, the one place in the house that the Wrysons, in their passion for neatness, had not put in order. It was crowded with leftover medicines from Dolly's trifling illnesses—cough syrups, calamine lotion for poison ivy, aspirin, and physics. And the mild pefume of these remnants and the tenderness she had felt for her daughter when she was ill—as if the door of the medicine cabinet had been a window opening onto some dazzling summer of the emotions—made her cry again. Among the bottles was one that said "Poison," and she reached for this and unscrewed the top, and shook into her left hand a pill for herself and one for the girl. She told the trusting child some gentle lie, and was about to put the pill between her lips when the ceiling of the bathroom collapsed and they stood knee deep in plaster and dirty water. She groped around in the water for the poison, but it was lost, and the dream usually ended in this way. And how could she lean across the breakfast table and explain her **pallor** to her husky husband with this detailed vision of the end of the world? He would have laughed his jackass laugh.

pallor: paleness

$\mathcal{D}$onald Wryson's oddness could be traced easily enough to his childhood. He had been raised in a small town in the Middle West that couldn't have had much to recommend it, and his father, an old-fashioned commercial traveler, with a hothouse rose in his buttonhole and buff-colored spats,[2] had abandoned his wife and his son when the boy was young. Mrs. Wryson had few friends and no family. With her husband gone, she got a job as a clerk in an insurance office, and took up, with her son, a life of **unmitigated melancholy** and need. She never forgot the horror of her abandonment, and she leaned so heavily for support on her son that she seemed to threaten his animal spirits. Her life was a Calvary,[3] as she often said, and the most she could do was to keep body and soul together.

unmitigated: unrelieved

melancholy: sadness

She had been young and fair and happy once, and the only way she had of evoking these lost times was by giving her son baking lessons. When the nights were long and cold and the wind whistled around the four-family house where they lived, she would light a fire in the kitchen range and drop an apple peel onto the stove lid for the fragrance. Then Donald would put on an apron and scurry around, getting out the necessary bowls and pans, measuring out flour and sugar, separating eggs. He learned the contents of every cupboard. He knew where the spices and the sugar were kept, the nutmeats and the citron, and when the work was done, he enjoyed washing the bowls and pans and putting them back where they belonged. Donald loved these hours himself, mostly because they seemed to dispel the oppression that stood unlifted over those years of his mother's life—and was there any reason why a lonely boy should rebel against the feeling of security that he found in the kitchen on a stormy night? She taught him how to make cookies and muffins and banana bread and, finally, a Lady Baltimore cake.[4] It was sometimes after eleven

> $\mathcal{S}$he never forgot the horror of her abandonment, and she leaned so heavily for support on her son that she seemed to threaten his animal spirits.

2 **spats:** fancy, old-fashioned shoes or leg coverings

3 **Calvary:** an experience of intense mental suffering; also the place in the Bible where Jesus was crucified

4 **Lady Baltimore cake:** a fluffy, layered cake filled with raisins, nuts, cherries, and sherry

The Wrysons

o'clock when their work was done. "We do have a good time together, don't we, son?" Mrs. Wryson would ask. "We have a lovely time together, don't we, you and me? Oh, hear that wind howling! Think of the poor sailors at sea." Then she would embrace him, she would run her fingers through his light hair, and sometimes, although he was much too big, she would draw him onto her lap.

All of that was long ago. Mrs. Wryson was dead, and when Donald stood at the edge of her grave he had not felt any very great grief. She had been **reconciled** to dying years before she did die, and her conversation had been full of **gallant** references to the grave. Years later, when Donald was living alone in New York, he had been overtaken suddenly, one spring evening, by a depression as keen as any in his adolescence. He did not drink, he did not enjoy books or movies or the theatre, and, like his mother, he had few friends. Searching desperately for some way to take himself out of this misery, he hit on the idea of baking a Lady Baltimore cake. He went out and bought the ingredients—deeply ashamed of himself—and sifted the flour and chopped the nuts and citron in the kitchen of the little walk-up apartment where he lived. As he stirred the cake batter, he felt his depression vanish. It was not until he had put the cake in the oven and sat down to wipe his hands on his apron that he realized how successful he had been in summoning the ghost of his mother and the sense of security he had experienced as a child in her kitchen on stormy nights. When the cake was done he iced it, ate a slice, and dumped the rest into the garbage.

The next time he felt troubled, he resisted the temptation to bake a cake, but he was not always able to do this, and during the eight or nine years he had been married to Irene he must have baked eight or nine cakes. He took extraordinary precautions, and she knew nothing of this. She believed him to be a complete stranger to the kitchen. And how could he at the breakfast table—all two hundred and sixteen pounds of him—explain that he looked sleepy because he had been up until three baking a Lady Baltimore cake, which he had hidden in the garage?

$\mathcal{G}$iven these unpleasant facts, then, about these not attractive people, we can dispatch them brightly enough, and who but Dolly would ever miss them? Donald Wryson, in his crusading zeal for upzoning, was out in all kinds of weather, and let's say that one night, when he was returning from a referendum in an ice storm, his car skidded down Hill Street, struck the big elm at the corner, and was demolished. Finis.[5] His poor widow, either through love or dependence, was inconsolable. Getting out of bed one morning, a month or so after the loss of her husband, she got her feet caught in the dust ruffle and fell and broke her hip. Weakened by a long convalescence, she contracted pneumonia and departed this life. This leaves us with Dolly to account for, and what a sad tale we can write for this little girl. During the months in which her parents' will is in probate,[6] she lives first on the charity and then on the **forbearance** of her neighbors. Finally, she is sent to live with her only relative, a cousin of her mother's, who is a schoolteacher in Los Angeles. How many hundreds of nights will she cry herself to sleep in bewilderment and loneliness. How strange and cold the world will seem. There is little to remind her of her parents except at Christmas, when, forwarded from Shady Hill, will come Greetings from Mrs. Sallust Trevor, who has been living in Paris and does not know about the accident; Salutations from the Parkers, who live in Mexico and never did get their lists straight; Season's Greetings from Meyers' Drugstore; Merry Christmas from the Perry Browns; Santissimas from the Oak Tree Italian Restaurant; A Joyeux Noël from Dodie Smith. Year after year, it will be this little girl's responsibility to throw into the wastebasket these cheerful holiday greetings that have followed her parents to and beyond the grave. . . . But this did not happen, and if it had, it would have thrown no light on what we know.

forbearance: patience; leniency

> *The* air smelled sweet. Sweating suddenly, the beating of her heart strained with terror, she realized that the end had come. What could that sweetness in the air be but atomic ash?

What happened was this: Irene Wryson had her dream one night. When she woke, she saw that her husband was not in bed. The air smelled sweet. Sweating suddenly, the beating of her heart strained with terror, she realized that the end had come. What could that sweetness in the air be but atomic ash? She ran to the window, but the river was empty. Half asleep and feeling cruelly lost as she was, she was kept from waking Dolly only by a healthy curiosity. There was smoke in the hallway, but it was not the smoke of any common fire. The sweetness made her feel sure that this was lethal ash. Led on by the smell, she went on down the stairs and through the dining room

---

5 Finis: Middle English for "the end"

6 probate: the process of legally determining if a last will and testament is genuine

into the lighted kitchen. Donald was asleep with his head on the table and the room was full of smoke. "Oh, my darling," she cried, and woke him.

"I burned it," he said when he saw the smoke pouring from the oven. "I burned the damned thing."

"I thought it was the hydrogen bomb," she said.

"It's a cake," he said. "I burned it. What made you think it was the hydrogen bomb?"

"If you wanted something to eat, you should have waked me," she said.

She turned off the oven, and opened the window to let out the smell of smoke and let in the smell of nicotiana and other night flowers. She may have hesitated for a moment, for what would the stranger at the gates—that intruder with his beard and his book—have made of this couple, in their nightclothes, in the smoke-filled kitchen at half past four in the morning? Some comprehension—perhaps momentary—of the complexity of life must have come to them, but it was only momentary. There were no further explanations. He threw the cake, which was burned to a cinder, into the garbage, and they turned out the lights and climbed the stairs, more mystified by life than ever, and more interested than ever in a good appearance.

Read and Think Critically

Analyze, Conclude, Infer

 1. **SATIRE** Analyze the use of **satire** in the story. What human vices and follies are satirized in this story? Support your answer with examples from the text.

2. Reread the three paragraphs that concern Irene Wryson's dream beginning on page 451. What can you conclude about her fears and obsessions?

3. The word *wry* means "ironically or grimly humorous." It is probably not an accident that the word is embedded in the Wrysons' name. In what way is the meaning of their name played out in the Wrysons' story?

4. In her dream, Irene Wryson checks on her sleeping daughter and "the force and purity of the love that she felt toward this fragrant child was an agony." What do you think can make a pure and strong love feel agonizing?

5. Why is Donald Wryson so secretive about baking cakes?

6. **THE AUTHOR'S STYLE** Cheever has the gift for revealing the psychology of **characters**, especially when the characters don't understand themselves. Choose either Irene or Donald Wryson. What can you infer about their character that they don't understand themselves? Use personality traits, fears, **motivations**, mannerisms, and attitudes mentioned explicitly in the text to support your **inferences**.

Before You Read

Kurt Vonnegut 1922–2007

About the Author

"As a kid I was a jokemaker," Kurt Vonnegut recalled of his boyhood in Indianapolis. "I was the youngest member of my family, and the youngest child in any family is always a jokemaker because a joke is the only way he can enter into adult conversation." (*Christian Century*)

The author's rollicking but edgy humor is one reason he is not only praised by critics but also popular with readers. Although much of what he wrote can be considered science fiction, an overall tone of black humor, absurdism, and satire transcends that label and puts his writing in the literary mainstream.

Before becoming a freelance writer in 1950, Vonnegut served as a soldier in World War II and worked at General Electric Company. Awarded a Purple Heart for his military service, Vonnegut and other prisoners of war were forced to take refuge in an underground meatlocker for several days during the firebombing of Dresden, Germany.

That experience became the basis of his hugely successful 1969 novel, *Slaughterhouse-Five*, which attracted a cultlike following. Other well-known works include a collection of short stories called *Welcome to the Monkey House* and the novels *Cat's Cradle* and *The Sirens of Titan*. The unpretentious writer once commented that he would rather have written the television show *Cheers* than anything he has written. Some of his works have been adapted for stage and screen.

****

The Author's Style

In many of Vonnegut's stories, the narrative tone is unemotional and nonjudgmental. This is a satirist's strategy for forcing us to respond to what we see because, at least on the surface, the author himself isn't taking any stands.

Generally, Vonnegut's stories and novels lean in the direction of fable rather than realistic fiction. His often-exaggerated characters and fantastic plots are meant to wake us up by taking us outside our own society, whose faults and attitudes we tend to overlook. In the novel *Slaughterhouse-Five*, for example, his use of the science fiction technique of time travel enables Vonnegut to deliver a biting critique not only of contemporary culture, but also of the Vietnam War, which was going on at the time the novel was published. Frequent Vonnegut targets include consumerism, ecology, and war.

Vonnegut sometimes discusses oppression as if he were resigned to it, but his ironic tone tells us that he is criticizing its tragic human cost. By making matter-of-fact statements about outrageous actions, the writer is forcing the reader to evaluate and decide what matters.

Harrison Bergeron

Kurt Vonnegut

LITERARY LENS: ABSURDISM The **absurdists** were a group of artists of the 1950s and 1960s who attempted to show the absurdity of the human condition and to satirize social attitudes and institutions. These authors used extreme illogic, black humor, and dark fantasy to expose what they felt to be the futility and despair of modern society. Watch for aspects of the absurd in this short story.

The year was 2081, and everybody was finally equal. They weren't only equal before God and the law. They were equal every which way. Nobody was smarter than anybody else. Nobody was better looking than anybody else. Nobody was stronger or quicker than anybody else. All this equality was due to the 211th, 212th, and 213th Amendments to the Constitution, and to the unceasing **vigilance** of agents of the United States Handicapper General.

vigilance: watchfulness; caution

Some things about living still weren't quite right, though. April, for instance, still drove people crazy by not being springtime. And it was in that clammy month that the H-G men took George and Hazel Bergeron's fourteen-year-old son, Harrison, away.

It was tragic, all right, but George and Hazel couldn't think about it very hard. Hazel had a perfectly average intelligence, which meant she couldn't think about anything except in short bursts. And George, while his intelligence was way above normal, had a little mental handicap radio in his ear. He was required by law to wear it at all times. It was tuned to a government transmitter. Every twenty seconds or so, the transmitter would send out some sharp noise to keep people like George from taking unfair advantage of their brains.

George and Hazel were watching television. There were tears on Hazel's cheeks, but she'd forgotten for the moment what they were about.

On the television screen were ballerinas.

A buzzer sounded in George's head. His thoughts fled in panic, like bandits from a burglar alarm.

"That was a real pretty dance, that dance they just did," said Hazel.

"Huh?" said George.

"That dance—it was nice," said Hazel.

"Yup," said George. He tried to think a little about the ballerinas. They weren't really very good—no better than anybody else would have been, anyway. They were burdened with sashweights[1] and bags of birdshot,[2] and their faces were masked, so that no one, seeing a free and graceful gesture or a pretty face, would feel like something the cat drug in. George was toying with the vague notion that maybe dancers shouldn't be handicapped. But he didn't get very far with it before another noise in his ear radio scattered his thoughts.

George winced. So did two out of the eight ballerinas.

Hazel saw him wince. Having no mental handicap herself, she had to ask George what the latest sound had been.

"Sounded like somebody hitting a milk bottle with a ball peen hammer,"[3] said George.

"I'd think it would be real interesting, hearing all the different sounds," said Hazel, a little envious. "All the things they think up."

"Um," said George.

"Only, if I was Handicapper General, you know what I would do?" said Hazel. Hazel, as a matter of fact, bore a strong resemblance to the Handicapper General, a woman named Diana Moon Glampers. "If I was Diana Moon Glampers," said Hazel, "I'd have chimes on Sunday—just chimes. Kind of in honor of religion."

---

1 **sashweights:** narrow lead weights

2 **birdshot:** lead that is inside shotgun shells

3 **ball peen hammer:** hammer with one rounded head, usually used for working with metal

"I could think, if it was just chimes," said George.

"Well—maybe make 'em real loud," said Hazel. "I think I'd make a good Handicapper General."

"Good as anybody else," said George.

"Who knows better'n I do what normal is?" said Hazel.

"Right," said George. He began to think **glimmeringly** about his abnormal son who was now in jail, about Harrison, but a twenty-one-gun salute in his head stopped that.

"Boy!" said Hazel, "that was a doozy, wasn't it?"

It was such a doozy that George was white and trembling and tears stood on the rims of his red eyes. Two of the eight ballerinas had collapsed to the studio floor, holding their temples.

"All of a sudden you look so tired," said Hazel. "Why don't you stretch out on the sofa, so's you can rest your handicap bag on the pillows, honeybunch." She was referring to the forty-seven pounds of birdshot in a canvas bag, which was padlocked around George's neck. "Go on and rest the bag for a little while," she said. "I don't care if you're not equal to me for a while."

George weighed the bag with his hands. "I don't mind it," he said. "I don't notice it anymore. It's just a part of me."

"You been so tired lately—kind of wore out," said Hazel. "If there was just some way we could make a little hole in the bottom of the bag, and just take out a few of them lead balls. Just a few."

"Two years in prison and two thousand dollars fine for every ball I took out," said George. "I don't call that a bargain."

"If you could just take a few out when you came home from work," said Hazel. "I mean—you don't compete with anybody around here. You just set around."

"If I tried to get away with it," said George, "then other people'd get away with it—and pretty soon we'd be right back to the dark ages again, with everybody competing against everybody else. You wouldn't like that, would you?"

> "All of a sudden you look so tired," said Hazel. "Why don't you stretch out on the sofa, so's you can rest your handicap bag on the pillows, honeybunch." She was referring to the forty-seven pounds of birdshot in a canvas bag, which was padlocked around George's neck.

glimmeringly:
intermittently;
unsteadily

And she had to apologize at once for her voice, which was a very unfair voice for a woman to use. Her voice was a warm, luminous, timeless melody.

"I'd hate it," said Hazel.

"There you are," said George. "The minute people start cheating on laws, what do you think happens to society?"

If Hazel hadn't been able to come up with an answer to this question, George couldn't have supplied one. A siren was going off in his head.

"Reckon it'd fall all apart," said Hazel.

"What would?" said George blankly.

"Society," said Hazel uncertainly. "Wasn't that what you just said?"

"Who knows?" said George.

The television program was suddenly interrupted for a news bulletin. It wasn't clear at first as to what the bulletin was about, since the announcer, like all announcers, had a serious speech impediment. For about half a minute, and in a state of high excitement, the announcer tried to say, "Ladies and gentlemen—"

He finally gave up, handed the bulletin to a ballerina to read.

"That's all right—" Hazel said of the announcer, "he tried. That's the big thing. He tried to do the best he could with what God gave him. He should get a nice raise for trying so hard."

"Ladies and gentlemen—" said the ballerina, reading the bulletin. She must have been extraordinarily beautiful, because the mask she wore was hideous. And it was easy to see that she was the strongest and most graceful of all the dancers, for her handicap bags were as big as those worn by two-hundred-pound men.

And she had to apologize at once for her voice, which was a very unfair voice for a woman to use. Her voice was a warm, luminous, timeless melody. "Excuse me—" she said, and she began again, making her voice absolutely uncompetitive. "Harrison Bergeron, age fourteen," she said in a grackle[4] squawk, "has just escaped from jail, where he was held on suspicion of plotting to overthrow the government. He is a genius and an athlete, is under-handicapped, and should be regarded as extremely dangerous."

A police photograph of Harrison Bergeron was flashed on the screen, upside down, then sideways, upside down again, then right side up. The

---

4 grackle: a large blackbird

picture showed the full length of Harrison against a background calibrated in feet and inches. He was exactly seven feet tall.

The rest of Harrison's appearance was Halloween and hardware. Nobody had ever borne heavier handicaps. He had outgrown **hindrances** faster than the H-G men could think them up. Instead of a little ear radio for a mental handicap, he wore a tremendous pair of earphones, and spectacles with thick wavy lenses. The spectacles were intended to make him not only half blind, but to give him **whanging** headaches besides.

Scrap metal was hung all over him. Ordinarily, there was a certain symmetry, a military neatness to the handicaps issued to strong people, but Harrison looked like a walking junkyard. In the race of life, Harrison carried three hundred pounds.

And to offset his good looks, the H-G men required that he wear at all times a red rubber ball for a nose, keep his eyebrows shaved off, and cover his even white teeth with black caps at **snaggletooth** random.

"If you see this boy," said the ballerina, "do not—I repeat, do not—try to reason with him."

There was the shriek of a door being torn from its hinges.

Screams and barking cries of consternation came from the television set. The photograph of Harrison Bergeron on the screen jumped again and again, as though dancing to the tune of an earthquake.

George Bergeron correctly identified the earthquake, and well he might have—for many was the time his own home had danced to the same crashing tune. "Oh, no—" said George, "that must be Harrison."

The realization was blasted from his mind instantly by the sound of an automobile collision in his head.

When George could open his eyes again, the photograph of Harrison was gone. A living, breathing Harrison filled the screen.

> Screams and barking cries of consternation came from the television set. The photograph of Harrison Bergeron on the screen jumped again and again, as though dancing to the tune of an earthquake.

Clanking, clownish, and huge, Harrison stood in the center of the studio. The knob of the uprooted studio door was still in his hand. Ballerinas, technicians, musicians, and announcers cowered on their knees before him, expecting to die.

"I am the Emperor!" cried Harrison. "Do you hear? I am the Emperor! Everybody must do what I say at once!" He stamped his foot and the studio shook.

"Even as I stand here—" he bellowed, "crippled, hobbled, sickened—I am a greater ruler than any man who ever lived! Now watch me become what I *can* become!"

Harrison tore the straps of his handicap harness like wet tissue paper, tore straps guaranteed to support five thousand pounds.

Harrison's scrap-iron handicaps crashed to the floor.

Harrison thrust his thumbs under the bar of the padlock that secured his head harness. The bar snapped like celery. Harrison smashed his headphones and spectacles against the wall.

He flung away his rubber-ball nose, revealed a man that would have awed Thor, the god of thunder.

"I shall now select my Empress!" he said, looking down on the cowering people. "Let the first woman who dares rise to her feet claim her mate and her throne!"

A moment passed, and then a ballerina arose, swaying like a willow. Harrison plucked the mental handicap from her ear, snapped off her physical handicaps with marvelous delicacy. Last of all, he removed her mask.

A moment passed, and then a ballerina arose, swaying like a willow. Harrison plucked the mental handicap from her ear, snapped off her physical handicaps with marvelous delicacy. Last of all, he removed her mask.

She was blindingly beautiful.

"Now—" said Harrison, taking her hand, "shall we show the people the meaning of the word dance? Music!" he commanded.

The musicians scrambled back into their chairs, and Harrison stripped them of their handicaps, too. "Play your best," he told them, "and I'll make you barons and dukes and earls."

The music began. It was normal at first—cheap, silly, false. But Harrison snatched two musicians from their chairs, waved them like batons as he sang the music as he wanted it played. He slammed them back into their chairs.

The music began again and was much improved.

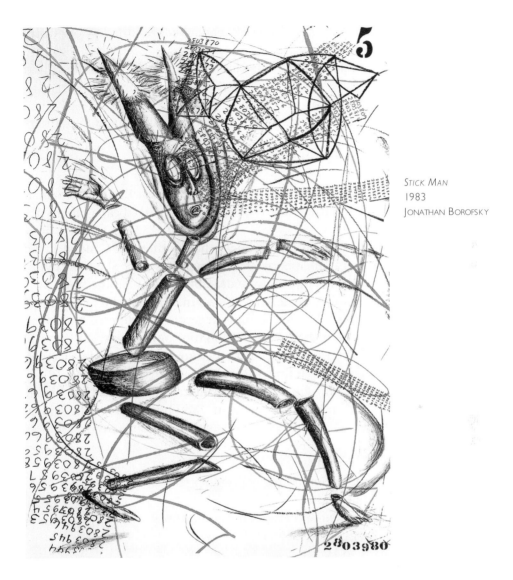

STICK MAN
1983
JONATHAN BOROFSKY

Harrison and his Empress merely listened to the music for a while—listened gravely, as though synchronizing their heartbeats with it.

They shifted their weight to their toes.

Harrison placed his big hands on the girl's tiny waist, letting her sense the weightlessness that would soon be hers.

And then, in an explosion of joy and grace, into the air they sprang!

Not only were the laws of the land abandoned, but the law of gravity and the laws of motion as well.

gamboled:
leapt; frolicked

They reeled, whirled, swiveled, flounced, capered, **gamboled**, and spun.

They leaped like deer on the moon.

The studio ceiling was thirty feet high, but each leap brought the dancers nearer to it.

It became their obvious intention to kiss the ceiling.

They kissed it.

And then, neutralizing gravity with love and pure will, they remained suspended in air inches below the ceiling, and they kissed each other for a long, long time.

It was then that Diana Moon Glampers, the Handicapper General, came into the studio with a double-barreled ten-gauge shotgun. She fired twice, and the Emperor and the Empress were dead before they hit the floor.

Diana Moon Glampers loaded the gun again. She aimed it at the musicians and told them they had ten seconds to get their handicaps back on.

It was then that the Bergerons' television tube burned out.

Hazel turned to comment about the blackout to George. But George had gone out into the kitchen for a can of beer.

George came back in with the beer, paused while a handicap signal shook him up. And then he sat down again. "You been crying?" he said to Hazel.

"Yup," she said,

"What about?" he said.

"I forget," she said. "Something real sad on television."

"What was it?" he said.

"It's all kind of mixed up in my mind," said Hazel.

"Forget sad things," said George.

"I always do," said Hazel.

"That's my girl," said George. He winced. There was the sound of a riveting gun in his head.

"Gee—I could tell that one was a doozy," said Hazel.

"You can say that again," said George.

"Gee—" said Hazel, "I could tell that one was a doozy."

Read and Think Critically

Explain, Brainstorm, Analyze

1. **ABSURDISM** From the story, detail at least one example of extreme illogic, black humor, or dark **fantasy**. Then explain why you think Vonnegut uses the device.

2. Why do you think the Handicapper General and others in charge want everyone to be equal?

3. "All people are created equal" is a basic tenet of American democracy. How is this notion exploited in "Harrison Bergeron"?

4. **Satirists** are quick to identify the evils and excesses of society and those in power, but they often don't have ready solutions to the problems they point out. What evil is Vonnegut satirizing? Brainstorm for possible solutions to the problem.

5. **THE AUTHOR'S STYLE** A *pessimist* is a person who generally considers reality to be dismal and expects the worst outcome; an *optimist* is just the opposite. Consider the quotation by Vonnegut below as you analyze the short story "Harrison Bergeron." Do you think Vonnegut leans more toward pessimism or optimism? Explain your response.

Laughter and Tears

Laughter and tears are both responses to frustration and exhaustion. I myself prefer to laugh, since there is less cleaning up to do afterward.

—Kurt Vonnegut,
Quotations to Cheer You Up When the World Is Getting You Down

---

Before You Read

Flannery O'Connor 1925–1964

About the Author

When Flannery O'Connor was growing up in Milledgeville, Georgia, she lived right across the street from the looming cathedral her family attended. Her intense Catholicism was to have a strong influence on her life and work.

Also influential was her parents' encouragement in developing her talents. O'Connor was a shy and talented only child who wrote, drew cartoons, and attended an experimental private school. The author showed ingenuity and a certain fascination with freakishness at a young age, when she taught a "frizzled" chicken (one whose feathers grew inward) to walk backwards. This fascination would later turn up in her writing.

O'Connor went to college in the South and published her first story in 1946. Not long after receiving her master's degree from the well-known University of Iowa Writers' Workshop, she was stricken with lupus, the chronic inflammatory disease that had killed her father. She returned home to live with her mother and raise peacocks on her family's ancestral farm while continuing to write until her death in 1964.

Remembered primarily as a short story writer, O'Connor's best-known works include the novel *The Violent Bear It Away* and the short story collections *A Good Man Is Hard to Find* and *Everything That Rises Must Converge*.

****

The Author's Style

O'Connor was a devout Catholic who lived in the South, a region historically intolerant toward her religion. Her stories focus on the need for salvation in a world that is beset by evil. O'Connor's characters often reveal through their manners and everyday behavior how obsessed they are by race and social class. Worse, they often think their wrongful actions and attitudes make them "good people."

These characters, who speak in the idiom of rural Georgia, often fail to see the moral implications of their own words. In the end, they are often shaken out of their narrow habits of mind by shocking, even violent, events.

When O'Connor's characters are saved from their meanness and shallowness, it is not through their own efforts. Instead, it is by mysterious events, sudden evidence of what O'Connor thought of as the grace of God. She is critical of the prideful and the smug—people who think they always know what is right—and these characters often pay a high price for the humbling insights they reach. O'Connor's stories sometimes read like modern parables of spiritual enlightenment. Bizarre characters, comical descriptions, and grotesque metaphors for the way things look or feel also mark her style. The physical deformities of her characters often reflect their moral shortcomings. Her stories often concern an individual's relationship to God.

Everything That Rises Must Converge

F L A N N E R Y   O ' C O N N O R

LITERARY LENS: MOTIF In literature, recurrent images, objects, phrases, or actions are called **motifs**. The repetition of such elements tends to unify a work of literature. Watch for motifs in this story.

*H*er doctor had told Julian's mother that she must lose twenty pounds on account of her blood pressure, so on Wednesday nights Julian had to take her downtown on the bus for a reducing class at the Y. The reducing class was designed for working girls over fifty, who weighed from 165 to 200 pounds. His mother was one of the slimmer ones, but she said ladies did not tell their age or weight. She would not ride the buses by herself at night since they had been integrated,[1] and because the reducing class was one of her few pleasures, necessary for her health, and *free*, she said Julian could at least put himself out to take her, considering all she did for him. Julian did not like to consider all she did for him, but every Wednesday night he

---

1 **since they had been integrated:** since blacks had been allowed to ride the same buses as whites

Morality Was Her Own, Daphne Confar

braced himself and took her.

She was almost ready to go, standing before the hall mirror, putting on her hat, while he, his hands behind him, appeared pinned to the door frame, waiting like Saint Sebastian for the arrows to begin piercing him.[2] The hat was new and had cost her seven dollars and a half. She kept saying, "Maybe I shouldn't have paid that for it. No, I shouldn't have. I'll take it off and return it tomorrow. I shouldn't have bought it."

Julian raised his eyes to heaven. "Yes, you should have bought it," he said. "Put it on and let's go." It was a hideous hat. A purple velvet flap came down on one side of it and stood up on the other; the rest of it was green and looked like a cushion with the stuffing out. He decided it was less comical than **jaunty** and pathetic. Everything that gave her pleasure was small and depressed him.

She lifted the hat one more time and set it down slowly on top of her head. Two wings of gray hair protruded on either side of her **florid** face, but her eyes, sky-blue, were as innocent and untouched by experience as they must have been when she was ten. Were it not that she was a widow who had struggled fiercely to feed and clothe and put

jaunty:
showy; stylish

florid:
flowery;
ornate in
style

---

2 **Saint Sebastian . . . piercing him:** Sebastian was tied to a tree and shot with arrows for being a Christian during the reign of Roman emperor Diocletian, 284–305 A.D.

him through school and who was supporting him still, "until he got on his feet," she might have been a little girl that he had to take to town.

"It's all right, it's all right," he said. "Let's go." He opened the door himself and started down the walk to get her going. The sky was a dying violet and the houses stood out darkly against it, **bulbous** liver-colored monstrosities of a uniform ugliness though no two were alike. Since this had been a fashionable neighborhood forty years ago, his mother persisted in thinking they did well to have an apartment in it. Each house had a narrow collar of dirt around it in which sat, usually, a grubby child. Julian walked with his hands in his pockets, his head down and thrust forward and his eyes glazed with the determination to make himself completely numb during the time he would be sacrificed to her pleasure.

The door closed and he turned to find the dumpy figure, surmounted by the atrocious hat, coming toward him. "Well," she said, "you only live once and paying a little more for it, I at least won't meet myself coming and going."

"Some day I'll start making money," Julian said gloomily—he knew he never would—"and you can have one of those jokes whenever you take the fit." But first they would move. He visualized a place where the nearest neighbors would be three miles away on either side.

"I think you're doing fine," she said, drawing on her gloves. "You've only been out of school a year. Rome wasn't built in a day."

She was one of the few members of the Y reducing class who arrived in hat and gloves and who had a son who had been to college. "It takes time," she said, "and the world is in such a mess. This hat looked better on me than any of the others, though when she brought it out I said, 'Take that thing back. I wouldn't have it on my head,' and she said, 'Now wait till you see it on,' and when she put it on me, I said, 'We-ull,' and she said, 'If you ask me, that hat does something for you and you do something for the hat, and besides,' she said, 'with that hat, you won't meet yourself coming and going.'"

The door closed and he turned to find the dumpy figure, surmounted by the atrocious hat, coming toward him. "Well," she said, "you only live once and paying a little more for it, I at least won't meet myself coming and going."

bulbous: round; resembling a bulb

Julian thought he could have stood his lot better if she had been selfish, if she had been an old hag who drank and screamed at him. He walked along, saturated in depression, as if in the midst of his martyrdom he had lost his faith. Catching sight of his long, hopeless, irritated face, she stopped suddenly with a grief-stricken look, and pulled back on his arm. "Wait on me," she said. "I'm going back to the house and take this thing off and tomorrow I'm going to return it. I was out of my head. I can pay the gas bill with that seven-fifty."

He caught her arm in a vicious grip. "You are not going to take it back," he said. "I like it."

"Well," she said, "I don't think I ought . . . "

"Shut up and enjoy it," he muttered, more depressed than ever.

"With the world in the mess it's in," she said, "it's a wonder we can enjoy anything. I tell you, the bottom rail is on the top."

Julian sighed.

"Of course," she said, "if you know who you are, you can go anywhere." She said this every time he took her to the reducing class. "Most of them in it are not our kind of people," she said, "but I can be gracious to anybody. I know who I am."

"They don't give a damn for your graciousness," Julian said savagely. "Knowing who you are is good for one generation only. You haven't the foggiest idea where you stand now or who you are."

She stopped and allowed her eyes to flash at him. "I most certainly do know who I am," she said, "and if you don't know who you are, I'm ashamed of you."

"Oh hell," Julian said.

"Your great-grandfather was a former governor of this state," she said. "Your grandfather was a prosperous landowner. Your grandmother was a Godhigh."

"Will you look around you," he said tensely, "and see where you are now?" and he swept his arm jerkily out to indicate the neighborhood, which the growing darkness at least made less dingy.

"You remain what you are," she said. "Your great-grandfather had a plantation and two hundred slaves."

"There are no more slaves," he said irritably.

"They were better off when they were," she said. He groaned to see that she was off on that topic. She rolled onto it every few days like a train on an open track. He knew every stop, every junction, every swamp along the way, and knew the exact point at which her conclusion would roll majestically into the station: "It's ridiculous. It's simply not realistic. They should rise, yes, but on their own side of the fence."

"Let's skip it," Julian said.

"The ones I feel sorry for," she said, "are the ones that are half white. They're tragic."

"Will you skip it?"

"Suppose we were half white. We would certainly have mixed feelings."

"I have mixed feelings now," he groaned.

"Well let's talk about something pleasant," she said. "I remember going to Grandpa's when I was a little girl. Then the house had double stairways that went up to what was really the second floor—all the cooking was done on the first. I used to like to stay down in the kitchen on account of the way the walls smelled. I would sit with my nose pressed against the plaster and take deep breaths. Actually the place belonged to the Godhighs but your grandfather Chestny paid the mortgage and saved it for them. They were in reduced circumstances," she said, "but reduced or not, they never forgot who they were."

He preferred its threadbare elegance to anything he could name and it was because of it that all the neighborhoods they had lived in had been a torment to him—whereas she had hardly known the difference.

"Doubtless that decayed mansion reminded them," Julian muttered. He never spoke of it without contempt or thought of it without longing. He had seen it once when he was a child before it had been sold. The double stairways had rotted and been torn down. Negroes were living in it. But it remained in his mind as his mother had known it. It appeared in his dreams regularly. He would stand on the wide porch, listening to the rustle of oak leaves, then wander through the high-ceilinged hall into the parlor that opened onto it and gaze at the worn rugs and faded draperies. It occurred to him that it was he, not she, who could have appreciated it. He preferred its threadbare elegance to anything he could name and it was because of it that all the neighborhoods they had lived in had been a torment to him—whereas she had hardly known the difference. She called her insensitivity "being adjustable."

"And I remember the old darky[3] who was my nurse, Caroline. There was

---

3 darky: derogatory term for a black person

no better person in the world. I've always had a great respect for my colored friends," she said. "I'd do anything in the world for them and they'd . . . "

"Will you for God's sake get off that subject?" Julian said. When he got on a bus by himself, he made it a point to sit down beside a Negro, in **reparation** as it were for his mother's sins.

reparation:
compensation;
atonement

"You're mighty touchy tonight," she said. "Do you feel all right?"

"Yes I feel all right," he said. "Now lay off."

vile:
foul; miserable

She pursed her lips. "Well, you certainly are in a **vile** humor," she observed. "I just won't speak to you at all."

They had reached the bus stop. There was no bus in sight and Julian, his hands still jammed in his pockets and his head thrust forward, scowled down the empty street. The frustration of having to wait on the bus as well as ride on it began to creep up his neck like a hot hand. The presence of his mother was borne in upon him as she gave a pained sigh. He looked at her bleakly. She was holding herself very erect under the **preposterous** hat, wearing it like a banner of her imaginary dignity. There was in him an evil urge to break her spirit. He suddenly unloosened his tie and pulled it off and put it in his pocket.

preposterous:
ridiculous

She stiffened. "Why must you look like *that* when you take me to town?" she said. "Why must you deliberately embarrass me?"

"If you'll never learn where you are," he said, "you can at least learn where I am."

"You look like a—thug," she said.

"Then I must be one," he murmured.

"I'll just go home," she said. "I will not bother you. If you can't do a little thing like that for me . . . "

Rolling his eyes upward, he put his tie back on. "Restored to my class," he muttered. He thrust his face toward her and hissed. "True culture is in the mind, the *mind*," he said, and tapped his head, "the mind."

"It's in the heart," she said, "and in how you do things and how you do things is because of who you *are*."

"Nobody in the damn bus cares who you are."

"I care who I am," she said icily.

The lighted bus appeared on top of the next hill and as it approached, they moved out into the street to meet it. He put his hand under her elbow and hoisted her up on the creaking step. She entered with a little smile, as if she were going into a drawing room where everyone had been waiting for her.

While he put in the tokens, she sat down on one of the broad front seats for three which faced the aisle. A thin woman with protruding teeth and long yellow hair was sitting on the end of it. His mother moved up beside her and left room for Julian beside herself. He sat down and looked at the floor across the aisle where a pair of thin feet in red and white canvas sandals were planted.

His mother immediately began a general conversation meant to attract anyone who felt like talking. "Can it get any hotter?" she said and removed from her purse a folding fan, black with a Japanese scene on it, which she began to flutter before her.

"I reckon it might could," the woman with the protruding teeth said, "but I know for a fact my apartment couldn't get no hotter."

"It must get the afternoon sun," his mother said. She sat forward and looked up and down the bus. It was half filled. Everybody was white. "I see we have the bus to ourselves," she said. Julian cringed.

"For a change," said the woman across the aisle, the owner of the red and white canvas sandals. "I come on one the other day and they were thick as fleas—up front and all through."

"The world is in a mess everywhere," his mother said. "I don't know how we've let it get in this fix."

"What gets my goat is all those boys from good families stealing automobile tires," the woman with the protruding teeth said. "I told my boy, I said you may not be rich but you been raised right and if I ever catch you in any such mess, they can send you on to the reformatory. Be exactly where you belong."

"Training tells," his mother said. "Is your boy in high school?"

"Ninth grade," the woman said.

"My son just finished college last year. He wants to write but he's selling typewriters until he gets started," his mother said.

The woman leaned forward and peered at Julian. He threw her such a **malevolent** look that she **subsided** against the seat. On the floor across the aisle there was an abandoned newspaper. He got up and got it and opened it out in front of him. His mother discreetly continued the conversation in a lower tone but the woman across the aisle said in a loud voice, "Well that's nice. Selling typewriters is close to writing. He can go right from one to the other."

"I tell him," his mother said, "that Rome wasn't built in a day."

Behind the newspaper Julian was withdrawing into the inner compartment of his mind where he spent most of his time. This was a kind of

malevolent: evil; spiteful

subsided: slumped; settled back

mental bubble in which he established himself when he could not bear to be a part of what was going on around him. From it he could see out and judge but in it he was safe from any kind of penetration from without. It was the only place where he felt free of the general idiocy of his fellows. His mother had never entered it but from it he could see her with absolute clarity.

The old lady was clever enough and he thought that if she had started from any of the right premises, more might have been expected of her. She lived according to the laws of her own fantasy world, outside of which he had never seen her set foot. The law of it was to sacrifice herself for him after she had first created the necessity to do so by making a mess of things. If he had permitted her sacrifices, it was only because her lack of foresight had made them necessary. All of her life had been a struggle to act like a Chestny without the Chestny goods, and to give him everything she thought a Chestny ought to have; but since, said she, it was fun to struggle, why complain? And when you had won, as she had won, what fun to look back on the hard times! He could not forgive her that she had enjoyed the struggle and that she thought *she* had won.

> *M*ost miraculous of all, instead of being blinded by love for her as she was for him, he had cut himself emotionally free of her and could see her with complete objectivity. He was not dominated by his mother.

What she meant when she said she had won was that she had brought him up successfully and had sent him to college and that he had turned out so well—good looking (her teeth had gone unfilled so that his could be straightened), intelligent (he realized he was too intelligent to be a success), and with a future ahead of him (there was of course no future ahead of him). She excused his gloominess on the grounds that he was still growing up and his radical ideas on his lack of practical experience. She said he didn't yet know a thing about "life," that he hadn't even entered the real world—when already he was as **disenchanted** with it as a man of fifty.

disenchanted: disillusioned; disappointed

The further irony of all this was that in spite of her, he had turned out so well. In spite of going to only a third-rate college, he had, on his own initiative, come out with a first-rate education; in spite of growing up dominated by a small mind, he had ended up with a large one; in spite of all her foolish views, he was free of prejudice and unafraid to face facts. Most miraculous of all, instead of being blinded by love for her as she was for him, he had cut himself emotionally free of her and could see her with complete objectivity. He was not dominated by his mother.

The bus stopped with a sudden jerk and shook him from his meditation. A woman from the back lurched forward with little steps and barely escaped falling in his newspaper as she righted herself. She got off and a large Negro got on. Julian kept his paper lowered to watch. It gave him a certain satisfaction to see injustice in daily operation. It confirmed his view that with a few exceptions there was no one worth knowing within a radius of three hundred miles. The Negro was well dressed and carried a briefcase. He looked around and then sat down on the other end of the seat where the woman with the red and white canvas sandals was sitting. He immediately unfolded a newspaper and obscured himself behind it. Julian's mother's elbow at once prodded insistently into his ribs. "Now you see why I won't ride on these buses by myself," she whispered.

The woman with the red and white canvas sandals had risen at the same time the Negro sat down and had gone further back in the bus and taken the seat of the woman who had got off. His mother leaned forward and cast her an approving look.

Julian rose, crossed the aisle, and sat down in the place of the woman with the canvas sandals. From this position, he looked serenely across at his mother. Her face had turned an angry red. He stared at her, making his eyes the eyes of a stranger. He felt his tension suddenly lift as if he had openly declared war on her.

He would have liked to get in conversation with the Negro and to talk with him about art or politics or any subject that would be above the comprehension of those around them, but the man remained entrenched behind his paper. He was either ignoring the change of seating or had never noticed it. There was no way for Julian to convey his sympathy.

His mother kept her eyes fixed reproachfully on his face. The woman with the protruding teeth was looking at him avidly as if he were a type of monster new to her.

"Do you have a light?" he asked the Negro.

Without looking away from his paper, the man reached in his pocket and handed him a packet of matches.

"Thanks," Julian said. For a moment he held the matches foolishly. A NO SMOKING sign looked down upon him from over the door. This alone would not have deterred him; he had no cigarettes. He had quit smoking some months before because he could not afford it. "Sorry," he muttered and handed back the matches. The Negro lowered the paper and gave him an annoyed look. He took the matches and raised the paper again.

His mother continued to gaze at him but she did not take advantage of his momentary discomfort. Her eyes retained their battered look. Her face seemed to be unnaturally red, as if her blood pressure had risen. Julian allowed no glimmer of sympathy to show on his face. Having got the advantage, he wanted desperately to keep it and carry it through. He would have liked to teach her a lesson that would last her a while, but there seemed no way to continue the point. The Negro refused to come out from behind his paper.

stolidly: dully; without emotion

Julian folded his arms and looked **stolidly** before him, facing her but as if he did not see her, as if he had ceased to recognize her existence. He visualized a scene in which, the bus having reached their stop, he would remain in his seat and when she said, "Aren't you going to get off?" he would look at her as at a stranger who had rashly addressed him. The corner they got off on was usually deserted, but it was well lighted and it would not hurt her to walk by herself the four blocks to the Y. He decided to wait until the time came and then decide whether or not he would let her get off by herself. He would have to be at the Y at ten to bring her back, but he could leave her wondering if he was going to show up. There was no reason for her to think she could always depend on him.

He retired again into the high-ceilinged room sparsely settled with large pieces of antique furniture. His soul expanded momentarily but then he became aware of his mother across from him and the vision shriveled. He studied her coldly. Her feet in little pumps dangled like a child's and did not quite reach the floor. She was training on him an exaggerated look of reproach. He felt completely detached from her. At that moment he could with pleasure have slapped her as he would have slapped a particularly obnoxious child in his charge.

He began to imagine various unlikely ways by which he could teach her a lesson. He might make friends with some distinguished Negro professor or lawyer and bring him home to spend the evening. He would be entirely justified but her blood pressure would rise to 300. He could not push her to the extent of making her have a stroke, and moreover, he had never been successful at making any Negro friends. He had tried to strike up an acquaintance on the bus with some of the better types, with ones that looked like professors or ministers or lawyers. One morning he had sat down next to a distinguished-looking dark brown man who had answered his questions with a sonorous **solemnity** but who had turned out to be an undertaker. Another day he had sat down beside a cigar-smoking Negro with a diamond ring on his finger, but after a few stilted pleasantries, the Negro had rung the buzzer and risen, slipping two lottery tickets into Julian's hand as he climbed over him to leave.

solemnity: seriousness; dignity

He imagined his mother lying desperately ill and his being able to secure only a Negro doctor for her. He toyed with that idea for a few minutes and then dropped it for a momentary vision of himself participating as a sympathizer in a sit-in demonstration. This was possible but he did not linger with it. Instead, he approached the ultimate horror. He brought home a beautiful suspiciously Negroid woman. Prepare yourself, he said. There is nothing you can do about it. This is the woman I've chosen. She's intelligent, dignified, even good, and she's suffered and she hasn't thought it *fun*. Now persecute us, go ahead and persecute us. Drive her out of here, but remember, you're driving me too. His eyes were narrowed and through the indignation he had generated, he saw his mother across the aisle, purple-faced, shrunken to the dwarf-like proportions of her moral nature, sitting like a mummy beneath the ridiculous banner of her hat.

> *She* was a giant of a woman. Her face was set not only to meet opposition but to seek it out.

He was tilted out of his fantasy again as the bus stopped. The door opened with a sucking hiss and out of the dark a large, gaily dressed, sullen-looking colored woman got on with a little boy. The child, who might have been four, had on a short plaid suit and a Tyrolean hat with a blue feather in it. Julian hoped that he would sit down beside him and that the woman would push in beside his mother. He could think of no better arrangement.

As she waited for her tokens, the woman was surveying the seating possibilities—he hoped with the idea of sitting where she was least wanted. There was something familiar-looking about her but Julian could not place what it was. She was a giant of a woman. Her face was set not only to meet opposition but to seek it out. The downward tilt of her large lower lip was like a warning sign: DON'T TAMPER WITH ME. Her bulging figure was encased in

> The vision of the two hats, identical, broke upon him with the radiance of a brilliant sunrise. His face was suddenly lit with joy. He could not believe that Fate had thrust upon his mother such a lesson.

a green crepe dress and her feet overflowed in red shoes. She had on a hideous hat. A purple velvet flap came down on one side of it and stood up on the other; the rest of it was green and looked like a cushion with the stuffing out. She carried a mammoth red pocketbook that bulged throughout as if it were stuffed with rocks.

To Julian's disappointment, the little boy climbed up on the empty seat beside his mother. His mother lumped all children, black and white, into the common category, "cute," and she thought little Negroes were on the whole cuter than little white children. She smiled at the little boy as he climbed on the seat.

Meanwhile the woman was bearing down upon the empty seat beside Julian. To his annoyance, she squeezed herself into it. He saw his mother's face change as the woman settled herself next to him and he realized with satisfaction that this was more objectionable to her than it was to him. Her face seemed almost gray and there was a look of dull recognition in her eyes, as if suddenly she had sickened at some awful confrontation. Julian saw that it was because she and the woman had, in a sense, swapped sons. Though his mother would not realize the symbolic significance of this, she would feel it. His amusement showed plainly on his face.

The woman next to him muttered something unintelligible to herself. He was conscious of a kind of bristling next to him, a muted growling like that of an angry cat. He could not see anything but the red pocketbook upright on the bulging green thighs. He visualized the woman as she had stood waiting for her tokens—the ponderous figure, rising from the red shoes upward over the solid hips, the mammoth bosom, the haughty face, to the green and purple hat.

His eyes widened.

The vision of the two hats, identical, broke upon him with the radiance of a brilliant sunrise. His face was suddenly lit with joy. He could not believe that Fate had thrust upon his mother such a lesson. He gave a loud chuckle so that she would look at him and see that he saw. She turned her eyes on him slowly. The blue in them seemed to have turned a bruised purple. For a moment he had an uncomfortable sense of her innocence, but it lasted only a second before principle rescued him. Justice entitled him to laugh. His grin hardened until it said to her as plainly as if he were saying aloud: Your punishment exactly fits your pettiness. This should teach you a permanent lesson.

Her eyes shifted to the woman. She seemed unable to bear looking at him and to find the woman preferable. He became conscious again of the bristling presence at his side. The woman was rumbling like a volcano about to become active. His mother's mouth began to twitch slightly at one corner. With a sinking heart, he saw **incipient** signs of recovery on her face and realized that this was going to strike her suddenly as funny and was going to be no lesson at all. She kept her eyes on the woman and an amused smile came over her face as if the woman were a monkey that had stolen her hat. The little Negro was looking up at her with large fascinated eyes. He had been trying to attract her attention for some time.

incipient: beginning

"Carver!" the woman said suddenly. "Come heah!"

When he saw that the spotlight was on him at last, Carver drew his feet up and turned himself toward Julian's mother and giggled.

"Carver!" the woman said. "You heah me? Come heah!"

Carver slid down from the seat but remained squatting with his back against the base of it, his head turned slyly around toward Julian's mother, who was smiling at him. The woman reached a hand across the aisle and snatched him back to her. He righted himself and hung backwards on her knees, grinning at Julian's mother. "Isn't he cute?" Julian's mother said to the woman with the protruding teeth.

"I reckon he is," the woman said without conviction.

The Negress yanked him upright but he eased out of her grip and shot across the aisle and scrambled, giggling wildly, onto the seat beside his love.

"I think he likes me," Julian's mother said, and smiled at the woman. It was the smile she used when she was being particularly gracious to an inferior. Julian saw everything lost. The lesson had rolled off her like rain on a roof.

The woman stood up and yanked the little boy off the seat as if she were snatching him from **contagion**. Julian could feel the rage in her at having no weapon like his mother's smile. She gave the child a sharp slap across his leg. He howled once and then thrust his head into her stomach and kicked his feet against her shins. "Be-have," she said vehemently.

contagion: spreading infection

The bus stopped and the Negro who had been reading the newspaper got off. The woman moved over and set the little boy down with a thump between herself and Julian. She held him firmly by the knee. In a moment he put his hands in front of his face and peeped at Julian's mother through his fingers.

"I see yoooooooo!" she said and put her hand in front of her face and peeped at him.

The woman slapped his hand down. "Quit yo' foolishness," she said, "before I knock the living Jesus out of you!"

Julian was thankful that the next stop was theirs. He reached up and pulled the cord. The woman reached up and pulled it at the same time. Oh my God, he thought. He had the terrible intuition that when they got off the bus together, his mother would open her purse and give the little boy a nickel. The gesture would be as natural to her as breathing. The bus stopped and the woman got up and lunged to the front, dragging the child, who wished to stay on, after her. Julian and his mother got up and followed. As they neared the door, Julian tried to relieve her of her pocketbook.

"No," she murmured, "I want to give the little boy a nickel."

"No!" Julian hissed. "No!"

She smiled down at the child and opened her bag. The bus door opened and the woman picked him up by the arm and descended with him, hanging at her hip. Once in the street she set him down and shook him.

Julian's mother had to close her purse while she got down the bus step but as soon as her feet were on the ground, she opened it again and began to rummage inside. "I can't find but a penny," she whispered, "but it looks like a new one."

"Don't do it!" Julian said fiercely between his teeth. There was a street-light on the corner and she hurried to get under it so that she could better see into her pocketbook. The woman was heading off rapidly down the street with the child still hanging backward on her hand.

"Oh little boy!" Julian's mother called and took a few quick steps and caught up with them just beyond the lamp-post. "Here's a bright new penny for you," and she held out the coin, which shone bronze in the dim light.

The huge woman turned and for a moment stood, her shoulders lifted and her face frozen with frustrated rage, and stared at Julian's mother. Then all at once she seemed to explode like a piece of machinery that had been given one ounce of pressure too much. Julian saw the black fist swing out with the red pocketbook. He shut his eyes and cringed as he heard the woman shout, "He don't take nobody's pennies!" When he opened his eyes, the woman was disappearing down the street with the little boy staring wide-eyed over her shoulder. Julian's mother was sitting on the sidewalk.

"I told you not to do that," Julian said angrily. "I told you not to do that!"

He stood over her for a minute, gritting his teeth. Her legs were stretched out in front of her and her hat was on her lap. He squatted down and looked her in the face. It was totally expressionless. "You got exactly what you deserved," he said. "Now get up."

He picked up her pocketbook and put what had fallen out back in it. He picked the hat up off her lap. The penny caught his eye on the sidewalk and he picked that up and let it drop before her eyes into the purse. Then he stood up and leaned over and held his hands out to pull her up. She remained immobile. He sighed. Rising above them on either side were black apartment buildings, marked with irregular rectangles of light. At the end of the block a man came out of a door and walked off in the opposite direction. "All right," he said, "suppose somebody happens by and wants to know why you're sitting on the sidewalk?"

She took the hand and, breathing hard, pulled heavily up on it and then stood for a moment, swaying slightly as if the spots of light in the darkness were circling around her.

She took the hand and, breathing hard, pulled heavily up on it and then stood for a moment, swaying slightly as if the spots of light in the darkness were circling around her. Her eyes, shadowed and confused, finally settled on his face. He did not try to conceal his irritation. "I hope this teaches you a lesson," he said. She leaned forward and her eyes raked his face. She seemed trying to determine his identity. Then, as if she found nothing familiar about him, she started off with a headlong movement in the wrong direction.

"Aren't you going on to the Y?" he asked.

"Home," she muttered.

"Well, are we walking?"

For answer she kept going. Julian followed along, his hands behind him. He saw no reason to let the lesson she had had go without backing it up with an explanation of its meaning. She might as well be made to under-stand what had happened to her. "Don't think that was just an uppity Negro woman," he said. "That was the whole colored race which will no longer take your condescending pennies. That was your black double. She can wear the

gratuitously:
unnecessarily;
unkindly

obsolete:
outdated;
useless

same hat as you, and to be sure," he added **gratuitously** (because he thought it was funny), "it looked better on her than it did on you. What all this means," he said, "is that the old world is gone. The old manners are **obsolete** and your graciousness is not worth a damn." He thought bitterly of the house that had been lost for him. "You aren't who you think you are," he said.

She continued to plow ahead, paying no attention to him. Her hair had come undone on one side. She dropped her pocketbook and took no notice. He stooped and picked it up and handed it to her but she did not take it.

"You needn't act as if the world had come to an end," he said, "because it hasn't. From now on you've got to live in a new world and face a few realities for a change. Buck up," he said, "it won't kill you."

She was breathing fast.

"Let's wait on the bus," he said.

"Home," she said thickly.

"I hate to see you behave like this," he said. "Just like a child. I should be able to expect more of you." He decided to stop where he was and make her stop and wait for a bus. "I'm not going any farther," he said, stopping. "We're going on the bus."

She continued to go on as if she had not heard him. He took a few steps and caught her arm and stopped her. He looked into her face and caught his breath. He was looking into a face he had never seen before. "Tell Grandpa to come get me," she said.

He stared, stricken.

"Tell Caroline to come get me," she said.

Stunned, he let her go and she lurched forward again, walking as if one leg were shorter than the other. A tide of darkness seemed to be sweeping her from him. "Mother!" he cried. "Darling, sweetheart, wait!" Crumpling, she fell to the pavement. He dashed forward and fell at her side, crying, "Mamma, Mamma!" He turned her over. Her face was fiercely distorted. One eye, large and staring, moved slightly to the left as if it had become

unmoored:
disconnected

unmoored. The other remained fixed on him, raked his face again, found nothing and closed.

"Wait here, wait here!" he cried and jumped up and began to run for help toward a cluster of lights he saw in the distance ahead of him. "Help, help!" he shouted, but his voice was thin, scarcely a thread of sound. The lights drifted farther away the faster he ran and his feet moved numbly as if they carried him nowhere. The tide of darkness seemed to sweep him back to her, postponing from moment to moment his entry into the world of guilt and sorrow.

Read and Think Critically

Analyze, Explain, Determine

1. **MOTIF** What **motifs** did you notice in this story? In what ways do these repeated elements unify the story?

2. Reread the first paragraph of the story. What do you know about Julian's mother from the very beginning?

3. Analyze the concept of martyrdom in the story. What sacrifices are made in this story, and by whom?

4. Explain the significance of the **title** of the story. Understanding that *converge* means "to come together and unite with a common focus," what in the story rises and therefore must converge?

5. It has been said that good literature raises more questions than it answers. O'Connor in particular is known for the profound questions her fiction poses. Determine some questions that O'Connor raises but purposely does not answer.

6. **THE AUTHOR'S STYLE** Many of O'Connor's stories contain unexpected, sometimes violent, actions. Read the quotation below by O'Connor and consider "Everything That Rises Must Converge" in light of her statement. What action or gesture do you think indicates the "real heart of the story"?

O'Connor on the Unexpected

I often ask myself what makes a story work, and what makes it hold up as a story, and I have decided that it is probably some action, some gesture of a character that is unlike any other in the story, one which indicates where the real heart of the story lies. This would have to be an action or a gesture which was both totally right and totally unexpected; it would have to be one that was both in character and beyond charac-ter; it would have to suggest both the world and eternity. . . . It would be a gesture that somehow made contact with mystery.

—Flannery O'Connor

Before You Read

John Updike   1932–2009

About the Author

As the recipient of two Pulitzer Prizes and a man who has twice been on the cover of *Time* magazine, John Updike is one of America's most celebrated authors.

Updike grew up in Shillington, Pennsylvania, on an 80-acre farm, a setting much like the American Protestant, small-town middle class he often uses as the backdrop for his work. President and co-valedictorian of his high school class, he worked summers at his home-town newspaper, *Reading Eagle*, before entering Harvard, where he wrote for the *Harvard Lampoon*. While studying art at Oxford University in England, Updike met E. B. White (author of *Charlotte's Web*). White offered him a position as a columnist at *The New Yorker*, where

Updike eventually published many stories.

Among Updike's best-known work is the "Rabbit" novel series, about a former star athlete who is unable to recapture the glory he knew in school when trapped by marriage and life in a small town. Updike was quoted in *Writers on Writing* as saying, "When I write, I aim in my mind not toward New York but toward a vague spot a little to the east of Kansas. I think of the books on library shelves, without their jackets, years old, and a countryish teen-aged boy finding them, and having them speak to him. The reviews, the stacks in Brentano's, are just hurdles to get over, to place the books on that shelf."

****

The Author's Style

Updike's fiction typically chronicles everyday incidents from middle-class lives. His stories often reflect the eventual influence of cultural movements or historical events, such as the Civil Rights marches or the Vietnam War, on the lives of his characters. Yet he is more interested in the way personal choices affect family relationships and how personal decisions and behavior change individual lives. For this reason, Updike shows us how characters think and feel through ordinary incidents rather than confrontations with catastrophe.

Often, Updike uses humor, irony, and pathos to suggest that people are not tragic figures but works in progress—especially when they are struggling through the difficulties of adolescence. His stories are gently realistic and pay careful attention to the nuances of personality. It is not uncommon for an Updike story to end with a sense that whatever a character has learned from a particular incident, there is more to come.

A&P

JOHN UPDIKE

 LITERARY LENS: VOICE Listen for the **voice** of the narrator in this story.

In walks these three girls in nothing but bathing suits. I'm in the third checkout slot, with my back to the door, so I don't see them until they're over by the bread. The one that caught my eye first was the one in the plaid green two-piece. She was a chunky kid, with a good tan and a sweet broad soft-looking can with those two crescents of white just under it, where the sun never seems to hit, at the top of the backs of her legs. I stood there with my hand on a box of HiHo crackers trying to remember if I rang it up or not. I ring it up again and the customer starts giving me hell. She's one of these cash-register-watchers, a witch about fifty with rouge on her cheekbones and no eyebrows, and I know it made her day to trip me up. She'd been watching cash registers for fifty years and probably never seen a mistake before.

By the time I got her feathers smoothed and her goodies into a bag—she gives me a little snort in passing, if she'd been born at the right time they would have burned her over in Salem[1]—by the time I get her on her way the girls had circled around the bread and were coming back, without a pushcart,

*S*he didn't look around, not this queen, she just walked straight on slowly, on these long white primadonna legs.

back my way along the counters, in the aisle between the checkouts and the Special bins. They didn't even have shoes on. There was this chunky one, with the two-piece—it was bright green and the seams on the bra were still sharp and her belly was still pretty pale so I guessed she just got it (the suit)—there was this one, with one of those chubby berry-faces, the lips all bunched together under her nose, this one, and a tall one, with black hair that hadn't quite frizzed right, and one of these sunburns right across under the eyes, and a chin that was too long—you know, the kind of girl other girls think is very "striking" and "attractive" but never quite makes it, as they very well know, which is why they like her so much—and then the third one, that wasn't quite so tall. She was the queen. She kind of led them, the other two peeking around and making their shoulders round. She didn't look around, not this queen, she just walked straight on slowly, on these long white primadonna legs. She came down a little hard on her heels, as if she didn't walk in bare feet that much, putting down her heels and then letting the weight move along to her toes as if she was testing the floor with every step, putting a little deliberate extra action into it. You never know for sure how girls' minds work (do you really think it's a mind in there or just a little buzz like a bee in a glass jar?) but you got the idea she had talked the other two into coming here with her, and now she was showing them how to do it, walk slow and hold yourself straight.

She had on a kind of dirty-pink—beige maybe, I don't know—bathing suit with a little nubble all over it and, what got me, the straps were down. They were off her shoulders looped loose around the cool tops of her arms, and I guess as a result the suit had slipped a little on her, so all around the top of the cloth there was a shining rim. If it hadn't been there you wouldn't have known there could have been anything whiter than those shoulders. With the straps pushed off, there was nothing between the top of the suit and the top of her head except just *her*, this clean bare plane of the top of her

---

I burned . . . Salem: refers to the women who were burned for allegedly practicing witchcraft in Salem, Massachusetts, in 1692

chest down from the shoulder bones like a dented sheet of metal tilted in the light. I mean, it was more than pretty.

She had a sort of oaky hair that the sun and salt had bleached, done up in a bun that was unravelling, and a kind of prim face. Walking into the A & P with your straps down, I suppose it's the only kind of face you *can* have. She held her head so high her neck, coming up out of those white shoulders, looked kind of stretched, but I didn't mind. The longer her neck was, the more of her there was.

She must have felt in the corner of her eye me and over my shoulder Stokesie in the second slot watching, but she didn't tip. Not this queen. She kept her eyes moving across the racks, and stopped, and turned so slow it made my stomach rub the inside of my apron, and buzzed to the other two, who kind of huddled against her for relief, and then they all three of them went up the cat-and-dog food-breakfast-cereal-macaroni-rice-raisins-seasonings-spreads-spaghetti-soft drinks-crackers-and-cookies aisle. From the third

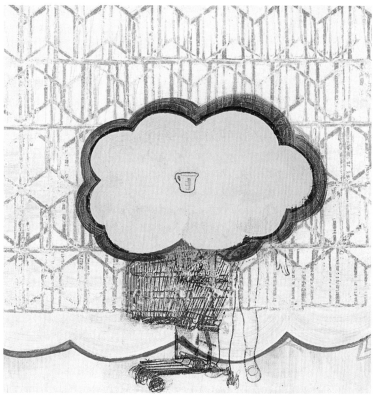

MEASURE, VICTOR MALDONADO

slot I look straight up this aisle to the meat counter, and I watched them all the way. The fat one with the tan sort of fumbled with the cookies, but on second thought she put the package back. The sheep pushing their carts down the aisle—the girls were walking against the usual traffic (not that we have one-way signs or anything)—were pretty hilarious. You could see them,

What he meant was, our town is five miles from a beach, with a big summer colony out on the Point, but we're right in the middle of town, and the women generally put on a shirt or shorts or something before they get out of the car into the street.

when Queenie's white shoulders dawned on them, kind of jerk, or hop, or hiccup, but their eyes snapped back to their own baskets and on they pushed. I bet you could set off dynamite in an A & P and the people would by and large keep reaching and checking oatmeal off their lists and muttering "Let me see, there was a third thing, began with A, asparagus, no, ah, yes, applesauce!" or whatever it is they do mutter. But there was no doubt, this jiggled them. A few houseslaves in pin curlers even looked around after pushing their carts past to make sure what they had seen was correct.

You know, it's one thing to have a girl in a bathing suit down on the beach, where what with the glare nobody can look at each other much anyway, and another thing in the cool of the A & P, under the fluorescent lights, against all those stacked packages, with her feet paddling along naked over our checker-board green-and-cream rubber-tile floor.

"Oh Daddy," Stokesie said beside me. "I feel so faint."

"Darling," I said, "Hold me tight." Stokesie's married, with two babies chalked up on his **fuselage** already, but as far as I can tell that's the only difference. He's twenty-two, and I was nineteen this April.

fuselage: central body portion of an airplane

"Is it done?" he asks, the responsible married man finding his voice. I forgot to say he thinks he's going to be manager some sunny day, maybe in 1990 when it's called the Great Alexandrov and Petrooshki Tea Company or something.

What he meant was, our town is five miles from a beach, with a big summer colony out on the Point, but we're right in the middle of town, and the women generally put on a shirt or shorts or something before they get out of the car into the street. And anyway these are usually women with six children and varicose veins mapping their legs and nobody, including them, could care less. As I say, we're right in the middle of town, and if you stand at our front doors you can see two banks and the Congregational church and the newspaper store and three real-estate offices and about twenty-seven old free-loaders tearing up Central Street because the sewer broke again. It's not as if we're on the Cape;[2] we're north of Boston and there's people in this town haven't seen the ocean for twenty years.

The girls had reached the meat counter and were asking McMahon something. He pointed, they pointed, and they shuffled out of sight behind a pyramid of Diet Delight peaches. All that was left for us to see was old McMahon patting his mouth and looking after them sizing up their joints. Poor kids, I began to feel sorry for them, they couldn't help it.

$\mathcal{N}$ow here comes the sad part of the story, at least my family says it's sad, but I don't think it's so sad myself. The store's pretty empty, it being Thursday afternoon, so there was nothing much to do except lean on the register and wait for the girls to show up again. The whole store was like a pinball machine and I didn't know which tunnel they'd come out of. After a while they come around out of the far aisle, around the light bulbs, records at discount of the Caribbean Six or Tony Martin Sings or some such gunk you wonder they waste the wax on, six-packs of candy bars, and plastic toys done up in cellophane that fall apart when a kid looks at them anyway. Around they come, Queenie still leading the way, and holding a little gray jar in her hand. Slots Three through Seven are unmanned and I could see her wondering between Stokes and me, but Stokesie with his usual luck draws an old party in baggy gray pants who stumbles up with four giant cans of pineapple juice (what do these bums *do* with all that pineapple juice? I've often asked myself) so the girls come to me. Queenie puts down the jar and I take it into my fingers icy cold. Kingfish Fancy Herring Snacks in Pure Sour Cream: 49¢. Now her hands are empty, not a ring or a bracelet, bare as God made them, and I wonder where the money's coming from. Still with that prim look she lifts a folded dollar bill out of the hollow at the center of her nubbled pink top. The jar went heavy in my hand. Really, I thought that was so cute.

*S*till with that prim look she lifts a folded dollar bill out of the hollow at the center of her nubbled pink top. The jar went heavy in my hand. Really, I thought that was so cute.

Then everybody's luck begins to run out. Lengel comes in from haggling with a truck full of cabbages on the lot and is about to scuttle into the door marked MANAGER behind which he hides all day when the girls touch his eye.

---

2 **Cape:** Cape Cod, Massachusetts

Lengel's pretty dreary, teaches Sunday school and the rest, but he doesn't miss that much. He comes over and says, "Girls, this isn't the beach."

Queenie blushes, though maybe it's just a brush of sunburn I was noticing for the first time, now that she was so close. "My mother asked me to pick up a jar of herring snacks." Her voice kind of startled me, the way voices do when you see the people first, coming out so flat and dumb yet kind of tony, too, the way it ticked over "pick up" and "snacks." All of a sudden I slid right down her voice into her living room. Her father and the other men were standing around in ice-cream coats and bow ties and the women were in sandals picking up herring snacks on toothpicks off a big glass plate and they were all holding drinks the color of water with olives and sprigs of mint in them. When my parents have somebody over they get lemonade and if it's a real racy affair Schlitz in tall glasses with "They'll Do It Every Time" cartoons stencilled on.

"That's all right," Lengel said. "But this isn't the beach." His repeating this struck me as funny, as if it had just occurred to him, and he had been thinking all these years the A & P was a great big dune and he was the head lifeguard. He didn't like my smiling—as I say he doesn't miss much—but he concentrates on giving the girls that sad Sunday-school-superintendent stare.

Queenie's blush is no sunburn now, and the plump one in plaid, that I liked better from the back—a really sweet can—pipes up, "We weren't doing any shopping. We just came in for the one thing."

"That makes no difference," Lengel tells her, and I could see from the way his eyes went that he hadn't noticed she was wearing a two-piece before. "We want you decently dressed when you come in here."

"We *are* decent," Queenie says suddenly, her lower lip pushing, getting sore now that she remembers her place, a place from which the crowd that runs the A & P must look pretty chummy. Fancy Herring Snacks flashed in her very blue eyes.

"Girls, I don't want to argue with you. After this come in here with your shoulders covered. It's our policy." He turns his back.

They keep right on going, into the electric eye; the door flies open and they flicker across the lot to their car, Queenie and Plaid and Big Tall Goony-Goony (not that as raw material she was so bad), leaving me with Lengel and a kink in his eyebrow.

That's policy for you. Policy is what the kingpins want. What the others want is juvenile delinquency.

All this while, the customers had been showing up with their carts but, you know, sheep, seeing a scene, they had all bunched up on Stokesie, who shook open a paper bag as gently as peeling a peach, not wanting to miss a word. I could feel in the silence everybody getting nervous, most of all Lengel, who asks me, "Sammy, have you rung up their purchase?"

I thought and said "No" but it wasn't about that I was thinking. I go through the punches, 4, 9, GROC, TOT—it's more complicated than you think, and after you do it often enough, it begins to make a little song, that you hear words to, in my case "Hello (bing) there, you (gung) hap-py *pee*-pul (*splat*)!"—the *splat* being the drawer flying out. I uncrease the bill, tenderly as you may imagine, it just having come from between the two smoothest scoops of vanilla I had ever known were there, and pass a half and a penny into her narrow pink palm, and nestle the herrings in a bag and twist its neck and hand it over, all the time thinking.

The girls, and who'd blame them, are in a hurry to get out, so I say "I quit" to Lengel quick enough for them to hear, hoping they'll stop and watch me, their unsuspected hero. They keep right on going, into the electric eye; the door flies open and they flicker across the lot to their car, Queenie and Plaid and Big Tall Goony-Goony (not that as raw material she was so bad), leaving me with Lengel and a kink in his eyebrow.

"Did you say something, Sammy?"

"I said I quit."

"I thought you did."

"You didn't have to embarrass them."

"It was they who were embarrassing us."

I started to say something that came out "Fiddle-de-do." It's a saying of my grandmother's, and I know she would have been pleased.

"I don't think you know what you're saying," Lengel said.

"I know you don't," I said. "But I do." I pull the bow at the back of my apron and start shrugging it off my shoulders. A couple customers that had been heading for my slot begin to knock against each other, like scared pigs in a chute.

Lengel sighs and begins to look very patient and old and gray. He's been a friend of my parents for years. "Sammy, you don't want to do this to your Mom and Dad," he tells me. It's true, I don't. But it seems to me that once you begin a gesture it's fatal not to go through with it. I fold the apron, "Sammy" stitched in red on the pocket, and put it on the counter, and drop the bow tie on top of it. The bow tie is theirs, if you've ever wondered. "You'll feel this for the rest of your life," Lengel says, and I know that's true, too, but remembering how he made that pretty girl blush makes me so scrunchy inside I punch the No Sale tab and the machine whirs "peepul" and the drawer splats out. One advantage to this scene taking place in summer, I can follow this up with a clean exit, there's no fumbling around getting your coat and galoshes, I just saunter into the electric eye in my white shirt that my mother ironed the night before, and the door heaves itself open, and outside the sunshine is skating around on the asphalt.

I look around for my girls, but they're gone, of course. There wasn't anybody but some young married[3] screaming with her children about some candy they didn't get by the door of a powder-blue Falcon station wagon. Looking back in the big windows, over the bags of peat moss and aluminum lawn furniture stacked on the pavement, I could see Lengel in my place in the slot, checking the sheep through. His face was dark gray and his back stiff, as if he'd just had an injection of iron, and my stomach kind of fell as I felt how hard the world was going to be to me hereafter.

---

3 **young married:** term for a young married woman

Read and Think Critically

Describe, Analyze, Predict

 1. **VOICE** Based on Sammy's narrative **voice**, describe his **character**. What specific phrases capture Sammy's personality?

2. Analyze the author's use of details in describing the **setting**. List and explain passages in the story that make you feel as if you really are in a grocery store.

3. Near the end of the story Sammy says, " . . . it seems to me that once you begin a gesture it's fatal not to go through with it." Do you agree? Explain why or why not.

4. Explain the last line of the story: ". . . my stomach kind of fell as I felt how hard the world was going to be to me hereafter." What do you think Sammy has learned from this incident? Make a prediction about some of the hard things Sammy will face in the world.

5. **THE AUTHOR'S STYLE** Updike is known for his skill at depicting the tensions and frustrations of small-town and suburban life in America. Explain the **conflicts** he explores in this story. Support your answer with specific details from the story.

Before You Read

Ernest J. Gaines 1933–

About the Author

Ernest J. Gaines dedicated his novel, *The Autobiography of Miss Jane Pittman*, to his handicapped aunt. She had not only inspired the book but also raised him in his birthplace of Louisiana after his parents moved to California. The author noted that although his aunt had never walked a day in her life, she taught him the importance of standing.

Gaines was picking cotton in plantation fields by the age of nine and attending a school where the sessions depended on the planting and harvesting seasons. African American children didn't go to school past eighth grade there, so at 15 he moved to San Francisco to join his mother and stepfather. He recalls, "I had a choice of going to three places—the library, the YMCA, and the movie house. I didn't have any money so I couldn't go to the movies. I went to the YMCA and I got beaten up by a guy who knew how to box, so I quit that and went to the library. Little old ladies can't hit that hard."

After graduating from San Francisco State University and spending two years in the army, Gaines was awarded a fellowship to Stanford University that enabled him to quit his job and devote himself to writing. One of his eight novels, *A Lesson Before Dying*, won the National Book Award in 1993.

★★★★★★★★★★★

The Author's Style

In his novels and stories, Gaines is concerned with the divisive and destructive effects of racial distinctions on American society—the values, priorities, and behavior of a troubled culture. Gaines' stories contain ordinary characters and everyday events set in southern Louisiana—people coming to terms with the rules and expectations that define their culture and shape their lives.

The author uses first-person narrators to make clear his characters' feelings, personalities, and social standing. Many of his narrators are men or young men, intent on understanding the nature and meaning of manhood. Using the dialect of their time and place, his African American characters describe their circumstances and explain the strategies they have developed for coping with them. Gaines reveals the effects of arbitrary racial distinctions not only through black-white interactions, as in his novel *The Autobiography of Miss Jane Pittman*, but also through interactions within African American families and communities. In the story you are about to read, "The Sky Is Gray," he gives us both.

The Sky Is Gray

Ernest J. Gaines

 LITERARY LENS: FIRST-PERSON POINT OF VIEW "The Sky is Gray" is narrated by an African American boy. As you read, consider why Gaines chose to use **first-person point of view**.

I

Go'n be coming in a few minutes. Coming round that bend down there full speed. And I'm go'n get out my handkerchief and wave it down, and we go'n get on it and go.

I keep looking for it, but Mama don't look that way no more. She's looking down the road where we just come from. It's a long old road, and far's you can see you don't see nothing but gravel. You got dry weeds on both sides, and you got trees on both sides, and fences on both sides, too. And you got cows in the pastures and they standing close together. And when we was coming out here to catch the bus I seen the smoke coming out of the cows's noses.

I look at my mama and I know what she's thinking. I been with Mama so much, just me and her, I know what she's thinking all the time. Right now it's home—Auntie and them. She's thinking if they got enough wood—if she left enough there to keep them warm till we get back. She's thinking if it go'n rain and if any of them go'n have to go out in the rain. She's thinking 'bout the hog—if he go'n get out, and if Ty and Val be able to get him back in. She always worry like that when she leaves the house. She don't worry too much if she leave me there with the smaller ones, 'cause she know I'm go'n look after them and look after Auntie and everything else. I'm the oldest and she say I'm the man.

I look at my mama and I love my mama. She's wearing that black coat and that black hat and she's looking sad. I love my mama and I want put my arm round her and tell her. But I'm not supposed to do that. She say that's weakness and that's crybaby stuff, and she don't want no crybaby round her. She don't want you to be scared, either. 'Cause Ty's scared of ghosts and she's always whipping him. I'm scared of the dark, too, but I make 'tend I ain't. I make 'tend I ain't 'cause I'm the oldest, and I got to set a good sample for the rest. I can't ever be scared and I can't ever cry. And that's why I never said nothing 'bout my teeth. It's been hurting me and hurting me close to a month now, but I never said it. I didn't say it 'cause I didn't want to act like a crybaby, and 'cause we didn't have enough money to go have it pulled. But, Lord, it been hurting me. And look like it wouldn't start till at night when you was trying to get yourself little sleep. Then soon 's you shut your eyes— ummm-ummm, Lord, look like it go right down to your heartstring.

"Hurting, hanh?" Ty'd say.

I'd shake my head, but I wouldn't open my mouth for nothing. You open your mouth and let that wind in, and it almost kill you.

I'd just lay there and listen to them snore. Ty there, right 'side me, and Auntie and Val over by the fireplace. Val younger than me and Ty, and he sleeps with Auntie. Mama sleeps round the other side with Louis and Walker.

I'd just lay there and listen to them, and listen to that wind out there, and listen to that fire in the fireplace. Sometimes it'd stop long enough to let me get little rest. Sometimes it just hurt, hurt, hurt. Lord, have mercy.

II

Auntie knowed it was hurting me. I didn't tell anybody but Ty, 'cause we buddies and he ain't go'n tell nobody. But some kind of way Auntie found out. When she asked me, I told her no, nothing was wrong. But she knowed it all the time. She told me to mash up a piece of aspirin and wrap it in some cotton and jugg it down in that hole. I did it, but it didn't do no good. It stopped for a little while, and started right back again. Auntie wanted to tell Mama, but I told her, "Uh-uh." 'Cause I knowed we didn't have any money, and it just was go'n make her mad again. So Auntie told Monsieur Bayonne, and Monsieur Bayonne came over to the house and told me to kneel down 'side him on the fireplace. He put his finger in his mouth and made the Sign of the Cross[1] on my jaw. The tip of Monsieur Bayonne's finger is some hard, 'cause he's always playing on that guitar. If we sit outside at night we can always hear Monsieur Bayonne playing on his guitar. Sometimes we leave him out there playing on the guitar.

Monsieur Bayonne made the Sign of the Cross over and over on my jaw, but that didn't do no good. Even when he prayed and told me to pray some, too, that tooth still hurt me.

"How you feeling?" he say.

"Same," I say.

He kept on praying and making the Sign of the Cross and I kept on praying, too.

"Still hurting?" he say.

"Yes, sir."

Monsieur Bayonne mashed harder and harder on my jaw. He mashed so hard he almost pushed me over on Ty. But then he stopped.

"What kind of prayers you praying, boy?" he say.

"Baptist," I say.

"Well, I'll be—no wonder that tooth killing him. I'm going one way and he pulling the other. Boy, don't you know any Catholic prayers?"

"I know 'Hail Mary,'" I say.

"Then you better start saying it."

"Yes, sir."

He started mashing on my jaw again, and I could hear him praying at the same time. And, sure enough, after while it stopped hurting me.

Me and Ty went outside where Monsieur Bayonne's two hounds was and we started playing with them. "Let's go hunting," Ty say. "All right," I say; and we went on back in the pasture. Soon the hounds got on a trail, and me and Ty followed them all 'cross the pasture and then back in the woods, too. And then they cornered this little old rabbit and killed him, and me and Ty made them get back, and we picked up the rabbit and started back home. But my tooth had started hurting me again. It was hurting me plenty now, but I wouldn't tell Monsieur Bayonne. That night I didn't sleep a bit, and first

---

1 **Sign of the Cross:** a Roman Catholic symbolic gesture that signifies the shape of the cross

The Sky Is Gray

thing in the morning Auntie told me to go back and let Monsieur Bayonne pray over me some more. Monsieur Bayonne was in his kitchen making coffee when I got there. Soon 's he seen me he knowed what was wrong.

"All right, kneel down there 'side that stove," he say. "And this time make sure you pray Catholic. I don't know nothing 'bout that Baptist, and I don't want to know nothing 'bout him."

III

Last night Mama say, "Tomorrow we going to town."

"It ain't hurting me no more," I say. "I can eat anything on it."

"Tomorrow we going to town," she say.

And after she finished eating, she got up and went to bed. She always go to bed early now. 'Fore Daddy went in the Army, she used to stay up late. All of us sitting out on the gallery or round the fire. But now, look like soon 's she finish eating she go to bed.

This morning when I woke up, her and Auntie was standing 'fore the fireplace. She say: "Enough to get there and get back. Dollar and a half to have it pulled. Twenty-five for me to go, twenty-five for him. Twenty-five for me to come back, twenty-five for him. Fifty cents left. Guess I get a little piece of salt meat with that."

"Sure can use it," Auntie say. "White beans and no salt meat ain't white beans."

"I do the best I can," Mama say.

They was quiet after that, and I made 'tend I was still sleep.

"James, hit the floor," Auntie say.

I still made 'tend I was asleep. I didn't want them to know I was listening.

"All right," Auntie say, shaking me by the shoulder. "Come on. Today's the day."

I pushed the cover down to get out, and Ty grabbed it and pulled it back.

"You, too, Ty," Auntie say.

"I ain't getting no teef pulled," Ty say.

"Don't mean it ain't time to get up." Auntie say. "Hit it, Ty."

Ty got up grumbling.

"James, you hurry up and get in your clothes and eat your food," Auntie say. "What time y'all coming back?" she said to Mama.

"That 'leven o'clock bus," Mama say. "Got to get back in that field this evening."

"Get a move on you, James," Auntie say.

I went in the kitchen and washed my face, then I ate my breakfast. I was having bread and syrup. The bread was warm and hard and tasted good. And I tried to make it last a long time.

Ty came back there grumbling and mad at me.

"Got to get up," he say. "I ain't having no teefes pulled. What I got to be getting up for?"

Ty poured some syrup in his pan and got a piece of bread. He didn't wash his hands, neither his face, and I could see that white stuff in his eyes.

"You the one getting your teef pulled," he say. "What I got to get up for. I bet if I was getting a teef pulled you wouldn't be getting up. Shucks; syrup again. I'm getting tired of this old syrup. Syrup, syrup, syrup. I'm go'n take with the sugar diabetes. I want some bacon sometime."

"Go out in the field and work and you can have your bacon," Auntie say. She stood in the middle door looking at Ty. "You better be glad you got syrup. Some people ain't got that—hard 's time is."

"Shucks," Ty say. "How can I be strong?"

"I don't know too much 'bout your strength," Auntie say; "but I know where you go'n be hot at, you keep that grumbling up. James, get a move on you; your mama waiting."

I ate my last piece of bread and went in the front room. Mama was standing 'fore the fireplace warming her hands. I put on my coat and my cap, and we left the house.

IV

I look down there again, but it still ain't coming. I almost say, "It ain't coming yet," but I keep my mouth shut. 'Cause that's something else she don't like. She don't like for you to say something just for nothing. She can see it ain't coming. I can see it ain't coming, so why say it ain't coming. I don't say it, I turn and look at the river that's back of us. It's so cold the smoke's just raising up from the water. I see a bunch of pool-doos[2] not too far out—just on the other side of the lilies. I'm wondering if you can

---

2 **pool-doos:** slang for mud-hens, or duck-like birds

*S*he went to the corner of the fence and broke the biggest switch over there she could find. I knelt 'side the trap, crying.

eat pool-doos. I ain't too sure, 'cause I ain't never ate none. But I done ate owls and blackbirds, and I done ate redbirds, too. I didn't want to kill the redbirds, but she made me kill them. They had two of them back there. One in my trap, one in Ty's trap. Me and Ty was go'n play with them and let them go, but she made me kill them 'cause we needed the food.

"I can't," I say. "I can't."

"Here," she say. "Take it."

"I can't," I say. "I can't. I can't kill him, Mama, please."

"Here," she say. "Take this fork, James."

"Please, Mama, I can't kill him," I say.

I could tell she was go'n hit me. I jerked back, but I didn't jerk back soon enough.

"Take it," she say.

I took it and reached in for him, but he kept on hopping to the back.

"I can't, Mama," I say. The water just kept on running down my face. "I can't," I say.

"Get him out of there," she say.

I reached in for him and he kept on hopping to the back. Then I reached in farther, and he pecked me on the hand.

"I can't, Mama," I say.

She slapped me again.

I reached in again, but he kept on hopping out of my way. Then he hopped to one side and I reached there. The fork got him on the leg and I heard his leg pop. I pulled my hand out 'cause I had hurt him.

"Give it here," she say, and jerked the fork out of my hand.

She reached in and got the little bird right in the neck. I heard the fork go in his neck, and I heard it go in the ground. She brought him out and helt him right in front of me.

"That's one," she say. She shook him off and gived me the fork. "Get the other one."

"I can't, Mama," I say. "I'll do anything, but don't make me do that."

She went to the corner of the fence and broke the biggest switch over there she could find. I knelt 'side the trap, crying.

"Get him out of there," she say.

Ernest J. Gaines   Unit 4

"I can't, Mama."

She started hitting me 'cross the back. I went down on the ground, crying.

"Get him," she say.

"Octavia?" Auntie say.

'Cause she had come out of the house and she was standing by the tree looking at us.

"Get him out of there," Mama say.

"Octavia," Auntie say, "explain to him. Explain to him. Just don't beat him. Explain to him."

But she hit me and hit me and hit me.

I'm still young—I ain't no more than eight; but I know now; I know why I had to do it. (They was so little, though. They was so little. I 'member how I picked the feathers off them and cleaned them and helt them over the fire. Then we all ate them. Ain't had but a little bitty piece each, but we all had a little bitty piece, and everybody just looked at me 'cause they was so proud.) Suppose she had to go away? That's why I had to do it. Suppose she had to go away like Daddy went away? Then who was go'n look after us? They had to be somebody left to carry on. I didn't know it then, but I know it now. Auntie and Monsieur Bayonne talked to me and made me see.

V

Time I see it I get out my handkerchief and start waving. It's still 'way down there, but I keep waving anyhow. Then it come up and stop and me and Mama get on. Mama tell me go sit in the back while she pay. I do like she say, and the people look at me. When I pass the little sign that say "White" and "Colored," I start looking for a seat. I just see one of them back there, but I don't take it, 'cause I want my mama to sit down herself. She comes in the back and sit down, and I lean on the seat. They got seats in the front, but I know I can't sit there, 'cause I have to sit back of the sign. Anyhow, I don't want sit there if my mama go'n sit back here.

They got a lady sitting 'side my mama and she looks at me and smiles little bit. I smile back, but I don't open my mouth, 'cause the wind'll get in and make that tooth ache. The lady take out a pack of gum and reach me a slice, but I shake my head. The lady just can't understand why a little boy'll turn down gum, and she reach me a slice again. This time I point to my jaw. The lady understands and smiles little bit, and I smile little bit, but I don't open my mouth, though.

They got a girl sitting 'cross from me. She got on a red overcoat and her hair's plaited in one big plait. First, I make 'tend I don't see her over there, but then I start looking at her little bit. She make 'tend she don't see me, either, but I catch her looking that way. She got a cold, and every now and then she h'ist that little handkerchief to her nose. She ought to blow it, but she don't. Must think she's too much a lady or something.

Every time she h'ist that little handkerchief, the lady side her say something in her ear. She shakes her head and lays her hands in her lap again. Then I catch her kind of looking where I'm at. I smile at her little bit. But think she'll smile back? Uh-uh. She just turn up her little old nose and turn her head. Well, I show her both of us can turn us head. I turn mine too and look out at the river.

The river is gray. The sky is gray. They have pool-doos on the water. The water is wavy, and the pool-doos go up and down. The bus go round a turn, and you got plenty trees hiding the river. Then the bus go round another turn, and I can see the river again.

I look toward the front where all the white people sitting. Then I look at that little old gal again. I don't look right at her, 'cause I don't want all them people to know I love her. I just look at her little bit, like I'm looking out that window over there. But she knows I'm looking that way, and she kind of look at me, too. The lady sitting 'side her catch her this time, and she leans over and says something in her ear.

"I don't love him nothing," that little old gal says out loud.

Everybody back there hear her mouth, and all of them look at us and laugh.

"I don't love you, either," I say. "So you don't have to turn up your nose, Miss."

"You the one looking," she say.

"I wasn't looking at you," I say. "I was looking out that window, there."

"Out that window my foot," she say. "I seen you. Everytime I turned round you was looking at me."

"You must have been looking yourself if you seen me all them times," I say.

"Shucks," she say. "I got me all kind of boyfriends."

"I got girlfriends, too," I say.

"Well, I just don't want you getting your hopes up," she say.

I don't say no more to that little old gal 'cause I don't want have to bust her in the mouth. I lean on the seat where Mama sitting, and I don't even look that way no more. When we get to Bayonne, she jugg her little old tongue out at me. I make 'tend I'm go'n hit her, and she duck down 'side her mama. And all the people laugh at us again.

VI

Me and Mama get off and start walking in town. Bayonne is a little bitty town. Baton Rouge is a hundred times bigger than Bayonne. I went to Baton Rouge once—me, Ty, Mama, and Daddy. But that was 'way back yonder, 'fore Daddy went in the Army. I wonder when we go'n see him again. I wonder when. Look like he ain't ever coming back home. . . . Even the pavement all cracked in Bayonne. Got grass shooting right out in the sidewalk. Got weeds in the ditch, too; just like they got at home.

It's some cold in Bayonne. Look like it's colder than it is home. The wind blows in my face, and I feel that stuff running down my nose. I sniff. Mama says use that handkerchief. I blow my nose and put it back.

We pass a school and see them white children playing in the yard. Big old red school, and them children just running and playing. Then we pass a café, and I see a bunch of people in there eating. I wish I was in there 'cause I'm cold. Mama tells me keep my eyes in front where they belong.

We pass stores that's got dummies, and we pass another café, and then we pass a shoe shop, and that bald-head man in there fixing on a shoe. I look at him and I butt into that white lady, and Mama jerks me in front and tells me stay there.

We come up to the courthouse, and I see the flag waving there. This flag ain't like the one we got at school. This one here ain't got but a handful of stars. One at the school got a big pile of stars—one for every state. We pass it and we turn and there it is—the dentist office. Me and Mama go in, and they got people sitting everywhere you look. They even got a little boy in there younger than me.

Me and Mama sit on that bench, and a white lady come in there and ask me what my name is. Mama tells her and the white lady goes on back. Then I hear somebody hollering in there. Soon 's that little boy hear him hollering, he starts hollering, too. His mama pats him and pats him, trying to make him hushup, but he ain't thinking 'bout his mama.

The man that was hollering in there comes out holding his jaw. He is a big old man and he's wearing overalls and a jumper.

"Got it, hanh?" another man asks him.

The man shakes his head—don't want to open his mouth.

"Man, I thought they was killing you in there," the other man says. "Hollering like a pig under a gate."

The man don't say nothing. He just heads for the door, and the other man follows him.

"John Lee," the white lady says. "John Lee Williams."

The little boy juggs his head down in his mama's lap and holler more now. His mama tells him go with the nurse, but he ain't thinking 'bout his mama. His mama tells him again, but he don't even hear her. His mama picks him up and takes him in there, and even when the white lady shuts the door I can still hear little old John Lee.

"I often wonder why the Lord let a child like that suffer," a lady says to my mama. The lady's sitting right in front of us on another bench. She's got a white dress and a black sweater. She must be a nurse or something herself, I reckon.

"Not us to question," a man says.

"Sometimes I don't know if we shouldn't," the lady says.

"I know definitely we shouldn't," the man says. The man looks like a preacher. He's big and fat and he's got on a black suit. He's got a gold chain, too.

"Why?" the lady said.

"Why anything?" the preacher says.

"Yes," the lady says. "Why anything?"

"Not us to question," the preacher says.

The lady looks at the preacher a little while and looks at Mama again.

"And look like it's the poor who suffers the most," she says. "I don't understand it."

"Best not to even try," the preacher says. "He works in mysterious ways—wonders to perform."

Right then little John Lee bust out hollering, and everybody turn their head to listen.

"He's not a good dentist," the lady says. "Dr. Robillard is much better. But more expensive. That's why most of the colored people come here. The white people go to Dr. Robillard. Y'all from Bayonne?"

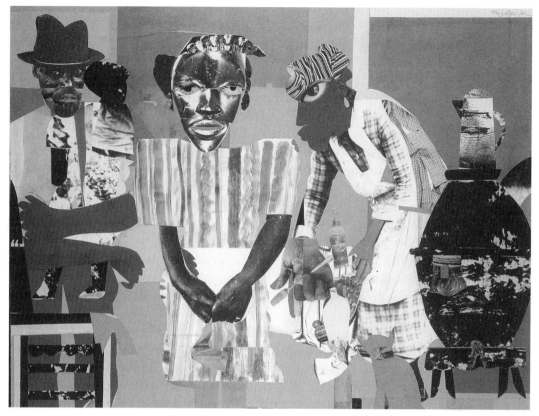

Sunday Morning Breakfast, Romare Bearden, 1967

"Down the river," my mama says. And that's all she go'n say, 'cause she don't talk much. But the lady keeps on looking at her, and so she says, "Near Morgan."

"I see," the lady says.

VII

"That's the trouble with the black people in the country today," some body else says. This one here's sitting on the same side me and Mama's sitting, and he is kind of sitting in front of that preacher. He looks like a teacher or somebody that goes to college. He's got on a suit, and he's got a book that he's been reading. "We don't question is exactly our problem," he says. "We should question and question and question—question every-thing."

The preacher just looks at him a long time. He done put a toothpick or something in his mouth, and he just keeps turning it and turning it. You can see he don't like that boy with that book.

"Maybe you can explain to me what you mean," he says.

"I said what I meant," the boy says. "Question everything. Every stripe, every star, every word spoken. Everything."

"It 'pears to me that this young lady and I was talking 'bout God, young man," the preacher says.

"Question Him, too," the boy says.

"Wait," the preacher says. "Wait now."

"You heard me right," the boy says. "His existence as well as everything else. Everything."

The preacher just looks across the room at the boy. You can see he's getting madder and madder. But mad or no mad, the boy ain't thinking 'bout him. He looks at that preacher just 's hard 's the preacher looks at him.

"Is this what they coming to?" the preacher says. "Is this what we educating them for?"

"You're not educating me," the boy says. "I wash dishes at night so that I can go to school in the day. So even the words you spoke need questioning."

The preacher just looks at him and shakes his head.

"When I come in this room and seen you there with your book, I said to myself, 'There's an intelligent man.' How wrong a person can be."

"Show me one reason to believe in the existence of a God," the boy says.

"My heart tells me," the preacher says.

"'My heart tells me,'" the boy says. "'My heart tells me.' Sure. 'My heart tells me.' And as long as you listen to what your heart tells you, you will have only what the white man gives you and nothing more. Me, I don't listen to my heart. The purpose of the heart is to pump blood throughout the body, and nothing else."

"Who's your paw, boy?" the preacher says.

"Why?"

"Who is he?"

"He's dead."

"And your mom?"

"She's in Charity Hospital with pneumonia. Half killed herself, working for nothing."

"And 'cause he's dead and she's sick, you mad at the world?"

"I'm not mad at the world. I'm questioning it with cold logic, sir. What do words like Freedom, Liberty, God, White, Colored mean? I want to know. That's why *you* are sending us to school, to read and to ask questions. And because we ask these questions, you call us mad. No sir, it is not us who are mad."

"You keep saying 'us'?"

"'Us.' Yes—us. I'm not alone."

The preacher just shakes his head. Then he looks at everybody in the room—everybody. Some of the people look down at the floor, keep from looking at him. I think of look 'way myself, but soon 's I know he done turn his head, I look that way again.

"I'm sorry for you," he says to the boy.

"Why?" the boy says. "Why not be sorry for yourself? Why are you so much better off than I am? Why aren't you sorry for these other people in here? Why not be sorry for the lady who had to drag her child into the dentist office? Why not be sorry for the lady sitting on that bench over there? Be sorry for them. Not for me. Some way or the other I'm going to make it."

"No, I'm sorry for you," the preacher says.

"Of course, of course," the boy says, nodding his head. "You're sorry for me because I rock that pillar you're leaning on."

"You can't never rock the pillar I'm leaning on, young man. It's stronger than anything man can ever do."

"You believe in God because a man told you to believe in God," the boy says. "A white man told you to believe in God. And why? To keep you ignorant so he can keep his feet on your neck."

"So now we the ignorant?" the preacher says.

"Yes," the boy says. "Yes." And he opens his book again.

The preacher just looks at him sitting there. The boy done forgot all about him. Everybody else make 'tend they done forgot the squabble, too.

Then I see that preacher getting up real slow. Preacher's a great big old man and he got to brace himself to get up. He comes over where the boy is sitting. He just stands there a little while looking down at him, but the boy don't raise his head.

"Get up, boy," preacher says.

The boy looks up at him, then he shuts his book real slow and stands up. Preacher just hauls back and hit him in the face. The boy falls back 'gainst the wall, but he straightens himself up and looks right back at the preacher.

"You forgot the other cheek," he says.

The preacher hauls back and hit him again on the other side. But this time the boy braces himself and don't fall.

"That hasn't changed a thing," he says.

The preacher just looks at the boy. The preacher's breathing real hard like he just run up a big hill. The boy sits down and opens his book again.

"I feel sorry for you," the preacher says. "I never felt so sorry for a man before."

The boy makes 'tend he don't even hear that preacher. He keeps on reading his book. The preacher goes back and gets his hat off the chair.

"Excuse me," he says to us. "I'll come back some other time. Y'all, please excuse me."

And he looks at the boy and goes out the room. The boy h'ist his hand up to his mouth one time to wipe 'way some blood. All the rest of the time he keeps on reading. And nobody else in there say a word.

VIII

Little John Lee and his mama come out the dentist office, and the nurse calls somebody else in. Then little bit later they come out, and the nurse calls another name. But fast 's she calls somebody in there, somebody else comes in the place where we sitting, and the room stays full.

The people coming in now, all of them wearing big coats. One of them says something 'bout sleeting, another one says he hope not. Another one says he think it ain't nothing but rain. 'Cause, he says, rain can get awful cold this time of year.

All round the room they talking. Some of them talking to people right by them, some of them talking to people clear 'cross the room, some of them talking to anybody'll listen. It's a little bitty room, no bigger than us kitchen, and I can see everybody in there. The little old room's full of smoke, 'cause you got two old men smoking pipes over by that side door. I think I feel my tooth thumping me some, and I hold my breath and wait. I wait and wait, but it don't thump me no more. Thank God for that.

I feel like going to sleep, and I lean 'gainst the wall. But I'm scared to go to sleep. Scared 'cause the nurse might call my name and I won't hear her. And Mama might go to sleep, too, and she'll be mad if neither one of us heard the nurse.

I look up at Mama. I love my mama. And when cotton come I'm go'n get her a new coat. And I ain't go'n get a black one, either. I think I'm go'n get her a red one.

"They got some books over there," I say. "Want read one of them?"

Mama looks at the books, but she don't answer me.

I love my mama. And when cotton come I'm go'n get her a new coat. And I ain't go'n get a black one, either. I think I'm go'n get her a red one.

"You got yourself a little man there," the lady says.

Mama don't say nothing to the lady, but she must've smiled, 'cause I seen the lady smiling back. The lady looks at me a little while, like she's feeling sorry for me.

"You sure got that preacher out here in a hurry," she says to that boy.

The boy looks up at her and looks in his book again. When I grow up I want to be just like him. I want clothes like that and I want to keep a book with me too.

"You really don't believe in God?" the lady says.

"No," he says.

"But why?" the lady says.

"Because the wind is pink," he says.

"What?" the lady says.

The boy don't answer her no more. He just reads in his book.

"Talking 'bout the wind is pink," that old lady says. She's sitting on the same bench with the boy and she's trying to look in his face. The boy makes 'tend the old lady ain't even there. He just keeps on reading. "Wind is pink," she says again. "Eh, Lord, what children go'n be saying next?"

The lady 'cross from us bust out laughing.

"That's a good one," she says. "The wind is pink. Yes sir, that's a good one."

"Don't you believe the wind is pink?" the boy says. He keeps his head down in the book.

"Course I believe it, honey," the lady says. "Course I do." She looks at us and winks her eye. "And what color is grass, honey?"

"Grass? Grass is black."

She bust out laughing again. The boy looks at her.

"Don't you believe grass is black?" he says.

The Sky Is Gray

The lady quits her laughing and looks at him. Everybody else looking at him, too. The place quiet, quiet.

"Grass is green, honey," the lady says. "It was green yesterday, it's green today, and it's go'n be green tomorrow."

"How do you know it's green?"

"I know because I know."

"You don't know it's green," the boy says. "You believe it's green because someone told you it was green. If someone had told you it was black you'd believe it was black."

"It's green," the lady says. "I know green when I see green."

"Prove it's green," the boy says.

"Sure, now," the lady says. "Don't tell me it's coming to that."

"It's coming to just that," the boy says. "Words mean nothing. One means no more than the other."

"That's what it all coming to?" the old lady says. That old lady got on a turban and she got on two sweaters. She got a green sweater under a black sweater. I can see the green sweater 'cause some of the buttons on the other sweater's missing.

"Yes ma'am," he says. "Words mean nothing. Action is the only thing. Doing. That's the only thing."

"Other words, you want the Lord to come down here and show Hisself to you?" she says.

"Exactly, ma'am," he says.

"You don't mean that, I'm sure?" she says.

"I do, ma'am," he says.

"Done, Jesus," the lady says, shaking her head.

"I didn't go 'long with that preacher at first," the other lady says; "but now—I don't know. When a person says the grass is black, he's either a lunatic or something's wrong."

"Prove it to me that it's green," the boy says.

"It's green because the people say it's green."

"Those same people say we're citizens of these United States," the boy says.

"I think I'm a citizen," the lady says.

"Citizens have certain rights," the boy says. "Name me one right that you have. One right, granted by the Constitution, that you can exercise in Bayonne."

The lady don't answer him. She just looks at him like she don't know what he's talking 'bout. I know I don't.

"Things changing," she says.

"Things are changing because some black men have begun to think with their brains and not their hearts," the boy says.

"You trying to say these people don't believe in God?"

"I'm sure some of them do. Maybe most of them do. But they don't believe that God is going to touch these white people's hearts and change things tomorrow. Things change through action. By no other way."

Everybody sit quiet and look at the boy. Nobody says a thing. Then the lady 'cross the room from me and Mama just shakes her head.

"Let's hope that not all your generation feel the same way you do," she says.

"Think what you please, it doesn't matter," the boy says. "But it will be men who listen to their heads and not their hearts who will see that your children have a better chance than you had."

"Let's hope they ain't all like you, though," the old lady says. "Done forgot the heart absolutely."

"Yes ma'am, I hope they aren't all like me," the boys says. "Unfortunately, I was born too late to believe in your God. Let's hope that the ones who come after will have your faith—if not in your God, then in something else, something definitely that they can lean on. I haven't anything. For me, the wind is pink, the grass is black."

IX

The nurse comes in the room where we are all sitting and waiting and says the doctor won't take no more patients till one o'clock this evening. My mama jumps up off the bench and goes up to the white lady.

"Nurse, I have to go back in the field this evening," she says.

"The doctor is treating his last patient now," the nurse says. "One o'clock this evening."

"Can I at least speak to the doctor?" my mama asks.

"I'm his nurse," the lady says.

"My little boy's sick," my mama says. "Right now his tooth almost killing him."

The nurse looks at me. She's trying to make up her mind if to let me come in. I look at her real pitiful. The tooth ain't hurting me at all, but Mama say it is, so I make 'tend for her sake.

"This evening," the nurse says, and goes on back in the office.

"Don't feel 'jected, honey," the lady says to Mama. "I been round them a long time—they take you when they want to. If you was white, that's something else; but we the wrong color."

Mama don't say nothing to the lady, and me and her go outside and stand 'gainst the wall. It's cold out there. I can feel that wind going through my coat. Some of the other people come out of the room and go up the street. Me and Mama stand there a little while and we start walking. I don't know where we going. When we come to the other street we just stand there.

"You don't have to make water, do you?" Mama says. "No, ma'am," I say.

We go up on the street. Walking real slow. I can tell Mama don't know where she's going. When we come to a store we stand there and look at the dummies. I look at a little boy wearing a brown overcoat. He's got on brown shoes, too. I look at my old shoes and look at his'n again. You wait till summer, I say.

Me and Mama walk away. We come up to another store and we stop and look at them dummies, too. Then we go on again. We pass a café where the white people in there eating. Mama tells me keep my eyes in front where they belong, but I can't help from seeing them people eat. My stomach starts to growling 'cause I'm hungry. When I see people eating, I get hungry; when I see a coat, I get cold.

A man whistles at my mama when we go by a filling station. She makes 'tend she don't even see him. I look back and I feel like hitting him in the mouth. If I was bigger, I say; if I was bigger, you'd see.

We keep on going. I'm getting colder and colder, but I don't say nothing. I feel that stuff running down my nose and I sniff.

"That rag," Mama says.

I get it out and wipe my nose. I'm getting cold all over now—my face, my hands, my feet, everything. We pass another little café, but this'n for white people, too, and we can't go in there, either. So we just walk. I'm so cold now I'm 'bout ready to say it. If I knowed where we was going I wouldn't be so cold, but I don't know where we going. We go, we go, we go. We walk clean out of Bayonne. Then we cross the street and we come back. Same thing I seen when I got off the bus this morning. Same old trees, same old walks, same old weeds, same old cracked pave—same old everything.

I sniff again.

"That rag," Mama says.

I wipe my nose real fast and jugg that handkerchief back in my pocket 'fore my hands gets too cold. I raise my head and I can see David's hardware store. When we come up to it, we go in. I don't know why, but I'm glad.

It's warm in there. It's so warm in there you don't ever want to leave. I look for the heater, and I see it over by them barrels. Three white men standing round the heater talking in Creole. One of them comes over to see what my mama want.

"Got any axe handles?" she says.

Me, Mama and the white man start to the back, but Mama stops me when we come up to the heater. She and the white man go on. I hold my hands over the heater and look at them. They go all the way to the back, and I see the white man pointing to the axe handles 'gainst the wall.

Mama takes one of them and shakes it like she's trying to figure how much it weighs. Then she rubs her hand over it from one end to the other end. She turns it over and looks at the other side, then she shakes it again, and shakes her head and puts it back. She gets another one and she does it just like she did the first one, then she shakes her head. Then she gets a brown one and do it that, too. But she don't like this one, either. Then she gets another one, but 'fore she shakes it or anything, she looks at me. Look like she's trying to say something to me, but I don't know what it is. All I know is I done got warm now and I'm feeling right smart better. Mama shakes this axe handle just like she did the others, and shakes her head and says something to the white man. The white man just looks at his pile of axe handles, and when Mama pass him to come to the front, the white man just scratch his head and follows her. She tells me to come on and we go on out and start walking again.

We walk and walk, and no time at all I'm cold again. Look like I'm colder now 'cause I can still remember how good it was back there. My stomach growls and I suck it in to keep Mama from hearing it. She's walking right 'side me, and it growls so loud you can hear it a mile. But Mama don't say a word.

X

When we come to the courthouse, I look at the clock. It's got quarter to twelve. Mean we got another hour and a quarter to be out here in the cold. We go and stand 'side a building. Something hits my cap and I look up at the sky. Sleet's falling.

I look at Mama standing there. I want stand close 'side her, but she don't like that. She say that's crybaby stuff. She say you got to stand for yourself, by yourself.

"Let's go back to that office," she says.

We cross the street. When we get to the dentist office I try to open the door, but I can't. I twist and twist, but I can't. Mama pushes me to the side and she twist the knob, but she can't open the door, either. She turns 'way from the door. I look at her, but I don't move and I don't say nothing. I done seen her like this before and I'm scared of her.

"You hungry?" she says. She says it like she's mad at me, like I'm the cause of everything.

"No, ma'am," I say.

"You want eat and walk back, or you rather don't eat and ride?"

"I ain't hungry," I say.

I ain't just hungry, but I'm cold, too. I'm so hungry and cold I want to cry. And look like I'm getting colder and colder. My feet done got numb. I try to work my toes, but I don't even feel them. Look like I'm go'n die. Look like I'm go'n stand right here and freeze to death. I think 'bout home. I think 'bout Val and Auntie and Ty and Louis and Walker. It's 'bout twelve o'clock and I know they eating dinner now. I can hear Ty making jokes. He done forgot 'bout getting up early this morning and right now he's probably making jokes. Always trying to make somebody laugh. I wish I was right there listening to him. Give anything in the world if I was home round the fire.

"Come on," Mama says.

We start walking again. My feet so numb I can't hardly feel them. We turn the corner and go on back up the street. The clock in the courthouse starting hitting for twelve.

The sleet's coming down plenty now. They hit the pave and bounce like rice. Oh, Lord; oh, Lord, I pray. Don't let me die, don't let me die, don't let me die, Lord.

XI

Now I know where we going. We going back of town where the colored people eat. I don't care if I don't eat. I been hungry before. I can stand it. But I can't stand the cold.

I can see we go'n have a long walk. It's 'bout a mile down there. But I don't mind. I know when I get there I'm go'n warm myself. I think I can hold out. My hands numb in my pockets and my feet numb, too, but if I keep moving I can hold out. Just don't stop no more, that's all.

The sky's gray. The sleet keeps on falling. Falling like rain now—plenty,

plenty. You can hear it hitting the pave. You can see it bouncing. Sometimes it bounces two times 'fore it settles.

We keep on going. We don't say nothing. We just keep on going, keep on going.

I wonder what Mama's thinking. I hope she ain't mad at me. When summer come I'm go'n pick plenty cotton and get her a coat. I'm go'n get her a red one.

I hope they'd make it summer all the time. I'd be glad if it was summer all the time—but it ain't. We got to have winter, too. Lord, I hate the winter. I guess everybody hate the winter.

I don't sniff this time, I get out my handkerchief and wipe my nose. My hands's so cold I can hardly hold the handkerchief.

I think we getting close, but we ain't there yet. I wonder where everybody is. Can't see a soul but us. Look like we the only two people moving round today. Must be too cold for the rest of the people to move round in.

I can hear my teeth. I hope they don't knock together too hard and make that bad one hurt. Lord, that's all I need, for that bad one to start off.

I hear a church bell somewhere. But today ain't Sunday. They must be ringing for a funeral or something.

I wonder what they doing at home. They must be eating. Monsieur Bayonne might be there with his guitar. One day Ty played with Monsieur Bayonne's guitar and broke one of the strings. Monsieur Bayonne was some mad with Ty. He say Ty wasn't go'n ever 'mount to nothing. Ty can go just like Monsieur Bayonne when he ain't there. Ty can make everybody laugh when he starts to mocking Monsieur Bayonne.

I used to like to be with Mama and Daddy. We used to be happy. But they took him in the Army. Now, nobody happy no more . . . . I be glad when Daddy comes home.

Monsieur Bayonne say it wasn't fair for them to take Daddy and give Mama nothing and give us nothing. Auntie say, "Shhh, Etienne. Don't let them hear you talk like that." Monsieur Bayonne say, "It's God truth. What they giving his children? They have to walk three and a half miles to school hot or cold. That's anything to give for a paw? She's got to work in the field rain or shine just to make ends meet. That's anything to give for a husband?" Auntie say, "Shhh, Etienne, shhh." "Yes, you right," Monsieur Bayonne say. "Best don't say it in front of them now. But one day they go'n find out. One day." "Yes, I suppose so," Auntie say. "Then what, Rose Mary?" Monsieur

Bayonne say. "I don't know, Etienne," Auntie say. "All we can do is us job, and leave everything else in His hand . . . "

We getting closer, now. We getting closer. I can even see the railroad tracks.

We cross the tracks, and now I see the café. Just to get in there, I say. Just to get in there. Already I'm starting to feel little better.

XII

We go in. Ahh, it's good. I look for the heater; there 'gainst the wall. One of them little brown ones. I just stand there and hold my hands over it. I can't open my hands too wide 'cause they almost froze.

Mama's standing right 'side me. She done unbuttoned her coat. Smoke rises out of the coat, and the coat smells like a wet dog.

I move to the side so Mama can have room. She opens out her hands and rubs them together. I rub mine together, too, 'cause this keep them from hurting. If you let them warm too fast, they hurt you sure. But if you let them warm just little bit at a time, and you keep rubbing them, they be all right every time.

They got just two more people in the café. A lady back of the counter, and a man on this side of the counter. They been watching us ever since we come in.

You see, one day, I'm go'n make all this up. I want say it now; I want tell her how I feel right now; but Mama don't like us to talk like that.

Mama gets out the handkerchief and count up the money. Both of us know how much money she's got there. Three dollars. No, she ain't got three dollars, 'cause she had to pay us way up here. She ain't got but two dollars and a half left. Dollar and half to get my tooth pulled, and fifty cents for us to go back on, and fifty cents worth of salt meat.

She stirs the money round with her finger. Most of the money is change 'cause I can hear it rubbing together. She stirs it and stirs it. Then she looks at the door. It's still sleeting. I can hear it hitting 'gainst the wall like rice.

"I ain't hungry, Mama," I say.

"Got to pay them something for they heat," she says.

She takes a quarter out the handkerchief and ties the handkerchief up again. She looks over her shoulder at the people, but she still don't move. I hope she don't spend the money. I don't want her spending it on me. I'm hungry, I'm almost starving I'm so hungry, but I don't want her spending the money on me.

She flips the quarter over like she's thinking. She's must be thinking 'bout us walking back home. Lord, I sure don't want walk home. If I thought it'd do any good to say something, I'd say it. But Mama makes up her own mind 'bout things.

She turns 'way from the heater right fast, like she better hurry up and spend the quarter 'fore she change her mind. I watch her go toward the counter. The man and the lady look at her, too. She tells the lady something and the lady walks away. The man keeps on looking at her. Her back's turned to the man, and she don't even know he's standing there.

The lady puts some cakes and a glass of milk on the counter. Then she pours up a cup of coffee and set it 'side the other stuff. She's looking real sad. I say to myself, I'm go'n make all this up one day. You see, one day, I'm go'n make all this up. I want say it now; I want tell her how I feel right now; but Mama don't like us to talk like that.

"I can't eat all this," I say.

They ain't got but just three little old cakes there. I'm so hungry right now, the Lord knows I can eat a hundred times three, but I want my mama to have one.

Mama don't even look my way. She knows I'm hungry, she knows I want it. I let it stay there a little while, then I get it and eat it. I eat just on my front teeth, though, 'cause if cake touch that back tooth I know what'll happen. Thank God it ain't hurt me at all today.

After I finish eating I see the man go to the juke box. He drops a nickel in it, then he just stand there a little while looking at the record. Mama tells me keep my eyes in front where they belong. I turn my head like she say, but then I hear the man coming toward us.

"Dance, pretty?" he says.

Mama gets up to dance with him. But 'fore you know it, she done grabbed the little man in the collar and done heaved him 'side the wall. He hit the wall so hard he stop the juke box from playing.

"Some pimp," the lady back of the counter says. "Some pimp."

The little man jumps up off the floor and starts toward my mama. 'Fore you know it, Mama done sprung open her knife and she's waiting for him.

"Come on," she says. "Come on. I'll gut you from your neighbo to your throat. Come on."

I got up to the little man to hit him, but Mama makes me come and stand 'side her. The little man looks at me and Mama and goes on back to the counter.

"Some pimp," the lady back of the counter says. "Some pimp." She starts laughing and pointing at the little man. "Yes sir, you a pimp, all right. Yes sir-ree."

XIII

"Fasten that coat, let's go," Mama says.

"You don't have to leave," the lady says.

Mama don't answer the lady, and we right out in the cold again. I'm warm right now—my hands, my ears, my feet—but I know this ain't go'n last too long. It done sleet so much now you got ice everywhere you look.

We cross the railroad tracks, and soon's we do, I get cold. That wind goes through this little old coat like it ain't even there. I got on a shirt and a sweater under the coat, but that wind don't pay them no mind. I look up and I can see we got a long way to go. I wonder if we go'n make it 'fore I get too cold.

We cross over to walk on the sidewalk. They got just one sidewalk back here, and it's over there.

After we go just a little piece, I smell bread cooking. I look, then I see a baker shop. When we get closer, I can smell it more better, I shut my eyes and make 'tend I'm eating. But I keep them shut too long and I butt up 'gainst a telephone post. Mama grabs me and see if I'm hurt. I ain't bleeding or nothing and she turns me loose.

I can feel I'm getting colder and colder, and I look up to see how far we still got to go. Uptown is 'way up yonder. A half mile more, I reckon. I try to think of something. They say think and you won't get cold. I think of that poem, "Annabel Lee." I ain't been to school in so long—this bad weather—I reckon they done passed "Annabel Lee" by now. But passed it or not, I'm sure Miss Walker go'n make me recite it when I get there. That woman don't never forget nothing. I ain't never seen nobody like that in my life.

I'm still getting cold. "Annabel Lee" or no "Annabel Lee," I'm still getting cold. But I can see we getting closer. We getting there gradually.

Soon's we turn the corner, I see a little old white lady up in front of us. She's the only lady on the street. She's all in black and she's got a long black rag over her head.

"Stop," she says.

Me and Mama stop and look at her. She must be crazy to be out in all this bad weather. Ain't got but a few other people out there, and all of them's men.

"Y'all done ate?" she says.

"Just finish," Mama says.

"Y'all must be cold then?" she says.

"We headed for the dentist," Mama says. "We'll warm up when we get there."

"What dentist?" the old lady says. "Mr. Bassett?"

"Yes, Ma'am," Mama says.

"Come on in," the old lady says. "I'll telephone him and tell him y'all coming."

Me and Mama follow the old lady in the store. It's a little bitty store, and it don't have much in there. The old lady takes off her head rag and folds it up.

"Helena?" somebody calls from the back.

"Yes, Alnest?" the old lady says.

"Did you see them?"

"They're here. Standing beside me."

"Good. Now you can stay inside."

The old lady looks at Mama. Mama's waiting to hear what she brought us in here for. I'm waiting for that, too.

"I saw y'all each time you went by," she says. "I came out to catch you, but you were gone."

"We went back of town," Mama says.

"Did you eat?"

"Yes, ma'am."

The old lady looks at Mama a long time, like she's thinking Mama might be just saying that. Mama looks right back at her. The old lady looks at me to see what I have to say. I don't say nothing. I sure ain't going 'gainst my Mama.

"There's food in the kitchen," she says to Mama. "I've been keeping it warm."

Mama turns right around and starts for the door.

"Just a minute," the old lady says. Mama stops. "The boy'll have to work for it. It isn't free."

"We don't take no handout," Mama says.

"I'm not handing out anything," the old lady says. "I need my garbage moved to the front. Ernest has a bad cold and can't go out there."

"James'll move it for you," Mama says.

"Not unless you eat," the old lady says. "I'm old, but I have my pride, too, you know."

Mama can see she ain't go'n beat this old lady down, so she just shakes her head.

"All right," the old lady says. "Come into the kitchen."

She leads the way with that rag in her hand. The kitchen is a little bitty little old thing, too. The table and the stove just 'bout fill it up. They got a little room to the side. Somebody in there laying 'cross the bed—'cause I can see one of his feet. Must be the person she was talking to: Ernest or Alnest—something like that.

"Sit down," the old lady says to Mama. "Not you," she says to me. "You have to move the cans."

"Helena?" the man says in the other room.

"Yes, Alnest?" the old lady says.

"Are you going out there again?"

"I must show the boy where the garbage is Alnest," the old lady says.

"Keep that shawl over your head," the old man says.

"You don't have to remind me, Alnest. Come, boy," the old lady says.

We go out in the yard. Little old back yard ain't no bigger than the store or the kitchen. But it can sleet here just like it can sleet in any big back yard. And 'fore you know it, I'm trembling.

"There," the old lady says, pointing to the cans. I pick up one of the cans and set it right back down. The can's so light, I'm go'n see what's inside of it.

"Here," the old lady says. "Leave that can alone."

I look back at her standing there in that door. She's got that black rag wrapped around her shoulders, and she's pointing one of her little old fingers at me.

"Pick it up and carry it to the front," she says. I go by her with the can, and she's looking at me all the time. I'm sure the can's empty. I'm sure she could've carried it herself—maybe both of them at the same time. "Set it on the sidewalk by the door and come back for the other one," she says.

I go and come back, and Mama looks at me when I pass her. I get the other can and take it to the front. It don't feel a bit heavier than the first one. I tell myself I ain't go'n be nobody's fool, and I'm go'n look inside this can to see just what I been hauling. First, I look up the street, then down the street. Nobody coming. Then I look over my shoulder toward the door. That little old lady done slipped up there quiet's mouse, watching me again. Look like she knowed what I was go'n do.

"Ehh, Lord," she says. "Children, children. Come in here, boy, and go wash your hands."

I follow her in the kitchen. She point toward the bathroom, and I go in there and wash up. Little bitty old bathroom, but it's clean, clean. I don't use any of her towels; I wipe my hands on my pants leg.

When I come back in the kitchen, the old lady done dished up the food. Rice, gravy, meat—and she even got some lettuce and tomato in a saucer. She even got a glass of milk and a piece of cake there, too. It looks so good, I almost start eating 'fore I say my blessing.

"Helena?" the old man says.

"Yes, Alnest?"

"Are they eating?"

"Yes," she says.

"Good," he says. "Now you'll stay inside."

The old lady goes in there where he is and I can hear them talking. I look at Mama. She's eating slow like she's thinking. I wonder what's the matter now. I reckon she's thinking 'bout home.

The old lady comes back in the kitchen.

"I talked to Dr. Bassett's nurse," she says. "Dr. Bassett will take you as soon as you get there."

"Thank you, ma'am," Mama says.

"Perfectly all right," the old lady says. "Which one is it?"

Mama nods toward me. The old lady looks at me real sad. I look sad, too.

"You're not afraid, are you?" she says.

"No ma'am," I say.

"That's a good boy," the old lady says. "Nothing to be afraid of. Dr. Bassett will not hurt you."

When me and Mama get through eating, we thank the old lady again.

"Helena, are they leaving?" the old man says.

"Yes, Alnest."

"Tell them I say good-bye."

"They can hear you, Alnest."

"Good-bye both mother and son," the old man says. "And may God be with you."

Me and Mama tell the old man good-bye, and we follow the old lady in the front room. Mama opens the door to go out, but she stops and comes back in the store.

"You sell salt meat?" she says.

"Yes."

"Give me two bits worth."

"That isn't very much salt meat," the old lady says.

"That's all I have," Mama says.

The old lady goes back of the counter and cuts a big piece off the chunk. Then she wraps it up and put it in a paper bag.

"Two bits," she says.

"That looks like awful lot of meat for a quarter," Mama says.

"Two bits," the old lady says. "I've been selling salt meat behind this counter twenty-five years. I think I know what I'm doing."

"You got a scale there," Mama says.

"What?" the old lady says.

"Weigh it," Mama says.

"What?" the old lady says. "Are you telling me how to run my business?"

"Thanks very much for the food," Mama says.

"Just a minute," the old lady says.

"James," Mama says to me. I move toward the door.

"Just one minute, I said," the old lady says.

Me and Mama stop again and look at her. The old lady takes the meat out of the bag and unwraps it and cuts 'bout half of it off. Then she wraps it up again and juggs it back in the bag and gives the bag to Mama. Mama lays the quarter on the counter.

"Your kindness will never be forgotten," she says. "James," she says to me.

We go out, and the old lady comes to the door to look at us. After we go a little piece I look back, and she's still there watching us.

The sleet's coming down heavy, heavy now, and I turn up my coat collar to keep my neck warm. My Mama tells me turn it right back down.

"You not a bum," she says. "You a man."

Read and Think Critically

Analyze, Explain, Compare and Contrast

1. **FIRST-PERSON POINT OF VIEW** Analyze the author's use of **first-person point of view**. How does this affect the **tone** of the story?

2. Every stop along the way in this trip to the dentist offers a lesson for James, the **protagonist**. Explain these lessons in detail.

3. By some standards, the mother's treatment of the boy appears harsh, even cruel. What is your opinion of the mother's treatment of the boy? Use specific examples to support your position.

4. Both "The Black Ball" in the previous unit and this story concern African American parents dealing with the effects of racial discrimination on their children. Use a chart like the one below to compare and contrast literary elements of the two stories. Consider **point of view**, tone, the **dénouement** (final outcome of the **plot**), and **themes** of the stories.

Literary Element	The Sky Is Gray	The Black Ball
Point of view	The story is told by the boy.	The story is told by the father.

5. The passage in the dentist's waiting room (pages 507–510) explores the themes of faith and reason. Summarize the positions of the preacher and the young man in the waiting room. Given the ending of the story, which position do you think James will adopt in life?

6. **THE AUTHOR'S STYLE** **Tone** is an important element of this story. Describe the tone, and then analyze how the author achieves it.

Responding to Unit Four

Key Ideas and Details

1. An integral part of the **conflict** of a story is its **resolution**, or the manner in which the main conflict is worked out. In some stories the conflict is resolved completely; in others, the author leaves an ambiguous ending, forcing readers to draw their own conclusions. Consider your experience reading the stories in this unit. In your opinion, which story has the most satisfying resolution? Explain your choice.

2. Some stories yield most of their pleasure on first reading. Others, like people, are harder to get to know but are well worth knowing. Which story in this unit did you like best on first reading, and which grew on you the most after examining it more closely? Explain.

Craft and Structure

3. "Barn Burning," "Angel Levine," and "Everything That Rises Must Converge" all contain images or references to wings or flight. Choose one of these stories and explain the **imagery** related to flight. In what ways does the author use the images?

4. Several writers in this unit use **satire** to communicate important **themes**. Choose a work of satire from this unit and analyze how the writer uses satire both to entertain and to inform.

Integration of Knowledge and Ideas

5. "Everything That Rises Must Converge" and "The Sky Is Gray" both deal with interactions between races. Analyze the themes related to race in each story.

6. Compare and contrast the attitudes the children in "The Veldt" and "Barn Burning" have toward their parents. What were the end results of these attitudes?

7. Harrison in "Harrison Bergeron" is a larger-than-life **protagonist**. Other characters, such as Sammy in "A & P" and Manischevitz in "Angel Levine," share qualities of the **antihero**. Of the two types of protagonists—larger-than-life or antihero—which do you think best represents the human condition? Use references to any of the stories you have read in this unit to support your evaluation.

Writing About the Literature

Comparing Styles

William Faulkner's style is often characterized as difficult and obscure. John Updike's style in "A & P," on the other hand, is very accessible, or easy to understand. Write a short essay in which you compare and contrast the styles of these two authors. What do you think are the strengths and weaknesses of each?

Universality

One of the hallmarks of good literature is that while it has a unique setting and compelling characters, it also deals with universal themes—emotions and problems that affect everyone. Pick your favorite story from this unit. Write an essay evaluating what elements make it both unique and universal.

Writing with Style

A Setting of Your Own

The setting of a story often influences its tone. For example, Gaines' description of the setting in "The Sky Is Gray" creates an almost oppressive tone, whereas Bradbury's description of the nursery in "The Veldt" creates an ominous tone. Select a location you know well, such as a store or a location in your school. Describe it in the tone of one of the short stories in this unit. Feel free to exaggerate the tone of your selected author. See if your classmates can guess the source of your "influence."

★★★

IN YOUR OWN STYLE

In "The Veldt," "Barn Burning," and "Everything That Rises Must Converge," parents and children have difficulty communicating. In your own style, write a scene that shows a parent and son or daughter struggling to understand each other. You will want to make choices about setting the scene, using dialogue, and showing nonverbal communication.

Unit Five

Voices of Diversity and Disillusionment 1970s and 1980s

Burger Chef, Ralph Goings, 1970

With the swing of history's pendulum, the seventies saw another war for Americans to grieve, more technological advances to marvel at, and changes in social structures that liberated some and frightened others. The nation was at war with itself over American involvement in the Vietnam War. Rallies and sit-ins turned into mass arrests and violence. Soldiers, once our heroes, came home without fanfare or thanks.

The modern women's movement also emerged in the seventies, flourishing on the ideas and energy of the Civil Rights era. Women sought equal pay with men and the chance to work any job. In the years that followed, our country saw its first female Supreme Court Justice, and Alice Walker became the first African American woman to win the Pulitzer Prize. Stories written by such writers as Walker, Bobbie Ann Mason, Louise Erdrich, and Amy Tan testified to the intensity and scope of change in female lives.

During this time of rapid change, the age of the personal computer dawned and the generation gap widened. The way teens dressed became a matter of public debate—and family stress. Families arriving from faraway countries worried about tossing their children into this bubbling melting pot. The following collection of short stories reflects the turbulence of the time, the diversity of our country, and the power of storytelling to heal.

The Power of Poetry and Perspective

Poet-novelists such as Alice Walker injected fiction with brilliant images, rich in metaphors that invested ordinary objects with powerful emotions. In "The Flowers," featured in this collection, Walker draws our attention to a corpse in a peaceful wood, a hanging noose, and a wild pink rose. In doing so, her short story speaks volumes about the heritage of slavery.

Like Walker, novelist and poet Louise Erdrich brought polished imagery and a reverence for nature to her stories. Erdrich also uses the narrative techniques of William Faulkner. Her novel *Love Medicine* is comprised of short, disjointed narratives that shift in time. Each story is told from the perspective of a different character, all of whom belong to a Native American reservation in North Dakota. Like her novels, her short stories show her talent for changing perspectives without "taking sides."

Amy Tan, another woman writer exploring her family heritage, devotes her pages to lyrical descriptions of the smells, tastes, and sounds of her Chinatown home—and on shifting points of view. In her bestselling novel, *The Joy Luck Club,* she explores the strained relationships of four Chinese American families by alternating first-person narratives between mothers and daughters. Her short story, "Rules of the Game," as much about life as about chess, shows Tan's ear for speech patterns. The halted English of a Chinese mother seems to battle against the defiant California slang of her American daughter.

Metafiction

While writing about his experiences as a soldier in Vietnam, Tim O'Brien experimented with "metafiction," in which the act of telling a story becomes part of the story. Other authors of the time were finding ways to draw the reader's attention to literary devices, and even make fun of them. O'Brien would sometimes suggest in his writing that part of a story wasn't real, unraveling the reader's suspension of disbelief. But instead of implying that his stories were fakes, O'Brien asked readers to consider the difference between the truth of fiction and the truth of facts. He suggested that the emotions produced by "story truth" might be truer than actual facts.

Minimalism

Postmodernist literature of the seventies and eighties reflected experimentation and a return to plainness in prose. Perhaps there is always someone, somewhere trying to emulate the crisp, straightforward sentences of Ernest Hemingway. Raymond Carver succeeded. He spurred a revitalization of the short story in the eighties, drawing a wave of writers to minimalism.

Minimalist writers gave straightforward descriptions of the surface of things, and left readers to imagine what lay beneath it. Minimalists hesitated to use adjectives, adverbs, or meaningless details. Early in Raymond Carver's career, an editor told him to write only fifteen words where there were once twenty-five, then five words instead of fifteen. His greatest influence was Anton Chekhov, the Russian writer who created the modern story a century before. Like Chekhov, Carver came from a family that knew hardship. Like Chekhov, he strived for truth in descriptions and objectivity throughout.

By wiping away unnecessary words from their stories, minimalist writers such as Carver, Bobbie Ann Mason, and Russell Banks created characters without attaching their own judgments or emotions. And yet, their stories have the power to stir great depths of emotion and understanding about people of all kinds.

★★

Before You Read

Isaac Bashevis Singer 1904–1991

About the Author

Born in Poland to a Jewish family, Isaac Bashevis Singer wrote in Yiddish all of his life, often supervising the translation of his work into English after he left his homeland for the United States. The son of a rabbi, he received a traditional rabbinical education in Poland but chose the life of a writer instead, moving to New York in 1935.

As a writer for *The Jewish Daily Forward*, Singer brought forth an astonishing number of stories under various pseudonyms. During his lifetime, he published fifty-five volumes of short stories, novels, plays, children's stories, and memoirs; five more volumes were published after his death. Among his best-known works are his novel, *The Family Moskat*, and a collection of short stories titled *Gimpel the Fool*.

Singer believed that the first job of literature is to entertain. He said many times, "A good writer is basically a storyteller, not a scholar or a redeemer of mankind."

★★★★★★★★★★★

The Author's Style

Singer's fiction reflects his roots; he grew up learning the tradition of the Yiddish folktale in his native Poland. His stories are allegories in which the fantastic and supernatural often come into play in the lives of people who find themselves in extreme situations. His style is to link lives of sad and earthly everyday reality with a world of mystery and superstition. Here demons, specters, and dreams have a real and permanent impact on human lives. Whether ordinary or fantastic, events in Singer's stories are described in simple, direct, matter-of-fact prose.

Singer's characters are often colorful and compelling exaggerations; they are overly stubborn, perhaps, or compulsive or gullible. They are often victimized by the deceptiveness and unkindness of others, their own imaginations, and the general unfairness of life. At times Singer draws a contrast between the cruel and disorienting modern world and an alternative life of mystical possibilities, peopled with both angels and demons.

Many of Singer's stories were written specifically for children, but because of the folk origins and fable-like appeal, his writing has always had a wide-ranging audience.

The Key

ISAAC BASHEVIS SINGER

 LITERARY LENS: SYMBOLISM A **symbol** is something that stands for, or represents, something else. As you read, consider how the author uses the key as a symbol.

At about three o'clock in the afternoon, Bessie Popkin began to prepare to go down to the street. Going out was connected with many difficulties, especially on a hot summer day: first, forcing her fat body into a corset, squeezing her swollen feet into shoes, and combing her hair, which Bessie dyed at home and which grew wild and was streaked in all colors—yellow, black, gray, red; then making sure that while she was out her neighbors would not break into her apartment and steal linen, clothes, documents, or just disarrange things and make them disappear.

Besides human tormentors, Bessie suffered from demons, imps, Evil Powers. She hid her eyeglasses in the night table and found them in a slipper. She placed her bottle of hair dye in the medicine chest; days later she discovered it under the pillow. Once, she left a pot of borscht[1] in the refrigerator, but the Unseen took it from there and after long searching Bessie came upon it in her clothes closet. On its surface was a thick layer of fat that gave off the smell of rancid tallow.[2]

What she went through, how many tricks were played on her and how much she had to wrangle in order not to perish or fall into insanity, only God knew. She had given up the telephone because racketeers and degenerates called her day and night, trying to get secrets out of her. The Puerto Rican milkman once tried to rape her. The errand boy from the grocery store attempted to burn her belongings with a cigarette. To evict her from the rent-controlled apartment where she had lived for thirty-five years, the company and the superintendent infested her rooms with rats, mice, cockroaches.

Her chin sprouted a little white beard. She wore a faded dress in a flowered print, a misshapen straw hat trimmed with wooden cherries and grapes, and shabby shoes.

Bessie had long ago realized that no means were adequate against those determined to be spiteful—not the metal door, the special lock, her letters to the police, the mayor, the FBI, and even the president in Washington. But while one breathed one had to eat. It all took time: checking the windows, the gas vents, securing the drawers. Her paper money she kept in volumes of the encyclopedia, in back copies of the *National Geographic*, and in Sam Popkin's old ledgers. Her stocks and bonds Bessie had hidden among the logs in the fireplace, which was never used, as well as under the seats of the easy chairs. Her jewels she had sewn into the mattress. There was a time when Bessie had safe-deposit boxes at the bank, but she long ago convinced herself that the guards there had passkeys.

At about five o'clock, Bessie was ready to go out. She gave a last look at herself in the mirror—small, broad, with a narrow forehead, a flat nose, and eyes slanting and half-closed, like a Chinaman's. Her chin sprouted a little white beard. She wore a faded dress in a flowered print, a misshapen straw hat trimmed with wooden cherries and grapes, and shabby shoes. Before she left, she made a final inspection of the three rooms and the kitchen.

---

1 **borscht:** hot or cold beet soup served with sour cream

2 **tallow:** white fat from cattle or sheep used in soap and candles

Everywhere there were clothes, shoes, and piles of letters that Bessie had not opened. Her husband, Sam Popkin, who had died almost twenty years ago, had liquidated his real-estate business before his death, because he was about to retire to Florida. He left her stocks, bonds, and a number of pass-books from savings banks, as well as some mortgages. To this day, firms wrote to Bessie, sent her reports, checks. The Internal Revenue Service claimed taxes from her. Every few weeks she received announcements from a funeral company that sold plots in an "airy cemetery." In former years, Bessie used to answer letters, deposit her checks, keep track of her income and expenses. Lately she had neglected it all. She even stopped buying the news-paper and reading the financial section.

In the corridor, Bessie tucked cards with signs on them that only she could recognize between the door and the door frame. The keyhole she stuffed with putty. What else could she do—a widow without children, rela-tives, or friends? There was a time when the neighbors used to open their doors, look out, and laugh at her exaggerated care; others teased her. That had long passed. Bessie spoke to no one. She didn't see well, either. The glasses she had worn for years were of no use. To go to an eye doctor and be fitted for new ones was too much of an effort. Everything was difficult—even entering and leaving the elevator, whose door always closed with a slam.

$\mathcal{B}$essie seldom went farther than two blocks from her building. The street between Broadway and Riverside Drive became noisier and filthier from day to day. Hordes of urchins ran around half-naked. Dark men with curly hair and wild eyes quarreled in Spanish with little women whose bellies were always swollen in pregnancy. They talked back in rattling voices. Dogs barked, cats meowed. Fires broke out and fire engines, ambulances, and police cars drove up. On Broadway, the old groceries had been replaced by supermarkets, where food must be picked out and put in a wagon and one had to stand in line before the cashier.

God in heaven, since Sam died, New York, America—perhaps the whole world—was falling apart. All the decent people had left the neighborhood and it was overrun by a mob of thieves, robbers, whores. Three times Bessie's pocketbook had been stolen. When she reported it to the police, they just laughed. Every time one crossed the street, one risked one's life. Bessie took a step and stopped. Someone had advised her to use a cane, but she was far from considering herself an old woman or a cripple. Every few weeks she painted her nails red. At times, when the rheumatism left her in peace, she took clothes she used to wear from the closets, tried them on, and studied herself in the mirror.

Opening the door of the supermarket was impossible. She had to wait till someone held it for her. The supermarket itself was a place that only the Devil could have invented. The lamps burned with a glaring light. People pushing wagons were likely to knock down anyone in their path. The shelves were either too high or too low. The noise was deafening, and the contrast between the heat outside and the freezing temperature inside! It was a miracle that she didn't get pneumonia. More than anything else, Bessie was tortured by indecision. She picked up each item with a trembling hand and read the label. This was not the greed of youth but the uncertainty of age. According to Bessie's figuring, today's shopping should not have taken longer than three-quarters of an hour, but two hours passed and Bessie was still not finished. When she finally brought the wagon to the cashier, it occurred to her that she had forgotten the box of oatmeal. She went back and a woman took her place in line. Later, when she paid, there was new trouble. Bessie had put the bill in the right side of her bag, but it was not there. After long rummaging, she found it in a small change purse on the opposite side. Yes, who could believe that such things were possible? If she told someone, he would think she was ready for the madhouse.

*W*hen Bessie went into the supermarket, the day was still bright; now it was drawing to a close. The sun, yellow and golden, was sinking toward the Hudson, to the hazy hills of New Jersey. The buildings on Broadway radiated the heat they had absorbed. From under gratings where the subway trains rumbled, evil-smelling fumes arose. Bessie held the heavy bag of food in one hand, and in the other she grasped her pocketbook tightly. Never had Broadway seemed to her so wild, so dirty. It stank of softened asphalt, gasoline, rotten fruit, the excrement of dogs. On the sidewalk, among torn newspapers and the butts of cigarettes, pigeons hopped about. It was difficult to understand how these creatures avoided being stepped on in the crush of passers-by. From the blazing sky a golden dust was falling. Before a storefront hung with artificial grass, men in sweated shirts poured papaya juice and pineapple juice into themselves with haste, as if trying to extinguish a fire that consumed their insides. Above their heads hung coconuts carved in the shapes of Indians. On a side street, black and white children had opened a hydrant and were splashing naked in the gutter. In the midst of that heat wave, a truck with microphones drove around blaring out shrill songs and deafening blasts about a candidate for political office. From the rear of a truck, a girl with hair that stood up like wires threw out leaflets.

It was all beyond Bessie's strength—crossing the street, waiting for the elevator, and then getting out on the fifth floor before the door slammed. Bessie put the groceries down at the threshold and searched for her keys. She used her nail file to dig the putty out of the keyhole. She put in the key and turned it. But woe, the key broke. Only the handle remained in her hand. Bessie fully grasped the catastrophe. The other people in the building had copies of their keys hanging in the superintendent's apartment, but she trusted no one—some time ago, she had ordered a new combination lock, which she was sure no master key could open. She had a duplicate key somewhere in a drawer, but with her she carried only this one. "Well, this is the end," Bessie said aloud.

There was nobody to turn to for help. The neighbors were her blood enemies. The super only waited for her downfall. Bessie's throat was so constricted that she could not even cry. She looked around, expecting to see the fiend who had delivered this latest blow. Bessie had long since made peace with death, but to die on the steps or in the streets was too harsh. And who knows how long such agony could last? She began to ponder. Was there still open somewhere a store where they fitted keys? Even if there were, what could the locksmith copy from? He would have to come up here with his tools. For that, one needed a mechanic associated with the firm which produced these special locks. If at least she had money with her. But she never carried more than she needed to spend. The cashier in the supermarket had given her back only some twenty-odd cents. "O dear Momma, I don't want to live anymore!" Bessie spoke Yiddish, amazed that she suddenly reverted to that half-forgotten tongue.

After many hesitations, Bessie decided to go back down to the street. Perhaps a hardware store or one of those tiny shops that specialize in keys was still open. She remembered that there used to be such a key stand in the neighborhood. After all, other people's keys must get broken. But what should she do with the food? It was too heavy to carry with her. There was no choice. She would have to leave the bag at the door. "They steal anyhow," Bessie said to herself. Who knows, perhaps the neighbors intentionally

> *The elevator went down and the man opened the door for her. She wanted to thank him, but remained silent. Why thank her enemies? These were all sly tricks.*

manipulated her lock so that she would not be able to enter the apartment while they robbed her or vandalized her belongings.

Before Bessie went down to the street, she put her ear to the door.

She heard nothing except a murmur that never stopped, the cause and origin of which Bessie could not figure out. Sometimes it ticked like a clock; other times it buzzed, or groaned—an entity imprisoned in the walls or the water pipes. In her mind Bessie said goodbye to the food, which should have been in the refrigerator, not standing here in the heat. The butter would melt, the milk would turn sour. "It's a punishment! I am cursed, cursed," Bessie muttered. A neighbor was about to go down in the elevator and Bessie signaled to him to hold the door for her. Perhaps he was one of the thieves. He might try to hold her up, assault her. The elevator went down and the man opened the door for her. She wanted to thank him, but remained silent. Why thank her enemies? These were all sly tricks.

When Bessie stepped out into the street, night had fallen. The gutter was flooded with water. The streetlamps were reflected in the black pool as in a lake. Again there was a fire in the neighborhood. She heard the wailing of a siren, the clang of fire engines. Her shoes were wet. She came out on Broadway, and the heat slapped her like a sheet of tin. She had difficulty seeing in daytime; at night she was almost blind. There was light in the stores, but what they displayed Bessie could not make out. Passers-by bumped into her, and Bessie regretted that she didn't have a cane. Nevertheless, she began to walk along, close to the windows. She passed a drugstore, a bakery, a shop of rugs, a funeral parlor, but nowhere was there a sign of a hardware store. Bessie continued on her way. Her strength was ebbing, but she was determined not to give up. What should a person do when her key was broken off—die? Perhaps apply to the police. There might be some institution that took care of such cases. But where?

There must have been an accident. The sidewalk was crowded with spectators. Police cars and an ambulance blocked the street. Someone sprayed the asphalt with a hose, probably cleaning away the blood. It occurred to Bessie that the eyes of the onlookers gleamed with an uncanny satisfaction. They enjoy other people's misfortunes, she thought. It is their only comfort in this miserable city. No, she wouldn't find anybody to help her.

She had come to a church. A few steps led to the closed door, which was protected by an overhang and darkened by shadows. Bessie was barely able to sit down. Her knees wobbled. Her shoes had begun to pinch in the toes and above the heels. A bone in her corset broke and cut into her flesh. "Well, all the Powers of Evil are upon me tonight." Hunger mixed with nausea gnawed at her. An acid fluid came up to her mouth. "Father in Heaven, it's my end." She remembered the Yiddish proverb "If one lives without a reckoning, one dies without confession." She had even neglected to write her will.

Bessie must have dozed off, because when she opened her eyes there was a late-night stillness, the street half-empty and darkened. Store windows were no longer lit. The heat had evaporated and she felt chilly under her dress. For a moment she thought that her pocketbook had been stolen, but it lay on a step below her, where it had probably slipped. Bessie tried to stretch out her hand for it; her arm was numb. Her head, which rested against the wall, felt as heavy as a stone. Her legs had become wooden. Her ears seemed to be filled with water. She lifted one of her eyelids and saw the moon. It hovered low in the sky over a flat roof, and near it twinkled a greenish star. Bessie gaped. She had almost forgotten that there was a sky, a moon, stars. Years had passed and she never looked up—always down. Her windows were hung with draperies so that the spies across the street could not see her. Well, if there was a sky, perhaps there was also a God, angels, Paradise. Where else did the souls of her parents rest? And where was Sam now? She, Bessie, had abandoned all her duties. She never visited Sam's grave in the cemetery. She didn't even light a candle on the anniversary of his death. She was so steeped in wrangling with the lower powers that she did not remember the higher ones. For the first time in years, Bessie felt the need to recite a prayer. The Almighty would have mercy on her even though she did not deserve it. Father and Mother might intercede for her on high. Some Hebrew words hung on the tip of her tongue, but she could not recall them. Then she remembered. "Hear, O Israel."[3] But what followed? "God forgive me," Bessie said. "I deserve everything that falls on me."

It became even quieter and cooler. Traffic lights changed from red to green, but a car rarely passed. From somewhere a Negro appeared. He staggered. He stopped not far from Bessie and turned his eyes to her. Then he walked

---

3 **"Hear, O Israel.":** the beginning of a common Jewish prayer

on. Bessie knew that her bag was full of important documents, but for the first time she did not care about her property. Sam had left a fortune; it all had gone for naught. She continued to save for her old age as if she were still young. "How old am I?" Bessie asked herself. "What have I accomplished in all these years? Why didn't I go somewhere, enjoy my money, help somebody?" Something in her laughed. "I was possessed, completely not myself. How else can it be explained?" Bessie was astounded. She felt as if she had awakened from a long sleep. The broken key had opened a door in her brain that had shut when Sam died.

The moon had shifted to the other side of the roof—unusually large, red, its face **obliterated**. It was almost cold now. Bessie shivered. She realized that she could easily get pneumonia, but the fear of death was gone, along with her fear of being homeless. Fresh breezes drifted from the Hudson River. New stars appeared in the sky. A black cat approached from the other side of the street. For a while, it stood on the edge of the sidewalk and its green eyes looked straight at Bessie. Then slowly and cautiously it drew near. For years Bessie had hated all animals—dogs, cats, pigeons, even sparrows. They carried sicknesses. They made everything filthy. Bessie believed that there was a demon in every cat. She especially dreaded an encounter with a black cat, which was always an **omen** of evil. But now Bessie felt love for this creature that had no home, no possessions, no doors or keys, and lived on God's bounty. Before the cat neared Bessie, it smelled her bag. Then it began to rub its back on her leg, lifting up its tail and meowing. The poor thing is hungry. I wish I could give her something. How can one hate a creature like this, Bessie wondered. O Mother of mine, I was bewitched, bewitched. I'll begin a new life. A treacherous thought ran through her mind: perhaps remarry?

The night did not pass without adventure. Once, Bessie saw a white butterfly in the air. It hovered for a while over a parked car and then took off. Bessie knew it was a soul of a newborn baby, since real butterflies do not fly after dark. Another time, she wakened to see a ball of fire, a kind of lit-up soap bubble, soar from one roof to another and sink behind it. She was aware that what she saw was the spirit of someone who had just died.

*B*essie had fallen asleep. She woke up with a start. It was daybreak. From the side of Central Park the sun rose. Bessie could not see it from here, but on Broadway the sky became pink and reddish. On the building to the left, flames kindled in the windows; the panes ran and blinked like the portholes of a ship. A pigeon landed nearby. It hopped on its

obliterated: wiped away; destroyed

omen: sign or symbol of future events

little red feet and pecked into something that might have been a dirty piece of stale bread or dried mud. Bessie was baffled. How do these birds live? Where do they sleep at night? And how can they survive the rains, the cold, the snow? I will go home, Bessie decided. People will not leave me in the streets.

Getting up was a torment. Her body seemed glued to the step on which she sat. Her back ached and her legs tingled. Nevertheless, she began to walk slowly toward home. She inhaled the moist morning air. It smelled of grass and coffee. She was no longer alone. From the side streets men and women emerged. They were going to work. They bought newspapers at the stand and went down into the subway. They were silent and strangely peaceful, as if they, too, had gone through a night of soul-searching and come out of it cleansed. When do they get up if they are already on their way to work now, Bessie marveled. No, not all in this neighborhood were gangsters and murderers. One young man even nodded good morning to Bessie. She tried to smile at him, realizing she had forgotten that feminine gesture she knew so well in her youth; it was almost the first lesson her mother had taught her.

She reached her building, and outside stood the Irish super, her deadly enemy. He was talking to the garbage collectors. He was a giant of a man, with a short nose, a long upper lip, sunken cheeks, and a pointed chin. His yellow hair covered a bald spot. He gave Bessie a startled look. "What's the matter, Grandma?"

Stuttering, Bessie told him what had happened to her. She showed him the handle of the key she had clutched in her hand all night.

"Mother of God!" he called out.

"What shall I do?" Bessie asked.

"I will open your door."

"But you don't have a passkey."

"We have to be able to open all doors in case of fire."

The super disappeared into his own apartment for a few minutes, then he came out with some tools and a bunch of keys on a large ring. He went up in the elevator with Bessie. The bag of food still stood on the threshold, but it looked depleted. The super busied himself at the lock. He asked, "What are these cards?"

Bessie did not answer.

"Why didn't you come to me and tell me what happened? To be roaming around all night at your age—my God!" As he poked with his tools, a door opened and a little woman in a housecoat and slippers, her hair bleached and done up in curlers, came out. She said, "What happened to you? Every time I opened the door, I saw this bag. I took out your butter and milk and put them in my refrigerator."

Bessie could barely restrain her tears. "O my good people," she said. "I didn't know that . . ."

The super pulled out the other half of Bessie's key. He worked a little longer. He turned a key and the door opened. The cards fell down. He entered the hallway with Bessie and she sensed the musty odor of an apartment that has not been lived in for a long time. The super said, "Next time, if something like this happens call me. That's what I'm here for."

Bessie wanted to give him a tip, but her hands were too weak to open her bag. The neighbor woman brought in the milk and butter. Bessie went into her bedroom and lay down on the bed. There was a pressure on her breast and she felt like vomiting. Something heavy vibrated up from her feet to her chest. Bessie listened to it without alarm, only curious about the whims of the body; the super and the neighbor talked, and Bessie could not make out what they were saying. The same thing had happened to her over thirty years ago when she had been given anesthesia in the hospital before an operation—the doctor and the nurse were talking but their voices seemed to come from far away and in a strange language.

Soon there was silence, and Sam appeared. It was neither day nor night—a strange twilight. In her dream, Bessie knew that Sam was dead but that in some **clandestine** way he had managed to get away from the grave and visit her. He was feeble and embarrassed. He could not speak. They wandered through a space without a sky, without earth, a tunnel full of debris—the wreckage of a nameless structure—a corridor dark and winding, yet somehow familiar. They came to a region where two mountains met, and the passage between shone like sunset or sunrise. They stood there hesitating and even a little ashamed. It was like that night of their honeymoon when they went to Ellenville in the Catskills and were let by the hotel owner into their bridal suite. She heard the same words he had said to them then, in the same voice and intonation: "You don't need no key here. Just enter—and *mazel tov.*"[4]

clandestine: secretive

---

4 *mazel tov:* a Hebrew expression for "best wishes" or "congratulations"

Read and Think Critically

Describe, Infer, Analyze

1. **SYMBOLISM** The key takes on symbolic significance in this story. Explain the **symbolism** of the key.

2. In literature, an **epiphany** refers to an event, sometimes mystical in nature, in which a **character** changes in profound ways due to the revelation of a simple yet powerful truth. Use a chart like the one below to describe the epiphany that Bessie experiences. First describe Bessie before the epiphany, then describe the revelation she experiences, and finally describe her after the event.

Before	Epiphany	After

3. Reread the first few paragraphs of the story. What does the text explicitly say about Bessie? Based upon this description, what can you infer about Bessie's character?

4. Critics often say Singer's work explores the weaknesses in human nature. What human weaknesses does Singer expose in this short story?

5. **THE AUTHOR'S STYLE** In this story, Singer shows the power of naming: what we choose to name something affects what we believe about it. For example, in the beginning of the story, when Bessie is fearful and paranoid, she refers to "Evil Powers." Analyze the changes in Bessie's language as her view of the world changes.

Before You Read

Alice Walker 1944–

About the Author

Born in Eatonton, Georgia, as the eighth child of sharecroppers, Alice Walker grew up poor in material goods but rich in values. After a long, hard day of labor in the fields, her mother worked in the family's backyard garden. Seeing this convinced the author that beauty is worth searching for, laboring for, and celebrating. She began to read and write poetry at the age of eight.

Valedictorian of her high school class, Walker attended Sarah Lawrence College in New York, from which she traveled to Africa as an exchange student. After graduation, she moved to Jackson, Mississippi, and married a Jewish civil rights lawyer whom she later divorced. They were said to have been the first married interracial couple in that city in 1967.

Known for using her writing as a vehicle for commentary on issues such as civil rights, human rights, and nuclear war, Walker has also worked to rediscover and honor African American authors who went before her. Perhaps her best known work is her novel *The Color Purple*, for which she won the Pulitzer Prize in 1983; it was made into a film in 1985.

****

The Author's Style

Walker's fiction reflects her awareness that racism and its appalling social impact take a particular toll on females. Walker addresses this issue in numerous stories in *You Can't Keep a Good Woman Down* and *In Love and Trouble*, in her acclaimed novel *The Color Purple* (written in the form of letters in black English vernacular), and in the essays in *In Search of Our Mothers' Gardens*. She refers to herself as a black feminist, or "womanist," and her stories involve girls and women who face injustice and struggle for change. The focus in "The Flowers," the story you are about to read, is on a single female figure. This approach follows the example of Zora Neale Hurston, an earlier African American woman writer whose life and work Walker finds inspirational.

Several of Walker's stories use objects or artifacts to illustrate her themes, the most familiar of which is a family quilt in the story "Everyday Use." Her use of key metaphors and striking imagery is also consistent with her work as a poet. Walker's tone is often one of irony shaded with sarcasm. Frequently, this is because her central character has begun to realize that she has been mistreated and that early signs of that were everywhere.

The Flowers

ALICE WALKER

 LITERARY LENS: MOOD Think about how the **mood** changes over the course of the story.

$\mathcal{I}$t seemed to Myop as she skipped lightly from hen house to pigpen to smokehouse that the days had never been as beautiful as these. The air held a keenness that made her nose twitch. The harvesting of the corn and cotton, peanuts and squash, made each day a golden surprise that caused excited little tremors to run up her jaws.

Myop carried a short, knobby stick. She struck out at random at chickens she liked, and worked out the beat of a song on the fence around the pigpen. She felt light and good in the warm sun. She was ten, and nothing existed for her but her song, the stick clutched in her dark brown hand, and the tat-de-ta-ta-ta of accompaniment.

Turning her back on the rusty boards of her family's sharecropper cabin, Myop walked along the fence till it ran into the stream made by the spring. Around the spring, where the family got drinking water, silver ferns and wildflowers grew. Along the shallow banks pigs rooted. Myop watched the tiny white bubbles disrupt the thin black scale of soil and the water that silently rose and slid away down the stream.

She had explored the woods behind the house many times. Often, in late autumn, her mother took her to gather nuts among the fallen leaves. Today she made her own path, bouncing this way and that way, vaguely keeping an eye out for snakes. She found, in addition to various common but pretty ferns and leaves, an armful of strange blue flowers with velvety ridges and a sweetsuds bush full of the brown, fragrant buds.

laden:
loaded;
burdened

By twelve o'clock, her arms **laden** with sprigs of her findings, she was a mile or more from home. She had often been as far before, but the strangeness of the land made it not as pleasant as her usual haunts. It seemed gloomy in the little cove in which she found herself. The air was damp, the silence close and deep.

Myop began to circle back to the house, back to the peacefulness of the morning. It was then she stepped smack into his eyes. Her heel became lodged in the broken ridge between brow and nose, and she reached down quickly, unafraid, to free herself. It was only when she saw his naked grin that she gave a little yelp of surprise.

He had been a tall man. From feet to neck covered a long space. His head lay beside him. When she pushed back the leaves and layers of earth and debris Myop saw that he'd had large white teeth, all of them cracked or broken, long fingers, and very big bones. All his clothes had rotted away except some threads of blue denim from his overalls. The buckles of the overalls had turned green.

Myop gazed around the spot with interest. Very near where she'd stepped into the head was a wild pink rose. As she picked it to add to her bundle she noticed a raised mound, a ring, around the rose's root. It was the rotted remains of a noose, a bit of shredding plowline, now blending benignly into the soil. Around an overhanging limb of a great spreading oak clung another piece. Frayed, rotted, bleached, and frazzled—barely there— but spinning restlessly in the breeze. Myop laid down her flowers.

And the summer was over.

Read and Think Critically

Explain, Interpret, Analyze

1. **MOOD** Readers experience a very abrupt break in this story. Identify where the break comes, describe what it does to the **mood** of the story, and explain how you responded to it.

2. What **foreshadowing** of the ending did you encounter? Cite examples from the text.

3. Why do you think Myop lays down her flowers?

4. How do you **interpret** the last line of the story: "And the summer was over"?

5. Walker has written, "Black women are called, in the folklore that so aptly identifies one's status in society, the 'mules of the world' because we have been handed the burdens that everyone else—*everyone* else—refused to carry." Based on what you can glean about Myop, what burdens do you think she will have to carry in life?

6. **THE AUTHOR'S STYLE** The work of Walker, who is a poet as well as a prose writer, is known for its rich **imagery**. Analyze the use of imagery in the story by picking the image from "The Flowers" that you think is the most memorable and telling how it contributes to the overall success of the story.

Before You Read

Tim O'Brien 1946–

About the Author

It has been said that in the Vietnam era, those in the White House and Pentagon who sent troops to Vietnam were concerned about the possibility of antiwar protests, but they couldn't have imagined the power of the literature written after the war. Tim O'Brien, who grew up in Minnesota, is an important contributor to that literature.

O'Brien admits his contributions stem from cowardice. In 1968, he graduated from Macalester College, where he had written antiwar editorials for the college newspaper and knocked on doors seeking support for the presidential candidacy of Eugene McCarthy, who opposed the war. After graduation he received his draft notice and intended to flee to

Canada but stopped just yards short of the border. He told a reporter, "My conscience told me to run, but I was ashamed of my conscience, ashamed to be doing the right thing. I was a coward. I went to Vietnam."

Upon his return to the United States, O'Brien attended Harvard University, where he worked on his graduate degree as one of the few student veterans there at the time. Since then, O'Brien has published many books and articles, including the novel *Going After Cacciato,* which won the National Book Award.

****

The Author's Style

O'Brien's experiences in the Vietnam War have inspired some of his best writing, including the novels *Going After Cacciato* and *The Things They Carried.* Both are composed of linked stories. The fear, confusion, and panic of combat make O'Brien's characters wish for safety and peace, and they often find themselves absorbed in nightmares and fantasies. These mental states are far from irresponsible attempts to escape reality and duty; instead, they are often shown to be unconscious or unavoidable strategies for survival.

O'Brien reveals his soldiers' humanity by showing their vulnerability to the brutality of war. He also shows us their survival strategies, including intentional and unintentional mental tricks for making it through the day. The plight of combat soldiers is at times so bleak that it seems like a bad joke. The soldiers often respond with irony and black humor of their own.

O'Brien's writing is often simple and direct, conveying the facts and ironic truths of the soldiers' lives. Frequently it develops through calculated repetition and simple figures of speech. At times his prose is reminiscent of Hemingway's.

Where Have You Gone, Charming Billy?

TIM O'BRIEN

🔍 **LITERARY LENS: SIMILES** The use of **similes** does much to establish the tone and the meaning of a story. Watch for them in this story.

$\mathcal{T}$he platoon of twenty-six soldiers moved slowly in the dark, single file, not talking.

One by one, like sheep in a dream, they passed through the hedgerow,[1] crossed quietly over a meadow and came down to the rice paddy.[2] There they stopped. Their leader knelt down, motioning with his hand, and one by one the other soldiers squatted in the shadows, vanishing in the primitive stealth of warfare. For a long time they did not move. Except for the sounds of their breathing, . . . the twenty-six men were very quiet: some of them excited by the adventure, some of them afraid, some of them exhausted from the long night march, some of them looking forward to reaching the sea where they would be safe. At the rear of

---

1 **hedgerow:** a thick hedge separating sections of land

2 **rice paddy:** a waterlogged field where rice is grown

the column, Private First Class Paul Berlin lay quietly with his forehead resting on the black plastic stock of his rifle, his eyes closed. He was pretending he was not in the war, pretending he had not watched Billy Boy Watkins die of a heart attack that afternoon. He was pretending he was a boy again, camping with his father in the midnight summer along the Des Moines River. In the dark, with his eyes pinched shut, he pretended. He pretended that when he opened his eyes, his father would be there by the campfire and they would talk softly about whatever came to mind and then roll into their sleeping bags, and that later they'd wake up and it would be morning and there would not be a war, and that Billy Boy Watkins had not died of a heart attack that afternoon. He pretended he was not a soldier.

In the morning, when they reached the sea, it would be better. The hot afternoon would be over, he would bathe in the sea and he would forget how frightened he had been on his first day at the war. The second day would not be so bad. He would learn.

There was a sound beside him, a movement and then a breathed: "Hey!"

He opened his eyes, shivering as if emerging from a deep nightmare.

"Hey!" a shadow whispered. "We're *moving*. . . . Get up."

"Okay."

"You sleepin', or something?"

"No." He could not make out the soldier's face. With clumsy, concrete hands he clawed for his rifle, found it, found his helmet.

The soldier-shadow grunted. "You got a lot to learn, buddy. I'd shoot you if I thought you was sleepin'. Let's go."

Private First Class Paul Berlin blinked.

Ahead of him, silhouetted against the sky, he saw the string of soldiers wading into the flat paddy, the black outline of their shoulders and packs and weapons. He was comfortable. He did not want to move. But he was afraid, for it was his first night at the war, so he hurried to catch up, stumbling once, scraping his knee, groping as though blind; his boots sank into the thick paddy water and he smelled it all around him. He would tell his mother how it smelled: mud and algae and cattle manure and chlorophyll,[3] decay, breeding mosquitoes and leeches as big as mice, the **fecund** warmth of the paddy waters rising up to his cut knee. But he would not tell how frightened he had been.

Once they reached the sea, things would be better. They would have their rear guarded by three thousand miles of ocean, and they would swim and

fecund:
fertile

---

3 chlorophyll: the green pigment found in plants

COME A LITTLE CLOSER, MICHAEL BROSTOWITZ, 1997, THE NATIONAL VIETNAM VETERANS ART MUSEUM

dive into the breakers and hunt crayfish and smell the salt, and they would be safe.

He followed the shadow of the man in front of him. It was a clear night. Already the Southern Cross[4] was out. And other stars he could not yet name—soon, he thought, he would learn their names. And puffy night

4 **Southern Cross:** a cross-shaped constellation of stars

clouds. There was not yet a moon. Wading through the paddy, his boots made sleepy, sloshing sounds, like a lullaby, and he tried not to think. Though he was afraid, he now knew that fear came in many degrees and types and peculiar categories, and he knew that his fear now was not so bad as it had been in the hot afternoon, when poor Billy Boy Watkins got killed by a heart attack. His fear now was **diffuse** and unformed: ghosts in the tree line, nighttime fears of a child, a boogieman in the closet that his father would open to show empty, saying "See? Nothing there, champ. Now you can sleep." In the afternoon it had been worse; the fear had been bundled and tight and he'd been on his hands and knees, crawling like an insect, an ant escaping a giant's footsteps and thinking nothing, brain flopping like wet cement in a mixer, not thinking at all, watching while Billy Boy Watkins died.

Now as he stepped out of the paddy onto a narrow dirt path, now the fear was mostly the fear of being so terribly afraid again.

He tried not to think.

There were tricks he'd learned to keep from thinking. Counting: He counted his steps, concentrating on the numbers, pretending that the steps were dollar bills and that each step through the night made him richer and richer, so that soon he would become a wealthy man, and he kept counting and considered the ways he might spend the money after the war and what he would do. He would look his father in the eye and shrug and say, "It was pretty bad at first, but I learned a lot and I got used to it." Then he would tell his father the story of Billy Boy Watkins. But he would never let on how frightened he had been. "Not so bad," he would say instead, making his father feel proud.

Songs, another trick to stop from thinking: *Where have you gone, Billy Boy, Billy Boy, Oh, where have you gone, charming Billy? I have gone to seek a wife, she's the joy of my life, but she's a young thing and cannot leave her mother,* and other songs that he sang in his thoughts as he walked toward the sea. And when he reached the sea he would dig a deep hole in the sand and he would sleep like the high clouds, and he would not be afraid any more.

diffuse: broad; nonspecific

> *T*hough he was afraid, he now knew that fear came in many degrees and types and peculiar categories, and he knew that his fear now was not so bad as it had been in the hot afternoon, when poor Billy Boy Watkins got killed by a heart attack.

$\mathscr{T}$he moon came out. Pale and shrunken to the size of a dime. The helmet was heavy on his head. In the morning he would adjust the leather binding. He would clean his rifle, too. Even though he had been frightened to shoot it during the hot afternoon, he would carefully clean the breech and the muzzle and the ammunition so that next time he would be ready and not so afraid. In the morning, when they reached the sea, he would begin to make friends with some of the other soldiers. He would learn their names and laugh at their jokes. Then when the war was over he would have war buddies, and he would write to them once in a while and exchange memories.

Walking, sleeping in his walking, he felt better. He watched the moon come higher.

Once they skirted a sleeping village. The smells again—straw, cattle, mildew. The men were quiet. On the far side of the village, buried in the dark smells, a dog barked. The graveyard had a perfumy smell. A nice place to spend the night, he thought. The mounds would make fine battlements, and the smell was nice and the place was quiet. But they went on, passing through a hedgerow and across another paddy and east toward the sea.

He walked carefully. He remembered what he'd been taught: Stay off the center of the path, for that was where the land mines and booby traps were planted, where stupid and lazy soldiers like to walk. Stay alert, he'd been taught. Better alert than **inert**. Ag-ile, mo-bile, hos-tile.[5] He wished he'd paid better attention to the training. He could not remember what they'd said about how to stop being afraid; they hadn't given any lessons in courage—not that he could remember—and they hadn't mentioned how Billy Boy Watkins would die of a heart attack, his face turning pale and the veins popping out.

inert: unable to move

Private First Class Paul Berlin walked carefully.

Stretching ahead of him like dark beads on an invisible chain, the string of shadow-soldiers whose names he did not yet know moved with the silence and slow grace of smoke. Now and again moonlight was reflected off a machine gun or a wrist watch. But mostly the soldiers were quiet and hidden and far-away-seeming in a peaceful night, strangers on a long street, and he felt quite separate from them, as if trailing behind like the caboose on a night train, pulled along by inertia, sleepwalking, an afterthought to the war.

---

5 **Ag-ile, mo-bile, hos-tile:** a chant reminding soldiers to be light on their feet, ready to move, and aggressive

So he walked carefully, counting his steps. When he had counted to three thousand, four hundred and eighty-five, the column stopped.

One by one the soldiers knelt or squatted down.

*T*he grass along the path was wet. Private First Class Paul Berlin lay back and turned his head so that he could lick at the dew with his eyes closed, another trick to forget the war. He might have slept. "I *wasn't* afraid," he was screaming or dreaming, facing his father's stern eyes. "I wasn't afraid," he was saying. When he opened his eyes, a soldier was sitting beside him, quietly chewing a stick of Doublemint gum.

"You sleepin' again?" the soldier whispered.

"No," said Private First Class Paul Berlin. . . .

The soldier grunted, chewing his gum. Then he twisted the cap off his canteen, took a swallow and handed it through the dark.

"Take some," he whispered.

"Thanks."

"You're the new guy?"

"Yes." He did not want to admit it, being new to the war.

The soldier grunted and handed him a stick of gum. "Chew it quiet— okay? Don't blow no bubbles or nothing."

"Thanks. I won't." He could not make out the man's face in the shadows.

They sat still and Private First Class Paul Berlin chewed the gum until all the sugars were gone; then the soldier said, "Bad day today, buddy."

Private First Class Paul Berlin nodded wisely, but he did not speak.

"Don't think it's always so bad," the soldier whispered. "I don't wanna scare you. You'll get used to it soon enough. . . . They been fighting wars a long time, and you get used to it."

"Yeah."

"You will."

They were quiet awhile. And the night was quiet, no crickets or birds, and it was hard to imagine it was truly a war. He searched for the soldier's face but could not find it. It did not matter much. Even if he saw the fellow's face, he would not know the name; and even if he knew the name, it would not matter much.

"Haven't got the time?" the soldier whispered.

"No."

"Rats. . . . Don't matter, really. Goes faster if you don't know the time, anyhow."

"Sure."

"What's your name, buddy?"

"Paul."

"Nice to meet ya," he said, and in the dark beside the path they shook hands. "Mine's Toby. Everybody calls me Buffalo, though." The soldier's hand was strangely warm and soft. But it was a very big hand. "Sometimes they just call me Buff," he said.

And again they were quiet. They lay in the grass and waited. The moon was very high now and very bright, and they were waiting for cloud cover.

The soldier suddenly snorted.

"What is it?"

"Nothin'," he said, but then he snorted again. "A bloody heart attack!" the soldier said. "Can't get over it—old Billy Boy croaking from a lousy heart attack. . . . A heart attack—can you believe it?"

The idea of it made Private First Class Paul Berlin smile. He couldn't help it.

"Ever hear of such a thing?"

"Not till now," said Private First Class Paul Berlin, still smiling.

"Me neither," said the soldier in the dark. ". . . Dying of a heart attack. Didn't know him, did you?"

"No."

"Tough as nails."

"Yeah."

"And what happens? A heart attack. Can you imagine it?"

"Yes," said Private First Class Paul Berlin. He wanted to laugh. "I can imagine it." And he imagined it clearly. He giggled—he couldn't help it. He imagined Billy's father opening the telegram: SORRY TO INFORM YOU THAT YOUR SON BILLY BOY WAS YESTERDAY SCARED TO DEATH IN ACTION IN THE REPUBLIC OF VIETNAM, **VALIANTLY SUCCUMBING** TO A HEART ATTACK SUFFERED WHILE UNDER ENORMOUS STRESS, AND IT IS WITH GREATEST SYMPATHY THAT . . . He giggled again. He rolled onto his belly and pressed his face into his arms. His body was shaking with giggles.

The big soldier hissed at him to shut up, but he could not stop giggling and remembering the hot afternoon, and poor Billy Boy, and how they'd been drinking Coca-Cola from bright-red aluminum cans, and how they'd started on the day's march, and how a little while later poor Billy Boy

valiantly: courageously

succumbing: giving in

stepped on the mine, and how it made a tiny little sound—*poof*—and how Billy Boy stood there with his mouth wide-open, looking down at where his foot had been blown off, and how finally Billy Boy sat down very casually, not saying a word, with his foot lying behind him, most of it still in the boot.

He giggled louder—he could not stop. He bit his arm, trying to stifle it, but remembering: "War's over, Billy," the men had said in **consolation**, but Billy Boy got scared and started crying and said he was about to die. "Nonsense," the medic said, Doc Peret, but Billy Boy kept bawling, tightening up, his face going pale and transparent and his veins popping out. Scared stiff. Even when Doc Peret stuck him with morphine,[6] Billy Boy kept crying.

consolation: sympathy; encouragement

"Shut up!" the big soldier hissed, but Private First Class Paul Berlin could not stop. Giggling and remembering, he covered his mouth. His eyes stung, remembering how it was when Billy Boy died of fright.

"Shut up!"

But he could not stop giggling, the same way Billy Boy could not stop bawling that afternoon.

Afterward Doc Peret had explained: "You see, Billy Boy really died of a heart attack. He was scared he was gonna die—so scared, he had himself a heart attack—and that's what really killed him. I seen it before."

So they wrapped Billy in a plastic poncho, his eyes still wide-open and scared stiff, and they carried him over the meadow to a rice paddy, and then when the Medevac helicopter[7] arrived they carried him through the paddy and put him aboard, and the mortar rounds[8] were falling everywhere, and the helicopter pulled up and Billy Boy came tumbling out, falling slowly and then faster, and the paddy water sprayed up as if Billy Boy had just **executed** a long and dangerous dive, as if trying to escape Graves Registration, where he would be tagged and sent home under a flag, dead of a heart attack.

executed: completed

"Shut up, . . . !" the soldier hissed, but Paul Berlin could not stop giggling, remembering: scared to death.

Later they waded in after him, probing for Billy Boy with their rifle butts, elegantly and delicately probing for Billy Boy in the stinking paddy, singing— some of them—*Where have you gone, Billy Boy, Billy Boy, Oh, where have you*

---

6 **morphine:** a drug used to soothe pain and induce calm

7 **Medevac helicopter:** Short for "medical evacuation," this helicopter was used to transport injured soldiers by air to medical facilities.

8 **mortar rounds:** shells fired from small cannons

ON THE ROAD TO CON THIEN, CHARLIE SHOBE, 1980, THE NATIONAL VIETNAM VETERANS ART MUSEUM

gone, charming Billy? Then they found him. Green and covered with algae, his eyes still wide-open and sacred stiff, dead of a heart attack suffered while—

"Shut up, . . . !" the soldier said loudly, shaking him.

But Private First Class Paul Berlin could not stop. The giggles were caught in his throat, drowning him in his own laughter: scared to death like Billy Boy.

Giggling, lying on his back, he saw the moon move, or the clouds moving across the moon. Wounded in action, dead of fright. A fine war story. He would tell it to his father, how Billy Boy had been scared to death, never letting on . . . He could not stop.

The soldier smothered him. He tried to fight back, but he was weak from the giggles.

The moon was under the clouds and the column was moving. The soldier helped him up. "You okay now, buddy?"

"Sure."

"What was so bloody funny?"

"Nothing."

"You can get killed, laughing that way."

"I know. I know that."

"You got to stay calm, buddy." The soldier handed him his rifle. "Half the battle, just staying calm. You'll get better at it," he said. "Come on, now."

He turned away and Private First Class Paul Berlin hurried after him. He was still shivering.

He would do better once he reached the sea, he thought, still smiling a little. A funny war story that he would tell to his father, how Billy Boy Watkins was scared to death. A good joke. But even when he smelled salt and heard the sea, he could not stop being afraid.

Read and Think Critically

Determine, Explain, Analyze

1. **SIMILES** This story contains numerous **similes**, such as "his boots made sleepy, sloshing sounds, like a lullaby." Find several more similes in this story. Determine what each comparison means.

2. Private Berlin's thoughts race wildly back and forth among scenarios of the past, present, and future. Using a chart like the one below, find an example of each. What impact does jumping around in time have on the reader?

Time	Example
Past	*Remembers going camping with his father*
Present	
Future	

3. Reread the imaginary telegram on page 555. Why do you think it makes Private Berlin laugh?

4. Both a chant ("Ag-ile, mo-bile, hos-tile") and the lyrics of the title song are used in this story. Explain what they add to the story.

5. **THE AUTHOR'S STYLE** **Repetition** is a striking feature of this story. For example, the name Private First Class Paul Berlin is repeated several times. And in the second paragraph, a form of the word "pretend" appears six times. Find other examples in the story. Analyze the use of repetition in the story and explain the overall effect.

Before You Read

Raymond Carver 1938–1988

About the Author

Raymond Carver was born in Oregon in 1938 during the postwar era that was a prosperous time for many Americans. For the Carver family, though, life was a tumultuous struggle with problems that included alcoholism, domestic abuse, mental illness, and unemployment. Married at age nineteen, Carver worked at various minimum-wage jobs, including one as a deliveryman. On a delivery one day, he was given a copy of *Poetry* magazine. This gave him a taste for literature, and Carver enrolled at Chico State College in California, where he took a creative writing course and met his mentor, the late author John Gardner. Under Gardner's guidance, Carver founded a college literary magazine and published his first story.

He later studied for a time at the University of Iowa Writers' Workshop but could not afford to finish his master's degree there. Instead he worked as a custodian and filed for bankruptcy several times, but eventually he began publishing stories such as "Will You Please Be Quiet, Please?" included in the 1967 edition of *The Best American Short Stories*. Personal troubles accompanied his professional success, however, including alcoholism, which he overcame in 1977. His short story collections include *What We Talk About When We Talk About Love*, *Cathedral*, and *Where I'm Calling From*. A heavy smoker, he died of lung cancer at the age of 50.

****

The Author's Style

Many of Carver's "minimalist" stories are unusually short with simple plots. In reading these stories it is good to look at what's left out—especially when the narrator is a main character. Carver's characters are often working-class people who have trouble expressing their feelings. Even so, Carver develops them with empathy and respect, writing stories about what happens when something in their lives is broken beyond repair. His characters' situations are often pathetic, and because he wants us to see how things got that way, he frequently has them attempt to tell their own stories.

Carver's use of concrete words and very short, declarative sentences make for an unemotional style many have compared to that of Hemingway. Typically, Carver's characters make simple observations that suggest there are unanswered questions and an inclination to cut off any discussion that might lead to unwelcome explanations. It is also typical of Carver to give us endings that are neither clear nor particularly happy—not necessarily "the end" of the characters' stories at all. Instead, he gives us a sense of their lives at a brief, crucial moment when everything else that has happened becomes clear.

Everything
Stuck to Him

RAYMOND CARVER

 LITERARY LENS: MINIMALISM As you read, consider the aspects of the story that reflect the sparse style of **minimalism**.

*S*he's in Milan for Christmas and wants to know what it was like when she was a kid.

Tell me, she says. Tell me what it was like when I was a kid. She sips Strega, waits, eyes him closely.

She is a cool, slim, attractive girl, a survivor from top to bottom.

That was a long time ago. That was twenty years ago, he says.

You can remember, she says. Go on.

What do you want to hear? he says. What else can I tell you? I could tell you about something that happened when you were a baby. It involves you, he says. But only in a minor way.

Tell me, she says. But first fix us another so you won't have to stop in the middle.

> The baby came along in late November during a cold spell that just happened to coincide with the peak of the waterfowl season. The boy loved to hunt, you see. That's part of it.

He comes back from the kitchen with drinks, settles into his chair, begins.

They were kids themselves, but they were crazy in love, this eighteen-year-old boy and this seventeen-year-old girl when they married. Not all that long afterwards they had a daughter.

The baby came along in late November during a cold spell that just happened to coincide with the peak of the waterfowl season. The boy loved to hunt, you see. That's part of it.

The boy and girl, husband and wife, father and mother, they lived in a little apartment under a dentist's office. Each night they cleaned the dentist's place upstairs in exchange for rent and utilities. In summer they were expected to maintain the lawn and the flowers. In winter the boy shoveled snow and spread rock salt on the walks. Are you still with me? Are you getting the picture?

I am, she says.

That's good, he says. So one day the dentist finds out they were using his letterhead for their personal correspondence. But that's another story.

He gets up from his chair and looks out the window. He sees the tile rooftops and the snow that is falling steadily on them.

Tell the story, she says.

The two kids were very much in love. On top of this they had great ambitions. They were always talking about the things they were going to do and the places they were going to go.

Now the boy and girl slept in the bedroom, and the baby slept in the living room. Let's say the baby was about three months old and had only just begun to sleep through the night.

On this one Saturday night after finishing his work upstairs, the boy stayed in the dentist's office and called an old hunting friend of his father's.

Carl, he said when the man picked up the receiver, believe it or not, I'm a father.

Congratulations, Carl said. How is the wife?

She's fine, Carl. Everybody's fine.

That's good, Carl said, I'm glad to hear it. But if you called about going hunting, I'll tell you something. The geese are flying to beat the band. I don't think I've ever seen so many. Got five today. Going back in the morning, so come along if you want to.

I want to, the boy said.

The boy hung up the telephone and went downstairs to tell the girl. She watched while he laid out his things. Hunting coat, shell bag, boots, socks, hunting cap, long underwear, pump gun.

What time will you be back? the girl said.

Probably around noon, the boy said. But maybe as late as six o'clock. Would that be too late?

The boy was a little in love with Sally, just as he was a little in love with Betsy, who was another sister the girl had.

It's fine, she said. The baby and I will get along fine. You go and have some fun. When you get back, we'll dress the baby up and go visit Sally.

The boy said, Sounds like a good idea.

Sally was the girl's sister. She was striking. I don't know if you've seen pictures of her. The boy was a little in love with Sally, just as he was a little in love with Betsy, who was another sister the girl had. The boy used to say to the girl, If we weren't married, I could go for Sally.

What about Betsy? the girl used to say. I hate to admit it, but I truly feel she's better looking than Sally and me. What about Betsy?

Betsy too, the boy used to say.

After dinner he turned up the furnace and helped her bathe the baby. He marveled again at the infant who had half his features and half the girl's. He powdered the tiny body. He powdered between fingers and toes.

He emptied the bath into the sink and went upstairs to check the air. It was overcast and cold. The grass, what there was of it, looked like canvas, stiff and gray under the street light.

Snow lay in piles beside the walk. A car went by. He heard sand under the tires. He let himself imagine what it might be like tomorrow, geese beating the air over his head, shotgun plunging against his shoulder.

Then he locked the door and went downstairs.

In bed they tried to read. But both of them fell asleep, she first, letting the magazine sink to the quilt.

*I*t was the baby's cries that woke him up.

The light was on out there, and the girl was standing next to the crib rocking the baby in her arms. She put the baby down, turned out the light, and came back to the bed.

He heard the baby cry. This time the girl stayed where she was. The baby cried fitfully and stopped. The boy listened, then dozed. But the baby's cries woke him again. The living room light was burning. He sat up and turned on the lamp.

I don't know what's wrong, the girl said, walking back and forth with the baby. I've changed her and fed her, but she keeps on crying. I'm so tired I'm afraid I might drop her.

You come back to bed, the boy said. I'll hold her for a while.

He got up and took the baby, and the girl went to lie down again.

Just rock her for a few minutes, the girl said from the bedroom. Maybe she'll go back to sleep.

The boy sat on the sofa and held the baby. He jiggled it in his lap until he got its eyes to close, his own eyes closing right along. He rose carefully and put the baby back in the crib.

It was a quarter to four, which gave him forty-five minutes. He crawled into bed and dropped off. But a few minutes later the baby was crying again, and this time they both got up.

The boy did a terrible thing. He swore.

For God's sake, what's the matter with you? The girl said to the boy. Maybe she's sick or something. Maybe we shouldn't have given her the bath.

The boy picked up the baby. The baby kicked its feet and smiled.

Look, the boy said, I really don't think there's anything wrong with her.

How do you know that? the girl said. Here, let me have her. I know I ought to give her something, but I don't know what it's supposed to be.

The girl put the baby down again. The boy and the girl looked at the baby, and the baby began to cry.

The girl took the baby. Baby, baby, the girl said with tears in her eyes.

Probably it's something on her stomach, the boy said.

The girl didn't answer. She went on rocking the baby, paying no attention to the boy.

The boy waited. He went to the kitchen and put on water for coffee. He drew his woolen underwear on over his shorts and T-shirt, buttoned up, then got into his clothes.

What are you doing? the girl said.

Going hunting, the boy said.

I don't think you should, she said. I don't want to be left alone with her like this.

Carl's planning on me going, the boy said. We've planned it.

I don't care about what you and Carl planned, she said. And I don't care about Carl, either. I don't even know Carl.

You've met Carl before. You know him, the boy said. What do you mean you don't know him?

That's not the point and you know it, the girl said.

What is the point? the boy said. The point is we planned it.

The girl said, I'm your wife. This is your baby. She's sick or something. Look at her. Why else is she crying?

I know you're my wife, the boy said.

The girl began to cry. She put the baby back in the crib. But the baby started up again. The girl dried her eyes on the sleeve of her nightgown and picked the baby up.

The boy laced up his boots. He put on his shirt, his sweater, his coat. The kettle whistled on the stove in the kitchen.

You're going to have to choose, the girl said. Carl or us. I mean it.

What do you mean? the boy said.

You heard what I said, the girl said. If you want a family, you're going to have to choose.

They stared at each other. Then the boy took up his hunting gear and went outside. He started the car. He went around to the car windows and, making a job of it, scraped away the ice.

He turned off the motor and sat awhile. And then he got out and went back inside.

The living-room light was on. The girl was asleep on the bed. The baby was asleep beside her.

The boy took off his boots. Then he took off everything else. In his socks and his long underwear, he sat on the sofa and read the Sunday paper.

The girl and the baby slept on. After a while, the boy went to the kitchen and started frying bacon.

The girl came out in her robe and put her arms around the boy.

Hey, the boy said.

I'm sorry, the girl said.

It's all right, the boy said.

I didn't mean to snap like that.

It was my fault, he said.

You sit down, the girl said. How does a waffle sound with bacon?

Sounds great, the boy said.

She took the bacon out of the pan and made waffle batter. He sat at the table and watched her move around the kitchen.

She put a plate in front of him with bacon, a waffle. He spread butter and poured syrup. But when he started to cut, he turned the plate into his lap.

I don't believe it, he said, jumping up from the table.

If you could see yourself, the girl said.

The boy looked down at himself, at everything stuck to his underwear.

I was starved, he said, shaking his head.

You were starved, she said, laughing.

He peeled off the woolen underwear and threw it at the bathroom door. Then he opened his arms and the girl moved into them.

We won't fight anymore, she said.

The boy said, We won't.

*H*e gets up from his chair and refills their glasses.

That's it, he says. End of story. I admit it's not much of a story. I was interested, she says.

He shrugs and carries his drink over to the window. It's dark now but still snowing.

Things change, he says. I don't know how they do. But they do without your realizing it or wanting them to.

Yes, that's true, only— But she does not finish what she started.

She drops the subject. In the window's reflection he sees her study her nails. Then she raises her head. Speaking brightly, she asks if he is going to show her the city, after all.

He says, Put your boots on and let's go.

But he stays by the window, remembering. They had laughed. They had leaned on each other and laughed until the tears had come, while everything else—the cold, and where he'd go in it—was outside, for a while anyway.

Read and Think Critically

Evaluate, Compare, Analyze

1. **MINIMALISM** After he tells the story, the father says, "I admit it's not much of a story." Evaluate this statement in light of the **minimalist** style. In what ways is the statement true of both the minimalist style and this short story? In what ways is this not true of the story?

2. Use a chart like the one below to compare the two **narrators** of this story. How would you describe these two narrators?

Points of Comparison	Frame Narrator	Story-within-the-story Narrator
Narrative **point of view**		
Attitude toward story		
Use of **dialogue**		
Description of **setting**		
Description of **character's** inner thoughts and feelings		

3. Analyze the **title**. What layers of meaning do you think the title might have? Support your ideas with evidence from the text.

4. Near the end of the story, the father says, "Things change . . . I don't know how they do. But they do without your realizing it or wanting them to." What changes do you think he is referring to?

5. **THE AUTHOR'S STYLE** Carver and other minimalist writers were influenced by Hemingway's terse style. Consider the Hemingway quotation below. What do you think makes up some of the seven-eighths of "Everything Stuck to Him" that is hidden or left uncertain?

> ### Hemingway's Principle of the Iceberg
>
> *I always try to write on the principle of the iceberg. There is seven-eighths of it underwater for every part that shows.*
>
> —Ernest Hemingway, *Paris Review*

Before You Read

Bobbie Ann Mason 1940–

About the Author

Bobbie Ann Mason grew up in rural Kentucky on a dairy farm doing chores before sunrise and more after school, but always finding time for her favorite Nancy Drew and Bobbsey Twins books. A shy "homebody," as she describes herself, she learned that it was her journeys away from home that most affected her appreciation of it.

After graduating from the University of Kentucky, Mason moved to New York City and made a living writing for movie magazines. She later received her Ph.D. in literature and moved to the woodlands of northern Pennsylvania with her husband, author Roger Rawlings.

Known particularly as a short story writer, among Mason's best-known works are her short story collection *Shiloh and Other Stories* and her novel *In Country*. In an interview in the book *Passion and Craft*, Mason agreed that she writes about people and places that do not seem very literary, adding, "I have my material, what's been allotted to me. And along with that comes a Southern defensive posture and a desire to reclaim a measure of pride and identity for my people."

****

The Author's Style

Many of Mason's stories deal sympathetically with the changing lives of people from rural Kentucky. Mason frequently writes from the viewpoints of women or girls who are undergoing changes that are confusing but often exhilarating. Her female characters try to understand both family relationships and the changing nature of their own expectations. Often her country people learn from confronting city life or "the mystery of travel."

Mason's prose style is simple and direct. Her characters experience and talk rather than ponder and write. She uses relatively short, declarative sentences that provide efficient descriptions of people and places and allow characters to reveal themselves without her interpretation or judgment.

Her stories reveal cultural differences and fascinating discoveries that her characters need to adjust to and understand. From adolescence on, Mason has followed American popular culture closely, and references to it often appear in her stories. Sometimes characters are inspired by learning how the acceptable way of doing things varies from place to place; sometimes they are confused or defeated. In "Detroit Skyline, 1949," which is both serious and comical, we see not only where people live and how they interact, but also how the adult world can create wonder and confusion for a child.

Detroit Skyline, 1949

BOBBIE ANN MASON

 LITERARY LENS: COMING-OF-AGE STORY In a **coming-of-age story**, the main character is initiated into adulthood through a life-changing experience or by gaining new knowledge about the world. In this story, consider what events cause the protagonist to change her view of life.

When I was nine, my mother took me on a long journey up North, because she wanted me to have a chance to see the tall buildings of Detroit. We lived on a farm in western Kentucky, not far from the U.S. highway that took so many Southerners northward to work in the auto industry just after World War II. We went to visit Aunt Mozelle, Mama's sister, and Uncle Boone Cashon, who had headed north soon after Boone's discharge from the service. They lived in a suburb of Detroit, and my mother had visited them once before. She couldn't get the skyscrapers she had seen out of her mind.

The Brooks bus took all day and all night to get there. On our trip, my mother threw up and a black baby cried all the way. I couldn't sleep for thinking about Detroit. Mama had tried in vain to show me how high the buildings were, pointing at the straight horizon beyond the cornfields. I had the impression that they towered halfway to the moon.

"Don't let the Polacks get you," my father had warned when we left. He had to stay home to milk the cows. My two-year-old brother, Johnny, stayed behind with him.

My aunt and uncle met us in a taxi at the bus station, and before I got a good look at them, they had engulfed me in their arms.

"I wouldn't have knowed you, Peggy Jo," my uncle said. "You was just a little squirt the last time I saw you."

"Don't this beat all?" said Aunt Mozelle. "Boone here could have built us a car by now—and us coming in a taxi."

"We've still got that old plug, but it gets us to town," said Mama.

"How could I build a car?" said Uncle Boone. "All I know is bumpers."

"That's what he does," my aunt said to me. "He puts on bumpers."

"We'll get a car someday soon," Uncle Boone said to his wife.

My uncle was a thin, delicate man with a receding hairline. His speckled skin made me think of the fragile shells of sparrow eggs. My aunt, on the other hand, was stout and tanned, with thick, dark hair draped like wings over her ears. I gazed at my aunt and uncle, trying to match them up with the photograph my mother had shown me.

"Peggy's all worked up over seeing the tall buildings," said Mama as we climbed into the taxi. "The cat's got her tongue."

"It has *not!*"

"I'm afraid we've got bad news," said Aunt Mozelle. "The city buses is on strike and there's no way to get into Detroit."

"Don't say it!" cried Mama. "After we come all this way."

"It's trouble with the unions," said Boone. "But they might start up before y'all go back." He patted my knee and said, "Don't worry, littlun."

"The unions is full of reds," Aunt Mozelle whispered to my mother.

"Would it be safe to go?" Mama asked.

> My uncle was a thin, delicate man with a receding hairline. His speckled skin made me think of the fragile shells of sparrow eggs. My aunt, on the other hand, was stout and tanned, with thick, dark hair draped like wings over her ears.

"We needn't worry," said Aunt Mozelle.

From the window of the squat yellow taxi, driven by a froglike man who grunted, I scrutinized the strange and vast neighborhoods we were passing through. I had never seen so many houses, all laid out in neat rows. The houses were new, and their pastel colors seemed peaceful and alluring. The skyscrapers were still as remote to me as the castles in fairy tales, but these houses were real, and they were nestled next to each other in a thrilling intimacy. I knew at once where I wanted to live when I grew up—in a place like this, with neighbors.

My relatives' house, on a treeless new street, had venetian blinds and glossy hardwood floors. The living room carpet had giant pink roses that made me think you could play hopscotch on them. The guest room had knotty-pine paneling and a sweet-smelling cedar closet. Aunt Mozelle had put His and Her towels in our room. They had dogs on them and were pleasurably soft. At home, all of our washrags came out of detergent boxes, and our towels were faded and thin. The house was grand. And I had never seen my mother sparkling so. When she saw the kitchen, she whirled around happily, like a young girl, forgetting her dizziness on the bus. Aunt Mozelle had a toaster, a Mixmaster, an electric stove, and a large electric clock shaped like a rooster. On the wall, copper-bottomed pans gleamed in a row like golden-eyed cats lined up on a fence.

"Ain't it the berries?" my mother said to me. "Didn't I tell you?"

"Sometimes I have to pinch myself," said my aunt.

Just then, the front door slammed and a tall girl with a ponytail bounded into the house, saying "Hey!" in an offhand manner.

"Corn!" I said timidly, which seemed to perplex her, for she stared at me as though I were some odd sort of pet allowed into the house. This was my cousin Betsy Lou, in bluejeans rolled up halfway to her knees.

"Our kinfolks is here," Aunt Mozelle announced.

"Law, you've growed into a beanpole," said Mama to Betsy Lou.

"Welcome to our fair city, and I hope you don't get polio," Betsy Lou said to me.

"Watch what you're saying!" cried her mother. "You'll scare Peggy Jo."

"I imagine it'll be worse this summer than last," said Mama, looking worried.

"If we're stuck here without a car, you won't be any place to catch polio," Aunt Mozelle said, smiling at me.

"Polio spreads at swimming pools," Betsy Lou said.

"Then I'm not going to any swimming pool," I announced flatly.

Aunt Mozelle fussed around in her splendid kitchen, making dinner. I sat at the table, listening to Mama and her sister talk, in a gentle, flowing way, exchanging news, each stopping now and then to smile at the other in disbelief, or to look at me with pride. I couldn't take my eyes off my aunt, because she looked so much like my mother. She was older and heavier, but they had the same wide smile, the same unaffected laughter. They had similar sharp tips on their upper lips, which they filled in with bright red lipstick.

> *S*uddenly I found myself watching a chubby girl in a lilac piqué playsuit zoom up and down the sidewalk on roller skates.

Mama said, "Boone sure is lucky. He's still young and ain't crippled and has a good job."

"Knock on wood," said Aunt Mozelle, rapping the door facing.

*T*hey had arranged for me to have a playmate, a girl my age who lived in the neighborhood. At home, in the summertime, I did not play with anyone, for the girls I knew at school lived too far away. Suddenly I found myself watching a chubby girl in a lilac **piqué** playsuit zoom up and down the sidewalk on roller skates.

piqué: durable, ribbed fabric

"Come on," she said, "It's not hard."

"I'm coming." Betsy Lou had let me have her old skates, but I had trouble fastening them on my Weather-Bird sandals. I had never been on skates. At home there was no sidewalk. I decided to try skating on one foot, like a kid on a scooter, but the skate came loose.

"Put both of them on," said the girl, laughing at me.

Her name was Sharon Belletieri. She had to spell it for me. She said my name over and over until it sounded absurd. "Peggy Peggy Peggy Peggy Peggy." She made my name sound like "piggy."

"Don't you have a permanent?" she asked.

"No," I said, touching my pigtails. "My hair's in plaits[1] 'cause it's summer."

"Har? Oh, you mean *hair?* Like air?" She waved at the air. She was standing there, perfectly balanced on her skates. She pronounced "hair" with two syllables. *Hayer.* I said something like a cross between *herr* and *harr.*

---

1 **plaits:** braids

Sharon turned and whizzed down the sidewalk, then skidded to a stop at the corner, twisted around, and faced me.

"Are you going to skate or not?" she asked.

$\mathscr{M}$y uncle smoked Old Golds, and he seemed to have excess nervous energy. He was always jumping up from his chair to get something, or to look outside at the thermometer. He had found his name in a newspaper ad recently and had won a free pint of Cunningham's ice cream. My aunt declared that that made him somewhat famous. When I came back that day with the skates, he was sitting on the porch fanning himself with a newspaper. There was a heat wave, he said.

"What did you think of Sharon Belletieri?" he asked.

"She talks funny," I said, sitting down beside him.

"Folks up here all talk funny, I've noticed that too."

Uncle Boone had been a clerk in the war. He told me about the time he had spent in the Pacific theater, sailing around on a battleship, looking for Japs.

"Me and some buddies went to a Pacific island where there was a tribe of people with little tails," he said.

"Don't believe a word he says," said my aunt, who had been listening.

"It's true," said Uncle Boone. "Cross my heart and hope to die." He solemnly crossed his hands on his chest, then looked at his watch and said abruptly to me, "What do you think of Gorgeous George?"[2]

"I don't know."

"How about Howdy Doody?"[3]

"Who's Howdy Doody?"

"This child don't know nothing," he said to my aunt. "She's been raised with a bunch of country hicks."

"He's fooling," said Aunt Mozelle. "Go ahead and show her, Boone, for gosh sakes. Don't keep it a secret."

He was talking about television. I hadn't noticed the set in the living room because it had a sliding cover over the screen. It was a ten-inch table model with an upholstered sound box in a rosewood cabinet.

---

2 **Gorgeous George:** George Wagner (1915–1963), professional wrestler known for his theatrical performances and outrageous fashion sense

3 **Howdy Doody:** a cowboy puppet who starred in the television show *Howdy Doody*

AMERICAN LANDSCAPE, CHARLES SHEELER, 1930, THE MUSEUM OF MODERN ART

"We've never seen a television," my mother said.

"This will ruin her," said my aunt. "It's ruined Boone."

Uncle Boone turned on the television set. A wrestling match appeared on the screen, and I could see Gorgeous George flexing his muscles and tossing his curls. The television set resembled our radio. For a long time I was confused, thinking that I would now be able to see all my favorite radio programs.

"It's one of those sets you can look at in normal light and not go blind," my aunt said, to reassure us. "It's called Daylight TV."

"Wait till you see Howdy Doody," said Uncle Boone.

The picture on the television set was not clear. The reception required some imagination, and the pictures frequently dissolved, but I could see Gorgeous George moving across the screen, his curls bouncing. I could see him catch hold of his opponent and wrestle him to the floor, holding him so tight I thought he would choke.

That night, I lay in the cedar-perfumed room, too excited to sleep. I did not know what to expect next. The streetlamps glowed like moons through the venetian blinds, and as I lay there, my guardian angel slowly crept into my mind. In *Uncle Arthur's Bedtime Stories*, there was a picture of a child with his guardian angel hovering over him. It was a man angel, and gigantic, with immense white feathery bird's wings. Probably the boy could never see him because the angel stayed in what drivers of automobiles call a blind spot. I had a feeling that my own guardian angel had accompanied the bus to Michigan and was in the house with me. I imagined him floating above the bus. I knew that my guardian angel was supposed to keep me from harm, but I did not want anyone to know about him. I was very afraid of him. It was a long time before I fell asleep.

In the North, they drank coffee. Aunt Mozelle made a large pot of coffee in the mornings, and she kept it in a Thermos so she could drink coffee throughout the day.

Mama began drinking coffee. "Whew! I'm higher than a kite!" she would say. "I'll be up prowling half the night."

"Little girls shouldn't ought to drink coffee," Uncle Boone said to me more than once. "It turns them black."

"I don't even want any!" I protested. But I did like the enticing smell, which awoke me early in the mornings.

My aunt made waffles with oleomargarine. She kneaded a capsule of yellow dye into the pale margarine.

"It's a law," she told me one morning.

"They don't have that law down home anymore," said Mama. "People's turning to oleo and it's getting so we can't sell butter."

"I guess everybody forgot how it tasted," said Aunt Mozelle.

"I wouldn't be surprised if that business about the dye was a Communist idea," said my uncle. "A buddy of mine at the plant thinks so.

He says they want to make it look like butter. The big companies, they're full of reds now."

"That makes sense to me," said Mama. "Anything to hurt the farmer."

It didn't make sense to me. When they talked about reds, all I could imagine was a bunch of little devils in red suits, carrying pitchforks. I wondered if they were what my uncle had seen in the Pacific, since devils had tails. Everything about the North was confusing. Lunetta Jones, for instance, bewildered me. She came for coffee every morning, after my uncle had left in a car pool. Lunetta, a seventh-grade teacher, was from Kentucky, and her parents were old friends of my aunt's, so Mozelle and Boone took a special interest in her welfare. Lunetta's life was tragic, my aunt said. Her sailor-boy husband had died in the war. Lunetta never spoke to me, so I often stared at her unselfconsciously. She resembled one of the Toni twins, except for her horsey teeth. She wore her hair curled tight at the bottom, with a fluffy topknot, and she put hard, precise *g*'s on the ends of words like "talking" and "going," the way both Sharon Belletieri and Betsy Lou did. And she wore elaborate dresses—rayon marquisette[4] dresses with Paris pockets, dresses with tiered tucks, others of tissue chambray,[5] with what she called "taffeta understudies." Sometimes I thought her dresses could carry her away on a frantic ride through the sky, they were so billowy and thin.

> *W*hen they talked about reds, all I could imagine was a bunch of little devils in red suits, carrying pitchforks. I wondered if they were what my uncle had seen in the Pacific, since devils had tails.

"Lunetta's man-crazy," my aunt explained to me. "She's always dressed up in one of them Sunday-go-to-meetin' outfits in case she might come across a man to marry."

Uncle Boone called her thick lipstick "man bait."

*T*he buses remained on strike, and I spent the days in the house. I avoided Sharon Belletieri, preferring to be alone, or to sit entranced before the television set. Sometimes the fading outlines of the characters on the screen were like ghosts. I watched Milton Berle, Morey Amsterdam, *Believe It Or Not*, *Wax Wackies*, and even *Blind Date*. Judy Splinters, a ventriloquist's dummy with pigtails like mine, was one of my favorites,

---

4 **marquisette:** a shear meshed fabric

5 **chambray:** a lightweight fabric

and I liked the magician Foodini on *Lucky Pup* better than Howdy Doody. Betsy Lou teased me, saying I was too old for those baby shows. She was away most of the time, out on "jelly dates." A jelly date was a Coke date. She had jelly dates with Bob and Jim and Sam all on the same day. She was fond of singing "Let's Take an Old-Fashioned Walk," although one of her boyfriends had a car and she liked to go riding in it more than anything else. Why couldn't he take us to Detroit? I wondered, but I was afraid to ask. I had a sick feeling that we were never going to get to see the buildings of the city.

In the mornings, when there was nothing but snow on television, and the women were gossiping over their coffee in the kitchen, I sat on the enclosed porch and watched the people and the cars pass. During the heat wave, it was breezy there. I sat on the rattan chaise lounge and read Aunt Mozelle's scrapbooks, which I had found on a shelf above the television set. They were filled with brittle newspaper clippings mounted in overlapping rows. The clippings included household hints and cradle notes, but most of the stories were about bizarre occurrences around the world—diseases and kidnappings and disasters. One headline that fascinated me read: TIBETAN STOMACH STOVE DECLARED CANCER CAUSE. The story said that people in Tibet who carry little hot stoves against their abdomens in winter frequently develop cancer from the irritation. I was thankful that I didn't live in a cold climate. Another story was about a boa constrictor that swallowed a horse blanket. And there were a number of strange stories about blue babies. When my aunt found me reading the scrapbooks, she said to me, "Life is amazing. I keep these to remind me of just how strange everything is. And how there are always people worse off." I nodded agreement. The porch was my favorite place. I felt secure there, as I read about these faraway wonders and afflictions. I would look up now and then and imagine I could see the tall buildings of Detroit in the distance.

*T*his is a two-tone gabardine spectator dress[6] with a low-slung belt in the back," said Lunetta one morning as she turned to model her new dress for us. Lunetta always had official descriptions for her extravagant costumes.

My mother said in a wistful voice, "Law me, that's beautiful. But what would I look like, feeding chickens in that getup?"

---

6 **gabardine spectator dress:** a dress of two contrasting colors in a twilled, durable fabric

*W*hen my uncle came home from work, I greeted him at the door and asked him bluntly, "Are you going to get fired because of the reds?"

"Just look at them shoes," Aunt Mozelle said.

Lunetta's shoes had butterfly bows and sling heels and open toes. She sat down and tapped her toes as Aunt Mozelle poured coffee for her. She said then, "Is Boone worried about his job now that they caught that red?"

"Well, he is, but he don't let on," said Aunt Mozelle, frowning.

Lunetta seized yesterday's newspaper and spread it out on the table. She pointed at the headlines. I remember the way the adults had murmured over the newspaper the day before. Aunt Mozelle had said, "Don't worry, Boone. You don't work for that company." He had replied, "But the plant is full of sympathizers." Now Lunetta said, "Just think. That man they caught could have given Russia all the plans for the power plant. Nothing's safe. You never know who might turn out to be a spy."

My mother was disturbed. "Everything you all have worked so hard for—and the reds could just come in and take it." She waved her hand at the kitchen. In my mind a strange scene appeared: a band of little red devils marching in with their pitchforks and taking the entire Kelvinator kitchen to hell. Later, it occurred to me that they would take the television set first.

When my uncle came home from work, I greeted him at the door and asked him bluntly, "Are you going to get fired because of the reds?"

He only laughed and twitched my plaits. "No, sugar," he said.

"That don't concern younguns," Aunt Mozelle told me. She said to her husband, "Lunetta was here, spreading ideas."

"Leave it to Lunetta," said Uncle Boone wearily.

That evening they were eager to watch the news on the television set. When the supervisor who had been fired was shown, my uncle said, "I hope they give him what-for."

"He was going to tell Russia about the power plant," I said.

"Hush, Peggy," said Mama.

That evening, I could hear their anxious voices on the porch, as I watched Arthur Godfrey,[7] wrestling, and the barbershop quartets. It seemed odd to me that my uncle did not want to watch the wrestling. He had told me wrestling was his favorite program.

---

7 Arthur Godfrey: (1903–1983), radio and television personality

Sharon Belletieri had a birthday party. Aunt Mozelle took Mama and me to a nearby Woolworth's, where I selected a coloring book for a present. The store was twice the size of ours at home. I also bought a souvenir of my trip—a pair of china dogs, with a label that read "Made in Japan." And my mother bought me a playsuit like Sharon's.

"It's Sanforized.[8] That's good," she said with an air of satisfaction, as she examined seams and labels.

My mother looked pale and tired. At breakfast she had suddenly thrown up, the way she had during our bus trip. "I can't keep anything down this early," she had said. My aunt urged her to drink more coffee, saying it would settle her stomach.

Sharon Belletieri lived with her parents in a famous kind of sanitary house where you couldn't get TB or rheumatic fever because it had no drafts. "You won't have to worry about polio," Betsy Lou had told me. The house had venetian blinds like my aunt's, and there was also a television set, an immense one, on legs. Howdy Doody was on, but no one was watching. I did not know what to say to the children. They all knew each other, and their screams and giggles had a natural continuity, something like the way my mother talked with her sister, and like the splendid houses of the neighborhood, all set so close together.

For her birthday, Sharon's parents gave her a Toni doll that took my breath away. It had a bolero sundress, lace-edged panties and slip, and white shoes and socks—an outfit as fine as any of Lunetta's. It came with a Play Wave, including plastic spin curlers and Toni Creme Rinse. The doll's magic nylon hair was supposed to grow softer in texture the more you gave it permanent waves. Feeling self-conscious in my new playsuit, I sat quietly at the party, longing to give that doll a permanent.

Eventually, even though I had hardly opened my mouth, someone laughed at my accent. I had said the unfortunate word "hair" again, in reference to the doll.

Sharon said, "*She's* from Kentucky."

Growing bold and inspired, I said, "Well, we don't have any reds in Kentucky."

Some of the children laughed, and Sharon took me aside and told me a secret, making me cross my heart and hope to die. "I know who's a red," she told me in a whisper. "My father knows him."

---

8 **Sanforized:** refers to fabric that has been preshrunk

"Who?"

"One of the men your uncle rides with to work. The one who drives the car on Thursdays. He's a red and I can prove it."

Before I could find out more, it was my turn to pin the tail on the donkey. Sharon's mother blindfolded me and spun me around. The children were squealing, and I could feel them shrinking from me. When I took the blindfold off, I was dizzy. I had pinned the donkey's tail on the wallpaper, in the center of a large yellow flower.

That evening Betsy Lou went out with a boy named Sam, the one with the car, and Lunetta came to play canasta[9] with the adults. During *Cavalcade of Stars*,[10] I could hear them in the kitchen, accusing each other of hiding reds, when they meant hearts and diamonds. They laughed so loudly I sometimes missed some of Jack Carter's[11] jokes. The wrestling came on afterward, but my uncle did not notice, so I turned off the television and looked at a magazine. I spent a long time trying to write the last line to a Fab jingle so that I could win a television set and five hundred dollars a month for life. I knew that life in Kentucky would be unbearable without a television.

Between hands, Uncle Boone and Lunetta got into an argument. My uncle claimed there were more reds teaching school than making cars, and Lunetta said it was just the opposite.

"They're firing schoolteachers too," he said to Lunetta.

"Don't look at *me*," she said. "I signed the loyalty oath."

"Hush your mouth, Boone," said Aunt Mozelle.

"I know who a red is," I said suddenly, coming to the table.

They all looked at me and I explained what Sharon had told me. Too late, I remembered my promise not to tell.

"Don't let anybody hear you say that," said Lunetta. "Your uncle would lose his job. If they even *think* you know somebody that knows somebody, you can get in trouble."

"You better not say anything, hon," said Uncle Boone.

"Peggy, it's past your bedtime," my mother said.

"What did *I* do?"

"Talk gets around," said Lunetta. "There's sympathizers even in the woodwork."

---

9 **canasta:** a form of the card game rummy

10 ***Cavalcade of Stars:*** a comedic showcase featuring skits, singing, and dancing that aired from 1949 to 1952

11 **Jack Carter:** the first emcee of *Cavalcade of Stars*

The next day, after a disturbing night in which my guardian angel did nothing to protect me from my terrible secret, I was glum and cranky, and for the first time I refused Aunt Mozelle's waffles.

"Are you burnt out on them?" she asked me.

"No, I just ain't hungry."

"She played too hard at the birthday party," Mama said knowingly to my aunt.

When Lunetta arrived and Mama told her I had played too hard at the birthday party, I burst into tears.

"It's nobody's business if I played too hard," I cried. "Besides," I shrieked at Mama, "you don't feel good at breakfast either. You always say you can't keep anything down."

"Don't be ugly," my mother said sharply. To the others, she said apologetically, "I reckon sooner or later she was bound to show out."

It was Sunday, and the heat wave continued. We all sat on the porch, looking at the Sunday papers. Betsy Lou was reading *Pleasant Valley* by Louis Bromfield. Uncle Boone read the Sunday comics aloud to himself. Actually, he was trying to get my attention, for I sat in a corner, determined to ignore everyone. Uncle Boone read "Abbie an' Slats," "The Gumps," and "Little Orphan Annie." He pretended he was Milton Berle as he read them, but I wouldn't laugh.

Lunetta and Uncle Boone seemed to have forgotten their argument. Lunetta had dressed up for church, but the man she planned to go with had gone to visit his mother's grave instead.

"That man sure did love his mother," she said.

"Why don't you go to church anyway?" asked Betsy Lou. "You're all dressed up."

"I just don't have it in me," said Lunetta. She was wearing a shell-tucked summer shantung[12] dress and raffia[13] T-strap sandals.

"Ain't you hot in that outfit?" asked my aunt. "We're burning up."

"I guess so." Lunetta seemed gloomy and distracted. I almost forgave her for upsetting me about the sympathizers, but then she launched into

---

12 **shantung:** a woven fabric with a slightly uneven surface

13 **raffia:** a durable fiber usually used in baskets and hats

a complicated story about a babysitter who got double-crossed. "This woman baby-sat for her best friend, who was divorced and had two little babies. And come to find out, the friend was going out on dates with the woman's own husband!"

"If that don't beat all," said Mama, her eyes wide. She was drinking her second cup of coffee.

"No telling how long that could have kept up," said my aunt.

"It made a big divorce case," Lunetta said.

"I never saw so many divorce cases," said Mama.

"Would you divorce somebody if you found out they were a Communist?" Lunetta asked.

"I don't know as I would," said Aunt Mozelle. "Depends."

"*I* would," said Mama.

"I probably would," said Lunetta. "How about you, Boone?"

> *M*ama was too much in pain to speak. Her face was distorted, her sharp-pointed lips stretched out like a slingshot. My aunt helped her to the bathroom, and a short while later, my aunt and uncle flew away with her in a taxi.

"If I found out Mozelle was a red?" Boone asked, grinning. "I'd probably string her up and tickle her feet till she hollered uncle."

"Oh, Boone," Lunetta said with a laugh. "I know you'd stick up for Mozelle, no matter what."

They sat around that morning talking like this, good-naturedly. In the light of day, the reds were only jokes after all, like the comics. I had decided to eat a bowl of Pep cereal, and "Some Enchanted Evening" was playing on the radio. Suddenly everything changed, as if a black storm had appeared to break the heat wave. My mother gave out a loud whoop and clutched her stomach in pain.

"Where does it hurt?" my aunt cried, grabbing at Mama.

Mama was too much in pain to speak. Her face was distorted, her sharp-pointed lips stretched out like a slingshot. My aunt helped her to the bathroom, and a short while later, my aunt and uncle flew away with her in a taxi. Mama had straightened up enough to say that the pain had subsided, but she looked scared, and the blood had drained from her face. I said nothing to her, not even good-bye.

Betsy Lou, left alone with me, said, "I hope she hasn't got polio."

"Only children get polio," I said, trembling. "She don't have polio."

The telephone rang, and Betsy Lou chattered excitedly, telling one of her boyfriends what had happened. Alone and frightened, I sat on the porch, hugging a fat pile of newspapers and gazing at the street. I could see Sharon Belletieri, skating a block away with two other girls. She was wearing a blue playsuit. She and her friends reminded me of those privileged children in the Peanut Gallery on *Howdy Doody*.

To keep from thinking, I began searching the newspaper for something to put in Aunt Mozelle's scrapbook, but at first nothing seemed so horrible as what had just happened. Some babies had turned blue from a diaper dye, but that story didn't impress me. Then I found an item about a haunted house, and my heart began to race. A priest claimed that mysterious disturbances in a house in Wisconsin were the work of an angelic spirit watching over an eight-year-old boy. Cryptic messages were found on bits of paper in the boy's room. The spirit manifestation had occurred fifteen times. I found my aunt's scissors and cut out the story.

Within two hours, my aunt and uncle returned, with broad smiles on their faces, but I knew they were pretending.

"She's just fine," said Aunt Mozelle. "We'll take you to see her after-while, but right now they gave her something to make her sleep and take away the pain."

"She'll get to come home in the morning," said my uncle.

He had brought ice cream, and while he went to the kitchen to dish it out, I showed my aunt the clipping I had found. I helped her put it in her scrapbook.

"Life sure is strange," I said.

"Didn't I tell you?" she said. "Now, don't you worry about your mama, hon. She's going to be all right."

*L*ater that day, my aunt and uncle stood in the corridor of the hospital while I visited my mother. The hospital was large and gray and steaming with the heat. Mama lay against a mound of pillows, smiling weakly.

"I'm the one that showed out," she said, looking ashamed. She took my hand and made me sit on the bed next to her. "You *were* going to have a little brother or sister," she said. "But I was mistaken."

"What happened to it?"

"I lost it. That happens sometimes."

When I looked at her blankly, she tried to explain that there wasn't *really* a baby, as there was when she had Johnny two years before.

She said, "You know how sometimes one or two of the chicken eggs don't hatch? The baby chick just won't take hold. That's what happened."

It occurred to me to ask what the baby's name would have been.

"I don't know," she said. "I'm trying to tell you there wasn't really a baby. I didn't know about it, anyway."

"You didn't even know there was a baby?"

"No. I didn't know about it till I lost it."

She tried to laugh, but she was weak, and she seemed as confused as I was. She squeezed my hand and closed her eyes for a moment. Then she said, "Boone says the buses will start up this week. You could go with your aunt to Detroit and see the big buildings."

"Without you?"

"The doctor said I should rest up before we go back. But you go ahead. Mozelle will take you." She smiled at me sleepily. "I wanted to go so bad— just to see those big fancy store windows. And I wanted to see your face when you saw the city."

That evening, *Toast of the Town* was on television, and then Fred Waring, and *Garroway at Large*.[14] I was lost among the screen phantoms—the magic acts, puppets, jokes, clowns, dancers, singers, wisecracking announcers. My aunt and uncle laughed uproariously. Uncle Boone was drinking beer, something I had not seen him do, and the room stank with the smoke of his Old Golds. Now and then I was aware of all of us sitting there together, laughing in the dim light from the television, while my mother was in the hospital. Even Betsy Lou was watching with us. Later, I went to the guest room and sat on the large bed, trying to concentrate on finishing the Fab jingle.

> Here's to a fabulous life with Fab
> There's no soap scum to make wash drab
> Your clothes get cleaner—whiter, too—

I heard my aunt calling to me excitedly. I was missing something on the

---

14 *Garroway at Large:* a musical variety show hosted by Dave Garroway that aired from 1949 to 1954

television screen. I had left because the news was on.

"Pictures of Detroit!" she cried. "Come quick. You can see the big buildings."

I raced into the living room in time to see some faint, dark shapes, hiding behind the snow, like a forest in winter, and then the image faded into the snow.

> *The reds had stolen the baby. They took things. They were after my aunt's copper-bottomed pans. They stole the butter.*

"Mozelle can take you into Detroit in a day or two," my uncle said. "The buses is starting up again."

"I don't want to go," I said.

"You don't want to miss the chance," said my aunt.

"Yes, I do."

That night, alone in the pine-and-cedar room, I saw everything clearly, like the sharpened images that floated on the television screen. My mother had said an egg didn't hatch, but I knew better. The reds had stolen the baby. They took things. They were after my aunt's copper-bottomed pans. They stole the butter. They wanted my uncle's job. They were invisible, like the guardian angel, although they might wear disguises. You didn't know who might be a red. You never knew when you might lose a baby that you didn't know you had. I understood it all. I hadn't trusted my guardian angel, and so he had failed to protect me. During the night, I hit upon a last line to the Fab jingle, but when I awoke I saw how silly and inappropriate it was. It was going over and over in my mind: *Red soap makes the world go round.*

On the bus home a few days later, I slept with my head in my mother's lap, and she dozed with her head propped against my seat back. She was no longer sick, but we were both tired and we swayed, unresisting, with the rhythms of the bus. When the bus stopped in Fort Wayne, Indiana, at midnight, I suddenly woke up, and at the sight of an unfamiliar place, I felt—with a new surge of clarity—the mystery of travel, the vastness of the world, the strangeness of life. My own life was a curiosity, an item for a scrapbook. I wondered what my mother would tell my father about the baby she had lost. She had been holding me tightly against her stomach as though she feared she might lose me too.

I had refused to let them take me into Detroit. At the bus station, Aunt Mozelle had hugged me and said, "Maybe next time you come we can go to Detroit."

"If there *is* a next time," Mama said. "This may be her only chance, but she had to be contrary."

"I didn't want to miss *Wax Wackies* and *Judy Splinters*," I said, protesting.

"We'll have a car next time you come," said my uncle. "If they don't fire everybody," he added with a laugh.

"If that happens, y'all can always come back to Kentucky and help us get a crop out," Mama told him.

The next afternoon, we got off the bus on the highway at the intersection with our road. Our house was half a mile away. The bus driver got our suitcases out of the bus for us, and then drove on down the highway. My father was supposed to meet us, but he was not there.

"I better not carry this suitcase," said Mama. "My insides might drop."

We left our suitcases in a ditch and started walking, expecting to meet Daddy on the way.

My mother said, "You don't remember this, but when you was two years old I went to Jackson, Tennessee, for two weeks to see Mozelle and Boone—came back before Boone was called overseas?—and when I come back the bus driver let me off here and I come walking down the road to the house carrying my suitcase. You was playing in the yard and you saw me walk up and you didn't recognize me. For the longest time, you didn't know who I was. I never *will* forget how funny you looked."

"They won't recognize us," I said solemnly. "Daddy and Johnny."

As we got to the top of the hill, we could see that our little white house was still there. The tin roof of the barn was barely visible through the tall oak trees.

Read and Think Critically

Analyze, Describe, Infer

 1. **COMING-OF-AGE STORY** Why do you think Peggy declines to see the Detroit skyline, saying at the end, "I understood it all"? In what way has Peggy grown in her understanding of the world? In what ways is her conclusion **ironic**?

2. Analyze the author's use of **setting** in "Detroit Skyline, 1949." What conclusions can you draw about the time, place, and **characters**? How does the setting contribute to the coming-of-age **theme**?

3. Mason allows the characters in the story to reveal themselves without providing much **interpretation** or judgment. Pick one character from the story. Describe what you know about the character based upon **inferences** from the text.

4. Coming from a small town, Peggy isn't used to city life. Describe some of the culture shocks she encounters.

5. At the end of the story, Peggy is certain her father and brother won't recognize her and her mother. Based upon the text, infer why Peggy feels this way.

6. **THE AUTHOR'S STYLE** Consider the quotation from Mason below. In it, she comments on her interest in the impact of rapid changes on the lives of working-class people. How do social forces affect the characters in this story?

My Version of Rock-and-Roll

Writing is my version of rock-and-roll . . . . I identify with Bruce Springsteen's songs, and of course I'm not alone in this. I like the way his songs are stories with characters. He writes about the disintegration of lives due to social forces. But his people keep striving, hoping.

—Bobbie Ann Mason, *Passion and Craft*

Before You Read

Louise Erdrich 1954–

About the Author

Louise Erdrich grew up in North Dakota, one of eight children of a German American father and an Ojibwa (Chippewa) Indian mother. Both her parents were teachers at a Bureau of Indian Affairs Boarding School. They encouraged her talents. Her grandfather, a tribal chair for the Turtle Mountain Reservation, used to give Erdrich a nickel for every story she wrote.

She went east to attend Dartmouth College and Johns Hopkins University, and married the late writer Michael Dorris, who collaborated with her on several works until his suicide.

Among her best-known works is her first novel, the award-winning *Love Medicine,* published in 1984. Erdrich followed the three families of characters that appeared in *Love Medicine* in her later novels *The Beet Queen*, *Tracks*, and *The Bingo Palace*.

In an interview with the *Chicago Tribune* in 1986, she commented, "My fondest hope is that people will be reading me in 10 or 20 years from now as someone who has written about the American experience in all of its diversity."

****

The Author's Style

Erdrich explores the mysteries of religion, culture, and family ties in her stories and novels. Often they are set in the flat, open spaces of North Dakota. Her heritage is part Ojibwa (Chippewa), and her stories focus on the impact on Indians of various aspects of the non-Indian world—for example, alcohol, Christianity, and the government. The Native Americans of Erdrich's stories struggle constantly for the survival of their cultural identity, always aware of betrayal and mistreatment in the past. An example is when Indian children were removed from their homes and sent to government-run "Indian schools" earlier in the 20th century.

Erdrich develops precise descriptions of bleak landscapes and reservation life. She is adept at characterization, conveying the personalities and relationships of her characters through alternating points of view. Her characters are aware of the ways language works in their lives, both for and against them. The use of dreams, visions, and miracles in Erdrich's fiction is one measure of the passionate intensity of her characters. It is also a constant reminder of her closeness to Native American culture. Erdrich also writes poetry, and the poet's eye for powerful images and complex metaphors can be found throughout her fiction.

American Horse

LOUISE ERDRICH

 LITERARY LENS: IMAGERY Watch for how Erdrich uses **imagery** in this story. Consider how the imagery complements or contrasts with the emotional events in the story.

The woman sleeping on the cot in the woodshed was Albertine American Horse. The name was left over from her mother's short marriage. The boy was the son of the man she had loved and let go. Buddy was on the cot too, sitting on the edge because he'd been awake three hours watching out for his mother and besides, she took up the whole cot. Her feet hung over the edge, limp and brown as two trout. Her long arms reached out and slapped at things she saw in her dreams.

Buddy had been knocked awake out of hiding in a washing machine while herds of policemen with dogs searched through a large building with many tiny rooms. When the arm came down, Buddy screamed because it had a blue cuff and sharp silver buttons. "Tss," his mother mumbled, half awake, "wasn't nothing." But Buddy sat up after her breathing went deep again, and he watched.

There was something coming and he knew it.

It was coming from very far off but he had a picture of it in his mind. It was a large thing made of metal with many barbed hooks, points, and drag chains on it, something like a giant potato peeler that rolled out of the sky, scraping clouds down with it and jabbing or crushing everything that lay in its path on the ground.

Buddy watched his mother. If he woke her up, she would know what to do about the thing, but he thought he'd wait until he saw it for sure before he shook her. She was pretty, sleeping, and he liked knowing he could look at her as long and close up as he wanted. He took a strand of her hair and held it in his hands as if it was the rein to a delicate beast. She was strong enough and could pull him along like the horse their name was.

He wanted to touch the satin roses sewed on her pink tee-shirt, but he knew he shouldn't do that even in her sleep. If she woke up and found him touching the roses, she would say, "Quit that, Buddy."

Buddy had his mother's and his grandmother's name because his father had been a big mistake.

"They're all mistakes, even your father. But *you* are the best thing that ever happened to me."

That was what she said when he asked.

Even Kadie, the boyfriend crippled from being in a car wreck, was not as good a thing that had happened to his mother as Buddy was. "He was a medium-sized mistake," she said. "He's hurt and I shouldn't even say that, but it's the truth." At the moment, Buddy knew that being the best thing in his mother's life, he was also the reason they were hiding from the cops.

He wanted to touch the satin roses sewed on her pink tee-shirt, but he knew he shouldn't do that even in her sleep. If she woke up and found him touching the roses, she would say, "Quit that, Buddy." Sometimes she told him to stop hugging her like a gorilla. She never said that in the mean voice she used when he oppressed her, but when she said that he loosened up anyway.

There were times he felt like hugging her so hard and in such a special way that she would say to him, "Let's get married." There were also times he closed his eyes and wished that she would die, only a few times, but still it haunted him that his wish might come true. He and Uncle Lawrence would be left alone. Buddy wasn't worried, though, about his mother getting married to somebody else. She had said to her friend, Madonna, "All men suck," when she thought Buddy wasn't listening. He had made an uncertain sound, and when they heard him they took him in their arms.

"Except for you, Buddy," his mother said. "All except for you and maybe Uncle Lawrence, although he's pushing it."

"The cops suck the worst though," Buddy whispered to his mother's sleeping face, "because they're after us." He felt tired again, slumped down, and put his legs beneath the blanket. He closed his eyes and got the feeling that the cot was lifting up beneath him, that it was arching its canvas back and then traveling, traveling very fast and in the wrong direction for when he looked up he saw the three of them were advancing to meet the great metal thing with hooks and barbs and all sorts of sharp equipment to catch their bodies and draw their blood. He heard its insides as it rushed toward them, purring softly like a powerful motor and then they were right in its shadow. He pulled the reins as hard as he could and the beast reared, lifting him. His mother clapped her hand across his mouth.

"Okay," she said. "Lay low. They're outside and they're gonna hunt."

She touched his shoulder and Buddy leaned over with her to look through a crack in the boards.

$\mathcal{T}$hey were out there all right, Albertine saw them. Two officers and that social worker woman. Vicki Koob. There had been no whistle, no dream, no voice to warn her that they were coming. There was only the crunching sound of cinders in the yard, the engine purring, the dust sifting off their car in a fine light brownish cloud and settling around them.

The three people came to a halt in their husk of metal—the car emblazoned with the North Dakota State Highway Patrol emblem which is the glowing profile of the Sioux policeman, Red Tomahawk, the one who killed Sitting Bull. Albertine gave Buddy the blanket and told him that he might have to wrap it around him and hide underneath the cot.

"We're gonna wait and see what they do." She took him in her lap and hunched her arms around him. "Don't you worry," she whispered against his ear. "Lawrence knows how to fool them."

Buddy didn't want to look at the car and the people. He felt his mother's heart beating beneath his ear so fast it seemed to push the satin roses in and out. He put his face to them carefully and breathed the deep, soft powdery woman smell of her. That smell was also in her little face cream bottles, in her brushes, and around the washbowl after she used it. The satin felt so unbearably smooth against his cheek that he had to press closer. She didn't push him away, like he expected, but hugged him still tighter, until he felt as close as he had ever been to back inside her again where she said he came from. Within the smells of her things, her soft skin and the satin of her roses, he closed his eyes then, and took his breaths softly and quickly with her heart.

They were out there, but they didn't dare get out of the car yet because of Lawrence's big, ragged dogs. Three of these dogs had loped up the dirt driveway with the car. They were rangy, alert, and bounced up and down on their cushioned paws like wolves. They didn't waste their energy barking, but positioned themselves quietly, one at either car door and the third in front of the bellied-out screen door to Uncle Lawrence's house. It was six in the morning but the wind was up already, blowing dust, ruffling their short moth-eaten coats. The big brown one on Vicki Koob's side had unusual black and white markings, stripes almost, like a hyena and he grinned at her, tongue out and teeth showing.

"Shoo!" Miss Koob opened her door with a quick jerk.

The brown dog sidestepped the door and jumped before her, tiptoeing. Its dirty white muzzle curled and its eyes crossed suddenly as if it was zeroing its cross-hair sights in on the exact place it would bite her. She ducked back and slammed the door.

"It's mean," she told Officer Brackett. He was printing out some type of form. The other officer, Harmony, a slow man, had not yet reacted to the car's halt. He had been sitting quietly in the back seat, but now he rolled down his window and with no change in expression unsnapped his holster and drew his pistol out and pointed it at the dog on his side. The dog smacked down on its belly, wiggled under the car and was out and around the back of the house before Harmony drew his gun back. The other dogs vanished with him. From wherever they had disappeared to they began to yap and howl, and the door to the low shoebox style house fell open.

"Heya, what's going on?"

Uncle Lawrence put his head out the door and opened wide the one eye he had in working order. The eye bulged impossibly wider in outrage when he saw the police car. But the eyes of the two officers and Miss Vicki Koob were wide open too because they had never seen Uncle Lawrence in his sleeping get up or, indeed, witnessed anything like it. For his ribs, which were cracked from a bad fall and still mending, Uncle Lawrence wore a thick white corset laced up the front with a striped sneakers lace. His glass eye and his set of dentures were still out for the night so his face puckered here and there, around its absences and scars, like a damaged but fierce little cake. Although he had a few gray streaks now, Uncle Lawrence's hair was still thick, and because he wore a special contraption of elastic straps around his head every night, two oiled waves always crested on either side of his middle part. All of this would have been sufficient to astonish, even without the most striking part of his outfit—the smoking jacket. It was made of black satin and hung open around his corset, dragging a tasseled belt. Gold thread dragons struggled up the lapels and blasted their furry red breath around his neck. As Lawrence walked down the steps, he put his arms up in surrender and the gold tassels in the inner seams of his sleeves dropped into view.

"My heavens, what a sight." Vicki Koob was impressed.

"A character," apologized Officer Harmony.

As a tribal police officer who could be counted on to help out the State Patrol, Harmony thought he always had to explain about Indians or get twice as tough to show he did not favor them. He was slow-moving and shy but two jumps ahead of other people all the same, and now, as he watched Uncle Lawrence's splendid approach, he gazed speculatively at the torn and bulging pocket of the smoking jacket. Harmony had been inside Uncle Lawrence's house before and knew that above his draped orange-crate shelf of war medals a blue-black German luger[1] was hung carefully in a net of flat-headed nails and fishing line. Thinking of this deadly exhibition, he got out of the car and shambled toward Lawrence with a dreamy little smile of welcome on his face. But when he searched Lawrence, he found that the bulging pocket held only the lonesome looking dentures from Lawrence's empty jaw. They were still dripping denture polish.

"I had been cleaning them when you arrived," Uncle Lawrence explained with acid dignity.

He took the toothbrush from his other pocket and aimed it like a rifle.

"Quit that, you old idiot." Harmony tossed the toothbrush away. "For once you ain't done nothing. We came for your nephew."

Lawrence looked at Harmony with a faint air of puzzlement.

"Ma Frere, listen," threatened Harmony amiably, "those two white people

---

1 **luger:** a pistol

in the car came to get him for the welfare. They got papers on your nephew that give them the right to take him."

"Papers?" Uncle Lawrence puffed out his deeply pitted cheeks. "Let me see them papers."

The two of them walked over to Vicki's side of the car and she pulled a copy of the court order from her purse. Lawrence put his teeth back in and adjusted them with busy workings of his jaw.

"Just a minute," he reached into his breast pocket as he bent close to Miss Vicki Koob. "I can't read these without I have in my eye."

He took the eye from his breast pocket delicately, and as he popped it into his face the social worker's mouth fell open in a consternated O.

"What is this," she cried in a little voice.

Uncle Lawrence looked at her mildly. The white glass of the eye was cold as lard. The black iris was strangely charged and menacing.

"He's nuts," Brackett huffed along the side of Vicki's neck. "Never mind him."

Vicki's hair had sweated down her nape in tiny corkscrews and some of the hairs were so long and dangly now that they disappeared into the zippered back of her dress. Brackett noticed this as he spoke into her ear. His face grew red and the backs of his hands prickled. He slid under the steering wheel and got out of the car. He walked around the hood to stand with Leo Harmony.

"We could take you in too," said Brackett roughly. Lawrence eyed the officers in what was taken as defiance. "If you don't cooperate, we'll get out the handcuffs," they warned.

One of Lawrence's arms was stiff and would not move until he'd rubbed it with witch hazel in the morning. His other arm worked fine though, and he stuck it out in front of Brackett.

"Get them handcuffs," he urged them. "Put me in a welfare home." Brackett snapped one side of the handcuffs on Lawrence's good arm and the other to the handle of the police car.

"That's to hold you," he said. "We're wasting our time. Harmony, you search that little shed over by the tall grass and Miss Koob and myself will search the house."

"My rights is violated!" Lawrence shrieked suddenly. They ignored him. He tugged at the handcuff and thought of the good heavy file he kept in his tool box and the German luger oiled and ready but never loaded, because of

Buddy, over his shelf. He should have used it on these bad ones, even Harmony in his big-time white man job. He wouldn't last long in that job anyway before somebody gave him what for.

"It's a damn scheme," said Uncle Lawrence, rattling his chains against the car. He looked over at the shed and thought maybe Albertine and Buddy had sneaked away before the car pulled into the yard. But he sagged, seeing Albertine move like a shadow within the boards. "Oh, it's all a damn scheme," he muttered again.

"I want to find that boy and salvage him," Vicki Koob explained to Officer Brackett as they walked into the house. "Look at his family life—the old man crazy as a bedbug, the mother intoxicated somewhere."

Brackett nodded, energetic, eager. He was a short, hopeful redhead who failed consistently to win the hearts of women. Vicki Koob intrigued him. Now, as he watched, she pulled a tiny pen out of an ornamental clip on her blouse. It was attached to a retractable line that would suck the pen back, like a child eating one strand of spaghetti. Something about the pen on its line excited Brackett to the point of discomfort. His hand shook as he opened the screen door and stepped in, beckoning Miss Koob to follow.

They could see the house was empty at first glance. It was only one rectangular room with whitewashed walls and a little gas stove in the middle. They had already come through the cooking lean-to with the other stove and washstand and rusty old refrigerator. That refrigerator had nothing in it but some wrinkled potatoes and a package of turkey necks. Vicki Koob noted that in her perfect-bound notebook. The beds along the walls of the big room were covered with quilts that Albertine's mother, Sophie, had made from bits of old wool coats and pants that the Sisters sold in bundles at the mission. There was no one hiding beneath the beds. No one was under the little aluminum dinette table covered with a green oilcloth, or the soft brown wood chairs tucked up to it. One wall of the big room was filled with neatly stacked crates of things—old tools and springs and small half-dismantled appliances. Five or six television sets were stacked against the wall. Their control panels spewed colored wires and at least one was cracked all the way across. Only the topmost set, with coathanger antenna angled sensitively to catch the bounding signals around Little Shell, looked like it could possibly work.

Not one thing escaped Vicki Koob's trained and cataloguing gaze. She made note of the cupboard that held only commodity flour and coffee. The unsanitary tin oil drum beneath the kitchen window, full of empty surplus pork cans and beer bottles, caught her eye as did Uncle Lawrence's physical and mental deteriorations. She quickly described these "benchmarks of alcoholic dependency within the extended family of Woodrow (Buddy) American Horse" as she walked around the room with the little notebook open, pushed against her belly to steady it. Although Vicki had been there before, Albertine's presence had always made it difficult for her to take notes.

"Twice the maximum allowable space between door and threshold," she wrote now. "Probably no insulation. 2–3 inch cracks in walls inadequately sealed with whitewash mud." She made a mental note but could see no point in describing Lawrence's stuffed reclining chair that only reclined, the shadeless lamp with its plastic orchid in the bubble glass base, or the three dimensional picture of Jesus that Lawrence had once demonstrated to her. When plugged in, lights rolled behind the water the Lord stood on so that he seemed to be strolling although he never actually went forward, of course, but only pushed the glowing waves behind him forever like a poor tame rat in a treadmill.

Brackett cleared his throat with a nervous rasp and touched Vicki's shoulder.

"What are you writing?"

She moved away and continued to scribble as if thoroughly absorbed in her work. "Officer Brackett displays an undue amount of interest in my person," she wrote. "Perhaps?"

He snatched playfully at the book, but she hugged it to her chest and moved off smiling. More curls had fallen, wetted to the base of her neck. Looking out the window, she sighed long and loud.

"All night on brush rollers for this. What a joke."

Brackett shoved his hands in his pockets. His mouth opened slightly, then shut with a small throttled cluck.

When Albertine saw Harmony ambling across the yard with his big brown thumbs in his belt, his placid smile, and his tiny black eyes moving back and forth, she put Buddy under the cot. Harmony stopped at the shed and stood quietly. He spread his arms wide to show her he hadn't drawn his big police gun.

"Ma Cousin," he said in the Michif dialect that people used if they were relatives or sometimes if they needed gas or a couple of dollars, "why don't you come out here and stop this foolishness?"

"I ain't your cousin," Albertine said. Anger boiled up in her suddenly. "I ain't related to no pigs."

She bit her lip and watched him through the cracks, circling, a big tan punching dummy with his boots full of sand so he never stayed down once he fell. He was empty inside, all stale air. But he knew how to get to her so much better than a white cop could. And now he was circling because he wasn't sure she didn't have a weapon, maybe a knife or the German luger that was the only thing that her father, Albert American Horse, had left his wife and daughter besides his name. Harmony knew that Albertine was a tall strong woman who took two big men to subdue when she didn't want to go in the drunk tank. She had hard hips, broad shoulders, and stood tall like her Sioux father, the American Horse who was killed threshing in Belle Prairie.

> She bit her lip and watched him through the cracks, circling, a big tan punching dummy with his boots full of sand so he never stayed down once he fell. He was empty inside, all stale air.

"I feel bad to have to do this," Harmony said to Albertine. "But for godsakes, let's nobody get hurt. Come on out with the boy why don't you. I know you got him in there."

Albertine did not give herself away this time. She let him wonder. Slowly and quietly she pulled her belt through its loops and wrapped it around and around her hand until only the big oval buckle with turquoise chunks shaped into a butterfly stuck out over her knuckles. Harmony was talking but she wasn't listening to what he said. She was listening to the pitch of his voice, the tone of it that would tighten or tremble at a certain moment when he decided to rush the shed. He kept talking slowly and reasonably, flexing the dialect from time to time, even mentioning her father.

"He was a damn good man. I don't care what they say, Albertine, I knew him."

Albertine looked at the stone butterfly that spread its wings across her fist. The wings looked light and cool, not heavy. It almost looked like it was ready to fly. Harmony wanted to get to Albertine through her father but she would not think about American Horse. She concentrated on the sky-blue stone.

Yet the shape of the stone, the color, betrayed her.

She saw her father suddenly, bending at the grill of their old grey car.

She was small then. The memory came from so long ago it seemed like a dream—narrowly focused, snapshot clear. He was bending by the grill in the sun. It was hot summer. Wings of sweat, dark blue, spread across the back of his work shirt. He always wore soft blue shirts, the color of shade cloudier than this stone. His stiff hair had grown out of its short haircut and flopped over his forehead. When he stood up and turned away from the car, Albertine saw that he had a butterfly.

"It's dead," he told her. "Broke its wings and died on the grill."

She must have been five, maybe six, wearing one of the boy's tee-shirts Mama bleached in hilex-water.[2] American Horse took the butterfly, a black and yellow one, and rubbed it on Albertine's collarbone and chest and arms until the color and the powder of it were blended into her skin.

"For grace," he said.

And Albertine had felt a strange lightening in her arms, in her chest, when he did this and said, "For grace." The way he said it, grace meant everything the butterfly was. The sharp delicate wings. The way it floated over the grass. The way its wings seemed to breathe fanning in the sun. The wisdom of the way it blended into flowers or changed into a leaf. In herself she felt the same kind of possibilities and closed her eyes almost in shock or pain she felt so light and powerful at that moment.

Then her father had caught her and thrown her high into the air. She could not remember landing in his arms or landing at all. She only remembered the sun filling her eyes and the world tipping crazily behind her, out of sight.

"He was a damn good man," Harmony said again.

Albertine heard his starched uniform gathering before his boots hit the ground. Once, twice, three times. It took him four solid jumps to get right where she wanted him. She kicked the plank door open when he reached for the handle and the corner caught him on the jaw. He faltered, and Albertine hit him flat on the chin with the butterfly. She hit him so hard the shock of it went up her arm like a string pulled taut. Her fist opened, numb, and she let the belt unloop before she closed her hand on the tip end of it and sent the stone butterfly swooping out in a wide circle around her as if it was on the end of a leash. Harmony reeled backward as she walked toward him swinging the belt. She expected him to fall but he just stumbled. And then he took the gun from his hip.

Albertine let the belt go limp. She and Harmony stood within feet of

---

2 **hilex-water:** "Hilex" is a brand of bleaching detergent.

each other, breathing. Each heard the human sound of air going in and out of the other person's lungs. Each read the face of the other as if deciphering letters carved into softly eroding veins of stone. Albertine saw the pattern of tiny arteries that age, drink, and hard living had blown to the surface of the man's face. She saw the spoked wheels of his iris and the arteries like tangled threads that sewed him up. She saw the living net of springs and tissue that held him together, and trapped him. She saw the random, intimate plan of his person.

She took a quick shallow breath and her face went strange and tight. She saw the black veins in the wings of the butterfly, roads burnt into a map, and then she was located somewhere in the net of veins and **sinew** that was the tragic complexity of the world so she did not see Officer Brackett and Vicki Koob rushing toward her, but felt them instead like flies caught in the same web, rocking it.

sinew: tendon; connective tissue

"Albertine!" Vicki Koob had stopped in the grass. Her voice was shrill and tight. "It's better this way, Albertine. We're going to help you."

Albertine straightened, threw her shoulders back. Her father's hand was on her chest and shoulders lightening her wonderfully. Then on wings of her father's hands, on dead butterfly wings, Albertine lifted into the air and flew toward the others. The light powerful feeling swept her up the way she had floated higher, seeing the grass below. It was her father throwing her up into the air and out of danger. Her arms opened for bullets but no bullets came. Harmony did not shoot. Instead, he raised his fist and brought it down hard on her head.

Albertine did not fall immediately, but stood in his arms a moment. Perhaps she gazed still farther back behind the covering of his face. Perhaps she was completely stunned and did not think as she sagged and fell. Her face rolled forward and hair covered her features, so it was impossible for Harmony to see with just what particular expression she gazed into the headsplitting wheel of light, or blackness, that overcame her.

*H*armony turned the vehicle onto the gravel road that led back to town. He had convinced the other two that Albertine was more trouble than she was worth, and so they left her behind, and Lawrence too. He stood swearing in his cinder driveway as the car rolled out of sight. Buddy sat between the social worker and Officer Brackett. Vicki tried to hold Buddy fast and keep her arm down at the same time, for the words she'd screamed at Albertine had broken the seal of antiperspirant beneath her arms. She was sweating now as though she'd stored an ocean up inside of her. Sweat rolled down her back in a shallow river and pooled at her waist and between her breasts. A thin sheen of water came out on her forearms, her face. Vicki gave an irritated moan but Brackett seemed not to take notice, or take offense at least. Air-conditioned breezes were sweeping over the seat anyway, and very soon they would be comfortable. She smiled at Brackett over Buddy's head. The man grinned back. Buddy stirred. Vicki remembered the emergency chocolate bar she kept in her purse, fished it out, and offered it to Buddy. He did not react, so she closed his fingers over the package and peeled the paper off one end.

The car accelerated. Buddy felt the road and wheels pummeling each other and the rush of the heavy motor purring in high gear. Buddy knew that what he'd seen in his mind that morning, the thing coming out of the sky with barbs and chains, had hooked him. Somehow he was caught and held in the sour tin smell of the pale woman's armpit. Somehow he was pinned between their pounds of breathless flesh. He looked at the chocolate in his hand. He was squeezing the bar so hard that a thin brown trickle had melted down his arm. Automatically, he put the bar in his mouth.

As he bit down he saw his mother very clearly, just as she had been when she carried him from the shed. She was stretched flat on the ground, on her stomach, and her arms were curled around her head as if in sleep. One leg was drawn up and it looked for all the world like she was running full tilt into the ground, as though she had been trying to pass into the earth, to bury herself, but at the last moment something had stopped her.

There was no blood on Albertine, but Buddy tasted blood now at the sight of her, for he bit down hard and cut his own lip. He ate the chocolate, every bit of it, tasting his mother's blood. And when he had the chocolate down inside him and all licked off his hands, he opened his mouth to say thank you to the woman, as his mother had taught him. But instead of a thank you coming out he was astonished to hear a great rattling scream, and then another, rip out of him like pieces of his own body and whirl onto the sharp things all around him.

Read and Think Critically

Analyze, Contrast, Conclude

 1. **IMAGERY** Analyze Erdrich's use of the **image** of the sharp thing coming out of the sky, which Buddy envisions throughout the story. Does this seem appropriate for Buddy's character?

2. Using a two-column chart like the one below, contrast the **characters**, imagery, and attitudes in this story that represent Native American culture on one side and non-Native American culture on the other. Then write a statement that summarizes the relationship between the two cultures.

Native American Culture	Non-Native American Culture

3. Reread pages 595–596 in which Vicki Koob records details about Uncle Lawrence's dwelling. What can you conclude about Koob's character based upon the details she writes down?

4. The focus of the narrative shifts several times between Buddy, Albertine, and Vicki Koob. Why do you think the author shifts the narrative focus in this way?

5. **THE AUTHOR'S STYLE** Read the quotation below. To use Erdrich's own words, how does "American Horse" rise, break, and fall?

Everything into a Story

The people in our families made everything into a story . . . . People just sit and the stories start coming, one after another. . . I suppose that when you grow up constantly hearing the stories rise, break, and fall, it gets into you somehow.

—Louise Erdrich, *Writer's Digest*

★★★

Before You Read

E. L. Doctorow 1931–2015

About the Author

E. L. Doctorow grew up in New York, where he attended Bronx High School of Science. He recalled, "I had no business being there. I was no good in science or math and was completely out of step with the other kids . . . so I drifted toward the school's literary magazine." It was there that he published his first fiction and poetry.

He went on to graduate from Kenyon College in Ohio and attend Columbia University, then worked in publishing as senior editor for the New American Library and editor in chief at Dial Press.

After a move to California, he published his

third novel, *The Book of Daniel*, in 1971. It firmly established him as a major writer. He is also known for *Ragtime*, a novel in which actual figures from American history mingle with characters of his own creation. Published in 1975, it was made into a film and musical. In *Writers on Writing* he was quoted as saying, "Good writing is supposed to evoke sensation in the reader—not the fact that it's raining but the feeling of being rained upon."

****

✎ The Author's Style

In many of his novels, the best known of which is probably *Ragtime*, Doctorow has illuminated what it means to succeed (or to try to succeed) in America. His characters are often preoccupied with money, property, social status, and other aspects of the American Dream. The unrecognized, unacknowledged tensions that lie beneath the surface of American life are central to Doctorow's purpose in writing. To reveal these tensions he often makes use of coincidence, highlights ironic connections between characters, and creates characters who are anxious to break

free from the restrictions imposed by family or culture.

Doctorow develops character not only through description, but also by means of dialogue. He is adept at rendering the idiom, accent, and verbal gestures of his characters. This is a way of both making them come to life as individuals and marking them as members of specific families, ethnic groups, or social classes. Like Eudora Welty, Bobbie Ann Mason, and Raymond Carver, one of his interests as a writer is how family members communicate with one another.

The Writer in the Family

E. L. DOCTOROW

 LITERARY LENS: THEME As you read, consider the **themes** of the story and how they interact to create a complex story.

*I*n 1955 my father died with his ancient mother still alive in a nursing home. The old lady was ninety and hadn't even known he was ill. Thinking the shock might kill her, my aunts told her that he had moved to Arizona for his bronchitis. To the immigrant generation of my grandmother, Arizona was the American equivalent of the Alps, it was where you went if you had the money. Since my father had failed in all the business enterprises of his life, this was the aspect of the news my grandmother dwelled on, that he had finally had some success. And so it came about that as we mourned him at home in our stocking feet, my grandmother was bragging to her cronies about her son's new life in the dry air of the desert.

My aunts had decided on their course of action without consulting us. It meant neither my mother nor my brother nor I could

My brother Harold and I didn't mind—it was always a nightmare at the old people's home, where they all sat around staring at us while we tried to make conversation with Grandma. She looked terrible, had numbers of ailments, and her mind wandered.

visit Grandma because we were supposed to have moved west too, a family, after all. My brother Harold and I didn't mind—it was always a nightmare at the old people's home, where they all sat around staring at us while we tried to make conversation with Grandma. She looked terrible, had numbers of ailments, and her mind wandered. Not seeing her was no disappointment either for my mother, who had never gotten along with the old woman and did not visit when she could have. But what was disturbing was that my aunts had acted in the manner of that side of the family of making government on everyone's behalf, the true citizens by blood and the lesser citizens by marriage. It was exactly this attitude that had tormented my mother all her married life. She claimed Jack's family had never accepted her. She had battled them for twenty-five years as an outsider.

A few weeks after the end of our ritual mourning my Aunt Frances phoned us from her home in Larchmont. Aunt Frances was the wealthier of my father's sisters. Her husband was a lawyer, and both of her sons were at Amherst.[1] She had called to say that Grandma was asking why she didn't hear from Jack. I had answered the phone. "You're the writer in the family," my aunt said. "Your father had so much faith in you. Would you mind making up something? Send it to me and I'll read it to her. She won't know the difference."

That evening, at the kitchen table, I pushed my homework aside and composed a letter. I tried to imagine my father's response to his new life. He had never been west. He had never traveled anywhere. In his generation the great journey was from the working class to the professional class. He hadn't managed that either. But he loved New York, where he had been born and lived his life, and he was always discovering new things about it. He especially loved the old parts of the city below Canal Street, where he would find ships' chandlers[2] or firms that wholesaled in spices and teas. He was a salesman for an appliance jobber with accounts all over the city. He liked to bring home rare cheeses or exotic foreign vegetables that were sold only in

---

1 **Amherst:** Amherst College in Massachusetts, a prestigious private college

2 **chandlers:** retailers who sell specialized items; in this case, items relating to ships

certain neighborhoods. Once he brought home a barometer,[3] another time an antique ship's telescope in a wooden case with a brass snap.

"Dear Mama," I wrote. "Arizona is beautiful. The sun shines all day and the air is warm and I feel better than I have in years. The desert is not as **barren** as you would expect, but filled with wildflowers and cactus plants and peculiar crooked trees that look like men holding their arms out. You can see great distances in whatever direction you turn and to the west is a range of mountains maybe fifty miles from here, but in the morning with the sun on them you can see the snow on their crests."

barren: lifeless

My aunt called some days later and told me it was when she read this letter aloud to the old lady that the full effect of Jack's death came over her. She had to excuse herself and went out in the parking lot to cry. "I wept so," she said. "I felt such terrible longing for him. You're so right, he loved to go places, he loved life, he loved everything."

*W*e began trying to organize our lives. My father had borrowed money against his insurance and there was very little left. Some commissions were still due but it didn't look as if his firm would honor them. There was a couple of thousand dollars in a savings bank that had to be maintained there

SOUTHERN ARIZONA, MAYNARD DIXON, 1941

---

3 **barometer:** an instrument used to measure atmospheric pressure, with the purpose of forecasting the weather

until the estate was settled. The lawyer involved was Aunt Frances' husband and he was very proper. "The estate!" my mother muttered, gesturing as if to pull out her hair. "The estate!" She applied for a job part-time in the admissions office of the hospital where my father's terminal illness had been diagnosed, and where he had spent some months until they had sent him home to die. She knew a lot of the doctors and staff and she had learned "from bitter experience," as she told them, about the hospital routine. She was hired.

I hated that hospital, it was dark and grim and full of tortured people. I thought it was **masochistic** of my mother to seek out a job there, but did not tell her so.

masochistic:
self-punishing

We lived in an apartment on the corner of 175th Street and the Grand Concourse, one flight up. Three rooms. I shared the bedroom with my brother. It was jammed with furniture because when my father had required a hospital bed in the last weeks of his illness we had moved some of the living-room pieces into the bedroom and made over the living room for him. We had to navigate bookcases, beds, a gateleg table,[4] bureaus, a record player and radio console, stacks of 78 albums,[5] my brother's trombone and music stand, and so on. My mother continued to sleep on the convertible sofa in the living room that had been their bed before his illness. The two rooms were connected by a narrow hall made even narrower by bookcases along the wall. Off the hall were a small kitchen and dinette and a bathroom. There were lots of appliances in the kitchen—broiler, toaster, pressure cooker, counter-top dishwasher, blender—that my father had gotten through his job, at cost.[6] A treasured phrase in our house: *at cost*. But most of these fixtures went unused because my mother did not care for them. Chromium[7] devices with timers or gauges that required the reading of elaborate instructions were not for her. They were in part responsible for the awful clutter of our lives and now she wanted to get rid of them. "We're being buried," she said. "Who needs them!"

So we agreed to throw out or sell anything inessential. While I found boxes for the appliances and my brother tied the boxes with twine, my mother opened my father's closet and took out his clothes. He had several suits because as a salesman he needed to look his best. My mother wanted us to

---

4 **gateleg table:** a table with sides that can be raised and supported by moveable legs

5 **78 albums:** records designed to be played at 78 revolutions per minute

6 **at cost:** strictly what it costs to make the product, without fees for labor, taxes, shipping, etc.

7 **chromium:** a metallic element

try on his suits to see which of them could be altered and used. My brother refused to try them on. I tried on one jacket which was too large for me. The lining inside the sleeves chilled my arms and the vaguest scent of my father's being came to me.

"This is way too big," I said.

"Don't worry," my mother said. "I had it cleaned. Would I let you wear it if I hadn't?"

It was the evening, the end of winter, and snow was coming down on the windowsill and melting as it settled. The ceiling bulb glared on a pile of my father's suits and trousers on hangers flung across the bed in the shape of a dead man. We refused to try on anything more, and my mother began to cry.

"What are you crying for?" my brother shouted. "You wanted to get rid of things, didn't you?"

A few weeks later my aunt phoned again and said she thought it would be necessary to have another letter from Jack. Grandma had fallen out of her chair and bruised herself and was very depressed.

"How long does this go on?" my mother said.

"It's not so terrible," my aunt said, "for the little time left to make things easier for her."

My mother slammed down the phone. "He can't even die when he wants to!" she cried. "Even death comes second to Mama! What are they afraid of, the shock will kill her? Nothing can kill her. She's indestructible! A stake through the heart couldn't kill her!"

When I sat down in the kitchen to write the letter I found it more difficult than the first one. "Don't watch me," I said to my brother. "It's hard enough."

"You don't have to do something just because someone wants you to," Harold said. He was two years older than me and had started at City College; but when my father became ill he had switched to night school and gotten a job in a record store.

"Dear Mama," I wrote. "I hope you're feeling well. We're all fit as a fiddle. The life here is good and the people are very friendly and informal. Nobody wears suits and ties here. Just a pair of slacks and a short-sleeved

> *T*he ceiling bulb glared on a pile of my father's suits and trousers on hangers flung across the bed in the shape of a dead man. We refused to try on anything more, and my mother began to cry.

shirt. Perhaps a sweater in the evening. I have bought into a very success-ful radio and record business and I'm doing very well. You remember Jack's Electric, my old place on Forty-third Street? Well, now it's Jack's Arizona Electric and we have a line of television sets as well."

I sent that letter off to my Aunt Frances, and as we all knew she would, she phoned soon after. My brother held his hand over the mouthpiece. "It's Frances with her latest review," he said.

"Jonathan? You're a very talented young man. I just wanted to tell you what a blessing your letter was. Her whole face lit up when I read the part about Jack's store. That would be an excellent way to continue."

"Well, I hope I don't have to do this anymore, Aunt Frances. It's not very honest."

Her tone changed. "Is your mother there? Let me talk to her."

"She's not here," I said.

"Tell her not to worry," my aunt said. "A poor old lady who has never wished anything but the best for her will soon die."

I did not repeat this to my mother, for whom it would have been one more in the family anthology of unforgivable remarks. But then I had to suf-fer it myself for the possible truth it might embody. Each side defended its position with **rhetoric**, but I, who wanted peace, rationalized the snubs and rebuffs each inflicted on the other, taking no stands, like my father himself.

Years ago his life had fallen into a pattern of business failures and missed opportunities. The great debate between his family on one side, and my mother Ruth on the other, was this: who was responsible for the fact that he had not lived up to anyone's expectations?

As to the **prophecies**, when spring came my mother's prevailed. Grandma was still alive.

One balmy Sunday my mother and brother and I took the bus to the Beth El cemetery in New Jersey to visit my father's grave. It was situated on a slight rise. We stood looking over rolling fields embedded with monuments. Here and there processions of black cars wound their way through the lanes, or clusters of people stood at open graves. My father's grave was planted with tiny shoots of evergreen but it lacked a headstone. We had chosen one and paid for it and then the stonecutters had gone on strike. Without a headstone my father did not seem to be honorably dead. He didn't seem to me properly buried.

My mother gazed at the plot beside his, reserved for her coffin. "They were always too fine for other people," she said. "Even in the old days on

rhetoric:
convincing words

prophecies:
mystical predictions

Stanton Street. They put on airs. Nobody was ever good enough for them. Finally Jack himself was not good enough for them. Except to get them things wholesale. Then he was good enough for them."

"Mom, please," my brother said.

"If I had known. Before I ever met him he was tied to his mama's apron strings. And Essie's apron strings were like chains, let me tell you. We had to live where we could be near them for the Sunday visits. Every Sunday, that was my life, a visit to mamaleh.[8] Whatever she knew I wanted, a better apartment, a stick of furniture, a summer camp for the boys, she spoke against it. You know your father, every decision had to be considered and reconsidered. And nothing changed. Nothing ever changed."

She began to cry. We sat her down on a nearby bench. My brother walked off and read the names on stones. I looked at my mother, who was crying, and I went off after my brother.

"Mom's still crying," I said. "Shouldn't we do something?"

"It's all right," he said. "It's what she came here for."

"Yes," I said, and then a sob escaped from my throat. "But I feel like crying too."

My brother Harold put his arm around me. "Look at this old black stone here," he said. "The way it's carved. You can see the changing fashion in monuments—just like everything else."

Somewhere in this time I began dreaming of my father. Not the **robust** father of my childhood, the handsome man with healthy pink skin and brown eyes and a mustache and the thinning hair parted in the middle. My dead father. We were taking him home from the hospital. It was understood that he had come back from death. This was amazing and joyous. On the other hand, he was terribly mysteriously damaged, or, more accurately, spoiled and unclean. He was very yellowed and debilitated by his death, and there were no guarantees that he wouldn't soon die again. He seemed aware of this and his entire personality was changed. He was angry and impatient with all of us. We were trying to help him in some way, struggling to get him home, but something prevented us, something we had to fix, a tattered suitcase that had sprung open, some mechanical thing: he had a car but it wouldn't start; or the car was made of wood; or his clothes, which had become too large for him, had caught in the

robust:
strong; vigorous

8 **mamaleh:** Yiddish for "mother"

> *H*e loved to walk. When I went walking with him he would say: "Hold your shoulders back, don't slump. Hold your head up and look at the world. Walk as if you meant it!"

door. In one version he was all bandaged and as we tried to lift him from his wheelchair into a taxi the bandage began to unroll and catch in the spokes of the wheelchair. This seemed to be some unreasonableness on his part. My mother looked on sadly and tried to get him to cooperate.

That was the dream. I shared it with no one. Once when I woke, crying out, my brother turned on the light. He wanted to know what I'd been dreaming but I pretended I didn't remember. The dream made me feel guilty. I felt guilty *in* the dream too because my enraged father knew we didn't want to live with him. The dream represented us taking him home, or trying to, but it was nevertheless understood by all of us that he was to live alone. He was this **derelict** back from death, but what we were doing was taking him to some place where he would live by himself without help from anyone until he died again.

derelict: good-for-nothing

At one point I became so fearful of this dream that I tried not to go to sleep. I tried to think of good things about my father and to remember him before his illness. He used to call me "matey." "Hello, matey," he would say when he came home from work. He always wanted us to go someplace—to the store, to the park, to a ball game. He loved to walk. When I went walking with him he would say: "Hold your shoulders back, don't slump. Hold your head up and look at the world. Walk as if you meant it!" As he strode down the street his shoulders moved from side to side, as if he was hearing some kind of cakewalk. He moved with a bounce. He was always eager to see what was around the corner.

*T*he next request for a letter coincided with a special occasion in the house. My brother Harold had met a girl he liked and had gone out with her several times. Now she was coming to our house for dinner.

We had prepared for this for days, cleaning everything in sight, giving the house a going-over, washing the dust of disuse from the glasses and good dishes. My mother came home early from work to get the dinner going. We opened the gateleg table in the living room and brought in the kitchen chairs. My mother spread the table with a laundered white cloth and put out her silver. It was the first family occasion since my father's illness.

I liked my brother's girlfriend a lot. She was a thin girl with very straight hair and she had a terrific smile. Her presence seemed to excite the air. It was amazing to have a living breathing girl in our house. She looked around and what she said was: "Oh, I've never seen so many books!" While she and my brother sat at the table my mother was in the kitchen putting the food into serving bowls and I was going from the kitchen to the living room, kidding around like a waiter, with a white cloth over my arm and a high style of service, placing the serving dish of green beans on the table with a flourish. In the kitchen my mother's eyes were sparkling. She looked at me and nodded and mimed the words: "She's adorable!"

My brother suffered himself to be waited on. He was wary of what we might say. He kept glancing at the girl—her name was Susan—to see if we met with her approval. She worked in an insurance office and was taking courses in accounting at City College. Harold was under a terrible strain but he was excited and happy too. He had bought a bottle of Concord-grape wine to go with the roast chicken. He held up his glass and proposed a toast. My mother said: "To good health and happiness," and we all drank, even I. At that moment the phone rang and I went into the bedroom to get it.

"Jonathan? This is your Aunt Frances. How is everyone?"

"Fine, thank you."

"I want to ask one last favor of you. I need a letter from Jack. Your grandma's very ill. Do you think you can?"

"Who is it?" my mother called from the living room.

"OK, Aunt Frances," I said quickly. "I have to go now, we're eating dinner." And I hung up the phone.

"It was my friend Louie," I said, sitting back down. "He didn't know the math pages to review."

The dinner was very fine. Harold and Susan washed the dishes and by the time they were done my mother and I had folded up the gateleg table and put it back against the wall and I had swept the crumbs up with the carpet sweeper. We all sat and talked and listened to records for a while and then my brother took Susan home. The evening had gone very well.

*O*nce when my mother wasn't home my brother had pointed out some-thing: the letters from Jack weren't really necessary. "What is this ritual?" he said, holding his palms up. "Grandma is almost totally blind, she's half deaf and crippled. Does the situation really call for a literary composition? Does it need **verisimilitude**? Would the old lady know the difference if she was read the phone book?

"Then why did Aunt Frances ask me?"

"That is the question, Jonathan. Why did she? After all, she could write the letter herself—what difference would it make? And if not Frances, why not Frances' sons, the Amherst students? They should have learned by now to write."

"But they're not Jack's sons," I said.

"That's exactly the point," my brother said. "The idea is *service*. Dad used to bust his balls getting them things wholesale, getting them deals on things. Frances of Westchester really needed things at cost. And Aunt Molly. And Aunt Molly's husband, and Aunt Molly's ex-husband. Grandma, if she needed an errand done. He was always on the hook for something. They never thought his time was important. They never thought every favor he got was one he had to pay back. Appliances, records, watches, china, opera tickets, any goddamn thing. Call Jack."

"It was a matter of pride to him to be able to do things for them," I said. "To have connections."

"Yeah, I wonder why," my brother said. He looked out the window.

Then suddenly it dawned on me that I was being **implicated**.

"You should use your head more," my brother said.

Yet I had agreed once again to write a letter from the desert and so I did. I mailed it off to Aunt Frances. A few days later, when I came home from school, I thought I saw her sitting in her car in front of our house. She drove a black Buick Roadmaster, a very large clean car with whitewall tires. It was Aunt Frances all right. She blew the horn when she saw me. I went over and leaned in at the window.

"Hello, Jonathan," she said. "I haven't long. Can you get in the car?"

"Mom's not home," I said. "She's working."

"I know that. I came to talk to you."

"Would you like to come upstairs?"

"I can't, I have to get back to Larchmont. Can you get in for a moment, please?"

I got in the car. My Aunt Frances was a very pretty white-haired woman,

---

verisimilitude: the appearance of truth

implicated: involved; drawn in

very elegant, and she wore tasteful clothes. I had always liked her and from the time I was a child she had enjoyed pointing out to everyone that I looked more like her son than Jack's. She wore white gloves and held the steering wheel and looked straight ahead as she talked, as if the car was in traffic and not sitting at the curb.

"Jonathan," she said, "there is your letter on the seat. Needless to say I didn't read it to Grandma. I'm giving it back to you and I won't ever say a word to anyone. This is just between us. I never expected cruelty from you. I never thought you were capable of doing something so deliberately cruel and perverse."

I said nothing.

"Your mother has very bitter feelings and now I see she has poisoned you with them. She has always resented the family. She is a very strong-willed, selfish person."

"No she isn't," I said.

"I wouldn't expect you to agree. She drove poor Jack crazy with her demands. She always had the highest aspirations and he could never fulfill them to her satisfaction. When he still had his store he kept your mother's brother, who drank, on salary. After the war when he began to make a little money he had to buy Ruth a mink jacket because she was so desperate to have one. He had debts to pay but she wanted a mink. He was a very special person, my brother, he should have accomplished something special, but he loved your mother and devoted his life to her. And all she ever thought about was keeping up with the Joneses."

I watched the traffic going up the Grand Concourse. A bunch of kids were waiting at the bus stop at the corner. They had put their books on the ground and were horsing around.

"I'm sorry I have to descend to this," Aunt Frances said. "I don't like talking about people this way. If I have nothing good to say about someone, I'd rather not say anything. How is Harold?"

"Fine."

"Did he help you write this marvelous letter?"

"No."

After a moment she said more softly: "How are you all getting along?"

"Fine."

"I would invite you up for Passover[9] if I thought your mother would accept."

I didn't answer.

---

9 Passover: the Jewish holiday commemorating the Hebrews' freedom from slavery in Egypt

She turned on the engine. "I'll say good-bye now, Jonathan. Take your letter. I hope you give some time to thinking about what you've done."

*T*hat evening when my mother came home from work I saw that she wasn't as pretty as my Aunt Frances. I usually thought my mother was a good-looking woman, but I saw now that she was too heavy and that her hair was undistinguished.

"Why are you looking at me?" she said.

"I'm not."

"I learned something interesting today," my mother said. "We may be eligible for a V.A. pension because of the time your father spent in the Navy."

That took me by surprise. Nobody had ever told me my father was in the Navy.

"In World War I," she said, "he went to Webb's Naval Academy on the Harlem River. He was training to be an ensign. But the war ended and he never got his commission."

After dinner the three of us went through the closets looking for my father's papers, hoping to find some proof that could be filed with the Veterans Administration. We came up with two things, a Victory medal, which my brother said everyone got for being in the service during the Great War, and an astounding

sepia:
brown-toned

sepia photograph of my father and his shipmates on the deck of a ship. They were dressed in bell-bottoms and T-shirts and armed with mops and pails, brooms and brushes.

"I never knew this," I found myself saying. "I never knew this."

"You just don't remember," my brother said.

I was able to pick out my father. He stood at the end of the row, a thin, handsome boy with a full head of hair, a mustache, and an intelligent smiling

countenance:
facial expression

countenance.

"He had a joke," my mother said. "They called their training ship the S.S. *Constipation* because it never moved."

> *W*e came up with two things, a Victory medal, which my brother said everyone got for being in the service during the Great War, and an astounding sepia photograph of my father and his shipmates on the deck of a ship.

Neither the picture nor the medal was proof of anything, but my brother thought a duplicate of my father's service record had to be in Washington somewhere and that it was just a matter of learning how to go about finding it.

CENTRAL NEVADA, MAYNARD DIXON, 1941

"The pension wouldn't amount to much," my mother said. "Twenty or thirty dollars. But it would certainly help."

I took the picture of my father and his shipmates and propped it against the lamp at my bedside. I looked into his youthful face and tried to relate it to the Father I knew. I looked at the picture a long time. Only gradually did my eye connect it to the set of Great Sea Novels in the bottom shelf of the bookcase a few feet away. My father had given that set to me: it was uniformly bound in green with gilt lettering and it included works by Melville, Conrad, Victor Hugo and Captain Marryat. And lying across the top of the books, jammed in under the sagging shelf above, was his old ship's telescope in its wooden case with the brass snap.

imperceptive: dense; undiscerning

I thought how stupid, and **imperceptive**, and self-centered I had been never to have understood while he was alive what my father's dream for his life had been.

On the other hand, I had written in my last letter from Arizona—the one that had so angered Aunt Frances—something that might allow me, the writer in the family, to soften my judgment of myself. I will conclude by giving the letter here in its entirety.

> Dear Mama,
>
> This will be my final letter to you since I have been told by the doctors that I am dying.
>
> I have sold my store at a very fine profit and am sending Frances a check for five thousand dollars to be deposited in your account. My present to you, Mamaleh. Let Frances show you the passbook.
>
> As for the nature of my ailment, the doctors haven't told me what it is, but I know that I am simply dying of the wrong life. I should never have come to the desert. It wasn't the place for me.
>
> I have asked Ruth and the boys to have my body cremated and the ashes scattered in the ocean.
>
> Your loving son
> Jack

Read and Think Critically

Explain, Interpret, Analyze

1. **THEME** A common **theme** for Doctorow is what it means to succeed, or try to succeed, in America. In what ways was the **narrator's** father both a failure and a success?

2. Consider the letters that Jonathan composed as the "writer in the family." Explain what these letters say about the interplay between lies and the truth in fiction.

3. If you were a psychologist, how would you interpret the dream on pages 609–610?

4. Aunt Frances thinks the final letter Jonathan writes is perverse and cruel. What is your evaluation of the letter?

5. **THE AUTHOR'S STYLE** Doctorow's works are often concerned with tensions between family members. What family tensions do you see in the story? Analyze how the themes of family tensions, success, and truth in fiction interact throughout the story.

Before You Read

Russell Banks 1940–

About the Author

Born in Massachusetts to a working-class family, Russell Banks was the eldest of four children and the first in his family to finish college. He intended to become a plumber like his father until his mother convinced him to go to college and study English. "The idea of being a writer was like the idea of being a butterfly," he has said.

Banks worked as a shoe salesman and window trimmer before becoming an editor, publisher, and writer. A world traveler who has lived in the Caribbean, he is perhaps best known for his novels *Continental Drift* and *Cloudsplitter*, both finalists for the Pulitzer Prize. Later novels *Affliction* and *The Sweet Hereafter* were adapted for the screen, the latter of which won the International Critics Prize at the 1997 Cannes Film Festival.

★★★★★★★★★★★

The Author's Style

The fiction of Banks usually involves people who confront bleak economic realities and are desperate for basic necessities and a better life. These characters are often part of conflicts involving race and social class. They are also affected by both their physical surroundings and the darker moods and motives behind human behavior.

Banks' characters are often feisty and resilient, but not particularly talkative or eloquent. They learn from experience about the terrible potential for disaster in everyday life and find themselves waiting, enduring, and trying to heal. Some Banks stories read like contemporary allegories or fables, suggesting broad implications from relatively simple events.

Banks conveys all this through concrete, factual descriptions and unemotional statements. He focuses on the gritty details of the physical world. The close attention he pays to the rough lives of working-class Americans has led some readers to compare his writing to that of other writers such as Raymond Carver, Bobbie Ann Mason, and Tobias Wolff.

The Fish

RUSSELL BANKS

LITERARY LENS: THE FABLE A **fable** is a brief tale featuring fantastic events meant to convey a useful truth or to satirize human foibles. Political satirists have been known to hide criticism of political leaders within a fable. Watch for elements of the fable in this unusual short story.

When Colonel Tung's first attempt to destroy the fish failed, everyone, even the Buddhists, was astonished. On the colonel's orders, a company of soldiers under the command of a young lieutenant named Han marched out from the village early one summer morning as far as the bridge. Departing from the road there, the soldiers made their way in single file through the bamboo groves and shreds of golden mist to a clearing, where they stepped with care over spongy ground to the very edge of the pond, which was then the size of a soccer field. Aiming automatic weapons into the water, the troopers waited for the fish to arrive. A large crowd from the village gathered behind them and, since most of the people were Buddhists, **fretted** and scowled at the soldiers, saying, "Shame! Shame!" Even some Catholics from the village joined the scolding, though it had been their complaints that first had drawn

fretted:
pestered

the colonel's attention to the existence of the huge fish and had obliged him to attempt to destroy it, for pilgrimages to view the fish had come to seem like acts of opposition to his administration. In great numbers, the Buddhists from other districts were visiting the Buddhists in his district, sleeping in local homes, buying food from local vendors, and trading goods of various kinds, until it had begun to seem to Colonel Tung that there were many more Buddhists in his district than Catholics, and this frightened him. Thus his opinion that the pilgrimages to view the fish were acts of political opposition, and thus his determination to destroy the fish.

Shortly after the soldiers lined up at the shore, the fish broke the surface of the water halfway across the pond. It was a silver swirl in the morning sun, a clean swash of movement, like a single brushstroke, for the fish was thought to be a reincarnation of Rad, the painter, an early disciple of Buddha. The soldiers readied their weapons. Lieutenant Han repeated his order: "Wait until I say to fire," he said, and there was a second swirl, a lovely arc of silver bubbles, closer to shore this time. The crowd had gone silent. Many were moving their lips in prayer; all were straining to see over and around the line of soldiers at the

Then there it was, a few feet out and hovering in the water like a cloud in the sky, one large dark eye watching the soldiers as if with curiosity, delicate fins fluttering gently in the dark water like translucent leaves. "Fire!" the lieutenant cried.

shore. Then there it was, a few feet out and hovering in the water like a cloud in the sky, one large dark eye watching the soldiers as if with curiosity, delicate fins fluttering gently in the dark water like **translucent** leaves. "Fire!" the lieutenant cried. The soldiers obeyed, and their weapons roared for what seemed a long time. The pond erupted and boiled in white fury, and when finally the water was still once again, everyone in the crowd rushed to the shore and searched for the remains of the fish. Even the lieutenant and his band of soldiers pushed to the mud at the edge of the water and looked for the fish, or what everyone thought would be chunks of the fish floating on the still surface of the pond. But they saw nothing, not a scrap of it, until they noticed halfway across the pond a swelling in the water, and the fish rolled and dove, sending a wave sweeping in to shore, where the crowd cried out joyfully and the soldiers and the young lieutenant cursed, for they knew that Colonel Tung was not going to like this, not at all.

translucent: see-through

They were correct. Colonel Tung took off his sunglasses and glared at the lieutenant, then turned in his chair to face the electric fan for a moment. Finally, replacing his glasses, he said, "Let us assume that in that pond an enemy submarine is surfacing at night to send spies and saboteurs[1] into our midst. Do you have the means to destroy it?" He tapped a cigarette into an ebony holder and lighted it. The lieutenant, like the colonel a man trained at the academy but rapidly adapting his skills to life in the provinces, said yes, he could destroy such an enemy. He would mine the pond, he said, and detonate the mines from shore. "Indeed," the colonel said. "That sounds like a fine idea," and he went back to work.

"*Let* us assume that in that pond an enemy submarine is surfacing at night to send spies and saboteurs into our midst. Do you have the means to destroy it?"

From a rowboat, the soldiers placed in the pond ten pie-sized mines connected by insulated wires to one another and to a detonator and battery, and when everything was ready and the area had been cleared of civilians, Lieutenant Han set off the detonator from behind a mound of earth they had heaped up for this purpose. There was a deep, convulsive rumble and the surface of the pond blew off, causing a wet wind that had the strength of a gale[2] and tore leaves from the trees and bent the bamboo stalks to the ground. Immediately after the explosion, everyone from the village who was not already at the site rushed to the pond and joined the **throng** that encircled it. Everything that had ever lived in or near the pond seemed to be dead and floating on its surface—carp, crayfish, smelts, catfish, eels, tortoises, frogs, egrets, woodcocks, peccaries, snakes, feral dogs, lizards, doves, shellfish and all the plants from the bottom, the long grasses, weeds, and reeds, and the banyans, mangroves and other trees rooted in the water and the flowering bushes and the lilies that had floated on the surface of the pond—everything once alive seemed dead. Many people wept openly, some prayed, burned incense, chanted, and others, more practical, rushed about with baskets, gathering up the unexpected harvest. The lieutenant and his soldiers walked intently around the pond, searching for the giant fish. When they could not find it, they rowed out to the middle of the pond and searched there. But still, amongst the hundreds of dead fish and plants, birds

throng: crowd

---

1 **saboteurs:** those who intend to sabotage, or damage

2 **gale:** a strong wind

> Soon the settlement surrounding the pond was as large as the village where the colonel's district headquarters was located. Naturally, this alarmed the colonel, for these pilgrims were Buddhists, many of them fanatics, and he, a Catholic, was no longer sure he could rule them.

obliquely: diagonally

and animals floating in the water, they saw no huge silver fish, no carcass that could justify such carnage. Then, as they began to row back toward shore, the lieutenant, who was standing at the bow, his hand shading his eyes from the milky glare of the water, saw before them once again the rolling, shiny side of the giant fish, its dorsal fin like a black knife slicing **obliquely** across their bow, when it disappeared, only to reappear off the stern[3] a ways, swerving back and suddenly heading straight at the small, crowded boat. The men shouted in fear, and at the last possible second the fish looped back and dove into the dark waters below. The crowd at the shore had seen it, and a great cheer went up, and in seconds there were drums and cymbals and all kinds of song joining the cheers, as the soldiers rowed slowly, glumly, in to shore.

The reputation of the fish and its miraculous powers began to spread rapidly across the whole country, and great flocks of believers undertook pigrimages to the pond, where they set up tents and booths on the shore. Soon the settlement surrounding the pond was as large as the village where the colonel's district headquarters was located. Naturally, this alarmed the colonel, for these pilgrims were Buddhists, many of them fanatics, and he, a Catholic, was no longer sure he could rule them. "We must destroy that fish," he said to the lieutenant, who suggested this time that he and his soldiers pretend to join the believers and scatter pieces of bread over the waters to feed the fish, as had become the custom. They would do this from the boat, he said, and with specially sweetened chunks of bread, and when the fish was used to being fed this way and approached the boat carelessly close, they would lob hand grenades painted white as bread into the water, and the fish, deceived, would swallow one or two or more whole, as it did the bread, and that would be that. Colonel Tung admired the plan and sent his man off to

---

3 stern: the rear end of a boat

implement it instantly. Lieutenant Han's inventiveness surprised the colonel and pleased him, though he foresaw problems, for if the plan worked, he would be obliged to promote the man, which would place Han in a position where he could begin to **covet** his superior's position as district commander. This damned fish, the colonel said to himself, may be the worst thing to happen to me.

It soon appeared that Lieutenant Han's plan was working, for the fish, which seemed recently to have grown to an even more gigantic size than before and was now almost twice the size of the boat, approached the boat without fear and rubbed affectionately against it, or so it seemed, whenever the soldiers rowed out to the middle of the pond and scattered large chunks of bread, which they did twice a day. Each time, the fish gobbled the chunks, cleared the water entirely and swam rapidly away. The throng on shore cheered, for they, too, had taken the bait—they believed that the soldiers, under the colonel's orders, had come to appreciate the fish's value to the district as a whole, to Catholics as much as to Buddhists, for everyone, it seemed, was profiting from its presence—tentmakers, carpenters,

implement:
carry out

covet:
envy; desire

RETURN TO THE BEGINNING, IN MEMORY OF GINGER, JOSEPH RAFFAEL, 1981

> "*If* this time we succeed in destroying the fish," a soldier said, "the people may not let us get back to shore. There are now thousands of them, Catholics as well as Buddhists, and but ten of us."

farmers, storekeepers, clothiers, woodchoppers, scribes, entrepreneurs of all types, entertainers, even, musicians and jugglers, and of course the manufacturers of altars and religious images and also of paintings and screens purported to have been made by the original Rad, the artist and early disciple of Buddha, now reincarnated as the giant fish.

When finally Lieutenant Han gave the order to float the specially prepared grenades out with the bread, several soldiers **balked**. They had no objections to blowing up the fish, but they were alarmed by the size of the crowd now more or less residing on the shore and, as usual, watching them in hopes of seeing the fish surface to feed. "If this time we succeed in destroying the fish," a soldier said, "the people may not let us get back to shore. There are now thousands of them, Catholics as well as Buddhists, and but ten of us." The lieutenant pointed out that the crowd had no weapons and they had automatic rifles that could easily clear a path from the shore to the road and back to the village. "And once the fish is gone, the people will go away, and things will settle back into their normal ways again." The soldiers took heart and proceeded to drop the grenades into the water with an equal number of chunks of bread. The fish, large as a house, had been lurking peacefully off the stern of the boat and now swept past, swooping up all the bread and the grenades in one huge swallow. It turned away and rolled, exposing its silver belly to the sun, as if in gratitude, and the crowd cried out in pleasure. The music rose, with drums, cymbals, flutes joining happily and floating to the sky on swirling clouds of incense, while the soldiers rowed furiously for shore. The boat scraped gravel, and the troopers jumped out, dragged the boat up onto the mud and made their way quickly through the throng toward the road. As they reached the road, they heard the first of the explosions, then the others in rapid succession, a tangled knot of bangs as all the grenades went off, in the air, it seemed, out of the water and certainly not inside the fish's belly. It was as if the fish were spitting the grenades out just as they were about to explode, creating the effect of a fireworks display above the pond, which must have been what caused the people gathered at the shore to break into sustained,

balked: hesitated; refused

awestruck applause and then, long into the day and the following night, song.

Now the reputation of the miraculous fish grew **tenfold**, and bus-loads of pilgrims began to arrive from as far away as Saigon and Bangkok. People on bicycles, on donkeys, in trucks and in oxcarts made their way down the dusty road from the village to the pond, where as many of them as could find a spot got down to the shore and prayed to the fish for help, usually against disease and injury, for the fish was thought to be especially effective in this way. Some prayed for wealth or for success in love or for revenge against their enemies, but these requests were not thought likely to be answered, though it surely did no harm to try. Most of those who came now took away with them containers filled with water from the pond. They arrived bearing bowls, buckets, fruit tins, jars, gourds, even cups, and they took the water with them back to their homes in the far corners of the country, where many of them were able to sell off small vials of the water for surprisingly high prices to those unfortunate neighbors and loved ones unable to make the long overland journey to the pond. Soldiers, too, whenever they passed through Colonel Tung's district, came to the pond and filled their canteens with the magical waters. More than once a helicopter landed on the shore, and a troop of soldiers jumped out, ran to the pond, filled their canteens and returned to the helicopter and took off again. Thus, when Lieutenant Han proposed to Colonel Tung that this time they try to destroy the fish by poisoning the water in the pond, the colonel demurred. "I think that instead of trying to kill the fish, we learn how to profit from it ourselves. It's too dangerous now," he observed, "to risk offending the people by taking away what has become their main source of income. What I have in mind, my boy, is a levy, a tax on the water that is taken away from this district. A modest levy, not enough to discourage the pilgrims, but more than enough to warrant the efforts and costs of collection." The colonel smiled slyly and set his lieutenant to the task. There will be no promotions now, he said to himself, for there are no heroics in tax collecting.

And so a sort of calm and orderliness settled over the district, which pleased everyone, Colonel Tung most of all, but also Lieutenant Han, who managed to collect the tax on the water so effectively that he was able without detection to cut a small percentage out of it for himself, and the soldiers, who felt much safer collecting taxes than trying to destroy a miraculous and

awestruck:
amazed; reverential

tenfold:
ten times

beloved fish, and the people themselves, who, because they now paid a fee for the privilege of taking away a container of pond water, no longer doubted the water's magical power to cure illness and injury, to let the blind see, the lame walk, the deaf hear, the dumb talk. The summer turned into fall, the fall became winter, and there were no changes in the district, until the spring, when it became obvious to everyone that the pond was much smaller in diameter than it had been in previous springs. The summer rains that year were heavy, though not unusually so, and the colonel hoped that afterwards the pond would be as large as before, but it was not. In September, when the dry season began, the colonel tried to restrict the quantity of water taken from the pond. This proved impossible, for by now too many people had too many reasons to keep on taking water away. A powerful black market operated in several cities, and at night tanker trucks edged down to the shore, where they sucked thousands of gallons of water out, and the next morning the surface of the pond would be yet another foot lower than before and encircling it would be yet another mud aureole[4] inside the old shoreline.

At last there came the morning when the pond was barely large enough to hold the fish. The colonel, wearing sunglasses, white scarf, and cigarette holder, and Lieutenant Han and the soldiers and many of the pilgrims walked across the drying mud to the edge of the water, where they lined up around the tiny pool, little more than a puddle now, and examined the fish. It lay on its side, half exposed to the sun. One gill, blood-red inside, opened and closed, but no water ran through. One eye was above water, one below, and the eye above was clouded over and fading to white. A pilgrim who happened to be carrying a pail leaned down, filled his pail and splashed the water over the side of the fish. Another pilgrim with a gourd joined him, and two soldiers went back to the encampment and returned with a dozen containers of various types and sizes, which they distributed to the others, even including the colonel. Soon everyone was dipping his container into the water and splashing it over the silvery side of the huge, still fish. By midday, however, the sun had evaporated most of the water, and the containers were filled with more mud than moisture, and by sunset they had buried the fish.

---

4 aureole: ring; circle

Read and Think Critically

Explain, Summarize, Analyze

1. **THE FABLE** The moral of this **fable** is not summarized at the end, as in more traditional fables. Explain the moral of the **tale**. If possible, try using Banks' satirical **tone** in stating your moral.

2. The fish means different things to different people and groups. Using a chart like the one below, summarize what the fish means to those listed. Then answer the question for yourself: What does the fish mean to you?

Person or Group	Meaning
The colonel	*The fish is a threat because it attracts Buddhists to the area of control.*
The pilgrims	
The soldiers	

3. What shortcomings of humankind does this story reveal?

4. The time and place of this story are kept somewhat vague, but many of the details point to Vietnam during the 20th century. Taking this into consideration, answer the following question: What possible meaning might the tale have if the **setting** were the Vietnam War?

5. **THE AUTHOR'S STYLE** At times, "The Fish" has a **surreal** (intense, irrational, and dreamlike) quality. Find examples of events in the story that could not happen in real life. Analyze how each of these surreal passages impacts the story.

Before You Read

Amy Tan 1952–

About the Author

Born in California to Chinese immigrant parents, Amy Tan wore a clothespin on her nose as a teenager in hopes of making it slimmer. She also hoped to have plastic surgery one day to make herself look more Western. As she matured, however, her Chinese heritage became an honored and important part of her work.

When Tan was an adolescent, both her brother and father died of brain tumors. Following the deaths, Tan, her mother, and her other brother moved to Switzerland, where she went to high school and found that the Swiss were more interested in her Asian heritage than her fellow Americans had been. After graduation she attended college back home in California and began work as a freelance writer. The short story you are about to read was originally written so that she could be accepted into a writer's workshop at Squaw Valley in California. Eventually it became part of her novel *The Joy Luck Club,* which won the National Book Award in 1989 and was made into a movie in 1993. In her free time, Tan sings in a garage band, The Rock Bottom Remainders, with novelist Stephen King and columnist Dave Barry; the group raises money for literacy and First Amendment rights groups.

★★★★★★★★★★★

The Author's Style

The interaction between Chinese immigrant and American cultures is a key concern of Tan's fiction. She is particularly interested in the impact this interaction has on individuals and families. An important focus is the mother-daughter relationship, especially the conflicts that arise from the relationship between culture and gender. Her young characters often struggle with what it means to be a Chinese American girl.

As Tan shows us through family dialogue, the effectiveness of mother-daughter communication often depends upon how well mothers and daughters use language themselves and how well they listen to each other. Both the mothers and the daughters attempt to express their identities by establishing their voices and stories within the family. Tan is particularly adept at capturing the choppy, uneven English of immigrant mothers and the breezy, California speech of their daughters. In *The Joy Luck Club,* she accomplishes this by conveying their first-person points of view in alternating sections.

Tan incorporates into her fiction the ways in which people work out what it might mean to be "American" and which set of "rules" ought to be followed. Her stories explore everyday aspects of culture such as food, language, and dating, showing how these can become the focus of tension and conflict. Characters in her stories often seem ambivalent about both cultures.

Rules of the Game

A M Y T A N

LITERARY LENS: CHARACTERIZATION Consider how Tan develops the **characters** of Waverly and her mother.

I was six when my mother taught me the art of invisible strength. It was a strategy for winning arguments, respect from others, and eventually, though neither of us knew it at the time, chess games.

"Bite back your tongue," scolded my mother when I cried loudly, yanking her hand toward the store that sold bags of salted plums. At home, she said, "Wise guy, he not go against the wind. In Chinese we say, Come from South, blow with wind—poom!— North will follow. Strongest wind cannot be seen."

The next week I bit back my tongue as we entered the store with the forbidden candies. When my mother finished her shopping, she quietly plucked a small bag of plums from the rack and put it on the counter with the rest of the items.

*M*y mother imparted her daily truths so she could help my older brothers and me rise above our circumstances. We lived in San Francisco's Chinatown. Like most of the other Chinese children who played in the back alleys of restaurants and curio shops,[1] I didn't think we were poor. My bowl was always full, three five-course meals every day, beginning with a soup of mysterious things I didn't want to know the names of.

We lived on Waverly Place, in a warm, clean, two-bedroom flat that sat above a small Chinese bakery specializing in steamed pastries and dim sum.[2] In the early morning, when the alley was still quiet, I could smell fragrant red beans as they were cooked down to a pasty sweetness. By daybreak, our flat was heavy with the odor of fried sesame balls and sweet curried chicken crescents. From my bed, I would listen as my father got ready for work, then locked the door behind him, one-two-three clicks.

At the end of our two-block alley was a small sandlot playground with swings and slides well-shined down the middle with use. The play area was bordered by wood-slat benches where old-country people sat cracking roasted watermelon seeds with their golden teeth and scattering the husks to an impatient gathering of gurgling pigeons. The best playground, however, was the dark alley itself. It was crammed with daily mysteries and adventures. My brothers and I would peer into the medicinal herb shop, watching old Li dole out onto a stiff sheet of white paper the right amount of insect shells, saffron-colored seeds, and pungent leaves for his ailing customers. It was said that he once cured a woman dying of an ancestral curse that had eluded the best of American doctors. Next to the pharmacy was a printer who specialized in gold-embossed wedding invitations and festive red banners.

Farther down the street was Ping Yuen Fish Market. The front window displayed a tank crowded with doomed fish and turtles struggling to gain footing on the slimy green-tiled sides. A hand-written sign informed tourists, "Within this store, is all for food, not for pet." Inside, the butchers with their bloodstained white smocks deftly gutted the fish while customers cried out their orders and shouted, "Give me your freshest," to which the butchers always protested, "All are freshest." On less crowded market days, we would inspect the crates of live frogs and crabs which we were warned not to poke, boxes of dried cuttlefish,[3] and row upon row of iced prawns,[4] squid, and

---

1 **curio shops:** shops containing novelty and gift items

2 **dim sum:** a variety of traditional Chinese foods

3 **cuttlefish:** 10-armed fish that are related to squid

4 **prawns:** large shrimp

slippery fish. The sanddabs[5] made me shiver each time; their eyes lay on one flattened side and reminded me of my mother's story of a careless girl who ran into a crowded street and was crushed by a cab. "Was smash flat," reported my mother.

At the corner of the alley was Hong Sing's, a four-table café with a recessed stairwell in front that led to a door marked "Tradesmen." My brothers and I believed the bad people emerged from this door at night. Tourists never went to Hong Sing's, since the menu was printed only in Chinese. A Caucasian man with a big camera once posed me and my playmates in front of the restaurant. He had us move to the side of the picture window so the photo would capture the roasted duck with its head dangling from a juice-covered rope. After he took the picture, I told him he should go into Hong Sing's and eat dinner. When he smiled and asked me what they served, I shouted, "Guts and duck's feet and octopus gizzards!" Then I ran off with my friends, shrieking with laughter as

GIRL WITH BANGS, MARY HEUSSENSTAM M

we scampered across the alley and hid in the entryway grotto of the China Gem Company, my heart pounding with hope that he would chase us.

My mother named me after the street that we lived on: Waverly Place Jong, my official name for important American documents. But my family called me Meimei, "Little Sister." I was the youngest, the only daughter. Each morning before school, my mother would twist and yank on my thick black hair until she had formed two tightly wound pigtails. One day, as she struggled to weave a hard-toothed comb through my disobedient hair, I had a sly thought.

I asked her, "Ma, what is Chinese torture?" My mother shook her head. A bobby pin was wedged between her lips. She wetted her palm and

---

5 **sanddabs:** fish that are a type of flounder

smoothed the hair above my ear, then pushed the pin in so that it nicked sharply against my scalp.

"Who say this word?" she asked without a trace of knowing how wicked I was being. I shrugged my shoulders and said, "Some boy in my class said Chinese people do Chinese torture."

"Chinese people do many things," she said simply. "Chinese people do business, do medicine, do painting. Not lazy like American people. We do torture. Best torture."

*M*y older brother Vincent was the one who actually got the chess set. We had gone to the annual Christmas party held at the First Chinese Baptist Church at the end of the alley. The missionary ladies had put together a Santa bag of gifts donated by members of another church. None of the gifts had names on them. There were separate sacks for boys and girls of different ages.

One of the Chinese parishioners had donned a Santa Claus costume and a stiff paper beard with cotton balls glued to it. I think the only children who thought he was the real thing were too young to know that Santa Claus was not Chinese. When my turn came up, the Santa man asked me how old I was. I thought it was a trick question; I was seven according to the American formula and eight by the Chinese calendar. I said I was born on March 17, 1951. That seemed to satisfy him. He then solemnly asked if I had been a very, very good girl this year and did I believe in Jesus Christ and obey my parents. I knew the only answer to that. I nodded back with equal **solemnity**.

solemnity:
seriousness;
earnestness

Having watched the older children opening their gifts, I already knew that the big gifts were not necessarily the nicest ones. One girl my age got a large coloring book of biblical characters, while a less greedy girl who selected a smaller box received a glass vial of lavender toilet water. The sound of the box was also important. A ten-year-old boy had chosen a box that jangled when he shook it. It was a tin globe of the world with a slit for inserting money. He must have thought it was full of dimes and nickels, because when he saw that it had just ten pennies, his face fell with such undisguised disappointment that his mother slapped the side of his head and led him out of the church hall, apologizing to the crowd for her son who had such bad manners he couldn't appreciate such a fine gift.

As I peered into the sack, I quickly fingered the remaining presents, testing their weight, imagining what they contained. I chose a heavy, compact one that was wrapped in shiny silver foil and a red satin ribbon. It was a twelve-pack of Life Savers and I spent the rest of the party arranging and rearranging the candy tubes in the order of my favorites. My brother Winston chose wisely as well. His present turned out to be a box of intricate plastic parts; the instructions on the box proclaimed that when they were properly assembled he would have an authentic miniature replica of a World War II submarine.

Vincent got the chess set, which would have been a very decent present to get at a church Christmas party, except it was obviously used and, as we discovered later, it was missing a black pawn and a white knight. My mother graciously thanked the unknown benefactor, saying, "Too good. Cost too much." At which point, an old lady with fine white, wispy hair nodded toward our family and said with a whistling whisper, "Merry, merry Christmas."

Vincent at first refused to let me play, but when I offered my Life Savers as replacements for the buttons that filled in for the missing pieces, he relented.

When we got home, my mother told Vincent to throw the chess set away. "She not want it. We not want it," she said, tossing her head stiffly to the side with a tight, proud smile. My brothers had deaf ears. They were already lining up the chess pieces and reading from the dog-eared instruction book.

I watched Vincent and Winston play during Christmas week. The chessboard seemed to hold elaborate secrets waiting to be untangled. The chessmen were more powerful than old Li's magic herbs that cured ancestral curses. And my brothers wore such serious faces that I was sure something was at stake that was greater than avoiding the tradesmen's door to Hong Sing's.

"Let me! Let me!" I begged between games when one brother or the other would sit back with a deep sigh of relief and victory, the other annoyed, unable to let go of the outcome. Vincent at first refused to let me play, but when I offered my Life Savers as replacements for the buttons that filled in for the missing pieces, he relented. He chose the flavors: wild cherry for the black pawn and peppermint for the white knight. Winner could eat both.

As our mother sprinkled flour and rolled out small doughy circles for the steamed dumplings that would be our dinner that night, Vincent explained the rules, pointing to each piece. "You have sixteen pieces and so do I. One king and queen, two bishops, two knights, two castles, and eight pawns. The pawns can only move forward one step, except on the first move. Then they can move two. But they can only take men by moving crossways like this, except in the beginning, when you can move ahead and take another pawn."

"Why?" I asked as I moved my pawn. "Why can't they move more steps?"

"Because they're pawns," he said.

"But why do they go crossways to take other men? Why aren't there any women and children?"

"Why is the sky blue? Why must you always ask stupid questions?" asked Vincent. "This is a game. These are the rules. I didn't make them up. See. Here in the book." He jabbed a page with a pawn in his hand. "Pawn. P-A-W-N. Pawn. Read it yourself."

My mother patted the flour off her hands. "Let me see book," she said quietly. She scanned the pages quickly, not reading the foreign English symbols, seeming to search deliberately for nothing in particular.

"This American rules," she concluded at last. "Every time people come out from foreign country, must know rules. You not know, judge say, Too bad go back. They not telling you why so you can use their way go forward. They say, Don't know why, you find out yourself. But they knowing all the time. Better you take it, find out why yourself. She tossed her head back with a satisfied smile.

I found out about all the whys later. I read the rules and looked up all the big words in a dictionary. I borrowed books from the Chinatown library. I studied each chess piece, trying to absorb the power each contained.

I learned about opening moves and why it's important to control the center early on; the shortest distance between two points is straight down the middle. I learned about the middle game and why tactics between two **adversaries** are like clashing ideas; the one who plays better has the clearest plans for both attacking and getting out of traps. I learned why it is essential in the endgame to have foresight, a mathematical understanding of all possible moves, and patience; all weaknesses and advantages become evident to a strong adversary and are **obscured** to a tiring opponent. I discovered that for the whole game one must gather invisible strengths and see the endgame before the game begins.

I also found out why I should never reveal "why" to others. A little knowledge withheld is a great advantage one should store for future use. That

adversaries:
opponents

obscured:
concealed

is the power of chess. It is a game of secrets in which one must show and never tell.

I loved the secrets I found within the sixty-four black and white squares. I carefully drew a handmade chessboard and pinned it to the wall next to my bed, where I would stare for hours at imaginary battles. Soon I no longer lost any games or Life Savers, but I lost my adversaries. Winston and Vincent decided they were more interested in roaming the streets after school in their Hopalong Cassidy cowboy hats.

$\mathcal{O}$n a cold spring afternoon, while walking home from school, I detoured through the playground at the end of our alley. I saw a group of old men, two seated across a folding table playing a games of chess, others smoking pipes, eating peanuts, and watching. I ran home and grabbed Vincent's chess set, which was bound in a cardboard box with rubber bands. I also carefully selected two prized rolls of Life Savers. I came back to the park and approached a man who was observing the game.

"Want to play?" I asked him. His face widened with surprise and he grinned as he looked at the box under my arm.

"Little sister, been a long time since I play with dolls," he said, smiling **benevolently**. I quickly put the box down next to him on the bench and displayed my **retort**.

Lau Po, as he allowed me to call him, turned out to be a much better player than my brothers. I lost many games and many Life Savers. But over the weeks, with each diminishing roll of candies, I added new secrets. Lau Po gave me the names. The Double Attack from the East and West Shores. Throwing Stones on the Drowning Man. The Sudden Meeting of the Clan. The Surprise from the Sleeping Guard. The Humble Servant Who Kills the King. Sand in the Eyes of Advancing Forces. A Double Killing Without Blood.

There were also the fine points of chess **etiquette**. Keep captured men in neat rows, as well-tended prisoners. Never announce "Check" with vanity, **lest** someone with an unseen sword slit your throat. Never hurl pieces into the sandbox after you have lost a game, because then you must find them again, by yourself, after apologizing to all around you. By the end of the summer, Lau Po had taught me all he knew, and I had become a better chess player.

A small weekend crowd of Chinese people and tourists would gather as I played and defeated my opponents one by one. My mother would join the

benevolently:
kindly

retort:
sharp reply

etiquette:
manners;
protocol

lest:
for fear that

crowds during these outdoor exhibition games. She sat proudly on the bench, telling my admirers with proper Chinese humility, "Is luck."

A man who watched me play in the park suggested that my mother allow me to play in local chess tournaments. My mother smiled graciously, an answer that meant nothing. I desperately wanted to go, but I bit back my tongue. I knew she would not let me play among strangers. So as we walked home I said in a small voice that I didn't want to play in the local tournament. They would have American rules. If I lost, I would bring shame on my family.

"Is shame you fall down nobody push you," said my mother.

During my first tournament, my mother sat with me in the front row as I waited for my turn. I frequently bounced my legs to unstick them from the cold metal seat of the folding chair. When my name was called, I leapt up. My mother unwrapped something in her lap. It was her *chang*, a small tablet of red jade which held the sun's fire. "Is luck," she whispered, and tucked it into my dress pocket. I turned to my opponent, a fifteen-year-old boy from Oakland. He looked at me, wrinkling his nose.

As I began to play, the boy disappeared, the color ran out of the room, and I saw only my white pieces and his black ones waiting on the other side. A light wind began blowing past my ears. It whispered secrets only I could hear.

"Blow from the South," it murmured. "The wind leaves no trail." I saw a clear path, the traps to avoid. The crowd rustled. "Shhh! Shhh!" said the corners of the room. The wind blew stronger. "Throw sand from the East to distract him." The knight came forward ready for the sacrifice. The wind hissed, louder and louder. "Blow, blow, blow. He cannot see. He is blind now. Make him lean away from the wind so he is easier to knock down."

"Check," I said, as the wind roared with laughter. The wind died down to little puffs, my own breath.

*M*y mother placed my first trophy next to a new plastic chess set that the neighborhood Tao society had given to me. As she wiped each piece with a soft cloth, she said, "Next time win more, lose less."

"Ma, it's not how many pieces you lose," I said. "Sometimes you need to lose pieces to get ahead."

"Better to lose less, see if you really need."

At the next tournament, I won again, but it was my mother who wore the triumphant grin.

"Lost eight piece this time. Last time was eleven. What I tell you? Better off lose less!" I was annoyed, but I couldn't say anything.

I attended more tournaments, each one farther away from home. I won all games, in all divisions. The Chinese bakery downstairs from our flat displayed my growing collection of trophies in its window, amidst the dust-covered cakes that were never picked up. The day after I won an important regional tournament, the window encased a fresh sheet cake with whipped-cream frosting and red script saying "Congratulations, Waverly Jong, Chinatown Chess Champion." Soon after that, a flower shop, headstone engraver, and funeral parlor offered to sponsor me in national tournaments. That's when my mother decided I no longer had to do the dishes. Winston and Vincent had to do my chores.

"Why does she get to play and we do all the work," complained Vincent.

"Is new American rules," said my mother. "Meimei play, squeeze all her brains out for win chess. You play, worth squeeze towel."

By my ninth birthday, I was a national chess champion. I was still some 429 points away from grand-master status, but I was **touted** as the Great American Hope, a child prodigy and a girl to boot. They ran a photo of me in *Life* magazine next to a quote in which Bobby Fischer said, "There will never be a woman grand master." "Your move, Bobby," said the caption.

touted: acclaimed

The day they took the magazine picture I wore neatly plaited braids clipped with plastic barrettes trimmed with rhinestones. I was playing in a large high school auditorium that echoed with phlegmy coughs and the squeaky rubber knobs of chair legs sliding across freshly waxed wooden floors. Seated across from me was an American man, about the same age as Lau Po, maybe fifty. I remember that his sweaty brow seemed to weep at my every move. He wore a dark, **malodorous** suit. One of his pockets was stuffed with a great white kerchief on which he wiped his palm before sweeping his hand over the chosen chess piece with great flourish.

malodorous: foul-smelling

In my crisp pink-and-white dress with scratchy lace at the neck, one of two my mother had sewn for these special occasions, I would clasp my hands under my chin, the delicate points of my elbows poised lightly on the table in the manner my mother had shown me for posing for the press. I would swing my patent leather shoes back and forth like an impatient child riding on a school bus. Then I would pause, suck in my lips, twirl my chosen piece in midair as if undecided, and then firmly plant it in its new threatening place, with a triumphant smile thrown back at my opponent for good measure.

$\mathcal{I}$ no longer played in the alley of Waverly Place. I never visited the playground where the pigeons and old men gathered. I went to school, then directly home to learn new chess secrets, cleverly concealed advantages, more escape routes.

But I found it difficult to concentrate at home. My mother had a habit of standing over me while I plotted out my games. I think she thought of herself as my protective **ally**. Her lips would be sealed tight, and after each move I made, a soft "Hmmmmph" would escape from her nose.

"Ma, I can't practice when you stand there like that," I said one day. She retreated to the kitchen and made loud noises with the pots and pans. When the crashing stopped, I could see out of the corner of my eye that she was standing in the doorway. "Hmmmmph!" Only this one came out of her tight throat.

My parents made many concessions to allow me to practice. One time I complained that the bedroom I shared was so noisy that I couldn't think. Thereafter, my brothers slept in a bed in the living room facing the street. I said I couldn't finish my rice; my head didn't work right when my stomach was too full. I left the table with half-finished bowls and nobody complained. But there was one duty I couldn't avoid. I had to accompany my mother on Saturday market days when I had no tournament to play. My mother would proudly walk with me, visiting many shops, buying very little. "This is my daughter Wave-ly Jong," she said to whoever looked her way.

One day after we left a shop I said under my breath, "I wish you wouldn't do that, telling everybody I'm your daughter." My mother stopped walking. Crowds of people with heavy bags pushed past us on the sidewalk, bumping into first one shoulder, then another.

"Aiii-ya. So shame be with mother?" She grasped my hand even tighter as she glared at me.

ally:
supporter;
collaborator

I looked down. "It's not that, it's just so obvious. It's just so embarrassing."

"Embarrass you be my daughter?" Her voice was cracking with anger.

"That's not what I meant. That's not what I said."

"What you say?"

I knew it was a mistake to say anything more, but I heard my voice speaking, "Why do you have to use me to show off? If you want to show off, then why don't you learn to play chess?"

My mother's eyes turned into dangerous black slits. She had no words for me, just sharp silence.

I felt the wind rushing around my hot ears. I jerked my hand out of my mother's tight grasp and spun around, knocking into an old woman. Her bag of groceries spilled to the ground.

"Aii-ya! Stupid girl!" my mother and the woman cried. Oranges and tin cans **careened** down the sidewalk. As my mother stooped to help the old woman pick up the escaping food, I took off.

careened: swayed

I raced down the street, dashing between people, not looking back as my mother screamed shrilly, "Meimei! Meimei!" I fled down an alley, past dark, curtained shops and merchants washing the grime off their windows. I sped into the sunlight, into a large street crowded with tourists examining trinkets and souvenirs. I ducked into another dark alley, down another street, up another alley. I ran until it hurt and I realized I had nowhere to go, that I was not running from anything. The alleys contained no escape routes.

My breath came out like angry smoke. It was cold. I sat down on an upturned plastic pail next to a stack of empty boxes, cupping my chin with my hands, thinking hard. I imagined my mother, first walking briskly down one street or another looking for me, then giving up and returning home to await my arrival. After two hours, I stood up on creaking legs and slowly walked home.

The alley was quiet and I could see the yellow lights shining from our flat like two tiger's eyes in the night. I climbed the sixteen steps to the door, advancing quietly up each so as not to make any warning sounds. I turned the knob; the door was locked. I heard a chair moving, quick steps, the locks turning—click! click! click!—and then the door opened.

"About time you got home," said Vincent. "Boy, are you in trouble."

He slid back to the dinner table. On a platter were the remains of a large fish, its fleshy head still connected to bones swimming upstream in vain

escape. Standing there waiting for my punishment, I heard my mother speak in a dry voice.

"We not concerning this girl. This girl not having concerning for us."

Nobody looked at me. Bone chopsticks clinked against the inside of bowls being emptied into hungry mouths.

I walked into my room, closed the door, and lay down on my bed. The room was dark, the ceiling filled with shadows from the dinnertime lights of neighboring flats.

In my head, I saw a chessboard with sixty-four black and white squares. Opposite me was my opponent, two angry black slits. She wore a triumphant smile. "Strongest wind cannot be seen," she said.

Her black men advanced across the plane, slowly marching to each successive level as a single unit. My white pieces screamed as they scurried and fell off the board one by one. As her men drew closer to my edge, I felt myself growing light. I rose up into the air and flew out the window. Higher and higher, above the alley, over the tops of tiled roofs, where I was gathered up by the wind and pushed up toward the night sky until everything below me disappeared and I was alone.

I closed my eyes and pondered my next move.

GRANT AVENUE
1992
MARTIN WONG

Read and Think Critically

Analyze, Describe, Judge

1. **CHARACTERIZATION** Using a chart like the one below, analyze the ways Tan reveals the differences and similarities of the two main **characters** in this story—Waverly and her Chinese-born mother. Consider **dialogue**, **motivation**, and any other elements of **characterization** you might find.

Characterization	Waverly	Waverly's Mother
Dialogue		
Motivation		

2. Besides chess, to what might "Rules of the Game" refer?

3. Why do you think the author spends so much time describing San Francisco's Chinatown before she gets into the action of the story?

4. Describe some of the ways Waverly attempts to establish her identity.

5. Most mothers and daughters have differences of opinion. Make a judgment about which mother-daughter problems depicted in the story are common in all cultures, and which are more specific to Chinese American families.

6. **THE AUTHOR'S STYLE** In conventional **plots**, the **conflict** is resolved one way or another by the end of the story. In this story, however, the plot remains unresolved. Why do you think Tan leaves the story so open-ended?

Responding to Unit Five

Key Ideas and Details

1. Write an objective summary of "The Sky Is Gray," "Everything Stuck to Him," and "American Horse." What is your reaction to each story's **realistic** portrayal of social problems such as alcoholism, racism, and divorce?

2. The solitary walk is the basis of many stories. On a deeper level, the solitary walk represents a rite of passage from childhood to maturity. Consider "The Flowers" and "The Key"—two stories in which the main **character** takes a solitary walk. Using a chart like the one below, compare the two journeys.

Main Character	The Flowers	The Key
State before walk		
What she encounters		
How she is changed		

Craft and Structure

3. In both "Everything Stuck to Him" and "Detroit Skyline, 1949," a seemingly ordinary event triggers a moment of clarity, or an **epiphany**. Pinpoint when the moment occurs in each story and interpret what the impact is on the character.

 4. The style and subject matter of O'Brien have been compared to that of Hemingway, whom you read in Unit 3. Whose style do you find more appealing, and why?

5. What elements in a story that examines a social problem distinguish it from a treatise or piece of **propaganda** on the same topic? Support your opinion with examples from this unit.

Integration of Knowledge and Ideas

6. Success is a common **theme** in literature. Using the **point of view** of the father in "The Writer in the Family" and the mother in "Rules of the Game," write two definitions of success in America.

7. The guardian angel is an important **image** in "Detroit Skyline, 1949" in this unit and in "Angel Levine" in the previous unit. Compare and contrast the way this **symbol** is handled in the two stories.

Writing About the Literature

The Real vs. the Fantastic

Realism and fantasy literature are often pitted against each other. Realism is often considered depressing; fantasy is often considered escapist. Consider one of the realistic stories you have read so far, such as "The Sky Is Gray" or "He," and one of the stories with elements of fantasy, such as "The Fish" or "The Veldt." Write a persuasive essay that tells which one you feel best succeeds at conveying its message.

Writing with Style

Choose one of these two assignments.

Are we there yet?

In the style of "Detroit Skyline, 1949," write an account of a trip taken in your own growing-up years. As Bobbie Ann Mason does, use details such as TV shows, songs, or historical incidents to evoke the era of your story.

The Carver Style

Raymond Carver's minimalist style often relies on the repetition of sentence openers. Consider these examples from the opening paragraphs of "Everything Stuck to Him."

> **Tell me**, she says. **Tell me** what it was like when I was a kid. . . .

> **That was** a long time ago. **That was** twenty years ago, he says. . . .

> **What** do you want to hear? he says. **What** else can I tell you?

Create your own Carveresque sentences by using the same technique.

IN YOUR OWN STYLE

Try your own hand at realistic literature by writing a fictional scene that deals with a social issue or an "ism"—for example, racism, sexism, ageism, war, or poverty.

Unit Six
Contemporary Voices 1990s and 2000s

THE READER, MAGGIE TAYLOR, 2002

The final decade of the 20th century and the first decade of the 21st brought new global triumphs as well as global fears. With the dissolution of the Soviet Union, Americans finally believed that the Cold War was over. Yet the world soon began to witness a rise in hijackings, car bombings, and terrorist attacks that amounted to a new undeclared war. Advances in technology brought increased international communication, commerce, and travel. Our friends—and our enemies—now seemed closer than ever. Many warned that our reliance on computers would be our downfall in the new millennium. In the last days of 1999, Americans prepared for a computer meltdown, due on January 1, 2000. They stocked up on water, food, and cash for the disaster that never came.

Realism and Gothic Literature Revisited

During the nineties, writers such as Tobias Wolff embraced Raymond Carver's minimalism. This "dirty realism" used spare prose to describe just the surface of everyday events and people. Simple dialogue and matter-of-fact descriptions allow readers to decide for themselves what lies beneath the surface and between the lines.

With her straightforward prose and focus on ordinary Americans, writer Barbara Kingsolver joined the literary tradition of great 20th-century writers such as John Steinbeck and John Updike. Kingsolver used her craft to draw attention to environmental problems and called on fellow writers to use their talents to bring about social change.

Though both Joyce Carol Oates and T. Coraghessan Boyle are known for the ability to write well in a variety of styles, perhaps they are best known for their tales of the bizarre. In Oates' modern Gothic tales, violence lurks behind a suburban facade. In "Ladies and Gentlemen:" she switches from a friendly to an ominous tone in a first-person narrative that satirizes America's consumerism. In his "Top of the Food Chain," Boyle also uses a first-person narrative. It is a wicked literary warning about environmental disaster.

Out of This World

Several authors in this collection have brought a global perspective to American literature. Robert Olen Butler, who worked in counter-intelligence and as a translator during the Vietnam War, has written numerous stories infused with his love for Vietnam and its people. In his short story "Letters from My Father," he uses the voice of a Vietnamese American adolescent girl to explore the impact of war and how language can both reveal and conceal feelings. Short story writer and novelist Paul Theroux has lived in England, Singapore, and Africa. He is also acclaimed for his nonfiction travel writing, which no doubt has heightened his ability to present a range of perspectives. Theroux captures how subtle shifts in language can change one's perspective.

Liar, Liar

Storytelling presents a terrific opportunity to lie. With fiction, you are *supposed* to make it up. But what if fiction is based on fact? Can writers change real events to make a story more interesting or more illuminating? Like metafiction writers of the eighties, some contemporary writers blur the line between fact and fiction.

In his novel *My Secret History,* Theroux was criticized for being too autobiographical, so he responded with another called *My Other Life.* The second novel was about a fictional Paul Theroux who did a lot of things the real Theroux did and a lot of things he *didn't* do. In "Charlie Hogle's Earring," the author continues to explore the shifting nature of identity and whether things can be real, even if they aren't true. The story shows how people can twist their own identity—or someone else's—until it's unrecognizable.

Tobias Wolff, whose father was a con man and a lifetime liar, also writes about truth and identity. His memoir, *This Boy's Life,* recounts his nomadic childhood and how he reinvented himself as a writer. Though it won numerous awards, critics questioned just how much of it was true. Like writers before him, Wolff could contend that, in storytelling, fact is *not* the same as truth. In his story "Mortals," you'll see how deception takes place in life and in death.

Post-postmodernism?

Many literary theorists believe that postmodernism was losing momentum in the late 1990s and that the terrorist attacks of September 11, 2001, closed the book on the movement. If postmodernism is out, what is in? It is too soon to say. We don't know which stories being written today will still be read decades from now or what literary label will best describe them. Still, some interesting names are popping up—post-postmodernism, remodernism, and post-millennialism. Some cultural observers see a shift away from postmodern irony and absurdist humor and toward art that tempers reason with spiritual concerns. Others warn that the nineties began our descent into a no-man's land of instant gratification. They predict that instant messaging, Facebook, and Twitter will strip us of our literature. This is not likely. The short story is adapting to our fast-paced lifestyles and shorter attention spans. Witness the advent in the last few years of short short stories, flash fiction, and nanofiction—a form that requires the writer to tell a complete story (with at least one character) in exactly 55 words.

No matter how long or how short, the short story will continue to help us discover who we are and where we are going.

Before You Read

Joyce Carol Oates 1938–

About the Author

Born in Lockport, New York, to a middle-class family, Joyce Carol Oates submitted her first manuscript for publication when she was 15. It was rejected, but at the age of 25 she published a collection of short stories, *By the North Gate*. Since then she has produced a flood of novels, stories, poems, and critical essays, averaging two or three books a year. Oates' speed is linked to her belief that much rewriting is avoidable and unnecessary.

Among her more important novels are *A Garden of Earthly Delights*, *THEM* (winner of a National Book Award) and *Do With Me What You Will*. A frequent contributor to periodicals such as *The New York Times*, Oates has also written suspense novels under the pseudonym Rosamond Smith. She teaches at Princeton University.

★★★★★★★★★★★

The Author's Style

One of the most prolific contemporary American writers, Oates often writes in the romantic tradition represented in American literature as early as the work of Edgar Allan Poe. Like Poe's tales, Oates' stories often develop from gothic situations involving hostile environments or isolated individuals. Her characters exhibit distorted physical or psychological extremes, and they often succumb to impulses and perversions that lead to dread and violence. Oates has been both criticized and praised for bringing the grotesque into the presumably safe havens of suburban, middle-class America.

The threatening aura of Oates' stories is created through the use of ironic situations, internal monologues that reveal the workings of her characters' minds, and the strategy of repeating words and phrases until they become ominous. She uses ellipses (. . .) to lead the reader to the verge of a disastrous event or appalling revelation. In many stories the ironic contrast between what characters believe (or want to believe) and what is actually taking place adds to the level of fear. In "Ladies and Gentlemen:" Oates' use of the second person intensifies a disturbing situation in which the captain seems not only to be addressing the cruise customers directly, but also the reader. The combination of grimness, helplessness, and bitterness turns many of her stories into dark fables.

Ladies and Gentlemen:

Joyce Carol Oates

LITERARY LENS: SATIRE Notice the **satire** in this story.

*L*adies and gentlemen: A belated but heartfelt welcome aboard our cruise ship S.S. *Ariel*. It's a true honor and a privilege for me, your captain, to greet you all on this lovely sun-warmed January day—as balmy, isn't it, as any June morning back north? I wish I could claim that we of the *Ariel* arranged personally for such splendid weather, as compensation of sorts for the— shall we say—somewhat rocky weather of the past several days. But at any rate it's a welcome omen indeed and bodes well for the remainder of the cruise and for this morning's excursion, ladies and gentlemen, to the island you see us rapidly approaching, a small but remarkably beautiful island the natives of these waters call the Island of Tranquility or, as some translators prefer, the Island of Repose. For those of you who've become virtual sailors with a keen eye for navigating, you'll want to log our longitude at 155 degrees East and our latitude at 5 degrees North, approximately twelve hundred miles north and east of New Guinea. Yes, that's right! We've come so far! And as this is a rather crucial morning, and your island adventure an important event not only on this cruise but in your lives, ladies and gentlemen, I hope you will quiet just a bit—just a bit!—and give me, your captain, your fullest attention. Just for a few minutes, I promise! Then you disembark.

As to the problems some of you have experienced: let me take this opportunity, as your captain, ladies and gentlemen, to apologize, or at least to explain. It's true for instance that certain of your staterooms are not *precisely* as the advertising brochures depicted them, the portholes are not quite so large; in some cases the portholes are not in evidence. This is not the fault of any of the *Ariel* staff; indeed, this has been a sore point with us for some years, a matter of misunderstandings and embarrassments out of our control, yet I, as your captain, ladies and gentlemen, offer my apologies and my profoundest sympathies. Though I am a bit your junior in age, I can well understand the special disappointment, the particular hurt, outrage, and dismay that attend one's sense of having been cheated on what, for some of you, probably, is perceived as being the last time you'll be taking so prolonged and exotic a trip—thus, my profoundest sympathies! As to the toilets that have been reported as malfunctioning or out of order entirely, and the loud throbbing or "tremors" of the engines that have been keeping some of you awake, and the **negligent** or even rude service, the overcooked or undercooked food, the high tariffs on mineral water, alcoholic beverages, and cigarettes, the reported sightings of rodents, cockroaches, and other vermin on board ship— perhaps I should explain, ladies and gentlemen, that this is the final voyage of the S.S. *Ariel* and it was the owners' decision, and a justifiably **pragmatic** decision, to cut back on repairs, services, expenses, and the like. Ladies and gentlemen, I am sorry for your inconvenience, but the *Ariel is* an old ship, bound for dry dock in Manila and the fate of many a veteran seagoing vessel that has outlived her time. God bless her! We'll not see her likes again!

Ladies and gentlemen, may I have some quiet—please, just five minutes more?—before the stewards help you prepare for your disembarkment? Thank you.

Yes, the *Ariel* is bound for Manila next. But have no fear, you won't be aboard.

negligent: careless; inattentive

pragmatic: practical; expedient

Ladies and gentlemen, *please*. This murmuring and muttering begins to annoy.

(Yet, as your captain, I'd like to note that, amid the usual whiners and complainers and the just plain bad-tempered, it's gratifying to see a number of warm, friendly, *hopeful* faces and to know that there are men and women determined to enjoy life, not quibble and harbor suspicions. Thank *you!*)

Now to our business at hand: ladies and gentlemen, do you know what you have in common?

You can't guess?

You *can* guess?

No? Yes?

No?

Well, yes sir, it's true that you are all aboard the S.S. *Ariel*; and yes, sir— excuse me, *ma'am*—it's certainly true that you are all of "retirement" age. (Though "retirement" has come to be a rather vague term in the past decade or so, hasn't it? For the youngest among you are in their late fifties—the result, I would guess, of especially generous early-retirement programs— and the eldest among you are in their mid-nineties. Quite a range of ages!)

Yes, it's true you are all Americans. You have expensive cameras, even in some cases video equipment, for recording this South Seas adventure; you have all sorts of tropical-cruise **paraphernalia**, including some extremely attractive bleached-straw hats; some of you have quite a supply of sun-protective lotions; and most of you have a considerable quantity and variety of pharmacological supplies. And quite a store of paperbacks, magazines, cards, games, and crossword puzzles. Yet there is one primary thing you have in common, ladies and gentlemen, which has determined your presence here this morning, at longitude 155 degrees East and latitude 5 degrees North: your fate, as it were. Can't you guess?

Ladies and gentlemen: *your children.*

Yes, you have in common the fact that this cruise on the S.S. *Ariel* was originally your children's idea and that they arranged for it, if you'll recall. (Though you have probably paid for your own passages, which weren't cheap.) Your children—who are "children" only technically, for of course they are fully grown, fully adult, a good number of them parents themselves (having made you proud grandparents—yes, haven't you been proud!)—these sons and daughters, if I may speak frankly, are *very* tired of waiting for their inheritances.

paraphernalia: gear

Yes, and *very* impatient, some of them, *very* angry, waiting to come into control of what they believe is their due.

Ladies and gentlemen, please! I'm asking for quiet, and I'm asking for respect. As captain of the *Ariel*, I am not accustomed to being interrupted.

I believe you did hear me correctly, sir. And you too, sir.

Yes and you, ma'am. And *you*. (Most of you aren't nearly so deaf as you pretend!)

candidly:
frankly

*L*et me speak candidly. While your children are in many cases, or at least in some cases, genuinely fond of you, they are simply impatient with the prospect of waiting for your "natural" deaths.

Let me speak **candidly**. While your children are in many cases, or at least in some cases, genuinely fond of you, they are simply impatient with the prospect of waiting for your "natural" deaths. Ten years, fifteen? Twenty? With today's medical technology, who knows; you might outlive *them*!

Of course it's a surprise to you, ladies and gentlemen. It's a *shock*. Thus you, sir, are shaking your head in disbelief, and you, sir, are muttering just a little too loudly, "Who does that fool think he is, making such bad jokes?"—and you, ladies, are giggling like teenaged girls, not knowing what to think. But remember: your children have been living lives of their own, in a very difficult, very competitive corporate America; they are, on the face of it, well-to-do, even affluent; yet they want, in some cases desperately need, *your* estates—not in a dozen years but *now*.

That is to say, as soon as your wills can be probated.

For, however your sons and daughters appear in the eyes of their neighbors, friends, and business colleagues, even in the eyes of their own offspring, you can be sure that *they have not enough money*. You can be sure that they suffer keenly certain financial jealousies and yearnings—and who dares **calibrate** another's suffering? Who dares peer into another's heart? Without betraying anyone's confidence, I can say that there are several youngish men, beloved sons of couples in your midst, ladies and gentlemen, who are nearly bankrupt; men of integrity and "success" whose worlds are about to come tumbling about their heads—unless they get money or find themselves in the position of being able to borrow money against their parents' estates, *fast*. Investment bankers, lawyers, a college professor or two—some of them already in debt. Thus they decided to take severe measures.

calibrate:
measure

Ladies and gentlemen, it's pointless to protest. As captain of the *Ariel*, I merely **expedite** orders.

expedite: carry out promptly

And you must know that it's pointless to express disbelief or incredulity, to roll your eyes as if *I* (of all people) were a bit cracked, to call out questions or demands, to shout, weep, sob, beg, rant and rave and mutter—"If this is a joke it isn't a very funny joke!" "As if my son/daughter would ever do such a thing to me/us!"—in short, it's pointless to express any and all of the reactions you're expressing, which have been expressed by other ladies and gentlemen on past *Ariel* voyages to the South Seas.

*Y*es, it's the best thing, to cooperate. Yes, in an orderly fashion. It's wisest not to provoke the stewards (whose nerves are a bit ragged these days—the crew is only human, after all) into using force.

Ladies and gentlemen, these *are* lovely **azure** waters—exactly as the brochures promised!—but shark-infested, so take care.

azure: sky-blue

As, yes, those dorsal fins slicing the waves, just beyond the surf: observe them closely.

No, we're leaving no picnic baskets with you today. Nor any bottles of mineral water, Perrier water, champagne.

For why delay what's inevitable? Why cruelly protract anguish?

Ladies and gentlemen, maybe it's a simple thing, maybe it's a self-evident thing, but consider: you are the kind of civilized men and women who brought babies into the world not by crude, primitive, anachronistic chance but by systematic deliberation. You planned your futures; you planned, as the expression goes, your parenthood. You are all of that American economic class called "upper middle"; you are educated, you are cultured, you are stable; nearly without exception, you showered love upon your sons and daughters, who knew themselves, practically in the cradle, privileged. The very best—the most exclusive—nursery schools, private schools, colleges, universities. Expensive toys and gifts of all kinds; closets of clothing, ski equipment, stereo equipment, racing bicycles; tennis lessons, riding lessons, snorkeling lessons, private tutoring, trips to the Caribbean, to Mexico, to Tangier, to Tokyo, to Switzerland; junior years abroad in Paris, in Rome, in London; yes, and their teeth were perfect, or were made to be; yes, and they had cosmetic surgery if necessary, or nearly necessary; yes, and you gladly paid for their abortions or their tuition for law school, medical school, business school; yes, and you paid for their weddings; yes, and you I

THE SPHINX AND THE
MILKY WAY
1946
CHARLES BURCHFIELD
MUNSON-WILLIAMS-
PROCTOR ARTS INSTITUTE,
MUSEUM OF ART, UTICA,
NY

oaned them money "to get started," certainly you helped them with their mortgages, or their second cars, or their children's orthodontic bills; nothing was too good or too expensive for them, for what, ladies and gentlemen, would it have been?

And always the more you gave your sons and daughters, the more you seemed to be holding in reserve; the more generous you displayed yourself, the more generous you were hinting you might be in the future. But so far in the future—when your wills might be probated, after your deaths.

Ladies and gentlemen, you rarely stopped to consider your children as other than *your* children, as men and women growing into maturity distinct from you. Rarely did you pause to see how patiently they were waiting to inherit their due—and then, by degrees, how impatiently. What anxieties **besieged** them, what nightmare speculations—for what if you squandered your money in medical bills? nursing home bills? the **melancholic impedimenta** of age in America? What if—worse yet!—addle-brained, suffering from Alzheimer's disease (about which they'd been reading suddenly, it seemed, everywhere) you turned against them, disinherited them, remarried someone younger, healthier, more cunning than they, rewrote your wills, as elderly fools are always doing?

> **besieged:** attacked
>
> **melancholic:** sad; depressing
>
> **impedimenta:** obstacles

Ladies and gentlemen, your children declare that they want only *what's theirs.*

They say laughingly, *they* aren't going to live forever.

(Well, yes: I'll confide in you, off the cuff, in several instances it was an *in-law* who looked into the possibility of a cruise on the S.S. *Ariel*; your own son/daughter merely cooperated, after the fact as it were. Of course, that isn't the same thing!)

Ladies and gentlemen, as your captain, about to bid you farewell, let me say I *am* sympathetic with your plight. Your stunned expressions, your staggering-swaying gait, your damp eyes, working mouths—"This is a bad joke!" "This is intolerable!" "This is a nightmare!" "No child of mine could be so cruel—inhuman—monstrous" et cetera—all this is touching, wrenching to the heart, altogether *natural.* One might almost say *traditional.* Countless others, whose bones you may discover should you have the energy and spirit to explore the Island of Tranquility (or Repose), reacted in more or less the same way.

Thus do not despair, ladies and gentlemen, for your emotions, however painful, are time-honored; but do not squander the few precious remaining hours of your life, for such emotions are futile.

*L*adies and gentlemen: the Island of Tranquility upon which you now stand shivering in the steamy morning heat is approximately six kilometers in circumference, ovoid in shape, with a curious archipelago of giant metamorphic rocks trailing off to the north, a pounding hallucinatory surf, and horizon, vague, dreamy, and distant, on all sides. Its soil is an admixture of volcanic ash, sand, rock, and peat; its jungle interior is pocked with treacherous bogs of quicksand.

habituated:
accustomed;
used to

ubiquitous:
unavoidable;
pervasive

iridescent:
lustrous;
rainbowlike

It *is* a truly exotic island, but fairly quickly most of you will become **habituated** to the ceaseless winds that ease across the island from several directions simultaneously, air intimate and warmly stale as exhaled breaths, caressing, narcotic. You'll become habituated to the **ubiquitous** sand flies, the glittering dragonflies with their eighteen-inch **iridescent** wings, the numerous species of snakes (the small quicksilver orange-speckled *baya* snake is the most venomous, you'll want to know); the red-beaked carnivorous macaw and its ear-piercing shriek; bullfrogs the size of North American jackrabbits; two-hundred-pound tortoises with pouched, intelligent eyes; spider monkeys playful as children; tapirs; tarantulas; and, most colorful of all, the comical cassowary birds with their bony heads, gaily-hued wattles, and stunted wings—these ungainly birds whom millions of years of evolution, on this island lacking mammal predators, have rendered flightless.

And orchids: some of you have already noticed the lovely, bountiful orchids growing everywhere, dozens of species, every imaginable color, some the size of grapes and others the size of a man's head, unfortunately inedible.

And the island's smells, are they fragrances or odors? Is it rampant, fresh-budding life or jungle-rancid decay? Is there a difference?

By night (and the hardiest among you should survive numerous nights, if past history prevails), you'll contemplate the tropical moon, so different from our North American moon, hanging heavy and luminous in the sky like an overripe fruit; you'll be moved to smile at the sport of fiery-phosphorescent fish frolicking in the waves; you'll be lulled to sleep by the din of insects, the cries of nocturnal birds, your own prayers perhaps.

Some of you will cling together, like terrified herd animals; some of you will wander off alone, dazed, refusing to be touched, even comforted, by a spouse of fifty years.

Ladies and gentlemen, I, your captain, speak for the crew of the S.S. *Ariel*, bidding you farewell.

Ladies and gentlemen, your children have asked me to assure you that they *do* love you—but circumstances have intervened.

Ladies and gentlemen, your children have asked me to recall to you those years when they were in fact *children*—wholly innocent as you imagined them, adoring you as gods.

Ladies and gentlemen, I now bid farewell to you as children do, waving goodbye not once but numerous times, solemn, **reverential**. Goodbye, goodbye, goodbye.

reverential:
expressing
profound
respect

★★

Read and Think Critically
Explain, Evaluate, Analyze

 1. **SATIRE** is a form of literature that exposes and condemns human vices. Explain the vice or vices satirized in this piece.

 2. Explain how Oates' choice of **narrator** (the captain of the ship) contributes to the satire.

 3. A *euphemism* is a figure of speech in which a name or term masks a more direct, or brutal, fact. For example, the phrase "senior citizens" is a euphemism for "old people." What euphemisms are employed in this story, and what truths do they mask?

 4. Evaluate the vision of American life presented in "Ladies and Gentlemen:." Do you think that this is in any way an accurate view of the American upper-middle class? Why or why not?

 5. **THE AUTHOR'S STYLE** Oates' stories often **juxtapose** the safe, daytime lives of the upper-middle class with the dark, nightmarish underside of American life. Using a chart such as the one below, analyze the elements of the story as well as aspects of Oates' style that contribute to the juxtaposition.

Safe, Daytime Life	Dark, Nightmarish Underside
Retirees are on a cruise.	The cruise ship is decrepit.

Before You Read

Barbara Kingsolver 1955–

About the Author

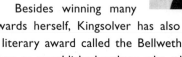

Born in Kentucky, Barbara Kingsolver has remained connected to her roots all of her life. The area where she grew up, "in the middle of an alfalfa field," is mentioned in many of her works. From an early age, however, she was a world traveler. Her father was a doctor who took his family along when he practiced medicine in the Congo (now called Zaire) and St. Lucia, a Caribbean island.

Always the keeper of a journal, Kingsolver traveled and studied biology and ecology for several years before writing her first novel. She wrote it in the middle of the night when she was suffering from insomnia during a pregnancy. *The Bean Trees* became a bestseller.

Besides winning many awards herself, Kingsolver has also established a literary award called the Bellwether, which is given to unpublished authors who address issues of social injustice in their writing. She says of her work, "I want an English professor to understand the symbolism while at the same time I want the people I grew up with—who may not often read anything but the Sears catalogue—to read my books."

****

The Author's Style

Kingsolver was born in eastern Kentucky but has also lived in Indiana and Arizona; she has lived in and written about Africa and the Congo. These experiences and her work as a biological researcher, an archaeologist, and a scientific writer incline her to see multiple points of view. She approaches the human dilemmas that are created by social, political, cultural, and personal differences with generous sympathy.

The emphasis in Kingsolver's fiction is on the personal relationships of families and communities. She focuses particularly on "average" people who find themselves in unusual or extreme situations but use love, endurance, and common sense in working toward solutions. She writes in straightforward, declarative prose, using down-to-earth language and figures of speech. Her particular emphasis is on the lives of girls and women, with female characters combining toughness, humor, and hopefulness to overcome anxiety and fear, especially after some catastrophic experience. They then carry on with their lives sensibly and responsibly. Her sensitive presentation of working-class people has led some readers to compare her writing to that of Bobbie Ann Mason and Russell Banks.

Fault Lines

BARBARA KINGSOLVER

LITERARY LENS: INTERIOR MONOLOGUE As you read, pay attention to Grace's **interior monologue**, or her unspoken thoughts and feelings.

*R*andall is moving away from his living wife. With the reckless, innocent grace of a liberated animal he scrambles toes-and-hands up the face of a huge rock; this must be Africa because none of the trees look right. The two boys are little and hold onto her hands, watching their father. When he straddles the top, Randall turns around to wave at the three of them. She's about to tell him to be careful, but then he jumps off, just jumps on purpose, as if he means to amuse the boys. It's much too high. His body bounces several times with a dull energy like an old tennis ball. He lies still, and then looks up at her sorrowfully because he knows he's going to die.

SAN FRANCISCO LANDSCAPE, WAYNE THIEBAUD, 1976

Grace wakes up with her breath quick in her throat. It's exactly 5:00 A.M. She gets up to check on the boys, who are breathing, as they've been doing steadily for more than a decade and will surely continue to do. She wishes she could believe it. Her new friends in California tell her to "trust the universe," but Grace sees nothing trustworthy about the universe; it's full of exploding stars. Randall didn't die in Africa but in Louisville, two miles from home, when a drill bit broke in the machine shop where he worked. His employer called it a freak accident. Grace considers it a freak accident that anyone ever makes it through life in one piece. When the life insurance came through she thought it would help her mind-set to get away from Kentucky, so they moved to Oakland. Now she has earthquakes to consider.

She goes back to bed but sits up against the headboard waiting for the sun to come up and the boys to stir and another day to happen. The blue shirt she hugs around herself is Randall's, going threadbare at the elbows, wearing out without him. Maybe she dreamed of Randall out of guilt, because she's going on her first date tonight. A blind date—the term alone sounds hazardous. A redhead named Fiona in her grieving group is setting

Grace up with her brother. Grace would rather pass, but Fiona has that California air of calling everything between here and New York "the Midwest," in a pitying way, and organizing your whole life for you over the phone before you know what's hit you. Fiona also likes to brag that her apartment is located exactly on the San Andreas Fault.

Grace's relatives have reminded her that Kentucky gets earthquakes too—in 1812 one hit that made the Mississippi run backward. "There's nothing new under the sun to worry about," her cousin Rita declared. Grace is amazed at the things people will say, supposedly to be helpful. When she was pregnant, both times, women would stop her in the grocery to describe their own pregnancies, always disastrous. "Don't do what I did," someone actually told her once in frozen foods at Kroger's. "I went into labor in the fifth month and had a boy that's blind and retarded. He's at the Lexington Shriner's Home." Grace was exactly five months along with Jacob then. It was Christmas Eve. She went straight home to bed, not daring to carry in the groceries from the car. When Randall got home the ice cream had melted into a huge puddle in the bottom of the trunk and then refrozen. He tried to make her laugh about it: he called it the Neapolitan skating rink. Randall always trusted the universe. And he ended up with a drill bit in his femoral artery. Grace wipes her eyes on his shirtsleeve. The people in her grieving group say she's in the denial phase, but she's not denying anything. She knows he's dead. She just wishes she could go back and start life over. She'd meet Randall again and they'd move into a safe-deposit box.

In the parking lot after work Grace has an attack of despair. Her job is not the cause. It's a position she secured with the help of her former boss, before moving here: she's a secretary for a company that sells high-pressure liquid chromatography systems to scientists everywhere. She's not clear on what high-pressure liquid chromatography is, but Kareema, the cheeky receptionist who shares the front office, has even less of an idea, and she's been there over a year. "Do I look like a rocket scientist?" she asks Grace.

She doesn't. She looks like an exotic paintbrush. She wears black tights and has dyed her hair fuchsia on the ends and somehow persuades it to reach for the stars. She gives Grace wardrobe tips and tells her she envies her petite figure and undamaged hair. This is one more concern Grace hasn't much considered before: hair damage. When she confided this afternoon that she had a date after work, Kareema offered the loan of her lucky earrings.

So Grace has a pair of little silver snakes biting her earlobes now, but she has no idea what good luck would bring her, if she came into any. She doesn't want to drive to U.C. Berkeley and fall in love tonight. She wants to go home and find Randall in the driveway shooting baskets, missing on purpose so Jacob can win a round of Horse. Puberty is turning Matthew's face into an exact replica of his father's. He'll never even know what they look like, she thinks. When he died they still had preteen baby faces, no jawbones, no real noses yet, just stamped-out cookie dough faces like all kids have till they've lived long enough to reveal their family secrets. She pulls the car off the street and crumples around the pain in her stomach. She thinks of Randall's face in her dream, so pleased, before he jumped. Why Africa? Where is he trying to take her? How can she hold back what happens next? She lies curled on the front seat, staring up at the darkening sky and a neon fish blinking its way to no particular reward. People have told her she's taking his death too personally. She wonders what options she has; if she were a plant, she'd take it like a plant. She sits up again, fixes her eyes, and drives.

> *P*eople have told her she's taking his death too personally. She wonders what options she has; if she were a plant, she'd take it like a plant. She sits up again, fixes her eyes, and drives.

*F*iona's brother Loren turns out to be fortyish and tall, with long black hair and pale blue eyes and a blue tattoo in Chinese that curls around his wrist like a suicide scar. If you saw this guy on the street, Grace thinks, you'd expect him to ask for a quarter or steal your purse, but now here he is, her date.

Parking is a problem so they leave her car in his reserved space at the university and walk to the restaurant. Grace never knows what to make of Berkeley's cleverness: a stationer's shop called Avant Card; a coffeehouse called Sufficient Grounds.

"In the town where I grew up," she confesses, "nobody would even get these jokes." It's true. Grace barely remembers what she once expected to find here: trolley cars and the ocean. Now she isn't sure whether she's come up in the world or just moved to a city of pretenders. If these people have the answers, why are they living on a fault line? Also, they're dying like crazy: a great, sad wave of them. Loren touches her arm and they both stop to let a blind young man pass by—his sight taken, Grace now understands, by AIDS. She's learned about retinitis and pneumocystis[1] and the other devastations from three different people in her grieving group; she often feels she's being introduced to her new home through the tragedy channel.

They arrive at their destination, the China Doll. The menu is printed in Chinese with hesitant-looking translations in pencil. Grace laughs at an item called "Funny-Tasting Eggplant." "Who'd order that?" she asks Loren. "It sounds like you'd get salmonella."

He smiles. "My sister forced you into this, didn't she?"

"No, it's okay. She's trying to help me take charge of my life. She thinks I'm lonely."

"Are you?" Loren watches her. Up close he's going a little gray and seems more respectable than she'd first thought.

"No. I've got two boys. Did she tell you that? Teenagers in the house are like living in a buffalo herd." His face registers a tiny shock. People here always do that, she's noticed. It's one more backward thing she's done with her life, had kids before she was twenty.

"I'm envious," he says. "My life is too quiet. Nothing ever happens. Maybe one of my books might fall off the shelf."

Grace doesn't believe for a minute that this man's life is too quiet. It dawns on her that the envies people claim on her—undamaged hair, rowdy teenagers—are stretching it; they're being nice to a widow from East Jesus Nowhere. She looks around the restaurant and wonders if everybody has already guessed this is a first date going on here. She and Loren are both practically glowing with miserable goodwill. "What kind of, what are you at the university?" she asks. "Fiona said an associate professor."

"Of Chinese history," he says, and her eyes inadvertently go to the tattoo on his wrist. He looks down too, then draws up his sleeve and displays it for her. "It says, Beware of funny-tasting eggplant."

Grace laughs, feeling grateful. Even if she never sees him again, she'll remember that he helped her get through this day. "So can you read this whole menu?" she asks.

They're interrupted by a peppy blond waiter wearing checked pants and a moppy haircut something like Dennis the Menace. "Can I answer any questions for you tonight?" he asks.

---

1 **retinitis . . . pneumocystis:** inflammation of the retina, or lining of the eye . . . a type of pneumonia that attacks weakened immune systems

> "*E*verything that happens to you is like a tattoo," Grace says quietly. "It might not show on the outside, but it's permanent."

"Sure," says Loren. "What is the meaning of life?"

"Enjoy it. You don't die with your assets; you die with your memories."

Grace is amazed. She doesn't think she'll ever be witty enough to live here. When the waiter is gone, she asks, "What does it really say? Your tattoo. I'll bet it's some girl."

"Worse than that. It's a quote from the I Ching that I considered momentous when I was seventeen."

"You don't die with your assets; you die with your memories?"

"Something along those lines. Never get a tattoo."

The waiter brings their wine and they stare into their glasses. Then they both glance up as the blind man who passed them earlier comes into the restaurant with a companion and is seated at a far table. "Everything that happens to you is like a tattoo," Grace says quietly. "It might not show on the outside, but it's permanent."

"Or it shows up later," Loren says.

Grace wonders if he's thinking of AIDS. "You know what I keep imagining? Whenever I come over here to Berkeley I see all these guys blinded, in wheelchairs, and I think they're home from some war nobody knows about."

"Everybody knows about it; they just wish they didn't."

"No, I don't think so. There's lots of little towns like the one I grew up in where they're still in the dark."

"They haven't heard?"

"Oh, they've *heard*. But they scrub behind their ears and go to church and count on being saved. My cousin told me somebody I used to know was back there visiting his mother and went swimming at the Country Club pool. After he'd left, the city council found out he was HIV positive. They revoked his mother's membership and drained the swimming pool."

Loren appears to choke, or laugh. "Drained the pool?"

"Yes. Can you imagine? They don't have any idea of how big a disaster it is. I guess they figure they had a near miss, but it's all under control now."

"People don't believe in disasters."

"I do," Grace vows.

"No, I mean real Cecil B. DeMille natural disasters, epidemics and floods and locust plagues. People believe in individual will. They think they can control what happens to them. Drain the pool, hell, drain the ocean. Uncontrollable **pestilence** and boils are things that happened a million years ago, to Moses, not to people who possess microchip technology."

"Right. Here's to pestilence and boils," Grace says, raising her glass. She's aware that this may be the unsexiest conversation in the history of dating.

pestilence: devastating, infectious disease

$\mathcal{M}$atthew is asleep when she gets home, but Jacob is still up working on an experiment with goldfish he's conducting for a science fair. Grace is amazed at the difference between Kentucky and California school systems. Last year Jacob pasted photos of endangered species on a poster and won first prize; this year he's worked every night for weeks to make something Grace thinks ought to go on *Nova*, and he says it's terrible— a lot of kids have better projects. It stuns her to realize she's brought her sons to a place where they'll grow up feeling second-rate, as she does. So many things in life she has failed to predict.

Jacob's experiment involves electricity, but he swears it doesn't hurt the goldfish. Grace believes it, because he's named them: Madonna and Goldilocks. Jacob has the softest heart of any fourteen-year-old she's ever heard of. He's been obsessed with endangered species all his life. *Jacob believes in disasters*, Grace knows. Adults walk around making jokes about the hole in the ozone, even Johnny Carson does, but Jacob looks up at the sky and chews the skin around his cuticles.

"They do this in Germany to test the drinking water," he explained to her on the day he brought home the fish and a box of electrodes. "They keep all these goldfish in a tank of city water downtown and they monitor the current. The fish give off so many electrical impulses per minute when the water's pure. If there's too much zinc or cadmium or stuff like that in it, then they give off less. It makes a power shortage, and that sets off an alarm at the headquarters."

Jacob's experiment only shows the electrical emissions from happy fish. His teacher told him he would need to show both control and polluted conditions for a chance at the prize, but Jacob said no. His room is papered with endangered cheetahs and great dying whales. He's not going to poison Madonna and Goldilocks with zinc.

On Saturday morning Grace feels an unsteadiness in her kitchen she suspects of being a tremor. Two minutes later the phone rings and she's pretty sure it will be Fiona telling her to go stand under a doorway. It's Fiona, all right, but she just wants a report on the date. Grace runs down the details, including the menu of China Doll; there's not a lot more to tell.

"No electricity," Fiona concludes, and Grace laughs, thinking of Jacob's goldfish. Maybe we're swimming through too much pollution, she thinks, and then on impulse decides to tell Fiona about her dream. "Your brother's sweet, but I'm still too attached to Randall to see another man," she says, describing how her heart was pounding, how she woke up feeling guilty.

"He *bounced* when he fell? That sounds almost whimsical."

"It wasn't whimsical," Grace says, shocked. "It was awful. He looked down at us and then he just jumped. On purpose."

"Sounds like you're holding him responsible for his death," Fiona says. Fiona has been through so much therapy she feels qualified to say things that normal people would consider extremely none of their business. She and her husband got a no-fault divorce and lived for one year as best friends before he died of a drug overdose. But this grieving group is only the latest of a long series of groups for Fiona.

"I don't hold him responsible," Grace says. "It was an industrial accident. I blame OSHA."[2]

"But you blame him for being there. You've told me yourself you wished he'd finished his night courses and been a CPA."[3]

Grace regrets bringing up the dream. She knows Fiona could be partly right. "I just feel abandoned sometimes. Not that it's his fault. Just mad that we got left behind."

"It's natural to want to blame somebody."

"I know. Your brother said people don't believe in disasters, they believe in individual will."

Fiona laughs. "Loren's a little intense. But it's true, it's the modern age—Grace, we all act like we were born with some certificate saying we're going to have perfect, happy lives, guaranteed. So if you slip on a bar of soap, you sue Procter and Gamble."

"I saw a show about that on *Oprah*," Grace says, hoping to change the subject. "This woman got window cleaner in her eye and went blind. She

---

2 **OSHA:** Occupational Safety and Health Organization

3 **CPA:** Certified Public Accountant

sued the window-cleaner company, and then she turned around and sued her maid for taking the day off."

"It's a totally American phenomenon," Fiona says. "We refuse to accept bad luck."

 After work on Monday, Grace drives into San Francisco to pick up Jacob from the science fair. Matthew will come home on the bus alone and log in a few more hours as a Latchkey Child. He's thirteen and seems tough beyond his years, with his spiked haircut and heavy high-topped sneakers, but Grace still worries.

"Mom, I think there's going to be an earthquake today," Jacob reports from the backseat as they're transporting Goldilocks and Madonna home. They won third prize.

"Why's that?" Grace asks, not doubting it a bit.

"All the experiments with white rats messed up today. They wouldn't go through the mazes or anything; they all just huddled up together in their boxes. It was lucky for me—that's the only reason I won a prize."

"You think white rats know when an earthquake's coming?"

"All mammals do. Except people. They can smell the positive ions that get released into the air."

"If that's so," Grace says, "They ought to have a big cage of rats downtown at the fire station, like your German goldfish."

"They do have rats downtown," Jacob says. "But nobody's keeping an eye on them."

Grace smiles. She believes Jacob is a near-genius, something she always felt about Randall too, even though he worked in an auto plant. He didn't want to be a CPA, he wanted to make cars. He just had his own crazy way of looking at the world. "So how come we can't smell the positive ions like other animals do?"

"I don't know," he says, and Grace can tell he's looking out the window thinking about this. They're approaching the eastbound on-ramp to the Bay Bridge. The double-decker traffic makes her nervous, with all those westbound commuters whizzing by above them, but both boys love crossing the water. She tries to relax and see the bridge as they do: an intricate forest of I-beams.

Finally he says, "I guess we're tracking so many other stimuli that we don't notice the positive ions. We're too busy doing our own stuff."

Isn't that the truth, Grace thinks, and then suddenly her car is out of control. "Oh God," she says. "Oh my God, I've got a flat tire. I've got *two* flat tires." She pulls as hard as she can on the steering wheel and the car sways less and less violently and finally comes to a stop as far over to the right as she can get on the cramped bridge. She jumps out and looks under the car. She can't see a thing wrong with the tires on this side. She walks around to the other side, and then sees Jacob getting out of the car, laughing. He points behind Grace and she turns around.

A hundred other cars are pulled over, a hundred other drivers all bent over staring at their tires. It's taking everybody quite a while to realize this isn't a personal problem.

She finds the scene hilarious. She thinks again of Randall, catching her eye, spreading his arms wide to embrace the air. It *is* whimsical; nobody knows what's going to happen next. That's where he's trying to take her—that far and no farther. There are only two choices in the "what happens next" department: to pretend it's your job to know or to admit you don't have a clue.

The steel cables over Grace's head hum strangely and then suddenly go slack. Somewhere the structure has broken. Lots of drivers have raised their hoods and are waiting for a tow truck, civilized salvation, hoping they still might make their appointments. For once Grace feels like the only person around who's getting the joke. It will be hours, if not tomorrow, before they're all off the bridge. "Forget it!" she says aloud. "Nobody's coming. This is the mess we're in."

The concrete is still trembling under her shoes and Grace laughs so hard she can't stop. There are stalled cars over her head and the dancing bay below and Jacob is hugging her. She decides to trust the universe.

Read and Think Critically

Infer, Analyze, Compare and Contrast

1. **INTERIOR MONOLOGUE** Consider how Kingsolver uses **interior monologue** to reveal Grace's **character**. Find several examples of Grace's thoughts. Explain what we can infer about Grace's character from each example.

2. Consider the **repartee** in the story. What do these exchanges reveal about Grace?

3. What is the obvious meaning of the **title**? What other meanings might the title have?

4. Kingsolver is adept at sketching minor characters in a line or two. Of Grace's friend, she writes, "Fiona also likes to brag that her apartment is located exactly on the San Andreas Fault." What does this tell you about the character of Fiona?

5. Analyze the way in which Kingsolver chooses to end the story. Consider the events of the story and the attitude of the main character.

6. **THE AUTHOR'S STYLE** "Fault Lines" might be seen as a story of ideas and attitudes toward life. Compare and contrast the different attitudes expressed in the story by the characters of Grace, Jacob, Randall, Loren, and Fiona. Which idea or attitude best sums up the central **theme** of the story?

Before You Read

T. Coraghessan Boyle 1948–

About the Author

T. Coraghessan Boyle stands a wiry six foot, three inches. His red hair spikes up from his head and out from his goatee, and he can usually be found in torn jeans, lots of earrings, and a wrinkled T-shirt that advertises the name of his latest book. Born in Peekskill, New York, the grandson of Irish immigrants, he studied English and history at the State University of New York at Potsdam.

He says that to avoid service in Vietnam, he taught for several years at his high school alma mater. Subsequently, he attended the University of Iowa Writers' Workshop. A flamboyant speaker, Boyle often goes on book tours and appears on talk shows. He is known for making comments that are outrageously immodest, such as this one in an interview for *Passion and Craft*: "I think all my novels are a complete and utter joy and I can't understand why everyone in America isn't reading them instead of John Grisham."

Among his best-known works are the short story collection *Greasy Lake* and the novels *The Road to Wellville*, which was made into a film, and *The Tortilla Curtain*.

****

The Author's Style

Boyle writes comic satire that provides an unforgiving look at human folly—the way supposedly smart people turn into pathetic fools and make victims of themselves and others in their pursuit of pleasure, comfort, security, and order. In Boyle's work, characters are undone by the fundamental human weaknesses of pride, greed, and anger. They also come to grief because of a smug belief that their intelligence, education, and money will protect them from harm.

Boyle is noted for his eerily inventive and sometimes quirky use of language. He has an ability to splice together the normal and the bizarre, the humorous and the horrifying.

The prevailing tone of Boyle's stories is irony; a typical mood is dread. He puts characters in extreme situations of which they are blissfully ignorant until it is too late. Since Boyle's characters are often unaware of their weaknesses and of the power of social, political, and natural laws and forces around them, they push forward almost obsessively, oblivious to warning signs—even as these signs become increasingly clear to the reader. At times their situations are calamitous to the point of absurdity, yet the characters are so hapless that they evoke laughter as well as sympathy.

Top of the Food Chain

T. Coraghessan Boyle

🔍 **Literary Lens: Tone** As you read, consider the **tone**, or the narrator's attitude toward the events in the story.

*T*he thing was, we had a little problem with the insect **vector** there, and believe me, your tamer stuff, your Malathion and pyrethrum[1] and the rest of the so-called environmentally safe products didn't begin to make a dent in it, not a dent, I mean it was utterly useless—we might as well have been spraying with Chanel No. 5 for all the good it did. And you've got to realize these people were literally covered with insects day and night—and the fact that they hardly wore any clothes just compounded the problem. Picture if you can, gentlemen, a naked little two-year-old boy so black with flies and mosquitoes it looks like he's wearing long johns, or the young mother so racked with the malarial shakes she can't even lift a diet Coke to her lips—it was

vector: disease-spreading organism

---

1 **Malathion and pyrethrum:** insecticides that are said to be nontoxic to mammals

pathetic, just pathetic, like something out of the Dark Ages. . . . Well, anyway, the decision was made to go with DDT. In the short term. Just to get the situation under control, you understand.

Yes, that's right, Senator, *DDT*: Dichlorodiphenyltrichloroethan.

Yes, I'm well aware of that fact, sir. But just because *we* banned it domestically, under pressure from the birdwatching contingent and the hopheads down at the EPA, it doesn't necessarily follow that the rest of the world—especially the developing world—is about to jump on the bandwagon. And that's the key word here, Senator: *developing*. You've got to realize this is Borneo we're talking about here, not Port Townsend or Enumclaw.[2] These people don't know from square one about sanitation, disease control, pest eradication—or even personal hygiene, if you want to come right down to it. It rains a hundred and twenty inches a year, minimum. They dig up roots in the jungle. They've still got headhunters along the Rajang River, for god's sake.

And please don't forget they *asked* us to come in there, practically begged us—and not only the World Health Organization, but the Sultan of Brunei and the government in Sarawak too. We did what we could to accommodate them and reach our objective in the shortest period of time and by the most direct and effective means. We went to the air. Obviously. And no one could have foreseen the consequences, no one, not even if we'd gone out and generated a hundred environmental-impact statements—it was just one of those things, a freak occurrence, and there's no defense against that. Not that I know of, anyway. . . .

Caterpillars? Yes, Senator, that's correct. That was the first sign: caterpillars.

But let me backtrack a minute here. You see, out in the bush they have these roofs made of thatched palm leaves—you'll see them in the towns too, even in Bintulu or Brunei—and they're really pretty effective, you'd be surprised. A hundred and twenty inches of rain, they've got to figure a way to keep it out of the hut, and for centuries, this was it. Palm leaves. Well, it was about a month after we sprayed for the final time and I'm sitting at my desk in the trailer thinking about the drainage project at Kuching, enjoying the fact that for the first time in maybe a year I'm not smearing mosquitoes all over the back of my neck, when there's a knock at the door. It's this elderly

---

2 **Borneo . . . Port Townsend . . . Enumclaw:** a large island near the Philippines; a port city on Washington's coast; an inland city in Washington

gentleman, tattooed from head to toe, dressed only in a pair of running shorts—they love those shorts, by the way, the shiny material and the tight machine-stitching, the whole country, men and women and children, they can't get enough of them. . . . Anyway, he's the headman of the local village and he's very excited, something about the roofs—*atap*, they call them. That's all he can say, *atap*, *atap*, over and over again.

It's raining, of course. It's always raining. So I shrug into my rain slicker, start up the 4 x 4 and go have a look. Sure enough, all the *atap* roofs are collapsing, not only in his village, but throughout the target area. The people are all huddled there in their running shorts, looking pretty miserable, and one after another the roofs keep falling in, it's bewildering, and gradually I realize the headman's **diatribe** has begun to feature a new term I was unfamiliar with at the time—the word for caterpillar, as it turns out, in the Iban dialect. But who was to make the connection between three passes with the crop duster and all these staved-in roofs?

diatribe: bitter complaint

Our people finally sorted it out a couple weeks later. The chemical, which, by the way, cut down the number of mosquitoes exponentially, had the unfortunate side effect of killing off this little wasp—I've got the scientific name for it somewhere in my report here, if you're interested— that preyed on a type of caterpillar that in turn ate palm leaves. Well, with the wasps gone, the caterpillars hatched out with nothing to keep them in check and chewed the roofs to pieces, and that was unfortunate, we admit it, and we had a real cost overrun on replacing those roofs with tin . . . but the people were happier, I think, in the long run, because let's face it, no matter how tightly you weave those palm leaves, they're just not going to keep the water out like tin. Of course, nothing's perfect, and we had a lot of complaints about the rain drumming on the panels, people unable to sleep and what-have-you. . . .

Yes, sir, that's correct—the flies were next.

Well, you've got to understand the magnitude of the fly problem in Borneo, there's nothing like it here to compare it with, except maybe a garbage strike in New York. Every minute of every day you've got flies everywhere, up your nose, in your mouth, your ears, your eyes, flies in your rice, your Coke, your Singapore sling and your gin rickey. It's enough to drive you to distraction, not to mention the diseases these things carry, from dysentery to typhoid to cholera and back round the loop again. And once the mosquito population was down, the flies seemed to breed up to fill in the gap—Borneo wouldn't be Borneo without some damned insect blackening the air.

Of course, this was before our people had tracked down the problem with the caterpillars and the wasps and all of that, and so we figured we'd had a big success with the mosquitoes, why not a series of ground sweeps, mount a fogger in the back of a Suzuki Brat and sanitize the huts, not to mention the open sewers, which as you know are nothing but a breeding ground for flies, chiggers and biting insects of every sort. At least it was an error of commission rather than omission. At least we were trying.

I watched the flies go down myself. One day they were so thick in the trailer I couldn't even *find* my paperwork, let alone attempt to get through it, and the next they were collecting on the windows, bumbling around like they were drunk. A day later they were gone. Just like that. From a million flies in the trailer to none. . . .

Well, no one could have foreseen that, Senator.

The geckos ate the flies, yes. You're all familiar with geckos, I assume, gentlemen? These are the lizards you've seen during your trips to Hawaii, very colorful, patrolling the houses for roaches and flies, almost like pets, but of course they're wild animals, never lose sight of that, and just about as unsanitary as anything I can think of, except maybe flies.

Yes, well don't forget sir, we're viewing this with twenty-twenty hindsight, but at the time no one gave a thought to geckos or what they ate—they were just another fact of life in the tropics. Mosquitoes, lizards, scorpions, leeches—you name it, they've got it. When the flies began piling up on the windowsills like drift, naturally the geckos feasted on them, stuffing themselves till they looked like sausages crawling up the walls. Where before they moved so fast you could never be sure you'd seen them, now they waddled across the floor, laid around in the corners, clung to the air vents like magnets—and even then no one paid much attention to them till they started turning belly-up in the streets. Believe me, we confirmed a lot of things there about the buildup of these products as you move up the food chain and the **efficacy**—or lack thereof—of certain methods, no doubt about that. . . .

efficacy:
effectiveness

The cats? That's where it got sticky, really sticky. You see, nobody really lost any sleep over a pile of dead lizards—though we did the tests routinely and the tests confirmed what we'd expected, that is, the product had been concentrated in the geckos because of the sheer number of contaminated flies they'd consumed. But lizards are one thing and cats are another. These people really have an affection for their cats—no house, no hut, no matter how primitive, is without at least a couple of them. Mangy-looking things, long-legged and scrawny, maybe, not at all the sort of animal you'd see here, but there it was: they loved their cats. Because the cats were functional, you understand—without them, the place would have been swimming in rodents inside of a week.

You're right there, Senator, yes—that's exactly what happened.

You see, the cats had a field day with these feeble geckos—you can imagine, if any of you have ever owned a cat, the kind of joy these animals must have experienced to see their **nemesis**, this ultra-quick lizard, and it's just barely creeping across the floor like a bug. Well, to make a long story short, the cats ate up every dead and dying gecko in the country, from snout to tail, and then the cats began to die . . . which to my mind would have been no great loss if it wasn't for the rats. Suddenly there were rats everywhere— you couldn't drive down the street without running over half-a-dozen of them at a time. They fouled the grain supplies, fell in the wells and died, bit infants as they slept in their cradles. But that wasn't the worst, not by a long shot. No, things really went down the tube after that. Within the month we were getting scattered reports of bubonic plague, and of course we tracked them all down and made sure the people got a round of treatment with antibiotics, but still we lost a few and the rats kept coming. . . .

It was my plan, yes. I was brainstorming one night, rats scuttling all over the trailer like something out of a cheap horror film, the villagers in a panic over the threat of the plague and the stream of nonstop hysterical reports from the interior—people were turning black, swelling up and bursting, that sort of thing—well, as I say, I came up with a plan, a stopgap, not perfect, not cheap; but at this juncture, I'm sure you'll agree, something had to be implemented.

We wound up going as far as Australia for some of the cats, cleaning out the SPCA[3] facilities and what-have-you, though we rounded most of them up in Indonesia and Singapore—approximately fourteen thousand in all. And yes, it cost us—cost us upfront purchase money and aircraft fuel and pilots' overtime and all the rest of it—but we really felt there was no alternative. It was like all nature had turned against us.

And yet still, all things considered, we made a lot of friends for the U.S.A. the day we dropped those cats, and you should have seen them, gentlemen,

nemesis:
formidable
rival

---

3 **SPCA:** Society for the Prevention of Cruelty to Animals

the little parachutes and harnesses we'd tricked up, fourteen thousand of them, cats in every color of the rainbow, cats with one ear, no ears, half a tail, three-legged cats, cats that could have taken pride of show in Springfield, Massachusetts, and all of them twirling down out of the sky like great big oversized snowflakes. . . .

It was something. It was really something.

Of course, you've all seen the reports. There were other factors we hadn't counted on, adverse conditions in the paddies and manioc fields—we don't to this day know what predatory species were inadvertently killed off by the initial sprayings, it's just a mystery—but the weevils and whatnot took a pretty heavy toll on the crops that year, and by the time we dropped the cats, well, the people were pretty hungry, and I suppose it was inevitable that we lost a good proportion of them right then and there. But we've got a CARE[4] program going there now, and something hit the rat population—we still don't know what, a virus, we think—and the geckos, they tell me, are making a comeback.

So what I'm saying is, it could be worse, and to every cloud a silver lining, wouldn't you agree, gentlemen?

THE TOP OF THE FOOD CHAIN, CATY BARTHOLOMEW, 1993

---

4 **CARE:** Cooperative for Assistance and Relief Everywhere

Read and Think Critically

Describe, Infer, Analyze

 1. **TONE** Describe the author's attitude toward the events in the story. What examples of **irony** do you find in his narration of the story?

2. Reread the first sentence of the story. What do you **infer** about the **narrator** and the situation that is about to unfold?

3. What is being **satirized** in "Top of the Food Chain"?

4. Some critics consider both Joyce Carol Oates and T. Coraghessan Boyle harsh and unforgiving judges of contemporary American morals and values. Discuss why you agree or disagree.

5. At one point, the narrator justifies sweeping the ground with a fog of pesticides this way: "At least it was an error of commission rather than omission. At least we were trying." If you were a member of the committee before which he is testifying, how would you respond?

6. Analyze the narrator's attitude toward the developing world. Support your analysis with examples from the text.

7. **THE AUTHOR'S STYLE** Boyle is said to have a gift for pairing the familiar with the frightening and the normal with the bizarre. Find two such pairings in "Top of the Food Chain." Explain what these pairings add to the story.

Before You Read

Robert Olen Butler 1945–

About the Author

Robert Olen Butler grew up in Granite City, Illinois, majored in theatre at Northwestern University, and then studied playwriting at the University of Iowa. In 1971, he went to Vietnam as a counter-intelligence special agent and later as a translator; he was fluent in Vietnamese because the army had sent him to language school the year before.

During an interview at Powells City of Books in Portland, Oregon, in 1996, he said that while serving in Vietnam, "My favorite thing in the world to do was to wander out into the back alleys of Saigon, where nobody seemed to sleep. I did this almost every night. In those back alleys I would crouch with the people and talk with

them. The Vietnamese people as a group are the most open and generous-spirited people in the world. Invariably they would invite me into their homes, their culture, and their lives."

Although Butler is known primarily for writing about Vietnam, he has written on a variety of topics, publishing nine novels and two volumes of short fiction, as well as screenplays and teleplays, since 1981. In 1993 his collection of short stories, *A Good Scent from a Strange Mountain*, was awarded the Pulitzer Prize. He is a professor at Florida State University.

****

The Author's Style

Butler served as an army linguist during the Vietnam War. His command of the language of Vietnam and his familiarity with its climate, geography, and people are central to much of his fiction. Butler's stories are concerned with individuals whose lives continue to be affected by their experiences in the war and by the sharp differences between American and Vietnamese culture. He is remarkably adept at conveying the language, tone, and points of view of both male and female characters and both Americans and Vietnamese. He has won an award from fellow

veterans for outstanding contributions to American culture by a Vietnam veteran.

His work makes clear many fascinating and appealing aspects of Vietnamese life. It also shows how frustratingly different that life can be from life in the United States. His characters' struggles with one or another aspect of American culture reveal why their postwar lives are characterized by both new opportunities and painful betrayals. The lasting emotional and physical wounds suffered by both civilians and former soldiers help explain the urgency behind the first-person stories they tell.

Letters from My Father

R O B E R T   O L E N   B U T L E R

LITERARY LENS: ANALOGIES AND COMPARISONS Look for the **analogies** and **comparisons** in this story.

*T*look through the letters my father sent to me in Saigon and I find this: "Dear Fran. How are you? I wish you and your mother were here with me. The weather here is pretty cold this time of year. I bet you would like the cold weather." At the time, I wondered how he would know such a thing. Cold weather sounded very bad. It was freezing, he said, so I touched the tip of my finger to a piece of ice and I held it there for as long as I could. It hurt very bad and that was after only about a minute. I thought, How could you spend hours and days in weather like that?

It makes no difference that I had misunderstood the cold weather. By the time he finally got me and my mother out of Vietnam, he had moved to a place where it almost never got very cold. The point is that in his letters to me he often said this and that about the weather. It is cold today. It is hot today.

Today there are clouds in the sky. Today there are no clouds. What did that have to do with me?

He said, "Dear Fran" because my name is Fran. That's short for Francine and the sound of Fran is something like a Vietnamese name, but it isn't really. So I told my friends in Saigon that my name was Trán, which was short for Hôn Trán, which means "a kiss on the forehead." My American father lived in America but my Vietnamese mother and me lived in Saigon, so I was still a Saigon girl. My mother called me Francine, too. She was happy for me to have this name. She said it was not just American, it was also French. But I wanted a name for Saigon and Trán was it.

I was a child of dust. When the American fathers all went home, including my father, and the communists took over, that's what we were called, those of us who had faces like those drawings you see in some of the bookstalls on Nguyen Huê Street. You look once and you see a beautiful woman sitting at her mirror, but then you look again and you see the skull of a dead person, no skin on the face, just the wide eyes of the skull and the bared teeth. We were like that, the children of dust in Saigon. At one look we were Vietnamese and at another look we were American and after that you couldn't get your eyes to stay still when they turned to us, they kept seeing first one thing and then another.

Last night I found a package of letters in a footlocker that belongs to my father. It is in the storage shack at the back of our house here in America. I am living now in Lake Charles, Louisiana, and I found this package of letters outside—many packages, hundreds of letters—and I opened one, and these are all copies he kept of letters he sent trying to get us out of Vietnam. I look through these letters my father wrote and I find this: "What is this crap that you're trying to give me now? It has been nine years, seven months, and fifteen days since I last saw my daughter, my own flesh-and-blood daughter."

This is an angry voice, a voice with feeling. I have been in this place now for a year. I am seventeen and it took even longer than nine years, seven months, fifteen days to get me out of Vietnam. I wish I could say something about that, because I know anyone who listens to my story would expect me right now to say how I felt. My mother and me were left behind in Saigon. My father went on ahead to America and he thought he could get some paperwork done and prepare a place for us, then my mother and me would be leaving for America very soon. But things happened. A different footlocker was lost and some important papers with it, like their marriage license and my birth certificate. Then the country of South Vietnam fell to the communists, and even those who thought it might happen thought it happened pretty fast, really. Who knew? My father didn't.

I look at a letter he sent me in Saigon after it fell and the letter says: "You can imagine how I feel. The whole world is let down by what happened." But I could not imagine that, if you want to know the truth, how my father felt. And I knew nothing of the world except Saigon, and even that wasn't the way the world was, because when I was very little they gave it a different name, calling it Hô´Chí Minh City. Now, those words are a man's name, you know, but the same words have several other meanings, too, and I took the name like everyone took the face of a child of dust: I looked at it one way and it meant one thing and then I looked at it a different way and it meant something else. Hô´Chí Minh also can mean "very intelligent starch-paste," and that's what we thought of the new name, me and some friends of mine who also had American fathers. We would meet at the French cemetery on Phan Thanh Gian´ Street and talk about our city—Hô´, for short; starch-paste. We would talk about our lives in Starch-Paste City and we had this game where we'd hide in the cemetery, each in a separate place, and then we'd keep low and move slowly and see how many of our friends we would find. If you saw the other person first, you would get a point. And if nobody ever saw you, if it was like you were invisible, you'd win.

The cemetery made me sad, but it felt very comfortable there somehow. We all thought that, me and my friends. It was a ragged place and many of the names were like Couchet, Picard, Vernet, Believeau, and these graves never had any flowers on them. Everybody who loved these dead people had gone home to France long ago. Then there was a part of the cemetery that had Vietnamese dead. There were some flowers over there, but not very many. The grave markers had photos, little oval frames built into the stone, and these were faces of the dead, mostly old people, men and women, the wealthy Vietnamese, but there were some young people, too, many of them dead in 1968 when there was much killing in Saigon. I would always hide over in this section and there was one boy, very cute, in sunglasses, leaning on a motorcycle, his hand on his hip. He died in February of 1968, and

I look at a letter he sent me in Saigon after it fell and the letter says: "You can imagine how I feel. The whole world is let down by what happened."

I probably wouldn't have liked him anyway. He looked cute but very conceited. And there was a girl nearby. The marker said she was fifteen. I found her when I was about ten or so and she was very beautiful, with long black hair and dark eyes and a round face. I would always go to her grave and I wanted to be just like her, though I knew my face was different from hers. Then I went one day—I was almost her age at last—and the rain had gotten into the little picture frame and her face was nearly gone. I could see her hair, but the features of her face had faded until you could not see them, there were only dark streaks of water and the picture was curling at the edges, and I cried over that. It was like she had died.

Sometimes my father sent me pictures with his letters. "Dear Fran," he would say. "Here is a picture of me. Please send me a picture of you." A friend of mine, when she was about seven years old, got a pen pal in Russia. They wrote to each other very simple letters in French. Her pen pal said, "Please send me a picture of you and I will send you one of me." My friend put on her white aó dài[1] and went downtown and had her picture taken before the big banyan tree in the park on Le´ Thánh Tôn. She sent it off and in return she got a picture of a fat girl who hadn't combed her hair, standing by a cow on a collective farm.

My mother's father was some government man, I think. And the communists said my mother was an agitator or collaborator. Something like that. It was all mostly before I was born or when I was just a little girl, and whenever my mother tried to explain what all this was about, this father across the sea and us not seeming to ever go there, I just didn't like to listen very much and my mother realized that, and after a while she didn't say any more. I put his picture up on my mirror and he was smiling, I guess. He was outside somewhere and there was a lake or something in the background and he had a T-shirt on and I guess he was really more squinting than smiling. There were several of these photographs of him on my mirror. They were always outdoors and he was always squinting in the sun. He said in one of his

---

I **aó dài:** a traditional Vietnamese dress

letters to me: "Dear Fran, I got your photo. You are very pretty, like your mother. I have not forgotten you." And I thought: I am not like my mother. I am a child of dust. Has he forgotten that?

One of the girls I used to hang around with at the cemetery told me a story that she knew was true because it happened to her sister's best friend. The best friend was just a very little girl when it began. Her father was a soldier in the South Vietnam Army and he was away fighting somewhere secret, Cambodia or somewhere. It was very secret, so her mother never heard from him and the little girl was so small when he went away that she didn't even remember him, what he looked like or anything. But she knew she was supposed to have a daddy, so every evening, when the mother would put her daughter to bed, the little girl would ask where her father was. She asked with such a sad heart that one night the mother made something up.

There was a terrible storm and the electricity went out in Saigon. So the mother went to the table with the little girl clinging in fright to her, and she lit an oil lamp. When she did, her shadow suddenly was thrown upon the wall and it was very big, and she said, "Don't cry, my baby, see there?" She pointed to the shadow. "There's your daddy. He'll protect you." This made the little girl very happy. She stopped shaking from fright immediately and the mother sang the girl to sleep.

The next evening before going to bed, the little girl asked to see her father. When the mother tried to say no, the little girl was so upset that the mother gave in and lit the oil lamp and cast her shadow on the wall. The little girl went to the wall and held her hands before her with the palms together and she bowed low to the shadow. "Good night, Daddy," she said, and she went to sleep. This happened the next evening and the next and it went on for more than a year.

Then one evening, just before bedtime, the father finally came home. The mother, of course, was very happy. She wept and she kissed him and she said to him, "We will prepare a thanksgiving feast to honor our ancestors. You go in to our daughter. She is almost ready for bed. I will go out to the market and get some food for our celebration."

So the father went in to the little girl and he said to her, "My pretty girl, I am home. I am your father and I have not forgotten you."

But the little girl said, "You're not my daddy. I know my daddy. He'll be here soon. He comes every night to say good night to me before I go to bed."

The man was shocked at his wife's faithlessness, but he was very proud, and he did not say anything to her about it when she got home. He did not say anything at all, but prayed briefly before the shrine of their ancestors and picked up his bag and left. The weeks passed and the mother grieved so badly that one day she threw herself into the Saigon River and drowned.

The father heard news of this and thought that she had killed herself from shame. He returned home to be a father to his daughter, but on the first night, there was a storm and the lights went out and the man lit the oil lamp, throwing his shadow on the wall. His little girl laughed in delight and went and bowed low to the shadow and said, "Good night, Daddy." When the man saw this, he took his little girl to his own mother's house, left her, and threw himself into the Saigon River to join his wife in death.

My friend says this story is true. Everyone in the neighborhood of her sister's friend knows about it. But I don't think it's true. I never did say that to my friend, but for me, it doesn't make sense. I can't believe that the little girl would be satisfied with the shadow father. There was this darkness on the wall, just a flatness, and she loved it. I can see how she wouldn't take up with this man who suddenly walks in one night and says, "I'm your father, let me tell you good night." But the other guy, the shadow—he was no father either.

When my father met my mother and me at the airport, there were people with cameras and microphones and my father grabbed my mother with this enormous hug and this sound like a shout and he kissed her hard and all the people with microphones and cameras smiled and nodded. Then he let go of my mother and he looked at me and suddenly he was making this little choking sound, a kind of gacking in the back of his throat like a rabbit makes when you pick him up and he doesn't like it. And my father's hands just fluttered before him and he got stiff-legged coming over to me and the hug he gave me was like I was soaking wet and he had on his Sunday clothes, though he was just wearing some silly T-shirt.

> When my father met my mother and me at the airport, there were people with cameras and microphones and my father grabbed my mother with this enormous hug and this sound like a shout and he kissed her hard and all the people with microphones and cameras smiled and nodded.

SEPARATION, LARRY YUNG

All the letters from my father, the ones I got in Saigon, and the photos, they're in a box in the back of the closet of my room. My closet smells of my perfume, is full of nice clothes so that I can fit in at school. Not everyone can say what they feel in words, especially words on paper. Not everyone can look at a camera and make their face do what it has to do to show a feeling. But years of flat words, grimaces at the sun, these are hard things to forget. So I've been sitting all morning today in the shack behind our house, out here with the tree roaches and the carpenter ants and the smell of mildew and rotting wood and I am sweating so hard that it's dripping off my nose and chin. There are many letters in my lap. In one of them to the U.S. government my father says: "If this was a goddamn white woman, a Russian ballet dancer and her daughter, you people would have them on a plane in twenty-four hours. This is my wife and my daughter. My daughter is so beautiful you can put her face on your dimes and quarters and no one could ever make change again in your goddamn country without stopping and saying, Oh my God, what a beautiful face."

I read this now while I'm hidden in the storage shack, invisible, soaked with sweat like it's that time in Saigon between the dry season and the rainy season, and I know my father will be here soon. The lawn mower is over there in the corner and this morning he got up and said that it was going to be hot today, that there were no clouds in the sky and he was going to have to mow the lawn. When he opens the door, I will let him see me here, and I will ask him to talk to me like in these letters, like when he was so angry with some stranger that he knew what to say.

Read and Think Critically

Examine, Analyze, Explain

1. **ANALOGIES AND COMPARISONS** Consider the unusual **analogies** and **comparisons** the **narrator** uses in telling her story. With a chart like the one below, examine several of these comparisons and what they mean to Fran. Then write a short description of Fran based on the analogies she uses.

Comparison	Meaning to Fran
Hô´ Chí Minh can mean "very intelligent starch-paste."	The name of the city could be taken the same way that some people take the faces of the children of dust.

2. Write an analysis of the character of Fran. What are some of the ways you see Fran struggling for her identity in this story?

3. What do you think is the significance of the game the children play at the cemetery in Vietnam?

4. Why do you think Fran became so attached to the girl whose photograph was framed on the headstone in the cemetery?

5. Do you think Butler, an adult American male, is convincing when writing in the **voice** of a young Vietnamese girl? Explain your reaction.

6. **THE AUTHOR'S STYLE** In telling Fran's story, Butler uses bits and pieces of her past such as photos, paintings, letters, memories, and even an urban legend. Which of these do you think best defines Fran's **character**?

Before You Read

Sherman Alexie 1966–

About the Author

A Spokane/Coeur d'Alene Indian, Sherman Alexie grew up on the Spokane Reservation in Washington but chose to attend high school in a nearby town. There, as he puts it, he was the only Indian except the mascot. After high school he went on to Washington State University, where he stumbled into a poetry class and found what he was looking for.

A stand-up comedian as well as a three-time world heavyweight poetry slam champion and writer of stories and novels, Alexie is a funny writer who is nonetheless very serious about his work and its focus on Indian concerns. In a

July 2, 1998, interview in *Salon*, he said, "I'm not trying to speak for everybody. I'm one individual heavily influenced by my tribe. And good art doesn't come out of assimilation—it comes out of tribalism." (*Assimilation* is the process of being absorbed into a culture or group.)

Alexie's best-known works include the poetry collection *The Business of Fancydancing* and *The Lone Ranger and Tonto Fistfight in Heaven*, a series of linked stories that won a Hemingway Foundation/PEN Award.

★★★★★★★★★★★

The Author's Style

Alexie writes with sensitivity and energetic wit about the everyday lives of Indians. One of his concerns is the interaction between traditional tribal culture and mainstream, contemporary American life. The dreams, hopes, and visions of his characters are linked to Native American oral storytelling and are in constant conflict with elements of the non-Indian world. His stories examine Indian stereotypes, dependence on government food and housing, and exploitation of Indian culture.

Alexie's stories and novels often use flashbacks and are written in brief sections or episodes that enable Alexie to point out the ironies of contemporary Indian life. Alexie's stories are marked by a poet's use of symbols and figures of speech.

Alexie is a comic writer in that his stories are simultaneously funny and sad; he is hopeful, but not optimistic. The quick dialogue and biting wit of his characters contain serious messages and have been successfully rendered in the film *Smoke Signals*. The film was adapted from *The Lone Ranger and Tonto Fistfight in Heaven*, which drew particularly from the story you are about to read.

This Is What
It Means to Say
Phoenix, Arizona

S HERMAN A LEXIE

LITERARY LENS: FLASHBACK Watch for the **flashbacks** (abrupt scene changes to earlier times) in this story.

*J*ust after Victor lost his job at the BIA,[1] he also found out that his father had died of a heart attack in Phoenix, Arizona. Victor hadn't seen his father in a few years, only talked to him on the telephone once or twice, but there still was a genetic pain, which was soon to be pain as real and immediate as a broken bone.

Victor didn't have any money. Who does have money on a reservation, except the cigarette and fireworks salespeople? His father had a savings account waiting to be claimed, but Victor needed to find a way to get to Phoenix. Victor's mother was just as poor as he was, and the rest of his family didn't have any use at all for him. So Victor called the Tribal Council.

---

1 **BIA:** Bureau of Indian Affairs, a federal government department that administers programs and policies for Native American people and reservations

"Listen," Victor said. "My father just died. I need some money to get to Phoenix to make arrangements."

"Now, Victor," the council said. "You know we're having a difficult time financially."

"But I thought the council had special funds set aside for stuff like this."

"Now, Victor, we do have some money available for the proper return of tribal members' bodies. But I don't think we have enough to bring your father all the way back from Phoenix."

"Well," Victor said. "It ain't going to cost all that much. He had to be cremated. Things were kind of ugly. He died of a heart attack in his trailer and nobody found him for a week. It was really hot, too. You get the picture."

"Now, Victor, we're sorry for your loss and the circumstances. But we can really only afford to give you one hundred dollars."

"That's not even enough for a plane ticket."

"Well, you might consider driving down to Phoenix."

"I don't have a car. Besides, I was going to drive my father's pickup back up here."

"Now, Victor," the council said. "We're sure there is somebody who could drive you to Phoenix. Or is there somebody who could lend you the rest of the money?"

"You know there ain't nobody around with that kind of money."

"Well, we're sorry, Victor, but that's the best we can do."

Victor accepted the Tribal Council's offer. What else could he do? So he signed the proper papers, picked up his check, and walked over to the Trading Post to cash it.

While Victor stood in line, he watched Thomas Builds-the-Fire standing near the magazine rack, talking to himself. Like he always did. Thomas was a storyteller that nobody wanted to listen to. That's like being a dentist in a town where everybody has false teeth.

Victor and Thomas Builds-the-Fire were the same age, had grown up and played in the dirt together. Ever since Victor could remember, it was Thomas who always had something to say.

Once, when they were seven years old, when Victor's father still lived with the family, Thomas closed his eyes and told Victor this story: "Your father's heart is weak. He is afraid of his own family. He is afraid of you. Late at night he sits in the dark. Watches the television until there's nothing but that white noise. Sometimes he feels like he wants to buy a motorcycle and ride away. He wants to run and hide. He doesn't want to be found."

Thomas Builds-the-Fire had known that Victor's father was going to leave, knew it before anyone. Now Victor stood in the Trading Post with a one-hundred-dollar check in his hand, wondering if Thomas knew that Victor's father was dead, if he knew what was going to happen next.

Just then Thomas looked at Victor, smiled, and walked over to him.

"Victor, I'm sorry about your father," Thomas said.

"How did you know about it?" Victor asked

"I heard it on the wind. I heard it from the birds. I felt it in the sunlight. Also, your mother was just in here crying."

"Oh," Victor said and looked around the Trading Post. All the other Indians stared, surprised that Victor was even talking to Thomas. Nobody talked to Thomas anymore because he told the same damn stories over and over again. Victor was embarrassed, but he thought that Thomas might be able to help him. Victor felt a sudden need for tradition.

"I can lend you the money you need," Thomas said suddenly. "But you have to take me with you."

"I can't take your money," Victor said. "I mean, I haven't hardly talked to you in years. We're not really friends anymore."

"I didn't say we were friends. I said you had to take me with you."

"Let me think about it."

Victor went home with his one hundred dollars and sat at the kitchen table. He held his head in his hands and thought about Thomas Builds-the-Fire, remembered little details, tears and scars, the bicycle they shared for a summer, so many stories.

𝒯homas Builds-the-Fire sat on the bicycle, waited in Victor's yard. He was ten years old and skinny. His hair was dirty because it was the Fourth of July.

"Victor," Thomas yelled. "Hurry up. We're going to miss the fireworks."

After a few minutes, Victor ran out of his house, jumped the porch railing, and landed gracefully on the sidewalk.

"And the judges award him a 9.95, the highest score of the summer," Thomas said, clapped, laughed.

"That was perfect, cousin," Victor said. "And it's my turn to ride the bike."

Thomas gave up the bike and they headed for the fairgrounds. It was nearly dark and the fireworks were about to start.

"You know," Thomas said. "It's strange how us Indians celebrate the Fourth of July. It ain't like it was *our* independence everybody was fighting for."

$\mathcal{H}$e counted his one hundred dollars again and again. He knew he needed more to make it to Phoenix and back. He knew he needed Thomas Builds-the-Fire.

"You think about things too much," Victor said. "It's just supposed to be fun. Maybe Junior will be there."

"Which Junior? Everybody on this reservation is named Junior."

And they both laughed.

The fireworks were small, hardly more than a few bottle rockets and a fountain. But it was enough for two Indian boys. Years later, they would need much more.

Afterwards, sitting in the dark, fighting off mosquitoes, Victor turned to Thomas Builds-the-Fire.

"Hey," Victor said. "Tell me a story."

Thomas closed his eyes and told this story: "There were these two Indian boys who wanted to be warriors. But it was too late to be warriors in the old way. All the horses were gone. So the two Indian boys stole a car and drove to the city. They parked the stolen car in front of the police station and then hitchhiked back home to the reservation. When they got back, all their friends cheered and their parents' eyes shone with pride. *You were very brave*, everybody said to the two Indian boys. *Very brave*."

"Ya-hey," Victor said. "That's a good one. I wish I could be a warrior."

"Me, too," Thomas said.

They went home together in the dark, Thomas on the bike now, Victor on foot. They walked through shadows and light from streetlamps.

"We've come a long ways," Thomas said. "We have outdoor lighting."

"All I need is the stars," Victor said. "And besides, you still think about things too much."

They separated then, each headed for home, both laughing all the way.

$\mathcal{V}$ictor sat at his kitchen table. He counted his one hundred dollars again and again. He knew he needed more to make it to Phoenix and back. He knew he needed Thomas Builds-the-Fire. So he put his money in his wallet and opened the front door to find Thomas on the porch.

"Ya-hey, Victor," Thomas said. "I knew you'd call me."

Thomas walked into the living room and sat down on Victor's favorite chair.

"I've got some money saved up," Thomas said. "It's enough to get us down there, but you have to get us back."

"I've got this hundred dollars," Victor said. "And my dad had a savings account I'm going to claim."

"How much in your dad's account?"

"Enough. A few hundred."

"Sounds good. When we leaving?"

*W*hen they were fifteen and had long since stopped being friends, Victor and Thomas got into a fistfight. That is, Victor was really drunk and beat Thomas up for no reason at all. All the other Indian boys stood around and watched it happen. Junior was there and so were Lester, Seymour, and a lot of others. The beating might have gone on until Thomas was dead if Norma Many Horses hadn't come along and stopped it.

"Hey, you boys," Norma yelled and jumped out of her car. "Leave him alone."

If it had been someone else, even another man, the Indian boys would've just ignored the warnings. But Norma was a warrior. She was powerful. She could have picked up any two of the boys and smashed their skulls together. But worse than that, she would have dragged them all over to some tipi and made them listen to some elder tell a dusty old story.

The Indian boys scattered, and Norma walked over to Thomas and picked him up.

"Hey, little man, are you okay?" she asked.

Thomas gave her a thumbs up.

"Why they always picking on you?"

Thomas shook his head, closed his eyes, but no stories came to him, no words or music. He just wanted to go home, to lie in his bed and let his dreams tell his stories for him.

*T*homas Builds-the-Fire and Victor sat next to each other in the airplane, coach section. A tiny white woman had the window seat. She was busy twisting her body into pretzels. She was flexible.

"I have to ask," Thomas said, and Victor closed his eyes in embarrassment.

"Don't," Victor said.

"Excuse me, miss," Thomas asked. "Are you a gymnast or something?"

"There's no something about it," she said. "I was first alternate on the 1980 Olympic team."

"Really?" Thomas asked.

"Really."

"I mean, you used to be a world-class athlete?" Thomas asked.

"My husband still thinks I am."

Thomas Builds-the-Fire smiled. She was a mental gymnast, too. She pulled her leg straight up against her body so that she could've kissed her kneecap.

"I wish I could do that," Thomas said.

Victor was ready to jump out of the plane. Thomas, that crazy Indian story-teller with ratty old braids and broken teeth, was flirting with a beautiful Olympic gymnast. Nobody back home on the reservation would ever believe it.

"Well," the gymnast said. "It's easy. Try it."

Thomas grabbed at his leg and tried to pull it up into the same position as the gymnast. He couldn't even come close, which made Victor and the gymnast laugh.

"Hey," she asked. "You two are Indian, right?"

"Full-blood," Victor said.

"Not me," Thomas said. "I'm half magician on my mother's side and half clown on my father's."

They all laughed.

"What are your names?" she asked.

"Victor and Thomas."

"Mine is Cathy. Pleased to meet you all."

The three of them talked for the duration of the flight. Cathy the gymnast complained about the government, how they screwed the 1980 Olympic team by boycotting.

"Sounds like you all got a lot in common with Indians," Thomas said.

Nobody laughed.

After the plane landed in Phoenix and they had all found their way to the terminal, Cathy the gymnast smiled and waved good-bye.

"She was really nice," Thomas said.

"Yeah, but everybody talks to everybody on airplanes," Victor said. "It's too bad we can't always be that way."

"You always used to tell me I think too much," Thomas said. "Now it sounds like you do."

"Maybe I caught it from you."

"Yeah."

Thomas and Victor rode in a taxi to the trailer where Victor's father died.

"Listen," Victor said as they stopped in front of the trailer. "I never told you I was sorry for beating you up that time."

"Oh, it was nothing. We were just kids and you were drunk."

"Yeah, but I'm still sorry."

"That's all right."

Victor paid for the taxi and the two of them stood in the hot Phoenix summer. They could smell the trailer.

"This ain't going to be nice," Victor said. "You don't have to go in."

"You're going to need help."

*V*ictor walked to the front door and opened it. The stink rolled out and made them both gag. Victor's father had lain in that trailer for a week in hundred-degree temperatures before anyone found him.

Victor walked to the front door and opened it. The stink rolled out and made them both gag. Victor's father had lain in that trailer for a week in hundred-degree temperatures before anyone found him. And the only reason anyone found him was because of the smell. They needed dental records to identify him. That's exactly what the coroner said. They needed dental records.

"Oh, man," Victor said. "I don't know if I can do this."

"Well, then don't."

"But there might be something valuable in there."

"I thought his money was in the bank."

"It is. I was talking about pictures and letters and stuff like that."

"Oh," Thomas said as he held his breath and followed Victor into the trailer.

*W*hen Victor was twelve, he stepped into an underground wasp nest. His foot was caught in the hole, and no matter how hard he struggled, Victor couldn't pull free. He might have died there, stung a thousand times, if Thomas Builds-the-Fire had not come by.

"Run," Thomas yelled and pulled Victor's foot from the hole. They ran then, hard as they ever had, faster than Billy Mills, faster than Jim Thorpe,[2] faster than the wasps could fly.

Victor and Thomas ran until they couldn't breathe, ran until it was cold and dark outside, ran until they were lost and it took hours to find their way home. All the way back, Victor counted his stings.

---

2 **Billy Mills . . . Jim Thorpe:** Native American Olympic athletes. Both were gold medalists—Thorpe in 1912 and Mills in 1964.

"Seven," Victor said. "My lucky number."

$\mathcal{V}$ictor didn't find much to keep in the trailer. Only a photo album and a stereo. Everything else had that smell stuck in it or was useless anyway.

"I guess this is all," Victor said. "It ain't much."

"Better than nothing," Thomas said.

"Yeah, and I do have the pickup."

"Yeah," Thomas said. "It's in good shape."

"Dad was good about that stuff."

"Yeah, I remember your dad."

"Really?" Victor asked. "What do you remember?"

Thomas Builds-the-Fire closed his eyes and told this story: "I remember when I had this dream that told me to go to Spokane, to stand by the Falls in the middle of the city and wait for a sign. I knew I had to go there but I didn't have a car. Didn't have a license. I was only thirteen. So I walked all the way, took me all day, and I finally made it to the Falls. I stood there for an hour waiting. Then your dad came walking up. *What the hell are you doing here?* he asked me. I said, *Waiting for a vision.* Then your father said, *All you're going to get here is mugged.* So he drove me over to Denny's, bought me dinner, and then drove me home to the reservation. For a long time I was mad because I thought my dreams had lied to me. But they didn't. Your dad was my vision. *Take care of each other* is what my dreams were saying. *Take care of each other.*"

Victor was quiet for a long time. He searched his mind for memories of his father, found the good ones, found a few bad ones, added it all up, and smiled.

"My father never told me about finding you in Spokane," Victor said.

"He said he wouldn't tell anybody. Didn't want me to get in trouble. But he said I had to watch out for you as part of the deal."

"Really?"

"Really. Your father said you would need the help. He was right."

"That's why you came down here with me, isn't it?" Victor asked.

"I came because of your father."

Victor and Thomas climbed into the pickup, drove over to the bank, and claimed the three hundred dollars in the savings account.

$\mathcal{T}$homas Builds-the-Fire could fly.

Once, he jumped off the roof of the tribal school and flapped his arms like a crazy eagle. And he flew. For a second, he hovered, suspended above all the other Indian boys who were too smart or too scared to jump.

"He's flying," Junior yelled, and Seymour was busy looking for the trick wires or mirrors. But it was real. As real as the dirt when Thomas lost altitude and crashed to the ground.

He broke his arm in two places.

"He broke his wing," Victor chanted, and the other Indian boys joined in, made it a tribal song.

"He broke his wing, he broke his wing, he broke his wing," all the Indian boys chanted as they ran off, flapping their wings, wishing they could fly, too. They hated Thomas for his courage, his brief moment as a bird. Everybody has dreams about flying. Thomas flew.

One of his dreams came true for just a second, just enough to make it real.

$\mathcal{V}$ictor's father, his ashes, fit in one wooden box with enough left over to fill a cardboard box.

"He always was a big man," Thomas said.

Victor carried part of his father and Thomas carried the rest out to the pickup. They set him down carefully behind the seats, put a cowboy hat on the wooden box and a Dodgers cap on the cardboard box. That's the way it was supposed to be.

"Ready to head back home," Victor asked.

"It's going to be a long drive."

"Yeah, take a couple days, maybe."

"We can take turns," Thomas said.

"Okay," Victor said, but they didn't take turns. Victor drove for sixteen hours straight north, made it halfway up Nevada toward home before he finally pulled over.

"Hey, Thomas," Victor said. "You got to drive for a while."

"Okay."

Thomas Builds-the-Fire slid behind the wheel and started off down the road. All through Nevada, Thomas and Victor had been amazed at the lack of animal life, at the absence of water, of movement.

"Where is everything?" Victor had asked more than once.

Now when Thomas was finally driving they saw the first animal, maybe the only animal in Nevada. It was a long-eared jackrabbit.

"Look," Victor yelled. "It's alive."

" $\mathcal{I}$ can't believe this," Thomas said. "You drive for a thousand miles and there ain't even any bugs smashed on the windshield. I drive for ten seconds and kill the only living thing in Nevada."

Thomas and Victor were busy congratulating themselves on their discovery when the jackrabbit darted out into the road and under the wheels of the pickup.

"Stop the damn car," Victor yelled and Thomas did stop, backed the pickup to the dead jackrabbit.

"Oh, man, he's dead," Victor said as he looked at the squashed animal.

"Really dead."

"The only thing alive in this whole state and we just killed it."

"I don't know," Thomas said. "I think it was suicide."

Victor looked around the desert, sniffed the air, felt the emptiness and loneliness, and nodded his head.

"Yeah," Victor said. "It had to be suicide."

"I can't believe this," Thomas said. "You drive for a thousand miles and there ain't even any bugs smashed on the windshield. I drive for ten seconds and kill the only living thing in Nevada."

"Yeah," Victor said. "Maybe I should drive."

"Maybe you should."

$\mathcal{T}$homas Builds-the-Fire walked through the corridors of the tribal school by himself. Nobody wanted to be anywhere near him because of all those stories. Story after story.

Thomas closed his eyes and this story came to him: "We are all given one thing by which our lives are measured, one determination. Mine are the stories which can change or not change the world. It doesn't matter which as long as I continue to tell the stories. My father, he died on Okinawa in World War II, died fighting for this country, which had tried to kill him for years. My mother, she died giving birth to me, died while I was still inside her. She pushed me out into the world with her last breath. I have no brothers or sisters. I have only my stories which came to me before I even had the words to speak. I learned a thousand stories before I took my first thousand steps. They are all I have. It's all I can do."

Thomas Builds-the-Fire told his stories to all those who would stop and listen. He kept telling them long after people had stopped listening.

$\mathscr{V}$ictor and Thomas made it back to the reservation just as the sun was rising. It was the beginning of a new day on earth.

"Good morning," Thomas said.

"Good morning."

The tribe was waking up, ready for work, eating breakfast, reading the
newspaper, just like everybody else does. Willene LeBret was out in her garden wearing a bathrobe. She waved when Thomas and Victor drove by.

"Crazy Indians made it," she said to herself and went back to her roses.

Victor stopped the pickup in front of Thomas Builds-the-Fire's HUD[3]
house. They both yawned, stretched a little, shook dust from their bodies.

"I'm tired," Victor said.

"Of everything," Thomas added.

They both searched for words to end the journey. Victor needed to
thank Thomas for his help, for the money, and make the promise to pay it
all back.

"Don't worry about the money," Thomas said. "It don't make any
difference anyhow."

"Probably not, enit?"

"Nope."

Victor knew that Thomas would remain the crazy story teller who talked
to dogs and cars, who listened to the wind and pine trees. Victor knew that
he couldn't really be friends with Thomas, even after all that had happened.
It was cruel but it was real. As real as the ashes, as Victor's father, sitting
behind the seats.

"I know how it is," Thomas said. "I know you ain't going to treat me any
better than you did before. I know your friends would give you too much
trouble."

Victor was ashamed of himself. Whatever happened to the tribal ties, the
sense of community? The only real thing he shared with anybody was a
bottle and broken dreams. He owed Thomas something, anything.

"Listen," Victor said and handed Thomas the cardboard box which contained half of his father. "I want you to have this."

Thomas took the ashes and smiled, closed his eyes, and told this story:
"I'm going to travel to Spokane Falls one last time and toss these ashes into
the water. And your father will rise like a salmon, leap over the bridge, over

---

3 **HUD:** Housing and Urban Development, the federal government department in charge of housing; here it means a
house built with HUD funds

me, and find his way home. It will be beautiful. His teeth will shine like silver, like a rainbow. He will rise, Victor, he will rise."

Victor smiled.

"I was planning on doing the same thing with my half," Victor said. "But I didn't imagine my father looking anything like a salmon. I thought it'd be like cleaning the attic or something. Like letting things go after they've stopped having any use."

"Nothing stops, cousin," Thomas said. "Nothing stops."

Thomas Builds-the-Fire got out of the pickup and walked up his driveway. Victor started the pickup and began the drive home.

"Wait," Thomas yelled suddenly from his porch. "I just got to ask one favor."

Victor stopped the pickup, leaned out the window, and shouted back. "What do you want?"

"Just one time when I'm telling a story somewhere, why don't you stop and listen?" Thomas asked.

"Just once?"

"Just once."

Victor waved his arms to let Thomas know that the deal was good. It was a fair trade, and that was all Victor had ever wanted from his whole life. So Victor drove his father's pickup toward home while Thomas went into his house, closed the door behind him, and heard a new story come to him in the silence afterwards.

Read and Think Critically

Conclude, Predict, Analyze

1. **FLASHBACK** In what ways does this "story" break the rules of the traditional **plot** structure of **exposition**, **rising action**, **climax**, and **resolution**? What can you conclude about the author's reasons for structuring the story this way?

2. Do you think the relationship between Victor and Thomas will change after this trip? Support your prediction with evidence from the text.

3. Critics often describe Alexie's writing as "energetic." Analyze and explain the writer's techniques that give this story its liveliness.

4. What do you think is the significance of the **title**?

5. In one sentence each, describe the relationship between Victor and his father and between Thomas and Victor's father. Cite examples from the text to support your answer.

6. **THE AUTHOR'S STYLE** This story about a storyteller is made up of many shorter stories told by either the **narrator** or by Thomas Builds-the-Fire. Reread one of these shorter stories and explain how it fits into both the meaning and beauty of the entire story.

Before You Read

Tobias Wolff 1945–

About the Author

Born in Birmingham, Alabama, Tobias Wolff had a difficult childhood and adolescence. His father was a con man and his parents divorced when he was young, his mother taking him to raise and his father taking his brother. He traveled with his mother, who moved frequently, finally settling in Seattle where she remarried an abusive man. Wolff recalls those experiences in *This Boy's Life: A Memoir*, which was made into a film in 1993.

After serving in Vietnam, Wolff was educated at Oxford University and Stanford University. He is known primarily as a writer of short stories; his collections of them include *In the Garden* of *North American Martyrs* and *Back in the World*.

In *Passion and Craft,* Wolff is quoted as saying, "All my stories are in one way or another autobiographical. Sometimes they're autobiographical in the actual events which they describe, sometimes more in their depiction of a particular character. In fact, you could say that all my characters are reflections of myself, in that I share their wish to count for something and their almost complete confusion as to how this is supposed to be done."

★★★★★★★★★★★

The Author's Style

Wolff has worked as a waiter, night watchman, high school teacher, and reporter. His fiction often involves ordinary people in everyday situations who make extraordinary discoveries about the role of morality in their lives. Wolff's stories are often character studies that turn on human impulse, weakness, loneliness, and betrayal—always with a sense that people's choices and actions have complex moral consequences, often unforeseen. In some stories the ending is inconclusive, suggesting that the full impact of events is yet to come. Lying and other forms of deception make up a consistent thematic thread in his fiction.

Wolff's writing is straightforward. His stories develop forcefully, but he is more interested in the circumstances and the complex consequences of people's actions than in using them to teach, warn, or judge. At times his stories reveal the flawed-but-funny aspects of experience that make us refer to life as the human comedy. The story you are about to read was inspired by an incident that occurred when Wolff was writing obituaries for the *Washington Post*.

Mortals

Tobias Wolff

Literary Lens: Morality Play In what ways do the characters in this story personify moral qualities, similar to in a **morality play**?

*T*he metro editor called my name across the newsroom and beckoned to me. When I got to his office he was behind the desk. A man and a woman were there with him, the man nervous on his feet, the woman in a chair, bony-faced and vigilant, holding the straps of her bag with both hands. Her suit was the same bluish gray as her hair. There was something soldierly about her. The man was short, doughy, rounded off. The burst vessels in his cheeks gave him a merry look until he smiled.

"I didn't want to make a scene," he said. "We just thought you should know." He looked at his wife.

"You bet I should know," the metro editor said. "This is Mr. Givens," he said to me, "Mr. Ronald Givens. Name ring a bell?"

"Vaguely."

"I'll give you a hint. He's not dead."

"Okay," I said. "I've got it."

"Another hint," the metro editor said. Then he read aloud, from that morning's paper, the obituary I had written announcing Mr. Givens's death. I'd written a whole slew of obits the day before, over twenty of them, and I

HARD AND SOFT FIGURES, SAUL STEINBURG, 1952

didn't remember much of it, but I did remember the part about him working for the IRS for thirty years. I'd recently had problems with the IRS, so that stuck in my mind.

As Givens listened to his obituary he looked from one to the other of us. He wasn't as short as I'd first thought. It was an impression he created by hunching his shoulders and thrusting his neck forward like a turtle. His eyes were soft, restless. He used them like a peasant, in swift measuring glances with his face averted.

He laughed when the metro editor was through. "Well, it's accurate," he said. "I'll give you that."

"Except for one thing." The woman was staring at me.

"I owe you an apology," I told Givens. "It looks like somebody pulled the wool over my eyes."

He wasn't as short as I'd first thought. It was an impression he created by hunching his shoulders and thrusting his neck forward like a turtle.

"Apology accepted!" Givens said. He rubbed his hands together as if we'd all just signed something. "You have to see the humor, Dolly. What was it Mark Twain said? 'The reports of my death—'"

"So what happened?" the metro editor said to me.

"I wish I knew."

"That's not good enough," the woman said.

"Dolly's pretty upset," Givens said.

"She has every right to be upset," the metro editor said. "Who called in the notice?" he asked me.

"To tell the truth, I don't remember. I suppose it was somebody from the funeral home."

"You call them back?"

"I don't believe I did, no."

"Check with the family?"

"He most certainly did not," Mrs. Givens said.

"No," I said.

The metro editor said, "What do we do before we run an obituary?"

"Check back with the funeral home and the family."

"But you didn't do that."

"No, sir. I guess I didn't."

"Why not?"

I made a helpless gesture with my hands and tried to appear properly stricken, but I had no answer. The truth was, I never followed those procedures. People were dying all the time. I hadn't seen the point in asking their families if they were really dead, or calling funeral parlors back to make sure the funeral parlors had just called me. All this procedural stuff was a waste of time, I'd decided; it didn't seem possible that anyone could amuse himself by concocting phony death notices and impersonating undertakers. Now I saw that this was foolish of me, and showed a radical failure of appreciation for the varieties of human pleasure.

> *I began to lose my nerve. I'd given up a lot for my writing, and it wasn't giving anything back—not respectability, nor money, nor love.*

But there was more to it than that. Since I was still on the bottom rung in metro, I wrote a lot of obituaries. Some days they gave me a choice between that and marriage bulletins, but most of the time obits were all I did, one after another, morning to night. After four months of this duty I was full of the consciousness of death. It soured me. It puffed me up with morbid snobbery, the feeling that I knew a secret nobody else had even begun to suspect. It made me wearily philosophical about the value of faith and passion and hard work, at a time when my life required all of these. It got me down.

I should have quit, but I didn't want to go back to the kind of jobs I'd had before a friend's father fixed me up with this one—waiting on tables, mostly, pulling night security in apartment buildings, anything that would leave my days free for writing. I'd lived like this for three years, and what did I have to show for it? A few stories in literary journals that nobody read, including me. I began to lose my nerve. I'd given up a lot for my writing, and it wasn't giving anything back—not respectability, nor money, nor love. So when this job came up I took it. I hated it and did it badly, but I meant to keep it. Someday I'd move over to the police beat. Things would get better.

I was hoping that the metro editor would take his pound of flesh and let me go, but he kept after me with questions, probably showing off for Givens and his wife, letting them see a real newshound at work. In the end I was forced to admit that I hadn't called any other families or funeral homes that day, nor, in actual fact, for a good long time.

Now that he had his answer, the metro editor didn't seem to know what to do with it. It seemed to be more than he'd bargained for. At first he just sat there. Then he said, "Let me get this straight. Just how long has this paper been running unconfirmed obituaries?"

"About three months," I said. And as I made this admission I felt a smile on my lips, already there before I could fight it back or dissemble it. It was the **rictus** of panic, the same smile I'd given my mother when she told me my father had died. But of course the metro editor didn't know that.

He leaned forward in his chair and gave his head a little shake, the way a horse will, and said, "Clean out your desk." I don't think he'd meant to fire me; he looked surprised by his own words. But he didn't take them back.

Givens looked from one to the other of us. "Now hold on here," he said. "Let's not blow this all out of proportion. This is a live-and-learn situation. This isn't something a man should lose his job over."

"He wouldn't have," Mrs. Givens said, "if he'd done it right."

Which was a truth beyond argument.

I cleaned out my desk. As I left the building I saw Givens by the newsstand, watching the door. I didn't see his wife. He walked up to me, raised his hands, and said, "What can I say? I'm at a loss for words."

"Don't worry about it," I told him.

"I sure as heck didn't mean to get you fired. It wasn't even my idea to come in, if you want to know the truth."

"Forget it. It was my own fault." I was carrying a box full of notepads and files, several books. It was heavy. I shifted it under my other arm.

"Look," Givens said, "how about I treat you to lunch. What do you say? It's the least I can do."

I looked up and down the street.

"Dolly's gone on home," he said. "How about it?"

I didn't especially want to eat lunch with Givens, but it seemed to mean a lot to him, and I didn't feel ready to go home yet. What would I do there? Sure, I said, lunch sounded fine. Givens asked me if I knew anyplace reasonable nearby. There was a Chinese joint a few doors down, but it was always full of reporters. I didn't want to watch them try to conjure up sympathy over my situation, which they'd laugh about anyway the minute I left, not that I blamed them. I suggested Tad's Steakhouse over by the cable car turnaround. You could get a six-ounce sirloin, salad, and baked potato for a buck twenty-nine. This was 1974.

"I'm not that short," Givens said. But he didn't argue, and that's where we went.

Givens picked at his food, then pushed the plate away and contemplated mine. When I asked if his steak was okay, he said he didn't have much appetite.

"So," I said, "who do you think called it in?"

His head was bent. He looked up at me from under his eyebrows. "Boy, you've got me there. It's a mystery."

"You must have some idea."

"Nope. Not a one."

"Think it could've been someone you worked with?"

"Nah." He shook a toothpick out of the dispenser. His hands were pale and **sinewy**.

"It had to be somebody who knows you. You have friends, right?"

"Sure."

"Maybe you had an argument, something like that. Somebody's mad at you."

"*Y*ou're sure it isn't one of your friends," I said. "It could be a little thing. You played cards, landed some big ones, then folded early before he had a chance to recoup."

He kept his mouth covered with one hand while he worked the toothpick with the other. "You think so? I had it figured for more of a joke."

"Well, it's a pretty serious joke, calling in a death notice on someone. Pretty threatening. I'd sure feel threatened, if it was me."

Givens inspected the toothpick, then dropped it in the ashtray. "I hadn't thought of it like that," he said. "Maybe you're right."

I could see he didn't believe it for a second—didn't understand what had happened. The words of death had been pronounced on him, and now his life would be lived in relation to those words, in failing opposition to them, until they overpowered him and became true. Someone had put a contract out on Givens, with words as the torpedoes. Or so it appeared to me.

"You're sure it isn't one of your friends," I said. "It could be a little thing. You played cards, landed some big ones, then folded early before he had a chance to recoup."

"I don't play cards," Givens said.

"How about your wife? Any problems in that department?"

"Nope."

"Everything smooth as silk, huh?"

He shrugged. "Same as ever."

"How come you call her Dolly? That wasn't the name in the obit."

"No reason. I've always called her that. Everybody does."

"I don't feature her as a Dolly," I said.

He didn't answer. He was watching me.

"Let's say Dolly gets mad at you, really mad . . . She wants to send you a message—something outside normal channels."

"Not a chance." Givens said this without **bristling**. He didn't try to convince me, so I figured he was probably right.

"You're survived by a daughter, right? What's her name again?"

"Tina," he said, with some tenderness.

"That's it, Tina. How are things with Tina?"

"We've had our problems. But I can guarantee you, it wasn't her."

"Well, hell's bells," I said. "Somebody did it."

I finished my steak, watching the show outside: winos, evangelists, out-patients, whores, fake hippies selling oregano to tourists in white shoes. Pure theater, even down to the smell of popcorn billowing out of Woolworth's. Richard Brautigan often came here. Tall and owlish, he stooped to his food and ate slowly, ruminating over every bite, his eyes on the street. Some funny things happened here, and some appalling things. Brautigan took it all in and never stopped eating.

I told Givens that we were sitting at the same table where Richard Brautigan sometimes sat.

"Sorry?"

"Richard Brautigan, the writer."

Givens shook his head.

I was ready to go home. "Okay," I said, "you tell me. Who wants you dead?"

"No one wants me dead."

"Somebody's imagining you dead. Thinking about it. The wish is father to the deed."

"Nobody wants me dead. Your problem is, you think everything has to mean something."

That was one of my problems, I couldn't deny it.

"Just out of curiosity," he said, "what did you think of it?"

"Think of what?"

"My obituary." He leaned forward and started fooling with the salt and pepper shakers, tapping them together and sliding them around like partners in a square dance. "I mean, did you get any feeling for who I was? The kind of person I am?"

I shook my head.

"Nothing stood out?"

I said no.

"I see. Maybe you wouldn't mind telling me, what exactly does it take for you to remember someone?"

"Look," I said, "you write obituaries all day, they sort of blur into each other."

"Yes, but you must remember some of them."

"Some of them—sure."

"Which ones?"

"Writers I like. Great baseball players. Movie stars I've been in love with."

"Celebrities, in other words."

"Some of them, yes. Not all."

"You can lead a good life without being a celebrity," he said. "People with big names aren't always big people."

"That's true," I said, "but it's sort of a little person's truth."

"Is that so? And what does that make you?"

I didn't answer.

"*If* the only thing that impresses you is having a big name, then you must be a regular midget. At least that's the way I see it." He gave me a hard look and gripped the salt and pepper shakers like a machine gunner about to let off a burst.

"That's not the only thing that impresses me."

"Oh yeah? What else, then?"

I let the question settle. "Moral distinction," I said.

He repeated the words. They sounded **pompous**.

pompous:
self-important

"You know what I mean," I said.

"Correct me if I'm wrong," he said, "but I have a feeling that's not your department, moral distinction."

I didn't argue.

"And you're obviously not a celebrity."

"Obviously."

"So where does that leave you?" When I didn't answer, he said, "Think you'd remember your own obituary?"

"Probably not."

"No probably about it! You wouldn't even give it a second thought."

"Okay, definitely not."

"You wouldn't even give it a second thought. And you'd be wrong. Because you probably have other qualities that would stand out if you were looking closely. Good qualities. Everybody has something. What do you pride yourself on?"

"I'm a survivor," I said. But I didn't think that claim would carry much weight in an obituary.

Givens said, "With me it's loyalty. Loyalty is a very clear pattern in my life. You would've noticed that if you'd had your eyes open. When you read that a man has served his country in time of war, stayed married to the same woman for forty-two years, worked at the same job, by God, that should tell you something. That should give you a certain picture."

He stopped to nod at his own words. "And it hasn't always been easy," he said.

I had to laugh, mostly at myself for being such a dim bulb. "It was you," I said. "You did it."

"Did what?"

"Called in the obit."

"Why would I do that?"

"You tell me."

"That would be saying I did it." Givens couldn't help smiling, proud of what a slyboots he was.

I said, "You're out of your ever-loving mind," but I didn't mean it. There was nothing in what Givens had done that I couldn't make sense of or even, in spite of myself, admire. He had dreamed up a way of going to his own funeral. He'd tried on his last suit, so to speak, seen himself rouged up and laid out, and listened to his own eulogy. And the best part was, he resurrected afterward. That was the real point, even if he thought he was doing it to throw a scare into Dolly or put his virtues on display. Resurrection was what it was all about, and this tax collector had gotten himself a taste of it. It was biblical.

"You're a caution, Mr. Givens. You're a definite caution."

"I didn't come here to be insulted."

"Relax," I told him. "I'm not mad."

He scraped his chair back and stood up. "I've got better things to do than sit here and listen to accusations."

I followed him outside. I wasn't ready to let him go. He had to give me something first. "Admit you did it," I said.

He turned away and started up Powell.

"Just admit it," I said. "I won't hold it against you."

He kept walking, head stuck forward in that turtlish way, navigating the crowd. He was slippery and fast. Finally I took his arm and pulled him into a doorway. His muscles bunched under my fingers. He almost jerked free, but I tightened my grip and we stood there frozen in contention.

"Admit it."

He shook his head.

"I'll break your neck if I have to," I told him.

"Let go," he said.

"If something happened to you right now, your obituary would be solid news. Then I could get my job back."

He tried to pull away again but I held him there.

"It'd make a hell of a story," I said.

I felt his arm go slack. Then he said, almost inaudibly, "Yes." Just that one word.

This was the best I was going to get out of him. It had to be enough. When I let go of his arm he turned and ducked his head and took his place in the stream of people walking past. I started back to Tad's for my box. Just ahead of me a mime was following a young swell in a three-piece suit, catching to the life his leading-man's assurance, the **supercilious** tilt of his chin. A girl laughed raucously. The swell looked back and the mime froze. He was still holding his pose as I came by. I slipped him a quarter, hoping he'd let me pass.

supercilious: arrogant

Read and Think Critically

Explain, Analyze, Describe

1. **MORALITY PLAY** A **morality play**—a once-popular kind of drama—is a stage piece in which characters are named for, and personify, moral or abstract qualities such as Charity, Greed, Death, and Youth. If you were to rewrite "Mortals" as a morality play, what titles would you assign the **narrator** and Givens?

2. Givens comments, "People with big names aren't always big people." The narrator concedes the point, adding "but it's a little person's truth." Explain what you think he means by "a little person's truth."

3. Analyze the **metaphor** found in the last paragraph on page 711. What two things are being compared? What does this metaphor mean?

4. What do you think the **title** "Mortals" means?

5. Reread the last paragraph of the story. What are some of the layers of meaning in the narrator's wish that the mime let him pass?

6. **THE AUTHOR'S STYLE** Consider the quotation from Wolff below. Describe ways in which the story opens people up to scrutiny.

Opening Up

There's no form you can prescribe for a short story. I would say that the stories that have stayed with me over the years are stories that make some unexpected use of the form, that open people up to scrutiny in a way that I haven't quite seen. I go case by case. Not why are stories good, but why is this story good.

—Tobias Wolff, *Stanford Today Online*

Before You Read

Paul Theroux 1941–

About the Author

Born in Massachusetts to a large family, Paul Theroux had this to say about his childhood in the book *The Powells.com Interviews*: "My earliest thought, long before I was in high school, was just to go away, get out of my house, get out of my city. I went to Medford High School, but even in grade school and junior high, I fantasized about leaving . . . . So I had the idea of being a traveler, of going to some exotic place, before I wanted to be a writer. Then the idea of writing began to absorb me."

Theroux has written travelogues, essays, and novels based on his travels, sometimes blurring the line between fact and fiction. After hearing claims that his 1989 novel, *My Secret History*, was a thinly disguised autobiography, he turned the tables by writing a novel, *My Other Life*, and calling it an autobiography. "It is a pack of lies that looks like it amounts to a sort of truth," he says. His best-known works include the travel book *The Great Railway Bazaar* and two novels, which have been adapted for the screen, *St. Jack* and *The Mosquito Coast*.

****

The Author's Style

Theroux is widely known as a nonfiction travel writer, but he has also written much fiction based on the experiences of visiting and living in other countries. His life of travel began in 1963, when he was an English teacher and Peace Corps volunteer in Africa. A consistent theme of his writing is that of the stranger who experiences discomfort in an unfamiliar situation. Theroux develops characters by having them make discoveries and gain understanding through their relationships with others in "foreign" places.

Since individuals reveal their character when they are under pressure, Theroux chooses his narrators carefully. He enjoys using point of view to reveal the significance of experiences and events. The narrator of his stories that are set in the London Embassy, a consul named Savage, tells stories in precise diplomatic language that conveys information in a safe, protected way.

The cultural contrasts in Theroux's stories create ironic situations, but he treats them with sympathetic humor as well as satirical criticism. Conflicts that arise from characters' responses to new places and unconventional people are intriguing and challenging—even threatening—and for this reason make for interesting stories.

Charlie Hogle's Earring

PAUL THEROUX

 LITERARY LENS: CONFLICT As you read, consider both the internal and external **conflicts** in this story.

*T*here is something athletic, something physical, in the way the most successful people reach decisions. The businessmen who plot take-overs, the upstarts who become board chairmen, the masterminds of conglomerates—they are often jocks who regard more thoughtful men as cookie-pushers, and who shoulder their way into offices and hug their allies and muscle in on deals. They move like swaggerers and snatchers, using their elbows when their money fails. And when they are in command they are puppetmasters.

Everett Horton, our number two, prized his football photograph (Yale '51) as much as he did his autographed portrait of the President. Here was another of him, posed with a Russian diplomat, each in white shorts, holding a tennis racket and shaking hands across a tennis net. And others: Horton golfing, Horton fishing,

Horton sailing. Horton had interesting ears—slightly swollen, and gristlier than the average, and they did not match: "Wrestling," someone said. It seemed innocent vanity that Horton thought of himself as a man of action. I suppose he was a man of action. He worked hard. He succeeded where Ambassador Noyes often failed.

Erroll Jeeps used to say: "Watch out for Horton's body English."

He could have sent me a memo, or phoned me, or we might have had lunch. But he had not become minister by sending memos. He was a hugger, a hand-shaker, a back-slapper—body English—and when something important came up he tore downstairs and interrupted whatever I was doing and said, "You're the only one around here who can straighten this out. You've been in the Far East, not in Washington, among the cookie-pushers!"

Today he hugged me. His sweet-whiskey fragrance of aftershave lotion stung my eyes. A file folder was tucked under his arm.

"Is that the problem?"

"That's his file," Horton said.

I tried to catch a glimpse of the name, but he tossed the file onto a chair and kicked my office door shut.

"Let me tell you about it. That'll be quicker than reading this crap." He sat on the edge of my desk and swung one heavy thigh over the other.

"Do you know Charlie Hogle from C and R?"

"I saw him once at your house—that reception you gave for me. I don't go down to the telex room."

"You let your *pyoon* do it, eh?" It was the Malay word for office lackey, and he was mocking me with it. He said, "You should get around more—you'd be amazed at some of the things you find."

"In the telex room?"

"Especially there," Horton said. "This fellow Hogle—very gifted, they say, if you can describe a telex operator in that way. Very personable. Highly efficient, if a bit invisible. He's been here almost three years. No trouble, no scandal, nothing." Horton stopped talking. He stared at me. "I was down there this morning. What do I find?" Horton watched me again, giving me the same dramatic scrutiny as before. He wanted my full attention and a little pause.

I said, "I give up—what did you find?"

agile:
nimble; graceful

"Hogle. With an earring." Horton sighed, slid off the desktop, and threw himself into a chair. He was remarkably **agile** for such a big man.

I said, "An earring?"

"Right. One of those gold . . . loops? Don't make me describe it." Horton suddenly seemed cross. "I don't know anything about earrings."

"Was he wearing it?"

"What a dumb question! Of course he was."

"I thought you were going to tell me that he stole it—that you found it on him."

"He's got a hole in his ear for it."

I said, "So he's had his ear pierced."

"Can you imagine? A special hole in his ear!"

I said, "What exactly is wrong, coach?"

He had encouraged us to use this ridiculous word for him. I had so far refrained from it, and though I felt like a jackass using it today, it seemed to have the right effect. It calmed him. He smiled at me.

I said, "What exactly is wrong, coach?"

He had encouraged us to use this ridiculous word for him. I had so far refrained from it, and though I felt like a jackass using it today, it seemed to have the right effect. It calmed him.

"Let's put it at its simplest. Let's be charitable. Let's not mock him," Horton said. "An earring is against regulations."

"Which ones?"

"Dress regulations. The book. It's as if he's wearing a skirt."

"But he's not wearing a skirt. It's jewelry. Is there a subsection for that?"

"Sure! In Muslim countries, Third World countries—"

"This is England, coach."

"And he's a guy! And he's got this thing hanging off his ear!"

"You're not going to get him on a technicality," I said. "All you can do is ask him to remove it. 'Would you mind taking off that earring, Mr. Hogle?'"

Horton did not smile. He began lecturing me. He said, "You act as if there's nothing wrong. Did you know there's no law against lesbianism in this country? Do you know why? Because Queen Victoria refused to believe that women indulged in that sort of behavior!"

"Hogle's earring is hardly in that category," I said.

"Bull! It's precisely in that category. That's how serious a violation it is. It's unthinkable for a man to turn up at work wearing an earring, so there's no legislation, nothing in the rulebook for earrings *per se*. But there's a paragraph on Improper Dress—"

"That covers lewd or suggestive clothes."

"What about Inappropriate Accessories?"

"Religious or racial taboos. Cowhide presents in Hindu countries, pig-skin suitcases in Muslim countries, the New York Philharmonic touring Israel and playing Wagner."

"What has Wagner got to do with Accessories?"

"You know what I mean. Earrings don't figure."

"There's something," Horton said. He came over to me and jerked my shoulder, giving me a hug. "It doesn't matter." He grinned. He was a big man. He hugged me sideways as we stood shoulder to shoulder. "There's always something—just find it."

"Why me?" I said. "You could do it more easily."

His eyes became narrow and dark as he said, "I'll tell you why I can't." He looked at the door suspiciously, as if he were about to bark at it. Then he made an ugly disgusted face and whispered, "When I saw Hogle with that thing in his ear, and the hole, and the implications, I felt sick to my stomach." He glanced darkly at the door again. "He's a nice clean-cut guy. I'd lay into him—I'd lose my temper. I know I would, and I want to spare him that. You'll be more rational. You know about these nutty customs. You've been in the Far East."

"Doesn't Hogle have a personnel officer?"

Horton gave me a disdainful look. His expression said I was letting him down, I was a coward, a weakling.

He said, "You don't want to do this, do you?"

"What I want is of no importance," I said. "I do what I'm told."

"Excellent!" he said. Horton stood up straight. The muddy green was gone from his eyes; he was smiling. "Now get down there and tell Hogle to **divest** himself."

I said, "That's his file, right?"

"Ignore the file for now. When you've settled this problem, stick a memo in here and hand it back to me. I also want to know why he's wearing it—that's important. And, by the way, this is strictly confidential, this whole matter—everything I've said."

I made a move toward the file.

"You don't really need that," he said.

"Maybe not," I said. "But I think I'll take it home and blow on it."

divest:
get rid of
something

$\mathcal{I}$ had a thought, *Why me?* But of course Horton was testing me as much as he was gunning for Hogle. He was trying to discover where my sympathies were: Would I give him an argument, or would I obey? Perhaps I was a latent earring-wearer? Horton's own reaction seemed to me extraordinary. He felt sick to his stomach. That may have been an exaggeration, but the fear that he would lose his temper was almost unbelievable in someone whose temper was always in check. Everett Horton—he wanted to be called 'coach'!—was a man of action. I could not understand his **reticence** now, unless I was right in assuming that I was the real subject of the inquiry.

I was new here—less than four months on the job. I had to play ball. And I must admit I was curious.

The file was thin. Charlie Hogle had come to us from the Army under a program we called Lateral Entry. He had been in the communications unit of the Signal Corps, running a C and R office in Frankfurt. He was twenty-nine, not married, a graduate—German major—of the University of Northern Iowa in Cedar Falls. He had been born and raised in nearby Waterloo, Iowa. His annual job evaluations from the State Department fault-finders were very good. In fact, one suggested—as a black mark—that Hogle had experienced "no negative situations." In other words, he was such a happy fellow he might prove to be a problem. I did not buy that naive analysis. Hogle was a well-adjusted, middle-level technician with a good record, and after looking through this worthy man's file I regretted what I had been ordered to do.

$\mathcal{H}$ogle was a well-adjusted, middle-level technician with a good record, and after looking through this worthy man's file I regretted what I had been ordered to do.

reticence:
restraint; hesitancy

$\mathcal{L}$unch with him was out: it was both too businesslike and too friendly. Anyway, I hated lunch as unnecessary and time-wasting. Lunch is the ritual meal that makes fat people fat. And dinner was out—too formal. I kept telling myself that this was a small matter. I could send for him. I pictured poor Hogle, clutching his silly earring, cowering in my office, awkward in his chair.

There was only one possibility left—a drink after work. That made it less official, less intimidating, and if I got bored I could plead a previous engagement and go home.

I met him at a large overdecorated pub called the Audley, on the corner of Mount and Audley Streets, not far from the Embassy. Hogle, whom I spotted as American from fifty feet away, was tall even by the generous standards of the Midwest. He was good-looking, with a smooth polite face and clear blue eyes. His blond eyelashes made him look completely frank and unsecretive. His hands were nervous, but his face was innocent and still. His voice had the plain splintery **cadences** of an Iowa Lutheran being truthful. I took him to be a muscular Christian.

cadences:
rhythms

"I kind of like these English beers," he was saying now. (Earlier we had talked about his Sunday school teaching.) "They're a little flat, but they don't swell you up or make you drunk, like lager. Back home—"

As he spoke, I glanced at his earring. It was a small gold hoop, as Horton had said, but Horton had made it seem like junk jewelry, rather vulgar and obvious—and embarrassing to the onlooker. I was surprised to find it a lovely earring. And it was hardly noticeable—too small to be a pirate's, too simple for a transvestite. I thought it suited him. It was the sort of detail that makes some paintings remarkable; it gave his face position and focus—and an undeniable beauty. It was the size, and it had the charm, of Shakespeare's **raffish** earring in the painting in the National Portrait Gallery.

raffish:
carelessly
unconventional

Charlie Hogle was still talking about beer. His favorite was the Colorado Coors brand, because it was made from—

This was ridiculous. We were getting nowhere. I said, "Is that an earring you're wearing?"

His fingers went for it. "Yes," he said. "What do you think of it?"

"Very nice," I said. He smiled. I said, "And unusual."

"It cost me twenty-two pounds. That's almost fifty bucks, but it included getting my ear pierced. I figure it was worth it, don't you?"

Was he trying to draw me?

"You've just," I said, "got the one?"

"One earring's enough!"

I said, "I'm not sure—"

"You think I should have *two*? Don't you think that'd be pushing it a little?"

"Actually," I said, and hated my tone of voice and dreaded what was coming, "I was wondering whether one earring might be pushing it, never mind two."

"You said it was nice." He looked at me closely, and sniffed. He was an honest fellow for whom a contradiction was a bad smell. "What do you mean, 'One earring might be pushing it'?"

"It *is* very nice," I said. "And so are those split skirts the secretaries have started to wear. But I wouldn't be very happy about your wearing a split skirt, Mr. Hogle."

He smiled. He was not threatened: he saw a joke where I had intended a warning. He said, "I'm not wearing a split skirt, sir."

"Yes," I said. "But you are wearing an earring."

"Is that the same as wearing a skirt?"

"Not exactly, but it's the same *kind* of thing."

"What—illegal?"

"Inappropriate," I said. This was Horton's line, and its illogicality was hideously apparent to me as I parroted it. "Like coming to work in your bathing suit, or dyeing your hair green, or—"

I couldn't go on. Hogle was, quite rightly, smiling at the stupidity of my argument. And now I saw that Horton's objection was really a form of abuse.

Hogle said, "I know those things are silly and inappropriate. I wouldn't come to work dressed like a slob. I'm no punk. I don't have green hair."

"Yes, I know."

"I've got a pretty clean record, sir. I got a commendation from the Consul in Frankfurt for hanging on and keeping the telex room open during a Red Army Faction riot. I'm not bragging, sir. I'm just saying I take my job seriously."

"Yes, it's mentioned in your file. I know about it."

"You've been looking in my file," he said. His face became sad, and his attention slackened. He had let go of his earring. "I get it—my ass is in a crack."

"Not yet."

"Sir, I could have bought a cheaper earring—one of those silver dangly ones. Instead I saved up. I bought a nice one. You said so yourself."

"I also said it's rather unusual."

"There's nothing wrong with 'unusual,' is there?"

"Some people think so."

He looked at me, with his lips compressed. He had now seen the purpose of this innocent drink. I had led him here on false pretext; I had deceived him. His eyes went cold.

He said, "Mr. Horton, the minister. It's him, isn't it?"

"It's the regulations," I said lamely.

"He was staring at me the other day, like the second louies used to stare at me when I was in the Army. Even though he was about fifty feet away I could feel his eyes pressing on my neck. You can tell when something's wrong." Hogle shook his head in a heavy rueful way. "I thought he used to like me. Now he's yanked my file and sent you to nail me down."

Hogle was completely correct. But I could not admit it without putting Horton into a vulnerable position and exposing him as petty and spiteful. After all, Horton's was the only objection to the earring. But Horton was boss.

I said, "Everyone thinks that it would be better if you dispensed with your earring."

"I still don't understand why."

"It's contrary to dress regulations. Isn't that obvious?"

He touched the earring, as if for luck. He said, "Maybe they should change the regulations."

"Do you think it's likely they will?"

He made a glum face and said no.

"Be a sport," I said. "I'm telling you this for your own good. Get rid of that thing and save yourself a headache."

Hogle had been staring at his glass of beer. Without moving his head, he turned his eyes on me and said, "I don't want to seem uncooperative, sir, but I paid good money for this earring. And I had a hole punched in my ear. And I like it, and it's not hurting anyone. So—no way am I going to get rid of it."

"What if we take disciplinary action?"

"That's up to you, sir."

"You could be suspended on half-pay. What do you say to that?"

"I wouldn't like it much," Hogle said.

"Mr. Hogle," I said, "does that earring represent anything? I mean, is it a sort of symbol?"

"Not any more than your tie clip is a symbol. You don't see many tie clips these days—and I think yours is neat. I think this earring is neat. That's the only reason. Don't you think that's a pretty good reason?"

> "Not any more than your tie clip is a symbol. You don't see many tie clips these days—and I think yours is neat. I think this earring is neat. That's the only reason. Don't you think that's a pretty good reason?"

TRACK JACKET, ALEX KATZ, 1956

I wished he would not ask me these questions. They were traps; they **incriminated** me; they tore me in two. I said, "What I think doesn't matter. I'm an employee. So are you. What you think doesn't matter either. There is nothing personal about this; there's no question about opinion or tolerance or flexibility. It's strictly regulations."

Hogle replied in a sort of wounded whisper. "I'd like to see the regulations, sir," he said. "I'd like to see in black and white which rule I've broken."

"It's a very general regulation concerning appropriate dress," I said. "And we can make it stick. We're going to give you a few days to decide which is more important to you—your earring or your job."

incriminated: proved guilty

I had lapsed into "we"—it is hard to use it and not seem cold and bullying; it can be a terrifying pronoun. And yet I had hoped this meeting would be friendly. It was, from my point of view, disastrously cold. His resentment made me **officious**; my officiousness made him stubborn. In the end I had simply pulled rank on him, used the scowling "we," and given him a crude choice. Then I left him. He looked isolated and lonely at the table in the pub, and that saddened me, because he was handsome and intelligent and young and a very hard worker. His earring distinguished him and made him look like a prince.

officious: prying; interfering

The next day I went to Horton's office. Seeing me, he rushed out and gave me a playful shove. He then helped me into the office with a hug, all the while saying, "Get in here and tell me what a great success you've been in the telex room."

I hated this fooling. I said, "I've had a talk with Hogle."

"With what result?"

"He's thinking about it."

"You mean, it's not settled? You let him *think* about it?"

I freed myself from his grasp. I said, "Yes."

"It's not a thinking matter," Horton said. "It's an order—didn't you tell him that?"

"I didn't want to throw my weight around. You said yourself there's no point making an issue out of it if it can be settled quietly."

Horton gaped at this. He became theatrical, imitating shock and incredulity with his exaggerated squint, and there was something of an actressy whine in his voice when he said, "So he's still down there, wearing that *thing* on his ear?"

I let him rant a bit more. Then I said, "I didn't want to put pressure on him. If he hasn't got the sense to see that our displeasure matters, then he's hardly any use to us."

"That's a point—I don't want any passengers in this Embassy, and I certainly won't put up with freaks." Horton's phone was ringing; it had the effect of sobering him and making him snappish. "I'll expect that file back by the end of the week—and I want a happy conclusion. Remember, if you can't get this chappie"—Horton wiggled his head on the word—"to remove his earring, you can hardly expect me to have much faith in your powers of persuasion."

"I'd like to drop the whole damned thing," I said.

Horton paused, and he peered at me with interest in spite of his nagging phone. "And why is that?"

"I don't see the importance of it," I said.

"It is very important," he said. "And of course I'm interested in your technique. You see, in this Embassy one is constantly trying to point out that there is a sensible, productive way of doing things—and there is the British way. Tactful persuasion is such an asset, whether one is dealing with a misunderstood aspect of NATO[1] or an infraction of the dress regulations by a serving officer—I mean, Hogle's earring. I hate even the word."

"I'll do it," I said. "But my heart isn't in it."

"That is precisely why I want you to do it," Horton said. "If nothing else, this should teach you that feelings have nothing to do with this job. Now, please, get it over with. It's starting to make me sick."

I chose the pub carefully. It was in Earl's Court and notoriously male; but at six-thirty it was empty and could easily have been mistaken for the haunt of darts players and polite locals with wives and dogs. Hogle was late. Waiting there, I thought that he might not turn up at all, just to teach me a lesson. But he came with an excuse and an apology. He had been telexing an urgent cable. Only he had clearance to work with classified material after hours, and the duty officer—Yorty, a newcomer—had no idea how to use a telex machine. So Hogle had worked late. As an ex-Army man he understood many of the military cables, and he had security clearance, and he was willing; I knew from his file that he didn't make mistakes. His obedience had never been questioned—that is, until Horton spotted the earring. I began to see why this detail worried Horton so much: Hogle, in such a ticklish job, had to be absolutely reliable.

He said, "I've been thinking over what you told me."

He looked tired—paler than he had three days ago. It was not the extra work, I was sure—he was worrying, not sleeping well. Perhaps he had already decided to resign on a point of principle, for in spite of his wilted posture and ashen skin, his expression was full of **tenacity**. I suppose it was his eyes. They were narrow, as though wounded, and hot, and seemed to say *No surrender*.

I said, "Don't say anything."

He had been staring into the middle distance. Now he looked closely at me. He winced, but he kept his gaze on me.

I said, "I've managed to prevail. I took it to the highest possible level. I think everyone understands now."

tenacity: perseverance; stubbornness

I **NATO:** North Atlantic Treaty Organization

"What do you mean, 'understands'?" There was a hint of anxiety in his voice.

"Your earring," I said.

"What's there to understand?"

"You've got nothing to worry about. We don't persecute people for their beliefs anymore. If that were the case I wouldn't be in the Foreign Service."

"Wearing an earring," Hogle said. "Is that a belief?"

"It depends on how naïve you are," I said. "But be glad it doesn't matter. Be glad you live in a free society, where you can dress any way you like, and where you can choose your friends, whether they're British or American, white or black, female or male—"

Hogle became very attentive.

I said, "I'm grateful to you. It's people like you who break down barriers and increase our self-awareness."

"I don't want to break down any barriers," he said. "I'm not even sure what self-awareness is all about."

"It's about earrings," I said. "The other day I told you your earring was nice. I was being insincere. May I call you Charlie?"

"Sure."

"Charlie, I think your earring is fantastic."

His hand went to his ear. He looked wary. He did not let go of the earring or his earlobe. He sat fixedly with his fingers making this plucking gesture on his ear.

"It's a very handsome accessory," I said. His fingers tightened. "A real enhancement." They moved again. "An elegant statement—"

I thought he was going to yank his ear off. His hand was trembling, still covering the earring. He said, "I'm not making a statement."

"Take it easy," I said, giving him the sort of blanket assurance of no danger that convinces people—and rightly—that they're in a tight spot. "You've got absolutely nothing to worry about!" He looked very worried. "You can relax with me." I ordered him a drink and told him there was no point in discussing the earring.

"To be perfectly honest," I said, "I rather like your earring."

"I'm certainly not making any kind of statement," Hogle said. The word worried him. It had implications of being unerasable and hinted of hot water. "I got the idea from one of the delivery men—an English guy. He wasn't making a statement. It looked neat, that's all."

"It looks more than neat," I said. "It has a certain mystery. I think that's its real charm."

He winced at this, and now he was pinching his earlobe. He lowered his eyes. He did not look up again.

"I feel funny," he said.

"Be glad you work with people who say yes instead of no."

I gave him a friendly punch on the shoulder, the sort of body English Horton would have approved. It made me feel uncomfortable and mannered and overhearty. It amazed me then to realize that Horton was always punching and hugging and digging in the ribs. Hogle was unresponsive, not to say wooden. His eyes darted sideways.

The night's clients had started to arrive in the pub—men in leather jackets, with close-cropped hair, and heavy chains around their necks, and tattooed thumbs, and sunglasses. Some were bald, some devilishly bearded; one wore crimson shoes; another had an enormous black dog on a leather strap. All of them wore earrings.

"Have another drink," I said.

Hogle stood up. "I have to go."

"What's the hurry?"

He was breathing hard. A man encased in tight black leather was hovering near us and staring at Hogle. The man had silver chains with thick links looped around his boots and they clanked as he came closer.

"No hurry," Hogle said. Now he was reassuring me in the way that I had reassured him earlier, giving me hollow guarantees as he backed away. "Hey, I had a good time." He stepped past the clanking man, whose leather, I swear, oinked and squeaked. "No kidding. It's just that"—he looked around—"I told this friend of mine, this girl I know, that I'd—I don't know, I'd give her a call." He looked desperate. "Hey, thanks a lot. I really appreciate everything you've done!"

Then he left, and then I removed my earring. That was easy enough to do—just a matter of unscrewing the little plunger and putting the foolish thing into my pocket. And I hurried out of the pub, hearing just behind me clanks and squeaks of **reproach**.

reproach:
disappointment; blame

Charlie Hogle's Earring

In my report for Charlie Hogle's file I recorded the earring incident as a minor infraction—Inappropriate Dress. I left it vague. What was the point in explaining? I noted the two meetings; I described Hogle as "compliant" and "reasonable." There was no **innuendo** in my report. I spared him any indignity. It sounded no worse than if he had come to work without a necktie.

innuendo: subtle implication

Indeed, it was no worse than if he had come to work without a necktie. I had had no objection to the earring, nor had any of Hogle's co-workers in the telex room. Horton had made it an issue; Horton was minister, so Horton was obeyed. And Hogle did not wear his earring again.

"It's for his own good," Horton said later, and he squeezed my arm. I was the team member who had just played well; he was the coach. He was proud of me and pleased with himself. He was beaming. "I feel a thousand times better, too! That really annoyed me—that kid's earring. I used to go down to the telex room a lot. I realized I was staying away—couldn't stand to look at it!"

"Aren't you being a little melodramatic?"

"I'm completely serious," he said. "That situation was making me sick. I mean sick. I got so mad the first time I saw that thing on his ear"—Horton turned away and paused—"I got so mad I actually threw up. Puked! That's how angry I was."

"You must have been very angry," I said.

"Couldn't help it. We can't have that sort of thing—" He didn't finish the sentence. He shook his head from side to side and then said, "You were too easy on him in your report. That kid had a problem. Incredible. I took him for a clean, stand-up guy!"

I said, "He may have feelings of which he's unaware. It's not that uncommon."

"No," Horton said. "I'll keep an eye on him."

"Fine," I said. "Anyway, everyone's safe now, coach."

He smiled and smacked my arm and sent me back to my office.

In the following weeks I saw scores of young men Hogle's age wearing earrings. They were English, and all sorts, and I was ashamed that I had been a success. It was not merely that I had succeeded by deceiving Hogle, but that I had made him think there was something dangerous and deviant in this trinket decorating his ear. And he never knew just how handsome that trinket made him. Hogle would be all right. But after what he had told me, I was not so sure about Horton.

Read and Think Critically

Analyze, Explain, Conclude

1. **CONFLICT** Analyze and explain the types of **conflict**—both internal and external—in the story.

2. One black mark in Charlie Hogle's file states that he never experienced "negative situations." How can his never having been in a "negative situation" be considered a black mark?

3. On several occasions in the story, the **narrator** is disgusted by his own actions. What do you think most bothers him about what he has been asked to do and how he does it?

4. At one point the narrator says, "I had lapsed into 'we'—it is hard to use it and not seem cold and bullying; it can be a terrifying pronoun." Explain what the author means by this statement.

5. **THE AUTHOR'S STYLE** Often, Theroux's fiction involves **characters** who are under pressure. The threats they face help them reveal their character. What can you conclude about the characters of Horton, Hogle, and the narrator based on the earring incident? Base your conclusions on details from the text.

Before You Read

A Collection of Short Shorts

About the Authors

JUSTIN KAHN has published stories in several online magazines, including *McSweeney's Internet Tendency*, a "zine" that publishes satirical and tongue-in-cheek articles and stories.

MARTHA WILSON is a writer, a performance artist, and the founding director of Franklin Furnace Archives, a museum of avant-garde art in lower Manhattan. "A Short Story About Nova Scotia" was a 2005 *storySouth* Million Writers Award Notable Story.

MATT BELL has published short stories in numerous online magazines. "An End to Efficient Vehicles" first appeared in *Rumble Magazine,* an online site devoted to micro fiction. Bell lives in Anne Arbor, Michigan, where he is working on his first novel and where he helps with the Dzanc Writer in Residence Program, a nonprofit organization committed to increasing youth literacy.

GABRIEL ORGREASE was raised in northern Appalachia and now resides on the south shore of Long Island. Orgrease has published short pieces in several online magazines. You can even see a handwritten rough draft of a piece he published on *Hit and Run Magazine,* a site that publishes the "raw materials of fiction, poetry and other creative work: scrap metal; index cards; napkin notes; etc."

★★★★★★★★★★★

A New Short Story Form?

Writers did not have to wait for the Internet to be drawn to the short short story form. Aesop used the short form for his fables. And one of the most powerful pieces of "flash fiction" was written by Ernest Hemingway well before the Internet was dreamed up: "For sale: baby shoes, never worn."

That said, the Internet has created a forum for shorter and shorter story forms. Since the late 1990s, zines devoted to short short stories—stories that can be read in the amount of time it might take to read an email message—have proliferated.

The four pieces that follow were found on Web sites that feature shorter story forms, forms with names that telegraph their length: flash fiction, micro-stories, nano fiction. The most recent piece, "Tree Reader," by Gabriel Orgrease, was typed into a PDA while the event described was taking place, like a stream-of-consciousness snapshot.

Technology has always had an impact on the stories we read (or listen to or watch). Improvements in printing and mail service, for example, led to the proliferation of magazines, which in turn led to the short story form. It is anyone's guess what the impact of flash fiction and related genres will have on the short story form and fiction in general. The fun will be in the reading (and the writing). Enjoy.

Models of Conflict in Literature,

Which I Think Justify My Beeping the Horn While Driving, Even If My Girlfriend Thinks Not.

JUSTIN KAHN

LITERARY LENS: STYLE As you read the pieces that follow, label each with the literary or stylistic term you think best represents the dominant element or force in the piece.

Character's struggle against nature

Hello, dog. You are going to move? Yes, yes, yes? No? I am human, you are canine. We are different, but know this: I will run you over if you don't get out of the street. Dog! Are you trying to bring me to a halt?! How often I forget that I can reconnect myself to the great web of life with just a simple message: BEEEEEEP, BEEEEEEEP.

Character's struggle against an antagonist

The thing is, I need to be at my dentist's appointment. If you don't let me turn left onto Cedar, I will be unable to make my appointment. Why are you going the exact same speed as me? I go 30, you go 30. I go 40, you go 40. I do an illegal U-turn, you do an illegal U-turn.

Perhaps if we were all going to the same place, I'd just go with the flow. But I've been going with the flow, trying to get in the left-hand-turn flow, and no one is letting me do it. And you, ma'am, are obviously doing everything you can to prevent me from getting to my personal destination. Hear me when I say this: BEEP, BEEP, BEEP, BEEEEEEP.

Character's struggle against society

The road has three lanes. The SUV is using two of them at any given moment. This raises a question, first raised by Plato in *The Republic*: What is justice? Specifically, when given a scarce resource (the road), how do you distribute the scarce resource among the potential recipients (the drivers)? This particular SUV is suggesting a reprisal of Thrasymachus's definition of justice: whatever is done by the powerful is what is just. Following Plato, I voice my dissent, by pressing hard on my horn for seven seconds, followed by three quick BEEP, BEEP, BEEPs.

Struggle between competing elements within the character

Sweet world, how much I have shared with you! I have withdrawn from you, wearied by my conflicts. I want peace. Will I be able to find it by withdrawing, thinking, eating, and driving?

As I withdraw from the world, I find it difficult to breathe.

One second I am savoring the taste of this BBQ chicken wing while driving, but now so very much of the chicken is stuck between my tonsils and the back part of my tongue. I can't breathe, I can't think clearly, all I can do is slump over as everything becomes very blurry. Thanks for hearing me out—BEEEEEEEEEEEEEEEEEEEP. BEEP. BEEEEEEEEEEEEEEEEEEEEEEEEEEEEEEP. BEEEEEEEEEEEEEEEEEEEEEEEEEEP.

A Short Story About
Nova Scotia

MARTHA WILSON

*T*his is the first sentence of my short story about Nova Scotia. The first sentence of any short story is easy enough to write; its function is to plunge the reader into the action of the story, and by reading the first sentence of this story the reader will have a fair idea of what kind of action to expect. I find the second sentence of a short story harder to write, because it hardens the style into Naturalism, Surrealism, Expressionism, Realism, Impressionism and so on. But in this story, as the reader can see by now, I am not particularly concerned with any of these styles. Such labels refer to various modes of reference to external nature. (My whole plan is to beguile you with the reference to Nova Scotia in the title, and then finish the story without resorting to description of it.)

The tone I have established might suggest that what I am really writing here is a pragmatic story. Wrong again. I am not interested in writing a short story about Nova Scotia with sociological, journalistic, philosophical, historical, or even pornographic intent. To treat any of these topics, I would have to be well-informed in a field besides English literature, and, as a child of specialization, I admit I am not.

It has been out of fashion to write with a moral intent since the 1860's, but this story might be a disguised diatribe, judging from the tone, which is ambiguous. I advise the reader to be on the lookout for covert references to an approved social norm. But the tone also does not eliminate the possibility that this story is intended as a joke, so I further advise that the reader try to keep a lookout both ways, to avoid embarrassment.

The lewd suggestion left over is that this story is really "art" appearing incognito as a short story without much point. I'll let this flattering idea flutter for the moment in the background while I try again to start this story out on another foot.

Here I am, making a clean slate of it again. In writing about Nova Scotia (as I said I would do in my title), regardless of what the tone suggests I do, it seems to me I must turn either inward or outward. I can write about "what Nova Scotia means to me", for example. This approach has the advantage of eliminating the need for knowledge about Nova Scotia in the technical sense. If I were going to write a short story like this, I would write about the wildflowers that appear in the St. Margaret's Bay area between May 1 and June 1, because I lived out there once and the wildflowers were incomparable. (I know I said I wouldn't do this, but my sympathy for the amateur botanists who might be reading this story is sufficiently strong that I'll briefly list the wildflowers I would have talked about in much detail if this were some other kind of story: Buttercup, Canadian Mayflower, Cinquefoil, Evening Primrose, Fireweed, Goldthread, Lupine, Violet.)

If I were to turn outward and write about Nova Scotia "objectively," I would still be limited by what I chose to be objective about. A compromise might be to try to prove by what I write that I really *am* in Nova Scotia, and am not an imposter, writing from New Brunswick. In either case, the assumption has to be made that there is an external reality I can refer to with some accuracy, and from which facts can be derived empirically. Most people don't question that the information they receive can be verified by sensory data. For example, if I say Peggy's Cove is notable for its exposed granite cliffs, whether they have been to Peggy's Cove or not, people will assume that if they go there, they will be able to perceive exposed granite. But the question of whether we know what's out there is too broad for short stories to treat. From my point of view as a short story writer, it would be vastly more interesting to make up everything I say about Nova Scotia. This would have the advantage of outraging everyone who thinks he knows something about Nova Scotia, and hoodwinking everyone else.

Back to the clean slate. My aim, in case it hasn't become obvious yet, is to write a short story without actually writing it. In other words, I'm trying to assemble about two thousand words that can make sense even if my personality doesn't exist, and even if Nova Scotia doesn't exist. I'm trying to create a self-conscious system analogous to a system of mathematics or philosophy. Any such system is based on presuppositions, so I will define them as best I can: This is a "short story," so it will be composed of enough words to fill several pages. It will have a focus, or problem to solve (besides getting itself written) that will be to answer the question implied in my stated aim: Why should anyone intend to write a short story without actually writing one?

To answer my question, I'll have to reconsider all those intents mentioned as possibilities in the beginning. If this story had a moral intent, for example, I would be writing with reference to some moral order. As far as morality is concerned, didactic stories always fail to influence sophisticated readers, so if I intend any moral at all, it should be conveyed by default. (The absence of moral judgment in this story, however, will be taken by some to be a comment on the absence of morality in the larger world; such a conclusion will then supply the reader with the incentive for reformed behaviour, or the incentive for licensed behaviour.) Sophistication makes moral stories pretty difficult to write nowadays. I certainly don't intend to worry about morality in this story. When the time comes for me to exert a moral influence over someone else, I'll do it by more direct means, such as spanking.

Lots of stories are pragmatic these days, but this one does not have a pragmatic intent. So far, I have not referred to Nova Scotia much, which might seem a travesty of my title. But I want to say as little about Nova Scotia as possible to prove that a short story doesn't need to communicate any external facts to exist. (Even though I want to avoid facts, just for my own amusement I will mention that fishermen in Nova Scotia are often non-swimmers, and drown if they fall out of their boats.)

Why I am trying to write a short story without actually writing one must be for a joke, or perhaps it really is for "art." The irony is that both of these possibilities boil down to the same thing, unless some kind of distinction can be drawn between them. "Amusement" I take to mean therapy or preoccupation with one's activity without regard for how this activity will fit into a larger system of activities. But if "amusement" is taken to mean activity (funny or not) that finally makes its way into a public system, then I think it is no longer therapy; it becomes "art." (It also becomes a "joke.") The act of writing a pointless short story can be seen as an affirmation or as a negation, depending on how the reader chooses to view it. My story exists now, so readers will think I think there is still need for short stories in the clean modern world, or they will take my short story as an epitaph for the short story form. But in either case, a public of some sort makes the judgment.

When I say that this story might be a joke, I mean that in order for it to be art or a joke, it must be public.

Before I finish writing this short story, I should try to convince the reader that it was worth reading. Given that this story is art and not therapy because it has found its public, is it good or bad art? Has the intention of this story been fulfilled? And was the intention itself worth the attempt? Since nothing I say to explain myself outside the limits of this story will reach the public, I will incorporate my explanations directly, and call them more art. I wanted to write a short story, and I have done so. The near-finished product describes little, does not proselytize, and is good for nothing, but it seems to have order; the sentences are intelligible, and follow one another logically. It is a self-conscious story, I think, and that is all it needed to be to fulfill my intention—to write a short story without actually writing a short story. Whether my readers are tickled or disgusted by having wasted so much time in reading an absent story, is not my concern. Now that I have made my attempt at nothing, posterity will have to decide if the effort has value in relation to all the other attempts like it in the past. The job remaining for me is to stop what I have started. Some readers will be asking how this story can keep going on, now that it is finished justifying itself. Others will wonder whether, if I have made it this far, I can keep going interminably. A pointless story is interesting up to a point, and then it really does become pointless. Even the short story writer who places value on doing pointless things can have enough, like the child with a new kite on a windy day. I will have to find a sentence to end my short story, but with the proper click; if it just fizzles out, it will not fulfill the demands of short story form, and all of this will have been written for nothing. So, this is almost the last sentence of my short story about Nova Scotia. Although I did not write it for "amusement" (as I have defined it), it will probably be called funny by all the point-seekers who have made it this far. I don't resent chuckles, or even snickers about my short story, because if someone laughs, at least I know someone is there.

An End to
Efficient
Vehicles

MATT BELL

*I*n the sky, invisible microwaves crisscross like jet trails, undetectable to us but disorienting to migrating birds, rearranging the V's of geese into characters from new, unknowable alphabets. I point and you follow my finger as we try together to read their messages. The V is an efficient vehicle, you say, its shape doubling the potential range of the geese.

I wonder if their new letters will be any better, or if all that will happen is that they will fall frightened from the sky, unable to tell their crashing families that they love them, the way I want to tell you and know I'll never be able to again. Instead we will move cautiously around each other, interference rendering impossible our old structures even as we become unable or unwilling to find the new shapes that might save us. I scream something, words you might never hear or understand, and then I too am plummeting downward, racing you headfirst towards the bottom.

Tree Reader

GABRIEL ORGREASE

*I*n furrowed bark of the old basswood tree as I read an older brother say ten with a younger sister on the train she was all over the place in and out of the seat she fell in the aisle and taunted him then bumped her elbows into commuters who smiled or winced or stared defiantly or shut their eyes to retreat to sleep if they saw nuisance or themselves reflected in their memory of childhood as a climber of trees as he said eat and they ate cold fries and paper wrapped hamburgers she yelped and whined they spilled dark-brown soda while all he wanted was his own seat to sit he pushed her down and off of his head where she grabbed the leaves away from his own room and as the commuter train slid on the iron line further East the passengers thinned out stop by station stop until eventually the young boy got to sit alone he fell over and slept and the ride fell quiet as it passed the old basswood tree in the lawn of the cemetery as I read in the metallic flicker of sunlight on the afternoon window.

Read and Think Critically

Analyze, Explain, Evaluate

1. **STYLE** Using a chart like the one below, analyze the **style** of each of the stories. List the stylistic or literary term(s) you feel best represents the dominant force in the story. You may want to refer to the Glossary of Literary Terms on pages 758–761. Be prepared to explain your list.

Title	Dominant Literary or Stylistic Element
Models of Conflict in Literature	
A Short Story About Nova Scotia	
An End to Efficient Vehicles	
Tree Reader	

2. In "An End to Efficient Vehicles," Matt Bell weaves together several comparisons. List the comparisons and then describe some **themes** of the story.

3. Gabriel Orgrease typed "Tree Reader" into a PDA while watching the events described. He did not have punctuation easily available as he typed. Read "Tree Reader" aloud. Rewrite the story, placing periods and commas where you feel they should go. Then decide what you think the **title** refers to.

4. Justin Kahn based his piece on the four types of **conflict**. Think back over the short stories you have read in this book. For each type of conflict Kahn models, select a short story that you feel represents the same type of conflict. You may want to review the table of contents. Be prepared to share your list and your rationale.

5. **AN AUTHOR'S STYLE** Which of the four pieces do you like the best? In a brief paragraph, evaluate your favorite piece, explaining the aspects of the piece that you find appealing.

Responding to Unit Six

Key Ideas and Details

1. A **moral** is a short statement that summarizes the main message of a fable. For example, "Slow and steady wins the race" is an example of a moral. Select two of the stories in this unit and write a moral for each story. Be prepared to explain your response.

2. It might be said that "This Is What It Means to Say Phoenix, Arizona" is a collage of stories. Analyze and explain the impact of the author's choice to relate the story in episodic style.

Craft and Structure

3. The **voices** of the **narrators** in "Ladies and Gentlemen:" and "Top of the Food Chain" are similar in some ways. Compare and contrast the two stories to find how the voices achieve different results.

4. Consider the story "Fault Lines," written in the **third-person point of view**, and "Mortals," written in **first-person point of view**. What do you think the advantages of each point of view are in making readers feel empathy for the main **characters**?

Integration of Knowledge and Ideas

5. The story "This Is What It Means to Say Phoenix, Arizona" was the basis for a book called *The Lone Ranger and Tonto Fistfight in Heaven,* which was made into a movie called *Smoke Signals.* Watch the movie and then write a comparison of the story and the movie. Consider ways in which the author adapted his story for a different medium.

6. Read Paul Theroux's response below to readers who want to know if the events in his fiction actually happened. Make a list of stories from this unit that seem closer to real-life situations and those that are obviously made up. Which stories impacted you most, or, as Theroux says, you "like it, remember it, dream about it"? Does your experience fit with Theroux's opinion? Why or why not?

> *It's a 'What if?' life. The question is not, 'Did it happen?' It is, 'Did it convince you? Did it hold you until the end? Did you like it?' Rather than, 'Is it true?' If all the other things happen—if you read it, like it, remember it, dream about it—in a way it doesn't matter if it's true or not.*
>
> —Paul Theroux

Writing About the Literature

Staying Power

Some of the relatively recent stories in this unit may be ignored by future readers, and others may gain staying power and appear over and over in anthologies like this one. Select the one that you think will last and one that, in your opinion, will be soon forgotten. Explain your choices in a short essay.

Writing with Style

Choose one of the following writing activities.

Found Story

Robert Olen Butler has been known to find inspiration for his stories in unusual places. For example, he wrote a story titled "*Titanic* Victim Speaks Through Waterbed" based on a headline of a supermarket tabloid. Develop a story line using a "found" object (a soft drink can, a piece of clothing—whatever you decide) or a "found" story (such as a newspaper account).

From Story to Film

While trying to find a studio to finance a movie version of "This Is What It Means to Say Phoenix, Arizona," Sherman Alexie was urged to use white actors for the two main characters. The movie *Smoke Signals* was finally produced using Native Americans. Refer to passages in "This Is What It Means to Say Phoenix, Arizona" that use dialogue, such as the exchanges on page 694. Then try your hand at writing in Alexie's style by making up a scene, in dialogue, in which Alexie meets with a white producer to discuss making the film.

IN YOUR OWN STYLE

Several of the stories in this unit involve a moral dilemma: whether to persuade Charlie Hogle to give up his earring in "Charlie Hogle's Earring," for example, or how Victor should treat Thomas in "This Is What It Means to Say Phoenix, Arizona." Now it's your turn. Try writing about any moral dilemma of your choosing—whether it actually happened or not—in your own style. Instinctive or deliberate, the choices you make about dialogue, point of view, and tone will help to shape your style.

Writing About Short Stories

"The answers you get from literature depend on the questions you pose."

Margaret Atwood

Almost everyone has a response after reading a story or poem or attending a play. Works of literature are meant to provoke an effect. Sometimes the effect is a fizzle, and sometimes it's volcanic—powerful enough to change a person's life.

Good literature expresses common experiences and emotions and universal truths. It raises important questions—ones it prefers you answer yourself. You may enjoy a story and appreciate the emotions it brings forth, but you shouldn't expect to understand it without asking a few questions of your own. Consider it a dialogue.

Reading Creatively

Reading is more than appreciating the "rare flavor" of a literary work. Like writing, reading is a creative process. As a reader, you help create the meaning of a literary work. No work has a single, correct meaning. Instead, the meaning grows out of the relationship between the writer's words and each reader's response.

Who you are, where you live, and what your life has been like so far may enable you to identify with a character, situation, or feeling in a work. When you identify with characters, you put yourself in their shoes; you see what they see and feel what they feel. The more closely you can identify with characters, the more enjoyment and meaning you may find in reading and writing about a literary work.

It's important to remember, however, that reading is a process of interpretation within an acceptable range. You can't say, willy-nilly, that a story means whatever you want it to mean.

Personal Response Strategies

If you own your own book, mark it up while you are reading. In order to note your first impressions, underline and highlight any words or passages that excite your interest in some way. Feel free to write in the margins as well. Briefly note any questions you have, things you are reminded of, or short points that you want to explore later. This marked-up text can be a valuable blueprint for the beginnings of your literary analysis.

Keep a reading journal. Use it to answer questions such as the following:

- Which character do you identify with most closely? Why? Do other characters remind you of people you know? If so, how?

- How does the work make you feel? Why?

- If you were a character in the work, would you have behaved differently? What behaviors in the story puzzle you?

- What experiences from your own life came to your mind as you read this work? How did you feel about those experiences?

Conclude with a personal response statement in which you summarize what the work means to you. In small discussion groups, share your responses to the work. As you listen to your classmates' reactions, refine your ideas. Afterward, write freely about how your ideas have evolved.

Responding from Literary Knowledge

As a reader, you not only respond to each work on the basis of your past experience and background, but you also apply your knowledge of other stories, poems, or plays that you have read. Through reading, you develop a deeper understanding of the characteristics that distinguish each genre. This knowledge helps you interpret a work and appreciate a writer's skill. When you respond to literature on the basis of your literary knowledge, you analyze its elements. For a quick review of literary elements, see the Glossary of Literary Terms, pages 758–761.

The elements of each genre contribute to the meaning of a work. The following list of questions can help you explore the meaning of a piece of literature.

Plot

- What actions happen?

- How does each event affect the main characters?

- What conflicts occur? What is their source?

- How do the events connect to each other and to the whole?

- Is the story told in chronological order, or are there flashbacks or flash forwards? If it is not told chronologically, what is the effect of its order on your response to the action?

- What foreshadowing did you detect when reading the story the first time? When you reread it?

- Do you detect a formula in this plot, or is it unpredictable?

- Would you characterize the story's ending as happy, unhappy, or something in between?

- What do the climax and the ending reveal about the theme?

Setting

- What does the setting contribute to the story?

- Does the setting influence the characters?

- What setting details are important in the development of the plot?

- How does the setting relate to the story's theme?

- Are scene shifts meaningful?

- Is the setting symbolic?

- Is the setting antagonistic to the characters—and part of the conflict?

- Could this story be set anywhere else?

Characters

- Who are the principal people in the story, and how do they interact? Who are the minor characters, and what do they contribute to the work?

- What do their words, thoughts, and actions reveal about their personalities and motivations, as well as the personalities of others?

- How does each character contribute to the development of the plot?

- Who is the protagonist; who is the antagonist?

- How do the characters relate to their setting?

- Are the characters symbolic—do they seem to stand for something in addition to themselves?

- How does the writer reveal character—for instance, by explicit comment or by letting us see the character in action? Does the writer use names, physical conditions, or family histories to convey character traits?

- Are they round (three-dimensional and capable of change)? Flat (two-dimensional and incapable of change)? Or are they stock characters—stereotypes such as the Mad Scientist, Town Drunk, or Computer Geek?

- With which characters do you sympathize? Does your response to them change over the course of the story? If so, what causes the change?

- Do the characters speak alike or differently? How would you characterize their speech—is it formal or informal? Does it reflect their geographical origins, education, or class status?

Point of View

- Who tells the story? Is the narrator a character, or does the narrator stand completely outside the story?

- What kind of person is he or she? Is this person reliable, or does he or she appear to be too emotional, mentally unstable, naive, ignorant, or biased to be trusted?

- Why do you think the writer chose to have this character tell the story?

- How does the story's point of view affect the characterizations? How much does the narrator really know?

- Does the author comment on the story?

- How would the story's effect be similar or different if someone else were the narrator?

Theme

- What is the theme, or underlying meaning, of the story? Is it stated explicitly or developed through some other element?

- What story elements contribute to the meaning?

- What passages and details in the story best express the main theme?

- What does the point of view contribute to the theme?

- How does the author communicate the theme through the development of setting, characters, and plot?

- What else have you read that has a similar theme?

- Does the theme challenge your values or reinforce them?

Language

- What is the significance of the story's title? Does it suggest anything about the plot, characters, setting, overall theme, or tone? Can you think of a better title?

- Are there motifs—repeated words or images? What special meaning do they take on?

- How would you characterize the tone—lighthearted, mysterious, sentimental, ironic, or objective?

- What symbols, if any, appear in the story? What do they stand for, and how do they add to your understanding of the story?

- How would you describe the word choice—formal or informal? Colorful or plain? Are the sentences characteristically long and complex, or short and concise?

- What kinds of imagery and figurative language does the author use, if any? Can you find figures of speech such as metaphors, similes, and personification? How do they contribute to the unity of the work?

Additional Questions for Analyzing Short Stories

- How does this story reflect the historical and cultural context in which it is set? Does it fit in, or does it conflict with that context?

- How do economic conditions affect the characters' lives? Does the story challenge or support the economic order?

- How are women's lives and relationships shown in the work? Do the women go along with or rebel against these roles? Does the work challenge or support traditional beliefs about women in society?

- Does this story remind you of anything else, such as a tale, myth, or story by someone else, or something from another time period or stylistic tradition? Does it contain any archetypes, such as a quest, initiation, or transformation?

- How does the author's biography affect the work? Do you recognize any characters or incidents in the story that figured in the writer's life? How might the writer's personal and political values affect the work?

- Is there anything about your own background, values, or way of thinking that affects your appreciation and understanding?

- Did you enjoy the short story? What especially pleased or displeased you about it?

Writing a Literary Analysis

Writing about a literary work helps you digest and appreciate it. Vladimir Nabokov describes the process this way:

> Literature, real literature, must not be gulped down . . . Literature must be taken and broken into bits, pulled apart, squashed . . . [T]hen, and only then, its rare flavor will be appreciated . . . and the broken and crushed parts will come together again in your mind.

Choosing and Limiting a Subject

As you respond to a short story by using both your personal experience and your literary knowledge, you will develop some definite ideas about the meaning of the work. Your understanding will then become the basis for choosing a subject for a literary analysis.

Unless your teacher has assigned you a specific topic, you will have a wide choice of possible subjects. When choosing a subject, jot down your initial responses to the story. Then narrow your choice by asking yourself the following questions.

Questions for Choosing a Subject

- What elements of the story would you like to understand better? What parts of the story puzzle you?

- What parts of the story do you find especially moving? Why?

- What images and details made a strong impression on you? What do they contribute to the story?

- With which character do you identify the most? Why?

- How do the characters relate to one another? How do their relationships affect the plot?

- What feeling, meaning, or message does the story convey to you? What insight or understanding have you gained?

Developing a Thesis

When you clearly focus your subject, you will discover the **thesis**, or main idea, for your literary analysis. By expressing your main idea in a complete sentence, you will have a working thesis statement on which to build. Your thesis is a proposition that you must defend by presenting evidence that will convince the reader that your interpretation is valid. Notice that the thesis statement is carefully worded. In a literary analysis, a thesis statement should be specific enough to be proven conclusively.

Focused Subject	qualities Mr. Ryder has that would make him a suitable spouse for the wife of his youth
Working Thesis	Despite his prejudices and snobbishness, Mr. Ryder has qualities that might make him a good husband for the wife of his youth.

Gathering Evidence

To prove the truth of your thesis, you must supply evidence. You automatically gather evidence when you read, whether you are aware of it or not. After you have stated your thesis, however, you should reread the story and look for specific details that will help you prove it. The kinds of details you will use include specific examples of description, narrative, dialogue, and action.

Skim the text from start to finish, looking for any elements that will directly contribute to proving your thesis. As you skim, jot down each supporting detail you find—either on a note card or on a separate sheet of paper.

Even if you are not sure a story detail supports your thesis, note it on a card or a sheet of paper. You can always discard it later if you decide it is not relevant.

Examples of such details are shown in the following chart.

Model: Kinds of Evidence in Literature

*(All quotations are from "The Wife of His Youth," by Charles W. Chesnutt, pages 179–192.)

Background Detail	Mr. Ryder had a "genius for social leadership."
Descriptive Detail	"His manners were irreproachable. . . . [he had] a poetic soul and . . . was economical."
Narrative Detail	In order to "fortify" himself for his ball, Mr. Ryder reread some favorite poems. He experienced "an appreciative thrill" when reading a love poem.
Dialogue Detail	"Ladies and Gentlemen . . . . Permit me to introduce to you the wife of my youth."
Action Detail	"He began by speaking of woman as the gift of Heaven to man."

How do I take notes?

Unless your teacher requires you to take notes a certain way, you can choose from several efficient methods. The time-honored way to take notes is on 3" × 5" index cards, with a key word to identify the source and the page number (if available) at the top. Here is a note card with a sentence from Chesnutt's story "The Wife of His Youth."

Chesnutt (p. 189 in <u>American Short Stories</u>)

"But perhaps the quality which most distin-guishes woman is her fidelity and devotion to those she loves."

Breaking information into small chunks makes it easier to organize and write your analysis. Identifying sources will help you give them proper credit within the paper and in the Works Cited page at the end of your paper.

Some people prefer to take notes on the computer. Information from electronic databases and Web sites can be saved as word processing files or cut and pasted into a document. If you save an entire article, indicate the material you expect to use by emphasizing it with highlighting or bold type, adding headings, or using the Comments feature in your word processor.

How do I keep track of my sources?

The easiest way to keep track of your sources is to write information about each source on a 3" × 5" index card. Record the author's name and publication information before you take a single note. Then you won't have to retrace your steps when you're trying to credit the sources you used for your presentation or paper.

What information do you need? Example citations of some commonly used sources are shown below. If your teacher wants you to follow the Modern Language Association (MLA) style, you can find more detailed examples in guides such as the *MLA Handbook for Writers of Research Papers.*

Sample MLA Documentation

Source	Example
Book	Melville, Herman. *Melville's Short Novels* (Norton Critical Editions). New York: Norton. 2001.
Article	Howells, W. D. "Mr. Charles W. Chesnutt's Stories." *Atlantic Monthly* 85 1900: 699–701
Article in a familiar reference work	"Melville, Herman." *The New Encyclopedia Britannica.* 1984 ed.
Web site	Mark Twain, "On the Decay of the Art of Lying," http://www.readbookonline.net/readOnLine/442/

How should I credit sources in my paper?

Here's a general rule for citing sources: When in doubt, give credit! To avoid plagiarism, you must acknowledge any words, facts, or ideas taken from other people's works. The only exceptions: facts or ideas that are so widely known they are considered common knowledge. For example, the statement that Willa Cather is a Nebraska writer appears in many sources and does not need to be credited. However, a critic's comment about Willa Cather needs to be credited.

Within your paper, acknowledge any source you use by giving the author's last name and page numbers inside parentheses following the quotation or idea you used in your paper. This is called *parenthetical documentation*. If your source is from the Web or an electronic database and has numbered paragraphs, use the abbreviation *par.* or *pars.* and give paragraph numbers instead of page numbers.

Every source mentioned in parenthetical documentation should be in included in a Works Cited page at the end of your paper. Center the heading "Works Cited" and list your sources in alphabetical order. You can find sample Works Cited pages in guides such as the *MLA Handbook for Writers of Research Papers* or Perfection Learning's *Write in Style*.

How can I avoid plagiarizing?

Using other people's words and ideas without acknowledging them is called *plagiarism*. When best-selling authors are accused of plagiarizing, they end up in court. When students are caught, penalties depend on the school. They range from loss of credit for the assignment to failing the course to expulsion.

There are several ways to avoid plagiarism: cite borrowed ideas and use quotation marks to indicate borrowed words. Using your own words for someone else's ideas is called *paraphrasing*. You still need to credit the source from which you took the paraphrase, but you do not need to use quotation marks. When you copy someone else's words, you must use quotation marks to acknowledge that you are using not just ideas, but exact words. Quote passages that are exceptionally well-stated. For example, if you are trying to disprove a critic's opinion, quoting the opinion will help your audience follow your argument.

While there's no question about when you need to use quotation marks, the line between plagiarism and paraphrasing is not always as clear. You may have no intention of stealing someone else's words. However, if your paraphrase is too close to the original, you may find yourself slipping into unintentional plagiarism. That means you've kept too much of the author's wording or organization.

These note-taking tips will help you avoid being too dependent on your sources.

- Take time to understand the material.
    - —Look up difficult words.
    - —Break long sentences into shorter parts.

—State the main point of what you have just read in your own words.

- Cover up the source as you take your notes. Then check to be sure that

   —your notes contain all the information you think you'll need.

   —your notes are accurate.

   —quotation marks set off any words you've taken directly from the source.

   —you've remembered to identify the source and location of the information (page numbers for printed material; paragraph numbers for Internet sources with numbered paragraphs).

Organizing Details into an Outline

For your literary analysis, you should group your details into categories. Then you can arrange your ideas and information in a logical order. You might arrange your details in the order in which they appear in the work.

The following chart shows examples of how different types of order may be appropriate for proving different kinds of theses.

Examples for Ordering Evidence

Kind of Thesis	Type of Order
To show how a character or elements of a plot change or develop over time	Chronological Order
To show similarities and differences between characters or to compare two different works of literature	Comparison/Contrast
To analyze a character's motivation or to explain the significance of the setting	Order of Importance or Cause and Effect
To draw a conclusion about the theme	Developmental Order

As you order your evidence, check to be sure each detail directly supports your thesis. Set aside note cards when the details seem irrelevant.

After you decide how to organize your ideas and evidence, you should make a list, chart, or outline to use as a guide for writing your literary analysis. When outlining, you may use either an informal outline—a simple listing, in order, of the points you wish to cover—or a formal outline.

Following is a simple outline for a literary analysis of "The Wife of His Youth" by Charles W. Chesnutt. Notice that the writer includes the ideas for the introduction and the conclusion. Because the details have equal importance in proving the thesis, they are placed in developmental order. In this order, information is arranged to lead up to a conclusion.

Sample Outline

I. Introduction

    A. Background details about Mr. Ryder

    B. Thesis Statement: Despite his history of social snobbery and prejudice, Mr. Ryder has qualities that will make him a fine husband for the wife of his youth.

II. Body

Qualities Mr. Ryder has that will make him a suitable spouse for the wife of his youth

    A. Social leadership (ability to persuade and lead others) ADD SUPPORTIVE DETAILS

    B. Sensitivity (his "poetic soul" and fine manners) ADD SUPPORTIVE DETAILS

    C. Nobility (his willingness to do the right thing when it would be easy to avoid doing so) ADD SUPPORTIVE DETAILS

III. Conclusion

Despite his past behavior, Mr. Ryder will make a fine husband for the wife of his youth. He distinguishes himself in the story by showing social leadership, a respect for right and wrong, and a strength of mind that will make him a loyal husband.

Drafting

When you are ready to draft your literary analysis, you may find the following guidelines helpful.

Guidelines for Drafting a Literary Analysis

- In the introduction, identify the title and author of the work you are discussing and include your thesis statement.

- In the body of your literary analysis, include clearly organized supporting details, using transitions to show how one detail relates to another. Use direct quotations from the work wherever they strengthen your thesis.

- In the conclusion, reinforce the main idea of your literary analysis by explaining how the details that you included prove your thesis.

- Add an interesting, appropriate title that suggests the focus of your literary analysis.

Guidelines for Using Quotations in a Literary Analysis

- Always support your assertions with quoted material from the text. Generally, use brief quotations—four lines or fewer for prose. Quotations should not be used to pad your paper but only as evidence to support your ideas.

- How does the quotation relate to your idea? Make the connection for the reader by introducing it in an informative way. For example, "One aspect of the black veil's symbolism is revealed when the minister says, . . ." You may also want to comment after the quotation.

- All spelling, mechanics, and other features should appear in the quotation exactly as they are in the source.

- If you need to add something to a quotation, perhaps to make it fit the grammar of your sentence, use brackets. "[Goodman Brown is] depicted as a highly strung and self-righteous young man."

- If you need to drop any words from the source quotation, use ellipses to show the omission. "Henry James's sentences are . . . rarely short."

- Document your sources—give credit for any ideas that are not completely your own. Don't worry that it will look like you've borrowed your material from others; in fact, you will probably make the opposite impression. By scrupulously citing your sources, you demonstrate your skills as a researcher and your ability to use and integrate supportive evidence. Most importantly, it establishes your credibility.

In writing a literary analysis, your primary source is the fictional work being discussed. Thus, it is important to know how to handle quotations because direct evidence is a necessity in a literary analysis. Your teacher will probably let you know how many (if any) secondary sources you can refer to, such as historical, biographical, and critical studies.

The chart on the following page provides guidelines for determining the credibility of these sources.

Criteria for Quality Secondary Sources

Timeliness	Is the information in this source outdated?
Completeness/ Accuracy	Does this source cover the topic thoroughly?
	How does information in this source compare to other sources on this topic?
Bias	Is this source objective?
	Does the source stand to profit from taking this position?
	Does this source include only evidence favorable to one side of a controversy?
	Does this source reflect the views of a particular time in history, such as empire builders' attitudes toward native peoples?
Credibility	What evidence do I have that this source is knowledgeable and believable?
	• academic or professional credentials
	• documentation, such as lists of references
	• recognition as an authority

Additional Evidence

If you have difficulty drafting your literary analysis, you may not have enough evidence to support your thesis statement. Go back to the story and look for evidence you may have missed. Review your note cards or create additional cards to support your thesis.

After completing your first draft, set it aside for a day or two so that you can return to it with a critical eye. You may want to share your literary analysis with a peer reader. Using your partner's comments and the following checklist, you should then revise your essay.

Revision Checklist

Checking Content

- Do you have a strong introduction that identifies the author and the work you will discuss?

- Does your introduction contain a clearly worded thesis statement?

- Does the body of your essay provide ample details from the work to strengthen your points?

- Does your conclusion summarize the details in the body and reinforce your thesis statement?

- Does your whole essay have unity, coherence, and clarity?
- Did you add an interesting, appropriate title that suggests the focus of your essay?

Checking Language Use

- Are your sentences varied and concise?
- Did you use vivid, precise words? active verbs? concrete nouns? specific details?
- Are your mechanics correct—your grammar, spelling, usage, and punctuation? Avoid creating a poor impression with a mistake-strewn paper.

Publishing

Using the correct manuscript form, produce a neat and presentable final draft of your literary analysis. Share it with your teacher, fellow students, family members, or someone else who would be interested in reading it. You might want to submit your essay to the school literary magazine. If you have a school Web site, consider publishing your paper there.

The Essay Exam

Students are often asked to write literary analyses in a different context—as shorter essays in the classroom or as take-home tests. These essays are usually short, concise, and directed squarely at the question(s) posed by the teacher. The following strategies include practical advice for writing successful essay exams.

Strategies for Writing Essay Exams

1. Never start writing before reading through the entire exam. In fact, don't even start *thinking* about the answers until you have read through the entire exam (not including studying for it, of course). Find out how many questions there are and how many you must answer.

2. Create a time budget, either mentally or on paper. Short-answer questions should not take up too much of your time and detract from longer essay questions. Some teachers helpfully provide time limits; if so, follow these! No matter how "tasty" a question and how impressively you can answer it, don't ever linger on one question. Your best strategy is to demonstrate your mastery of all the subject matter, not just your special understanding of one area.

3. Some students like to start with the easiest questions, others with the most difficult. It really shouldn't matter as long as you are sticking to your time budget.

You don't ever want to get in the position of running out of time because you have spent too much time on easy, low-point questions.

4. When you settle down to answer the questions, read each one at least twice. Underline key words, such as the instructions: *describe, analyze, compare and/or contrast, evaluate, define, explain,* and so forth. Underline important noun phrases and anything important to help you focus your answer: *Romantic movement, realism, existentialism, modernism.* Underline or mark other critical instructions, such as "*give two specific examples*" or "*conclude in one or two sentences . . . .*"

5. Make brief notes or a simple list or outline of what you plan to cover in your essay. *Do not lose any time copying the question.* Some teachers allow you to bring outlines to an essay exam, but you may not bring one without permission.

6. Begin by answering the question directly. You may want to start with a thesis statement that includes both the question and an indication of how you intend to respond to it. "Kurt Vonnegut's 'Harrison Bergeron' is a good example of postmodern absurdism, which I will show in two features of the story: the narrative voice and the plot." Remember that each generalization you make will require evidence. The general statement "Vonnegut uses a deadpan narrative style" would require support in the form of a specific example of that style. Keep a tight focus and make your answers direct. Any digressions will look like padding.

7. Unless you are asked to do so, avoid summarizing unnecessarily or defining familiar terms, such as *symbol* or *theme.* Also avoid pointing out knowledge that would be obvious to any reader of the work; for example, "The main character of 'Harrison Bergeron' is Harrison Bergeron." Focus on the elements of the questions you have underlined at the start of the exam.

8. Avoid wordiness. English instructors especially are familiar with verbal "bloat" and will downgrade you accordingly.

9. Keep your personal opinions to a minimum. Too many *I*'s will lend your answer an air of too much subjectivity. It can also look as if you are finessing your lack of knowledge about the work being tested.

10. Always give yourself extra time to proofread and to add any additional details that are relevant and worthy. Review all the mechanics and search for better words and phrases if you have time. Cross out anything that looks redundant or irrelevant, or which lacks support or credibility.

Types of Essay Questions

1. **Description** Sometimes your teacher simply wants you to describe the details and nature of a situation, setting, character, or other element in a story. Your task is to make sure your description is specific and precise and encompasses every detail that is important. A typical question might be, "Describe the setting in Kate Chopin's story, 'A Pair of Silk Stockings.'" It might or might not have a follow-up question that asks you to think critically about that setting, e.g., whether it adds meaning to her story or not.

2. **Definition** This asks you to explain what a term means and then point out how the work in question fits (or does not fit) the definition. For example, "Define minimalism. In what ways does Raymond Carver's story 'Everything Stuck to Him' represent this literary style?"

3. **Explication** This simply means to explain in detail each line or passage in a work of prose or poetry (most often poetry). You are asked to put into plain English elements of diction (word choice), metaphors, similes, symbolism, or other language elements. This directive is a good way for your teacher to see if you have found the meaning in an author's literary language.

4. **Analysis** This is one of the most common types of literary essay questions. Here you look at specific elements, such as symbolism or imagery, in a body of work and examine their effect on the whole. For example, "Analyze the importance of color imagery in Stephen Crane's story 'The Bride Comes to Yellow Sky.'" You must find several examples of these images in the story and decide what their overall effect is.

5. **Cause and Effect Analysis** How does *x* cause (or not cause) *y*? In literature, analyzing causes and effects is not always a cut-and-dried business. However, it is a good way to test your skills of perception and logic. A sample exam question might be, "Why does Paul in 'Paul's Case' make his teachers angry? What are some of the results of his attitude?" In your essay, you would examine the known and possible causes of his attitude and state the known and possible effects.

6. **Comparison and Contrast** This common essay question asks you to discuss the similarities and/or differences between stories, authors, or other literary elements. For example, you might be asked to compare the realism evident in a story by Mark Twain with the realism in a story by Henry James.

Glossary of Literary Terms

absurdism writing that reflects the idea that the universe is irrational and meaningless

allegory a literary work in which characters, objects, and events stand for abstract qualities outside the story such as goodness, pleasure, or evil

allusion a reference to an artistic, historical, or literary figure, work, or event

analogy a description of an unfamiliar thing made by comparing it to something more familiar

anecdote a short incident or story that illustrates a point; anecdotal stories usually have an informal storyteller's tone

antagonist a character who opposes the hero or main character of the story

antihero a protagonist who displays traits opposite to the qualities usually associated with a traditional hero

aphorism a saying that teaches a lesson

appeal to emotion a persuasive technique that encourages others to act based on emotions rather than facts; *see also* propaganda

archetype an image, character, symbol, plot, or other literary device that appears frequently enough in myths, folktales, and other literary works so as to become an important part of a culture

character a person or animal in a story

characterization the manner in which an author creates and develops a character utilizing exposition, dialogue, and action

climax the high point of a plot; sometimes coincides with the turning point or defining moment; some stories do not have a clear climax

coincidence when significant events happen simultaneously

colloquialism a local or regional expression

coming-of-age story a story in which the protagonist is initiated into adulthood through gaining experience and/or knowledge about the world

concrete universal a universal concern (one that applies to everyone, everywhere) addressed through a concrete (local) setting

conflict the struggle between opposing forces; **external conflict** involves an outer force such as nature or another character, while **internal conflict** exists inside a person, say between a hero's sense of duty and desire for freedom

connotation the emotional associations surrounding a word

denotation the dictionary definition of a word

dénouement literally "the untying"; the part of a plot in which the conflict is "untied" or resolved; usually follows the climax

dialect the way in which people from a certain region or group speak that differs from standard pronunciation

dialogue conversation between characters in a literary work

diction the way in which a writer uses words, phrases, figures of speech, and sentence structure

epiphany an event, sometimes mystical in nature, in which a character changes in profound ways due to the revelation of a simple yet powerful truth; also called a **defining moment, moment of clarity**, or **moment of truth**

eulogy a formal expression of praise, usually about the dead

existentialism a philosophy that stresses a person's free will and responsibility for his or her actions

exposition information or background that is directly conveyed or explained, usually by the narrator

fable a short story or tale that demonstrates a **moral** or truth; frequently contains fantasy elements such as talking animal characters

fairy tale a story involving fairies, elves, giants, and other make-believe characters; such tales are characterized by familiar types of characters, settings, and patterns of events

falling action the events of a plot that follow the climax; also referred to as the **dénouement** or **resolution**

fantasy stories that contain characters, settings, and objects that could not exist, such as dragons or magic swords; often heroic in nature and sometimes based on myths and legends

farce a type of humor based on exaggeration and unlikely situations; includes rapid shifts in action and slapstick comedy

figurative language any of several techniques such as imagery, metaphor, or analogy that describe an object or character through comparison to something else

figure of speech an expression that conveys meaning or increases an effect, usually through figurative language

first-person point of view *see* point of view

flashback an interruption of the normal chronological order of a plot to narrate events that happened earlier

foil a character whose actions and values contrast with those of another character (usually the protagonist)

folktale a narrative, usually originating in an oral tradition, with a timeless and placeless setting and archetypal plot elements and characters; may contain elements of fantasy as well

foreshadowing the use of hints or clues about what will happen later in a plot

frame narrator a narrator of a story in which other narrators may appear to tell stories within the story; *see also* narrator

genre a distinctive type or category of literature, such as the epic, comedy, tragedy, short story, novel, science fiction, or mystery

Gothic a type of writing that focuses on the macabre, grotesque, mysterious, and/or violent; Southern Gothic refers to stories that have these elements and are set in the American South

hyperbole an overstatement or ridiculous exaggeration, e.g., "I'm so hungry I could eat a horse."

idiom an expression that is peculiar to a group or community; often difficult to translate

imagery vivid and striking descriptions of objects and details in a literary work, often through figurative language; **color imagery** uses references to light and color to create images

inference a reasonable conclusion drawn by the reader based on clues given in a literary work

in media res literally, "in the midst of things"; refers to a type of plot that begins at a high point of the action and fills in the exposition

interior monologue the presentation in a literary work of the unspoken thoughts and feelings of a character

interpretation an explanation of the meaning of a piece of literature, dependent in part on the perspective of the reader

irony a recognition and heightening of the difference between appearance and reality; **situational irony** occurs when events turn out differently from what is expected; **dramatic irony** occurs when the audience has important knowledge that a main character lacks

juxtaposition two or more things placed side by side, generally in an unexpected combination

local color a style of writing that developed just after the Civil War and that strives to reveal the peculiarities of a particular place and the people who live there; *see also* regionalism

metafiction fiction that contains references to the process of writing fiction

metaphor a figure of speech that implies a similarity between two unlike things

minimalist a spare, pared down style of writing made popular in the 1970s

mood the overall atmosphere of a work

moral a practical lesson drawn from a story, often used in **fables** and **parables**

morality play a play in which the characters personify moral or abstract qualities such as Charity or Death

motif a recurring element in a story such as an object, image, or situation

motivation the reasons or forces that cause characters to act as they do

mysticism the belief that knowledge of God, truth, or reality can be gained through intuition or insight

myth a traditional story, often one that explains a belief or natural phenomenon

narrator a teller of a story; an **unreliable narrator** makes incorrect conclusions and biased assumptions; a **naïve narrator** does not fully understand the events he or she narrates; *see also* frame narrator

naturalism a philosophy that informed the dominant literary movement of the 20th century. Writers in the naturalist tradition believe that all events can be explained in terms of the sciences, especially the premise of cause and effect; thus, they deny the existence of the miraculous or supernatural. In addition, naturalists do not believe in free will, but rather that people's actions are ruled by their heredity and environment.

neologism a newly-coined word

oral tradition legends, folktales, and stories that were initially told orally

parable short story that illustrates a moral lesson or principle

paradox a statement or situation that seems contradictory, but may in fact be true

parody a humorous imitation of another work

pathos an element of literature that evokes pity or compassion

personification a figure of speech in which human characteristics are given to nonhuman things

plot the events of a story

point of view the perspective from which a story is narrated: in **first-person** point of view, the narrator is a character in the story and uses the personal pronoun "I"; in **third-person limited** point of view, the narrator is outside the story but presents the story through the thoughts and feelings of one character; in **third-person omniscient** point of view, the narrator is outside the story and knows the thoughts and feelings of all characters and can comment on any part of the story

propaganda writing that presents a subject in a one-sided or biased manner

protagonist the main character of a story

realism a literary movement that emphasizes ordinary people in everyday experiences

realistic fiction fiction that attempts to describe the world in a realistic fashion

regionalism literature with an emphasis on locale or other local characteristics such as dialect; *see also* local color

repartee quick, witty exchanges of dialogue

repetition a technique in which words or phrases are repeated to stress a theme or give unity to a story

resolution the point at which the chief conflict or complication is worked out

rising action the events leading up to the climax of a plot

Romanticism a literary movement that valued the individual and intuition over society's rules and logic. Romantic writers used imaginative, figurative language and often the themes of spirituality, intellectual pride, and an attraction to the forbidden

satire writing that uses humor or ridicule to point out human shortcomings and follies

scenario a plot outline; one of many ways in which a story could be worked out

sensory details descriptive elements based on the five senses: taste, touch, smell, sight, and hearing

setting the time and place of the action of a story

simile comparison of one thing to another that uses "like" or "as"

stream of consciousness the flow of internal impressions—visual, auditory, psychological, intuitive—that represent the mind and heart of a character

subtext a hidden meaning, often symbolic or metaphorical, that must be inferred from the text

surprise ending an unexpected plot twist at the end of a story

surrealism a literary and artistic movement emphasizing the expression of the subconscious through dreamlike imagery

symbol an object that stands for or represents a more abstract concept, such as an eagle for freedom or a rose for love

symbolism writing that makes use of symbols

tale a series of facts or events either told or written

tall tale a story with exaggerated situations and characters such as Paul Bunyan and Johnny Appleseed

theme the underlying meaning or message of a literary work

third-person limited point of view *see* point of view

third-person omniscient point of view *see* point of view

title the name of a piece of writing

tone the author or narrator's attitude toward the subject of a work; for example, an author's attitude might be ironic, humorous, sarcastic, serious, or deadpan

Transcendentalism a philosophical movement in the mid-19th century based in the belief that wisdom comes in part from within oneself. Transcendentalist beliefs emphasized intuition, self-reliance, the intellect, and living close to nature

universality the quality of having feelings, thoughts, emotions, themes, or problems that cross all times and cultures

voice an author or character's distinctive way of expressing himself or herself

worldview the background, attitudes, and values of a society or individual

Index of Titles and Authors

Acknowledgments

Text Credits

"A & P" by John Updike from *Pigeon Feathers and Other Stories*. Copyright © 1962, renewed 1990 by John Updike. Used by permission of Alfred A. Knopf, a division of Random House, Inc.

"American Horse" by Louise Erdrich. Copyright © 1983 by Louise Erdrich. Reprinted by permission of The Wylie Agency, Inc.

"Angel Levine" by Bernard Malamud from *The Magic Barrel*. Copyright © 1950, 1958, renewed 1977, 1986 by Bernard Malamud. Reprinted by permission of Farrar, Straus & Giroux, LLC.

"Babylon Revisited" by F. Scott Fitzgerald from *The Short Stories of F. Scott Fitzgerald*. Copyright 1931 by Curtis Publishing Company, renewed © 1959 by Frances Scott Fitzgerald Lanahan. Reprinted with permission of Scribner, a division of Simon & Schuster, Inc.

"Barn Burning" by William Faulkner from *Collected Stories of William Faulkner*. Copyright © 1950 by Random House, renewed 1977 by Jill Faulkner Summers. Used by permission of Random House, Inc.

"The Black Ball" by Ralph Ellison from *Flying Home and Other Stories*. Copyright © 1996 by Fanny Ellison; Introduction copyright © 1996 by John F. Callahan. Used by permission of Random House, Inc.

"Charlie Hogle's Earring" by Paul Theroux from *Collected Stories of Paul Theroux*. Copyright © 1969, 1970, 1971, 1972, 1975, 1977 by Paul Theroux, Copyright © 1980, 1982, 1983, 1996, 1997 by Cape Cod Scriveners. Used by permission of Viking Penguin, a division of Penguin Putnam Inc.

"The Chrysanthemums" by John Steinbeck. Copyright 1937, renewed © 1965 by John Steinbeck. Used by permission of Viking Penguin, a division of Penguin Putnam Inc.

"Detroit Skyline, 1949" by Bobbie Ann Mason from *Shiloh & Other Stories*. Copyright © 1982 by Bobbie Ann Mason. Reprinted by permission of International Creative Management.

"An End to Efficient Vehicles" by Matt Bell as appeared at <http://rumble.sy2.com/stories/vehicles.html>. Reprinted by permission of the author.

"Everything Stuck to Him" by Raymond Carver from *What We Talk About When We Talk About Love*. Copyright © 1981 by Raymond Carver. Reprinted by permission of International Creative Management.

"Everything That Rises Must Converge" by Flannery O'Connor from *Complete Stories*. Copyright © 1971 by the Estate of Mary Flannery O'Connor. Reprinted by permission of Farrar, Straus & Giroux, LLC.

"The Far and the Near" by Thomas Wolfe. Copyright 1935 by Charles Scribner's Sons;

★★

"Sucker" by Carson McCullers from *The Mortgaged Heart*. Copyright © 1971 by Floria V. Lasky, Executrix of the Estate of Carson McCullers. Reprinted by permission of Houghton Mifflin Company. All rights reserved.

"This Is What It Means to Say Phoenix, Arizona" by Sherman Alexie from *The Lone Ranger and Tonto Fistfight in Heaven*. Copyright © 1993 by Sherman Alexie. Used by permission of Grove/Atlantic, Inc.

"Top of the Food Chain" by T. Coraghessan Boyle from *Without a Hero*. Copyright © 1993 by T. Coraghessan Boyle. Used by permission of Viking Penguin, a division of Penguin Putnam Inc.

"Tree Reader" by Gabriel Orgrease as appeared at <http://www.elimae.com/2009/02/Reader.html>. Composed on smart phone. Reprinted by permission of Gabriel Orgrease.

"The Veldt" by Ray Bradbury, originally published in *The Saturday Evening Post*. Copyright 1950 by Curtis Publishing Company, renewed © 1977 by Ray Bradbury. Reprinted by permission of Don Congdon Associates, Inc.

"Where Have You Gone, Charming Billy?" by Tim O'Brien from *Redbook*, 1975. Copyright © 1975, 1978 by Tim O'Brien. Reprinted by permission of the author.

"Why I Live at the P. O." from *A Curtain of Green and Other Stories*. Copyright 1941, renewed © 1969 by Eudora Welty. Reprinted by permission of Harcourt, Inc.

"The Writer in the Family" by E. L. Doctorow from *Lives of the Poets*. Copyright © 1984 by E. L. Doctorow. Used by permission of Random House, Inc.

"The Wrysons" by John Cheever from *The Stories of John Cheever*. Copyright © 1978 by John Cheever. Used by permission of Alfred A. Knopf, a division of Random House, Inc.

Every reasonable effort has been made to properly acknowledge ownership of all material used. Any omissions or mistakes are not intentional and, if brought to the publisher's attention, will be corrected in future editions.

Photo and Art Credits

Page 18: Smithsonian American Art Museum, Washington D.C. / Art Resource, NY. Page 22: The Norman Rockwell Art Collection Trust, The Norman Rockwell Museum at Stockbridge, Massachusetts. Reproduced by permission of the Norman Rockwell Family Agency, Inc. Page 46: Collection of the Heckscher Museum of Art, Huntington, New York. August Heckscher Collection. Page 49: Yale University Art Gallery, Mabel Brady Garvan Collection. Page 54: Perfection Learning Corporation. Page 56: *Augusta Porter Woodbury*, 1828, by Sarah Goodridge. Watercolor miniature on ivory, Neville-Strass Collection. Page 63: © Ken O'Brien Collection/CORBIS. Page 70: Library of Congress. Page 78: Perfection Learning Corporation. Page 87: Horace Bundy, *Vermont Lawyer*, Gift of Edgar William and Bernice Chrysler Garbisch, Image © Board of Trustees, National Gallery of Art, Washington. Page 97: © Bettmann/CORBIS. Page 111: © CORBIS.

Page 118: Art Resource, NY. Page 122: Perfection Learning Corporation. Page 128: The Granger Collection, New York. Page 130: Perfection Learning Corporation. Page 132: The Granger Collection, New York. Page 139: Alan Ball, Cool Dude Productions. Page 142: Perfection Learning Corporation. Page 146: © Bettmann/CORBIS. Page 153: Erich Lessing / Art Resource, NY. Page 162: Bildarchiv Preussischer Kulturbesitz / Art Resource, NY. Page 167: Erich Lessing / Art Resource, NY. Page 173: Réunion des Musées Nationaux / Art Resource, NY. Page 176: The Granger Collection, New York. Page 181: The Granger Collection, New York.

Page 186: The Granger Collection, New York. Page 191: The Granger Collection, New York. Page 194: Perfection Learning Corporation. Page 200: Snark / Art Resource, NY. Page 205: © Royalty-Free/Corbis. Page 208: Clipart.com. Page 213: Erich Lessing / Art Resource, NY. Page 220: The Granger Collection, New York. Page 222: © CORBIS. Page 226: National Portrait Gallery, Smithsonian Institution / Art Resource, NY. Page 232: Clipart.com. Page 238: © PoodlesRock/CORBIS.

Page 244: © The Metropolitan Museum of Art / Art Resource, NY. Page 248: ©The Nobel Foundation. Page 251: ©CORBIS. Page 256: Papers of Katherine Anne Porter, Special Collections, University of Maryland Libraries. Page 258: ©Horace Bristol/CORBIS. Pages 266 and 267: Andrew Wyeth, *Public Sale*, 1943. Tempera, 22 × 48 in. The Philadelphia Museum of Art. Page 275: Florine Stettheimer, *The Cathedrals of Broadway*, 1929. Oil on canvas, 60 1/8 × 50 1/8 in. The Metropolitan Museum of Art, gift of Ettie Stettheimer, 1953. Page 297: Thomas Hart Benton, *Train on the Desert*, 1926-28. Oil on canvas, 13 1/4 × 19 1/4 in. ©T. H. Benton and R. P. Benton Testamentary Trusts/Licensed by VAGA, New York. Page 300: United Press International. Page 309: Andrew Wyeth, *Winter*, 1946. Tempera on board, 31 3/8 × 48 in. The North Carolina Museum of Art, Raleigh. Purchased with funds from the State of North Carolina. Page 312: ©The Nobel Foundation. Page 322: Rinaldo Cuneo, *Earth Patterns*, c. 1932. Oil on canvas, 30 × 36 in. Gift of Howard E. Johnson, Oakland Museum of California. Page 326: Gil Ford Photography. Page 337: Walker Evans, *Interior of Negro Preacher's House*, Florida, 1934. ©Walker Evans Archive, The Metropolitan Museum of Art, 1994. (1994.258.326). Page 339: Walker Evans, *Frame Houses in Virginia*, 1936. ©Walker Evans Archive, The Metropolitan Museum of Art, 1994. (1994.258.311). Page 342: AP Photo. Page 346: Ruth Marten. Page 354: United Press International. Page 356: Roy Lichtenstein, *Blam*, 1962. Oil on canvas, 5 ft. 8 in. × 6 ft. 8 in. Yale University Art Gallery. Gift of Richard Brown Baker, B.A. 1935. Page 362: Courtesy of Laurence J. Hyman. Page 365: Grant Wood, *Stone City, Iowa*, 1930. Oil on wood panel, 30 1/4 × 40 in. Joslyn Art Museum, Omaha, NE. Page 374: ©Hulton-Deutsch Collection/CORBIS. Page 379: Fairfield Porter, *Katie in an Armchair*, 1954. Used with permission.

Page 392: Digital Image © The Museum of Modern Art / Licensed by SCALA / Art Resource, NY. Page 396: Christine Rose Photography. Page 412: J. R. Colfield. Pages 414 and 415: Andrew Wyeth, *Hay Ledge*, 1957. Tempera on panel, 21 1/2 × 45 1/4. Greenville County Museum of Art, museum purchase in honor of Greenville philanthropists, Holly and Arthur Magill with major funding from the Museum Association, Inc. Page 434: ©David Lees/CORBIS. Page 442: Archibald Motley, Jr., *Blues*, 1929. Oil on canvas, 36 × 42 in. Collection of Archie Motley and Valerie Gerrard Browne. Page 448: ©David Lees/CORBIS. Page 451: Fairfield Porter, *Jane and Elizabeth*, 1967. Oil on canvas, 55 1/8 × 48 1/8 in. The Parrish Art Museum, Southhampton, NY. Gift of Jan Freilicher, (1979.13.2). Page 458: United Press International. Page 465: Jonathan Borofsky, *Stick Man*. ©1983, Jonathan Borofsky and Gemini G.E.L., Los Angeles. Page 468: AP Photo. Page 470: Daphne Confar, *Morality Was Her Own*. Oil on copper, 6 × 4.5 in. Courtesy Pepper Gallery, Boston. Page 486: United Press International. Page 489: Victor Maldonado, *Measure*, 2001. Acrylic, xerography, wax, 12 × 12 in. Courtesy of Froelick Gallery, Portland, OR. Page 496: Brad Kemp/AP Photo. Page 507: Romare Bearden, *Sunday Morning Breakfast*, 1967. Collage on masonite, 44 × 56 in. ©Bearden Foundation/Licensed by VAGA, New York.

Page 528: Ralph Goings, Burger Chef, 1970, Oil on canvas, 40 × 56 in. Photo courtesy of O. K. Harris Works of Art, New York. Page 532: Kathy Willens/AP Photo. Page 544: Noah Berger/AP Photo. Page 548: Jerry Bauer. Page 551: Michael Brostowitz, *Come a Little Closer*, 1997. Oil on board, 15 1/4 × 19 3/4 in. The National Vietnam Veterans Art Museum. Page 557: Charlie Shobe, *On the Road to Con Thien*, 1980. Oil on canvas, 24 × 18 in. National Vietnam Veterans Art Museum. Page 560: Chester Higgins/The New York Times. Page 568: Roger Rawlings. Page 574: Charles Sheeler, *American Landscape*, 1930. Oil on canvas, 24 × 31 in. Gift of Abby Aldrich Rockefeller (166.1934). The Museum of Modern Art, New York. Copyright The Museum of Modern Art/Licensed by SCALA/Art Resource, New York. Page 588: ©Marc Norberg/The Wylie Agency. Page 602: ©Bettmann/CORBIS. Page 605: Maynard Dixon, *Southern Arizona*, 1941. Pen and ink, 14 × 12 1/2 in. Private Collection. Page 615: Maynard Dixon, *Central*

Nevada, 1941. Pen and ink, 14 x 12 1/2 in. Private Collection. Page 618: ©Nathan Farb. Page 623: Joseph Raffael, *Return to the Beginning, In Memory of Ginger,* 1981. Watercolor on paper, 33 1/2 x 41 in. Private collection. Photo courtesy of Nancy Hoffman Gallery, New York. Page 628: ©Reuters NewMedia, Inc./CORBIS. Page 631: Mary Heussenstamm, *Girl with Bangs.* Watercolor. Page 640: Martin Wong, *Grant Avenue, San Francisco,* 1992. Acrylic on linen, 108 x 42 in. Private Collection. Photo courtesy Pilkington-Olsoff Fine Arts, Inc., New York.

Page 644: ©Maggie Taylor. Page 648: AP Photo. Page 654: Charles Burchfield, *The Sphinx and the Milky Way,* c. 1946. Watercolor, 52 5/8 x 44 3/4 in. Munson-Williams-Proctor Arts Institute, Museum of Art, Utica, NY (48.45). Page 658: ©2000 Steven L. Hopp. Courtesy of HarperCollins. Page 660: Wayne Thiebaud, *San Francisco Landscape,* 1976. Oil on canvas, 12 x 14 in. ©Wayne Thiebaud/Licensed by VAGA, New York. Page 670: Jim Cooper/AP Photo. Page 676: Caty Bartholomew. Page 678: ©Philip Gould/CORBIS. Page 685: Larry Yung, *Separation.* Latex, acrylic, plaster, chalk on plywood, 89 x 84 in. Page 688: Jim Cooper/AP Photo. Page 702: Dagmar Logie. Page 704: Saul Steinberg, *Hard and Soft Figures,* 1952. ©2002 The Saul Steinberg Foundation/Artists Rights Society (ARS) New York. *The New Yorker* magazine original source of publication. Page 714: ©Jonathan Torgovinik/CORBIS SYGMA. Page 723: Alex Katz, *Track Jacket,* 1956. Oil on masonite, 24 x 18 in. Colby College Museum of Art, gift of the artist. (1995.062) ©Alex Katz/Licensed by VAGA, New York.